THE BIG BOOK OF MARKETING

Lessons and Best Practices From the World's Greatest Companies

edited by **Anthony G. Bennett**

New York   Chicago   San Francisco
Lisbon   London   Madrid   Mexico City   Milan
New Delhi   San Juan   Seoul   Singapore
Sydney   Toronto

ISBN 978-0-07-162125-0
MHID   0-07-162125-3

Mark Ting Cartoons
Copyright by Anthony G. Bennett
Illustrated by Joe Sutliff, President Crawdad Communications, www.cdad.com

This publication is designed to provide accurate and authoritative information in regard to the subject matter covered. It is sold with the understanding that neither the author nor the publisher is engaged in rendering legal, accounting, or other professional service. If legal advice or other expert assistance is required, the services of a competent professional person should be sought.

—From a Declaration of Principles jointly adopted by a Committee of the American Bar Association and a Committee of Publishers

Contents

24. Store Retailing 424

Fifth Avenue Saks / Costco / Sears / Patagonia / Trader Joe's

25. Internet Retailing 442

Lulu.com / Staples.com / Toysrus.com / Bloomingdales.com

Preface

ABOUT THE BOOK

The goal of *The Big Book of Marketing* is to provide students, small business owners, marketing professionals, and entrepreneurs with the best source of marketing strategies available in order to help them craft a successful marketing plan, launch a successful product, and help grow a successful business.

The Big Book of Marketing is the most comprehensive and authoritative book on marketing ever published. This approach provides a real-world perspective that explains the How and Why essentials to understanding today's fast-paced marketing environment.

The Big Book of Marketing is a unique marketing book with chapters and case studies written by experts from 110 of the world's most successful companies.

The editor developed the chapter outlines based on an extensive review of over 1,200 marketing books. The outlines were then reviewed by 47 major associations prior to submission to the contributing companies.

The authors—acknowledged experts in their industry—were selected through recommendations by associations, trade journals, government agencies, and other professionals in their fields. The 110 contributing companies represent an exciting range of organizations covering goods and services, high-tech and low-tech, industrial and consumer, and are located in every region of the United States. These companies are the most successful in the world, have been leaders in their field of expertise for decades, and most rank in the Fortune 100.

ABOUT THE AUTHORS

Respective corporate profiles and author biographies are detailed at the end of each chapter.

ABOUT THE EDITOR

Anthony G. Bennett has worked in marketing for over 30 years, including sales account executive with AT&T, international marketing research analyst with Union Camp (now International Paper), general manager/vice president for Hunt-Marmillion Public Relations (now Ogilvy Action), entrepreneur and inventor of two products that sold nationally, special assistant promoting solar energy in the first Bush administration, registered lobbyist on behalf of the solar energy industry, and marketing consultant. Mr. Bennett has taught marketing as an adjunct lecturer for ten years, the last seven years at Georgetown University in Washington, D.C. Mr. Bennett received his BBA and MBA from George Washington University.

Part 1
Introduction

1 MARKETING OVERVIEW

by Anthony G. Bennett

INTRODUCTION

Why does anyone choose to buy one product instead of another? Why does one product succeed (making billions of dollars) and another languish (losing money)? Product providers of goods and service are constantly in search of new tools to make their product the successful product, the one that sells. These tools are collectively called *marketing*. A dynamic marketing effort can make the difference for a product and propel a company into the billion-dollar category.

Why did customers around the world, who typically watch action films, flock to see Paramount Picture's *The First Wives Club*, a romantic comedy? Why did customers who were happy using steel tennis rackets buy Wilson's new carbon fiber racket? Why did customers who were buying regular paper by the ton start buying International Paper's new more expensive paper? How, after customers had been using green money in the United States for decades, did Burson-Marsteller help remove skepticism for using the new money with the purple ink? Why are customers who love bananas, America's favorite fruit, drawn to Safeway?

The answer is that each of these companies understood the needs and wants of their customers and supplied a product (goods or services) that met those needs. Understanding this demand and supply through the eyes of the customer is a process called marketing.

- *Demand* is the desire to possess something (goods, services, ideas, information) combined with the ability to purchase/accept it.
- *Supply* is the thing (goods, services, ideas, information) available to meet the demand.

Marketing is a process that starts with identifying and understanding the needs and wants of the customer (demand) and then fulfilling those needs and wants (supply). An effective marketing plan offers a solution to fulfill the needs and wants of society (individuals and organizations), while achieving the goals of the organization. In addition, marketing can create new needs or reformat existing needs.

MARKETING DEFINITIONS

Multifaceted and evolving, marketing encompasses a wide array of activities. As such, defining marketing has always been difficult. The following definitions can serve as a starting point.

- "Marketing is the activity, set of institutions, and processes for creating, communicating, delivering, and exchanging offerings that have value for customers, clients, partners, and society at large."[1]
- "Marketing is a process of facilitating exchanges in which buyers exchange something of value (typically money) for something of equal value to them (goods or services)." (common usage)

- "Marketing is all activities after manufacturing that promote and deliver the good or service to the customer." (common usage)
- "Marketing is the process by which resources are brought to bear against opportunities and threats."[2]

MARKETING — CHANGING PERSPECTIVES

Yesterday

In the Pre-Industrial Age, products were custom-made, and while they could be custom-tailored to each individual, they were expensive on a per-unit basis and varied in quality.

In the Industrial Age, mass production and specialization could make a higher-quality, more uniform, and less expensive product. Unfortunately, individual consumer needs were often a secondary consideration to the manufacturing processes. Sell what was made was the order of the day. The "one size fits all" concept was exemplified by Henry Ford who said in 1909, "Any customer can have a car painted any color that he wants, so long as it is black."

Starting in the 1960s and 1970s, customers realized that they did not want to be "sold to." They wanted to be listened to as individuals (or as groups known as *market segments*), and they wanted their wants and needs to be met. Marketers had to compete with other companies and convince the potential consumer that their company's goods or services were worth the customer's consideration. A true marketing orientation was coming of age.

Today

Today, in 2009, Henry Ford would be proud to know that his company offers customers 60 different colors of paint for their cars. The field of marketing has become extremely important and is applicable to every individual and organizational endeavor. Globally, consumers desire to be free to choose what they want, when and where they want it, and how much they are willing to pay. Marketing helps these consumers make the best and most informed choices.

Tomorrow

In the future, it will be incumbent upon marketers to understand that life will be more complex and increasingly global. There will be more sophisticated customers, more sophisticated competitors, and fewer natural resources. As more countries' economies become increasingly sophisticated and more trading opportunities emerge, marketing will be key in reaching customers globally. As the world matures, so will marketing. In addition, marketing will increasingly lead organizations toward ethical, social, and environmental responsibility.

MARKETING GOALS

Both customers (demand) and organizations (supply) have objectives. Customers' goals are to satisfy their needs and wants. Organizations' goals are to supply a good or service that provides value or is useful to customers and to provide employment for employees and profit to shareholders. In the case of nonprofit organizations, marketing success may be measured by the public's response rather than by profitability. In each instance, marketing management must ensure that these goals are met. Idealistically, value is provided to the customer, and the organization benefits.

Marketing provides the customer with choices, and, hopefully, the superior product stands out and

---

A business is not defined by the company's name, statutes, or articles of incorporation. It is defined by the want the customer satisfies when [he/she] buys a product or service. To satisfy the customer is the mission and purpose of every business.

Peter Drucker, *Management: Tasks, Responsibilities, Practices*[3]

succeeds. However, just as important as what marketing can do is what it cannot do. It cannot overcome an inferior product or offset a noncompetitive marketing situation. If competitors provide important benefits that are not matched by the inferior product, no amount of promotion will be able to maintain sales for the inferior product for long. If a product is overpriced versus the competition, consumers will eventually notice and switch brands. If consumers cannot find a product in stores, then the product cannot be purchased. If consumers are not aware of a product or its benefits, special promotional offers will not motivate purchases. And, if a product does not live up to its claims, promotion can actually accelerate the decline of a brand because it will make customers notice the deficiencies faster.

PROVIDING VALUE TO THE CUSTOMER

Customers feel they must receive some value or utility from a good or service that satisfies their needs or demand objectives, and thus have a reason to make the purchase or act in accord with the marketer's persuasive suggestions. In order to be successful, marketers must understand customer values. Customer value or utility has four aspects:

- *Form* is *what* the customer needs or wants, as either a good or a service.
- *Place* is the availability of this good or service *where* the customer needs it.
- *Time* is the availability of this good or service *when* the customer needs it.
- *Ownership* is the customer taking *possession* (transfer of title from seller to buyer).

Organizations contribute to the fulfillment of demand objectives and provide utility to the consumer through the use of all the marketing elements.

VALUE STREAM		
Manufacturer →	Marketing →	Consumer

MARKETING AND CONSUMPTION

Marketing facilitates the satisfaction of consumer and business demands or needs, typically by promoting the use or consumption of goods or services considered to be beneficial. However, marketing elements also are used to reduce the demand for products or services perceived as harmful or negative (liquor, cigarettes, addictive drugs) and to reduce the demand for something in short supply (gas during an oil crisis, water during a drought). These marketing efforts generally are initiated or promoted by government organizations or public interest groups.

MARKETING ELEMENTS (THE MARKETING MIX)

Various marketing elements, or functions, are used to satisfy the needs and wants of the customer and achieve the goals of the organization. Each element is studied separately, but in practice they are performed simultaneously to provide an optimal approach to both demand and supply objectives in what is known as the *marketing mix* or *integrated marketing*.

Traditionally, the marketing mix has been described as the "the four Ps": *Product, Price, Promotion,* and *Place*. This book groups the various marketing elements according to the business and economic concepts of demand and supply. Each of the marketing elements listed below are discussed in the indicated chapters.

Marketing Planning Elements (Chapters 2–5)

- **Corporate Responsibility (ethical, social, environmental)** moves the company in a direction that helps the company, employees, shareholders, and the community.
- **Strategic Planning** is the management and coordination of the marketing mix to allow customer needs to be fulfilled and organizational goals to be met.
- **Branding** determines the essence of the company.

- **Marketing Research** determines and implements the appropriate methods of researching the actual and potential customer base.

Demand Elements (Chapters 6–7)

- **Consumer Purchasing Behavior** understands the consumers' needs and wants and their buying habits.
- **Organizational Purchasing Behavior** understands business and organizations' needs and wants and their buying habits.

Marketing Communications Elements (Chapters 8–14)

Demand promotion management, known as marketing communications, attempts to reach the appropriate customers and communicate with them in order to promote demand and increase sales. When all demand management elements are performed in a coordinated approach, the effort is called *integrated communications*.

- **Personal Selling** is one-on-one selling between a sales representative and a buyer.
- **Advertising** is the mass communications of information through paid media.
- **Public Relations** provides information and third-party endorsements to assure the customer of the organizations' goodwill and quality products.
- **Promotional Marketing** is a variety of marketing tactics (coupons, free samples, trial periods of services/subscriptions) designed to overcome buying hesitancy.
- **Direct Marketing** creates messages specifically designed and delivered to targeted buyers and potential buyers.
- **Brand Ambassadors** are employees who embody the spirit and enthusiasm of the company.

Supply Elements (Chapters 15–19)

Supply management develops the appropriate products (goods and services) and pricing mechanisms in response to customer demand.

- **Product Management** controls brand legal protection and product life-cycle strategies.
- **Product Development** is the idea creation, research and development, and product design.
- **Product Packaging and Labeling** protects and promotes the product.
- **Product Pricing** determines strategies and factors that affect pricing strategies.
- **Product Quality** oversees quality strategies.

Supply Chain Elements (Chapters 20–25)

- **Supply Chain Management** manages the supply chain (wholesaling, warehousing, transportation, retailing) that delivers products to the customer.
- **Wholesaling** creates transaction economies of scale for the manufacturer and the retailer.
- **Warehousing** is the storing and distribution of the product.
- **Transportation** is the physical movement of the products.
- **Retailing** creates ease of purchase and transaction economies of scale for the customer.
- **Internet retailing** is buying and selling by computer.

MARKETING APPLICABILITY

Marketing targets individual consumers and organizations (businesses, governments, institutions, and nonprofits). In turn, organizations, governments, individuals, and geographic entities use marketing to establish a mutually beneficial relationship with their own customers.

Organizations

- Profit orientation
  - For profit (Pepsi expanding its beverage lines)
  - Not-for-profit (the Red Cross promoting a blood drive)
- Size orientation
  - Large (General Motors selling a fleet of electric cars to the government)
  - Small (local, family-owned restaurant)

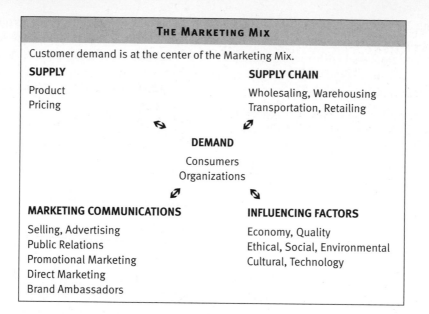

- Individual entrepreneur (a new singer pitching her first demo tape to a recording company)
- Product offering: Goods or services
  - Goods (Kodak introducing a new digital camera)
  - Services (United Airlines promoting vacation packages)

Governments

- Federal (a national program to explore space that results in NASA spending billions on new technology from companies such as Boeing)
- State (a governor promoting higher pay for teachers)

- Local (a mayor promoting citywide recycling efforts)

Individuals

- Celebrities (an actor promoting his or her new movie)
- Sports stars (enhancing their community image)
- Political candidates (running for office)
- Employees (trying to get a promotion)

Geographic Entities

- States ("Virginia is for Lovers")
- Cities ("I Love NY")
- Countries ("It's better in the Bahamas")

Marketing is so basic that it cannot be considered a separate function within the business, on a par with others such as manufacturing or personnel. Marketing requires separate work, and a distinct group of activities. But it is, first, a central dimension of the entire business. It is the whole business seen from the point of view of its final result, that is, from the customer's point of view. Concern and responsibility for marketing must, therefore, permeate all areas of the enterprise.

Peter Drucker, *Management: Tasks, Responsibilities, Practices*[4]

MARKETING'S PLACE IN THE ORGANIZATIONAL STRUCTURE

Each business function (any of which may be provided by in-house staff or by outside companies) is essential to an organization's success. A typical corporate organization includes many functions, as shown in the organizational chart in Figure 1.1. Each function must interrelate smoothly with all of the other functions in order for the company to operate and compete effectively.

NOTES

1. The American Marketing Association, 2007. Printed with permission.
2. *A New Brand World* by Scott Bedbury, Penguin, 2002, p. 153. Printed with permission.
3. Peter Drucker, *Management: Tasks, Responsibilities, Practices,* Harper, 1973, p. 79. Reprinted by permission of HarperCollins Publishers, Inc.
4. Ibid., p. 63.

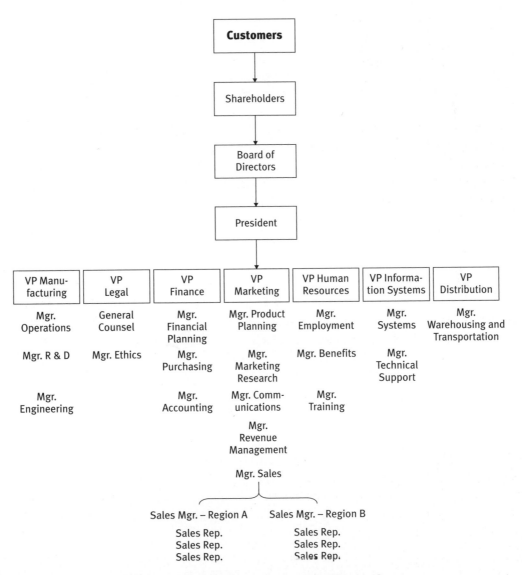

Figure 1.1 Typical Corporate Organizational Chart

Part 2
Planning

2 ORGANIZATIONAL RESPONSIBILITY

by Bristol-Myers Squibb, Pfizer, SC Johnson, Tenet Healthcare, Texas Instruments, Inc., Verizon, Weyerhaeuser, and Xerox

> *That which is not good for the bee-hive cannot be good for the bees.*
> Marcus Aurelius, Roman Emperor
> (A.D. 121–180)

ORGANIZATIONAL RESPONSIBILITY
by Weyerhaeuser

Introduction

The legal, ethical, social, and environmentally responsible aspects of marketing are important because of marketing's immense influence on society. These aspects can pose restraints on, and opportunities for, marketing efforts. The impetus for corporate responsibilities came from culture, religions, scientific reasoning, political structure, and the economic structure.

Historically, business has been held in relatively high esteem. The current focus on business ethics by the corporate, government, and public sectors began to change during the 1970s when foreign bribery and illegal campaign financing scandals attracted increased attention. By the mid–1980s, a *Wall Street Journal* front-page story called business ethics "an oxymoron, a contradiction in terms like jumbo shrimp."[1] However, little more than a decade later, a national survey found that 60 percent of the American public believed that business and ethics can coexist, and that ethical dilemmas in the workplace can and should be reduced.[2]

The public has become more demanding of ethical and socially responsible behavior in businesses and business leaders. Organizations that are strategically positioned to gain customer trust will succeed in the marketplace.

As with society, as marketing organizations mature, their level of responsibility increases. These increases in responsibility form a hierarchy: economic, legal, ethical, social, and environmental.

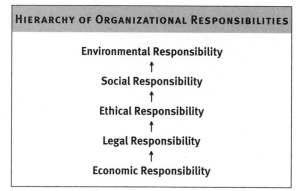

HIERARCHY OF ORGANIZATIONAL RESPONSIBILITIES

Environmental Responsibility
↑
Social Responsibility
↑
Ethical Responsibility
↑
Legal Responsibility
↑
Economic Responsibility

Economic Responsibility

Organizations have economic responsibilities to their customers, shareholders, and employees. Companies must perform their marketing tasks well in order to succeed and be profitable. This will provide goods and services to the customers, jobs for the employees, and profits for the shareholders.

Legal Responsibility

Organizations have a legal responsibility to adhere to the laws of society. This is for the good of all and ensures economic fair play and freedom from unsafe work practices. Marketing programs must incorporate a company's responsibility to conduct all business operations in accordance with the highest legal standards. It is very difficult for a marketing communications campaign to overcome a well-publicized infraction. The continued goodwill of a clean record directly assures a customer base that has many alternatives from which to choose. In addition, there are local, state, and federal governments, and international agencies that promulgate literally thousands of codes, laws, and regulations concerning marketing. These laws pertain to everything from toy safety to consumer credit. There are specific legal aspects to each element of the marketing mix, and it is important to note that the marketing professional should seek legal counsel for guidance on each marketing element.

ETHICAL RESPONSIBILITY
by Weyerhaeuser

It is imperative that organizations work proactively in facing new ethical challenges. This is important, not because of fear of punishment, but because it is the right thing to do. Virtually all large U.S.-based corporations have a written ethics and compliance document. A majority of U.S. corporations have an ethics training program, and more than one-third have an ethics officer or a senior manager who is responsible for implementing and overseeing the organization's internal ethics, compliance, or business conduct programs.[3]

Marketing ethics aspects include ethics definition, specific marketing issues, and ethics accountability methods.

Ethics Definition

Business ethics are the practices, policies, and programs that ensure consistently high standards of behavior with employees, suppliers, customers, shareholders, and the communities in which businesses operate. Ethics is the right thing to do.

The society designs standards or establishes goals so as to promote the highest quality of life. Business and trade help create a better standard of living for all. Business ethics helps the system work to establish its maximum value. All players have a responsibility to adhere to these rules in order to allow the greatest number of people to achieve their maximum potential, thus improving the system and creating yet more potential. Breaking these rules hurts the system and denies the benefits of the system to all. For example, bribery is wrong, not just because you will get caught, but because it creates a benefit for only one, while hindering everyone else in the system.

Marketing Elements Ethics Issues

Organizations usually are confronted on a daily basis with a wide variety of ethics issues. These issues can be divided into five broad categories: personal conduct, protection of company assets, fair dealings, international business activities, and government interactions.

There are specific ethical aspects to each element of the marketing mix. The following are the main representative examples.

Planning
The main ethical concern in planning is prioritizing loyalties to customers, employees, and shareholders.

Marketing Research
The primary ethical issue in marketing research is privacy or confidentiality. Privacy should be balanced with the genuine need for information. For example, it is important to separate individual survey information from data that later will most likely be linked to database marketing. Respondents should not be directly affected by marketing or sales efforts after participating in a survey. The Council of American Survey Research Organizations (CASRO) mandates that all its members

subscribe to the industry-accepted CASRO Code of Standards and Ethics for Survey Research. Some unethical sales companies have used the premise of selling under the guise of research.

Consumer Purchasing Behavior

The main ethics issues in the understanding of consumer behavior are the overzealous drive to gather information concerning individuals leading to privacy concerns and an overzealous approach to hype the consumers' needs and wants in a manner that is confusing to the customer.

Organizational Purchasing Behavior

Because external perceptions of a company's purchasing personnel are so important in building a firm's reputation, most organizations include in their policy manuals numerous statements about conflicts of interest, personal obligations, and fairness. Buyers and other members of the procurement system who deal with present and potential suppliers must recognize their responsibilities as agents. Buyers know of major procurement contracts that may affect the performance of the supplier and the purchasing company ahead of the financial markets and therefore have been occasional targets of insider trading.

Personal Selling

Illegal pyramid schemes may confuse some people by a surface resemblance to hierarchical sales force infrastructures in the direct-selling industry. The distinguishing difference is that pyramid schemes collect their profits up front on the high-cost sale of the business opportunity to the gullible recruit, whereas legitimate direct-selling companies typically require very little or no capital investment, and entry costs are usually limited to a kit of start-up product samples and supplies. The pyramid scheme may offer products or paybacks for a time in order to establish credibility or hold out the hope that investors may rise to the top and get rich by bringing in other new recruits, but ultimately the business opportunity evaporates as the pyramid collapses, and victims lose their investment and/or get stuck with substantial inventory. In an effort to ensure high integrity in the direct-selling industry, the industry's professional trade organization, the

Direct Selling Association's Code of Conduct sets and polices ethical standards among its member companies. The customer should always be dealt with in good faith. However, occasionally, there are cases where the financial rewards of the sale tempt the salesperson to resort to unethical practices. Examples include overexaggeration of product performance, overzealous commitment to delivery schedules, or, in rare instances, bribery to achieve the sale. Some aspects of bribery are still legal in a few countries; however, it is becoming regulated more and more. Sales *puffery*, which is stating overly generalized positive aspects of a product ("This is the world's best car!") is legal, although unethical.

Advertising

What constitutes ethical and acceptable advertising is a matter of constant debate and is dictated generally by evolving social standards and behavior. For example, advertising that appears on programming with controversial levels of sex and violence is frequently criticized even though the advertising itself may not have any controversial content. This debate presents tough choices for advertisers and their agencies. The advertiser is anxious to reach the maximum number of potential customers via the mass audiences attracted to such programming, but, at the same time, the advertiser should be careful not to alienate consumers who regard such programming as inappropriate.

Sensitivity to the particular vulnerability of children is another ethical challenge facing the advertising community. Children do not yet have the mental ability to fully understand the difference between the show or magazine's content and the ad and can't make a reasoned choice. Overzealously promoting a product to children violates the core of the social system. The government and consumer protection groups often carefully monitor advertising on children's programming. However, even though the advertising may deal with a product that can only be legally purchased by adults, such advertising may have some exposure to children. Advertisers must evaluate the extent to which they should modify their message and its presentation to accommodate this unintended audience.

In general there also is the ongoing debate as to persuasion versus manipulation, and overzealous and misleading claims versus free speech rights.

Public Relations

Managers, who have inside information about such matters as mergers, new products, profitability, and other commercial knowledge, are restricted about what they can say about their organizations. Lobbying and political influence is increasingly coming under scrutiny.

Promotional Marketing

The most important ethical issue with promotional marketing is to ensure the honest and straightforward design of promotional offers and the way in which they are communicated. Too often, promotional programs are developed with complicated or obscure restrictions that deceive consumers. Doing so is always counterproductive because dissatisfied customers tell others, find competitive alternatives in the future, and sometimes even sue the offending company. All are costly to companies in the long term.

Direct Marketing

The Direct Marketing Association established Guidelines for Ethical Business Practice in 1960, and constantly updates them to reflect consumer and regulatory concerns, as well as new marketing techniques. The self-regulatory guidelines are intended to provide individuals and organizations involved in direct marketing in all media with generally accepted principles of conduct. The DMA's Committee on Ethical Business Practice, an industry peer review committee, implements the guidelines. Other trade associations, as well as most major corporations, have also instituted guidelines and policies for consumer protection and customer service. One of the major current ethics issues for direct marketers is privacy. Consumers should be informed of how companies collect and use information and should have choices about how information about them is used. Marketing to children deserves special mention. Children cannot make the same types of informed purchase decisions as adults. Because of this, children can be more easily

deceived and disappointed. Certain marketing practices, such as gathering personal information from a child online, can be both illegal and unethical.

Product Management

Product managers should have as a major ethical focus the promotion of product safety and disclosure of usage risks. They also should seek to eliminate planned obsolescence, industrial espionage, product knock-offs (particularly products produced in foreign countries that may violate patent, copyright, and trademark protections), and overzealous product claims.

Product Packaging and Labeling

Product labeling issues include full disclosure, accuracy, and truth in advertising and label knock-offs (confusingly similar product packaging/labeling).

Product Pricing

In a free market, corporations are encouraged to compete in an ethical, yet vigorous, manner. This provides customers with the best product while providing assurances that they may purchase that product at a fair price. Many companies and industries have adopted a set of guidelines to answer any ethical issues (price fixing, price gouging, full disclosure of needed additional costs) they may encounter. For example, in 1994, the major airlines submitted a consent decree to the U.S. Department of Justice outlining certain rules of conduct regarding fair and open pricing that the major airlines are still following today.

Product Quality

Because of the growing emphasis on quality, companies now are more assured that they are doing what is right and thus are more open to outside inspection.

Supply Chain Management

Supply chain partners should be aware of exerting undue control over other supply chain participants. Dual-channel conflicts arise when the expectation of channel exclusivity is met instead with competition. Another ethical issue regards the duty of a third-party logistics provider or distributor within the supply chain to maintain inventory at sufficient levels so that there are no lost sales due to sudden surges in customer demand.

Wholesaling

Wholesalers usually represent multiple suppliers and may have the issue of promoting one supplier over another, which may infrequently promote favoritism or kickbacks. When wholesale sales reps make recommendations to customers, the sales reps should not promote excessive claims for either product performance, service performance, or misrepresent product availability. When a requested product is unavailable, a substitution of product should not be done without the customers' knowledge. Employee shrinkage (theft) is a concern in wholesale as it is in retail.

Warehousing

When a product arrives at the warehouse below quality standards, it must be destroyed or returned to the factory. However, occasionally, these products may be listed as having been destroyed but end up being sold for a profit.

Transportation

Transportation managers should refrain from promising delivery schedules that they know are unrealistic.

Retailing

Some unethical retailers resort to bait and switch and selling of private mailing lists. Many companies have had to reduce their liberal return policies due to occasional consumer return fraud. Friendly customer service must also include asking for identification to prevent fraudulent checks. Consumer ethics issues also include shoplifting (both consumer and employee theft) amounting to over $98 billion per year globally in retail losses,[4] which marketers must recoup through higher consumer prices.

ETHICS—ACCOUNTABILITY
by Verizon

Ethics Accountability (External)

Organizations are held accountable for their actions by several forces, including society, government, and business.

Society's Role in Marketing Ethics

Society has both individual and group norms that hold business to a higher ethical standard than that of the individual. Business relies on the consumer for its livelihood and makes its best efforts to be a good corporate citizen. Individuals and consumer groups are ever watchful of any lapse of ethics in business or marketing. Current corporate practice incorporates the advice of individuals (whether they be customers or stakeholders or neither) and consumer groups as to how businesses may act more responsibly.

Individuals or consumer groups who feel that a certain business is not acting in an ethical manner have several courses of action, including:

- Contact the company directly, usually through complaint-reporting channels set up by the company.
- Contact any number of business and professional groups that represent a particular industry.
- Report any alleged wrongdoing to the government, traditional media, and new media.
- Form consumer boycotts.

Government's Role in Marketing Ethics

Many of the first formal ethics and compliance programs, which reflect the style that is common today, were developed in conjunction with the 1986 *Defense Industry Initiative on Business Ethics and Conduct* (DII). During the 1980s, 18 major defense contractors were being investigated for waste, fraud, and abuse. These contractors accepted the DII Commission's challenge as an opportunity to improve corporate ethics and as a methodology to avoid additional regulations. The contractors agreed to promote ethical business conduct through the implementation of policies, procedures, and programs such as the creation of codes of ethics. They also vowed to develop and deliver ethics training to create avenues for internal reporting of allegations of misconduct, and to implement internal systems to monitor compliance. The DII signatory companies also agreed to allow public audits of their ethics and compliance programs and to share best practices with one another.

In 1991, new federal regulations known as the *U.S. Sentencing Guidelines for Organizations* were designed to ensure that organizations that were found to be in violation of federal law would receive uniform sentencing. The guidelines enabled organizations to greatly reduce fines levied against them by cooperating with investigators and creating ethics and compliance programs.

Importantly, the guidelines applied to all types and sizes of organizations, not just large government contractors. The guidelines included a summary of the steps that organizations should take in order to have an effective internal ethics and compliance program. The specific steps outlined in the guidelines were largely based on the experiences of the DII companies.

According to the Organizational Guidelines, an effective program includes the following:

- Established standards and procedures that are reasonably capable of reducing the prospect of criminal conduct
- Specific individual(s) at high levels within the organization who are assigned responsibilities to oversee compliance with such standards
- Steps to communicate the standards and procedures to all employees and agents by "requiring participation in training programs or by disseminating publications that explain in a practical manner what is required"
- A monitoring and auditing system(s) designed to detect criminal conduct and an internal reporting system that employees and others can use to report criminal conduct "without fear of retribution"
- A record of consistent enforcement of the standards
- A plan to respond appropriately to prevent similar offenses from recurring

It is clear that the business ethics and compliance landscape has been shaped in significant ways by the DII and by the 1991 Organizational Guidelines. The guidelines prompted many organizations that had been slow to join the ethics movement to review their policies and practices.

They also provided an impetus for many companies to create an ethics office.

Business Community's Role in Marketing Ethics

Peer review of ethical behavior is a constant factor for every business. It is in an industry's best interest to alter the behavior of those businesses that tarnish an industry's reputation. Shareholders, professional associations, industry associations, and trade journals all investigate ethical lapses.

ETHICS AND BUSINESS

In a survey of 120 business executives, whose company sales volume ranged between $1–250 million, the following desirable *personal characteristics* of managers were ranked, highlighting the need for ethical behavior:

1. Personal moral / ethical integrity
2. Ability to work with others
3. Ability to listen
4. Tolerance of individual differences
5. Perseverance
6. Ability to follow instructions
7. Leadership
8. Confidence
9. Decisiveness
10. Ability to work alone

Compiled by: A. G. Bennett
Source: Survey conducted by Mr. Shotaro, MBA, in conjunction with The College of William and Mary's Bureau of Business Research.

Ethics Accountability (Internal)

Many corporations have responded to the global and economic changes of business against the backdrop of heightened social scrutiny and governmental initiatives. An important part of their response has been the creation of a formal ethics office and formal internal corporate ethics programs, chiefly designed to prevent and detect violations of both law and company standards and policies. Increasingly, they also are being seen as tools to communicate and develop shared values within organizations and to help employees make responsible choices in the workplace.

Office of Ethics and Business Conduct

Ethics officers are responsible for particular activities within an organization.[5]

- Preparation of a Code of Conduct
- Ethics training design
- Oversight of hotline/internal misconduct reporting
- Assessing/reviewing vulnerabilities
- Overseeing investigations of wrongdoing
- Assessing/reviewing successes

Ethics officers also coordinate with legal, human resources, security, and finance. In order for ethics and compliance programs to be effective, compliance must be viewed as a marketing management function rather than a policing and/or legal function. A commitment to good management practices, such as those that encourage two-way communications and enable employees to take responsibility for their actions, is proving to be the most reliable indicator of successful compliance practices.

The creation of an ethics office can either reflect the existing values of an organization or can serve as the cornerstone of a new direction for a corporation. In either case, an ethics office usually is based on the following:

- Common ethical standards for the corporation
- Ethical awareness, training, and ongoing education of employees
- An avenue for communication and dialogue with employees and customers

One of the most important purposes of an organization's ethics office is to give employees a formal channel to voice their concerns and report wrongdoing. The ethics office can underscore an organization's commitment to ethical behavior and reinforce an organization's core values. The ethics office can serve as a resource to all employees by providing guidance and interpretation of actual or potential issues. The ethics office typically responds daily to questions and issues from employees and management.

Many organizations give ethics a high priority in the daily operations of the marketing elements.

Some companies facilitate this by including the ethics office in the development of the organization's strategic business plan, which is aligned with corporate strategy and supported by the executive team. The ethics office of any organization typically is part of the larger goal of maintaining a business environment where all employees are encouraged and reinforced to act in accordance with an organization's ethical standards. To facilitate this role, many companies have established *integrity* as one of the organization's core values. To put this value into action, it is important that all executives have a hand in establishing the business conduct standards.

An organization's ethics officer usually reports directly to the most senior members of management or the Board of Directors' Audit Committee on activities, results, and strategic recommendations. Companies view this reporting relationship as critical to providing an objective and confidential resource for employees.

Ethics Programs

Ethics programs consist of five major areas: a code of conduct, communicating ethics standards, employee ethics training, ethics risk assessment, and an ethics complaint resolution process.

- **Establish Corporate Ethics Code of Conduct.** The organization's ethics office usually is responsible for establishing and updating an organization's ethics standards, known as the *Ethics Code of Conduct*. The Code of Conduct typically contains guidelines for the following areas of marketing conduct: antitrust; company funds; conflict of interest; employment practices; environmental responsibility; government affairs; inside information; relationships with suppliers, contractors, and customers; marketing communications; and trade secrets and intellectual property.
- **Communicate the Ethics Standards.** To ensure that employees have the knowledge to make decisions and take actions in accordance with an organization's ethics and compliance standards, many companies use numerous strategies and resources to put the right information

at their employees' disposal. Ongoing communication is seen as essential. A communication strategy to convey corporate ethics goals will typically focus on conveying subject matter that reaches all employees, stakeholders, and business suppliers. This communication may be made available in the company newsletter and on the company Intranet.

- **Employee Ethics Training.** The ethics office typically develops corporatewide training programs that raise and reinforce ethics awareness. The ethics office may also offer targeted courses that address specific needs. In addition to ongoing ethics training, many companies have mandatory ethics or Code of Conduct training as part of the new employee orientation process.
- **Ongoing Ethics Risk Assessments.** An organization's ethics office may perform ongoing manage-by-prevention actions that encourage proactive disclosure of activities or relationships that may create the appearance of impropriety or conflicts of interest. These programs are for individuals and organizations.

Many organizations distribute a Conflict of Interest Questionnaire to all of its higher management worldwide on an annual basis and update as needed.

Before many organizations enter into any potential partnership, the ethics office may conduct an assessment of the potential business partner's values and standards through a thorough, formalized Ethics Risk Assessment process. This process includes outside research on litigation and scandalous or high-risk activities.

- **Ethics Complaint Resolution Processes.** There are quite a few steps in an ethics complaint resolution process.

1. Promoting awareness of process
2. Providing reporting channels
3. Complaint examination
4. Conduct investigation
5. Determining cause
6. Enacting preventive measures
7. Taking corrective measures

ETHICAL RESPONSIBILITY— INTERNATIONAL
by Texas Instruments, Inc.

As U.S.-based organizations increasingly incorporate international marketing into their activities, as well as establish non-U.S. operations, it is extremely important to align ethics with a company's global business strategy.

International Ethical Aspects

The reputation of any organization depends on the actions, decisions, and choices made on its behalf by those who represent it. That reputation can be either enhanced or damaged by the nature of these actions. A company that has earned a reputation for business competency and for being highly ethical is attractive to potential customers and investors. It is reliable and predictable because it makes every effort to honor its commitments. By minimizing the time required to gain trust, the company can do more business and do it quickly. In regions of the world where corruption and bribery have been well documented, companies with strong reputations can provide a comfort zone of ethical consistency for suppliers and customers. There is an increasing understanding worldwide that ethical shortcuts have a distorting impact on the free market by displacing sound business decisions with personal incentives and conflicts of interest. Companies that can deliver maximum value back to their customers through high-integrity business relationships are being recognized as attractive business partners worldwide.

Global Approach
Company relationships with other companies have now become so intertwined that a company may be dealing with another company as a customer, supplier, competitor, or an alliance partner. Irrespective of their geographic location, employees are expected to understand their ethical and legal obligations.

Communicating an organization's ethical and legal expectations and requirements in today's global market presents both opportunities and challenges. Opportunities are there for those who learn how to operate ethically under a variety of different cultural and legal environments. However, companies are presented with serious risks if they focus too heavily on respecting local customs because locations within a multinational corporation are not isolated from regulations imposed by other parts of the world. For example, in the United States, the concept of informal relationships is promoted to create open and candid communications, something that is viewed as a primary attribute for enhancing the ethics of the workplace. This concept is not viewed as appropriate in many cultures where respect for authority and organizational hierarchy are very important.

Local Approach

Companies cannot simply extend home country ethics principles outward. A company should implement a global ethical strategy and deploy it effectively on a local basis by using a four-level approach:

- Comply with all legal requirements, especially focusing on local laws.
- Understand how these local requirements or practices may impact coworkers in other parts of the world.
- Understand when practices need to be adapted based on local laws and customs of a particular locality.
- Anticipate the points of friction and proactively address the dissonance employees may experience.

Developing a Global Code of Ethics

Companies provide the tools with which worldwide employees make informed decisions and take actions quickly and correctly both in the office and on the factory floor. A set of policies or rules can never be comprehensive enough for all employees to deal with all of the issues that will inevitably arise. Individual actions and decisions can be guided only through basic core values.

There are several steps to developing a company's code of ethics:

- Determine the common cultural themes and values in the global organization.
- Draft an ethics document incorporating core ethics policies.
- Disseminate to company employees worldwide for review and comment.
- Discuss individually with the top management
- Review by the Board of Directors.
- Distribute to employees worldwide in appropriate languages and train employees on their responsibilities.

Attributes of an Effective International Ethics Program

- Align the values and principles to the business objectives of the company. In many cultures it is important to equate individual efforts to overall objectives.
- The core values that drive the conduct and behavior of an organization must be sourced from headquarters. The local and country implementation becomes a shared or deployed responsibility.
- Focus on positive statements. For example, the words *avoid* or *never* are viewed as negative in Asian cultures.
- If translated, have the document interpreted back into the original language to be certain that the core message has been retained.

SOCIAL RESPONSIBILITY
by Pfizer

In the next level above corporate ethical behavior is socially responsible behavior. Social responsibility (SR) is important in order to improve the quality of life in the community at large. Marketing organizations are paying more attention to their role and influence in the world, and many now have social responsibility programs. In addition, many investors are investing in socially responsible funds and impose selective screens on investments. Similarly, stockholders, employees, and consumers have exerted pressure on corporations to help advance a number of socially responsible causes. Social responsibility issues include work/family benefits, environmental protection, time for worker community outreach, charitable giving, women and minority advancement, worker health/safety, full information disclosure, and job security.

Recipients of charitable contributions may be individuals, communities, research labs, cause-related marketing sponsorships, or even countries. Corporate giving typically is done through charities that represent the local community or segments of the world community.

Companies may differentiate themselves in the marketplace by promoting their social programs in advertising or packaging and have become very successful. For example, Ben & Jerry's (1% for peace), Newman's Own (100% of after-tax profits go toward education and charitable purposes), Reebok (Amnesty International Concert Tour), and Star Kist Tuna (Dolphin safe).

These programs have worked, in large part, due to the corporate commitment at senior levels, which typically then permeates to all employees.

Definition

Corporate social responsibility (also known as *corporate citizenship*) is a comprehensive set of policies and practices that organizations adopt in order to demonstrate respect for ethical values, people, communities, and the environment, thereby enhancing corporate value for customers, investors, and employees.

Reasons for Social Programs

There are three main reasons why an organization institutes a social responsibility policy.

- It is the right thing to do, and responds to the needs of individuals and the community.
- It promotes a positive image of the company, creates corporate identity differentiation, and promotes goodwill to various audiences, such as consumers, governments, the business/financial community, and suppliers/vendors. Recipients of corporate giving programs may be selected in order to appeal to a specific customer base. For example, donations to breast cancer research appeal to women and sponsorships of Alzheimer's research appeal to the elderly.
- It promotes a corporate culture of caring and a customer first attitude among employees.

Methods for Community Involvement

Organizations give in three ways: financial, employee time, and in-kind.

- **Financial donations.** Known as philanthropy, provide needed funding for new or existing programs. Marketing communications typically promote these contributions by stating that the organization is "a proud sponsor of" a program such as the Race for the Cure or the Special Olympics.
- **Employee time donations.** Known as volunteerism, provide support through contributions of individual skills. The employee, and thus the organization, is seen interacting in the community through events such as Habitat for Humanity or Red Cross disaster relief. These events may be company organized or employee chosen.
- **In-kind donations.** Specific corporate goods or services, are matched up with and provided to a specific need. For example, Intel, Hewlett Packard, Microsoft, and Premio provided $500 million worth of computers, software, and technical assistance to "Teach to the Future," a program designed to train teachers in computer skills.

Organizing a Cause-Related Partnership

There are several steps involved in coordinating a marketing relationship:

1. Determine corporate giving and marketing goals.
2. Determine which community or charitable organization has the most need or best fits with the organization's goals.
3. Determine a formal legal agreement, including responsibilities, amounts of giving, liabilities, and codes of conduct.

4. Manage the SR program.
5. Communicate involvement in the program.
6. Evaluate marketing results. In many cases a program will succeed and a long-term partnership is formed. In some instances, the need may diminish and the corporation may then move on to another cause. The public is quick to see hypocritical marketing efforts, and if these efforts are not working, the program should be either enhanced or dropped.

SOCIAL RESPONSIBILITY— INTERNATIONAL
by Texas Instruments, Inc.

Social responsibility, on an international basis, addresses a variety of different topics such as human rights issues, environmental stewardship, philanthropy, and governance. Global companies now are being held accountable for their business practices, and many desire to certify and promote their acceptable practices, seeking to differentiate themselves from companies that do not have acceptable workplace conditions. Similar in nature to ISO 9000 and ISO 14000 is the social accountability certification program SA8000, developed by the Council on Economic Priorities Accreditation Agency. SA8000 is a third-party standardized program that assesses and monitors the social accountability of suppliers, manufacturers, and vendors. SA8000 certifies corporate performance in the following areas: child labor, forced labor, health and safety, freedom of association, discrimination, disciplinary practices, working hours, and compensation. Increasingly, corporations are requested to produce more CSR-related information for public consumption. Investors and customers frequently include publicly available information in their investing and purchase decision models. The Global Reporting Initiative (GRI) framework has become a generally accepted framework for setting CSR-related goals and reporting CSR results.

In several instances, individual industry associations have taken steps to address industry-specific challenges with more specific standards that apply to their industry, for example, textiles and electronics. Tailoring a benchmark on a specific area can provide a standard by which similarly situated suppliers and customers understand the generally accepted variables that apply to the business models in their marketplace.

ENVIRONMENTAL RESPONSIBILITY
by Xerox and SC Johnson

Introduction/Environmental Issues

Throughout the first half of the twentieth century, during the age of global industrialization, the developed world grew at a rapid pace with little regard for lasting impacts on the earth and its resources. Few considered the implications of industrial waste disposal into the environment or the possibility that the materials needed to fuel continued global growth might someday be in short supply.

In the 1970s and 1980s, the previous lack of awareness of the environment began to change. A series of environmental disasters, such as Love Canal, Bhopal, and the *Valdez,* triggered closer scrutiny of industry practices and led to tighter government regulation and controls of pollution outputs at manufacturing facilities. Many viewed further industrial development as a choice between continued economic expansion and environmental protection.

In 1992, at the Earth Summit in Rio de Janeiro, Brazil, world leaders from the public and private sectors promoted the concept of sustainable development to emphasize that environmental and economic goals not only could be, but had to be, reached together.

Environmental marketing can indicate a comparative advantage and enhance the company's image for those companies that embrace sustainable development through environmental product development, environmental cost-based pricing structures, and providing environmentally oriented information through marketing communications.

- Global population growth, coupled with current consumption patterns around the world, make resource scarcity a growing and costly concern for the world's consumers. Sustainable development both acknowledges and provides the opportunity for business to assume a leadership role in addressing the burden that human occupancy places on the earth's resources. The economic power, technological assets, and marketing savvy wielded by global industrial giants may place them in a unique position to contribute to the world's economy. At the same time, these companies can minimize their impact on the environment and win consumer support for their efforts. Recognition of this opportunity is what drives the integration of sustainability thinking into business strategy.
- *Sustainable development* is broadly defined as meeting consumer needs today without compromising the ability of future generations to meet their needs.
- *Environmental marketing* provides that all participants in the commerce chain produce, consume, dispose, and promote the use of resources so that the world economy expands to support the needs of the world's population without sacrificing the environment.

Environmental Factors

To understand environmental concerns and their impact on marketing, it is important to understand environmental factors such as expanding population, expanding consumption, and the earth's finite resources.

Supply ⟷ Environmental Factors ⟷ Demand

Expanding Population

The world's population now stands at approximately six billion people, with expectations that that number will double by 2039. Productive areas are the most severely affected. For example, agriculturally rich drylands already are turning into deserts, forests into poor pastures, and freshwater wetlands into salty dead soils. As ecosystems are degraded, the biological diversity and genetic resources they contain could be lost permanently.

Expanding Consumption

The overuse and misuse of consumed resources often are accompanied by the pollution of the atmosphere, water, and soil with substances that continue to harm the environment for long periods.

Earth's Finite Resources

Much of the earth's natural resources are finite. Even though it is difficult to predict how long they will last, they will run out. Metals and minerals are the most finite of the world's resources, including all the fossil fuels. These resources are being depleted relatively rapidly and are extracted and used almost as soon as they are found. The amount of resources extracted depends on market prices and the rate at which technical innovation allows increasingly difficult sources to be tapped.

In most cases, easily found, high-quality finite resources are becoming scarce, and companies search in increasingly environmentally sensitive areas. For example, companies now search for oil under the sea, in hostile arctic regions, and in tropical forests. As these materials become more costly to find and extract, their price increases.

In the face of finite resource depletion, many industries around the world are turning to substitution. The U.S. telecommunications industry, for example, now uses fiber optics based on ubiquitous silicone (sand) instead of copper. Canada's largest electrical utility has embarked on the development of renewable energy resources, such as solar, wind, and biomass, to replace fossil fuel. British Petroleum's efforts to shift to renewable sources of energy are the main focus of their advertising campaigns.

The Global Response to Environmental Factors

Consumers

Successful environmental marketing campaigns are designed around understanding and meeting the needs of the marketplace. Increasingly, consumers are expressing their demand for products and services that are effective, competitively priced, and not harmful to the environment. Clean air and safe drinking water are among the top concerns of families around the world today. According to a 1997 survey conducted by the Global Environmental Monitor (GEM), the environment and the effect of pollution on human health are strong and growing global concerns among a representative sampling of 60 percent of the world's total population. While individuals are generally aware of the global implications of environmental protection, most are primarily interested in what happens locally.

Consumer environmental needs are being promoted by environmental groups, nongovernmental organizations, governments, and international organizations. These groups are challenging companies to think globally, while acting locally. Multinational enterprises with offices and manufacturing facilities around the world find benefits and marketing opportunities by working toward sustainable operations within each host community, and following the regulations and reporting requirements of the local government.

According to the 1997 Green Gauge Report from Roper-Starch, 81 percent of Americans find environmental marketing acceptable. According to recent polls reported in the *International Herald Tribune,* the environment is among the top five factors influencing U.S. consumers' purchasing decisions. Women, minorities, and parents with young children tend to be the most environmentally minded in their purchasing decisions.

The consumer usually will not buy a green product unless that product is price-worthy and performs the same function as a product without green claims. This is especially true for fast-moving consumer goods. For example, when Procter & Gamble (P&G) introduced a hair spray that used hand-pumped air rather than an aerosol as the propellant, the company suffered poor sales. P&G concluded that customers are not willing to accept the inconvenience of hand pumping just to gain an environmental benefit. However, in 1997–1998, surveys of electrical utility customers in Texas indicated that the average customer would pay 10 percent more for their electric utility bill if a significant portion of the power was generated by renewable energy sources.

Environmental Groups

Increasingly, companies are working together with environmental groups to find solutions for corporate environmental issues, while at the same time marketing these proenvironmental efforts to consumers. One example is the partnership between McDonald's Corporation and the Environmental Defense Fund to cut waste and improve recycling efforts. In another example, British Petroleum (BP) has initiated renewable energy programs and is working with the Environmental Defense Fund to develop voluntary emissions trading systems for greenhouse gases.

Governments

Governments can assist businesses to progress faster toward sustainable development goals. Governments can influence corporate environmental strategies through government regulatory requirements, government-driven market programs, and the promotion of industry self-regulation.

Government Regulatory Requirements

Environmental engineers are now expected to design manufacturing emission treatment/control technologies to ensure compliance with environmental laws and/or regulations. The government's move to eliminate toxic materials in the manufacturing process has become a factor in product design. Manufacturers have realized they can avoid manufacturing costs most effectively in the design stage. In addition, these design efforts can provide a mechanism for differentiating products in the marketplace.

The Federal Trade Commission (FTC) has issued *Guides for the Use of Environmental Marketing Claims.* These guides represent administrative interpretations of laws administered by the FTC for the guidance of the public in conducting its affairs in conformity with legal requirements. These guides apply to environmental claims included in labeling, advertising, promotional materials, and all other forms of marketing, whether asserted directly or by implication, through words, symbols, emblems, logos, depictions, and product brand names. Environmental claims typically include the areas of: biodegradability, compostability, recyclability, recycled content, source reduction, refillability, ozone safety, and ozone friendliness.

The guidelines state that an environmental marketing claim should not be presented in a manner that overstates the environmental attribute or benefit, expressly or by implication. Marketers should avoid implications of significant environmental benefits if the benefit is in fact negligible. For example, if a package is labeled, "50% more recycled content than before," and the manufacturer increased the recycled content of its package from 2 to 3 percent recycled material, the claim is technically true, but it conveys the false impression that the advertiser has significantly increased the use of recycled material.

Government Market Programs

Procurement requirements listing environmental specifications are the most powerful government-driven mechanism for the achievement of environmental goals. For some products, the federal and state governments are the largest purchasers, and their purchasing power can create economies of scale. Therefore, compliance with government environmental specifications makes economic sense for most suppliers. Once the government procures an environmentally friendly product and an economically justified price is reached, then, and only then, is it likely that other smaller purchasing entities will adopt the use of the product. For example, the U.S. government now mandates a minimum 30 percent recycled content in office paper. In 1996 the federal government purchased 20.9 billion sheets of copy paper, so it is obviously a major influence in promoting the growth of the recycled paper industry.

While these programs effectively define environmental responsibility in the business market, they do not necessarily create a pull in the consumer marketplace. The hope is that with economies of scale and a good marketing campaign, these companies will effectively translate business products and services to the consumer marketplace. For example, after the federal requirement for recycled paper took effect, Union Camp (subsequently acquired by International Paper) introduced the Great White brand of office paper in 1993. This brand was one of only a few recycled-content copy papers available from a high-volume manufacturer. It was positioned as an everyday copy paper that had the appearance, performance, and price of regular, nonrecycled content paper. This enabled Union Camp to quickly obtain shelf space in retail channels and rapidly increase market share. During its first five years on the market, Great White sales volume grew 10 times faster than the total retail market for copy paper.

Government Promotion of Industry Programs

While regulations and enforcement of environmental policies are getting tougher, there has been a greater emphasis among some governments to promote innovation in the private sector by focusing on voluntary methodologies. Many governments are encouraging self-regulation in business and pacts with government agencies, rather than new and costly environmental laws and command-and-control policies.

International Organizations

With the globalization of corporations, the new manufacturing environmental performance standards are expanding across the globe. Many in industry are adopting voluntary environmental management standards to drive continuous improvement beyond local compliance requirements.

The International Standards Organization (ISO), headquartered in Switzerland, has developed global voluntary standards in an effort to bring greater uniformity to management systems and reporting. Similar to the ISO 9000 quality standards, ISO 14000 is a series of standards addressing environmental management. Many companies use ISO environmental standards to market and promote their products.

ISO		
ISO 14000	→	a series of environmental standards
ISO 14001	→	internal systems for corporations to achieve the standards[7]

Source: ISO (International Organization for Standardization)

Multilateral Environmental Agreements (MEAs) are international treaties negotiated among countries to address environmental concerns. MEAs can serve as important environmental objectives. International conventions, such as the Montreal Protocol, the Biodiversity Convention, and the Climate Convention, recognize that global problems warrant global solutions.

The Montreal Protocol has led to the phasing-out of ozone-depleting substances. This phaseout was done in conjunction with industry as businesses worked to develop environmentally friendly substitute products that would meet consumers' needs.

Organizational Response to Environmental Concerns

The general increase in public awareness of environmental issues has provided a marketing opportunity to shift industry's perceived role from problem creator to solutions provider. Whereas regulation traditionally has been used to address environmental market failure, regulators and policy makers are now leveraging increased public environmental awareness to drive environmental improvement through voluntary market-based incentive programs. Businesses are participating in government-sponsored voluntary programs as well as using environmental attributes to capture market share.

There is a growing corporate awareness that the environment can provide an opportunity for revenue generation. Companies that have integrated environmental thinking into their business processes can capture competitive advantages. For example, Xerox realized that solid waste from the return of leased copiers was their largest environmental issue. Xerox undertook an aggressive

program to recover parts from returned products as reusable assets. Designing new products with asset recovery in mind has enabled Xerox to be positioned for mandatory product take-back legislation in Europe.

As with any other marketing strategy, it is important to quantify the potential market value of an environmentally friendly product or service through market research, direct customer request, or competitor activities. The preferred approach is to identify the opportunity before the competition does. For example, Xerox developed its print/copy and toner cartridge return programs in direct response to customer requests. SC Johnson responded to its customers' desires and introduced numerous lower environmental impact products and processes, including Raid Flea Trap, a noninsecticidal flea control device that was redesigned in the concept stage to cut plastic use by 25 percent.

Corporate Financial/Environmental Goals

While eco-efficiency has helped industry make significant strides in reducing pollution and waste, it often fails to address another important aspect of sustainability: the potential for economic market growth through sustainable technology development. DuPont, Monsanto, SC Johnson, and Xerox were among the first U.S. corporations to recognize the critical link between environmental and financial performance. These companies began to focus less on the cost to the business of environmental compliance and more on the potential for profit in environmental innovation. For example, from 1992 to 1998, SC Johnson eliminated over 420 million pounds of waste material from its products and processes and, as a result, saved over $125 million.

Environmental marketing strategies are dependent on the type of goods or services being marketed and the end user. For example, in the office equipment market, where the purchasing decision makers are not necessarily the end users of the product, there are fewer environmental-based marketing opportunities than for the consumer products marketplace.

Implementing an environmental management system and auditing the system's performance will aid in ensuring sustainable environmental performance. International recognition and acceptance have resulted in many companies choosing to implement the ISO 14001 environmental management system. This type of system drives a company to understand the environmental impact of its operations and products, work toward reducing those impacts, and comply with applicable environmental laws and regulations.

An environmental audit gauges how a company manages itself against compliance requirements and its own policies and practices. Compliance with national and state environmental regulations is sometimes the lowest common denominator as companies start to aim higher to meet international requirements, to comply early with the next level of government requirements, and to appeal to a growing consumer base that expects corporate environmentalism. An environmental audit reviews every aspect of the company including research and development, suppliers, the manufacturing process, all aspects of physical distribution, and all aspects of the supply chain.

Environmental performance-based standards measure energy/material input versus product output, life cycle impacts, disposal costs, durability, and toxicity. Performance indicators should be specific, numeric, and include timelines. Companies should apply these indicators uniformly to provide comparability from year to year, among companies within the industry and across industries.

Corporate Green Marketing and the Marketing Mix

Credibility is built on market recognition and public perception that a company is a good environmental corporate citizen and is maintained through a clean environmental record coupled with continuous environmental performance improvement.

In its simplest form, green or eco-marketing might add terms like "phosphate free," "recyclable," "refillable," and "ozone-friendly" to product advertising. Sustainable marketing goes much further than this by incorporating product stewardship into the business planning process. *Product*

stewardship is the management of a product by both economic and environmental standards. Thus, sustainable marketing includes continuous product improvement for greater safety, efficiency, and environmental effectiveness.

The application of sustainable business strategies to product development not only improves a product's environmental friendliness but also may offer a significant marketing advantage. Being the first to market a product that is highly effective and less harmful to the environment can capture consumer loyalty.

Incorporating sustainable thinking into product development can require turning thoughts into actions. For example, SC Johnson organized workshops for multifunction product development teams designed to raise awareness of the financial benefits of reducing waste at the point of product design. SC Johnson introduced a computer tool, Success Through Environmental Progress (STEP), to provide a comprehensive way of internally measuring environmental improvement in products and processes. This tool enabled SC Johnson to gain information that it could then translate into a consumer-friendly format for marketing purposes.

When communicating with a target audience, companies should differentiate themselves in order to increase sales. This can be done by promoting the company's environmental image and assuring that product attributes are presented in a way that the consumer can understand. In some cases, the communication of environmental attributes may require an education campaign to influence consumer understanding of, and preference for, certain environmental benefits.

For example, at SC Johnson, educational programs on two fronts help to create pull from the marketplace for the company's products. First, to clarify consumer misconceptions about aerosols and the upper ozone layer, the company includes a CFC-free (chlorofluorocarbons) message on product packages and in advertising, and sponsors an education campaign with the Consumer Aerosol Products Council (CAPCO) to raise the public's awareness that today's aerosols do not contribute to upper ozone depletion. Second, SC Johnson partnered with other industrial companies, including the Steel Recycling Institute, to promote the acceptance of empty aerosol cans in community recycling programs.

Each element of the marketing mix both affects the environment and can be used to differentiate companies that embrace environmental stewardship.

Marketing Research

It is important to know consumers' attitudes toward the environmental impact of their needs before developing and marketing new offerings.

Most people say they are pro-environment. However, observational marketing research techniques can be very insightful to determine which consumers actually put this attitude into practice. One research group even dug up garbage from a city dump to determine actual product usage patterns, which showed that more products were thrown away than were claimed in consumer surveys.

Organizational Purchasing

Most companies and many governmental agencies are beginning to incorporate some environmental aspects into their purchasing requirements. For example, since the early 1990s, the federal government has mandated by executive order the use of recycled content in various items purchased such as paper, tires, and motor oil.

Sales

Companies market product-specific environmental attributes both proactively and by using competitive strategies. Typically, these attributes translate into aspects of the product that address a customer environmental need. Proactive approaches promote new features, functions, and/or services provided by the supplier. Salespeople often travel great distances either by car or by plane. Both methods of travel rely on fossil fuels that are harmful to the environment. Telephones, videoconferencing, and the Internet provide more environmentally friendly methods of delivering sales messages.

Advertising

After the first Earth Day in 1970, many products were advertised touting environmental benefits. Unfortunately, not all of these advertisements were true. Consumers became wary of the hype. Nevertheless, according to recent polls reported in the *International Herald Tribune,* 10 to 15 percent of all new products now make some kind of environmental claim in their labeling and advertising.

Products will never have a zero impact on the environment, but a company may advertise its commitment to continuous environmental practices improvement, environmentally aware product ingredients, how to use the product in an environmentally safe way, and how to properly recycle or dispose of the product.

General terms such as "ozone friendly," "recycled," and "recyclable" cannot be used unless specifically qualified as to what is meant by the claim. For example, when claiming a product is "recycled," the manufacturer must indicate the percent of the product that is recycled and whether this recycled material is preconsumer or postconsumer. If this claim is on the package, it must further clarify whether it pertains to the product or to the package.

Public Relations

Companies use public relations to communicate a consistent leadership role in their environmental efforts and seek dialogue with targeted publics. Most publishing organizations give full support to articles written about the company's environmental activities, processes, and products. The socially responsible ethic of a company promotes image building. Partnering with environmental groups is another strategy companies can use to promote an environmentally conscious image.

Promotional Marketing

Promotional programs may be blamed for excessive packaging or excessive use of materials related to in-store promotional offers. When selecting premiums or the packaging in which they are delivered to consumers, promotional marketers should attempt to use renewable resources and minimize waste.

Direct Marketing

The direct marketing community actively supports environmental protection in many ways, including programs that promote recycling, tree replanting, solid waste management, and environmental education. Shopping from catalogs and other forms of direct mail saves gasoline and cuts pollution.

Many direct marketers, including JCPenney, The Body Shop, and National Wildlife Federation, print portions or all of their catalogs on paper made with recycled content. Some companies contribute to tree replanting programs. In addition, companies are encouraged to use the Direct Marketing Association's Mail Preference Service and to have their own in-house name-suppression services so that they do not send mail to consumers who do not wish to receive it, thereby cutting down on resources used.

Product Development

Realizing that environmental research and development (R&D) proposals will be competing with other investment proposals, it is critical to develop a strong business case. When considering R&D investments, there are two marketing aspects to consider. The first is specifically developing a technology that will solve a customer environmental problem. For example, SC Johnson determined that many institutional cleaning employees could not read the direction labels on cleaning products. As a result, many solvents were improperly mixed, thus leading to expensive, environmentally degrading, and potentially harmful waste. Consequently, SC Johnson developed a color-coded, mechanical mixing system for its clients.

The second R&D aspect is to market the environmental applications of new technologies being developed that the customer does not yet realize will be a benefit. For example, in DuPont's basic research laboratories, new plastics have been developed that are easier to recycle than previous versions. Marketing was then responsible for determining a market and creating a demand for the new technology.

Product Design

One of the first tools implemented in industry efforts to operate more sustainably is eco-efficiency. The World Business Council for Sustainable Development (WBCSD), a coalition of some 130 leading multinational corporations committed to advancing environmental protection and sustained economic growth, defines *eco-efficiency* as designing a product that uses fewer but more efficient materials and less energy in production. The end result is a product manufactured with less waste and a lower environmental impact that also costs less to produce and may avoid potential environmental liabilities.

Product Packaging

Packaging was one of the first product-oriented environmental considerations in the marketplace, because it contributed significant volume to landfills. It is important that marketing incorporates consumer environmental concerns into waste management and packaging. Packaging efforts fall into three main categories: reduce, reuse, and recycle.

- **Reduce.** Lightweight or streamlined packaging reduces use of materials at the source. For example, the soft drink bottlers have made great strides in reducing the amount of material used in their containers: the weight of aluminum cans was reduced by 35 percent, PET plastic bottles by 28.5 percent, and glass bottles by 25 percent.
- **Reuse.** Reusable or refillable packages minimize resource utilization. For example, a longtime favorite of kids, the Welch's grape jelly jars, can be reused as glassware.
- **Recycle.** Packaging that is recyclable or has recycled content cuts down on the use of virgin materials. Mail Boxes Etc., a private mailbox and shipping company, promotes its acceptance and reuse of foam shipping peanuts.

Product Labeling

Environmental labels were created to provide a simple way for purchasers of the products to select those that are environmentally preferable. The labels provide the credibility of an independent endorsement. Environmental labeling programs typically focus on a single environmental characteristic, such as the U.S. Energy Star program that focuses on energy efficiency. Alternatively, some labeling programs may include multiple criteria spanning the product life cycle.

Pricing

Additional costs caused by environmental efforts should be reflected in a product's price. However, business customers generally balk at paying more for products even if they are environmentally oriented. Public opinion polls indicate that the general public is willing to spend only a small percentage more for environmental products. Consequently, pricing is dependent on the company's target market strategy. If the strategy is to capture the extremely environmentally sensitive niche market, a price premium may be appropriate. Otherwise, the focus should be on positioning environmental aspects as the deciding factor where cost, quality, and features are equal. Some business companies will price new products at a premium and offer remanufactured goods at a discount. Other companies, such as Xerox, will incorporate remanufactured/recycled parts into new products, offer the new products at a slightly reduced rate to incorporate lower parts cost, and warranty the products as new products (as the recycled parts are identical to new parts).

Wholesaling

Wholesaling as a process has little environmental impact; however, certain products handled by wholesalers, such as hazardous materials and chemicals, require extra care when handling, storing, shipping, and sorting. Occupational Safety and Health Administration (OSHA) requirements and Material Safety Data Sheet (MSDS) documentation requirements should be strictly adhered to. Marketing communications in trade magazines and internal publications such as newsletters should stress the importance of safety.

Warehousing

An important environmental concern in warehousing is the handling and storage of hazardous materials and chemicals. Companies should have a rigorous communications policy regarding these environmental issues due to community right-to-know regulations and worker safety concerns.

The land around a warehouse typically is three to four times the area of the warehouse and may be entirely paved. This large paved area creates rainwater runoff that causes erosion and carries oil contaminants. Used packing and handling materials such as pallets, peanuts, and shrink-wrap often are not recycled.

Transportation

Transportation users and providers are confronted with a number of issues that potentially impact the environment, yet the transportation sector rarely has used environmental issues as a differentiating marketing tool. In the near future, as technologies such as electric or natural gas delivery trucks come into use, this environmentally sound delivery practice could become a sought after point of differentiation in the supply chain.

Concentrated products, such as Concentrated Tide, require less delivery fuel per unit, are both environmentally and economically sound, and can be marketed as a differentiating benefit. In addition, proposed take-back requirements to recycle used products would mean never returning to the factory with an empty truck, thus not wasting fuel.

Retailing

The retail industry has minimal environmental impact in general. However, there are several specific environmental areas that should be addressed. These include excessive use of energy for heating, cooling, and lighting; parking lot rainwater runoff for shopping centers; ground storage leakage for retail gas stations; overpackaging of products; and overproviding of shopping bags. Retailers are likely to become the return point for a variety of recycled product programs (as they currently are for glass bottles and automobile batteries). Some retailers, such as Ben & Jerry's Ice Cream, have found success in using an environmental approach to differentiate themselves from their competition. Other retailers are finding that having environmentally sound operational practices, such as installing efficient lighting that uses less energy, can be financially advantageous. Security is a big concern among retailers, as theft accounts for profit loss of approximately 10 percent. Music stores and music departments in department stores were using excessively large plastic packaging of cassettes to deter theft of the otherwise small product. Several musical groups, including the Grateful Dead, were instrumental in bringing about the voluntary ban on excessive packaging in the retail music industry.

ENVIRONMENTAL RESPONSIBILITY— INTERNATIONAL
by Bristol-Myers Squibb

There is a growing consensus worldwide among scientists, consumers, and policy makers that protecting the natural environment is critical to the world's economic and environmental vitality. Companies are working with shareholders, lawmakers, regulators, environmental groups, and consumers to clean up their processes and products. Companies recognize that doing business in an environmentally conscious or sustainable manner encourages marketing innovation and is essential to developing and maintaining a competitive advantage in the international marketplace.

Innovative companies have developed management systems that integrate environmental responsibility across international organization lines and drive companies beyond pollution control to sustainable business innovations. For example, Monsanto, a major chemical manufacturer, is designing bioengineered potatoes and cotton that are protected from insects and viruses. As a result, farmers in any country will not need to use pesticides, thereby protecting land and water from chemical applications. This will reduce human exposure to chemicals and eliminate the need to use energy and raw materials to manufacture, package, and distribute the pesticides.

The participation of marketing personnel on international-multifunctional teams will help strike a balance between the potential conflicting requirements of product needs versus environmental sensitivity and the impact of products throughout their environmental life cycle: research and development, marketing, procurement, manufacturing, packaging, sales, distribution, consumer use, and ultimate disposal.

Marketing personnel are able to communicate the company's accomplishments and develop the company's image as an environmental leader. For example, marketers at Clairol determined that international consumers had preferences for natural products with sound environmental attributes, including a biodegradable formula, natural plant-derived ingredients, and recycled and recyclable packaging. Clairol launched *Herbal Essences* in 1995, and by 1997 the product line was being sold in more than 40 countries and was on its way to becoming a billion-dollar franchise.

Marketing contributes to environmental protection by considering how the international customer will use the product. Most companies are committed to reducing the pollution created by their laboratories, manufacturing sites, distribution, products, and packaging. If a product design cannot fully avoid possible health or environmental impacts, consumer information should provide instructions on safe use and disposal, in the language of the country where the product will be sold. With the growing emphasis on environmental progress and responsibility, providing these tools is more than just good citizenship, it is essential to gaining a competitive edge. For example, a Bristol-Myers Squibb facility in Germany has developed two instructional tools in German for its business customers: a booklet on the basics of handling hazardous drugs, including precautions that should be taken by home health care attendants, and a notebook on the safe use and disposal of oncology products for physicians, hospitals, and pharmacists.

Marketers are marketing not only a product or product line but the whole corporation. Environmental responsibility is a growing aspect of the corporate persona. The current trend is not to place environmental requirements on specific products, but rather on suppliers of those products and whether the supplier has adopted an environmental management system. Companies often place a requirement on their suppliers to be certified to ISO 14000, an assurance to the buyer that the supplier meets its environmental performance criteria. This requirement for certification may extend throughout the entire supply chain.

Although the United States has more environmental regulations than any other country, the rest of the world is catching up to and, in some instances, outpacing, the United States with regulatory and nonregulatory requirements that will affect a company's ability to market products. For example, in Sweden, the government health system requires companies to report on their environmental programs as part of their business licensing. The benefits of environmental leadership go beyond risk avoidance, regulatory compliance, and cost savings; in some markets it may become the price of admission to do business.

Marketing's focus on building and maintaining market share for the product line has now expanded beyond the traditional customer requirements of cost, convenience, and quality, and encompasses the growing environmental concerns of consumers,

investors, and governments. Through ingenuity, companies can achieve both economic growth and environmental progress. Marketers will be at the forefront in making the business decisions that will transform responsible environmental management into competitive advantage.

Environmental Labels

A standard international environmental label would make all consumers aware of the environmental features and benefits of a product. However, currently, most countries have their own approach. The most successful environmental label programs are in Germany, Sweden, Canada, the United States, and the Nordic countries. Other label programs are being developed in Japan, France, Spain, Singapore, and the European Union. Most international labeling programs include multiple environmental criteria spanning the product life cycle, such as the German Blue Angel label. European label programs are designed to target the top 10 to 20 percent of environmental performers. Label specifications become progressively more aggressive as more products are able to meet the certification requirements.

ORGANIZATIONAL RESPONSIBILITY – CASE STUDY

by Tenet Healthcare

Company: Tenet Healthcare
Case: Ethical Responsibility

A decade ago, National Medical Enterprises (NME) was beset by a federal investigation into allegations that certain NME psychiatric hospitals had committed ethical and legal violations in their marketing practices, overbilled Medicare, and violated federal antikickback statutes. In fact, FBI agents had descended on the headquarters of the company to seize documents related to the company's psychiatric hospital division. To help rebuild its reputation and its business, the company put together an ethics and compliance program that has become recognized as a model in the health care industry.

Ten years later, the company, renamed Tenet Healthcare in 1995, found itself once again in the middle of a federal investigation concerning certain Medicare billing practices. And, more than ever, it is counting on the ethics and compliance program that helped it so much in 1993 to help it regain a position of leadership and integrity in the industry.

Health care is one of the most regulated industries in the United States, subject to multiple reviews by federal, state, and local agencies. Almost every day, news stories report on industry investigations. So Tenet's predicament was not unique, but the harm to its reputation was very real.

In 1994, a year later, NME had negotiated a settlement with the federal government that included an agreement to sell the psychiatric hospital division and pay a $375 million fine, at that time the largest such penalty ever for a health-care provider. A little noticed, but far more important, component of the settlement was a Corporate Integrity Agreement that mandated an ethics and compliance program.

This program became the foundation on which Tenet, which now operates 53 general hospitals and various related health-care facilities in 12 states, worked hard to rebuild its reputation. With its new challenges, the company has committed to enhancing and strengthening the program to help it engineer a corporate culture in which ethics plays a central role in company decision-making.

Tenet's ethics and compliance program has several components:

- Mission and values statements
- Standards of Conduct
- A training program
- Ethics Action Line
- Ethics and Compliance Department
- Quality, Compliance, and Ethics Committee of the Board of Directors
- Corporate Compliance Committee

The above components are integrated into a closely knit system that guides the program, establishes priorities, and evaluates the results. By virtue of the program permeating the entire company and its culture, it created an awareness and sensitivity, both internally and externally, that no one envisioned. For example, the existence of the program became a positive factor in recruiting employees, in making Tenet hospitals more visible in the communities served, and in the marketing of services in the competitive health industry.

The Ethics and Compliance Program has become a part of the Tenet company culture. Examples include numerous additional evaluation techniques, including assessments by trainees, instructors, and managers of company procedures. Also, all employees are encouraged to evaluate the program periodically by completing a comprehensive questionnaire. About 60 percent of Tenet's more than 62,000 employees respond.

The Ethics Action Line has responded to calls since its inception over 14 years ago. Evaluation of the patterns and types of calls indicates that about half of the calls received are related to human resources issues and the remaining half include requests for clarification of company policy or other ethics concerns. This is attributed to the effective handling of the calls by a staff of company employees, who receive training on how to encourage callers to share information needed for appropriate follow-up. In a recent company survey, 95 percent of participating employees responded that issues are investigated when reported. An average of 400 calls is received monthly.

The Ethics Action Line provides advice on a variety of issues, many related to compliance and ethics allegations and others involving human resources problems. As Tenet's ethics and compliance program has matured, the number of alleged wrongdoing as a percentage of the total number of employee ethics calls has decreased, while the percentage of calls requesting information or consultation has increased. Many of these calls come from managers who are sensitive to the company's

(Continued)

desire to have employees seek advice on ethical issues before taking an action that they may later regret. Tenet's program emphasizes that it is more appropriate to seek permission than make a mistake and then hope for forgiveness.

Tenet's ethics training program has several aspects that go beyond what was required in the agreement with the federal government. For example, instead of using just a videotape, as many ethics training programs do, all of Tenet's ethics training is conducted in classrooms by a Hospital Compliance Officer. The Hospital Compliance Officers who lead the training sessions are full-time compliance officers who are part of the Tenet Ethics and Compliance Department. One of the strengths of Tenet's Ethics and Compliance Program is its independent reporting structure. Each Hospital Compliance Officer reports to Regional Compliance Directors who report to the Tenet Chief Compliance Officer. The Tenet Chief Compliance Officer reports to the Quality, Compliance and Ethics Committee of the Tenet Board of Directors. The Ethics and Compliance Department works collaboratively with the company's operations but maintains its independence from company operations and the company's Law Department so that it can provide objective advice on ethics and compliance matters.

Most significantly, Tenet opted to continue its ethics program even though it was no longer required to do so after its Corporate Integrity Agreement with the federal government expired in 1999. Tenet's ethics and compliance program has created a consciousness among its employees that emphasizes doing the right thing. It has fostered a commitment among employees to report possible wrongdoing without fear of retaliation. Today, Tenet's employees routinely indicate how comforting it is to work for a company that encourages and supports their efforts to make sound ethical decisions. Although the value of the ethics and compliance programs is difficult to quantify, Tenet's experience has been very positive, and most employees believe the program has made a major contribution to the company's success.

The development of a strong and highly visible ethics and compliance program also has served as a positive factor when Tenet expresses interest in acquiring other hospitals. Although this is a subjective measure, hospitals seeking new ownership clearly value an acquirer with a proven record in ethics, especially given the scrutiny of the health-care industry by the government and others. Tenet's ethics program is an asset to both the company and those with whom it conducts business.

In 2006, Tenet entered into a comprehensive settlement agreement with the U.S. Department of Justice to resolve allegations regarding Medicare billing and coding and financial arrangements with physicians. In connection with the settlement, Tenet entered into a five-year Corporate Integrity Agreement with the Office of Inspector General of the U.S. Department of Health and Human Services. The agreement will be in effect for five years and reflects Tenet's agreement to act honestly and openly with the federal government—one of Tenet's key customers. The Corporate Integrity Agreement reflects the ethics and values that the company already adheres to and requires Tenet to continue its Ethics and Compliance Program and to periodically submit reports to the federal government on program activities. It also requires that every Tenet employee participate in ethics and compliance training and certify that he or she will abide by the Tenet Standards of Conduct. Tenet and its hospitals are also subject to internal and external audits of its operations to determine compliance.

by Pfizer

Company: Pfizer
Case: Social Responsibility (2009)

As a research-based, global pharmaceutical company, Pfizer's most important contribution to society remains discovering, developing, and bringing to market new medicines. But producing even a great treatment is not enough. What is also essential is how responsibly we use our skills and resources to invest in health around the world. Pfizer's corporate responsibility is an expression of the company's mission: working together for a healthier world.

A principal focus of corporate responsibility at Pfizer has been improving health care and access to health care around the world. To do this requires a commitment on many fronts: engaging and educating health-care providers and patients about diagnosis and treatment, building health-care capacity, delivering the medicines where they need to be, and partnering effectively with organizations treating patients on the ground.

Today, Pfizer is a corporate leader in global health, whose $1.7 billion in contributions in 2008 ranked us one of the top corporate donors in the United States.[6] Our philanthropy is focused on investing the full scope of the company's resources—people, skills, expertise, and funding—to broaden access to medicines and strengthen health-care delivery for underserved people around the world. Our philanthropy platform, *Pfizer Investments in Health*, offers a coordinated approach to contribute to society beyond medicines:

Treat. Improving access to medicines and health-care services

Teach. Increasing patient education and health-care worker training on disease prevention and treatment options

Build. Strengthening the capacity of health-care organizations to support prevention, diagnosis, treatment, and care

Serve. Advocating and sharing best practices to improve health care for the underserved

Through direct engagement and collaboration with local nongovernmental organizations (NGOs), multilateral organizations (MLOs), governments, and private-sector partners, we strive to implement sustainable programs and impact global health outcomes.

The International Trachoma Initiative (ITI) was founded in 1998 by Pfizer and the Edna McConnell Clark Foundation to treat and prevent trachoma, the world's leading cause of preventable blindness. Trachoma plagues the developing world, particularly rural populations with limited access to clean water and health care. According to the World Health Organization (WHO), 63 million people suffer from trachoma infection and 8 million people are visually impaired or blind as a result of trachoma. Globally, the disease results in an estimated $2.9 billion in lost productivity per year.[7]

ITI supports the implementation of the WHO recommended SAFE strategy, a comprehensive public health approach that combines treatment with prevention, involving sight-saving surgery, mass treatment with the Pfizer-donated antibiotic Zithromax®, facial cleanliness, and environmental improvement to increase access to clean water and improved sanitation.

(Continued)

One dose of this medicine once a year has proven effective in treating active trachoma infection, a major advance from the standard treatment. Through Pfizer's donation of Zithromax, health-care workers are able to greatly simplify the process of getting treatment to those with trachoma and to increase compliance with the treatment regimen.

Since 1998 ITI has administered 94 million treatments of Zithromax in 16 countries and supported over 399,000 sight-saving surgeries to treat trichiasis, the advanced and blinding stage of trachoma. With the support of the ITI, Morocco became the first country to complete the campaign for trachoma control in 2006, and is now working toward WHO certification to signify that blinding trachoma has been eliminated as a public health problem.

Pfizer's commitment to global health and communities around the world goes beyond providing medicines and aims to build capacity and strengthen health-care systems in areas hardest hit by disease. Pfizer sends its highly skilled employees to serve on the front lines of health challenges in developing countries. Their goal is simple: to improve basic health-care infrastructure by loaning Pfizer employees to local nonprofit organizations and health service providers.

Since 2003, 171 Pfizer Fellows in 34 countries have worked with and transferred skills to local partners and nongovernmental organizations during three- to six-month assignments to share knowledge, learn new skills, and explore solutions to improving health care. Pfizer Global Health Fellows include physicians, nurses, lab technicians, marketing managers, financial administrators, and health educators from the United States, Europe, Latin America, Australia, Canada, and Asia. Assignments range from helping hospitals improve data collection and information technology to providing clinical training for health-care workers and supporting the expansion of services of local clinics.

The program delivers benefits for both the local nonprofit organizations and Pfizer. Studies find Global Health Fellows have a profound impact on partner organizations. A study by Boston University's Center for International Health and Development reveals that 100 percent of partners report Pfizer Fellows accelerated sustainable change, and 86 percent of partners stated that Fellows' performance exceeded initial expectations. Pfizer's program goals initially focused strictly on creating high social impact, but over time Fellows demonstrated business impact as well, by bringing back a broader world vision, a renewed focus on their work at Pfizer, and new ideas for innovation.

International Trachoma Initiative and the Pfizer Global Health Fellows programs are both flagships of Pfizer's corporate responsibility efforts and have received impressive awards and recognition from diverse audiences. These programs also are important because they are key examples of what makes Pfizer employees proud to work for Pfizer. Corporate responsibility continues to be a major part of Pfizer's corporate identity and a motivator for its workforce.

by Xerox

Company: Xerox
Case: Environmental Responsibility

The Xerox Corporation has developed and implemented a comprehensive, corporatewide Environmental Leadership Program (ELP). The ELP program's goals are to manufacture waste-free products in waste-free factories. In addition to the environmental benefit, this approach was designed to improve Xerox's productivity and capture substantial cost savings in manufacturing. Xerox believes that both the environmental improvements and the cost savings could result in a more satisfied customer and improve Xerox's global competitiveness. Components of ELP include product recycling management, facility waste reduction and recycling, cartridge return program, designing of environmental products, and environmental marketing. Employee involvement is key to the integration of the program across the corporation. The ELP is coordinated by a steering committee and includes participation by senior management from all aspects of the company.

Xerox's primary motivation to establish the program was its desire to manage products that were returned at the end of a customer lease program in a cost-effective and environmentally responsible manner. Large volumes of these returned products had accumulated and were costing the corporation significant investment in storage fees. External factors for establishing the program included the developing public interest in producer responsibility and potential product take-back legislation in Europe. The public had already accepted the notion of recycling and was starting to consider the purchase of recycled content products.

The first step in developing the program was to understand the customers' requirements. Using marketing research techniques such as surveys and customer focus groups, Xerox collected customer data on environmental preferences and practices. Product recycling management was one of the primary topics of research, as this program would result in incorporating reprocessed parts/assemblies into products. Customer perception of this practice was critically important. Would customers think that Xerox products were inferior if built with reprocessed parts? The findings indicated that what customers really cared about was getting a high-quality reliable product; they did not care how Xerox managed to achieve this. Customers' concerns about this new approach also were allayed because the products would continue to carry the total satisfaction guarantee.

The second step was enlisting senior management whose support was critical to the success of the program. This was accomplished by detailing the environmental benefits and quantifying the potential cost the program would save the corporation.

The third step in developing the ELP was to incorporate asset recycle design into the product development process. Prior to this program, asset recycling was only considered after products had been returned.

(Continued)

The fourth step was to develop an effective product return process. Getting products back was fundamental to recovering asset value and to effectively managing manufacturing inventory. Xerox first applied the product recycling management design approach to toner cartridges. Substantial investment in the new design of the recyclable cartridges meant that used cartridges needed to be recovered for remanufacturing; otherwise the company would lose the additional value designed into the cartridges. Xerox realized that to optimize cartridge recovery they had to make it easy and cost-free for customers to return the cartridges. The return process includes providing a new cartridge in a container, with a prepaid postage label included, in which the old cartridge can be returned. Xerox then disassembles and remanufactures returned cartridges. Currently, this return process has reached a 65 percent cartridge return rate.

Establishing supplier partnerships was critical to the program's success. Xerox relies on its suppliers to reprocess the parts and assemblies they originally supplied as new. Optimizing the asset value of recovered products is dependent upon incorporating environmental principles into Xerox product design to extract value. The greatest value is recovered in remanufacturing returned products. The next option is to add features and functions to meet new market requirements. When products are not remanufacturable, parts are stripped for the machine, repaired, and reused in other products. Finally, nonreusable parts are recycled for material content. The ultimate objective of the entire process is to prevent waste.

Xerox has developed innovative signature analysis technologies for ensuring the quality and reliability of its parts. Signature analysis works on the basis that parts have unique characteristics that indicate the performance and remaining life of the part. This technology enables Xerox to sort out parts that may fail so that only reliable parts are reused.

The product recycling management program has delivered impressive results both financially and environmentally. The program saves Xerox over $200 million each year and decreases the amount of Xerox parts destined for waste landfills by 74 percent.

Of note is that our product design efforts are in context of our overall strategy, which focuses on where we have the greatest opportunity to reduce impact along the value chain. We strive to focus efforts on where we can make a measurable difference and not waste efforts on the relatively small aspects.

CORPORATE PROFILES AND AUTHOR BIOGRAPHIES

BRISTOL-MYERS SQUIBB

Bristol-Myers Squibb, headquartered in New York City, is a global biopharmaceutical company whose mission is to extend and enhance human life. Visit Bristol-Myers Squibb at www.bms.com.

Thomas M. Hellman

Thomas M. Hellman formerly was Vice President, Environment Health & Safety, and the Corporate Quality Officer for Bristol-Myers Squibb. Dr. Hellman received his BA from Williams College and his Ph.D. from Pennsylvania State University.

PFIZER

Pfizer, headquartered in New York City, is the largest pharmaceutical company in the United States by sales. Founded in 1849, it has 84,000 employees. Visit Pfizer at www.pfizer.com.

Rich Bagger

Rich Bagger heads Worldwide Public Affairs and Policy for Pfizer, with responsibility for public policy, government relations, international public affairs, corporate responsibility, philanthropy, and stakeholder advocacy.

SC JOHNSON

SC Johnson is one of the world's leading manufacturers of household cleaning products and products for home storage, air care, personal care, and insect control. Visit SC Johnson at www.scjohnson.com.

Cynthia A. Georgeson

Cynthia Georgeson formerly was the Director, Corporate Public Affairs—Worldwide for SC Johnson.

TENET HEALTHCARE

Tenet Healthcare, through its subsidiaries, owns and operates acute care hospitals and related ancillary healthcare businesses, which include ambulatory surgery centers and diagnostic imaging centers. Visit Tenet at www.tenethealth.com.

Audrey Andrews

Audrey Andrews serves as Tenet's Chief Compliance Officer. Ms. Andrews is responsible for the company's ethics and compliance program. She received her BA in government and her JD in law from the University of Texas at Austin.

TEXAS INSTRUMENTS, INC.

Texas Instruments is a global semiconductor company and the world's leading designer and supplier of digital signal processing and analog technologies. Visit Texas Instruments at www.ti.com.

Carl Skooglund

Carl Skooglund is the former Vice President and Ethics Director for Texas Instruments. Mr. Skooglund received his BS from Pennsylvania State University.

David Reid, CPA

David Reid is Vice President and Ethics Director for Texas Instruments. Mr. Reid received his BBA in accounting from the University of Texas at Austin and his MA in behavioral management from the University of Texas at Dallas.

VERIZON

Verizon Communications Inc., headquartered in New York City, is a leader in delivering broadband and other wireline and wireless communication innovations to mass market, business, government, and wholesale customers. Visit Verizon at www.verizon.com.

Greg Miles

Greg Miles, Director of Verizon's Office of Ethics and Business Conduct, is charged with administering and enforcing Verizon's Code of Conduct and other compliance programs. Mr. Miles has a BS from Virginia State University. He also holds professional certifications from Cornell University, The Wharton School, Bentley College, and the Center for Creative Leadership—Leadership Excellence Program.

WEYERHAEUSER

Weyerhaeuser Company, one of the world's largest forest products companies, is principally engaged in the growing and harvesting of timber; the manufacture, distribution, and sale of forest products; and real estate construction, development, and related activities. Visit Weyerhaeuser at www.weyerhaeuser.com.

Nancy Thomas-Moore

Nancy Thomas-Moore is Weyerhaeuser's Director of Ethics and Business Conduct, and is responsible for the development and implementation of companywide ethics education, review and modification of the code of conduct, and resolution of business conduct issues. Ms. Thomas-Moore received her BA degree in Biblical Literature from Simpson College and her MBA from Pacific Lutheran University.

XEROX

Xerox is a multinational corporation, offering the broadest array of document products and services in the industry—copiers, printers, fax machines, scanners, desktop software, digital printing and publishing systems, supplies, and comprehensive document-management services—from the running of in-house production centers to the creation of networks. Visit Xerox at www.xerox.com.

Patricia Calkins

Patricia Calkins, Manager Environmental Market Leadership for Xerox Corporation, is responsible for establishing the company's strategic direction for environment, health, and safety. Ms. Calkins received her BA in Biology from Merrimack College, her MS in Civil/Environmental Engineering from Tufts University, and certificates from Northwestern University and Columbia University.

Additional information was provided by:

Tim Mazur, COO, The Ethics and Compliance Officer Association (ECOA).

NOTES

1. *Wall Street Journal,* May 5, 1983.
2. 1997 survey "Sources and Consequences of Work Place Pressure" by the Ethics and Compliance Officers Association (ECOA) and the American Society of Chartered Underwriters and Chartered Financial Consultants.
3. Ethics and Compliance Officers Association.
4. 2007 study by the Centre for Retail Research in England.
5. Ethics and Compliance Officers Association.
6. *The Chronicle of Philanthropy,* 2008.
7. World Health Organization, 2008.

3 STRATEGIC PLANNING

SHH! HE'S WORKING ON A LONG TERM STRATEGY!

MARKETING DIR.

by General Electric and ExxonMobil

PLANNING
by GE

Introduction

Every organization that intends to be successful should conduct marketing planning because it anticipates market opportunities and problems and allows time for a proper approach or solution to be attained.

Definition

Marketing planning is a detailed process of managing the organization's marketing mix, or elements of marketing, in order to accomplish the goals of the organization. This process entails researching potential options for the functional-, geographical-, and product-specific areas of the company and assigning responsibilities, budgets, and timelines. It comprises planning of all the activities involved in the development, design, creation, production, launch, distribution, advertising, promotion, public relations, and sale of a product (good or service).

Goals of Marketing Planning

Marketing goals evolve from general, long-term corporate goals. Effective marketing planning will allow for the successful realization of these goals. Marketing is responsible for planning activities that will increase the value of the business through outcomes, such as increasing sales and profits, improving quality, and reducing risk.

For example, General Electric's Equipment Financial Services has a marketing goal to create "targeted selling models for Construction Finance, facilitate greater sales efficiency by improved prioritization and improve the scalability of the sales model across both the direct and indirect value chain, and to rationalize and harmonize our value propositions to the target segments." This is directly linked to the corporate goal of increased sales and profits.

Increase Sales and Profit

Companies should set targets for *Operating Profits* (OP) and for unit and value share. OP describes the percentage of revenue after costs have been deducted. *Unit share* is the percentage of the total number of individual units sold in a given market. *Value share* is the percentage of total sales dollars generated by a product category in a given market. These percentages are frequently different from each other. For example, in a market in which 1,000 male shaving systems are sold, Gillette sells 500 of them, or 50 percent of the unit share. However, the Gillette system may sell at a higher retail price than competitive products, meaning that they achieve 60 percent of the value share in that category.

Improve Quality

Companies should constantly improve their product and service offerings. There are many ways to manage and measure quality improvements (described in detail in Chapter 19, "Product Quality"). Quality improvement goals include new features or upgrading performance, such as an increase in power or speed. Generally, a company will set quality goals based on a performance deficiency or upon improvements in competitors' products. A typical quality improvement goal includes the removal of negatives associated with product manufacturing and customer-oriented performance, such as the reduction of customer product returns and reduction of product failures in the field.

Reduce Risk

Risk is the possibility of suffering financial loss, such as loss of sales or loss of business. Planning helps to understand the organization's markets, product offerings, potential business climate, and so forth. Systematically creating a knowledge base will allow for more reliable choices, thus reducing the risk of failure.

Planning Perspective

The start-up of a company or the reinvention of a company could well begin in marketing. When looking beyond the current product range and served markets, it is important to ask several planning questions:

> "What might we sell (given our market access)?"
> "What new customers could we approach (given our capabilities)?"
> "What new product/service capabilities could we develop or acquire?"

Speedy competitive introduction of new products will continue to shorten planning timelines. Businesses will seek to gain competitive advantage by creating products and services that are unique and difficult to copy or reproduce. Businesses will continue to expand their operations worldwide in pursuit of growth through entry into new markets. This will put global marketing skills and the ability to create products and services that succeed worldwide at a premium. Companies will need to collaborate on marketing planning with people from a wide variety of cultures and disciplines. And it will be just as important to consider the requirements of three competing factors equally: the customer, the shareholder, and the employee.

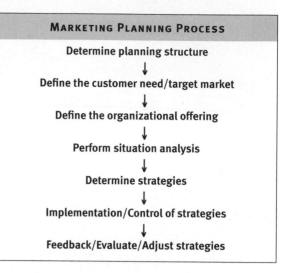

MARKETING PLANNING PROCESS

Determine planning structure
↓
Define the customer need/target market
↓
Define the organizational offering
↓
Perform situation analysis
↓
Determine strategies
↓
Implementation/Control of strategies
↓
Feedback/Evaluate/Adjust strategies

1. Determine Planning Structure

The planning structure consists of planning approaches or methods, planning time frames, and the planning participants.

Planning Methods

There are three basic methods to the planning process: top-down, bottom-up, and the team approach.

- **Top-down Planning.** Marketing plans are formulated by the senior executives and communicated to the rest of the staff who execute the plans. Advantages of top-down planning are a long-term, companywide perspective and the speed and ease of administrating the process. The disadvantage is the distances between the senior executive and the customer and the senior executive and the product development/manufacturing process.
- **Bottom-up Planning.** Marketing plans are formulated by people working at the operations and field level, then presented to and approved by senior executives. The advantage of bottom-up planning is that field and

operations personnel are closer to the customer and often have a better feel for the market. The disadvantage is the field level person's lack of overall company understanding.

- **Team Approach Planning.** There is early and continual interaction among various departments, such as marketing research, sales, manufacturing, and finance. The major advantage of team approach planning is the assurance that everyone associated with managing the business shares the same vision. The disadvantage is the cumbersome process of meetings.

Planning Time Frames
There are three basic time frames considered in planning: long-term, short-term, and continuous. Most businesses use a combination of the three.

- **Strategic (Long-Term) Planning.** The technology, capacity, personnel, and capital requirements of a company are forecast and typically focus on a three- to five-year outlook. For some industry segments, the product development cycle can be as long as seven years for industry-changing innovations such as using plastic to replace steel in some automobile parts. As part of this process, marketing takes an in-depth look at the market possibilities and the potential for new products. This activity is focused on understanding the needs, challenges, trends, and vulnerabilities of each industry, and assessing them in a competitive context. Formerly, some businesses attempted ultra long-range planning, from 15 to 20 years, but found that the business and competitive environment were changing too rapidly for this effort to be effective.
- **Tactical (Short-Term) Planning.** The operating plan is prepared for one year. The following year's opportunities usually are set by long-term development cycles, with effective implementation being the key to delivering results. Competitive shortcomings or new opportunities determined through the situation analysis process may change the short-term marketing possibilities. The advantage of short-term

planning is the ability to be flexible and react quickly to market changes and opportunities. The disadvantage is that the short-term outlook does not budget for long-term research, which may uncover new areas in which the company is not currently participating.

- **Continuous Planning.** The participants meet regularly, usually weekly or monthly. The representatives of the planning group meet or have a teleconference with the field marketing leaders to exchange information, ideas, and requirements, and to agree on action plans. These discussions can be wide-ranging and/or very specific in nature, depending entirely upon the needs and characteristics of each situation. The advantage of this dialogue is that the product and service requirements needed to solve problems, retain business, and gain sales are determined early. The disadvantage is the time spent in meetings that disrupts work schedules.

Planning Participants
Different planning methods and time frames require participants from different areas and levels of expertise.

- **Strategic Planning.** The corporate mission, objectives, and goals are part of the input. The following individuals are usually involved: the Chief Executive Officer (CEO), the Chief Financial Officer (CFO), the Chief Operating Officer (COO), the Chief Marketing Officer (CMO), as well as Executive Vice Presidents.
- **Tactical Planning.** Marketing objectives, goals, and strategies are discussed. The following people are usually involved: the Vice President of Marketing, Sales Director, Public Relations Director, Advertising Director, and the Marketing Research Director. For operational planning, where execution, implementation, and tasks are discussed, the following levels are usually involved: district sales managers, senior account supervisors, and senior sales representatives.
- **Continuous Planning.** Input comes from sev-

eral areas within the company. These cross-functional teams are comprised of personnel from the different areas listed above plus headquarters marketing and field marketing.

2. Define Customer Needs/Target Market Segmentation

It is essential that customer needs be clearly and succinctly defined. These are determined through marketing research with an understanding of consumer and organizational needs and buying behavior.

Not every consumer or organization will have identical needs. Therefore, the next step is to break the total market into potential customer segments that have similar needs. In marketing, the fundamental unit of planning is the market segment, or target market. A *target market* or *market segment* is comprised of a set of actual and potential users of a product or service. *Segmentation* allows for a more precise response to customer needs, a more precise tracking of the performance of an individual product in the market, and a reasonable marketing budget that does not include all consumers and/or companies. Defining customer segments is accomplished through marketing research. There are many market segments with the list changing from time to time, but not very rapidly. The target market generally may be defined as mass or niche, consumer or organizational, or core/new.

Mass Marketing/Niche Marketing

Planners should decide through marketing research and an analysis of the core competencies whether their company will target a mass market or a niche market.

- **Mass Market.** This is the largest possible grouping of potential users of the product or service. There are some products/services that virtually all customers use, such as clothing, food, tissue paper, or mattresses. The advantages of marketing to such a large audience are the potential for large sales revenue and economies of scale in production. The disadvantage is the immense competition for the same market. For example, GAP attempts to sell khakis to all people, and their ads reflect a broad cross-section of consumers.

- **Niche market.** A subset of the mass market, niche markets are determined by demographics or customer needs. Consumers may have a need for inexpensive tissue paper versus the desire for lanolin and antibiotic impregnated tissue paper. Businesses may have a need for more flexible terms and conditions, or broader service support, such as 24/7 × 365. The advantage of this approach is the potential for higher per unit profits as customers pay incrementally higher amounts to satisfy specific needs, as well as the benefit of less competition. The disadvantage is the smaller market and lower overall profit potential. For example, Buckle stores sell trendy clothes to teens in rural settings.

Consumer Market/Organizational Market

The consumer and organizational markets are described in detail in Chapters 6 and 7.

- **Consumer Market.** May be segmented by demographics (age, income, gender) and psychographics (values, lifestyles, beliefs). For example, a record company may target teens by advertising on MTV and target retirees by advertising on the History Channel.

- **Organizational Market.** May be segmented by businesses (manufacturing, wholesale, retail, transportation), governments (federal, state, local, international), institutions (schools, hospitals, prisons), and organizational size (small businesses, large businesses). For example, in the manufacturing market, there are three types of customers: companies that purchase products (Original Equipment Manufacturers or OEMs), companies (such as engineering and consulting firms) that specify the use of products to end users, and companies that participate in the supply chain (such as subassemblers and distributors).

Core/New Markets

- **Core Market.** One in which the applications are established and form the heart of the current business. This does not imply that these segments are static in their product development possibilities or in the needs of the existing product applications. There are frequently new (and revolutionary) applications available in markets that are well-established users of a product. For example, GE Mining's vertical strategy integrates several business offerings from the Water, Energy, Motors, Transportation, and Enterprise Solutions Organization, to create two mining division segments or core markets: operations and transport.

- **New Market.** One in which the cost or performance case for the product or service has yet to be introduced or widely accepted and established by actual practice. New markets may be determined by applying accepted products to new customers or finding new uses for existing products. (See Chapter 15, "Product Management.") Generally more time and resources are required to create product demand in new markets, because the company has to become familiar with the needs of the new client base and the client base has to become more familiar with the new product.

3. Define Organizational Offering

Companies must determine what goods or services they will offer to their customers to fulfill their needs. Defining the organizational offering (goods or services) has three steps: define core competencies, match core competencies with customer needs, and define the value proposition and differentiation features/benefits.

Define Core Competencies

The first step involves gathering data on the company's core competencies. A *core competency* is that which a company does best and its major reason for business success. Business is very competitive and those companies that can concentrate on one area and do it better than all competitors have a better chance of succeeding. This step should include inputs from a cross section of the company's departments/functions. Core competencies may include brand name recognition, technological product quality, manufacturing capacity, pricing strategies, after-the-sale service capabilities, or special distribution networks. For example, GE Transportation's core technical competencies are in engineering high-performance locomotives, parts and services, and signaling.

Some companies have too broad a focus and overextend management, marketing, and financial capabilities. These companies may eventually shut down or sell off divisions resulting in loss of sales and jobs. For example, NCR, in order to avoid being overextended, decided to concentrate on software development and data-warehousing services, and sold several manufacturing operations.

Some companies have too narrow a focus, relying too heavily on current product lines, and may miss growth opportunities from new products/ services or new customers and therefore may lose business or fail altogether. For example, the leaders of the vacuum tube industry did not become leaders in the transistor industry. Similarly, the leaders of the transistor industry did not become leaders in the microchip industry. A specific example of broadening perspectives is the shift of BP, the oil and gas company, to encompass the renewable energy business.

Match Core Competencies with Customer Needs

The next step is to match the core competencies against customer requirements to determine the product offering. Marketing research should collect and analyze data on the targeted market, competitor strengths and weaknesses, existing product feature trends and gaps (if any), major customer segments, customers' buying habits/preferences, and customer critical-to-quality factors (CTQs). Customer CTQs include both hard performance-oriented expectations (such as material properties for a polymer) plus soft performance-oriented expectations (such as a positive sales and service follow-up experience). The ultimate product offering needs to be designed to maximize customer satisfaction. From this data, planners can assess what features a company should offer that will fill important feature gaps and/or address a key competitor weakness for specific customer segments. For example, GE Oil & Gas products fill a customer's need for oil extraction capabilities at a higher rate of barrels per day.

Define Value Proposition/Product Differentiation

The next step, and a primary company objective, is to be the best at satisfying a particular customer need and therefore deliver a specific customer benefit. A company must determine a *value proposition*, or define their strategic reason why a customer would choose their company brand in general or their product specifically. This value proposition of a product offering is what sets the good or service apart, or differentiates it, from the competition. Brand managers set the company's brand apart from the competition in order to meet customers' needs. For example, Wal-Mart promoted lower prices and Target aired hip ads, and both have been successful. Kmart never broke out of the middle and ended up filing for bankruptcy.

Differentiation determines a unique set of features or benefits that will appeal to the target market's needs. *Features* are the physical element of a product or service, such as seat belts. *Benefits* are the met needs of the customer, such as reduced injury during an automobile collision. Differentiation can be achieved through any (or a combination) of the elements of the marketing mix.

The offerings that satisfy customer needs will form the basis for the company goal of relationship marketing. *Relationship marketing* is the ability of a company to offer something of value to the customer, which the customer feels most comfortable purchasing from that particular company. The product or service specifically meets the customer's needs as determined through continuous dialogue between the customer and the company.

4. Perform Situation Analysis

The next step is to perform an analysis or evaluation of the business itself and the business and social environment in which the company is operating in order to determine how these factors impact the customers' needs and wants and the company's ability to satisfy these needs. In general, this step is an ongoing process.

Supply → External/Internal Variables → Demand

Internal Variables

An internal variable originates within the organization or stems from an organization's activities, and generally is thought of as being within the control of the organization. Internal variables primarily consist of the current corporate mission, the current marketing mix, and the current business capabilities.

- **Corporate Mission and Marketing Objectives.** In a start-up company, establishing corporate mission and objective statements is a first step in the planning process. Marketing planning should be accomplished in light of the overall corporate mission and objectives, such as financial goals for shareholders, employment goals

PRODUCT DIFFERENTIATION		
Marketing Element	Differentiating Aspect	Example
Product	Quality	GM Cadillac
	Uniqueness	L.L. Bean boots
Pricing	Lowest	Costco
	Highest	Tiffany
Promotion	Attention getting	Pedigree Dog Adoption ads
	Desire creating	Saks ads
Distribution	Right place	7-Eleven locations everywhere
	Right time	1–800flowers.com available 24/7

for employees, and need fulfillment goals for customers. Specific marketing goals that follow typically include increased customer satisfaction, increased sales, improved brand image, and increased market share. For example, the mission of the Gillette Company "is to achieve or enhance clear leadership worldwide in the existing or new consumer categories in which they choose to compete." That means that the marketing plans must be formulated to ensure that category leadership is achieved or enhanced. In support of the overall mission, a company should set both general and specific objectives. A company may wish to increase sales by a certain percentage each year, introduce a certain number of new products, or increase their involvement in their community. For example, Gillette "seeks to increase its pace of new product development, so that a certain percentage of the company's sales derives from products introduced within the previous five years." L.L. Bean's mission is to "sell good merchandise at a reasonable profit, treat your customers like human beings, and they will always come back for more."

- **Current Marketing Mix.** The *marketing mix* consists of products, pricing, marketing communications, and the supply chain.

  ○ *Products.* Any marketing activity should be planned within the context of the company's current *product mix* (also known as *portfolio* or *basket*) and where each is located in its product life cycle (discussed in the "Product Management," Chapter 15). Often, a good or service is introduced or repositioned in order to fill a gap in a company's product line. Every change in a company's offering is likely to affect every other offering. For example, when Gillette introduces a new, improved shaving system, the company expects and desires that the new product will take market share away from its older, existing product. This intentional act, known as *cannibalism*, allows greater marketing emphasis and budgeting to be placed on the new product.

  ○ *Pricing.* The price of a product is determined by the costs required to develop and manufacture the product, the sales and profit objectives established for the product, the projected lifetime of the product, and the competitive market conditions. Determining the optimum price for a product is key to achieving its success. This requires assessing the product costs, forecasting the unit sales over a given period of

---

DSC LOGISTICS PARTNERSHIP STATEMENT

Vision:
It is the parties' shared vision to leverage our capabilities in teamwork, technology, manufacturing, logistics, and information resources. Integrating our capabilities under a process of continuous improvement, we will achieve operational excellence and exceptional products and services at the lowest system cost.

Mission:
To successfully leverage integrated manufacturing and logistics capabilities, and to ensure continuing competitive advantage in a rapidly changing marketplace and deliver outstanding products and services and minimum system costs.

Goals:
Provide service which exceeds customer requirements.
Continually lower systems costs.
Develop a framework that emphasizes ease of operation.
Provide the opportunity to capitalize on value-added services.
Work cooperatively to achieve expanded market share.
Establish and monitor benchmarks to assure the partnership's performance.

Source: DSC Logistics

time, setting a desired profit margin, and setting a unit price accordingly. Some products may be priced below typical retail in order to attract new customers, service existing ones, or enter new markets. Some products that have substantial competitive advantage may be priced at a substantial premium, and the profits may carry other underperforming products in the company's portfolio. For example, Gillette sells its flagship male shaving systems at a premium because the company considers that their products deliver clear and perceptible benefits to the consumer and sets the appropriate corporate image.

◦ *Marketing Communications.* Marketing planning involves the provision for communications among a number of constituencies both inside and outside the corporation. Effective communications are essential between company personnel and external parties, including partners, suppliers, distributors, and sales outlets. It is important that key internal groups have effective means of communicating and sharing information among themselves. A plan for which groups should be in communication with other groups, and at what points in any given process, is often developed as a *flow chart* or *process diagram*.

◦ *Supply Chain/Distribution.* Planning considers the various supply chain partners for the optimal distribution and delivery of products to the customer.

• **Current Business Capabilities.** These include manufacturing, research and development, suppliers, financial resources, and personnel resources.

◦ *Manufacturing.* Manufacturing is responsible for the technology and manufacturing of the company's products, and there is continual comparison of the two perspectives: marketing and manufacturing. A marketing viewpoint starts with the customers' needs

and applications (*pull marketing*) whereas a manufacturing viewpoint starts with product properties and production capabilities and their potential to satisfy customer needs (*push marketing*). This interaction is continual and designed to maximize the value to the customer.

◦ *Research and Development.* It is important to know the research and prototyping capabilities of the company's research and development (R&D) labs. This process can be done in-house or outsourced. For example, GE has capabilities for full prototyping at its appliance division but can only test subassemblies at its jet engine facility. In addition, R&D should be consulted for new product ideas and potential new product features.

◦ *Suppliers.* As companies focus on their core competencies, push into new geographic markets, and seek to outsource activities that are not profitable for them or in which they have no special expertise, the role of the supplier and partner has become increasingly important. Very often, a supplier is responsible for delivering a critical aspect of a product or service. For example, a vehicle manufacturer may work with a design firm to create a new car design, and an advertising agency may work with freelance directors to create television commercials. Marketing planning, therefore, should take into account those activities that will be accomplished in-house and those that will be outsourced. Partners and suppliers should be managed so that they understand the company's objectives, cost constraints, schedules, and other requirements.

◦ *Financial Resources.* Every marketing activity will be constrained by the amount of financial resources available. Even a company with large amounts of capital available must weigh the optimum use of that capital for marketing. For example, Gillette will commit substantial capital to the development and launch of its key male shaving products ($750 million was spent to bring the MACH3 razor to market). Other companies, such as fashion retailers, will commit large amounts of capital to product advertising and promotion, and relatively little to product development.

○ *Personnel Resources.* Most companies today operate with as few layers of authority as possible. The result is that most jobs are complex and employees tend to work on multiple projects and assignments at all times. In addition, people with specialized skills, such as computer programmers, multilingual human resource professionals, and top executives are generally in high demand within the organization. Marketing planning should therefore take into account the personnel required for any marketing project or task, when the people will be needed, and for how long. It may be necessary to hire new staff or reassign people within the company to accomplish a specific goal.

External Variables

An external variable affects the organization from outside its control. External variables include the competition, societal norms/culture, the economy, government regulations, and technological change.

- **Competition.** The company's competitors must be well understood. A determination should be made of the competitor's capabilities, particularly regarding the types of offerings where the competition is strongest. For example, the U.S. automobile industry constantly researches the quality of Japanese cars.

- **Societal Norms/Culture.** Marketing takes place within the context of the society in which the company's products or services are sold. Many products are highly affected by sociocultural factors and require constant planning, such as

toys, clothing, computers, and cars. Some products are designed to respond to the most basic and long-term needs of a society, such as food staples or building materials, and are less affected by short-term events or national trends. However, even these products gradually change as a result of cultural shifts, and marketing planners should periodically review and research these products. An example is the long-term trend toward natural foods.

Also, many products are designed for selling in more than one geographic market. This requires very careful understanding and testing of how a product will be perceived, accepted, and used in each market. For example, because male shaving habits show little variation from market to market, Gillette is able to create a single product that meets the needs of men worldwide.

Occasionally, products fail in a specific country because of a lack of planning for cultural differences, such as a product name that means something odd in the local language, or features that do not respond to local customer needs. For example, sales of the Chevrolet Nova, which means "brightness" in English, were slow in Latin America until General Motors realized that *no va* means "it does not go" in Spanish.

CHANGING SOCIETAL NORMS

What percentage of U.S. households consist of only one person? Today, over one quarter of all U.S. households consist of only one person. These households consist of: the young single person, the older divorced parents whose children have moved out, and widows and widowers, who are increasing in number because of longer life expectancies. Football is the most watched sport on American TV. What sport is #2? It is ice skating. Since the last Winter Olympics, ice skating has become an enormously popular spectator sport in the United States.

Source: Colgate Palmolive

- **The Economy.** Marketing planning should take into account the economic conditions of the markets into which the company's products or services will be sold. Economic conditions include current and projected conditions. A number of economic variables are usually considered, including rate of economic growth, employment, interest rates, inflation rates, availability of investment capital, availability of skilled labor, national debt, and the national mood usually expressed through retail sales or consumer confidence levels.
- **Government Regulations.** These are issued at the federal, state, local, and international levels. Changes in regulations can create opportunities or threats. For example, changes in environmental performance requirements for an industry could open up new markets for the first manufacturer that meets the new codes. A continual monitoring of regulatory activity is necessary. It often is possible to help shape these regulations, through government relations, as part of the marketing activity.
- **Technological Change.** Company growth may rely on new products or improvements in existing products. Company decline may result from a competitor's technological improvement. Technology changes rapidly, and planning should incorporate reviews of industrial, governmental, and academic laboratory reports.

5. Determine Marketing Strategies

There are never enough resources to research in great detail and sell to every market. The goal is to prioritize and sell to those markets that represent the majority of the current business and/or provide the most significant growth opportunities. For example, GE Aviation's approach has always been to stimulate core markets to innovate, which requires considerable understanding of the nature of an industry, the forces at work within it, and the places and applications where change is most likely. The long-term planning process categorizes markets and leads to the determination of what level of coverage is appropriate to achieve what is necessary in that market. There are some market segments for which there is no marketing development, but rather only selling to the segment upon their request.

No strategy can achieve every marketing objective. The optimum strategy is the one that best supports the corporate objectives, that has the highest probability of being successful, and that best utilizes the company's resources.

Strategic Business Plan

Each organization creates its own *strategic business plan* (SBP) that includes extensive detail about objectives, market conditions, expected financial performance results, financial performance targets, product plans, organizational structure, budgets, schedules, and critical success factors. These plans typically are developed by a committee comprised of the executives of each operating unit, and presented to the chairman or president each year for approval or adjustment.

Strategic Business Unit

Companies typically form separate units of their organization centered around separate products or markets, each called a *strategic business unit* (SBU). SBUs are set up to facilitate planning, budgeting, and market focus. Companies or SBUs determine the best mix of strategies for products/service offerings, pricing, marketing communications, and supply chain management through management expertise and planning tools.

Positioning

Positioning is the targeting of product attributes and demand promotion toward a definable target audience segment that yields the greatest profits. Planners should *position* each product relative to the competition so that the customer's perspective finds the product offering superior to the competitor's brand. The product's best features and benefits should be strengthened to be superior to the competition's and then promoted in marketing communications to the customer.

Each customer chooses a product based on preference for a combination of price and quality.

The more customers that agree on a specific combination, the greater the value to the company of positioning their products to meet that particular customer demand. Depending on the company's capabilities, some niches on the customer choice grid may be more profitable than others (see Figure 3.1).

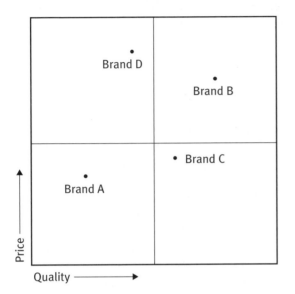

Figure 3.1 Positioning on the Customer Choice Grid.

Marketing Mix Strategies
Each element of the marketing mix has several strategy options, which are detailed in this book. These factors depend on the financial resources available and the skill qualities of the management team.

- Target Market Demand (consumer, organization)
- Demand Promotion / Marketing Communications (advertising, public relations, promotional marketing, direct marketing, brand ambassadors)
- Product – goods and services (quality, uniqueness, design looks, functionality)
- Pricing (high, low, image, corporate need)
- Distribution (wholesaling, warehousing, transportation, retailing, internet retailing)

Marketing Strategy Planning Tools
There are several planning tools that can be used to facilitate the creation of marketing mix strategies, including product grid, Six Sigma, SWOT, and market share matrix.

- **Product Grid.** This shows all the products that all the divisions of a company will launch in a given time period. For example, Gillette plans its new product development on a five-year grid. It identifies potential synergies among operating units that could be leveraged for joint-product development (such as Gillette's Braun unit, which makes small household appliances, and Duracell, which makes batteries). It also classifies each new product as *incremental* (a minor improvement to an existing product) or as a *breakthrough* (usually involving a new technology and warranting a new product name).
- **Design for Six Sigma.** An analysis tool used for marketing opportunity and innovation is called Design for Six Sigma. The objective of this tool is to produce a high-quality business opportunity design through the use of statistical analysis. Use of data-driven decisions is the general practice for engineers designing new products. Marketing and business development functions can apply a similar practice to select new market opportunities, define new products, track market behavior after product launch, and to improve sales efforts.
Sigma is a letter of the Greek alphabet used as a symbol by statisticians to mark a *bell curve* showing the likelihood that something will vary from the *norm*. The statistical definition of Six Sigma is 3.4 defects per 1 million opportunities, or 99.9997 percent perfect. Most good companies operate at less than four sigma, which is 99 percent perfect. For perspective, operating at only three or four sigma means 20,000 lost articles of mail per hour, unsafe drinking water almost 15 minutes each day, 5,000 incorrect surgical operations per week, and 200,000 wrong drug prescriptions each year. The goal is to move the marketing capabilities to Six Sigma.

The Six Sigma approach has five major steps:

- *Define.* Identify the market opportunity and general technical scope based on existing knowledge and secondary research.
- *Measure.* Focus the primary data gathering within the context of business opportunity through the use of cross-functional teams to translate the voice of the customer into measurable customer needs and expectations. The use of more nontraditional data gathering tools, such as customer site visits, team-based market research, and end-user research, is encouraged.
- *Analyze.* Analyze the data to generate a concept design (market segmentation, product concept) and to define the most attractive product opportunity using mathematical transfer functions to calculate customer expectation measures versus design variables.
- *Design.* Evaluate the impact of alternative strategies and concepts. Develop a detailed design for the most attractive approach using system cost model, product scorecard (quantitative measure against customer expectations, wants).
- *Verify.* Determine that the opportunity is real through business case studies, such as prelaunch focus groups, which verify cost and quality targets.

The key deliverables include a business model and forecast, a prioritized list of customers' expectations and needs, and a top-level product or service configuration plan.

- **SWOT.** *SWOT* is an acronym for the process of analyzing a company's *Strengths*, *Weaknesses*, *Opportunities*, and *Threats*. This process is done in conjunction with the process of determining the internal and external situation analysis and helps to determine a company's planning focus. When a company's internal strength, such as a technical patent, matches an external opportunity, such as a competitor's possible sale, the company should plan to *leverage* the strength by taking advantage of the opportunity, such as acquiring the company and making use of its idle manufacturing facilities. When opportunities are present and the company cannot respond due to a weakness, such as lack of capital, the company is *restrained* from taking advantage of the opportunity. The company should plan to reverse this particular weakness. When there is a new threat (such as a new competitor) to an existing strength, the company should focus on this new *vulnerability*, typically by reinforcing the strength. When there is a threat to a weak area it is called a problem, and the company should plan to make the weak area a strength or consider divestiture.

Typical marketing opportunities include the development of a breakthrough product, technology, or service; the failure of a competitive product; identification of a new demographic or geographic market; identification of a new application or use for a product or service; a potential tie-in with an event or activity; and a new law or regulation.

SWOT		
Strengths		**Opportunities**
Good product quality		New markets
Promotion quality		New products
Good name recognition		New technology
Low costs		
Weaknesses		**Threats**
Poor name recognition		Loss of customer base
Poor product quality		New competitors
Weak promotion capabilities		Regulatory restraints
High costs		

Typical marketing threats include the loss of market share, the emergence of a new competitor or competitive product, inability to manufacture enough products to meet demand, excess on-hand inventory, price-cutting in the marketplace, slow sales, labor disputes or strikes, poor product distribution, and poor product or service positioning.

- **Market Share Matrix.** Often called the *Boston Consulting Group Matrix*, the market share matrix gives planners a simple methodology for allocating corporate resources toward their products/services offering. "The first objective of corporate strategy is protection of the cash generators. Only the largest two or three competitors in any product-market segment can reasonably expect to avoid being a cash trap. However, there are usually several times that number of active competitors."[1] Market growth or attractiveness is correlated against a company's product strength or market share.

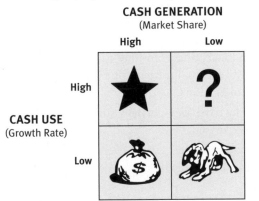

Figure 3.2 Market Share Matrix

Source: The Boston Consulting Group. Reprinted with permission.

- ○ **High growth/High competitive advantage (Stars).** A few products are self-sufficient in cash flow. A strategy is to reinvest in the product to keep ahead of large competitive base.
- ○ **Low growth/High competitive advantage (Cash Cows).** A few products generate far more cash than they can profitably reinvest. A strategy is to use the profits to reinforce other products or to grow new products.

- ○ **High growth/Low competitive advantage (Question Marks).** Many products require far more cash input than they can generate. A strategy is to invest enough to grow the product or to withdraw the product.
- ○ **Low growth/Low competitive advantage (Dogs/Cash Traps).** Many products generate very little cash flow even though they use very little. Profits probably will always need to be reinvested. A strategy is to withdraw or to sell the product.

6. Implementation/Control of Strategies

After an optimum strategy has been selected, the next step is the control process that is necessary to assure successful implementation. The control process includes establishing goals, responsibilities, and activity schedules; delegating tasks; and motivating personnel.

Establish Goals/Budgets/Timelines

A marketing plan includes descriptions of all tasks that must be accomplished, detailed budgets for each task and activity, and schedules that include start and end points, with critical milestones along the way. This is coordinated between the marketing department and the sales department. The planning gets down to the level of individual accounts, ensuring that there is the right level of resource behind each account.

Establish Responsibilities/Performance Indicators

The marketing plan should establish management responsibilities. A common problem in organizations is that personnel do not have clearly defined responsibilities and roles. As a result, they may devote time to tasks that are not within their scope of responsibility, neglect tasks that need attention, or waste time trying to define what they should be doing.

The marketing plan also should set performance goals for each individual, so that he or she knows what is expected of him or her. There are many kinds of performance goals, including the achievement of a sales target, the successful management of a budget, the completion of a project, the launch of a new project, the reduction of costs, the training of personnel, or the acquisition of a new skill. An employee's performance evaluation should be based on whether the employee achieved these predetermined goals.

Performance indicators can be objective or subjective:

- **Quantitative, or objective, performance indicators.** These can be determined numerically. Generally, they are linked to the objectives established at the beginning of the planning process and include objectives for unit sales, market share, value share, stock price, number of customers, number of shipments, productivity, and speed-to-market. The advantages of objective performance indicators are that they are impartial and easy to administer.
- **Qualitative, or subjective, performance indicators.** These are extremely varied and include those areas that cannot be specifically quantified. Subjective indicators include corporate or product image, customer satisfaction, and industry influence. The advantage of these indicators is the overall sense of customer needs and marketing direction.

Establish Activity Schedules/Operating Plans

An activity schedule adds more detail to the overall timeline, shows the specific tasks that must be accomplished, and indicates the order in which they must be completed. Activities that can be conducted simultaneously, in order to save time, also are indicated.

Delegate Tasks/Assign Authority

Each of the tasks identified must be delegated to a department, operating unit, group, team, or individual. The person selected will have authority to make unilateral decisions (sign-off authority) and will have the ultimate decision-making authority in the case of a dispute or disagreement.

Lead/Motivate

Once the marketing plan is complete, execution and implementation may begin. The role of the marketing executive or manager is to ensure that the plan is executed as designed, or, in the case of changes or unforeseen circumstances, to adjust the plan as needed. In most organizations today, the manager is expected to help people understand their responsibilities, secure resources, solve problems, resolve disputes, and provide encouragement and support, with the goal of executing the plan so that the objectives are met on time and within budget.

7. Feedback/Evaluate/Adjust Strategies

After the marketing plans have been implemented, it is essential to receive feedback indicating actual performance. The plan should be evaluated by comparing the selected performance indicators against actual performance. Once the marketing plan has been executed and evaluated, it should be adjusted to make any necessary improvements.

- The marketing plan may be sufficiently successful to be continued for a second time with few alterations.
- It may have been partially successful and need to be revised.
- It may be judged to have been a failure and discontinued altogether.

THE BUSINESS PLAN/MARKETING PLAN

The primary challenge in marketing is to convert a product or service idea into a successful business. Every great idea needs a business and marketing plan to bring the idea to market. The objective of the business and marketing plan is to detail a strategy or blueprint for running the business and act as a vehicle to attract sufficient capital to finance the plan. The business plan outlined below lists the elements typically found in a request for funding.

BUSINESS PLAN

I.   **Business Opportunity**
   A.   Consumer needs
   B.   Product/service description
   C.   Potential for growth

II. **Executive Summary**
   A.   Description of business
   B.   Funding needs analysis (% equity, % debt)
   C.   Projected return to investors
   D.   Timetable for use of funds and repayment of loan
   E.   Key personnel

III. **Business Description**
   A.   Location and description of business
   B.   Legal form of business and tax status election
   C.   Products/services provided (companywide)
   D.   Competition
   E.   Personnel policies and incentives
   F.   Company advantages (patents, resources)

IV. **Management Expertise**
   A.   Key personnel and related experience
   B.   Board of Directors
   C.   Officers
   D.   Organization chart

V.   **Products or Services (specific to the business plan)**
   A.   Full description of products or services
   B.   Manufacturing process
   C.   Competition (product specific)

VI. **Marketing Plan**
   A.   Source of customer base (target segment, size)
   B.   Product sales strategy/goals
   C.   Packaging
   D.   Pricing strategy and factors affecting
   E.   Promotional strategies (advertising, PR, promotional marketing, DM)
   F.   Distribution (transportation modes, warehousing)
   G.   Marketing research capabilities

VII. **Financial Detail**
   A.   Financial statements (historical)
   B.   Financial statements (projected)
   C.   Uses of funds (specific)
   D.   Projected return to investors
   E.   Collateral
   F.   Exit strategy (eventual sale of business)

Source: A. G. Bennett, Compiled from major banks.

PLANNING—INTERNATIONAL
by ExxonMobil

The international marketplace is dominated by products, services, and brand names that have migrated across the borders of every developed country and many developing countries around the globe. The ubiquity of these products, services, and brand names attests to the current sophistication of international marketing. A large part of this sophistication hinges on the planning and organization of a corporation's international marketing efforts. A corporation's planning and organizational structure directly influences its competitive advantage.

Planning

Marketing planning includes defining objectives, assessing resources, formulating marketing mix strategies, and determining operational plans. International planning adds the assessment of international opportunities and risks and international trade entry strategies.

Opportunity Assessment

International marketing provides many opportunities for companies, including:

- Sales growth from exports to new markets
- Sales growth from new product imports
- New product and service ideas
- New production and distribution methods

Risk Assessment

There also are many risks for companies involved in international marketing, including:

- Financial (tariffs, nontariff barriers, cash flow, currency conversion, profit repatriation, tax considerations)
- Political (nationalization/property seizure, buy local edicts)
- Military (insurrection, war)
- Cultural (language, religious differences)
- Legal (intellectual property rights, product dumping, industrial espionage, contract abrogation)
- Infrastructure standards (metric measurements, left side driving, electrical standards)

International Trade Entry Strategies

If a company decides that the opportunities outweigh the risks, there are several strategies for entering the international trade arena. These include:

- **Product Export.** The advantages of exporting are the control of product quality, economies of scale from existing plants, and expansion of local jobs. Disadvantages are the cost of shipping and potential difficulty of changing manufacturing to accommodate foreign product specifications.
- **Foreign Licensing/Royalty Agreements.** The advantage of foreign licensing is the additional profit with no additional infrastructure costs involved. The disadvantage is disclosing sources and processes to a potential future competitor.
- **Joint Venture.** The advantages of a joint venture are the sharing of costs and the immediate addition of outside infrastructure or capabilities. The disadvantage may be the political requirement of a joint venture where a major investment is given for a small return.
- **Direct Investment in Foreign Facilities.** The advantages of direct investment are the quicker responsiveness to foreign customer needs and the attainment of local host country visibility. The disadvantages are the cost of additional infrastructure and the time spent on siting and constructing facilities.

Organizational Structure

Companies such as GM, Ford, IBM, and Coca-Cola that continually reevaluate their organizational structures and planning processes thrive in the global marketplace. Those that are fixed to old paradigms and do not incorporate new global structuring, such as Gulf and Tennaco, cease to exist.

In order to optimally organize and manage international operations, it is important to understand the larger influences and constraints of the international marketplace. A competitive international organization must take into account a myriad of issues such as regional differences, governmental issues, and transcontinental distances while being organizationally structured to provide customers with clear expectations of its goods, the greatest value, and a reasonable cost. International organizations encounter two opposing organizational approaches: integration and variation.

Organizational Approaches/Influences

- *Integration* centralizes the organization by giving corporate headquarters tight control over marketing, product development, and operations. This is done in order to minimize costs and maximize focus on the corporation's primary strategic objectives. Companies increasingly require integration of their worldwide operations in order to achieve economies-of-scale while meeting consumer demand on a global or regional basis.
- The international marketplace encompasses a wide *variation* in consumer preferences and in economic development. This creates a need to accommodate variation and leads to decentralization of the organization. Control is disseminated to local regions. Local subsidiaries in a decentralized organization are able to accommodate the need for more local differentiation and responsiveness to the fast-changing opportunities and threats of individual country markets. International market differences in consumer taste, market structure, and governmental regulation require close monitoring and finely tuned responses. Often, headquarters finds itself too distant from the regional issues to keep up with them and implement responses.

Organizational Models

As corporations have organized in order to respond to these two opposing needs, three organizational models have evolved: the domestic market extension model, the multidomestic market model, and the global market model.

- **Domestic Market Extension Model.** This model is chosen when the domestic marketing mix is centralized and extended unchanged to foreign markets. The advantage of market extension is its ease of administration. The disadvantage of market extension is the difficulty responding to diverse worldwide demands in a timely and effective manner. For example, Coca-Cola withdrew their two-liter bottle from Spain because few consumers owned refrigerators that would accommodate the large bottles. Hallmark cards initially failed in France because the French prefer writing their own cards and disliked the sentiments that Hallmark cards contained.
- **Multidomestic Market Model.** This model is chosen when control is spread to local affiliates that are loosely held together by corporate headquarters. This decentralized organizational structure tailors the marketing mix to suit the individual characteristics of each foreign market. The advantage is increased responsiveness to the individual market. The disadvantages may be duplication of efforts, inefficiencies in operations, and barriers to learning across the organization. For example, when IBM first began to market computers overseas in the late 1940s, it set up an affiliate structure consisting of autonomous units in 58 key markets around the world. Each subsidiary was responsible for marketing IBM products and executing marketing research and development. This structure enabled IBM to establish a firm foothold in critical markets and to develop strong relationships with vendors and distributors. However, this level of decentralization made it impossible for IBM to quickly identify and react to industry trends. By the 1980s, the company was lagging behind its competition in pricing, service, and the rate of technological innovation. In 1995, IBM unified its subsidiaries into a global marketing strategy that aligned all marketing communications around the world while allowing for a level of local customization. This overhaul had dramatic results; today IBM is considered one of the top 10 global brands.

- **Global Market Model.** This model integrates the simultaneous demands of integration and variation by creating a master marketing mix to suit large sets of varying markets around the world, with local subsidiaries adapting strategies that are cost-effective and culturally appropriate. The global market model, or integrated network structure, is an organization that concentrates control, coordination, and strategic decision processes at a corporation's headquarters whereas technology, finances, people, and materials flow between interdependent corporate units in foreign countries.

Within a global market strategy, headquarters sets the primary strategic direction for the corporation, determines the direction of the brand, and coordinates the strategic objectives and operating policies across businesses, functions, and geographic units. Headquarters also ensures that flows of supplies, components, and funds are coordinated throughout the organization. The marketing manager ensures the transfer of knowledge, skills, responsibilities, and resources to the local unit to develop its contribution to the larger organization.

At the country or regional level, subdivisions must implement and adapt corporate directives and policies while sensing and responding to the demands and opportunities of the local market. The country manager communicates opportunities and threats in the local market to corporate headquarters, advocates the country organization's interests, and implements the corporate strategy.

The global market strategy has a number of advantages. First, corporations can realize economies of scale in production and marketing. For example, Ford estimates that it can save up to $2 billion a year in product development, purchasing, and supply activities by adopting a global orientation. Secondly, a global orientation allows for a greater transfer of experience and know-how across countries. Finally, the global orientation supports a uniform global brand image.

In the integrated networks of many corporations, national units are no longer viewed simply as delivery pipelines for company products, the implementers of centrally defined strategies, or local adapters of corporate approaches. Instead, they are viewed as sources of ideas, skills, capabilities, and knowledge that can be harnessed for the benefit of the entire organization.

NOTES

1. *The Boston Consulting Group on Strategy,* 2nd ed., edited by Carl W. Stern and Michael S. Deimier, (Hoboken, NJ: John Wiley & Sons, 2006).

CORPORATE PROFILES AND AUTHOR BIOGRAPHIES

GE (NYSE: GE)

GE (General Electric) is a diversified global infrastructure, finance and media company that is built to meet essential world needs, from energy, water, transportation, and health to access to money and information. Visit GE at www.ge.com.

Jacqueline Woods

Jacqueline Woods is GE's head of GTM Segmentation and Customer Experience. Ms. Woods is responsible for driving the company's customer-centric focus through the execution of global growth initiatives for its product and service portfolio of Finance, Media, and Infrastructure representing over $175 billion in revenue. She received her BS in Managerial Economics from the University of California at Davis and her MBA from the University of Southern California.

EXXONMOBIL

ExxonMobil Corporation is engaged in oil and gas exploration, production, refining, and marketing. Visit Exxon at www.exxon.com.

James S. Carter

James S. Carter was Regional Director of ExxonMobil Fuels Marketing Company, which is responsible for the marketing, sales, and distribution of ExxonMobil's fuels in the United States. Mr. Carter received his BS in mechanical engineering from Clemson University in 1970. Following service in the U.S. Army, Mr. Carter received his MBA from Tulane University in 1974.

Additional information was provided by:

Karl Fink, Vice President of Marketing, Exxon Company International.

4 BRANDING

by Landor Associates, Fleishman-Hillard, Under Armour, HOLT CAT, and Paramount Pictures

THE ESSENTIALS OF BRANDING
by Landor Associates

Introduction

It is incredibly rare for a product or organization to be without a brand. There are museum brands (Guggenheim, Smithsonian), people brands (Martha Stewart, David Beckham), political brands (Obama versus McCain, Labour versus Conservatives), destination brands (Australia, Hong Kong), sport brands (Manchester United, New York Yankees, Super Bowl), nonprofit brands (Red Cross, Oxfam, RED), branded associations (YMCA, PGA, Association of Zoos and Aquariums), along with the product, service, and corporate brands with which we are all familiar. Many old marketing textbooks talk about brands versus commodities (no-name products), but in today's world very few true commodities are left. Even basic foodstuffs have some sort of identifier on them, whether it is a private-label store brand such as Walmart's Great Value salt or a major brand such as Morton Salt.

Brands help people make a choice, a choice among salts, financial institutions, political parties, and so on, and the choices are increasing. The number of brands on grocery store shelves, for example, tripled in the 1990s from 15,000 to 45,000.[1] The purpose of branding is to ensure that your product or service is the preferred choice in the minds of your key audiences (whether customers, consumers, employees, prospective employees, fans, donors, or voters). The way in which the brand affects business performance is shown below.

Business performance is based on the behavior of customers, whether they choose to buy a particular product or service. And that behavior is based a great deal on the perception customers have of the brand: how relevant it is to them and how differentiated it is from the other brands in the same category. In turn, customers derive their perceptions of a brand from the interactions they have with it. Finally, that customer experience, ideally, is informed by a brand idea—what the brand stands for: the promise it is willing to make and keep in the marketplace. If the first part of this chain of cause and effect is indistinct or irrelevant to customers, there is little chance the rest of the chain will work, and the brand will not affect the business's bottom line. Yet, despite the proliferation of brands and their inextricable link to business performance, it is not easy to define what a brand is, along with how to create, manage, and value it.

Brand Idea	→	Customer Experience	→	Brand Perception	→	Customer Behavior	→	Business Performance

The Difference between a Brand and Branding

Most experts define what a brand is in one of two ways. The first focuses on some of the elements that make up a brand:

I. "The intangible sum of a product's attributes: Its name, packaging and price, its history, its reputation, and the way it's advertised."[2]

II. "A name, sign, or symbol used to identify items or services of the seller(s) and to differentiate them from goods of competitors."[3]

The second set of definitions describes the associations that come to mind when people think about a brand:

III. "Products are made in the factory, but brands are created in the mind."[4]

IV. "A brand is a person's gut feeling about a product, service or company. ... It's a person's gut feeling, because in the end the brand is defined by individuals, not by companies, markets, or the so-called general public. Each person creates his or her own version of it.[5]

What do we mean by "created in the mind"? When we think of Coke, we may think of the time we went to Disney World years ago. It was an incredibly hot day, and we drank an ice-cold Coke from the iconic glass Coke bottle and there was nothing more refreshing. When we think about the can, we might think red. Today perhaps we think of *American Idol* (and wonder whether they are really drinking Coke in those plastic cups). We think of how that Christmas polar bear ad made us smile. Those of us who are old enough may remember the "I'd like to teach the world to sing" commercial. These personal Coke brand associations are neither positive nor negative, they just come to mind. Coke has worked incredibly hard at implanting some of these brand associations in our minds: the idea and delivery of refreshment (and the supply management and distribution that are behind this), prod-

uct placement, the color red, the association with a popular TV program, and the advertising all make us feel good about the brand. Coke has not controlled the buildup of these associations, but it has tried, at every stage of our experience with the brand, to positively influence them.

Accepting the second set of definitions poses more of a challenge. The first definition suggests that the brand is the purview of the marketing department—just get the name, logo, design, and advertising right and you have your brand. The second shows how the brand is inextricably linked to the business. The creation of the brand may begin in the marketing department, but the experience of the brand has to be driven through all parts of the organization. Every interaction, or touchpoint, in a customer's experience of a brand makes a difference.

If you consider Apple, the quintessential brand success story, the most powerful parts of the customers' experience of the brand are not confined to traditional brand elements, such as the logo, the name, or the advertising. It is the environment of the Apple stores that encourages you to stay and explore (and upgrade) and interact with its products and its genius bar. It is iTunes as much as the iPod, the applications as much as the iPhone. It is Apple's customer service and tone of voice that are seamless, from the instruction manuals to the real-time chat in the support section of the online store. The brand is driven throughout this whole experience, throughout every interaction.

But if a brand exists in an individual's mind, and if it is delivered by the business, what is the role of branding? Branding cannot control what people think of a brand, it can only influence. A brand can put some of the elements in place that will help people understand why they should choose or prefer a particular good, service, organization, or idea over another. Branding, and the related marketing disciplines covered in this book, can help influence and explain how many of these associations in our minds have been built, and whether they were built through advertising, PR, employee behavior, supply chain management, and so on.

Branding is about signals—the signals people use to determine what you stand for as a brand. Signals create associations.

Allen Adamson, *Brand Simple*[6]

The bulk of this chapter will explain the process that determines the foundational signals of a brand: what a brand stands for (the brand idea); the attitude it projects (the brand personality); its name and how it talks (the verbal identity); what it looks like (the visual identity); and what it feels and sounds like (the sensory identity). Creating these foundational signals is the core business of a branding agency.

Before foundational signals are created, however, a certain amount of groundwork needs to be done to ensure that the best conditions for success are in place. The first section of this chapter explains this essential preparation. The second section describes the creation of the foundational signals. The final two sections focus on what to do next with these foundational signals once they have been created, looking at brand management and measuring the performance and value of brands.

STARTING A BRANDING PROJECT

Starting a branding project includes finding the right reason, commitment, and strategy; analyzing brand equity; and uncovering insights and opportunities.

Start with the Right Reason

Take care to get born well.

George Bernard Shaw, playwright

Fundamentally, there are two reasons a business needs branding. Either a new product or company has been created or there is a desire to change an existing brand to better reflect new business objectives (most often called a *rebrand*). There must be a solid business reason to change, or refresh, a brand and a brand idea. Without a solid business objective and brand idea, the judging of brand change becomes purely subjective. Suffice it to say, when you embark on a rebrand it is critical to ensure that you are rebranding for the right *business* reason, and if there is a desire to alter some visual or verbal elements, a clearly defined brand idea is essential for guiding this change.

Start with the Right Commitment

It is critical to have the right steering committee before starting a branding process. Because the brand idea reflects what a company says it stands for and its vision for the future, the CEO must be 100 percent in agreement with it. And because a brand is inextricably linked to the business, all branding initiatives need to involve the business leaders, not at every stage of managing the project, but at every stage that a significant decision needs to be made, particularly in the early stages when the brand idea and personality are being defined.

The areas of the business that interact with the target audience need to be represented on the brand steering committee to ensure that the brand idea will be delivered. If this means that the steering committee increases to more than eight to ten people, then "buy-in" stages are needed in the process to keep decision making manageable while ensuring that the areas of the business responsible for living up to the brand are committed to the process.

Finally, experts in the field of branding will also be essential partners in the process. Branding agencies are usually hired as partners and guides in the process, since they are in the business of helping to create and manage this kind of change. The best agencies show strong strategic and creative thinking and output and have relevant expertise (not necessarily expertise in the same industry or product category, but experience in handling similar problems for similarly sized organizations and products, or with similar target audiences).

The foundational signals of a brand need to last at least a decade, and creating them is costly, so investing in the right advice is important at both the macro level ("How do we align our business with the brand idea?") and the micro level ("What should we do about our printers to ensure the new brand color reproduces well around the world?"). Because creating a new brand or undertaking a rebrand requires significant investment and signals change, there is really only one opportunity to do it; so it must be done right.

Start with the Right Business Strategy

Good branding cannot save a poor product or business. In fact, the desire to rebrand can sometimes mask a fundamental business problem and can distract managers from actually addressing it. Before you brand anything, it is important to have a strong, clear answer to three simple questions: (1) What are we selling? (2) Who is it intended for? and (3) What is the benefit to customers?

What Are We Selling?

In a very practical sense, selling involves making tough decisions about the market you are in, such as Intel's decision to abandon manufacturing computer memory chips and focus on microprocessors. Or it can be about deciding how you intend to describe the product or service being offered. In *Welcome to the Creative Age*, Mark Earls tells the story of working for Clarks, one of the leading shoe companies in the United Kingdom, and spending time in focus groups. His agency hit on an idea that resonated well: not a reexpression of the brand but a reevaluation of what Clarks was selling. Clarks had defined the business of selling shoes as a "replacement business"—replacing shoes that were worn out. The new model was about selling pleasure—buying new shoes that give you a lift.

Who Is It Intended For?

The more specific and targeted the answer to this question, the better. For example, rather than focusing on "moms," target "moms who put their careers on hold and are now back in the workforce trying to juggle career advancement with guilt about not having the time or energy to puree homemade baby food every evening."

For corporate brands, it is more difficult to focus on a single audience; at a minimum, both customers and employees need to be considered. But for both product and corporate brands, it is important to understand insights into these audiences to ensure that the brand idea resonates.

What Is the Benefit to Customers?

A company should be able to articulate clearly, in a few words, the unique aspect that differentiates its product from the competition and provides a benefit to its customers. This is also called the *unique selling proposition*, the *dominant selling idea*, the *unique value proposition*, or the *universal guarantor of performance*.

Start with the Right Focus: Customers

One of the most important first steps in a branding project is to create a framework that identifies and compares all possible interaction points where a customer experiences the brand. This is often called *a customer journey*, and the interactions are sometimes referred to as *touchpoints*. These interactions can be physical, such as in a supermarket, at an airline check-in desk, or in a showroom. They can be digital, such as through a download from a company Web site or on social media sites like Twitter or YouTube. Interactions can be analog, such as on the phone, via advertising on TV, or through promotional events.

The important thing is to create the framework from the customers' point of view and not simply compile a list of all things currently being executed to build the brand. Doing only the latter will not help you discover a new interaction that could better connect the customer to your brand. Creating the full framework, however, will foster understanding of where you are delivering the brand promise, where you are failing to keep it, where you need to innovate to improve the experience, and where you should spend your marketing dollars to generate the most impact.

Analyze the Brand's Equity

When a rebrand is undertaken, or if a new brand has another brand attached to it (for example, through a parent brand endorsement), it is important to understand where current brand equity lies to avoid inadvertently losing key elements that are actively building consumer recognition and relevant brand associations. To be clear, we are not talking about the broadest definition of "equity"—the accumulated value of a company's brand assets, both financially and strategically, which comprises the overall market strength of a brand. Rather, we are talking about the equity inherent in the brand signals to help answer questions such as "Should we keep the logo?" "Should the brand still be red?" "Should we continue to use the same brandline?"

When embarking on a rebrand, provided it is not occurring for a predominantly negative reason, you will often hear people within a company speak about the strong equity inherent in the current brand signals. "We can't get rid of the tagline. We've had it for five years. It has a lot of equity." "People love the logo. It's who we are. You can't change that." "Don't get rid of 'green.' It's a core brand color." Employees are likely to have some emotional attachment to certain brand signals. But often, impartial brand equity research must be conducted to truly understand where real equity lies and whether it remains relevant moving forward.

For the redesign of the Gatorade packaging in 2002, PepsiCo and Landor conducted equity research with customers who were asked to draw the bottle. This was a simple exercise, but one that resulted in a marked consistency of output. The lightning bolt seemed to be the most important and distinctive design element associated with the brand; it was recalled and drawn many times, and consumers associated it with a "spark of energy." Other aspects (orange cap, brand colors, bottle shape) also had strong recall, but did not evoke the same emotional responses.

But equity is not simply about awareness—it is also about relevance. The reason that Gatorade increasingly focused on the bolt in subsequent package designs and other marketing communications was not simply because people recalled it, but because they associated it with the difference Gatorade made to their athletic performance. In 2009, however, facing increasing pressure from Coke's VitaminWater and other competitors like Powerade, PepsiCo instituted a dramatic redesign for Gatorade that minimized the bolt and emphasized a somewhat collegiate-looking serif-type letter *G* as the prominent label graphic. Apparently, PepsiCo made this decision without conducting extensive packaging research and, at this writing, the results at point of sale have been mixed. It will be interesting to see whether this dramatic rebranding helps turn the brand's fortunes around.

Consider also the spate of brands such as Atari and Mini that have recently returned from the dead to take up residence at retail once more. Part of a phenomenon dubbed "dormandize" by consumer trend spotters at trendwatching.com, these brands hope to capitalize on residual brand equity to leapfrog competitors. Of course these revived brands get a head start on awareness, but with brands such as Atari, much more work needed to be done to bring the brand out of eight-bit graphics and give it relevance in the world of PlayStation and Xbox. As Steven Mallas wrote, "Atari's brand equity doesn't have that differentiated, maverick feel of yesteryear when it was always associated with the cutting edge of video game technology and was worshipped by hardcore players at the forefront of the video game revolution. Nowadays, it is an all-purpose distributor that finds intense competition in the likes of Electronic Arts and Activision."[7] Atari's fiscal losses ($38.6 million in 2004, a significant reversal of $17.4 million profit in 2003) seem to affirm the point. Just because people recognize a brand does not mean they have positive impressions about it or that they will purchase it.

Overemphasizing recognition in the brand equity equation is a quick way to get an immensely distorted picture of a brand's value. Ultimately, it can have the effect of making a company think that everything is so good there is no need to change anything. Yet if people know about the brand, but it does not reflect what you want it to stand for in their minds, then it is not relevant to keep. GE walked away from the ubiquitous tagline "We bring good things to life" because it no longer encapsulated what it stood for as a business.

A rebrand is a marker of change. It should be undertaken for a business reason.

Uncover Insights and Identify Opportunities

From an agency's point of view, the process of creating a new brand or a rebrand usually starts with a *situation analysis*, often called an *audit*, or what Scott Bedbury calls a "big dig."[8] Even in the creation of a new brand you are never starting with a completely clean slate. This big dig can be as small or as large as you want to make it, and there are various models and ways to structure it. It often involves consumer and/or customer research, whether primary or secondary (see Chapter 5, "Marketing Research," for an explanation).

The most important thing to keep in mind about situation analysis, however, is that the ultimate purpose is not to gather information. Its purpose is to assemble *insights* about customers, the category, competitors, or the brand itself in order to identify an opportunity that will shape the brand idea.

What is an insight? Professor Mohanbir Sawhney describes it as "a not yet obvious understanding that can be the basis of a competitive advantage."[9] Insights can be about a business, brand, category, or customer. These insights come from interpreting information available in a creative and analytical way, often using a framework, model, or map. And opportunities are usually identified through a combination of insights that connect multiple areas such as competition; category; customers; product or organization; heritage, ambition, and stories; and brand architecture.

THE BRAND STRATEGY

Creating the brand signals includes defining the brand idea, brand architecture, and brand personality, and producing the creative brief.

Defining the Brand Idea

A good situation analysis leads to insights and identifies areas of opportunity for a brand, but a stake must then be placed in the ground to define the *brand idea:* what you want the brand to stand for. There is no magic formula or model for this. It takes smart people, clarity, and creativity of thought,

debate, and sometimes more research to determine the right brand idea.

The most important thing about your brand idea is that it is differentiated from the competition and relevant to your target audience. It is essential to give the target audience a reason to choose your brand over all others. If there is nothing different about your brand, there is no reason to purchase it; if you are different but that difference is not important or meaningful to consumers, it is equally unlikely your brand will be purchased.

Creating the brand idea also requires a leap of faith to articulate something that captures the good about the present state of the brand, and, more importantly, a vision for its future. Mark Earls talks about the brand idea having to create "a longer-term trajectory for your business and your working life. It is rooted in a dream of the world as it should be. A dream that you feel and believe in with your whole being, rather than the small part of yourself that business normally connects with."[10]

The more visionary this idea, the more it can inspire the people who are tasked to deliver it. And the more relevant and differentiated it is, the better the outcome. This idea of having a noble purpose above and beyond the commercial or product equation seems to be gaining more traction in the Internet age. Consider Dove's *Campaign for real beauty*, or Ikea's purpose being defined as *Creating a better everyday life for the many*. Brands that claim a higher purpose in their brand ideas, and those that do it earlier than their competitors may connect better with consumers in the long run.

However, the limits of differentiation are important to note. The brand idea does not have to be, nor is it likely to be, different from any other idea that has ever been expressed by a brand before. Difference is a relative term and is proportional to a brand's competition: other brands the target audience might choose instead of yours. For example, if the proposed brand idea for a child's new toy is "stimulating imagination," this should not be disregarded because GE also stands for "imagination at work." The child or parent is not going to be making a choice between the toy and a GE steam-assisted gravity drainage produced water evaporator.

Similarly, you want the brand idea to be ownable; not in the sense of patenting the idea or the words, but rather in the sense of delivering the idea, relentlessly and with commitment. This way, the idea becomes so well associated with a given brand that any competitor would be foolish to invest time and money claiming it stands for the same thing.

Many models can be used to help encapsulate the brand idea. Consumer goods companies with large marketing departments usually have their own models; branding agencies have theirs. Companies often want to incorporate a vision statement, mission statement, and sometimes add a brand positioning statement.

The most valuable piece of any of these models is getting to a short, memorable phrase that encapsulates the core of what the brand is about. This is not a brandline or tagline, although it could become one. Rather, the brand idea defines what the brand is about at its most basic level. For example:

- BP is about *going beyond*.
- GE is about *imagination at work*.
- Nike is about *authentic athletic performance*.
- eBay aspires to be the *global online marketplace*.
- Ikea seeks to *create a better everyday life for the many*.

These simple articulations can be fleshed out into a paragraph, a positioning statement, a mission statement, or a vision statement, but if the core brand idea is not clear, then all elements emanating from it will be even weaker. Content will be spun off (PR messages, ad copy, Web sites, leadership speeches, recruitment specs, blogs), and without a clear idea to link back to, the brand will quickly become disparate, hard to manage, and not associated with anything distinct in the consumer's mind. The brand idea acts as a strategic filter for the future; it is a waste of time to fill in models or craft mission statements without spending time clarifying the brand idea first.

Defining the Brand Architecture

One component of developing a brand strategy requires establishing a clear structure and relationship among brands in a portfolio. This process is usually called brand architecture. Fundamentally, *brand architecture* is about deciding what you want to show as your face to the market and how to present your goods and services to your target audience. Many models and a great deal of marketing terminology are used to describe different approaches to brand architecture. But all fall somewhere among three strategies:

- A *monobrand strategy* (sometimes called a *branded house*), in which one brand is applied across everything. Examples are GE, Virgin, and IBM.
- An *endorsed or subbrand strategy,* in which the organization owns a variety of brands that include the parent name in some way. Examples are Nestlé, Cadbury, and Marriott.
- A *multibrand strategy* (*or house of brands*), in which a company uses many different brands with no parent endorsement. Examples are Procter & Gamble (P&G), Diageo, and GlaxoSmithKline (GSK).

Almost all brands, particularly those that have been around for a while and have gone through various mergers and acquisitions, sit somewhere in the messy, real-life middle with a *hybrid strategy*. For example, Starwood Hotels has a Sheraton brand that itself endorses Four Points by Sheraton. It owns stand-alone hotel brands, such as W Hotels, Westin, and St. Regis, and yet shows its face to the market as Starwood in its loyalty program that spans all its hotels. Toyota endorses the Prius, Corolla, Tacoma, and RAV4 brands (along with others) but not its luxury brand, the Lexus.

As these examples show, determining the best portfolio strategy is often difficult and rife with tradeoffs. It is important to remember that brand architecture is not about internal organizational structure. Well-designed architecture will be consumer-oriented and help customers make choices between one product or brand and another. It will use the minimum number of brands to cover the maximum number of market opportunities, while clearly differentiating among brands. Not only will good brand architecture reflect the strategic vision of the firm, but it should also improve financial performance by helping organizations direct resources to the best bets for future growth by minimizing redundancy among brands and cutting underperforming brands.

Brand architecture should not just rationalize an existing portfolio and stretch the remaining brands into new areas, as tempting as that may be. It is important to be careful with assumptions about how far current brands can stretch to cover future growth areas by understanding what each brand stands for in customers' minds. For example, when Polaroid began selling conventional camera film under the Polaroid label, this brand extension did not work because in the minds of consumers Polaroid stood for *instant* photography, not *generic* photography. The consumer's idea of Polaroid would not stretch enough to accommodate the new meaning.

In contrast, because Virgin stands for something so broad (essentially the idea of challenging convention), and because Virgin delivers its promise so relentlessly, the company has extended successfully into categories as diverse as financial services, mobile phones, airlines, beauty products, beverages, and space travel.

Although a very rational and analytical process, brand architecture often becomes an emotional topic for a company because it is mistaken for an attempt to change the organizational structure. For example, when a company decides not to create a subbrand for a business unit and instead uses the master brand (for example, going to market as "Deloitte" rather than as "Deloitte Tax"), employees can feel that their role is being downplayed, or even in jeopardy. Such strategic decisions must therefore be carefully and clearly managed to help employees understand that brand architecture is not about restructuring the internal organizational chart (which addresses optimizing delivery and costs), but rather about the company's face to its markets (which concerns maximizing revenue). One is not a mirror image of the other.

Defining the Brand Personality

Many brand strategists may be uncomfortable with the following statement: There are *not* an infinite number of brand ideas in the world, and many brands occupy very similar territories. If you look across the list of global Fortune 500 companies, the statements about what the organizations stand for generally use some combination of the words in Table 4.1.

We need not be downhearted by this. If, as Christopher Booker says, there are only "seven stories in the world,"[11] yet tens of millions of books, films, and plays tell these stories differently, the opportunity for relevant differentiation remains strong. BP and Toyota both focus their ideas on a sense of progress. However, nobody would say these brands are the same. One way they differ is through personality, and defining this is the next important element in building a brand.

The premise behind Rohit Bhargava's book *Personality Not Included* illustrates how critical it is for companies to move beyond being faceless organizations and express authentic personalities in order to thrive in the social media era. Given that functional attributes and benefits are not unique or long lasting enough to build a brand around, and that benefit areas are not infinite in number, defining

TABLE 4.1 POPULAR BRANDING WORDS	
Company Description	**Purpose**
Superior, leading, pace setting, number one, world class, trusted, innovative, inspirational, creative, passionate, customer focused	Enhance, improve, grow, success, performance, progress, quality, value, peace, harmony

the personality and expressing it across all interactions with customers is an important way to differentiate a brand and build relevance with customers. But a discussion around brand personality can be a difficult one to have in a boardroom. Brand personality is usually seen as an accepted part of what helps to differentiate a smoothie or chips brand. But a financial institution? A petroleum company? A parcel delivery firm? Not so acceptable. Yet often it is these types of companies that could benefit most by appearing more human.

Bhargava describes personality as "the unique, authentic, and talkable soul of your brand that people can get passionate about."[12] Defining company values is often the way large corporations try to articulate this. But when working on the creation of a brand idea, agencies are often told: "Don't touch the values." This may be because the client has already gone through a huge program internally to define them (or, just as likely, a group of senior executives crafted a values statement in a board meeting years ago) or the values have been in place since the founding of the firm and are an inextricable piece of "who we are." But when we look at values across an industry they are often remarkably similar. Consider the big four accountancy firms: If we take out *integrity, respect, collaboration*, and *leadership* (since at least three of the big four share these values, which do nothing to help differentiate the firms), we are left with very little: some *energy and enthusiasm* from Ernst & Young; *seeking facts* and *providing insight* from KPMG; and *getting strength from cultural diversity* from Deloitte. Not exactly the foundations of a brand personality to get passionate about.

One way of building internal passion for brands is through the creation of stories. For example, James Dyson's inventiveness and tenaciousness are hallmarks of the Dyson brand personality. When BP defined its *Beyond Petroleum* strategy, one of the first activities it undertook was to conduct hundreds of interviews with employees within the organization to get at these stories. The output was something called the "BP scroll" that was literally rolled out in a board meeting to help demonstrate

that the audacious brand idea and personality being proposed for the brand had roots in the passion and actions of employees. Along with the brand idea of *going beyond*, BP has four values—performance, progressive, innovation, and green—and people inside the company truly embrace them; they can be expressed authentically in communications.

Producing the Creative Brief

Once a brand idea and personality are in place, the core visual and verbal symbols can be developed. They are usually encapsulated in a *creative brief*, literally a short document that a creative team will work from as it designs and generates names, brandlines, and visual and sensory identities. A good brief is succinct (often only one page), uses words and pictures to help stimulate creativity, and has the brand idea and personality at its core. It also reflects learning about competitors and market categories from the situation analysis (for example, by including a section with things to avoid such as a color that a competitor uses consistently). Obtaining client sign-off on the brief is a critical part of managing expectations when it comes to reviewing work. Client sign-off should help to guide discussions around the work at every stage.

Along with the brief, the meeting itself is very important. This is often the first time a creative team will come into contact with a business or product and its challenges. It pays to take time to inspire and educate team members and involve them in discussions about the business challenges and the brand idea. Most brand signals need to last at least a decade, so bringing the team charged with creating them into the process early, and agreeing on the brief together rather than simply handing it to the agency team, will provide the best, most engaged start.

CREATING THE BRAND EXPERIENCE

Creating the brand experience involves crafting the verbal identity, designing the visual and sensory identities, and testing the verbal and visual identities.

Crafting the Verbal Identity

Naming

A new brand needs a name whereas a rebrand rarely has a name change. Indeed, changing a name signals that something significant has happened in the business, through forced circumstances, through a merger and acquisition, or through a negative event. A company that changes its name is expected to change the way it does business, too, so a name change should never be undertaken lightly.

Names can take many forms. They can be acronyms: IBM, BP, NBC. They can take the form of existing words or phrases: Shell, Apple, Twitter. They can be names constructed from other words: Spudulike, Kwik Save, Accenture. They can be coined: Avensis, Aventis, Avertis. And they can derive from the names of specific people or families: Ferrari, Hershey, Mercedes-Benz. See Table 4.2 for more examples.

Ideally, a name should be the pure encapsulation of the brand idea and, along with this audacious goal, should meet other key criteria:

- Be easy to pronounce in every language
- Be memorable (being brief also helps)
- Help people understand what the business is about
- Be able to stretch into other categories and areas in the future
- Have no negative connotations in other languages
- Be ownable and protectable as a trademark in all countries in which you want to operate
- Have an available domain name

These criteria are often given to an agency before it begins to generate names. But how many brand names can you think of that actually live up to all these criteria? Coke? BlackBerry? Facebook? Audi? Google? CNN? Target?

Name creation is an incredibly difficult business. It demands an immense amount of creativity, coupled with a heavy dose of practicality since most of the names created will not be legally available. In fact, almost 90 percent of names created will have to be rejected due to copyright considerations. And this is the most important thing to understand: A name is only one small part of a brand. Its power to build positive associations is limited when it is viewed in isolation. It only really gains meaning over time and in combination with all other brand signals.

Some brands create more than a name. They create a *naming device* that allows them to link a series of products together under a similar naming convention. The iMac spawned the iPod, iPhone, and iTunes. The iPod spawned the podcast. People tweet on Twitter and use devices such as Power Twitter to improve their brand experience. A good name will likely meet some of the criteria above, though not all; fortunately, there are many other brand signals to work with to help build a more complete picture of what you want your brand to stand for. It is most critical to make sure that the name is legally protected and that due diligence has been applied to check for negative connotations in other languages.

Furthermore, prepare to develop a hard skin at the launch of your new name. The media like nothing

TABLE 4.2 NAMES OF BRANDS		
Name Types	**Real**	**Coined**
Abstract	Apple	Google
	Twitter	Kodak
	Egg	Avaya
Associative	Lucent	Agilent
	Oracle	Clarica
	Sprint	Visteon
Descriptive	British Airways	FedEx
	America Online	Microsoft
	Computer Associates	Wikipedia

more than a name change they can react to, and their reaction is almost never positive. A name only becomes imbued with true meaning postlaunch. So as long as the homework has been completed up front, it pays to be patient and focus on constructing all of the many other signals that will help to support and give weight to this meaning.

Brandline

Because names can only do so much, brandlines are often developed in conjunction with the name to help signal what the brand stands for. Brandlines are often called taglines; however, taglines suggest a sign-off at the bottom of a piece of communication, and they can change as different marketing campaigns change. A brandline is developed as a permanent brand element to be used across different channels, often everywhere the logo appears. For example, FedEx's brandline is *The world on time*. It appears consistently on FedEx trucks, planes, and packaging and has been in place since 1995. Since then, however, FedEx has had many advertising campaigns that have featured different taglines, such as *When it absolutely, positively has to be there overnight* and *Relax, it's FedEx*.

Taglines can change (they are tactical), but brandlines remain the same unless a significant rebrand occurs. PricewaterhouseCoopers' brandline, *Connected thinking*, is at the heart of what the company says it stands for as an organization. *Beyond Petroleum* works cleverly to change associations with the name of the company from British Petroleum to something that implies what the firm wants to be about as a brand—*going beyond*. GE's *Imagination at work* captures the driving mission of the company. The brand overhaul of Citroën saw an end to the tagline *Just imagine what Citroën can do for you* and replaced it with a brandline that captures its business strategy: *Créative technologie*.

Creating a brandline presents many of the same challenges as creating a name (for example, it needs to be legally protectable and often needs to work in different countries), which may be why so many brands eschew a brandline altogether. Other brands seem to feel that a brandline is mandatory but create something that does not work hard enough to help to differentiate them. Look at PwC's competitors: KPMG locks up three words with its logo: *Audit. Tax. Advisory*. It tells people what the firm does but nothing about why it is different from its competitors (who are already perceived as very similar). There is already very little differentiation in this category, and KPMG's brandline does nothing to help. Ernst & Young is stuck with a legacy line from the immediate post-Enron days, *Quality in everything we do*; surely a given for one of the most regulated industries in the world. It focuses on an unspecific parity point (quality) with Ernst & Young's competitors rather than something that differentiates the organization. Deloitte has chosen not to use one, which, according to *Brandweek*, is an increasing trend. Perhaps some companies are finding that if you cannot have a good one (that is, one that focuses on your differentiation and relevance), it is better not to have one at all.

Tone of Voice

Tone of voice is another means of conveying what a brand stands for. Tone of voice is not messaging or writing; it is about *how* you say things rather than what you say. For example, a brand's voice can be friendly, informative, precise, grounded, real, honest, daring, playful, irreverent, emotional, or witty. The brand voice can express the personality of a friend or teacher, a geek or gamer, a leader or an advocate, a visionary or a knowledge seeker, a magician or an engineer. When tone of voice is consistent, it gives the consumer another means of recognizing the brand and its promise.

When you consider how many people within a company use words to communicate with a target audience on a daily basis, tone of voice would appear to be an incredibly important part of branding. Yet, compared with the development of a visual identity, creating tone of voice is less common. Whatever the reason, many brands do not have a consistent tone of voice, or their tone of voice is not considered when creating the foundational signals for a brand. Even brands that have crafted a tone of voice often do very little to train people on how and where to use it, or to promote its use on an ongoing basis.

A few brands are known for their tone of voice, and they deliver it consistently and memorably. For example, tone of voice helps differentiate maverick brands such as Virgin, as well as staid brands such as the BBC and the *Economist*. Southwest Airlines has a tone of voice that links strongly to its brand personality. The Southwest style is fresh and immediate, expressing respect and warm regard for people in general:

Although we cannot predict what external, uncontrollable events might transpire during 2003, we can forecast with considerable certainty that our valorous, caring, nimble, good-hearted, and resilient people will ensure that Southwest ends 2003 just the way it ended 2002—at the forefront of our industry.

Southwest 2002 *Annual Report*

To help an organization understand tone of voice and its implications for business communications, a common step is to take some current pieces of communication and rewrite them in the new tone. It is better to show than to tell, and focusing on high-profile, visible pieces of communication helps ensure that the new brand voice is noticed. Getting people to act on tone of voice is more difficult, however.

Designing the Visual and Sensory Identities

Great design gives people the shorthand markers of identification and engagement with a product, service, or organization: It stops us in our tracks to think again about our usual choices. It helps us find coffee, aids us in sending urgent documents in an unfamiliar city, or can make us feel part of a smarter or more stylish community. As we sit at the neighborhood Starbucks, typing on a MacBook, wearing Uggs or Adidas, minding a baby asleep in a Bugaboo stroller, we may suddenly realize that all these brands stand for something singular, that all of them have a personality, and that all of them use their visual and sensory identities to create powerful associations that we connect with.

Logo

There is something revered about the logo, and it is probably the first thing that comes to mind when we think about branding. It can mistakenly be where the desire to rebrand begins ("The new CEO doesn't like our logo") and is often where emotions can ride high in a branding project. It may have to do with the fact that the logo becomes personal on our business cards, or perhaps it has acquired such hallowed status that its role in branding is often overemphasized.

A logo becomes a visual shorthand for the meanings people attach to a brand, but it is not the only strong visual symbolism. As with a name, a logo will play up some aspects of the brand but will not be able to communicate others. However, it is also often undervalued, and stories about logos being "drawn on a napkin over a pint" abound, suggesting there is nothing difficult about their creation.

Most logos (also called *brandmarks*, *brand identities*, or *corporate identities*) are made up of several components: the *wordmark* (usually the name of the company), a *symbol* (a graphic device placed within, adjacent to, or around the logo), and the *colors* chosen to reflect the brand. Some logos comprise only a wordmark (such as Kiehl's, Virgin, Google, FedEx, IBM); a few use just a symbol (Nike, Apple, Prince); and others combine a symbol and a wordmark (The Body Shop, UBS, BP).

Some of the most memorable logos communicate myriad meanings, breaking new ground while respecting heritage. For example, the BP sunflower symbol (officially called the Helios mark) is a highly effective encapsulation of the core values of the brand. It is notably progressive and innovative—no other petroleum brand had done anything like the sunflower symbol at the time it was created—and it successfully represents BP's brand idea of *going beyond* to become an environmental leader and a truly great company. Incorporating green, a heritage color for BP, the symbol captures the feeling of pure energy, and its solar power initiative represented in the sunburst flame evokes broader environmental meanings for BP's future.

Some logos add essential communication that is missing from the name alone. For instance, a literal visualization of the word *Amazon* would take you to rainforests or Greek mythology. But instead, Amazon.com's logo helps suggest the range of products available (the arrow points from *a* to *z*) and forms a smile to communicate a sense of the welcoming, helpful, customer-friendly nature of the brand. The FedEx logo incorporates a hidden (negative space) arrow to subtly imply its speed and guarantee that packages will always get there on time. Evoking a story within the brand symbol presents not only a visual metaphor for the brand, but also a word-of-mouth communication campaign. Over the years, many people have recounted the story of discovering the arrow in the FedEx logo as an amusing "aha" moment.

While virtually no brand identity can convey everything about a product, service, or company, a logo must be evaluated on its ability to communicate at least one or two important concepts about the brand. The brief should incorporate these concepts, guiding both the creative team and the client in appraising the recommended designs.

Logos were once designed as purely static, two-dimensional devices with strict rules around usage that no one could distort or change in any way, on any application. This is still the case in many instances, but there are some logos that are designed to be more fluid. This trend started with the MTV logo in 1981, but it can also be seen with brands such as Google, which creates new designs within its wordmark and encourages its audiences to engage in the practice as well. The RED logo builds the brand by associations with others (iPod, Bono) and was created to work with brands as diverse as Dell, American Express, Gap, Hallmark, Converse, and Emporio Armani.

The Olympic 2012 logo created a negative media frenzy when launched in the United Kingdom. Its purpose was to be used in conjunction with other brands, allowing partners to adapt the logo to their own brand colors. But even this flexibility did not go far enough for some who felt that the logo had been "foisted on" the United Kingdom without properly involving members of the community it would represent.

By contrast, in creating the branding for Worldeka (a social-networking platform that brings together citizens who aim to change the world), Landor provided some brand structure—including the simplification of Worldeka to WE, the key insight that encapsulates the brand's collective voice—but decided along with the client to let the online community own the logo and the brandline. This encouraged a multitude of design executions that expanded the visual and verbal language (such as allowing various interpretations of WE: Wrestling Evil, Working Effectively, or World Engaged).

This kind of "open branding" is not appropriate for all brands, but what these examples highlight is that there is no one-size-fits-all approach to logo usage, and tools like animation, customization, and flexibility need to be considered along with colors, fonts, and symbols.

Color

Logos are not designed in black and white. The creation of a logo always introduces other core aspects of the brand. For some brands, color is one of the most important associations they have: for example, the Tiffany robin's-egg blue box, ING's orange versus the blue and red of other financial institutions, and Coca-Cola's red.

There is much written about color theory and the meaning of color in different societies. While white is traditionally the color of death or mourning in Asia, yellow means caution in the United States, and red is the color the eye is drawn to most—differing meanings of color should not be the overriding reason to either choose or discount these colors for a given brand. It is more important to go back to the brand idea and personality, and the situation analysis, to ensure that a color palette is chosen that first and foremost differentiates the brand from the competition and is relevant to what it is trying to stand for. Without doing this, designers face the inevitable risk of designing a logo and then being asked, "Can we just see it in red/blue/yellow/pink/aqua?" This exercise should rarely be necessary. If you plot your competitors on a color wheel and are clear about how color theory relates to your brand idea, the choice of colors will be limited.

Look and Feel or House Style

Other graphic elements that make up the visual identity can help create something that becomes differentiated and communicates the right associations about the brand. Some agencies call this collection of elements the "look and feel," others the "house style." They consist of the color palette (main and supporting colors), fonts, photography, imagery style, and any other graphic element.

A successful rebrand can occur without ever touching the logo, name, or brandline. Ernst & Young's rebrand is a case in point. Its brand idea is about *achieving potential*, implying a personality that is dynamic, optimistic, and always striving to move forward. The yellow beam powerfully translates this brand idea and personality into a graphic element that allows an organization of more than 130,000 people to create diverse communications that nonetheless look and feel like they came from one brand—Ernst & Young. Absolut used a graphic element derived from its unique bottle shape as a symbol that became far more important than the actual logo in identifying its brand. Target's use of the bull's-eye makes its communications so distinctive that the name Target is unnecessary. These graphic elements are all part of a visual toolbox that help these brands become differentiated and memorable.

Occasionally, however, the use of another graphic element can detract from your brand idea. Snoopy, although now associated with MetLife insurance, is an icon created independently of this organization and one also used by other, albeit nonfinancial products. Yet the Peanuts canine character has become virtually synonymous with MetLife owing to long and extensive awareness-building efforts (and expenditures) while technically having little, if anything, to do with the original brand idea or personality of MetLife. Rather, Snoopy's relationship to MetLife began as an advertising idea, intended to add warmth and borrowed interest to an otherwise somber and impersonal industry.

Packaging

A package may have only half a second to engage with a consumer, yet it has a laundry list of functions to fulfill. For example, the structure needs to respect shelf space, sustainability, and safety considerations; the graphics need to include legal information such as weight, nutritional facts, and bar codes, along with names (parent brand, sub-brand, flavor names, unique ingredient names), illustrations, photography, icons, logos, and the list goes on. Great package design manages to serve the brand first and foremost, while working within the mandatory limits of legal and structural constraints.

It is important to understand what the brand idea and personality are and project these associations onto the packaging. Innocent smoothies are a much-cited case of packaging success in the United Kingdom. Every aspect of Innocent packaging gets across its brand, from tone of voice and copy, to its recycling efforts, to its name and logo design. Moreover, Innocent packaging does not follow category conventions. Its labels do not show photographs or illustrations of cranberries or raspberries—these images are not a means of differentiation. Breaking traditional category conventions is a simple way to stand apart, but few brands have the courage to do it.

Another way of differentiating packaging is by taking cues from innovation and design in other categories. When Landor designed the packaging for Crest Vivid White toothpaste, it took inspiration from the cosmetic category. The package's vertical orientation, sans serif font, embossing, and clean side panel clearly define a cosmetic product, appealing to consumers who consider oral care part of their beauty regimen. But the design speaks just as loudly to consumers more focused on health care. In the first three months following its launch, Crest Vivid White exceeded sales forecasts by nearly 300 percent, and Vivid White was the top-selling oral care item in Target stores in the United States during the first quarter of 2006. According to Mary Zalla, managing director of both the Cincinnati and Chicago offices of Landor Associates, "Just because no company had ever designed a cosmetic-looking oral care package didn't mean it should never be done. What *has* been done will only get you so far. Great design is about what *can* be done."[13]

Packaging is usually created before all other marketing communications, which may be why, when there is something new to say, a branding violator is added to the front of a pack to link it to a current promotion or ad campaign. Why not use the pack more creatively to link better to these other brand associations that consumers are picking up elsewhere? When U.K. laundry detergent brand Ariel launched Ariel Cool Clean, it was the second in a series of innovative brand-led approaches to on-pack promotion. The goal was to advocate Ariel's effectiveness at 30°C and its inherent energy cost savings to consumers by washing at a lower temperature. One of Ariel Cool Clean's challenges was to overcome perceptions that lower temperatures have reduced cleaning power. The idea was to make the promotion the actual pack design. The "Turn to 30°C" message is reinforced visually by placing the Ariel logo on a washing machine dial that mirrors the act of physically turning the dial down. This concept maintains Ariel brand equities while pushing the boundaries of promotional packaging. Following the launch, Ariel became the market leader.

As noted, package design is connected to both graphics and structure. Branding has usually been reserved for the former, while packaging structure and materials are often unfortunately designed before the brand idea and personality have been

defined. A missed opportunity, but one some iconic brands have fully grasped. Martin Lindstrom calls this the "smash your brand" principle, explaining, "Nearly a century ago, when the first-ever Coca-Cola bottle was in the planning stages, the designer received his marching orders. Company executives wanted him to develop a bottle so distinctive that if you smashed it against a wall, you would still be able to recognize the pieces as part of a Coke bottle. The designer obviously lived up to the requirement, and to this day it works."[14] But how many brands could you smash today and still identify—Coke, Heinz Tomato Ketchup, Marmite in the United Kingdom, Gatorade, Absolut? And then it gets harder.

The deliberate use of structure to build brand differentiation varies even within product categories. Perrier, Johnnie Walker, Smirnoff, and other drink brands use bottle shape as a distinctive brand element, while graphics in the canned-drinks market are generally the only differentiator. In another sector, Ferrero Rocher chocolates' gold wrapping and clear container are essential parts of the brand experience, while a low-cost chocolate product's propylene flow wrap is designed purely to grab attention at the point of sale. Apple is expert at designing packaging that engages us even after we have penetrated the first layer, as anyone who has opened an iPod Nano box will attest.

Great package design will only become more important as differentiation on-shelf gets harder. Couple this with the increasing consumer interest in ecofriendly options and better functionality, and the stakes rise dramatically. In the 2008 Image-Power® Green Brands Survey, one of the most notable trends that surfaced is the attention consumers are giving to sustainable packaging. In 2008, Amazon launched a Frustration-Free Packaging initiative to make it easier for customers to liberate products from their packages, focusing on two kinds of items: those enclosed in hard plastic cases known as "clamshells" (said to cause "wrap rage," as anyone who has tried to open one will attest), and those secured with plastic-coated wire ties, commonly used in toy packaging. These types of packaging pose a challenge for brick-and-mortar retailers attempting to prevent incidents of theft. Green and frustration-free are two other aspects to juggle in the development of future packaging that can create positive brand associations.

Smell

Smell is one of the most powerful senses. Memories, imagination, old sentiments, and associations are more readily reached through the sense of smell than through any other channel. In humans there are four genes for vision, whereas there are 1,000 allocated to scent, which means we have the ability to differentiate more than 10,000 odors. According to the Sense of Smell Institute, 75 percent of all emotions we generate are due to what we smell.[15]

Some brands are synonymous with a smell. Johnson's has become the baby smell. The smell of Crayola crayons is instantly recognizable and can take most of us on a nostalgic trip back to childhood. In fact, Crayola's smell is ranked 18 among the 20 most recognizable smells in the United States. Kentucky Fried Chicken now regards its signature aroma as one of its key "brand ambassadors."[16]

Scent branding is a relatively new field, but more and more companies are realizing the power of scent to build brand experiences. In 2003, about $30 million was spent on aroma marketing around the world; by 2010, that figure is set to reach $220 million.[17]

Some brands, such as Victoria's Secret and Starbucks, have used scents to connect with their consumers for years. Singapore Airlines, which regularly achieves top ranking as the world's most preferred airline, incorporates the Stefan Floridian Waters scent in perfume worn by its flight attendants, on hot towels, and in numerous other elements of service.

Besides food, fashion retailers, and the occasional airline, scent has been underused as a branding symbol. Things are changing, however: breathe in Westin Hotels' white tea signature fragrance or the mandarin orange and vanilla scent in the Sony Style stores. Furthermore, scent branding does not need to be limited to a retail, service, or product experience. Most corporations have office spaces

and lobbies into which prospective clients walk, and where events, meetings, and interviews are held. The effective use of positive scent could have a potentially dramatic impact on employees and customers alike.

Choosing the right scent for your brand should link back to the brand idea and personality attributes. Alex Moskvin, director of BrandEmotions at International Flavors & Fragrances, says he studies the DNA of the brand and its relationship to consumers to figure out what resonates olfactorily. In designing a hotel fragrance, for example, Moskvin wants to know if the chain is trying to stand for family-friendly hostelry (think chocolate chip cookies) or a haute couture Zen-like retreat (think sandalwood or hinoki). "We want to capture a smell that makes people feel part of the club," he says.[18]

Sound

Sonic brand identity, like its visual counterpart, has many components. Sound can be used as an identifier of a brand, the equivalent of a sonic logo (like the Intel chime, McDonald's "I'm lovin' it," Nokia's ring tone, Yahoo's yodel), or on the device itself to accompany certain actions (such as the always-welcome sound of Microsoft Windows and Apple operating systems booting up). A longer piece of music can also be used to create positive brand associations (United Airlines uses Gershwin's *Rhapsody in Blue*). These identifying sounds have been a prominent signal of brand experience since the invention of radio (such as the NBC chimes), but in today's cluttered, multimedium, audiovisual, and online world, *sonic branding* has evolved into an increasingly serious business.

Originally used as a one-off piece of music for a British Airways ad, Leó Delibes's "The Flower Duet" from the opera *Lakmé* became so connected to its brand that when the airline dropped the music in 2000, it received such a volume of complaints that it was reinstated. Today British Airways nurtures its accidental sonic brand: even Dave Stewart from the Eurythmics has worked on one of the many British Airways–commissioned versions of the song. However, trying to appropriate a famous song for your brand, rather than composing something original, is costly and often unsuccessful. In France some years ago, a David Bowie song was used to dramatize the Vittel brand. After a few months, consumers remembered David Bowie but forgot Vittel. In essence, Vittel was asking consumers to remember two brands, David Bowie and Vittel, but the connection was strictly promotional and the stronger brand dominated recall.

Although it may take time to build recall, composing a sonic identity or longer piece of music based around a brand idea is a very efficient way to create differentiation and identifiable associations with your brand. Sounds are less likely to exacerbate cultural differences than words and images, particularly in a short sonic identity, and most contain only a few notes that can become relevant across most of the world.

Testing Verbal and Visual Identities

Once you have established a direction for a brand's verbal, visual, and sensory identities, the next step is to test leading concepts on targeted consumers to learn whether the brand signals effectively communicate the intended idea and have the desired impact. Research can be used in two main ways to inform and optimize the design process: insight and equity understanding before design and post-design validation. Preferably, both should be incorporated into a branding project because you learn different things at each stage.

Many different methodologies for testing brand signals are appropriate, depending on your goals, the category, geography, and whether you are introducing a new brand or a rebrand. Here are some lessons and principles to remember when undertaking a design or naming a research project:

- **People are skeptical about things that are different**. Brand signals are designed to be different. Skepticism is magnified in a group situation. Focus groups are therefore not the right choice for design research. Be creative. Talk to individuals; find them where they shop.
- **Research should be designed to inform your decisions**. Do not aim to pick winners and losers from brand signal research. Use it instead to understand attributes people associate with the signals and assess how well they match what you intend to communicate in your brand idea and personality. Do not expect every signal to communicate everything equally well. Understand strengths and weaknesses and make decisions with the whole picture in mind.
- **Think laterally and metaphorically**. Our brains are programmed this way. Use images, metaphors, and cross-category analogies to help consumers help you. If you want to communicate a sense of indulgence for a chocolate bar name, ask about the name's appropriateness in another indulgent category, such as spas or retail stores specializing in cashmere.[19]
- **Consumers are not namers or designers**. Consumers live in the real world, not the conceptual world. Put the names and designs in as real a context as possible. Let the designers do the designing and the consumers the reacting.
- **Familiarity is a powerful force**. New designs are usually less findable on a shelf than ones with which people are already familiar. Because of this, the strength of a new design must be evaluated on more than just "shelf pop." And new designs often underperform current ones in research; consumers often need time to adjust to new strategies and may not immediately like a new design.
- **Place more importance on emotional rather than rational responses.** Use the research to help you understand them. Do not underestimate emotional identification that cannot be rationalized. Try harder to understand it.

DELIVERING THE BRAND EXPERIENCE

It is important to stress that only in combination do brand signals make an impact on a customer's experience of a brand. And only when they are deployed boldly, with courage and single-mindedness, will they create impact in the cluttered world of brands we live in. You might notice the logo of an airline first, but it is your experience buying a ticket, waiting in line, flying in the cabin, and interacting with service people that will form your opinion of that airline brand. Red Bull may have a distinctive can, but its sponsorship and events probably imprint the idea of the Red Bull brand most firmly in our minds. Consumers derive their perception of a brand from the sum of interactions they have with it. And delivering the promise of that idea is the work of an entire organization, not just the marketing department.

Only through a deep understanding of its customers can airlines, soft drink companies, or financial institutions deliver a brand promise that lives up to the brand idea. Occasionally, the brand idea will be so well understood that an organization can hit on something that has the power to generate viral communications and amplify the brand idea. For example, Virgin Atlantic's head massage service got everyone talking about how amazing the Virgin experience was. In truth, it was one of the smallest parts of a holistic brand experience, but it generated buzz and marked the Virgin experience as remarkable.

In a world that gets noisier and more complex by the day, a company can design a relevant and differentiated brand and *still* not cut through the clutter to capture public imagination. If you can add a single catalyst, or power application, to the mix and ignite consumer excitement, the entire brand will be elevated by it. Finding this powerful interaction with customers can significantly stretch your marketing dollars and the impact of your brand.

MANAGING A BRAND

Once the foundational signals are in place for a new or refreshed brand, the next step is to begin the process of codifying and communicating these to all the people who will use them. This very involved process takes a long time. You may read about a firm undertaking a rebrand in July of one year, but not actually see it until a year later. It is not usually the production of the visual identity elements that generally takes the most time (and money) but the implementation. This can include media testing, the creation of templates (for specific applications such as presentations, business cards, stationery suites, brochures, internal Web sites, country-specific home pages), the design of packaging mechanicals (printer-ready files created to printer's specifications), and so on. Implementing a brand requires developing a plan for every touchpoint on the customer journey. It inevitably means creating guidelines: visual identity guidelines, verbal identity guidelines, digital guidelines, and print guidelines. Often these are translated into other languages for online accessibility.

An implementation process might involve updating training modules and brand resource centers. Some organizations develop help centers, particularly in the months pre- and postlaunch, and create brand modules for new recruits to educate them on exactly what the brand stands for and how to use and "live" it. The implementation process also needs to factor in all the other communications partners and their work (advertising, marketing, Facebook sites, screensavers, press releases, leadership speeches, conferences, events, exhibitions, offices, chairs, pens).

This process is typically seen as a key part of *brand management*, which is generally interpreted as the means of controlling your brand and keeping its expression consistent. It jars significantly with some of the other key aspects of branding: the two-way interactions with customers on their journey, the continually evolving impressions of a brand in people's minds, and the use of social media channels to develop a dialogue with customers rather than push out a stock message.

Brand management used to be about limiting external influences. Rigidity was the means to consistency, and consistency emphasized scale and professionalism. But the Internet and the democratization of image creation have made everything public property. (Is there really such a thing as internal and external communications today?) Today we create brand ideas that transcend the need to impose discipline by inviting partnerships with people, inside and outside an organization, who want to be part of the idea. Brands are no longer about one-way communication; they are about dialogue between the brand and its customers. Indeed, brand implementation can often incorporate cocreation with the consumer; the MyStarbucksIdea Web site and Dell's IdeaStorm are examples of this.

Brand management today should be about determining what cannot change and what must change. Advertising agency DDB talks about the 70/30 rule: 70 percent consistency but 30 percent flexibility. The 30 percent portion relates to language and cultural differences, buying behavior nuances, insights into the target market and its preferences for media consumption, and so on. For example, this understanding of the balance of consistency and flexibility allows McDonald's to offer a teriyaki burger in Japan and porridge in the United Kingdom, yet still deliver a consistent set of expectations for the familiar golden arches.[20]

Consider the role of the brand launch. Rather than seeing it as the way to push out tools and information, brand managers should make sure that it fully engages employees with the brand idea so that they are inspired to be part of delivering a customer experience that expresses the brand. Brand management in the future should not be about policing standards but rather about nurturing and developing the ongoing brand experience.

MEASURING THE PERFORMANCE OF A BRAND

Tracking Brand Strength

Building a brand based on differentiation and relevancy is not simply common sense; its success can be proven. In the mid–1980s it was recognized that all brands, regardless of category, country, or target, seemed to live by certain rules. To understand those rules and describe the strongest brands, Landor Associates developed ImagePower®, the first cross-category, multicountry study of brands. In the early 1990s, the ImagePower study was expanded from a few key measures of brand stature to the largest study of brands in the world, the BrandAsset® Valuator (BAV).

BAV stands apart from other brand studies because it is predictive, highlighting leading indicators of brand strength. Moreover, it is an incredible diagnostic tool, illustrating how a brand is performing against not only direct competitors but also against all other major brands in different categories. In this way it replicates a consumer's real experience of brands in the very cluttered brandscape. (You wake up to a Sony alarm clock, eat Kellogg's cereal for breakfast, watch the CNN morning news, turn on your iPhone, get in a Toyota car, and drive to a Safeway supermarket to use the HSBC ATM inside.)

To date, BAV has been fielded in 48 countries, covers some 30,000 brands, has conducted interviews with more than 500,000 consumers, and includes dozens of brand metrics and attitudinal questions. BAV is currently run by Young & Rubicam Brands, a consortium of companies that includes Landor, itself a WPP company.

BAV posits a proven model on how brands are built that is based on the interrelationship of four brand dimensions, known as the four pillars:

1. *Differentiation:* What makes your brand stand apart
2. *Relevance:* How appropriate this difference is to the audience you want to reach
3. *Esteem:* How well regarded your brand is in the marketplace
4. *Knowledge:* How well consumers know and understand your brand

This model shows how brands are built one pillar at a time, with differentiation being the first, most critical step. A strong brand has high levels of differentiation and relevance. The healthiest brands have greater differentiation than relevance, which gives them room to grow. When a brand has a higher degree of relevance to differentiation it is in danger of being seen as a commodity; Energizer, Bic, and Saran Wrap are examples of this.

Esteem and knowledge, the other two pillars, make up a brand's stature. A brand with a higher level of esteem than level of knowledge is a brand that has a good reputation, although people may not know much about it. This puts a brand in a great position to convince consumers to get to know it better. Brands such as Coach and Movado fit this mold. Too much knowledge and not enough esteem is an uncomfortable place to be, however.

In the case of leadership brands, such as Disney, Coca-Cola, Sony, and IBM, all four pillars are strong. A successful new brand, or a successfully relaunched brand, will demonstrate a desirable step-down pattern of pillars, from differentiation as the highest to knowledge as the lowest, indicating that the brand has found a meaningful way to differentiate itself in people's minds. It is ready to intensify its marketing efforts in order to expand its knowledge base. JetBlue and Ikea were in this situation early on and only grew stronger from there. In the early 1990s Starbucks had this profile, moved to a balanced pillar leadership profile, and now is beginning to show slight declines in differentiation.

Measuring Brand Value

There is a natural desire to understand how much a brand is worth—to have a tangible means to measure what is fundamentally an intangible asset. However, just as absolute control in brand management is not an achievable goal, neither is there a widely accepted, definitive way to accord value to a brand in financial terms.

Nonetheless, several approaches and models have been developed to create estimates for brand value. The application of these numbers falls broadly into two categories: *brand rankings* published in the business press and *brand valuations* that provide more serious support for business decisions.

The lack of consensus over valuation techniques is most clearly seen in the widely divergent value estimates for brands in published rankings and, for many people, calls into question the usefulness of such estimates for more serious purposes.

However, there is good academic and practical evidence that certain approaches provide more robust results than others. *Brand value models* generally differ in two areas: their structural approach to valuation and the degree of subjectivity used in determining their primary inputs. On one hand, several models employ expert judgment to assess structural factors such as the role of brand in driving business results, and the brand risk that is reflected in the rate used to discount a business's branded cash flows to determine value. In many people's minds, this subjectivity casts doubt on the reliability of the valuations such models produce. On the other hand, more rigorous approaches use statistical models built on objective market data for brand strength and financial performance, to assess the value contribution of a brand to a company's financial success.

For example, significant progress has been made with BAV, the research database that employs a well-established approach to measuring brand strength. In one study, partnering with Stern Stewart, a financial consulting firm, BAV was used to show a correlation between brand differentiation and operating margins. The study found that those firms whose brand differentiation grew tended to have an operating margin of 10.5 percent, while those that saw differentiation decline had an average operating margin of 7 percent.[21] Longer term, BAV has been used to track how declines in differentiation often set a precedent for a long-term decline in business performance.

Another brand strength methodology, Millward Brown Optimor's BrandZ, is as expansive as BAV (more than 23,000 brands across 31 countries). BrandZ uses a pyramid model that plots increasing levels of rational and emotional engagement of consumers over six levels. The top of the pyramid, the level called bonding (where, on average, 8 percent of customers sit), contributes, along with claimed purchasing data, to a *Voltage score*, a one-number summary of the growth potential of a brand. Millward Brown Optimor has mapped this score against market share and has proved that brands with strong Voltage scores are more likely to grow market share. Ogilvy and Mather and consultant A.T. Kearney have done further work with these Voltage scores in the United States and the United Kingdom, linking them not only to market share growth but also to profit, total shareholder returns, and levels of business risk.[22]

Three companies publish annual rankings of brand value. The longest-running global study is Interbrand's Global Brand Scorecard, published annually in conjunction with *BusinessWeek*. It assigns a brand value, measured in billions of U.S. dollars, to the world's top 100 brands and plots this against past-year results to show the year-on-year change in brand value. Arguably the best-known and most publicized approach, the scorecard includes qualitative judgments to assign relative weight to contributing factors. It also includes a range of inputs such as analysts' projections, companies' financial reports, and Interbrand's own qualitative and quantitative analysis.

Millward Brown Optimor first launched its list of top 100 global brands in 2005, establishing a methodology based purely on market data that looks both at financials (a brand's reported earnings and assets) and the results of surveys that assess consumers' perceptions of the brands versus their competition.

Another approach, used by U.K. consultancy Brand Finance, aims to forecast the top 500 global brands and focuses its reporting on a number that is said to signify future brand earnings.

Unsurprisingly, there are differences in these rankings. In 2008, Interbrand identified Coca-Cola, IBM, Microsoft, GE, Nokia, Toyota, Intel, McDonald's, Disney, and Google in its top 10. Millward Brown Optimor's BrandZ included Google, GE, Microsoft, Coca-Cola, China Mobile, IBM, Apple, McDonald's, Nokia, and Marlboro. Brand Finance selected Coca-Cola, Microsoft, Google, Walmart, IBM, GE, HSBC, HP, Nokia, and Citi. More significant, as well as differing top 10 lists, the single-number evaluations of brand worth also diverge considerably. For example, in the 2008 studies, Millward Brown Optimor suggested that the Google brand is worth more than three times what Interbrand reported ($86.057 billion versus $25.590 billion).

Clearly, brand valuation scores are not as definitive as other measures of financial performance, but the better models going forward will be those that take into account objective measures of brand strength based on consumer perception. After all, if we go back to what a brand is, and if we believe it is ultimately held in the minds of consumers, brand valuation models that do not factor consumer perceptions into their results may be seriously flawed.

Brand value is perhaps still best understood in hindsight, by looking at the price that companies are prepared to pay for brands. P&G bought Gillette in 2005 for $57 billion, and the value that P&G put on the Gillette brand was 17 percent higher than its stock market value.

Although measuring the ultimate worth of a brand is still evolving as a discipline, what is firmly accepted is the importance of brands to business performance the world over. Creating a strong brand is an even more complicated task than valuing one, and it is never actually complete. The stronger the foundation, however, the more chance there is that all the "scraps and straws" that consumers pick up along the way will accumulate into strong preference and long-term affinity for a brand.

BRANDING — INTERNATIONAL
by Fleishman-Hillard

Seems unusual that change associated with marketing and communication—where "new" is so valuable—has not affected the longevity or importance of branding. In fact, it grows in application and influence.

It is a testimony to the basic concept of branding that it has held up over the years to varied interpretations by so many experts. Whether a brand is described by its platform, foundation, pillar, core, essence, or personality, branding will continue despite the rapidly changing environment in which the concept functions.

The order and organization that branding provides are more important now than ever. Marketers recognized the opportunity (or need) to broaden the target audience for products and services around the world so a disciplined tool became necessary. It is important to understand two critical and interrelated international dynamics that influence the art and science of your branding process: one is geographical understanding and the other is technology.

As the world grew flatter and consumers in locations around the world were more frequently exposed to the brand, the need for a global brand strategy became obvious. Since product names, formulations, packaging, and marketing were modified for local idiosyncrasies of key stakeholders—especially consumers—country by country, the transfer of recognition and loyalty was challenged. Everything about the brand's relevance would literally need to be translated to different cultures and languages.

The second dynamic, technology, can help to develop successful brands. Touch, smell, sound, visual symbols, memories, emotions, and so on, all still guide product and package design, advertising, public relations, and merchandising. But technology is changing that; now everything is global, instant, and online. Marketers are learning that the more interactions with a brand, the faster and more intense the affinity. The global branding process embraces the new technology as it provides new ways to analyze and connect to the target audience that is faster, broader, and less expensive.

The key tools of a global branding process include common vocabulary; an action plan with goals, responsibilities, deliverables, deadline, and budget; consistent information to allow comparisons; empowered team with a leader; priorities (especially objectives) outlined; exchange of information that results in next steps; universally accepted messages; internal buy-in; roll-out strategy; programs that appeal to the target audiences delivered by media they use (not just "see"); and evaluating outcomes.

The branding process typically follows a four-phased approach. It is regularly modified to accommodate the ever-changing environment in which companies, their products/services, and the key audiences must operate to be successful. The process has gone from local to national to multinational, then global, and now, because of social media, to personal. A branding process must drive the development of brand strategies that impact performance: sales, employee productivity, and shareholder satisfaction.

Phase One Is Discovery

It is simply finding everything you need to know. At least, know what you don't know. With a global marketplace, it can take time, talent, and resources. Getting it right pays off. You must learn about the targeted stakeholders, both qualitatively and quantitatively, what is relevant to them, current attitudes, and all about the competition. It is important to develop key sources of information that help determine the emotional triggers that lead to advocacy. Sometimes, it seems the variations are infinite as you factor in all audiences in all places around the world. However, occasionally, a brand attribute resonates in the same way through the same vehicles everyplace, just the language is different. The outcome of this phase is a clear foundation for the brand. All the information is synthesized into manageable statements. A brand position forms the basis for all the further work. Since the brand has to be relevant for the audiences to allow it into their world, you must get this right.

Phase Two Is Translate

Now the verbal and visual elements of the brand are developed based on the position. A structure is developed to manage the brand in all its environments with all its audiences. Call it the "brand architecture." Included is messaging, logo development, guidelines, and toolkits for implementation. Testing is key. You have to resolve legal, cultural, and language issues. Your defined direction must be received as desired by key stakeholders. The best way to find out is to show and tell. Be prepared for the compromises required when input from around the world is processed. How far from the language, colors, design, or tagline must you go in certain places and still be true to the desired position? The outcome is an overall communications system. It is the road map for the elements basic to the global brand initiative.

Phase Three Is Execute

Based on the business and communications objectives, you now develop an overall plan. Objectives are quantified; key audiences are identified; strategies are outlined; creative program elements are prioritized; budgets and timelines are set. The plan must ensure that authority and responsibility are factored against the dynamic of central and/or local control. Each interaction must be reinforcing. The outcome is an effective and efficient delivery of actions that indicates the planning paid off. The inevitable need for modifications for optimum results is part of the plan.

Phase Four Is Evaluation

The plan must include measurement protocols in order to prove you have met or exceeded the metrics outlined. If not, explain why and what you are doing about it. There are a variety of ways to seek feedback—not all have to be costly or time-consuming. Certain geographies may be more important or sensitive; therefore, they deserve more comprehensive research. Ideally, you have access to tools that allow you to quantify the value of your brand. There is no better way to generate support. Everyone appreciates seeing that value increase as the elements are executed in more places and ways. The outcome here is proof that your planning paid off. You base your future planning on real data that makes the program all the more valuable.

The white paper *The Authentic Enterprise* summarized the challenge of the current environment: "The converging forces of technology, global integration, multiplying stakeholders and the resulting greater need for transparency are the most important communications challenges facing 21st century companies."[23] All can be managed confidently and leveraged successfully with a commitment to a global branding system. In fact, because a branding process leverages geography and technology, the borderless marketplace, and credible opinions expressed instantly by stakeholders, it is impossible to hide a strong brand. Why would you want to?

BRANDING—CASE STUDY

by Under Armour

Company: **Under Armour**
Case: **Company Start-up**

Brand Philosophy

We always say that we treat the Under Armour Brand like a book. Every chapter must carry on the story from the one before it and set up the next chapter to advance the story further. If you follow the story line, and do not skip pages or chapters, you take your loyal brand fanatics on a journey with you as you evolve and as they grow as well.

In theory, it all sounds easy enough, but building a brand and meeting the growth goals set forth by a red hot, publicly held company do not always mesh with the brand goals of staying true to the core consumer and the niche that established the company in the first place.

First, there is the challenge of competition. Once the niche brand is strong enough, and decides to expand, the larger mainstream corporations take notice. Sometimes for Under Armour, flying

(Continued)

under the radar was its best asset in the early days. But in the world of sports, where billion-dollar marketing budgets are the norm and even mediocre athletes can demand million-dollar endorsement deals, it does not bode well for a brand like Under Armour. We take great pride in providing apparel and footwear that athletes choose to wear for the benefits the garments provide during competition, not because there is a check coming to them in the mail. And lastly, there is the price at retail. If a brand like Under Armour that makes its product with the very best microfiber, moisture-wicking products never dilutes itself with nonperformance products, how do we succeed when other companies go cheaper on fabrics and sell at a discount or even a loss just to try to gain market share?

The answer to all these scenarios was the same. We blew up the old marketing model; we refused to pay athletes for the "honor" to have them wear our gear, and to this day we have never, ever compromised our brand integrity by making anything less than the very best performance apparel and footwear in the world. Simple answers, but the execution was not (and is not) always easy. But then again, building a brand takes time. And hard decisions. And great timing.

How the Brand Started

Kevin Plank, a 23-year-old former special teams captain on the University of Maryland football team, founded Under Armour in 1996 by solving one simple problem for athletes. Why do we accept wearing a heavy, sweat-soaked cotton T-shirt beneath our uniforms. Isn't there something better?

Through his testing done at major textile universities, he did discover that microfiber and fabric blends could be put together, as in biking shorts, to create a mixture of compression, stretch, and, most importantly, a silky, hydrophilic texture that would refuse to absorb sweat or other moisture. Where some players could weigh a sweat-soaked T-shirt at 2 to 3 pounds near the end of the game, an Under Armour prototype weighed mere ounces.

So using credit card advances to make 50 prototypes, Plank set up shop in the basement of his grandmother's townhouse in Washington, D.C., and sold them from locker room to locker room out of the back of his beat-up Ford Bronco.

Branding Rationale

The strength of a brand can be measured by the fact that its name defines the entire category or becomes synonymous with the entire category, such as Band-Aid, iPod, Coke, Kleenex, Under Armour. In fact, many sporting goods retailers still label the entire section of performance apparel and base layer "Under Armour." While market share in performance apparel for UA is still well over 80 percent, the telling sign for strength of a brand is hearing straight from the retail store sales associates who work on the floor. "No one asks for the 'moisture wicking compression shirts'; they say, 'Where's your Under Armour?'"

Typically, a company has to be The First or The Biggest to gain the status as the brand that defines the category. However, being first is often enough power to capture the market only for the time being, and being big does not always mean you can buy your way into consumers' hearts either. When Under Armour launched its first commercial campaign, WE MUST PROTECT THIS HOUSE, it was not only the tagline, but the rallying cry. We said nothing about the technology in the gear and did not even show a field or a ball. We had two simple goals. Establish Under Armour as the creator of the performance apparel category, and, secondly, create a tagline that athletes could replicate in their own world of sports, something that would take off long after the 30-second ad was over.

So, while Under Armour did create the Performance Apparel category, we had a three-pronged strategy to build the brand: (1) We started by seeding the product to the right influencers, the best athletes in the world. (2) We made sure our story was told clearly and succinctly online and in stores. (3) We built our brand not on the great looks of our T-shirts and mock turtlenecks but on the platform of performance.

Getting the Influencers

For Under Armour that meant getting it to the right players, the highly visible players, the best athletes in the world who showed up on televised games every Saturday and Sunday and on ESPN SportsCenter highlights every day and night. Not having any capital to follow suit of the big sports companies and pay athletes for endorsement deals, Plank relied on his network of friends who had gone on from college to play professionally in the National Football League (NFL) or Major League Baseball (MLB).

He also had those 50 high-tech Under Armour HeatGear prototype T-shirts, which he sent out to some of those former teammates, including the likes of prep school buddy and Heisman trophy winner Eddie George. Plank's only request was to put the shirts through the pro rigors and give some feedback.

To a man, each player asked for more of the silky, stretchy tight T-shirts. Many of the players asked for extras to hand out to their teammates who wanted to try the Under Armour Advantage. The other added benefit was that Under Armour shirts were so distinctive in their appearance, almost like superhero costumes, one athlete remarked. The tight long sleeves could be seen on television, the UA logo on the mock turtleneck poked above the jersey sometimes, and the large Under Armour chest logo was easily seen in the locker room. In fact, the original logo on the shirt was larger and raised higher on the chest, almost to the shoulder, so that it would get more exposure on postgame interviews.

The influencer role played heavily here since Under Armour could not be purchased in every sporting goods store yet, and having the UA logo meant you were authentic, a real player. Word of mouth spread from athlete to athlete. A problem they did not even know they had was now solved by a single layer underneath their pads. Plus they looked great in the muscle-enhancing shirts. So as long as players continued to wear those crazy new shirts on televised games, and as long as equipment managers would provide them for their top pro and collegiate teams, the influencers, then every other athlete around the globe, would know that if Under Armour could make the best running back in the world a little bit better, then it sure could help their game.

Telling the Story

We shaped the technology story not around what it did or how it did it, but focused marketing on what it would mean for an athlete's game. Imagine a T-shirt that keeps you cool (or warm), dry, and

(Continued)

two-to-three pounds lighter throughout the course of a game or workout. Now recall the alternative from the not-so-distant past, pre-Under Armour: a sweat-soaked cotton T-shirt and the equivalent of a two-pound weight bouncing around your neck.

In the world of sports, where a fraction of a second or one inch can mean the difference between winning and losing, it is not hard to understand why athletes—men and women, boys and girls— go out of their way to purchase Under Armour even if it costs four or five times more than its regular, heavier cotton alternative.

Building the Platform

The turning point for the brand came early on four years into business. We took the hard stance that we could not put our logo on anything that was not best in class—even trade show promotions and monogrammed golf balls for our annual golf tournaments. These cotton items and trinkets used at store openings and even sold online contradicted our platform of performance, even though they represented our biggest and easiest logo exposure.

Much like a simple red cross represents first aid in almost any language, we decided the interlocking UA logo that had become so hot in sporting goods was now the Universal Guarantee of Performance. Product would never again be built around the logo; the product would have to be good enough to earn it! That way, whether it was a new UA bag, a hat, or launching Under Armour footwear, athletes would know that if it had a UA logo, the Universal Guarantee of Performance (UGOP) was built in. And because of strict adherence to the UGOP, the question now, for any new Under Armour product, be it a padded hockey shirt, a football cleat, or a running shoe, will always be "What does it do?" The answer in broadest terms is "It's Under Armour; it makes you better."

Branding Philosophy Conclusion

If the product does not do what the advertising says it will, then the marketing is merely smoke and mirrors. The brand loyalty is built through delivering a promise. The performance on the field is the real reason why athletes choose to wear Under Armour. It is also why Under Armour, the brand known for its high-powered, intense commercials, will always be relied on to keep athletes cool, dry, light, and, at the very least, a step or two faster.

Still, the consumers need to know. And as easy as it is for another brand to outspend Under Armour in marketing, they cannot buy the brand equity. The brand is the loyalty we have established by making great products that make you better (the UGOP). The brand is the connection we have with athletes, so that when the athletes in our commercials scream "We Must Protect This House!", the athletes who see that advertising take it back to their field, their game, their teams, and make it their own.

Under Armour went from $17,000 in sales that first year to more than $700 million in 2008 as the hottest brand in sports. The brand is a story, and while the temptation is always there to skip to the later chapters, we have many, many pages to write before the story is finished.

by HOLT CAT

Company: HOLT CAT
Case: Company Rebranding with Values-Based Leadership

When Peter Holt took over HOLT CAT as CEO in the 1980s, he found a company that was unclear about its identity, which resulted in poor communications among management, employees, and customers. This lack of communication brought about mistrust, attrition, lack of focus, low morale, low productivity, and low sales. HOLT CAT was experiencing growing pains. At the same time, the petroleum and construction industries in Texas were in the middle of their downward spiral, and both industries were very important to the business of HOLT CAT. As a result, Holt's employees were depressed and pointing fingers at each other. Holt said, "I felt that the company and I needed a revolutionary approach in the way we operated." The challenge was to convey a corporate belief to customers and employees alike.

Through a process of exploring personal and organizational values, Peter Holt developed a vision of a company driven by what it values, not driven solely by bottom-line results. He wanted a company where employees wake up in the morning, eagerly come to work, and truly believe in the important contribution that they, and the company's products and services, provide to customers and the community.

Peter Holt evaluated his company to determine how to reenergize the company and revolutionize a values-based leadership approach in his business. Then, beginning in 1988, HOLT CAT adopted a new method of operating. Holt quit its "how much" and "how many" management style and began to operate on the basis of "shared company values."

HOLT CAT reflected a philosophy that values-based leadership and development are an ongoing journey, not a quick-fix program. The process of determining shared company values at HOLT CAT started by a rigorous discussion and selection of a set of core values that would be used to direct and drive key decisions. This process took several months for HOLT CAT to complete and eventually became known as Holt's Values-Based Leadership© program (also known as VBL). In the case of HOLT CAT, five core values were identified and prioritized. They include:

- **Ethical.** Doing the right thing
- **Success.** Consistently achieving targeted goals
- **Excellence.** Continually getting better
- **Commitment.** Being here to stay
- **Dynamic.** Pursuing strategic opportunities

Ethical is the first of the five stated values, and it comes before success. It means doing the right thing, being honest, showing integrity, being consistent, and being fair. This value, along with the others, defines the culture of HOLT CAT and guides individual and organizational actions. Putting "ethical" as the first core value was a very conscious decision. The spirit of the core values is captured in HOLT CAT's Vision Statement that reads:

We manage by our business values to provide a safe, productive, fulfilling work environment for employees, legendary service for customers, enhanced value for shareholders, and mutually beneficial outcomes for all stakeholders.

(Continued)

Peter Holt sees the CEO's role as one of "steward and guardian" of HOLT CAT's values. He monitors the values-development process, checking constantly to see that both his and the companies' actions are in alignment with the values. Holt also developed several supporting processes and training programs that were put in place to monitor and measure alignment with the stated values. HOLT CAT also established an ongoing and systematic evaluation system to identify gaps between what is said and what is done.

HOLT CAT's growth and success since 1988 has been phenomenal. The employee base has grown, turnover has declined, and customer satisfaction has increased. Sales and profits have increased substantially as the company grew beyond the $1 billion mark. Today, HOLT CAT is the largest Caterpillar dealer in North America. A spirit of shared responsibility and collaboration has accompanied these very tangible results. Peter Holt attributes these successes to the Holt Values-Based Leadership process.

Holt's unique brand of leadership has led it to influence many other companies. In 1994, Holt Development Services, Inc. (HDSI) was formed to share Holt's model, and success, with other organizations. They offer organizational and leadership development facilitation and products to organizations throughout North America, and have helped many begin their own values journey.

BRANDING—CASE STUDY

by Paramount Pictures

Company: Paramount Pictures
Case: Rebranding *The First Wives Club* for the International Market

Background

On Friday, September 20, 1996, Paramount Pictures released *The First Wives Club*, a $40 million romantic comedy starring Goldie Hawn, Diane Keaton, and Bette Midler. By the following Monday morning, the film had grossed $20.1 million, landing it firmly atop the weekend box office chart and setting the all-time record (up until then) for any September or October opening. From there, the film quickly went on to gross over $100 million in North America, a rare accomplishment. The studio had the makings of a major hit in the domestic market and quickly needed to decide whether to roll out the film internationally, and if so, how.

A classic comedy, *The First Wives Club* is the story of three college girlfriends reunited some 20 years later in the midst of strikingly similar mid-life crises. Having lost touch after graduation, each of them went on to marry seemingly decent men who all turned out to be of loathsome and failing character. As the three women reunite, it emerges that all three have been divorced in favor of younger trophy wives.

The film features a distinguished cast of three award-winning actresses in the starring roles: Bette Midler (Oscar nominations for *The Rose* and *For the Boys*); Diane Keaton (Academy Award for her role in *Annie Hall*); and Goldie Hawn (Academy Award for her role in *Cactus Flower*).

The domestic marketing campaign drew heavily on the star appeal of the cast. The poster art prominently featured all three women, seated triumphantly with legs crossed and their hands clutching champagne flutes and cigars. Marketing efforts trained the public's attention on the hilarity of three down-and-out wives getting back at their rich husbands, a theme captured in the movie's tagline (spoken by Ivana Trump in the movie): "Don't get mad. Get everything."

International Film Potential

It is commonplace today to believe that foreign markets represent a kind of rich bonus which is automatically allocated to films that have proved themselves in the United States. However, this is hardly the case. *Clueless*, which did extremely well in the United States and even spawned a successful spin-off series on television, earned less than half its domestic box office in foreign release. Howard Stern's *Private Parts* and *Beavis and Butt-Head Do America* were solid hits in the United States, but did not perform well overseas. Generally speaking, very few U.S. films do as well abroad as they do at home. The films that do well internationally tend to do so for two main reasons: big stars or big action.

However, data from 1996–1998, showed that foreign revenues began to exceed domestic revenues. For example, the breakout success of the film *Titanic*, which was released in late 1997, earned $1.2 billion overseas, twice its domestic box office. Movie studios live from the profits of their hit films. This is why Paramount had no choice but to release *First Wives* internationally.

International Film Issues

Whereas foreign revenues fluctuated relative to the domestic box office in the era preceding *First Wives*, the costs of releasing a film internationally continued to steadily increase. Today it is not uncommon for the international release of a film to cost $25 million (promotional costs). Unlike traditional consumer products that can be test-marketed, recalled, altered, postponed, or "strategically deployed," releasing a movie is basically an all-or-nothing proposition.

Given the considerable expense of international release, films that fail commercially in the domestic market are rarely released internationally. In the case of *First Wives*, Paramount had a success. However, it also had a comedy with all-female stars, which typically fell into a statistical category of motion pictures that have little significance. With the exception of action films, there is little consistency in the ratio of foreign box office to domestic box office in other genres.

Successful films were heavily skewed toward the action genre or star vehicles. For *First Wives*, a well-executed marketing strategy would have to fill the breach. If anything can be said of all films, it is this: until it opens, a film is largely what one tells the public it is. Empirically speaking, *Gone with the Wind* was a drama set against the backdrop of racial oppression in the post-civil war South. Of course no one thinks of it as such, because the film was advertised to the public as an epic romance.

Marketing Strategies

For Paramount Pictures and the motion picture industry, undeniably Bette, Goldie, and Diane are major stars. What the international marketing department was really concerned about was: Could the film be promoted abroad as a star vehicle or could the U.S. cultural experience of this film be replicated elsewhere?

Up to this point, the successful films that had dealt with the subject matter of divorce had mostly treated the topic dramatically (*Kramer vs. Kramer*, *The Goodbye Girl*, *Ordinary People*). America instantly liked *First Wives*, but would the rest of the world really laugh as hard as America had?

(Continued)

How would the film play, for instance, in such major territories as:

- France, where few men choose divorce when they can simply take a mistress
- Japan, where although divorce is technically an option, it is scarcely a topic for discussion
- Korea, where marriages are still arranged
- Predominantly Catholic nations of Latin America where, if it is more commonplace than it is in Asia, divorce is nonetheless nothing to be made light of

Paramount decided on a wide international release for *First Wives*. Within two months of opening in the United States, *First Wives* debuted in the next-largest territories: the United Kingdom and Germany, followed in rapid succession by France, Spain, Italy, and Japan.

Each time a studio releases a film abroad, numerous focus groups and test screenings are instituted in order to gauge viewer reaction and develop a sense for how the film should be positioned in a particular market. One of the chief benefits of this additional research is its ability to suggest an effective pattern for allocating marketing dollars to radio, television, or print advertising.

Despite the fact that, in the case of *First Wives*, international prerelease research largely confirmed trends witnessed in North America, the international marketing campaign was hardly a clone of the North American campaign. While it preserved some of the core features of the domestic release, the foreign campaign was varied and regionalized in a way that is not typically part of marketing a movie at home.

It also is important to realize that film marketers, particularly the international team, do not have carte blanche to dream up an entirely new campaign, as this would be prohibitively expensive. Domestic campaigns for major releases are now averaging almost $30 million, a fact that forces a certain amount of budgetary discipline on international marketers and compels them to incorporate as much of what has already been paid for as they possibly can. In the case of *First Wives*, the key poster art with the champagne and the cigars had to be changed for regulatory reasons, given that outdoor alcohol and tobacco advertising are severely restricted outside the United States. The tagline, on the other hand, was changed only out of creative necessity. In Germany, the title of the film was *Club der Teufelinnen* ("The She-Devils' Club") and the tagline, "Jede Scheidung hat ihren Preis" literally means "every divorce has its price."

Five general principles applied to the marketing of *First Wives*:

1. The film's success in the United States became a marketing instrument in itself. Publicists could more easily entice journalists to cover the film, and advertisements were able to invite audiences to "come see the film that took America by storm."
2. Marketers tended to rebrand the film as "a classic tale of revenge" rather than focusing on the more specific (and trickier) notion of divorce. Some campaigns directly catered to a "soak-the-rich" or similarly motivated revenge instinct and would, for instance, ask radio listeners or newspaper readers to share any personal experiences related to the movie's theme. This approach proved highly successful in building awareness about the picture. Radio stations in particular welcomed the promotion as a chance to build their own audiences. Similarly, television news magazines would do spin-off stories based on women who called in with similar experiences or related, interesting stories.
3. Managers carefully rebranded *First Wives* as *the* comedy alternative in a field of action films and dramas. Because *First Wives'* international release placed the film in a crowded field (which was not the case during the U.S. run), foreign marketers were forced to clearly differentiate the

film from the moment they brought it to the public's attention. For example, in cutting film trailers down to 20- and 30-second television commercials, editors selected the best liked moments of physical humor in the film.

4. Media buying targeted women primarily, in the belief they would drag the men with them. They did. Numerous promotional efforts created awareness among the core demographic: beauty salon giveaways and luxury spa weekends in connection with radio call-in contests; in Spain, marketers teamed up with Moschino accessories and Gianni Versace toiletries; in Korea, they partnered with Toblerone chocolates. Despite the fact that promotional efforts were exclusively focused on women, exit polls consistently showed audiences to be evenly mixed, male to female.

5. The number of advance screenings was significantly increased in an effort to build word-of-mouth. If hype is the most expensive way to open a film, word-of-mouth is the cheapest way to sustain one. Screening polls showed that nearly all women who enjoyed the film also liked it enough to actively recommend it to a friend. In many countries, special screenings were added for influential women, such as in Hungary, where 200 female VIPs attended; in Poland, celebrity divorcées were invited to a special gala opening.

On a territory-by-territory basis, campaigns naturally diverged in interesting ways. Brazil actually already had its own club of divorcées and was able to benefit accordingly. Prerelease interest in the film was so strong in other countries that it actually led to a First Wives' Club being founded, and in Hungary, actor Sandor Friderikusz even called for the creation of the First Husbands' Club.

Results

The film completed its international theatrical run on July 4, with a total of approximately $82 million in receipts, one of the best titles in foreign release for all of 1996.

by Landor Associates

Company: BP
Case: Delivering the Brand Promise

The BP story is one of the most famous corporate brand transformations in recent memory. It began with a clear vision from a strong leader, Lord John Browne, who wanted to forge a new kind of company from the merger of several well-established brands, chief among them British Petroleum, Amoco, Castrol, and bits and pieces of major oil and gas companies such as Mobil and Arco. Like all good visions, it was a serious stretch for the organization. Lord Browne and his team did not set out to be merely one of the best petroleum companies in the world; they wanted BP to be one of the best *companies* in the world, period.

This meant redefining itself from being primarily a refiner of hydrocarbons to a provider of complete energy solutions. It also meant evolving from a British corporation to becoming a diverse global

(Continued)

citizen organized around a clear brand idea and personality. With BP's upstream and downstream markets spanning over 100 countries, the challenge was to find an idea that could resonate meaningfully and credibly across multiple audiences while differentiating the brand from competitors. Through work with Ogilvy & Mather and Landor, the *Beyond Petroleum* brand idea became the mantra that championed both a vision and a promise for the future.

The brand idea was expanded into a Brand Driver™ platform consisting of the core brand idea, articulated as a verbal brand driver and statement of relevant differentiation (essentially a brand promise); personality, expressed in terms of brand beliefs (performance, progressive, innovation, and green); and an added tool Landor calls a visual Brand Driver, which is a metaphorical set of images the creative and consulting team develops with the client to help bridge the brand idea and the visual identity.

From the Brand Driver platform came the Helios logo and other aspects of the visual identity symbolizing energy and environmental sensitivity. The logo in particular became an external representation of the brand idea and a powerful internal symbol. But the real transformation came from the inside. The branding process involved creating a series of tools including Web sites, CDs, brand movies, newsletters, and all manner of company-branded items that emphasized not only the excitement of the new visual identity but, more importantly, the idea behind it. Indeed it was the *story* of the brand and its promise that BP focused on telling.

Brand champion workshops were organized to train trainers, generating ownership among individuals within the company who then evangelized the mission to others. In all, more than 1,400 brand champions were trained in 19 countries over the initial two months following the launch in July 2000. This was viral marketing at its best: from the inside. The impact was also measured, revealing that by the ninth month postlaunch, 97 percent of all BP employees were aware of the *Beyond Petroleum* brand idea and new identity.

Awareness and action, of course, are two different things. BP leadership knew that to engage the hearts and minds of employees over the long term, the brand transformation would have to be about more than flag waving. The result, among other initiatives, was the creation of the Helios awards. This annual program honors those employees who have contributed to the company and their respective communities through actions judged to be on-brand: performance, progressive, innovation, and green. In this way, leadership communicates that *Beyond Petroleum* is to be a way of life at BP, not a transient tagline.

Of course, it is all well and good to get the foundations in place, but, in the end, deeds count for more than words. BP chose its initial actions carefully. Early on, it committed publicly to reducing greenhouse emissions 10 percent by 2010, the equivalent of taking 18 million cars off the road. It initiated partnerships with leading auto manufacturers in the pursuit of more efficient engines and practical alternative fuels. BP quickly became one of the world's largest producers of solar panels and solar power, and the second-largest provider of natural gas. In the summer of 2005, the company announced an $8 billion investment in alternative energy.

These were among the many clear indicators that BP was committed to: achieving its goal of taking the promise of *Beyond Petroleum* seriously and becoming one of the world's greatest companies. But did this have any impact on the bottom line? That, too, was impressive. Retail sales at convenience stores increased 23 percent within one year of the rebranding effort.[24] Overall sales, and sales of lubricants and fuels, increased steadily between 5 and 10 percent above market growth through

2004. Profits were exceptional at $91.3 billion in 2005, enabling BP to fund new initiatives to drive its business.

These actions have been well noted by the public and press. *Fortune* magazine consistently ranks BP a Most Admired Company and as one of the 10 most improved brands in terms of brand equity value. Indeed, if we apply BAV metrics and Stern Stewart's Economic Value Added analytics, BP's brand assets alone were quantified as having increased by more than $7 billion between 2001 and 2005 while competitors declined in value.[25] In the intervening years, economic, competitive, and professional ups and downs have plagued all companies of BP's scale, but its brand continues to be regarded as one of the most respected and progressive in the world. And no other company comes close to owning BP's green positioning in its industry.

BP is still clearly committed to keeping and delivering its brand idea. As Lord Browne himself said: "In a global marketplace, branding is crucially important in attracting customers and business. It is not just a matter of a few gasoline stations or the logo on pole signs. It is about the identity of the company and the values that underpin everything that you do and every relationship that you have."[26]

CORPORATE PROFILES AND AUTHOR BIOGRAPHIES

FLEISHMAN-HILLARD

Fleishman-Hillard, one of the world's leading public relations firms, specializes in strategic communications that delivers what clients value most: meaningful, positive, and measurable impact on business performance. Visit Fleishman-Hillard at www.fleishman.com.

Rich Jernstedt

Rich Jernstedt has a 40-year career in public relations with a focus on brand and reputation management. Mr. Jernstedt received his BA in journalism from the University of Oregon. He is active in the major public relations organizations.

HOLT CAT

Benjamin Holt invented the first practical track-type tractor in 1904 and gave it the name Caterpillar. His firm, Holt Manufacturing Company, merged with a competitor in 1925 to form the Caterpillar Tractor Company. Visit HOLT CAT at www.holtcat.com.

Dan Norris, CMCT

Dan Norris is the Director of Training for Holt Development Services, Inc., the developmental training group of HOLT CAT. Mr. Norris specializes in the science of ethical influence.

Additional input by:

Larry Axeline.

LANDOR ASSOCIATES

Landor Associates is one of the world's leading strategic brand consulting and design firms. Landor is part of WPP, one of the world's largest global communications services companies. Visit Landor at www.landor.com.

Sarah Wealleans

Sarah Wealleans is consultant and former senior client director with Landor Associates, responsible for leading strategy development and managing projects. Ms. Wealleans received her BA in modern European history from the University of Warwick and received her MA in Japanese studies from the University of London.

PARAMOUNT PICTURES

Paramount Pictures is one of the original motion picture studios and is a leading producer and distributor of feature films with more than 2,500 titles including *The Ten Commandments, The Godfather,* and *Titanic*. Visit Paramount at www.viacom.com.

Robert G. Friedman

Robert Friedman was Vice Chairman of the Motion Picture Group and COO of Paramount Pictures. He was responsible for worldwide acquisition, marketing, and distribution of feature films and videos. Mr. Friedman was responsible for the U.S. marketing of *Titanic*, the highest grossing film in history.

Thomas B. McGrath

Thomas McGrath was Executive Vice President, Viacom Entertainment Group, which includes Paramount Pictures and Paramount Television. Mr. McGrath received his BA *cum laude* and his MBA from Harvard.

David L. Molner

David Molner was Senior Vice President, Worldwide Corporate Business Development for Viacom Entertainment Group and was responsible for the expansion and development of Paramount Pictures' ancillary businesses including online ventures, multiplex cinemas, theme parks, licensing, merchandising, music publishing, and television. Mr. Molner received his BA from Trinity College.

Additional input by:

The authors would like to extend their special thanks to Mr. Paul Oneile, chairman of United International Pictures (UIP), and Ms. Joanna Johnson, Vice

President of International Marketing in the Paramount Pictures Motion Picture Group, as well as the many field managers and executives at UIP who helped put together this case study.

UNDER ARMOUR

Under Armour, founded in 1996, is a leading developer, marketer, and distributor of branded performance apparel, footwear, and accessories. The brand's moisture-wicking synthetic fabrications are engineered in many different designs and styles for wear in nearly every climate. Visit Under Armour at www.under armour.com.

Stephen (Steve) J. Battista

Steve Battista, Senior Vice President of Brand, oversees all aspects of domestic and international communications, including brand marketing, advertising, public relations, marketing communications, product integration, events, and sponsorships. Mr. Battista and his team serve as the "Voice of the Brand" to ensure authenticity and find innovative ways to tell the Under Armour story to millions of athletes around the world. Mr. Battista received his BA from Towson University in 1996 and received his MFA from Johns Hopkins University in 2000.

NOTES

1. McKinsey & Company, "Strike Up the Brands,"
2. David Ogilvy, primary.co.uk/viewpoints.
3. *Dictionary of Business and Management*, Oxford University Press.
4. Walter Landor, founder of Landor Associates.
5. Marty Neumeier, *The Brand Gap*.
6. Allen Adamson, *BrandSimple* (New York: Palgrave Macmillan, 2007).
7. Steven Mallas, Motley Fool (May 7, 2004).
8. Scott Bedbury and Stephen Fenichell, *A New Brand World: Eight Principles for Achieving Brand Leadership in the Twenty-First Century.* (New York: Penguin Putnam, 2003).
9. "Insights into Customer Insights," kellogg.northwestern.edu/faculty/.
10. Mark Earls, *Welcome to the Creative Age*, (Hoboken, NJ: Wiley, 2002).
11. Christopher Booker, *The Seven Basic Plots: Why We Tell Stories.* (London, UK: Continuum, 2006).
12. Rohit Bhargava, *Personality Not Included. (New York: McGraw-Hill, 2008).*
13. Mary Zalla, *Packaging Design* magazine, April 2009.
14. www.martinlindstrom.com.
15. Linda Tischler, *Fast Company*, December 19, 2007.
16. Reena Amos Dyes, *Emirates Business*, June 20, 2008.
17. Ibid.
18. Linda Tischler, *Fast Company*, December 19, 2007.
19. Gerald Zaltman, *How Customers Think.* (Watertown, MA: Harvard Business Press, 2003)
20. ddb.com, October 2007.
21. Jon Miller and David Muir, *The Business of Brands.*
22. Ibid.
23. The Arthur Page Society.
24. *Wall Street Journal,* July 2002.
25. Al Ehrbar, *Fortune* magazine, October 31, 2005.
26. *Chicago Business Journal,* April 3, 2000.

5 MARKETING RESEARCH

by Colgate-Palmolive, Synovate, ACNielsen, and Sports and Leisure Research Group

First get your facts; then you can distort them at your leisure.

Mark Twain, American Author, 1835–1910

THE ESSENTIALS OF MARKETING RESEARCH
by Colgate-Palmolive

Introduction

Marketing research is the element of marketing that provides information about current and potential customers to management in order to reduce uncertainty and improve the quality of management's decision making and marketing planning. The needs of individual consumers and many organizations are often extremely diverse. Marketing research can help identify groups of customers who are homogeneous in some respects. By understanding and quantifying the nature and magnitude of these distinct groups and their needs, marketers can take advantage of unique and profitable marketing opportunities.

Marketing research gives companies insights into the influences of market demand and allows companies to see how well their products or services compare with the competition. It identifies which segments of the market to target, how to best reach and communicate with these targets, and how to design and price products or services to meet the needs of these target customers. Marketers who understand and anticipate customers' needs will often outperform their competition.

Companies want to make marketing decisions quickly in order to act decisively in the marketplace. Any time spent researching an issue is time that might be lost in generating sales and profits. Whenever marketing research is commissioned, companies must weigh the benefits of gaining specific information against the costs of the research and the time required to obtain useful answers. Occasionally, marketing research will be unable to provide exactly the kind of information needed within a reasonable timetable or budget.

Marketing research may be unnecessary if a company already knows its target market well. For example, many small personal service organizations, such as lawyers, accountants, and child-care workers, have exceptionally close relationships with relatively few clients and are able to understand, anticipate, adjust, and respond to their client base. However, as the number of customers gets larger—many companies manage brands with millions of international customers—the organization's ability to know its customers diminishes, and there is a need for marketing research.

For example, Nike is an effective user of marketing research. During the decade of the 1980s, America was characterized by a profound interest in health and fitness. Running shoes and sports clothing became the hottest-selling apparel. Yet by the mid–1980s, marketing research indicated that the momentum behind the hard-body craze was beginning to shift. The fastest growing outdoor activity was gardening, not exactly a high-energy sport. Nike listened to marketing research and was able to anticipate changing customer needs. They introduced a broad array of walking shoes and shoes targeted to specific sports beyond jogging. As a result, Nike was able to achieve a larger share of the footwear market in the 1990s.

Marketers drive innovation, introduce products, and make brands grow. Often marketers are the only people in the organization who have a clear vision of what a brand can or should be. However, marketers may risk becoming overly convinced by their own advocacy. Research provides an important check to this natural optimism. Research often is used as an objective control or audit mechanism against which marketers can gauge progress or success.

Definition

Marketing research is the element that links the customer to the marketer through information used to identify and define marketing opportunities and problems; generate, refine, and evaluate marketing actions; and monitor marketing performance. Marketing research involves problem definition, research design, sampling methodology definition, data collection, data analysis, statistical inferences, and reporting of results that aid corporate marketing decisions in a way that makes it possible for the corporation to profitably act upon it.

MARKETING RESEARCH LINKS CUSTOMERS AND ORGANIZATIONS

Goods/Services/Ideas

Organizations → Customers

Marketing information
Regarding needs/wants

TYPES OF FIRMS

The marketing research industry includes the following separate, yet interlocking, entities: advertisers/marketing organizations, marketing communications agencies, and marketing research companies/institutes.

Advertisers/Marketing Organizations

All organizations need information concerning their customers, markets, and competition. Organizations that use marketing research services are manufacturers of products, suppliers of services, and government agencies.

A typical marketing research project begins with a marketer who has a need for information about a problem or opportunity. The corporate marketing research manager has responsibility for identifying an appropriate research response to the information need or problem. He or she may contact a research institute or an agency to discuss alternative solutions. A research institute may employ a project director to design the research approach, manage a research project, analyze the results, and present them to the marketer. The project director will have professional support in the form of sampling statisticians, field interviewers, data processing professionals, database analysts, statistical analysts, production/printing experts, and graphics specialists.

Marketing Communications Agencies

Promotional agencies, such as advertising, public relations, promotional marketing, and direct marketing, share responsibility for effectively communicating marketing messages and producing advertising and other promotional marketing materials. Agencies tend to focus much of their research spending on communications effectiveness.

Marketing Research Companies/Institutes

Most of the marketing research survey and analysis work is conducted by research institutes or their subcontractors. Research institutes include qualitative research companies, syndicated quantitative research companies, and custom marketing research survey companies. Their subcontractors include field services that do interviewing work (personally, or via mail, telephone, or Internet), data entry or keypunch shops that convert questionnaire information from paper form into machine-readable data, tab houses that do large-scale cross-tabulations of data, and database modeling companies that prepare sample lists and develop predictive models. Consulting companies have become increasingly important generators of marketing research data.

Research companies can provide syndicated or nonsyndicated (custom) research.

- **Syndicated Research.** A syndicated research service is one in which a research company splits the costs of the research by selling the same data to multiple underwriters or clients. The largest amount of evaluative research spending is used for syndicated research services. For example, a typical consumer packaged-goods company may spend approximately 70 percent of their annual marketing research budget on syndicated research. The advantage of syndicating is that a data collection process that would be too expensive for any one company can be offered at a reasonable price to many underwriters. A disadvantage is that all underwriters have access to the same information.
- **Custom Research.** Marketing research companies also provide proprietary data. This research is very specific to the client's products or services. The advantages are the ability to tailor the questions to the company and specify the time and locations of the research. The disadvantage is the additional cost.

RESEARCH NEEDS

In 1975, in the United States, the stereotypical consumer target of most brands was a woman, 18 to 49 years old, with an average of 2.5 kids, in a high-consumption household. However, the world is becoming increasingly complex, and the traditional consumer target is changing. Today, this stereotypical household represents less than 20 percent of

U.S. households. Through marketing research, companies can better understand consumer behavior, and structure their efforts toward fulfilling demand opportunities. For example, Disney used to target their ads exclusively to kids; however, now they appeal to a much broader audience and spend a significant percentage of their promotion budget targeting adults.

Marketing research should consider general or macro market demand and consumer trends and integrate this with specific brand information. *Macro trends* are the forces that influence consumer behavior at the broadest level. These trends may lead to important implications for a company's brands. Macro trends include economics, social habits, values, lifestyles, demographics, and technology. These observations must be acted on and are not just theoretical or nice to know.

For example, because of the increase in women going to work, in many households, kids and teens started preparing meals as well as eating at separate times from other family members. This led to the development of high-quality convenience foods because adults wanted convenient but satisfying meals even if it meant paying a premium. The result was a success for Stouffer's and the birth of a major new product segment (high-quality frozen meals). Frozen pizza makers also caught on to this trend and have enjoyed success.

Consumer Studies

It is important to know in specific detail what, why, and how consumers use products. This kind of learning can lead to the identification of new consumer segments with products specifically designed to meet their needs. There are three main types of consumer studies: habits and practices, attitude and usage, and equity studies.

Habits and Practices
Habits and practices studies describe *what* consumers do, both reported and actual. For example, a study may be conducted to determine how people brush their teeth. People differ in how long they brush, although most overestimate the actual

amount of time they brush when asked. It is important to know the actual time the average person brushes because a company may need to reformulate a minty toothpaste flavor so that it will not burn within the average time period. The amount of time people brush also is critical for formulas that fight cavities and other problems.

Examples of habits and practices questions include:

Do consumers rinse their brush before brushing?
Do consumers brush their tongue?
Do consumers use cold water or hot water?
Do consumers rinse with water or mouthwash after brushing?

HABITS AND PRACTICES		
M&M Mars found out through a habits and practices study that consumers were putting their Snickers chocolate bars in the freezer, because it tastes good and provides a nice consistency. The company acted on this information with the outcome being the Snickers Ice Cream Bar.		
Source	Information	Outcome
Habits and Practices Research	Some consumers put chocolate bars in freezer.	Snickers Ice Cream Bars

Attitude and Usage

Attitude and usage studies describe *why* consumers behave a certain way and why they make certain brand choices. Companies should study attitudes separately because people do not always do what they say. Behaviors cannot always be fully described: it may be too complex or there may be inaccurate memory. The only way to be sure of getting the facts is by researchers observing consumers or by consumers filling out a diary right after performing the task of interest. For example, if everyone really flossed as often as they say they do, the floss market would be about six times bigger than it really is.

Examples of attitude and usage questions include:

Which brands are consumers aware of?
Why do consumers use certain brands?

How many consumers mainly seek therapeutic benefits in a toothpaste: protection from cavities, tartar, and gum problems?
How many mainly seek cosmetic benefits: whiter teeth and fresher breath?
What brands do consumers use, and why?

ATTITUDE AND USAGE		
Colgate found out through an attitude and usage study that consumers wash hands in order to kill germs. The company acted on this information with the outcome being the antibacterial Hand and Dish Liquid, one of Colgate's biggest successes.		
Source	Information	Outcome
Attitude and Usage Research	Killing germs is #1 reason for washing hands.	Palmolive Anti-Bacterial Hand and Dish Liquid

Equity Studies

Equity studies seek to understand *how* consumers think and feel about a particular brand. These studies seek to get at the attributes, characteristics, and personality of a brand and identify triggers and barriers to brand acceptance.

EQUITY STUDIES		
Irish Spring discovered through an equity study that users and nonusers had very divergent feelings about the brand. The company acted on this information with the outcome being a successful new ad campaign used to attract nonusers to the brand.		
Source	Information	Outcome
Equity Research	Irish Spring user feels that the soap means "Green, fresh, outdoors, and active." Irish Spring nonuser feels that the soap means "Harsh, masculine, too strong, and applies to heavy dirt."	Change in advertising

Consumer insight should influence product development; technology alone should not be the motivating force of a company's marketing activity. Unfortunately, sometimes companies try to promote new products that the consumer does not really want.

For example, Colgate Gum Protection was a technology-driven product that promoted superior gum-protection benefits; however, it was a sales disappointment, selling only $35 million a year. Consumers who saw themselves needing gum protection were a small group of people who suffer from gum disease. The same product was relaunched as Colgate Total, appealing to a much broader group needing tooth cleaning, tartar control, and gum protection. The result was that Colgate Total became a $200 million brand.

Marketing Research Process

1. Opportunity/Problem Definition

The marketing research process begins with a marketing opportunity or problem and a need for information to assess the options or solutions. The marketing researcher needs to understand the entire context of the problem in order to determine the proper research scope. For example, the brand manager for Jello may need to know how many people feel full after a meal.

2. Cost-Benefit Analysis (Initial Budgetary Considerations)

Research that does not result in action is largely wasted. A marketing research budget should be in proportion to the magnitude of the opportunity or problem. The cost of making marketing mistakes can be very high and should be roughly quantified in financial terms. When the benefit of additional information is low and the cost is high, perhaps research is not called for. When the opportunity is great, such as the soft drink market, the value of information that reduces the risk or increases the opportunity may be correspondingly higher. However, marketing research needs to realize a very high return on its expenditures for it to be a good business investment, typically at least a 20:1 relationship. In addition, there is a risk of revealing to competitors what is being tested.

Marketing research can be simple and inexpensive, such as when marketers talk directly to a few of their customers. It can be simple and expensive, such as when Honda Motor Company sends its senior Japanese marketing executives to different export market countries to keep in touch with their dealers and customers. It also can be highly complex and expensive. For example, Yankelovich Partners recently conducted a $1.8 million study of credit card customers that involved segmentation, forecasting, and market response modeling.

3. Research Hypothesis

If research is deemed beneficial and cost-effective, then the next step is to create a research hypothesis. The research hypothesis presupposes an association or causation between customer behavior and the marketing opportunity or problem. By attempting to prove or disprove the hypothesis, this forces a very specific direction to the research and eliminates wasteful side-issue research. For example, a researcher might hypothesize the following: "We believe school-age kids are the primary drivers of fruit-flavored soda purchases." Marketing research will determine the possible outcomes of the hypothesis. A company should set up an action standard to determine what it will do if this hypothesis is true versus if it is false, such as whether it will focus its advertising on school kids, teenagers, young adults, or parents.

To test the hypothesis, the researcher must specify what types of information, questions, data collection methods, sample designs, and questionnaires are needed.

4. Specify Information/Data Needs

Information needs are specified to give the researchers direction. They include amount and detail, time-series, and demographic/psychographic.

Amount and Detail

The amount and detail of marketers' data needs can be small and simple or expansive and detailed, depending on the product's characteristics, such as taste, consumer familiarity, and technical complexity. This decision also is dependent on time and budget constraints.

Time-Series

Researchers should determine whether the surveys will be a one-time test or longitudinal (repeated over time). Multiple time-period surveys give a more complete reading of the market but take significantly more time and cost more money.

Demographic/Psychographic

It is important to understand who is contributing answers to the research in order to have more projectable results and to understand their rationale. Consumer backgrounds are determined by demographic and psychographic data.

- **Demographic.** Demographic information is that which provides an *external identification* of the individual. This data includes age, gender, income, race, location of residence, make of car, and years of schooling. This information is helpful in depicting a typical consumer and therefore selecting appropriate media and a spokesperson for promotional efforts. This information is relatively easy to determine; however, it is of decreasing importance as product and service usage crosses demographic boundaries. For example, determining household composition or income levels would be useful for a regional ad campaign. The U.S. Census determines consumer income levels in order to know where to spend social program funding.

- **Psychographic.** Psychographic information is that which provides an *internal identification* of the consumer and their rationale for making product or service selections. This data includes an individual's values, beliefs, and attitudes (described in Chapter 6, "Consumer Purchasing Behavior"). These variables are difficult to determine and usually are indicated through *proxy or indicator variables* such as type of magazines read, television shows watched, brand of clothing worn, and age of car. For example, finding out whether an individual is introspective or extroverted would help an organization determine whether to market books on philosophy through a direct mailing or books on travel through telephone solicitation.

5. Specify Type of Questions/Type of Research

Based on the information needed, the next step is to select the appropriate research type: evaluative, generative, or predictive. This will determine how the results are presented.

- **Evaluative Research.** Evaluative research analyzes marketing activity performance (for example, how big, how good, or how much). Most research studies are evaluative in nature. Evaluative research examines results relative to a standard or an objective, often called an *action standard*. Having an action standard implies that the results will be acted upon depending on their relation to the standard of measurement. Marketing objectives often are set relative to marketplace measurement action standards, for example, market share objectives or sales objectives. Evaluative research provides the standard measurement, such as share, sales, preference, satisfaction, or level of response for marketing actions.

  Typical evaluative questions are

  "Which of these two advertisements works better?"

  "By how much can I decrease the costs of ingredients and still have a product that satisfies my customers?"

  "How satisfied are my customers compared to my competitors' customers?"

  Evaluative research areas include retail sales; copy testing services; product, concept, and package testing; customer satisfaction tracking; and advertising tracking for awareness and usage.

- **Generative Research.** Generative research identifies opportunities by determining how and why results occur. Generative research tries to move from specific observations about the consumer and the marketplace to general principles about how people make brand choice decisions. Knowing these principles allows marketers to predict results, rather than rely on trial and error. Generative research techniques, including everything from focus groups to sophisticated mathematical market response models, often employ the scientific method. The *scientific method* begins with an observation, which leads to a hypothesis that is then tested through experiments.

Typical generative research questions are

"How can I make my customers more loyal?"

"How can I make my advertising message work better?"

"Will my brand increase sales more if I increase my spending on advertising or if I put the same amount of money into promotion spending?"

Generative research areas include in-depth personal interviews, market experiments, market segmentation research (broad-scale surveys that examine the nature and composition of the customer base for an industry), and product optimization research (which uses an experimental design to systematically test alternative product configurations in order to identify the optimal product offering).

- **Predictive Research.** Predictive research analyzes behavior and market response. Predictive research is most concerned with forecasting sales. By attempting to forecast, marketers can set production targets, spending budgets, and sales goals. Typically, predictive research is dependent upon a quantitative model of consumer processes or marketplace channels.

Typical predictive research questions are

"How much can I decrease spending and still maintain my market share?"

"How much impact will my competitor's new marketing program have on my business?"

"What is the forecast volume for my product line over the next six months?"

Predictive research techniques include new product forecasting services (which offer an estimate of the first-year sales likely to be generated), sales forecasting models (which examine the historical sales data and the factors associated with higher or lower sales), consumption models (which examine store or consumer inventories relative to sales to try to predict the sell-through of products), and vulnerability models (which predict the likelihood of customers remaining in the franchise over time).

6. Specify Data Collection Method

Data is the information collected through marketing research and used to make marketing decisions.

Much of the art of marketing research is in making design tradeoffs among different data sources to obtain information of sufficiently high quality within an appropriate time-frame for decision making and at a reasonable cost. The best data quality may be too expensive to be worthwhile, or it may take too long to generate an answer. There are two main components of data collection methods: characteristics and sources.

Characteristics of Data Collection Methodology

Data quality can be assessed using six factors: reliability, validity, projectability, relevance, sensitivity, and practicality (see Table 5.1). Before making any major changes in marketing programs, it is important to evaluate the quality of new information. Increases in data quality usually are accompanied by increases in time spent and costs.

- **Reliability.** Reliability assesses the data collection method's ability to collect the same data again and get the same results. The goal is to reduce sources of error and make sure any differences in data are not due to the collection method. Reliability can be increased by repeated observations. Data quality improves in research surveys as more observations are added. Therefore, increasing the sample size will improve the reliability of the answer. For example, if three surveys from different cities report the same information, the company will have more confidence in the data.

- **Validity.** Validity assesses whether the data actually measures what it purports to measure. Validity is enhanced through the use of multiple measurements. Rather than depending upon a single observation of an attitude or behavior, the market researcher prefers to see convergence across multiple measurements. For example, the results obtained when asking people how much time they spend watching Public Television are not always valid. Most consumers in the United States believe that it is socially desirable to watch Public Television because the content is educational. Therefore, more people will claim to watch Public Television than will be observed behaviorally.

- **Projectability.** Projectability assesses whether the data is a fair representation of the entire market. It is important to know if one observation is a sufficient basis to project the results upon the entire business base. The most projectable result would be one where everyone in the market is interviewed; however, a census of the entire population is impractical. Some form of sampling is used to extract a representative cross-section of members of the market population. For example, a test with positive results in an area with a large retired population may not project onto a national sales program with a younger target audience.
- **Relevance.** Relevance assesses whether the collected information is appropriate to the marketing decisions to be made. Information should be relevant to the context and not only of casual interest. Lack of relevance is one of the leading problems of marketing research when little thought is given to what will be the decision impact of this expensive information. For example, knowing what type of automobile a typical consumer of a brand of cereal drives may be interesting but not relevant to cereal sales.
- **Sensitivity.** Sensitivity assesses the susceptibility to how small a difference can be detected between two alternative conditions. Sensitivity determines how easily a difference is likely to be noticeable to the consumer. If the difference needed to substantially affect a business is small, a much more sensitive measurement is needed. On the other hand, if the difference between success and failure requires a huge difference in marketplace measures, a very sensitive test will not be needed to determine success or failure, such as rating intent-to-purchase on a 1:100 scale versus a 1:10 scale.
- **Practicality (Specific).** Practicality assesses the cost and time required for each data collection method. The most practical data is that which can be acquired immediately and with no cost.

The more specific and comprehensive the data needs to be, the more expensive it will be to obtain the information and the more time it will take.

Sources of Data

Data can be derived through primary and secondary sources.

- **Secondary Data.** Secondary data is generated by some other individual or organization and is common, generic, and preexisting. Secondary data is found in journals, trade periodicals, databases, syndicated services, and government sources. The advantages of secondary data are that it is relatively quick and inexpensive to acquire and is helpful background information. The disadvantages are the lack of specific fit with organizational research needs and it is typically noncurrent. Examples of secondary data sources include building permits, new car registrations, retail sales, electricity consumed, and newspaper advertising lineage.
- **Primary Data.** Primary data is information collected directly from the consumer or marketplace, and is original, specific, and proprietary. Primary data can be internally or externally generated. Internal primary data is generated by an organization as it does business and includes sales call reports, sales orders, shipment information, inventory, and production information. External primary data is data that a company collects, or pays to have collected, from outside sources specifically for the company.

Primary data is collected through qualitative or quantitative methods. *Qualitative research* methods use discussions with individuals in small focus groups, in-depth interviews, or laboratory settings to gain insight into consumers' thoughts about nonquantifiable areas such as trust, integrity, idea generation, concept screening, and reaction to initial exposure. Typically companies start with qualitative research, then perform quantitative research. *Quantitative research* asks questions for which there are specific answers from a much larger database, often in the hundreds or thousands, in order to determine the feedback from a more projectable quantity of individuals. Quantitative methods include telephone interviews, mail interviews, Internet interviews, intercept interviews, and observation. The advantage of primary data is that it is specific to a company's current needs and the exact source of the data is known. The disadvantage is the additional time and cost to acquire the data.

Qualitative Research Methods

- **Focus Groups.** The most common type of qualitative marketing research—a focus group—involves a group of individuals, typically 8 to 12, with similar characteristics recruited to participate in a one- or two-hour discussion about a product, service, or idea. A *group moderator* leads the discussion and elicits input, such as opinions and beliefs, from each individual. Focus groups should only be viewed as generative research. Focus groups are conducted for two reasons: to generate hypotheses (later to be quantitatively verified) and to gather consumer language and views regarding a subject area. Focus groups have several advantages. Having several people in the discussion allows the respondents to talk in their own words and to build on each other's ideas. Additionally, the sponsor of the research can hear and see firsthand the group feedback through a one-way mirror without affecting the research. The disadvantage of a focus group is that the results are not projectable onto the total universe because of the usually low number of respondents, negative group dynamics such as teaming up or a leader emerging and influencing the others, and the subjective analysis phase. A number of companies are now using the Internet to conduct chat sessions using traditional qualitative research techniques, with very good success. These reduce the cost and time required to conduct exploratory research; however, there are fewer controls on content, and participants

may be more inclined to exaggerate or misreport their feelings or behavior.

- **In-Depth Interviews.** This qualitative research technique uses nonstructured, one-on-one discussions for several hours in order to fully understand the individual's behavior and motivations. The advantages of in-depth interviews are that they provide a lot of information not obtainable in short quantitative approaches, eliminate the biases inherent in focus group dynamics, can be used for sensitive subject matter, and can be conducted with relative confidentiality. The disadvantages are that they take a long time to perform, have a high cost per interview, and only a few people are involved.

Quantitative Research Methods

- **Telephone Interviews.** The most common type of quantitative marketing research, telephone interview information is derived from those individuals answering phones in a home or business setting called by *outbound telephone representatives*. The advantages of telephone interviewing are that it is inexpensive due to low cost of staff, has a quick response, and can generate a high-quality representation of the marketplace (telephone penetration is 97 percent in the United States), and there is low interviewer bias. Telephone interviewing has several disadvantages, such as samples have short attention spans and are unlikely to finish a lengthy questionnaire since neither the interviewer nor visual presentation is present. In addition, telephone interviews are most appropriate when interest in the question area is high and respondents are likely to be knowledgeable. When low-involvement categories are surveyed, cooperation rates are poor and the quality of answers obtained is often weak. For example, people with no children usually do not want to participate in a 30-minute telephone interview about diaper services.
- **Mail Interviews.** Information comes from *response cards* mailed to specific individuals or

attached to purchased products. The advantages of mail interviews are the possible wide distribution and no interviewer bias. In addition the recipient can see visual stimuli, can answer at their leisure, provide deeper psychographic information, and have less concern with privacy issues. The disadvantages are the low and slow response rate, no follow-on questions can be asked, and only those interested in the subject matter may respond.

- **Internet Interviews.** These interviews can range from *qualitative ad hoc chat rooms to random quantitative surveys* where text is instantly available for analysis. The advantages are the speed of response, the low cost, and the large sample size. The disadvantages are the self-selection of the recipients, usually with strong points of view, and the lack of randomness, usually with the young and educated online. Internet interviewing is the fastest growing form of survey research today and is characterized by extremely large sample sizes and poor sample control.

- **Intercept Interviews.** An example of an intercept interview would be attempting to talk with consumers while the behavior in question, usually shopping, is fresh in their minds. This usually is accomplished by having the interviewer walk directly up to the respondent in a central location, usually as the respondent walks between stores in a mall. The advantages are that consumer recollection is current because the consumer is currently engaged in relevant purchasing behavior. The disadvantages are that many shoppers may be too busy to participate, the high cost of trained personnel, length of time involved to intercept enough respondents, and the content of the questionnaire must be short to entice participation.

- **Personal Interviews.** Also known as *door-to-door* or *in-home interviews*, they involve an interviewer asking questions of the respondent one-on-one. Advantages of personal interviews are the smallest error rates, the highest-quality,

and the most projectable data. Personal interviews usually have a dialogue between the interviewee and interviewer that allow for flexibility and additional input. For example, personal interviewing should be selected when stimuli are present such as tasting products, showing advertising, and testing concepts. Disadvantages include their high cost, low response rates, long execution time in the field, the extra time and personnel required to obtain information in sparsely settled areas of the country, and they may be difficult to conduct in high-crime areas. They require careful control of interviewers who must execute the block-level sampling plans, making the required calls at the required times.

- **Laboratory Test Method (LTM).** The LTM research technique creates a simulated store-buying environment. Typically, consumers are shown advertising and then permitted to shop in a simulated store. Their subsequent purchasing activity in the laboratory is incorporated into a marketing model. This model can then be used, for example, to predict the total year-one sales of new products prior to their actual introduction in the market. Corporations can use this model to estimate the demand for new products, determine whether to introduce them, and test and fine-tune new product entries before spending millions of dollars on a new product launch.

- **Observation.** Researchers watch consumers' behavior unbeknownst to the individuals being observed. This is done because people often specify one type of behavior to researchers and actually do something different. Typically, observation research is done by observing in-store shopping behavior. An unusual method is to study actual garbage outside someone's home to see what products and in what amounts have been used. The main advantage of the observation method is the high validity of the research. The disadvantages are the length of time involved, the high cost, and privacy issues.

7. Specify Sampling Design

Once a data source has been selected, data quality is directed by the sampling design. It is too expensive to ask every member of the target audience about their preferences; therefore, a small sample is used. The basic principle of *sampling* is that every person within the target market should have an *equal probability* of being selected to participate in the survey. It is important to use a *random sample*, because it allows for a more accurate representation of the target audience and it is only possible to make statistical projections from a random sample. *Statistical projection* means that the results from the people who are questioned can be projected to the rest of the people in the target market.

When designing a sample, four critical issues must be addressed:

- **Target Market.** Determine the target market. Typically this is already specified.
- **Sampling Frame.** This is the specific source of target members from which the sample will be extracted. Sampling frames may include groupings such as telephone number listings,

TABLE 5.1 DATA COLLECTION METHODS AND SELECTION CRITERIA

Source	Reliability	Validity	Sensitivity	Projectability	Relevance	Cost	Time
Focus Groups	Low	Low	Low	Low	High	Moderate	Moderate
In-Depth Interviews	Low	Low	Moderate	Low	High	Moderate	Moderate
Central Location Intercept Interviews	Moderate	Moderate	Depends on Sample Size	Low	Depends on Question Asked	Moderate	Slow
Mall Interviews	Moderate	Moderate	Moderate	Moderate	Depends on Question Asked	Moderate	Slow
Telephone Interviews	High	High	Depends on Sample Size	Highest if Random Digit Dialing Employed	Depends on Question Asked	Low	Fast
Personal Door-to-Door Interviews	Highest	Highest	Depends on Sample Size	Moderate to High	Depends on Question Asked	Expensive	Slow
Internet Interview	High	Low	High	Good for Internet Products	Best for Technology Response	Cheap	Fast
Observation	Low	High	Moderate	Low	High	Costly	Fast
Lab Test	High	High	Moderate/Low	Moderate/High	High	Costly	Slow
Secondary Sources	Low	Low	Low	Low	Moderate	Cheap	Fast

Source: Colgate-Palmolive

street addresses, employee ID numbers, and demographic groupings. The sampling frame will dictate the repeatability and reliability of the research.

- **Sampling Method.** This is the technique of selecting the individuals from within the sampling frame to participate in the research survey. For example, a sampling method could select every "*N*th" name from the telephone book or every "*N*th" person who walks into a mall or store.
- **Sample Size.** Marketing research based upon samples has a small, but real, chance of giving an inaccurate reading of the target market when sample sizes are small. When decisions are critical to business success, it may be worth the additional cost to have a larger sample size to reduce the risk that results will be affected by sampling error.

Sampling error is one of the major risks with qualitative research, such as focus groups. Interviewing groups of 8 to 10 people in a market may provide an understanding of the group; however, the groups may or may not represent the true perspective of the total target market. When companies hear a consumer say something in a focus group, they tend to presume that these attitudes are projectable, or extendible, to the rest of the target market customer base. Yet, even with a large sample size, there is some risk that the results from a sample are going to be different than the rest of the target market population.

For most consumer survey interviews, telephone book databases have been replaced by *random digit dialing (RDD) samples*. RDD samples, generated by computers, are the only way unlisted households can be sampled via a telephone interview. Other types of random sampling include door-to-door sampling (very expensive, but may reach certain segments of the population who have less access to telephones), random shopper sampling (intercepts at point-of-purchase), and random database samples. For example, random samples often include self-selected or self-response questionnaires on the Internet, mail-in magazine survey forms, on-pack/in-pack questionnaires, and in-room guest surveys.

SAMPLING

Reliance on a self-selected sample also may lead to wrong marketing decisions. For example, Nestle Foods wanted to cut marketing research costs by using a less expensive data collection method. Comparing results from an in-pack survey to a random survey in the same markets was proposed. The product evaluated was a new freeze-dried soup product under the Crosse & Blackwell label. The freeze-drying process allowed extremely high quality. However, they were extremely expensive soups. Nestle included postage-paid survey forms within each box of soup sold in the test market and, at the same time, conducted an RDD product satisfaction and forecasting study in the same test market. At the end of six months, the Crosse & Blackwell soups were doing poorly from a sales perspective. Yet, when in-pack survey responses were examined, there were over 10,000 survey responses that were nearly uniformly positive. Nestle could have incorrectly concluded from the survey responses that the soup was a total winner, suitable for national introduction. The random survey of soup purchasers in the test market allowed Nestle to examine the attitudes of people who were aware of the Crosse & Blackwell soups, but had not tried them. The company was able to project these results to the target market and concluded that they would never have enough buyers at that price to profitably introduce the brand.

---

8. *Determine Questionnaire Layout*

After a decision has been made to conduct primary consumer survey research, the next step is determining the questions that need to be answered, and how to best ask the questions in order to get the most useful information. Every question in the questionnaire takes time to administer. Careful questionnaire development will manage the information flow, obtain only the specific information needed to address the marketing issues, make it easy for the respondent to answer and for the interviewer to administer, and minimize biased responses.

- **Wording Clarity.** Question wording needs to be clear and concise, particularly if the data collection occurs over the telephone, so that information is not misunderstood.
- **Questionnaire Order.** Questionnaire order, also known as *scaling*, refers to the proper order of questions. Question content should move from general (product category) to specific (purchase

behavior, specific brand evaluations). Most survey questionnaires will have specific information areas that are more critical to the decision processes. Where possible, these should be asked earlier in the questionnaire to avoid respondent fatigue.

- **Bias Reduction.** It is important to avoid biasing respondents toward or away from particular answers. There are several types of biases.
  - *Wording bias.* Often is done unconsciously, simply from the way questions are asked. For example, wording a question a certain way may influence or annoy some respondents.
  - *Sponsor bias.* May occur if respondents are influenced by knowledge of or experience with the sponsor of the survey. Respondents might be positively or negatively influenced.
  - *Order bias.* May influence respondents by the order in which they see things. It often is important to control the order and the context within which stimuli are presented. Some people tend to prefer the thing they see first (*primacy bias*) whereas others tend to prefer the one they saw last (*recency bias*). The exposure order should be controlled, and the evaluation standardized across research subjects.
  - *Interviewer bias.* May be introduced by characteristics of the interviewer, the style of questioning, or overall demeanor. These characteristics can be either personal looks (too attractive or too unattractive) or the style of questioning (too meek or too harsh). They may cause interviewees to rush their answers and limit their responses or try to become too informative and waste time.
- **Instructions to Respondents.** Respondents are not used to being interviewed. Their closest analogy is being tested in school. This leads them to presume that there are right answers that the interviewer seeks. It is important to reassure respondents that the survey is only interested in their opinions, and that there are no right or wrong answers.
- **Self-Administered Format.** If a questionnaire is to be self-administered, it is particularly important to make the questionnaire fun and give clear instructions in order to encourage correct responses and timely return. Game-playing situations and pictures add interest to the questionnaire, increase respondent involvement, and consequently increase the quality of their information.

9. Data Collection

After the research design has been completed, the next step is for the interviewer team to collect the research data. This task may take a few hours, days, or weeks.

10. Data Input

Research data input involves aggregating and tabulating consumer responses. Consumer responses to a survey need to be translated into a computer-readable form. A number of technologies are used for research data input, including *optical character recognition* of responses on a paper questionnaire, *handwriting recognition software*, *mark-sense readers* of card markings, or *keypunching* of paper-based interviews. Telephone interviewing is nearly universally conducted via *CATI* (*computer-assisted telephone interviews*), and many mall locations use *CASI* (*computer-assisted self-administered interviews*) where the data is directly captured in a computer. Once the information is in hand, it is put into a *marketing research database*. This treats each respondent as a record with each piece of information from the survey treated as a *data field*. Every question results in a *field value* that is entered into the data field based upon the respondent's answer to that question.

11. Research Analysis

Researchers analyze the collected data to test the hypothesis. The primary analysis tool is *cross-tabulation*, whereby a standardized set of subgroups are profiled against all of the survey questions. Research companies use *frequency distribution software* that transforms information from the database into charts and graphs, and organizes the data around a standardized reporting framework to make analysis as simple as possible. Increasingly, marketers are using research results to feed complex *marketing models*.

A new type of analysis tool has emerged on the Internet called *Application Service Providers (ASPs)*. Instead of buying an entire forecasting project from a research institute, a corporation may do its own data collection and rent the forecasting application from an ASP Web site to model the results and evaluate alternative business scenarios from the results.

12. Reporting and Recommendations

Results reporting is communicating the research results to marketing decision makers. Typically there is a hierarchy of information in any study. Reports should first focus on the most important measures and use other measures to support overall conclusions. Presentations should take into account the specific needs of the end users of the information, using either pictures, words, or numbers. Recommendations also should include areas that need further study or where results of the immediate study can be used by other groups or brands. Most managers in organizations are too busy to read extensive research reports. Increasingly, results are being delivered via corporate Intranets, or as Web sites organized hierarchically using HTML hyperlinked text. The Web site may show a few key findings from the research. By clicking a mouse on any of the findings or keywords, a corporate user can drill down to see the data supporting the finding, and even perform a reanalysis of the data using attached "what if" models.

13. Results Implementation

The final step in the research process is to develop an action plan for integrating the research results into the marketing decision process. Most marketing research is part of an ongoing process within a corporation, and although the information is targeted to a specific decision, the results become part of a corporate database used on a daily basis to make ongoing marketing decisions.

ORGANIZATIONAL MARKETING RESEARCH

Organizations typically need to know about current competitors, potential competitors, and acquisition candidates to determine product quality, pricing, raw material sources, and service levels. Determining competitors' actions early allows a company to react in an appropriate time frame.

Sources of Organizational Information

- Trade associations
- Trade shows
- Delphi sampling (panel of client decision makers)
- Business publications
- Patent activity
- Industry experts, specialists, consultants
- Regulatory agencies and offices of elected officials
- Reports from industry suppliers
- Former competitive personnel
- Former competitive supply chain partners
- Help wanted ads
- Shop in competitors' stores
- Use competitors' products
- Visually watch a plant's activities
- Aerial reconnaissance photographs

MARKETING RESEARCH—INTERNATIONAL
by Synovate

Even though the fundamentals of international market research are the same as domestic U.S. research, there are both process and content issues that need to be considered, especially around adapting for multiple and differing environments.

Objectives and End Product Remain the Same

International research begins the same way as domestic research—by defining the business or marketing issue that needs to be addressed and determining the desired outcomes. This information is needed to help reduce the uncertainty of key decisions.

It also ends identically, with analysis and synthesis of the findings to provide the user with practical insight into consumer behavior and attitudes. This must be presented in a manner that allows the user to address the original business or marketing issue.

What happens in between will differ. Clear research hypotheses or objectives are required, good questions and a representative sample design are needed, the questionnaire must be laid out, and an appropriate method of obtaining the answers and processing the results need to be specified. What will differ is the process of how this is done.

Data Collection Is More Varied

What differs most is how the data is collected, as research design needs to be sensitive to the representativeness and cost efficiency of a wider array of methods. In the United States, more and more research is conducted online while door-to-door interviewing was long ago abandoned. The same is true in most developed markets, and online research is common in the European Union (EU), Japan, and Australia. However, in most developing markets, face-to-face and phone interviewing dominate as they are both more representative (given lower online penetration) and still economical. For example, in India, door-to-door interviewing can be cheaper and faster than online, and it reaches a much broader audience. In China, phone interviewing still works, as the volume of calls has not reached the annoyance level it has in the United States, so people still answer the telephone and will cooperate.

What this means is that the researchers are more likely to require a variety of methodologies when working in multiple countries. To reach affluent consumers in apartment complexes, phone interviews are often needed, as security precludes a door-to-door approach. Mall or street intercept interviewing can efficiently reach other audiences while door-to-door interviewing is usually required for low-income groups as phone penetration can be quite limited. For example, in Argentina, one-third of households do not have a telephone, so home visits are the most widely used.

Because the research methods are more likely to be in person, it is also important to be sensitive to the representativeness of interviews. In many situations, it will be important to have a good sense of the target market demographics and to set quotas or weight the results. While this may sound simple, in many cases it is not. In most developed countries, government census and other public data is both plentiful and reliable. But in the developing world this is often not the case, and care must be taken in evaluating the accuracy of market data.

It is also key to survey across different regions, as the responses in a capital city might differ significantly from elsewhere. For example, research in India routinely covers over a dozen languages and regions. In China it is common to cover both Tier 1, 2, and 3 cities (and sometimes rural areas where 600 million lower-income people live) while also covering the north, south, east, and central regions, since habits and attitudes differ substantially across both.

In addition, local habits will lead to differences in how research is conducted. In many Muslim countries, it is necessary to have males interview males and females interview females, as cross-gender interviewing is socially unacceptable. Likewise, differences in holidays affect when interviewing can be done as the holiday season impacts response rates and is believed to lead to potentially atypical responses. For example, research activity declines in the United States between Thanksgiving and Christmas; no researcher wants to be in the field in China during Chinese New Year (and elsewhere such as Korea where it is called the Lunar New Year). The same is true in the Middle East during Ramadan, when daytime fasting and late evening meals impact both the feasibility and accuracy of results.

Rural interviewing can also provide unique challenges, particularly in communal societies, where friends and neighbors will gather around the interviewer and respondent and often provide input. To address this, it is sometimes necessary to pair interviewers, so that one interviewer conducts the real interview while the other interviews the crowd, allowing for an undisturbed interview.

Meaning, Not Just Language, Must Be Considered

Attention must also be paid to language, to make sure questions are understood in the proper context and the translation is accurate. In many cases this can be addressed with *back translation*, where the questionnaire is translated into the local language and then translated back into English (by a different translator), to check if the meaning is clear and unambiguous. In many cases it is not, and further attention is necessary to clarify the meaning. For example, in Korea a meal includes rice so if you ask someone who ate a Big Mac, fries, and a shake at 1 P.M. if he had a meal, he will say "no." Ask him if he ate food and he will readily agree.

There are also instances where more work needs to be done to ensure that the respondents' answers are interpreted correctly. For example, Mexicans find it hard to say "no"—a cultural predilection that can lead to misunderstandings. On a personal level, this means that a dinner party host should repeatedly seek confirmation that a guest is really going to attend before actually setting a place at the table. With marketing research, this shows that any findings must be interpreted with care.

Sometimes the questionnaire must be considerably reworked due to differences in the local environment. For example, whereas about 15 percent of Korean women smoke, it is considered culturally unacceptable and most women smokers will deny they smoke. Therefore, tobacco research in Korea is done only among men. Similarly, the consumption of alcohol is prohibited among Muslims so asking about their drinking habits will return misleading results and is therefore avoided.

Practically, it is also important to consider the interview length after translation. English is a very efficient language as a result of having more words than any other language, by a significant factor. Therefore translated questionnaires can often be 50 percent longer in a local language than in the English original.

Finally, there are some topics or ideas that just do not translate well (or are forbidden). It is against the law to discuss politics in China or the Royal Family, especially the King, in Thailand. Some languages do not have genders, so feminine and masculine terms are more difficult to convey (while others have the opposite issue—there are nuanced

versions of Japanese so that men and women speak differently). Chinese actually has no word for *yes*. The most commonly used translation means more like "can," a more active term than the passive *yes*, while the Japanese *hai* really means "I hear you" not "I agree."

Interpreting the Results Can Be Difficult

Even though we can ask the same question around the world, interpreting what the answers mean raises additional issues. Cultural differences exist in how people use scales. Some cultures are very polite, like Thailand, where negative answers, even if true, would be considered rude. In others, there is greater willingness to try new products but conversion to regular usage is less certain. Finally, the ability of the marketer to build awareness via media and achieve access via distribution varies considerably. All of this will impact the interpretation of research findings.

There is active debate among research professionals about how best to address this issue. Some will use *calibration factors*, derived from outside sources or *benchmarks* from previous research. Others maintain that the differences are less cultural and more the impact of different local environments and do not require adjustment.

Besides comparability, interpretation can also require proper context. It can be difficult for someone in New York or Chicago to understand outcomes driven by macro habits. For example, one analyst's report assumed that the lower rate of beverage spending in China versus other developing markets was due to lower prices. While prices may explain some of the difference, what likely had a greater impact was the category definition. In the United States most liquid consumption is via beverages. But beverages are not the only form of liquid consumption—another is soup. Although soup may not play a big role in overall liquid consumption in the United States, in China it is part of almost every meal, suggesting that the different findings are due in part to different eating and drinking habits and a substitution of drinks with soup.

Quality Matters

In the EU, Japan, and many other countries, quality standards are consistent and strong; it is likely the results reflect accurate consumer feedback. But in much of the world this is not a given, and care must be taken to assure that adequate quality control procedures are in place. For example, when conducting high-end automotive focus groups in China, the incentive can lead some to lie about their ownership of a certain vehicle. To avoid this, respondents are asked to drive to the group in their vehicle and to then produce ownership papers in their name (as sometimes people borrow a vehicle to qualify). Unfortunately, the same care must sometimes be taken with interviewers, who have been known to fake the results.

Although the above can seem daunting, it need not be. There are many international research agencies whose networks cover the world. Working with them can help the marketer identify the issues that need to be addressed and then leverage their experience and local colleagues to provide the needed guidance.

MARKETING RESEARCH—CASE STUDY

by ACNielsen

Company: Unilever
Case: Frequent Shopper Program Analysis (2002)

The explosion of U.S. retailers implementing frequent shopper programs and their demands for manufacturers to financially participate in rewarding their loyal consumers have led organizations such as Unilever to analyze the return on investment for these growing promotion programs.

ACNielsen provides clients, such as Unilever, with consumer insights through its Homescan Panel, which equips 62,000 households nationwide with an in-home scanner, capturing purchasing data from all UPC-marked products from all outlets. These households are nationally projectable and demographically balanced to ensure local, regional, and national views. Promotional activity, such as feature ads, store coupons, and freestanding inserts from manufacturers also are cross-referenced with the household's purchasing data.

In 2001, shopper survey data found that 78 percent of all U.S. households participate in some frequent shopper program (with some markets such as Chicago hitting a participation rate of 96 percent) and 63 percent of all households participate in two or more programs. This raised the hypothesis that these programs only heighten promotional marketing sensitivity and do not build loyalty for the retailer or a manufacturer.

Unilever, with annual sales over $50 billion, is one of the world's largest consumer packaged goods companies. Unilever produces and markets a wide range of foods, beverages, and home and personal care products, such as Dove beauty bar, Lipton tea, Breyers ice cream, Hellmann's mayonnaise, Promise margarine, Vaseline and Pond's skin care products, Eternity perfume, and Sauve beauty care products. Historically, Unilever had completed several loyalty marketing projects using retailer-specific frequent shopper databases as well as geodemographic profiles to identify the optimal targets for comarketing efforts. These comarketing efforts link Unilever's brand promotions with a specific retailer, providing consumer incentives for the Unilever product to be purchased exclusively in that retailer's stores. Now, Unilever wanted a more complete national assessment. However, an analysis of every retailer's data would be far too expensive.

(Continued)

Unilever determined that the ACNielsen Homescan market in Boston would be the optimal market to analyze for a national perspective for two reasons: the retailer landscape was considered to be typical of an average U.S. market and frequent shopper membership was prevalent (85 percent of Boston households participated in such programs).

The analysis spanned two years of purchasing behavior from Boston Homescan panelists for the calendar years 1997 and 1998. Unilever wanted to specifically segment the heavy oral care buyers, as their mission was to convert toothpaste and toothbrush buyers to their Mentadent, Close-Up, and Aim brands.

The ACNielsen analysis illustrated some eye-opening purchasing dynamics of the oral care consumer. The heavy buyer classification of households represented 30 percent of the category buyers, but accounted for 70 percent or more of the category sales. Heavy oral care buyers in Boston represented 912,000 households of a total of 2.7 million oral care households in the entire marketplace. These heavy oral care households, on average, shopped in roughly 3.4 retailers over the two-year time frame.

The largest allocation of their oral care purchases was bought at Stop & Shop at a 16.7 percent share, followed by CVS at 15.4 percent. However, in comparison to all oral care buyers, the heavy oral care consumers' volume allocated to these two dominant retailers was somewhat average, indexing a 96 for CVS and 104 for Stop & Shop (with 100 being the average). Heavy oral care consumers in the Boston market were disproportionately buying oral care products in Shaws, BJ's Warehouse Club, and in Kmart.

Further segment analysis of heavy oral care consumers was based upon their shopping behavior by retailer. Consumers were grouped into frequent shoppers, medium shoppers, and light shoppers. This study cross-referenced the heavy oral care category purchasing dynamics with frequent shopping patterns, thereby identifying which retailers were the prime candidates for comarketing efforts. Heavy oral care buyers that also were classified as frequent shoppers to Shaws or Stop & Shop allotted over 60 percent of their oral care dollars to the respective chain. Unilever saw this as an opportunity to use these retailer frequent shopper databases to develop consumer promotions that would encourage brand switching to Mentadent, Aim, or Close-Up. Unilever would show a stronger return on investment for their organization, as well as for the retailer, by developing programs that entice these highly desirable consumers to switch retailers in a concerted effort to allocate more dollars to these chains.

The proliferation of the channels in which its products is distributed, along with the maturing U.S. market for consumer packaged goods, has led marketers such as Unilever to assess the financial ramifications of loyalty programs. The frequent shopper phenomenon is going to gain strength with the quest for one-to-one marketing becoming a reality. The directive Unilever has for its brands is to build profitable growth, rather than growth at any expense. This analysis was on the forefront of assessing which specific retailers would provide the most promise in building profitability through the utilization of frequent shopper information.

by Sports and Leisure Research Group

Company: Renaissance Cruises

Case: Itinerary Development and Positioning Research (2001)

The highly competitive leisure travel industry has seen price achievement (yields) undergo significant stress during periods of global conflict and economic hardship. The confluence of these factors along with a marked ramp-up in capacity exacerbated the need for niche travel marketers like Renaissance Cruises to pursue innovative offerings for past guests and prospective new customers. Comprehensive marketing research programs became a critical element in assessing potential consumer demand, price elasticities, and in determining the optimum marketing messaging to draw brand trial and loyalty.

Boutique full-service research firms like Sports and Leisure Research Group provide clients, like Renaissance Cruises, with both a means to test and assess the impact of various marketing strategies and communications platforms directly with best customers and prospective guests. Category-focused research firms combine skills in both classic marketing research methodology and an intimate understanding of the dynamics of a particular industry to offer not only marketing data, but tactical direction and strategy recommendations, drawn directly from the research.

At the turn of the new century, the high-end luxury cruise segment was confronted with burgeoning capacity growth coupled with a saturation of the core U.S. passenger cruise market. At the time, roughly only 9 percent of all U.S. households had cruised previously. With political instability in various foreign markets and a mild recession domestically, this time period was a particularly challenging environment for cruise lines as they sought greater new customer volume as well as repeat business from past guests to fill their growing fleets.

Earlier research into the cruise consumers' mindset had demonstrated that travelers typically chose a cruise vacation for several reasons including the all-inclusive nature of the experience, the ability to visit multiple exotic destinations without having to pack and repack, the allure of being on the open sea, and a welcome environment for relaxation around intensive touring. This phenomenon led to the launch of many new vessels by major players in the cruise industry, particularly Carnival, Royal Caribbean, and their various brands. These ships were often categorized as floating cities, with capacities of 2,500+ passengers and onboard amenities that included rock climbing walls, skating rinks, large theaters, and extensive shopping and dining choices. Characterized by some as floating parties, they met many of the expressed needs of U.S.-based cruise guests, but fell woefully short for others.

Niche players like Renaissance Cruises sought to develop alternative offerings for a more discerning and older clientele. It was evident by 2000 that demand for the South Pacific sailings, even among Renaissance's loyal past guests, was not meeting expectations. Because Renaissance Cruises had committed to French Polynesian itineraries, redeploying the vessels was not an option. The executive management team sought marketing research to uncover both potential objections to the French Polynesian sailings as well as to identify best prospective customers to target for the sailings and the optimal messaging to pique potential interest.

Renaissance Cruises wanted to remain a premium brand and did not want to resort to the rampant discounting that was proliferating in other areas of the cruise market. So the research team sought out a dual methodology of qualitative research to first tap into and identify key objections and expectations, followed by a rigorous and projectable quantitative study, conducted online, to test the hypotheses raised by the qualitative work and gauge their magnitude among key customer groups.

(Continued)

The researchers took great care in isolating several different groups of samples so as to be able to perform gap analysis against these targets and determine if needs and objections varied among different groups. The research studied past guests who had already sailed on the South Pacific itinerary to determine overall satisfaction and to identify strengths of the cruise offering that could be potentially accentuated in marketing communications. The more impactful propositions were then developed into a variety of direct marketing collateral (both e-mail and print) that were tested against samples of both past Renaissance guests who had not yet sailed the South Pacific as well as prospective cruise guests in the company's database that had been unresponsive to itinerary-specific marketing. Prior to the concept testing, respondents were questioned about their vacation habits, their specific desires for a cruise vacation, as well as their perceptions of a cruise to the South Pacific and price expectations for the same.

Among the more significant findings of the research was that those who had rejected the South Pacific cruise offer exhibited great concern about the ease of travel into the region, and duration and cost of transportation to the ship. This insight led directly to a variety of tactical product innovations by Renaissance that included the more subtle use of various maps and graphics that showed French Polynesia's proximity to the west coast of the United States and the Hawaiian Islands. The research and marketing teams also used this insight to creatively package a variety of inclusive airfares and discounted charter flights into the region. This combination of adjustments to both the product offering and its promotion enabled Renaissance to stay away from potentially devaluing the core cruise offering and tarnishing the brand through discounting, while addressing potential customer concerns about the destination's accessibility and affordability by enhancing the air offering.

Bookings for the itinerary and overall satisfaction did increase, after the above enhancements and others suggested by the research were implemented.

CORPORATE PROFILES AND AUTHOR BIOGRAPHIES

ACNIELSEN

ACNielsen is the global leader in providing business information, analysis, and insights to consumer packaged goods companies, their brokers, and retail organizations. Visit ACNielsen at www.acnielsen.com.

John O'Donnell

John O'Donnell was formerly Senior Vice President, Strategic Accounts, managing six of ACNielsen's largest clients in the United States, including Unilever, Pillsbury, Quaker, and Best Foods. Mr. O'Donnell received his B.S. in General Management from Purdue University.

COLGATE-PALMOLIVE

Colgate-Palmolive is the second largest consumer products company in the United States. Visit Colgate-Palmolive at www.colgate.com.

James S. Figura

Jim Figura, Vice President, Consumer Research North America, is responsible for all facets of consumer research and providing marketing with consumer insights. Mr. Figura received his BS in Business Administration and MS in Industrial Management from Carnegie Mellon University.

SPORTS AND LEISURE RESEARCH GROUP

For more than 20 years, the principals of Sports and Leisure Research Group have coupled an acute understanding of the sports, travel, and leisure markets with a classical marketing research approach to combine market insights with actionable strategies. Visit SLRG at www.sportsandleisureresearch.com.

Jon Last

Jon Last is founder and President of Sports and Leisure Research Group. Last received his BA, magna cum laude, from Tufts University. He received his MBA from The Wharton School of the University of Pennsylvania.

SYNOVATE

Synovate, founded in 2003, is one of the world's largest (and most curious) custom marketing research firms. Synovate has over 6,000 employees and annual revenue of $867 million (2007). Visit Synovate at www.synovate.com.

Mike Sherman

Mike Sherman is the Global Director, Knowledge Management & Insights. Mr. Sherman received his MBA from Harvard Business School.

Part 3
Demand

6 CONSUMER PURCHASING BEHAVIOR

by Kimberly-Clark, Frito-Lay, Kraft,
Discovery Communications

THE ESSENTIALS OF CONSUMER BEHAVIOR
by Kimberly-Clark

Introduction

After consumers acquire money through work, inheritance, or luck, they have two options: spend their money or save/invest it. Consumers typically spend over 97 percent of their earnings.[1] And these same individuals spend one-third of their day sleeping, one-third at work, and it would seem, the other third spending their money. Understanding consumer purchasing behavior allows a company to more easily provide for consumers' needs and more easily promote the company's products and services. Understanding consumer behavior leads to marketing success. Consumer behavior is constantly changing, and companies should identify consumer trends before their competitors do in order to strengthen the organization's sales. Companies focus on consumers because consumer demand, or spending, is approximately two-thirds of the gross national product.

Definitions

Consumer behavior is "the dynamic interaction of affect and cognition behavior and the environment by which human beings conduct the exchange aspects of their lives."[2]

Consumer behavior is "the exchange process involved in acquiring, consuming, and disposing of goods, services, experiences, and ideas."[3]

When organizations sell to individual consumers, the selling process is known as "business-to-consumer" or "B to C."

Consumer Purchasing Process

Marketers should understand the process that consumers follow to purchase their goods and services in order to successfully use all elements of the marketing mix. Consumers typically follow a purchasing process sequence of steps. Depending on the situation, such as attitudes, financial status, or the level of involvement in the product or services purchased, a step in the process may take only an instant or it may require a lengthy process in itself. Marketers attempt to influence each of these steps through the marketing mix (product development, pricing, distribution, and marketing communications). This process is repeated countless times in a consumer's lifetime. The goal of marketing is to influence this process so that each step ultimately narrows down a consumer's choice of competing options to one product brand.

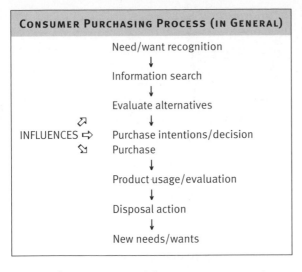

CONSUMER PURCHASING PROCESS (IN GENERAL)

Need/want recognition
↓
Information search
↓
Evaluate alternatives
↓
INFLUENCES ⇒ Purchase intentions/decision
Purchase
↓
Product usage/evaluation
↓
Disposal action
↓
New needs/wants

archy of relative prepotency [in an effort] to become everything that one is capable of becoming."

HIERARCHICAL MODEL OF CONSUMER NEEDS/WANTS	
5. Self actualization	(fulfilling personal goals or dreams, peace of mind)
	↑
4. Esteem	(being respected by the community, confidence)
	↑
3. Love	(belongingness, being liked or loved by an individual, family, friends)
	↑
2. Safety	(free from physical threats by man or nature)
	↑
1. Physiological	(hunger, sex, thirst, sleep)

Source: A. H. Maslow, Dominance, Self-Esteem, Self-Actualization, Brooks/Cole Publishing, 1973. Used with permission.

1. Need/Want Recognition

The first step in the consumer purchasing process occurs when a consumer recognizes the presence of a need or want. The recognition step can be influenced by marketing efforts when companies understand consumer needs ("I am thirsty") and then promote products ("Drink our soft drink") that meet those needs. Researchers have determined that there are several needs and wants that motivate human behavior. These needs range from basic biological necessities to a desire for inner happiness. There are two main models of needs and wants: the hierarchical model and the simultaneous model.

Hierarchical Model of Needs and Wants

A basic premise of this research is that the lower or most basic needs must be fulfilled before an individual can concentrate on fulfilling higher or more complicated needs. Another theory holds that humans never reach the apex of satisfaction, but constantly strive to do so. By striving or aspiring to reach each new level, in theory, each person will be better off. This hierarchy of needs has been depicted as having from 2 (wants and needs) to 12 levels. Researcher Abraham H. Maslow's five-level hierarchy is a commonly accepted approach. Maslow states that, "Human needs are organized into a hier-

The need to satisfy one of these needs motivates a consumer to procure a product or service. The marketing process seeks to address existing and aspirational needs with an appropriate product. Product development and the supply chain are geared to create ever better (price and quality) products to allow consumers to achieve their needs. Demand promotion (marketing communications) is geared to informing the consumer of these products and how they can fulfill a consumer's needs or wants.

This hierarchical approach may be depicted as an inverted pyramid in developed societies (with a narrow base for needs and a broad top for wants). Conversely, less developed societies have a greater requirement for basic needs; thus their hierarchy may be depicted as a pyramid. For example, in a developed country, a neighborhood Starbucks Coffee shop may position itself to not only satisfy thirst with better tasting coffee but also satisfy a "belongingness" need with a convivial atmosphere. Marketers of Gatorade associate their brand with professional athletes for "esteem" needs.

Simultaneous Model of Needs and Wants
Dr. John C. Mowen's model of consumer motivation states that people need to protect and/or enhance four fundamental resource needs: the body, material possessions, information, and social resources. Mowen's research indicates that both safety needs (the desire to protect a resource) and self-actualization needs (the desire to enhance a resource) can operate simultaneously. For example, consumers may simultaneously seek to protect their bodies from harm by purchasing and consuming a healthy diet and attempt to enhance their bodies through purchasing exercise equipment and vigorously exercising.

The marketing process often begins with a global assessment of how many people have a particular need or want. By calculating the number of people who have the need or want identified, the marketing person can quantify the financial opportunity being explored. Once adequate numbers of people exhibit the behavior under study, research is conducted to better understand the need to be satisfied.

For example, beverage manufacturers conduct market segmentation studies to understand the need and wants that people have when trying to satisfy their thirst. These studies will typically investigate the context of the various times in each day when people are thirsty. Further study may classify the various types of thirst that people exhibit. The product solutions that satisfy the thirst that people might have after an hour of full court basketball (Gatorade) varies from the thirst that occurs when we rise in the morning (coffee or tea). Once the marketing person can identify the need, quantify the opportunity or incidence of this need, and classify the different ways it manifests itself, new products can be developed or existing products repositioned. For example, the soft drink manufacturers were able to successfully encourage noncoffee drinkers to drink Coke or Pepsi with breakfast.

2. Information Search
In order to resolve the newly recognized need or want, consumers need information with which to make an appropriate evaluation and purchase decision. There are three main factors regarding the information search process: the amount of information needed, the sources of the information, and the learning process itself.

Amount of Information
The amount of information needed and the effort put into an information search and evaluation process is contingent upon several factors, including:

- Level of involvement with the product (importance, usage frequency, image, etc.)
- Price
- Complexity of the product
- Number of times the product has been purchased before
- Consequences of making a poor choice

Marketers should provide the appropriate amount of information, such as brochures, sales training, or advertising, for each product situation. For example, more research is needed in an involved purchase, such as for a new audio system, than for a routine purchase, such as toothpaste. Best Buy thus provides literature, and trained sales reps to provide information to the potential consumer of a new stereo.

Sources of Information
For ease, consumers will first search their own knowledge for how to resolve their problem, and if they cannot find a satisfactory solution, they will search external sources.

- **Internal Search.** The internal search is based in the consumer's memory of pleasant and unpleasant usage experiences and of marketing communications. This creates a key opportunity for a company's brand. In the interest of saving time and stress, consumers want to recall that a specific brand meets their needs and recall how to easily obtain this brand. Thus a company should strive to make consumer experiences consistently pleasant and use marketing communication, such as advertising and public relations, to reinforce this experience.

Three factors work in tandem here. They are product consistency, brand equity, and the consumer's historical product experience. By producing the product consistently and carefully limiting product changes, marketers ensure that the historical comfort and satisfaction expected from the brand are maintained. Consumers buy brands for this consistency and to avoid the risk associated with change.

For example, over the past century, Heinz has maintained its ketchup category leadership worldwide by consistently manufacturing the "thick, rich one," or the "slowest ketchup in the East, West, North, and South." The product and its characteristic bottle and label represent consistent quality. Consumers expect this quality every time and therefore are willing to pay more.

- **External Search.** If a consumer's internal knowledge is uncertain (or if there is no specific brand recall), then the consumer searches for external information. An external search can review many sources, including the news media; friends; a trusted advisor (such as a pharmacist); informational sources such as *Consumer Reports* magazine or the Internet; and marketing communications, such as a salesperson, labels on the product or packaging, and advertising.

  For example, a consumer may have Tylenol in memory for a headache remedy but not have any memory for a sleeping aid. When examining the shelf, the consumer may notice Tylenol P.M. (a sleeping aid) and generalize his or her trust in that brand to this item. Marketers need to have consistent elements in their branding and package graphics so that consumers can quickly recognize their brand. It is critical for a company to understand consumers' external information sources so they can provide the right communication. For example, since consumers tend to trust pharmacists' objective opinions of nonprescription products, many companies advertise and provide samples to pharmacists.

The Learning Process

Psychologists speculate that humans have innate mental faculties that enable us to create culture. It would be impossible to influence these innate abilities, and thus marketers attempt to influence the customer's process of learning about culture, needs and wants, and product selection. *Learning* is the process of gaining information and comprehension through study or experience. Understanding the consumer learning process helps marketers devise more accurate marketing communications programs. Marketing researchers have developed several learning process models. One important model developed by social psychologist William J. McGuire, retired from Yale, is included in Table 6.1.

3. Evaluate Alternatives

Once the research step is completed, consumers can then evaluate the alternatives that have been determined. The goal of the consumer is to select the option that results in the greatest reward. Consumer evaluative criteria of the product or service attributes are impacted by internal influences, such as existing beliefs and attitudes, and external influences, such as marketing attempts and group norms.

Marketers attempt to understand consumers' evaluative criteria in order to segment the market based on consumer benefits. For example, in the late 1970s, the Beecham Products Company learned from a benefit segmentation study of the toothpaste market that there were three consumer segments or groups differentiated by their level of interest in the following benefits: cavity prevention, fresh breath, or the combination of the two. Beecham introduced Aquafresh toothpaste, which contained separate layers of toothpaste and gel, positioned as having all of the cavity prevention of the leading paste and all of the breath freshening of the leading gel. Aquafresh achieved over a 10 percent share of the market by addressing the evaluation criteria of this combination segment.

4. Purchasing Intentions/Decision

Consumers develop purchasing intentions, the subjective probability for purchasing an alternative, based on favorable research and favorable influences

TABLE 6.1 LEARNING PROCESS MODEL

Learning Process	Explanation
Stimuli ↓ ↓	Communications: advertising, public relations, and so on. A well-defined target (demographics, life stage, attitudes) enables the advertising agency to select the media so the target consumers will be "exposed" to the advertising.
Exposure ↓	Opportunity for a consumer to see and/or hear a message (stimuli). The more communications consumers are exposed to, the more likely they will perceive and retain the input. Therefore, marketers attempt to furnish optimum exposure by using all media methods (advertising, public relations, promotional marketing, direct marketing, and personal selling).
Attention ↓	Ability of message to gain consumers' attention. The marketer needs to develop a selling message or promise that meets a consumer need and attracts their attention (to avoid the clutter of other stimuli).
Comprehension/ Perception ↓	Interpretation of the message. Consumers tend to absorb concepts that fit with their beliefs and attitudes, and those ideas that conflict with their convictions are filtered out. It is the marketer's challenge to identify these beliefs and attitudes and present information to overcome them. This message should be clear and simple so consumers can comprehend it.
Acceptance ↓	Extent to which consumers are persuaded by message. The marketer should provide a reason or demonstrate a benefit for consumers to accept the message.
Retention ↓	Transfer of message into long-term memory. Unfortunately for marketers, humans tend to recall little of what is perceived and less of what they are exposed to. Marketers typically respond to this by providing a constant stream of information and reminder advertising. The marketer should communicate a consistent message and image that will reinforce awareness and build the brand's value over time.
Memory	Integration of message into consumers' belief system. The marketer's objective is for target consumers to "retain" and incorporate the brand-related selling message in their long-term "memory" and belief system.

Source: William J. McGuire, Yale University. Printed with permission.

(both internal and external). Marketers often question consumers about their purchasing intention as inputs to forecasting sales. In development of new products, marketers will show consumers a concept or description of a new product and ask their purchasing intention.

A consumer's purchasing intentions often lead to a purchasing decision, which may be immediate or postponed, depending on the situation. The situation may be influenced by many smaller factors, such as the weather, time constraints of the shopping trip, availability of cash, product availability, and competitive offers. Marketers use promotion and sales tactics to influence purchase decisions. These offers can influence a consumer to purchase a new item or stimulate purchase of an impulse item. Retailers stock impulse items, such as candy and film, near the cash register to increase the size of a consumer's overall purchase.

5. The Purchase Act

In order to save time and minimize stress, consumers want the purchase transaction to be as quick and simple as possible. Consumers do not like to wait in lines, on the telephone, or on the Internet. Marketers can develop competitive advantages (or eliminate a disadvantage by matching the service) with innovative ways to simplify purchase transactions. Examples include express checkout at hotels, credit card transactions at the gas pump, and car rental services that process the consumer's bill as he or she steps out of the car.

6. Product Usage/Evaluation

After the purchase, consumers use the product and evaluate its effectiveness in fulfilling their needs against their expectations, which can affect their beliefs about a particular brand. There are two outcomes of a purchase: satisfaction or dissatisfaction.

This information is stored in consumers' memory, which affects future purchasing behavior and their desire to disseminate information about the brand to influence others.

Marketers use several means to measure consumer satisfaction. This can be as simple as a waiter asking how a customer liked his or her meal. Many marketers prominently display toll-free telephone numbers and e-mail addresses to encourage consumers to report any questions or concerns. Studies have shown that if marketers promptly address a consumer's dissatisfaction, they are much more likely to continue repurchasing the brand. It is much more cost-efficient to retain a customer than to obtain a new one.

Sometimes consumers have second thoughts about their purchase, known as *buyer's remorse* or *post-purchase dissonance*, which could cause a consumer to return a purchase. This may happen as a result of any of several reasons, including lack of comparison shopping, hearing about a better deal, or acknowledging a poor impulse purchase. Marketers use several means to reduce post-purchase dissonance. A waiter can compliment a person's entrée selection or a sales clerk can compliment how well the buyer looks in a new outfit or pair of glasses. Many automobile salespeople check with the consumer a week or so after purchase to solidify in the customer's mind the wisdom of the purchase. Marketing has an important role to convince buyers they made the right purchase and strengthen their beliefs to encourage future repurchase.

7. Product Disposal Action

After use, consumers look for a quick and simple disposal of products and packaging. Consumers generally want to be responsible about the environment and recycle, if it does not take too much of their time. Common examples are recyclable aluminum cans and plastic bottles. Marketers can develop competitive advantages by reducing the amount of material that needs to be disposed of or by making disposal or recycling easier.

8. Continuous Needs/Purchasing Cycle

Consumers will always have needs and wants to resolve, and thus will always continue the purchasing process. Therefore, there will always be an opportunity for marketing to influence these purchases (see Table 6.2).

INTERNAL INFLUENCES ON CONSUMER BEHAVIOR

The reason why a consumer chooses one product over another lies in the make-up or core of the person who initiates the purchase. The actual decision process is often internalized by the consumer, and there are several factors that influence the consumer's purchasing behavior. It is important for the marketer to understand these influences in order to provide for the consumer's needs and then accurately promote a company's products and services. These influences include life stage, income/spending capacity, and values/beliefs attitudes.

Life Stage

There are several stages that an individual goes through in his or her lifetime. Each stage has unique behavior patterns, and consumers' needs can be monitored and targeted by marketers at each stage. The stage in a consumer's life cycle, coupled with household income, has an important influence on consumer purchasing. For example, newlyweds purchase more furniture and durable goods, and the addition of a new baby causes most consumers to reconsider their purchase of many categories. Couples with no children, known as "empty nesters," tend to have more discretionary personal income and are attractive customers for travel and other leisure goods. The younger the audience, the greater the ability to influence purchasing behavior over time. By age nine, 90 percent of children have shopped independently.[4] However, very young individuals are impressionable and impulsive, therefore ethically limiting this audience as a target. See Table 6.3 for stages and examples of needs in different life cycles.

Age plays a role in consumer behavior, and it is often used in marketing research to understand trends of target groups. Using American birth years 1961 to 1981, the Generation X market accounted,

TABLE 6.2 CONSUMER PURCHASING PROCESS (PURCHASE FUNNEL)

Consumer Purchasing Process	Purchase Funnel*	Branding Pyramid**
Need / Want Recognition		
↓		
Information Search	Brand Awareness	"I've heard of you."
↓	↓	↓
	Brand Familiarity	"I know who you are"
	↓	↓
Evaluate Alternatives	Brand Opinion	"I know what you stand for."
↓	↓	↓
	Brand Consideration	"You are a brand I would consider buying."
	↓	↓
	First Choice Intention	"You are my current top choice."
	↓	↓
	Shopping/Trial	"Show me what you can do."
	↓	↓
Purchase Decision / Purchase	Purchase	"You have met my expectations."
↓		↓

Consumer choice Grid

Price / Quality

Usage / Evaluation	Expectations Reinforcement	"Did I make the right decision?"
↓	↓	↓
	Satisfaction / Brand Equity	"I like you."
	↓	↓
	Referral	"I'll tell my friends to try you."
	↓	
Disposal Action		
↓		
New Needs / Wants	Repeat Purchase	

* GK Automotive Purchase Funnel ®, 2009 © GK Custom Research North America.
   www.gfkamerica.com

** Ronald S.Luskin, creator of the "Branding Pyramid," has over twenty-five years of experience in the marketing, advertising, and public relations profession. ronluskin@ids.net

TABLE 6.3 LIFE STAGES AND TYPICAL CONSUMER NEEDS	
Young dependent pre-teen	Games, food, movies, toys, clothes
Young dependent teen	Car, dates, music, movies, clothes, food
Young adult single	Dates, apartment, simple furniture, better car
Young married/ no children	Bigger apartment, better furniture, travel
Young married/ with children	House, baby stuff, yard equipment, insurance
Middle-aged/ with children	Financial security, bigger house, more insurance
Middle-aged/ children in college	College tuition, travel
Middle-aged/children out of college	Smaller house, better car, travel
Older married/single	Medical attention, retirement living

in 1995, for 79.4 million people. This fact will exacerbate marketers to develop a product and service mix for this growing target group. For example, Oldsmobile changed their advertising to include the phrase, "This isn't your father's Oldsmobile." The median American age is getting older, 35.2 years in July 1998 compared to 32.8 years in July 1990. Americans over 50 years of age, the "graying market," represent 64 million consumers, one out of every three adults. Therefore, a strategy is to create products and services such as maintenance-type pharmaceutical products and retirement communities for America's aging population.

Income/Spending Capacity

Individual purchasing behavior in a developed society is dependent on the capacity to exchange money for need satisfaction. Household income limits the amount of consumer purchasing, and is delineated by disposable and discretionary income.

- **Disposable Income.** Consumers cannot spend all of their income because they generally must pay taxes to government units. The remaining income, disposable personal income, is the amount available for spending and saving and

is an important statistic for marketers comparing opportunities across markets and over time.

- **Discretionary Income.** Another important statistic is discretionary personal income, which is the income available after outlays for necessities such as housing, insurance, and food. Marketers typically favor lower taxes to allow greater disposable income to be spent for their products.

Values/Beliefs/Attitudes

Psychographics are the consumers' learned predispositions, either positive or negative, that affect their purchasing behavior. Understanding these predispositions helps marketers to determine how a consumer will react to a product or marketing communications. There are three levels of orientations based on their importance and conviction: values, beliefs, and attitudes.

values → beliefs → attitudes → purchase intent

Values

A *value* is a pattern of behavior within a culture, which the members of that society hold in high regard and around which individuals integrate societal goals.[5] Examples include freedom, justice, and education. For instance, parents may have a value such as placing importance for their child being successful in school or of having more opportunities than they had. Companies must design products and communications with an understanding of consumer values, such as marketers of educational computer software incorporating the value of education and learning into their marketing communications.

Beliefs

A *belief* is an emotional acceptance of some proposition or doctrine.[6] Consumers develop purchasing beliefs over time based on product experience, input from reference groups, and marketing communications. Experience leads to a belief that an alternative is either the best choice, an acceptable choice, or an unacceptable choice. For example, a consumer may have a belief that "you generally get what you pay for" and therefore infer that higher-priced brands must have higher quality.

Attitudes

An *attitude* is an internal orientation toward intended action. This encompasses the idea that this orientation is *cognitive* (consciously held), *evaluative* (feelings either positive or negative), and *conative* (indicating disposition for action).[7] Thus attitudes denote a person's current disposition or feelings about a company or product and impacts the buying decision process.

EXTERNAL INFLUENCES ON CONSUMER BEHAVIOR

A complete marketing plan should incorporate the external influences on consumer behavior, which include culture, opinion leaders, the environment (physical/technological), product value, and marketing communications/demand promotion.

Culture

Culture is the behavior and customs that are passed down through generations socially, rather than genetically. Culture is a multifaceted concept that ties together attitudes, beliefs, and habits. Each consumer's individual needs are relatively similar from person to person. However, groupings of individuals do have some differences from other groupings. For example, each country has its own way of doing things, such as American or French culture. Culture is defined by various attributes of the way these groups act in a somewhat homogeneous manner. Cultural elements include time, space, self, honor, values, possessions, gender, and laws. Each of these elements affects or influences the individual's behavior.

People in a particular culture have similar behaviors and views. A marketing plan will define itself with a specific culture in mind. The United States has become a credit society where purchases are not necessarily a reflection of income. This direction has spurred buying patterns that were previously untracked through marketing research.

A culture's legal system influences behavior through its framework of socially approved conduct. It can be said that values are a derivative of society's laws; however, values also incorporate the effect of religious and upbringing beliefs and ideas. For the marketer, certain products deemed acceptable in America, such as the *Jerry Springer Show*, may be deemed inappropriate in another culture.

In addition to cultural behavior patterns, subcultures influence consumer behavior and are important to research and influence in a marketing environment. Subcultures include national origin/ethnicity, education, geography, and occupation. Many consumers are now receptive to mixing food, music, and fashion across subcultures and are more open to ethnic groups maintaining the traditions and customs of their heritage. Marketers should understand how these subcultures are consistent with the mass market and their product offerings. This will assist them in developing appropriate communications approaches and specific products. For example, many companies in the United States, such as Old El Paso, have developed packaged foods that cater to the tastes of those who grew up preferring spicy foods.

Opinion Leaders

Opinion leaders are people that the consumer looks to for information about an upcoming decision. Opinion leaders are divided into two groups: influencers and personal reference groups.

Influencers

Influencers are opinion leaders that the consumer does not know personally. A political leader may persuade the individual to think a certain way about a social or tax issue. A movie critic may persuade an individual to see or not see a movie.

Personal Reference Groups

Reference groups are sources of information, and they influence consumer purchasing behavior. Reference groups are groups of people that the individual personally knows, frequently contacts, and whose opinions and approval are valued. There are several types including family, friends, neighbors, and affiliations (work, clubs, churches). Desiring to gain approval or acceptance from a group is an attempt to be perceived as normal (fitting into the group norm).

Within each of these groups, there are influential individuals whose behavior can shape the perceptions and ultimately the purchases of the group itself. For example, the female head of household has been long regarded as the opinion leader in charge of most family purchases. This authoritative position is earned through many years of successful purchases. In this role, most family members are trained to make purchases according to the behavior of this gatekeeper. In like manner, these gatekeepers now extend their authority to include members of their extended family in need of their expertise. It is now common for these gatekeeper family members to influence health-care decisions, large capital purchases, and even exert control over their elderly parents. Finding and influencing a gatekeeper to become loyal to a company's products can have a dramatic impact on sales.

Organizations such as Weight Watchers have thrived by tapping into the power of personal reference groups. By providing a safe haven where a group of people can discuss their common challenges, such as losing weight, millions of people have been served. The successful sitcom *Cheers* demonstrated this power with the theme "where everybody knows your name."

Teenagers who would outright reject the idea of school uniforms may, nonetheless, purchase clothing to associate with reference groups. Some brands, such as Nike, Tommy Hilfiger, and Abercrombie & Fitch, show their trademarks boldly on the outside of clothing to facilitate these associations and show groups of people in their advertising.

The Environment

Both the physical and technological environment influence consumer behavior.

Physical Environment

The physical environment is another aspect that influences consumer behavior. Elements of physical environment influences include weather, geography, and time. Examples of weather and seasonal influences are the sales of snowblowers during the winter and lawn mowers in the spring and summer. Geographic influences are diminishing as mass communications is creating a more homogeneous society. Regional aspects are giving way to the more dominant differentiation between urban and rural lifestyles. Activities reliant upon different geographic settings, such as skiing in the Rocky Mountains, will always influence consumer purchases such as air transportation.

Technological Environment

Technology, such as automobiles, telephones, computers, refrigerators, and plastic food containers, influences how consumers behave and what they purchase. Many technological innovations contribute to an easier, more productive, and healthier life, and therefore are sought after by consumers. Each in turn influences behavior.

Product Value

Product value traditionally was the ability to satisfy needs as a function of quality and price. Now, many of today's consumers are busy working longer hours, spending more time in longer commutes to work, and caring for children or older parents and are concerned with the additional need for personal and family safety. As a result, many consumers have expanded their value equation beyond their traditional trade-off of quality and price to include time savings and a feeling of security.

> Product Value = Quality/Price/Time/Security

Most consumers want to shorten their purchasing processes. One example is fast-food restaurants, which now derive over half of their business from drive-through service. Other retail outlets are adding this service, such as drugstores with drive-through pharmacy service. Dominos created a fast-food segment by delivering pizzas. And one-hour photo developing will soon be too slow compared to digital camera processing using in-home computers and printers.

Most consumers want to shop when it is convenient for them, which is often not during normal business hours. As a result, many retail outlets are open extended hours or 24 hours to meet these consumer demands. Banks, which once had restricted bankers' hours, now have Saturday hours and automatic teller machines in convenient locations that are open 24 hours. Many consumers now shop any time of the day or night by Internet, catalog, and through toll-free telephone numbers.

Marketing Communications/ Demand Promotion

It is one of marketing's basic principles to satisfy consumer needs by providing appropriate products. Companies influence the consumers' desire for these products through marketing communications (described in Part 4 "Marketing Communications," beginning with Chapter 8). Marketing communications (sales, advertising, public relations, promotional marketing, and direct marketing) provides persuasive information and imagery. Understanding consumer needs helps the marketer to determine the appropriate tone and appeal of various promotional approaches. Satisfaction of current and striving needs is a common theme in the promotion of products and services, and is referred to as *aspirational marketing*. Marketing communications uses slogans to make references to a product's ability to satisfy an individual's needs.

Marketers use *marketing communications devices*, such as advertising and public relations, to communicate their idea/product/service message in an attempt to influence learning and consumer purchasing behavior. Because of both the potential increase to sales and the cost of communications, marketers need to understand how the communications process influences consumer behavior. Marketers use marketing communications to impart information, or cues, to influence the learning process. The cues stimulate a response: a purchase. If the purchase is satisfactory, the response is reinforced and a loyal customer is created. If the purchase is unsatisfactory, the customer is potentially lost.

MARKETING COMMUNICATIONS SLOGANS TOUTING CONSUMER NEEDS/WANTS
5. Self actualization "Just do it." (Nike) "Be all that you can be." (U.S. Army)
4. Esteem "If your friends could see you now." (Carnival Cruises) "Selected by James Bond." (Omega watches)
3. Love/Belongingness "Be a hero." (FTD flowers) "A diamond is forever." (DeBeers)
2. Safety "A house is not a home until it's safe." (Brinks Home Security) "I want my car to be as protective as I am." (Ford)
1. Physiological "Hungry? Grab a Snickers." (M&M Mars) "Good for your bones." (Ocean Spray Cranberry Juice Cocktail Plus with calcium) "You gotta eat." (Checkers)
Source: Compiled by A. G. Bennett

Marketing research has found that increasing advertising spending (and presumably all marketing communications spending) increases sales for a time, although further increases in advertising spending beyond a certain point do not contribute to further increases in sales. That is, the target consumers have seen the message and reacted. A marketer should continuously conduct marketing research in order to understand the consumers' level of response, and thus guide promotional strategies and budgets. See the illustration in Figure 6.1.

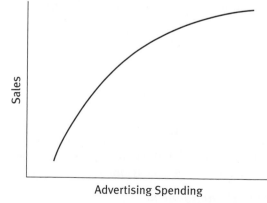

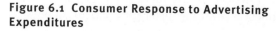

Source: Kimberly-Clark

Figure 6.1 Consumer Response to Advertising Expenditures

CONSUMER SEGMENTATION

The internal and external influences on consumer purchasing result in different consumer behavior patterns. Understanding these patterns helps the marketer to develop appropriate products and determine more accurate communications approaches. Consumer purchasing behavior can be quantified by marketing research and segmented into various groupings that are more easily and efficiently serviced or targeted. Consumers may be segmented by psychographics and demographics.

Psychographics

Psychographic segmentation has three primary types: timing of product adoption, shopping attitudes, and lifestyles.

New Product Adoption Patterns

An *adoption pattern* is the length of time it takes for a consumer to purchase a product after its introduction. When developing new products or services, marketers need to understand which consumers will first try a new product, how they might inform other consumers about the product, and the rate of adoption of the product in the society as a whole. The incremental purchasing process of consumers is known as the community's "diffusion of innovation". Dr. Everett M. Rogers, a leading academic at the University of New Mexico, defined *diffusion* as the process by which an innovation (a new product or idea) is communicated through certain channels among the members of a social system over time.

Consumers are classified according to the time at which they typically adopt a new product relative to other consumers. The first consumers to adopt are called innovators, followed in order by early adopters, early majority, late majority, and then laggards. The timing patterns differ by product, marketing effort, pricing levels, competition, economic conditions, and so forth. And each consumer may not follow the same adoption pattern each time.

- **Innovators and Early Adopters.** Marketers' understanding of this societal purchasing process and research among these innovators help them establish marketing strategies targeted to innovators during introduction. Distribution initially is made through a manageable and limited distribution channel known to the innovators. Initially, a high-pricing strategy may be used because innovators tend to be higher-income consumers who can afford expensive interests and purchase new products. Communications budgets can be smaller if the innovators like the product and inexpensive word-of-mouth allows for adequate dissemination of information.

For example, golf equipment manufacturers introduce new technologically advanced golf equipment at professional golf shops at a premium price. Later, they may sell the same items through discount golf shops, catalogs, and the Internet at a lower price.

But not all innovators fall into the same category. Some athletic shoe and clothing companies consider urban youth as innovators, and the diffusion moves from the inner city to the suburbs. Computer usage diffuses from children (exposed through schools and their friends) to their parents and grandparents.

Once the innovator market has been saturated, companies shift their focus to the larger markets of the early adopters and the early majority with the goal of increased sales. Reaching these markets requires a larger promotional budget and wider distribution.

- **Majority.** Most consumers fall into this category. Some consumers already are satisfied and have no need for a new product. Some may be influenced by the old adage of waiting until the bugs are worked out of newly introduced products. Improved products or lower prices may move this group to purchase.
- **Laggards.** This category is primarily influenced by price. These consumers wait for price reductions brought about by competition, economies of scale, or sales of product closeouts before they purchase.

Shopping Attitudes

Consumers may be segmented based on their attitude toward shopping (and thus their potential purchasing behavior). These attitudes may be defined as elite, strategic, or value.

- **Elite Shopper.** This segment of upscale shoppers demands prestige products and personal service, for whom price is of little or no concern. The retailers and services that cater to the elite shopper train their salespeople to refer to the shopper by name and to learn and anticipate his or her personal preferences. For example, companies such as Hertz offer these shoppers personal pickup at the airport and the preferred car is waiting and warmed up. Hertz has also altered the purchase process to reduce the waiting time in the pickup and return of the car.
- **Strategic Shopper.** There is a large segment of shoppers who either do not mind or enjoy the challenge of shopping to find the lowest price for specific products. They tend to have average or better than average incomes and education. These consumers know which retailers (prestige shops, outlet stores, and Internet) have the best prices and sales. This shopper might use a broker from the Internet to locate the best price for a BMW and then drive it to Sam's Club to purchase staple items at the lowest price. Note that a shopper can be elite for selected products and services and strategic for most other items. This type of shopper uses word of mouth and the Internet for information sources.
- **Value Shopper.** There is a large segment of shoppers with average or lower incomes who shop in outlets and discount stores that provide value in lower prices on a regular basis. Since this is a large segment of the population, about 40 percent according to Roper Reports, there is substantial opportunity for companies and retailers to service this market. Examples of successful retailers serving this segment are Wal-Mart and Family Dollar Stores that has opened 1,588 new stores during the last 10 years.

Lifestyles

Lifestyle is another classification that marketers use to think about the people who may buy their products. Lifestyle clustering emerged as a popular segmentation tool in the early 1980s as marketers learned to use the enormous pool of data that emerges from the U.S. Census each decade. Lifestyle combines the homogeneous beliefs and aspirations that groups have with the resulting purchases they generate. With the help of software, Census data is aggregated and zip codes identify where the majority of the population exhibits wide similarities in lifestyle. Lifestyle clusters can center on a variety of factors, such as economic status, educational level, or preferences for either the arts or sports. This is helpful in determining locations for direct-mail campaigns and advertising in specific lifestyle magazines or separate sections of the newspaper. For example, subscribers to *Outdoor* magazine would be good targets for a direct-mail campaign to raise funds for The Nature Conservancy.

Demographics

Demographic segmentation primarily includes income, age, and ethnicity.

Income

Over most of the past 50 years, marketing efforts were generally directed toward the large middle class. Consumers generally purchased identical television sets, telephone services, and watched the same network television programs. Since the 1980s, consumers have been dividing into two income tiers, as the wealthiest 20 percent of the population has seen its income grow by 21 percent while wages for the bottom 50 percent have stagnated or declined, according to Census Bureau data. This widening gap in incomes has changed how marketers are developing, advertising, and selling products and services.

For example, the automobile industry keeps introducing a more expensive sports utility vehicle (SUV) to meet the demands of higher-income consumers, while AutoNation and others are targeting refurbished used cars to lower-income households, who cannot afford a new car. The telecommunications industry has tailored its services to the two tiers, such as satellite telephone service for traveling executives and prepaid telephone cards to consumers who want the added convenience or cannot afford credit cards or telephone service.

Age

Age is the single most predictable aspect of consumer behavior. Age dictates life stage, which is predictive of needs and wants, which in turn influence product usage and therefore product development, distribution, and marketing communications strategies. As the most predictable aspect of consumer behavior, age is also among the most actively used segmentation method. Life stages usually correspond with distinct product and service needs.

Advertising communication options such as television, newspapers, magazines, and direct mail can easily be purchased with age as a selection criterion. Television is purchased almost exclusively in age breaks with gender as the only other primary classification. Marketing people, to further leverage age as a clustering tool, can use the many factors that have shaped each generation or captured the headlines.

PRODUCT CONSUMPTION PROJECTIONS

Product Use by Age × Population Projections by Age = Future Product Consumption

Source: Colgate-Palmolive

Ethnicity

Another powerful segmentation tool is ethnicity. Generational influences over a culture establish beliefs, attitudes, and images that are strongly linked to the diverse group of ethnic cultures that comprise a country's population. At times, by understanding these common influences, marketers can leverage common preferences to shape communications or develop desirable products and services. Many Latin cultures, for example, retain family values and cohesiveness as a fabric for their lives. Marketers need to both respect and mirror these values if they wish to be successful with these groups.

For example, American Hispanics are projected to comprise a third of the U.S. population in the near future. In some markets, they are already the largest population segment. In Los Angeles, Hispanic radio stations have the largest listening audience of any stations in this tremendous population center. Companies cannot successfully market a mass appeal product in LA without fully understanding the wants and needs of the Hispanic population.

However, stereotyping ethnic consumer behavior can often lead to wrong decisions. Companies must take a multidimensional approach that combines many of the segmentation options to remain successful. Marketing departments also fall into the trap of thinking that they can conduct an occasional relationship with an ethnic group when the available dollars exist in any year's budget. The commitment to conduct ethnic marketing should be viewed as long term and carry the desire for a long-term relationship. Anything less will become quickly transparent to the audience targeted, and damage the image and reputation of a company.

CONSUMER BEHAVIOR— INTERNATIONAL
by Frito-Lay

Across international markets, the foundations of consumer purchasing behavior are very similar. Wants and needs hierarchies, adoption patterns, and other purchasing behavior patterns influence consumers in every country. Companies manage unique and standard international marketing programs that will promote similar consumer purchasing behavior (trial, repeat, long-term frequency). It is the similarity in consumers worldwide that make global brands possible and multinational businesses profitable. The challenge in understanding and influencing international purchasing behavior is in developing mechanisms for measuring behavior. Unlike the U.S. market, many international markets lack the infrastructure needed to track consumer behavior. Companies need to analyze and respond to behaviors based on the level of information that is available.

There are several product *key performance indicators* that are used to continually measure consumer purchasing behavior. These measures provide benchmarks of a brand's relationship to its consumer and give direction as to any corrective actions needed. These measures are applicable in most countries, and include price/value needs, consumer quality needs, product availability, and consumer awareness.

Price/Value Needs

Value as it relates to price is a critical decision point in many international markets. Many markets have unstable fluctuating economies in which a consumer's economic situation can change overnight. Monitoring the affordability of a company's products relative to the competition on a frequent basis is very important. Companies should monitor changes in the consumer's economic situation so products designed to be priced affordably do not become premium items. Companies also should monitor competitors' costs as they can change rapidly based on changes in suppliers, manufacturing principles, and marketing strategy. It is important to know prior to setting a price increase whether the perceived value of a brand warrants those changes. A brand that is perceived by consumers as declining in value is likely to suffer revenue declines in the face of higher prices. In contrast, a brand with increasing perceived value may warrant increases in price and continue to flourish once they are initiated.

Packaging also plays a key role in how consumers view a product's value. For example, metalized or high-barrier packaging is often more expensive, but improves shelf life in high humidity climates and in countries where length-to-market is high. However, regardless of the benefits or higher costs, consumers in some cultures simply prefer the looks of the metalized packaging and purchase the product.

Consumer Quality Needs

Quality also is a key influence in consumer purchasing, and maintaining quality is particularly challenging internationally. Product quality differentials can change abruptly with emerging international competitors and changes in competitors' manufacturing capabilities. Local materials often fail to meet the specifications needed to make a quality product. Supply chains are set up to ensure that quality can be maintained at affordable costs. Quality is now so critical in most countries that companies use the entire supply chain to ensure that quality is maintained from the initial moment after manufacturing to the time that the product enters the marketplace. Handling specifications and shelf life dates can contribute to maintaining quality after long length-to-market shipments.

Product Availability

Most consumers desire to purchase products that are easy to find and are available on a continuous basis, although, in some countries, seeking out new products and price bargaining are an enjoyable part of the shopping experience. Therefore, distribution is another critical element in a new product's success. Without commercial availability, the best marketing promotions and advertising campaigns cannot create a sustainable business. In international markets, building distribution for a small brand can be difficult if there is not sufficient marketing spending behind that brand. It is often easier to build a brand's business using alternative trade channels such as small kiosk stores or individual retail outlets that may literally only be a grass hut with 10 products on a table. These alternative channels are easy to penetrate and can lead to great gains in building new markets for unknown products.

Consumer Awareness

Media, packaging, and point-of-purchase materials work together to create a brand's image internationally, just as they do in the United States. However, promotions and outdoor advertising often play more important roles in consumer awareness internationally. Promotions, such as inserted toys or games, often add greater perceived value. Unfortunately, consumers can become so addicted to promotions that the brand value becomes tied to continuing these promotions.

Branding is a critical factor in international consumer purchasing decisions. Each company's approach to branding will differ based on company culture and consumers' similarity around the world in particular categories. Most multinational companies pursue a strategy of global concepts with local execution. That is, brands have one positioning, one package design, and one name worldwide, while each market determines the appropriate marketing communications (both in terms of message content and appropriate marketing plan for product launch). Product innovation is a strong local marketing option as each country has a slightly different approach to variety within each category. For example, the consumer desire for snack food is very similar on a global basis, and Lay's potato chips use a common package design throughout the world. However, the name may change from country to country. See Table 6.3 for salty snack consumption in various countries.

CONSUMER BEHAVIOR—CASE STUDY

by KRAFT Foods, Inc.

Company: Kraft Pizza Company
Case: Influencing the Consumer Learning Process—DiGiorno Pizza

What do you do if you've figured out a way to make a frozen pizza that tastes as good as those delivered by the big retail chains, only you're pretty sure no one will believe you? That was the situation the Kraft Pizza Company found itself in during the mid–1990s when it was time to introduce its newly developed DiGiorno Rising Crust Pizza.

Kraft knew what it was getting into; it had the leading entries in the frozen pizza market: Tombstone, and Jack's, a strong regional brand. Both were healthy, but growth had been limited to modest gains in the $1.6 billion a year frozen pizza segment. Kraft had never grabbed pizza's brass ring: volume from the rest of the $24 billion category, dominated by Pizza Hut, Domino's, and Little Caesars. But this attempt would be different. In DiGiorno Rising Crust Pizza, Kraft finally had a product that delivered the quality consumers expected from the carry-out and delivery (CO/D) companies.

The trouble was a tangle of consumer beliefs and behaviors that would make it hard to build awareness and initial purchase/trial, including:

- **Skepticism.** Consumers had heard this pitch before. Other brands in the frozen segment had promised a frozen pizza that would taste as good as CO/D. But the products did not deliver, leaving a consumer perception that the quality gap was probably too wide to cross.
- **Price Deals.** Over the years, the frozen pizza case at the grocery store had become a battleground where frequent and deep discounts had trained consumers to wait for deals or to buy whatever

(Continued)

was on sale among their preferred set of brands. Along the way, this dynamic helped erode brand loyalty and increased the perception that frozen pizza was a commodity product. Would consumers be willing to fork over the unheard-of price of $5.49 for a frozen pizza when they could buy other frozen pizzas on a "three for $7" deal?

- **Purchase Routine.** Beyond looking for sales, frozen pizza users had little involvement with the category, and spent little or no time looking over the options in the aisle. It was not at all a given that consumers would notice a new product on the shelf.
- **User and Product Imagery.** To take volume from the CO/D brands, Kraft was going to have to attract a new kind of user to the frozen pizza aisle: a more affluent, urban, and adult-oriented pizza lover who was used to spending about $10 to have a pizza delivered. But the target market's perception of frozen pizza was negative. Focus group comments included: "Bad crust," "Skimpy toppings," and "Just for the kids." How could Kraft convince these consumers that DiGiorno could deliver a pizza with fresh-baked taste from the freezer case?

Kraft knew it needed to influence the learning process in order to shake up this consumer skepticism and complacency by driving home one key message to the target consumer: DiGiorno is as good as a CO/D pizza. To achieve this, the company saw to it that every element of the marketing mix worked to change the consumer perceptions about frozen pizza.

Kraft started with the box it came in. A slice-shaped hole was die-cut in the front so consumers could see the dramatic difference in the product right at the shelf. They could see huge toppings, bright and crisp-looking like the food in the produce aisle, and a heavy-gauge plastic vacuum seal locking in the freshness, preventing the freezer burn typical on frozen pies.

Kraft also took a risk and bucked the category's traditional retail promotional marketing by spending only a fraction of its marketing budget on retail pricing discounts. This put a strong focus on building real consumer equity from day one.

In order to begin generating the awareness needed to get consumers to pay attention at the shelf, Kraft and its advertising agency, Foote, Cone & Belding, then launched the "It's not delivery" campaign. They surrounded the target consumers with a marketing program featuring a strong television presence, magazine insertions, and a range of transit and outdoor advertising. The hallmarks of the campaign worked to address the consumers' negative image of frozen pizza and to reinforce the DiGiorno's-as-good-as-CO/D message:

- The campaign showed consumers who were fooled by DiGiorno's appearance and taste into believing it must be a carry-out or delivery pizza. If these people were pleasantly surprised, the thinking went, you could be, too. Each spot featured the line, "It's not delivery, it's DiGiorno," as did the print and outdoor advertising.
- The centerpiece of each commercial was a demonstration of DiGiorno's star attribute: a rising crust that was not prebaked like ordinary frozen pizzas but "baked up fresh like pizzeria pizza." This demonstration was a real influence on consumers' belief that DiGiorno was *different*.
- Finally, the situations in each spot were the kinds of occasions when one might have ordinarily ordered a pizza for delivery: throwing a casual party, a relaxing night at home for a young couple, or watching a pay-per-view boxing match on television with friends.

As good as the product, message, and advertising were, however, Kraft knew that many skeptics might see it and remain unconvinced. Although the rising crust was new, these target consumers had been promised CO/D quality before. So the company embarked on a massive sampling program, based on consumer research that revealed that over 50 percent of consumers who tried DiGiorno would repeat the purchase. Two "Travelin' Pizzerias" were built, which roamed from town to town offering consumers the fresh-baked taste of DiGiorno. The units were decked out in the brand's colors and graphics and carried the "It's not delivery…" theme line from the advertising.

Before the year was out, it became clear that consumers were accepting that DiGiorno was reinventing frozen pizza. Brand awareness and trial were climbing past initial forecasts. The repeat purchase rate was high. But the ultimate proof of the brand's success came from data on sources of volume. Over 50 percent of DiGiorno's business was from outside the frozen pizza category. Kraft went back to get a deeper understanding of consumers' perceptions of the brand and how they were using it.

The focus group research revealed shifts in attitudes about frozen pizza:

- Consumers described DiGiorno as a "fresh pizza in the freezer case, not frozen pizza."
- They said DiGiorno looked like it was "handmade, not mass-produced."
- They felt it was made with adults in mind: "This is not just for the kids."
- They saw CO/D pizzas as the benchmark for value: "It's a $12 pizza for $5."

Kraft also noted that its efforts behind DiGiorno were changing behavior:

- Consumers were substituting DiGiorno for CO/D on some occasions: "We used to order out. Now we just open the freezer." "Hey, it costs less to buy DiGiorno than a restaurant pizza."
- Some were buying DiGiorno for themselves and "the cheaper ones" for the kids.

Consumer reactions like these were a sign that the brand was fulfilling its promise. By the end of the 18-month rollout, the business was breaking Kraft records for successful new product launches. Even the northeastern United States, the region with the deepest skepticism rankings and the lowest use of frozen pizza, was posting record share gains. DiGiorno, followed by its inevitable rising crust competition, has established a new kind of grocery store pizza: "real pizza that just happens to be frozen."

CONSUMER BEHAVIOR—CASE STUDY

by Discovery Communications, Inc.

Company: Discovery Communications, Inc.
Case: Consumer Needs Are Universal—"Watch with the World"

Discovery Communications, Inc. (DCI) is the number-one nonfiction media company in the world, devoted to helping people explore their world and satisfy their natural curiosity. Marketing research had shown that there was a similarity of desire among consumers in different countries to see informative and entertaining programming. The Discovery Channel, launched as a single U.S. cable network serving 156,000 subscribers 23 years ago, now satisfies consumer needs in 170 countries.

Discovery's integrated promotion campaign aims to build awareness for global programming. The "Watch with the World" initiative is built around the concept of a "same day, same primetime,

(Continued)

same network" airing of Discovery programming in then 155 countries and 33 languages with corresponding content and merchandise opportunities through online, retail, and consumer product platforms. The marketing campaign takes advantage of Discovery's unique ability to deliver an international goal: a multiplatform event that brings a global audience the same programming during a shared prime-time viewing experience.

Raising the Mammoth was a two-hour never-before-seen television special recounting the discovery of the first nearly intact 20,000-year-old woolly mammoth in Siberia. The special showed the mammoth from its initial discovery in the spring of 1997 by reindeer herders, to its October 1999 excavation and airlift to an ice cave 200 miles away. For the show, Discovery created a two-tiered marketing strategy.

The first phase was the successful expedition to excavate the woolly mammoth. Coverage of the expedition online with live updates from Siberia allowed people to experience the expedition and pique their interest about the program five months ahead of its air date. Teasers for the program also began to run at this time, helping bridge the gap between the expedition and actual airing of the event, keeping audiences interested, and maximizing the marketing opportunities.

The second tier focused on tune-in as well as the promotion of *Raising the Mammoth* as a major cinematic event leveraging all of the marketing assets of DCI for one single event. No other cable or broadcast network had ever attempted this type of international strategy for a television program.

The Discovery Channel built expedition awareness and "Watch with the World" tune-in momentum by rolling out in phases over the last few months before airing, including "Mammoth Moments" vignettes with program sponsorship, online information, and "March Is Mammoth" countdown spots. These vignettes had a global reach through international and domestic use on the Discovery Channel as well as other Discovery networks: TLC, Animal Planet, and the Travel Channel.

In the style of theatrical releases, Discovery launched its first program-specific theatrical trailer to run in almost 300 theaters in 11 major U.S. markets. Featuring a fully animated mammoth and expedition footage, and scored by a 60-piece orchestra, the trailer maximized the large screen impact with powerful and dramatic sound and imagery. Discovery Channel India and Singapore also ran this movie trailer in their native languages.

Discovery developed free promotional materials specifically for *Raising the Mammoth* including plush mammoths, fleece parkas, and "Mammoth Munch" ice cream. Made by Kemps Dairy, this flavor is a premium fudge ripple with a chocolate-covered mammoth cookie buried deep within the pint of ice cream just waiting to be "excavated."

Discovery Channel and Discovery.com created a *Raising the Mammoth* sweepstakes inviting online consumers to experience a similar expedition. After watching *Raising the Mammoth* on Discovery Channel, consumers were able to enter and win a trip to a dinosaur dig in South Dakota with paleontologist Dr. Larry Agenbroad, who participated in the Mammoth expedition or an expedition to Russia that included a first-class journey through Siberia on the Trans-Siberian Railway.

Online marketing efforts included animated tune-in banners and ads that linked the *Raising the Mammoth* online feature content and sweepstakes and interactive banners that delivered mammoth-related facts.

Internationally, Discovery Channel Germany created an online initiative with sweepstakes, interactive game and banners, while Discovery Channel Europe created a feature event site, promoted on-air, with online stories, quick facts, discussions with experts, sweepstakes, and video clips. Discovery

Channel Asia promoted *Raising the Mammoth* through an on-air/off-air sweepstakes competition with a grand prize trip to Washington, D.C., with local stops at the Smithsonian Museums.

Discovery Channel U.S. and international ad sales teams secured extensive global sponsorship packages for *Raising the Mammoth*, including on-air, retail, in-flight, home video, poster, and online areas for several major companies. Participating international markets included Asia, Europe, and Latin America and involved additional customized regional marketing elements.

Retail stores showcased prehistoric-themed merchandise in Discovery and Nature Company stores, including mammoth plush toys, branded T-shirts, archeological dig kits, Discovery's *Atlas of the Prehistoric World*, as well as other related books and videos. The in-store promotional designs featured the same look and feel of the network's marketing elements for *Raising the Mammoth*.

Additional consumer marketing elements exclusive to New York City included a "fur-wrapped" commuter "Big Woolly Bus" that traveled around the city.

On Sunday, March 12, 2000, *Raising the Mammoth* drew a remarkable 7.8 rating in the United States. Those results made *Raising the Mammoth* not only the most watched program in the history of Discovery Communications, Inc., but also the most highly rated documentary in U.S. cable television history. In Canada, it drew the largest single audience for any program in Discovery's five-year history. In the United Kingdom, it earned the highest adult rating for all satellite channels that night. And, in the total 147 countries in which it aired, *Raising the Mammoth* drew over 30 million households in its first screening. *Raising the Mammoth* also proved to be the highest-trafficked Discovery.com feature, measured in a seven-day period, with over 3.75 million page views over the week. Approximately 919,000 page views were registered the day after *Raising the Mammoth* aired, which is the second highest one-day page view record to date for Discovery.com.

CORPORATE PROFILES AND AUTHOR BIOGRAPHIES

KIMBERLY-CLARK CORPORATION

Kimberly-Clark Corporation is a leading global manufacturer of tissue, personal care, and health-care products. Visit Kimberly-Clark at www.kimberly-clark.com.

Jeff Drake

Jeff Drake was formerly Director of Marketing Research for Kimberly-Clark Corporation (KCC). Mr. Drake led the marketing research function at KCC for over 10 years. He received his BS in Marketing from Wright State and his MBA from the University of Cincinnati.

FRITO-LAY

Frito-Lay North America is the $11 billion convenient foods business unit of PepsiCo. Visit Frito-Lay at www. frito lay.com.

Dwight R. Riskey

In 2002, Dwight Riskey was Senior Vice President of Global Marketing for Frito-Lay and has since retired from the company. Dr. Riskey received his bachelor's, master's, and doctorate degrees from the University of California, Los Angeles.

KRAFT FOODS, INC.

Kraft, headquartered in Northfield, Illinois, is the world's second largest food company. Visit Kraft at www.kraftfoods.com.

Mary Kay Haben

Mary Kay Haben was formerly Executive Vice President and President, Kraft Cheese Division. Ms. Haben received her BBA from the University of Illinois and her MBA from the University of Michigan.

DISCOVERY COMMUNICATIONS, INC.

Discovery Communications, headquartered in Silver Springs, Maryland, is the world's number-one nonfiction media company. Visit Discovery at www.discoverycommunications.com.

David C. Leavy

David Leavy is Executive Vice President of Global Communications and Corporate Affairs. Mr. Leavy received his BA from Colby College.

Additional information was provided by:

John C. Mowen who is a Regents Professor of Business Administration at Oklahoma State University.

NOTES

1. U.S. Department of Commerce, 1999.
2. Peter D. Bennett, *Dictionary of Marketing Terms* (Chicago, IL: American Marketing Association, 1995), p. 59.
3. *Consumer Behavior*, 5th ed., by John C. Mowen and Michael Minor.
4. Snack Food & Wholesale Bakery, Sept. 1999, p. 9.
5. Arthur S. Reber, *The Penguin Dictionary of Psychology*, Penguin, 1985.
6. Ibid.
7. Ibid.

7 ORGANIZATIONAL PURCHASING BEHAVIOR

by Boeing, Snap-on, IBM, and DuPont

THE ESSENTIALS OF ORGANIZATIONAL PURCHASING
by Boeing

Introduction

Of the consumers in the United States, 300 million account for two-thirds of demand (sales or GNP) and only 23 million organizations account for approximately one-third of demand. Organizational purchasing is conducted by individuals who have a specific buying behavior when involved in the process of purchasing products and services in large quantities. There can be several types of products procured through industrial purchasing, such as raw materials, components, subassemblies, equipment, or finished products. These products are then turned into products and services that are sold to end consumers. Organizational purchasing agents are concerned with buying the right quality, in the right quantity, at the right price and time, and from the right sources. The quality of the organizational finished product in turn leads to the organization having a competitive advantage.

Definition

Organizational purchasing is the identification, acquisition, access, positioning and management of resources and related capabilities the organization needs or potentially needs in the attainment of its strategic objectives, "a business process responsible for acquisition of required material, services, and equipment."[1] (Institute for Supply Management) Organizational purchasing also is known as *procurement* or *industrial purchasing (IP)*. When organizations sell to other organizations, the selling process is known as "business-to-business."

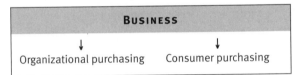

BUSINESS	
↓	↓
Organizational purchasing	Consumer purchasing

CHARACTERISTICS OF ORGANIZATIONAL DEMAND

Organizational, or business, demand is derived from a company's needs, and depends on the type of product or service that is being purchased. There are several characteristics of business demand including derived demand, dependent/independent demand, stability of demand, and competitive demand.

Derived Demand

Derived demand occurs when business product needs are derived from consumer needs. For example, a consumer may need a pair of in-line skates, and the roller blade company will then need to purchase plastic, metal buckles, ball bearings, and so forth. Virtually all business demand is based on consumer demand. Purchasing agents must pay attention to consumer trends as well as industrial needs. This is why manufacturers of component parts will team up with consumer manufacturers on advertising designed to stimulate consumer demand.

Dependent and Independent Demand

Dependent demand occurs when a product's use is directly dependent on the scheduled production of a larger component or parent product. For example, in a plant that produces automobile engines, the demand for engine block castings is a dependent demand; once the production schedule for a group of engines is established, the planner knows with certainty that one block will be required for each engine.

Independent demand occurs when an item's use is not directly correlated to a production schedule. For example, the demand for oil used by the machines on the assembly line cannot be calculated accurately from the production schedule; therefore, oil is said to have an independent demand. Generally, in an assembly or fabrication-type operation, most production inventory items will have a dependent demand, whereas maintenance items will have an independent demand.

Stability of Demand

A business typically has a continuous demand for the raw materials or components that it uses in its daily operations. Organizational purchasing agents become experts in their fields by buying items on a daily basis. In turn, purchasing agents count on other businesses to provide stability of supply.

Competitive Demand

Markets may be segmented into four economic conditions: perfect competition, imperfect competition, oligopoly, and monopoly. Knowledge of the competitive supply structure helps the buyer and seller know how prices are set, whether price concessions may be possible, and how to get the best terms and conditions.

Perfect Competition

In a *perfect competition* industry, the abundance of suppliers prevents any one supplier from determining the price. Under this condition, the marketplace, or the actions of all the organizational buyers, dictates the price of products. The buyer needs to continually research what is happening in the marketplace in order to determine the best value. Examples are agricultural commodities and the current large variety of business computers such as Hewlett Packard, IBM, Dell, and Gateway.

Imperfect Competition

In an *imperfect competition* industry, there are many sellers that have some control over price, each with differentiated products, The organizational buyer should concentrate on pricing and product quality and service. Examples are soap manufacturers, cereal companies, and television broadcast companies.

Oligopoly

In an *oligopolistic* industry, there are a few sellers of an identical, or nearly identical, product. Each seller can have some effect on prices. It is very difficult to get price concessions in an oligopolistic setting, especially if the product is standardized. This happens because, if a supplier's competitors hear about a price reduction, all competitors tend to reduce prices to meet the competition, resulting ultimately in lost profits for the oligopolistic industry. Examples of oligopolies are the steel, paper, hotel, and airline industries. The buyer should concentrate on service standards, such as performance, quality, and delivery.

Monopoly

In a *monopolistic* industry there is one seller with a unique or proprietary product. The company will have no direct competition and the purchaser will have no control over the price. A monopolistic setting occurs when a company is first to market with a new product. A company may be granted an exclusive ability to sell their product by the government, such as through a patent on a new drug. Also, a company may be granted an exclusive ability to operate its business in a given area, such as utilities or a cable television company, through a business license. In this case, the company prices are regulated by the government and given a rate that will yield a fair return on investment to the investors. However, the selling company in a monopolistic segment has no control over alternative products or services.

SEGMENTING ORGANIZATIONAL DEMAND

Organizational markets may be segmented, as in consumer markets, to more accurately satisfy specific needs in a cost-effective manner. Each of these organizational markets has industry-specific purchasing agents. One method of determining specific target companies within an industry is the *North American Industry Classification System (NAICS)*. NAICS classifies and lists industries by product and service in the United States, Canada, and Mexico by six-digit categories. The old system was formerly known as the Standard Industrial Classification system (SIC). Business-to-business sales managers and representatives spend many months or years learning about their specific target market in an effort to better serve their target clients. There are many types of organizational markets, including commercial, governmental, institutional, and trade.

Commercial

Commercial markets involve purchasing materials and services used for internal consumption or for conversion into other products or services. Commercial markets consist of industrial manufacturers such as automobiles and furniture, resource producers such as farming and mining, and service providers such as transportation and legal services. Most commercial companies provide differentiated products and therefore require high quality or specific inputs to their manufacturing or service processes. Purchasing managers who buy materials and services for these markets typically are called *industrial buyers*. Industrial buyers participate in determining what products and services

their company should make; what components or parts the company should manufacture; what services the company should provide; and what components, parts, or services should be purchased from outside suppliers. They correlate their purchasing actions with sales forecasts and production or demand schedules. They select suppliers from whom purchases can be made on a continuing and mutually profitable basis. Since many purchased items are technical in nature, they integrate the efforts of their departments with those of the other departments of the company. Also, because many items are extremely expensive, there is a need for the business-to-business sales rep to offer financing for these products. An example of a highly technical industrial purchase is high-quality silicon that will become part of a solar panel.

Governmental

Government buyers include procurement authorities from city, state, county, and federal governments. The purchasing principles are generally the same as business markets. However, the governmental documentation, procedures, and regulations are more detailed because of the large size of typical contracts, the sovereignty of the government, and the source of the funding which requires the trust of the taxpayers. The U.S. government has its own set of comprehensive federal regulations affecting procurement. Most notably are the Federal Agency Regulations (FAR) and the Defense Federal Agency Regulations (DFAR). Government purchasing managers typically seek low cost (low bidder), detailed product specifications, and the capability to deliver large quantities on time. Examples of products specified might be hundreds of miles of paved roads for a multistate highway project or new guidance systems for a jet fighter.

Institutional

Institutional buyers include universities, schools, hospitals, churches, and prisons. Due to the size of the institution, buyers typically purchase large quantities of goods and services and, therefore, often have specific rules and internal regulations governing the purchasing process. Purchasing managers seek low cost due to the typically low budgets of institutions. Quality often is not a primary requirement because end users of the purchased items have few if any competitive options and are considered to be a captive audience. However, quality requirements are improving as competition increases among institutions. For example, many colleges and hospitals now tout their improved food offering.

Trade (Wholesale/Retail)

The trade segment consists of wholesale and retail. Trade buyers purchase essentially finished products that may require some assembly, reprocessing, or repackaging. *Value-added resellers (VARs)* buy basic products from *original equipment manufacturers (OEMs)*, add various items such as hardware, software, and services, and then resell them to various business niches. Many items are purchased in bulk and therefore the buyers' primary concerns are quality and price. Purchasers buy with the knowledge that the items will go to the end user, and therefore are in constant touch with the consumer market through trade shows, marketing research, and business-to-business sales representatives. Space constraints may require a small retail purchaser to buy in small lots from a wholesale distributor, despite the higher cost. For example, Costco, a large store, chooses to buy directly from the manufacturer for most of its purchases because of the sheer volume of its purchases, its extensive distribution system, and the price discounts. Many retail buyers will seek unique or exclusive merchandise in an effort to provide a differentiating factor for their store. Many purchasing systems require a manufacturer or distributor to carry an entire line of products rather than just one item to set up an account with the buyer and achieve economies of scale in purchasing.

ORGANIZATIONAL BUYERS / PURCHASING DEPARTMENT

Each organizational market segment has a purchasing department. These departments interact with the sales force of supplying companies. The size of a company's purchasing department, including the number of buyers, often depends on the size and complexity of the products, commodities, and services being procured. Typically one or two buyers from a company will work with a supplier on the daily management issues of a contract. The supplier, often referred to as a *business-to-business sales representative*, will work with the buyer to provide important information. The role of buyers is to ensure that all parties involved adhere to any unique or special business provisions and the general corporate terms and conditions of the purchase contract. Buyers also are responsible for the coordination and communication of any activity with other groups within the organization, including the technical, finance, and legal departments; quality assurance; and customer service. It is imperative to have open and regular communications among these groups to ensure that the right product is delivered at the right time and at the right cost.

Marketers should understand the consumers of the business community, known collectively as *purchasing decision makers*. They may be individuals, buying teams, design-build teams, or buying consortiums, and are the people with whom supplier companies' sales managers and sales representatives should strive to form long-term business relationships.

Individuals

Individual decision makers often make the final decision in the procurement process. These individuals can either be part of the purchasing staff, the manager of the purchasing department, or a member of the group that will be using the product or service. The advantages of individual buyers are the ability to have knowledge and responsibility in one person and the faster response of one individual.

Buying Teams

Most companies use buying teams in the procurement process. A typical buying team consists of representatives from the purchasing, finance, legal, and engineering departments. The advantage of buying teams is the additional knowledge imparted by additional personnel.

Design-Build Teams

In some instances, design-build teams (DBTs) are used to facilitate communication among customers, manufacturers, and organizations in the supply chain. These teams typically will codevelop the requirements for a new product. Taking advantage of the expertise of the manufacturer and the supply base, and coupling that with the experience of the end user will help alleviate last-minute production changes and disruptions that ultimately will drive up the cost of the product.

Buying Consortiums

Consortium buying is defined as a group of companies that collaborate to leverage their procurement clout.

Types of Organizational Purchasing

Organizational purchasing usually is identified as centralized or decentralized. Although these terms sometimes are used to refer to the physical location of purchasing staff within a company, it is more commonly referred to as the location of the purchasing authority. Neither completely rigid centralization nor loose decentralization of purchasing seems to meet the needs of all companies. The solution to the problems presented by either extreme structure often is found in a centralized corporate staff control of purchasing policies and administration, with decentralization of purchasing operations. For example, the policies and strategic initiatives of some companies are derived at a central procurement division whereas the procurement operations are carried out in the decentralized manufacturing and operating facilities.

- **Centralized.** Centralized organizational purchasing exists when the responsibility for the purchasing function is assigned to a single group and its manager. This structure works quickly and efficiently if a company has a single operating facility. However, with the scattering of plants and diversification of products, the problems of purchasing departments become increasingly complex with additional demands on communications.
- **Decentralized.** Decentralized, or departmentalized, organizational purchasing exists when operations, marketing, finance, engineering, or other functional area personnel do their own buying. Decentralization provides quick response to local needs; however, this structure tends to produce duplication of effort and inefficiency.

Purchasing Process

Organizational buyers typically follow a formatted purchasing process. This process assures that all of an organization's needs are met. Marketers attempt to influence each of these steps through the marketing mix (product development, pricing, distribution, and marketing communications). The goal of marketing is to influence this process so that each step ultimately narrows down the organizational buyer's choice of competing options to one product brand. See the box that illustrates the Organizational Purchasing Process.

1. *Determine Needs*

The need for a purchase typically originates in one of an organization's operating departments or in its inventory control section. These needs can be for several types of products and services.

Installations/Structures
Installations or *structures* are buildings and equipment attached to buildings, such as heating and cooling equipment. Structures include manufacturing, utilities, mining operations, roads, dams, and airports. These are generally the most expensive of any business purchase and are therefore purchased infrequently and involve many people. In some instances, installations are leased rather than purchased owing to the large capital outlays needed. In many instances, state governments may be involved in promoting one installation site over

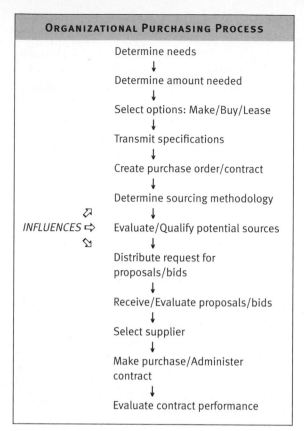

ORGANIZATIONAL PURCHASING PROCESS

Determine needs
↓
Determine amount needed
↓
Select options: Make/Buy/Lease
↓
Transmit specifications
↓
Create purchase order/contract
↓
Determine sourcing methodology
↓
INFLUENCES ⇨ Evaluate/Qualify potential sources
↓
Distribute request for proposals/bids
↓
Receive/Evaluate proposals/bids
↓
Select supplier
↓
Make purchase/Administer contract
↓
Evaluate contract performance

another, as jobs follow the selection and purchase of installations. For example, Mercedes Benz had several states competing for the site of a new automobile assembly plant.

Capital Equipment

Capital equipment has four components: industrial, information processing equipment, transportation equipment, and accessory/general-purpose equipment.

Parts and Components

Parts and *components* are defined as the materials supplied to the manufacturer during the manufacturing process that are then incorporated into the finished product. For example, when Boeing signs contracts with airlines to manufacture airplanes, the contract usually specifies certain customer variables for a particular aircraft that is unique to that airline. These may include such added components as the interior configuration, seats, in-flight entertainment, or other specific hardware that the buyer

perceives will give it a competitive advantage. In some instances, the buyer may supply these unique components, known as "buyer-furnished equipment."

Raw Materials

Raw materials are commodities that will be converted into production materials that are then converted into end items. Examples of raw materials include steel sheets, plastic resins, rubber compounds, and aluminum ingots. Purchasing raw materials and commodities is different from buying services, component parts, or fully manufactured products. Raw materials must meet the needs of many processing technologies, as the material passes through the manufacturing process. For example, to produce a steel fabrication the material must be formed, welded, and perhaps finished. Each of these process technologies may require different material characteristics for optimal processing. To achieve the lowest total cost, a buyer needs to work across all process technologies required to produce a product, including the design stage.

Maintenance, Repair, Operating Supplies

Maintenance, repair, and operating supplies (MRO) are materials that are purchased for the support of manufacturing or operations. These supplies are expendable items and do not become part of a product. Some examples are hand tools, cleaning materials, and office supplies. Service organizations such as hospitals, schools, and banks usually buy large volumes of MRO supplies. Typically, 80 to 85 percent of an organization's purchase orders are for MRO supplies; however, only 15 to 20 percent of the total purchasing dollars are spent for MRO items.

Services

Services provide skilled labor that does not produce a tangible good. Services range from architectural, engineering, advertising, and software development, to the maintenance and repair of production equipment. Procurement of services may represent more than 25 percent of an organization's expenditures. As outsourcing increases, expenditures on services increase each year. Specifying service quality levels can be one of a purchasing department's most challenging responsibilities.

Standardized versus Custom/Unique Goods and Services

Products or services obtained through procurement can be categorized as either standardized or unique.

The advantages of standardized products are the ease of purchase and known capabilities to the end consumer. The disadvantage is the inability to differentiate based on these parts or products.

The advantage of using custom parts or products is the ability to serve a consumer need and the potential for additional revenue. The disadvantage is the additional time and cost to purchase unique products.

2. Determine Amount Needed

The next step is to determine the amount of the product needed. Organizational buyers can make purchases of an item ranging from one to millions of the item. The advantages of purchasing many items at once is the lower cost of order processing. Typically the administrative cost is the same regardless of the amount ordered, thus repeating the same process can be very expensive. The disadvantage of purchasing large quantities at the same time is the excessive inventory carrying costs (detailed in "Warehousing," Chapter 22). Determining the correct amount to order is known as the *economic order quantity (EOQ)*. The goal of EOQ is to determine the order size that minimizes the total cost.

3. Select Options: Make/Buy/Lease

There are three options that a buyer considers when deciding whether to purchase a product or service. The buying company can make the product or provide the service internally, buy the product from another company, or lease the product or service from another company.

Make/Buy

Traditionally, a company will utilize a *make/buy* committee to determine if a product or service should be provided from within a company, or

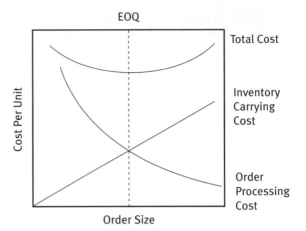

Figure 7.1 Determining the Economic Order Quantity

whether it should be procured from a supplier. This make/buy decision usually is made with input from the purchasing, technical, and finance departments.

A company conducts an internal analysis to determine whether the costs will be less if the product or service is produced internally or externally. Costs, the company's long-range plans, and managerial expertise usually establish that some parts and components of the company's products will be made internally and that others will be purchased from outside suppliers. Within this framework, make-or-buy determinations can originate in one of several ways:

- **New Product Development.** The development of a new product or the major modification of an old one are typical situations requiring make-or-buy determinations. Every major part of the new product should be studied well in advance to determine the most advantageous production and sourcing decisions.
- **Unsatisfactory Supplier Performance.** Unsatisfactory supplier performance for certain purchased parts and components may also trigger make-or-buy determinations. It may stem from the supplier's inability to perform certain complex production operations or from unstable quality performance.
- **Changing Sales Demand.** Periods of significant sales growth or sales decline also generate

situations that initiate make-or-buy determinations. Reduced sales result in reduced production activity, thus leaving company-owned plant facilities and workers underutilized. Rising sales require a rapid expansion of production capacity that cannot be met through plant expansion.

Lease

An operating lease is used by an organization to facilitate financial convenience and flexibility, usually when a firm has a need to use the assets but is not interested in owning them. This may be due to the risks and responsibilities that are associated with owning the asset or the potential cost of upkeep on the equipment. Most operating leases are for a short, fixed period of time, usually considerably less than the life of the equipment being leased. For example, companies may lease computers or a fleet of corporate automobiles.

4. Transmit Specifications

The operating departments within the organization will specify to the buyers the type of product or service and the quantity, quality, price, and time needed. Transmission of the specifications to the purchasing department usually is accomplished in one of four ways:

- **Standard Purchase Requisition.** This is an internal document, in contrast with a purchase order that usually is an external document. Most companies use a standard, serially numbered purchase requisition form for requests originating in the operating departments. The essential information on the form includes a description of the material, quantity, date required, estimated unit cost, operating account to be charged, date, and authorizing signature.
- **Traveling Purchase Requisition.** This type of requisition is used to communicate to the purchasing department the material needs that originate in the inventory control sections. When the stock level drops to the reorder point in a manual system, an inventory clerk takes the traveling requisition from the file, notes the current stock level and the desired quan-

tity and date, and sends it to the purchasing department.
- **Bill of Materials.** *A bill of materials (BOM)* is a structured list of materials that is used to create a particular part. The BOM, along with a production schedule, can be sent directly to the purchasing department as notification of the need for materials. Total requirements are obtained by calculating the BOMs for the production quantity scheduled.
- **Computerized Production/Inventory Control Systems.** Many companies use computerized production and inventory control systems to produce a complete requirements schedule for a given time period, containing most of the information needed by the buyer.

5. Create Purchase Orders/Contracts

Once the determination is made to purchase or lease, a contract is needed to initiate a new purchase. A *new purchase* is a new purchasing/leasing requirement that has been developed by the manufacturer's new specifications. Purchase contracts for small dollar amounts, usually under $1,000, with standard terms and conditions are typically called *purchase orders. Purchase contracts* are for larger amounts with nonstandard terms and conditions. The vendor or supplier sales representative should be aware of any potential new purchase decisions and assist in determining specifications and requirements.

6. Determine Sourcing Methodology

The purchasing department will determine the two main options for sources for contract fulfillment: sole source or multisource competitive bidding.

Sole Source

Sometimes a buyer will ask only one company to bid on a contract, known as a *sole source* or a *noncompetitive contract*. There are several reasons why sole sourcing may be used: only one source is available for a particular product (replacement parts for a specific computer), only one supplier has the specialized technical expertise, there is a time limitation, or a company has a special relationship with a particular supplier. An advantage of sole sourcing is the speed of contract fulfillment. The disadvantages of sole source contracts are the lack of competition and difficulty of negotiating terms. A negotiated contract may be used when there is only one supplier. This is typically used to attempt to secure favorable terms and conditions for the purchaser despite being in a sole source setting.

Multisource Competitive Bidding

Bids are sales proposals in writing from the supplier or vendor. There are several competitive purchasing options, including closed bid, open bid, negotiated contracts, two-step bidding, and online auction bidding. The advantage of competitive bidding usually is the negotiation of preferred terms. The disadvantage is the length of time taken to secure the contract. No legal requirements compel a private firm to award a contract to the lowest bidder; however, the competitive-bidding process itself implies that the highest-qualified and lowest-priced bidder will get the contract. Competitive bidding practices demand that a buyer be willing to do business with every vendor from whom he or she solicits a bid. Whenever the lowest bidder does not receive the contract, the buyer is required to explain the decision. Government contracts usually require competitive bidding.

- **Closed Bid.** A *closed bid* is a formal method for acquiring goods and services in which a main requirement is to use the lowest bidder. Bids are submitted in sealed envelopes, to prevent dissemination of its contents, before a strict deadline. For example, a city may use a closed bid for the highly competitive selection of a contract for city recycling. Advantages are that the process is fair and ethical to all bidders. The disadvantage is that this system prevents the development of a long-term, cooperative relationship.
- **Open Bid.** An *open bid* is a method for acquiring goods and services in which discussions or negotiations may be conducted with offerors who submit proposals in the competitive range. Open bidding is less formal; may be conducted in person, by phone, or by fax; and

generally is of a smaller dollar value than closed bidding. For example, a city with a requirement for a new ballfield facility may select two or three landscaping companies and invite them in for formal negotiations to determine which can provide the best service at the most reasonable price. Advantages are the ease of administration and the short time needed for responses. The disadvantage is the potential for unethical dealings.

- **Negotiated Bid.** A *negotiated bid* is a bargaining or discussion process between two or more parties, each with its own viewpoints and objectives, seeking to reach a mutually satisfactory agreement on, or settlement of, a matter of common concern. For example, a grocery store chain may come to a city with a proposal to buy and develop a parcel of the city's property to construct a new store. Through continuous talks and negotiations, the city may decide that the proposal has a mutually acceptable agreement and enter into a contract with the company to proceed with the project.
- **Two-Step Bidding.** *Two-step bidding* is used when not enough initial product or service specifications are available to start a formal bidding process. The first step seeks technical compliance, and the second step seeks price bids. The advantage of this process is the time saved in lieu of waiting until all specifications are ready. The disadvantage is the setting of parameters by the supplying vendors. An example was the need for a solution to the Y2K computer problem that required starting the debugging process immediately and working out the contract requirements later.
- **Online Auction Bidding.** *Online auction bidding* uses the Internet to receive bids from as many sources as possible. This method usually is used by private industry for nonstrategic, spot buys. The advantages are the lower prices, ranging in savings from 2 to 25 percent, and the quick response for receiving bids. The disadvantage is the lack of source loyalty.

7. Evaluate/Qualify Potential Sources

If multiple source bidding is selected, then companies typically will rate suppliers against established criteria and then rank the results. Suppliers that are not financially sound or do not meet the quality criteria set forth by the buyer generally will be excluded from the bidding process. Some companies require that their suppliers or vendors have strict quality systems in place and are certified to ISO 9000 requirements. The *International Standards Organization*, headquartered in Switzerland, helps determine quality standards worldwide. Many vendors or suppliers are selected only when they meet all the requirements in several determining categories and are then ranked in the top level of all vendors. The process of achieving the top-level status takes an average of 1.6 years and can range from three months to five years.[2] Companies may assist suppliers in improving their qualifications by providing communications regarding expectations or problems, training, and plant visits or audits. Many companies use quantifiable ratings charts to qualify sources. Companies utilize both quantitative and qualitative criteria when choosing a supplier. Many companies try to minimize the subjective influences in a procurement process through a process of checks and balances and through a strict segregation of the technical, financial, and legal analysis of a bid.

Quantitative Criteria

Quantitative influences or criteria that affect purchasing include quality, on-time delivery, cost, technological capabilities, after-market service, continuity of supply/financial stability, reciprocity, geographic location, and government guidelines. For example, a buyer may give preference to suppliers that are geographically close or that have the lowest cost.

Qualitative Influences

Qualitative or subjective influences that affect purchasing include the reputation of a particular company and its management team, friendships between supplier and buyer, and the security in knowing a supplier well.

8. Distribute Request for Proposals/Bids

Once the list of potential bidders/suppliers has been approved, they will be sent an *invitation for bids (IFB)* or a *request for proposal (RFP)*. An IFB or RFP is a formal request to prospective vendors soliciting price quotations or bids and consists of a description of the item or service required, information on quantities, required delivery schedules, special terms and conditions, and standard terms and conditions. The IFB typically has more predetermined specifications and primarily is concerned with the bid price. The RFP may seek input from the bidding company regarding suppliers and methodology.

9. Receive/Evaluate Bid Responses

Once the RFP bids from all qualified bidders are received, the company will conduct an evaluation. Generally, this evaluation consists of an independent review of the relevant portions of the RFP by the technical, finance, and legal departments. Typically, the bidders with a technically acceptable bid and the lowest cost will be selected for negotiation of a contract. When one or more bidders is brought in for final negotiations, the representative from the procurement department will usually lead the negotiations, with assistance from relevant departments. Usually procurements above a certain level will require authority from a member of senior management to finalize the contract.

Occasionally, a soliciting company may not proceed with the evaluation process for any of several reasons, such as reduced funding capacity, a decision to make the product in-house, or the cancellation of a larger project. In this case it is important to notify the bidding companies as soon as possible to prevent them from performing unnecessary bidding tasks.

Not every company capable of bidding will bid. They may be overbooked with other work or this particular bid may not be economically justified. Suppliers may be kept out of the bidding by submitting late bids, bids with errors, or by having employees with conflicts of interest with the soliciting company.

In many instances, one prospective supplier is obviously superior to its competition, and the selection is a simple matter. However, the choice is not always so clear. In these cases, a numerical weighted-factor rating system can facilitate the decision process. A weighted-factor system calls for both the development of evaluation criteria and the assignment of criteria weighting.

Evaluation Criteria
The first step is to identify the key factors to be considered in the selection, along with their respective weights. Typically, this is accomplished by a committee of individuals involved in the purchasing process. Factors that are evaluated include the supplier's technical approach; understanding of the technical problem; production facilities; operator's requirements; maintenance requirements; price, managerial, financial, and technical capabilities; product quality; ability to meet schedules; and legal compliance with terms and conditions.

Criteria Weighting
The second step requires the assignment of numerical ratings for each of the competing firms. These assessments are based on the collective judgments of the evaluators after studying all the data and information provided by the potential suppliers, as well as that obtained in field investigations.

10. Select Supplier
The selection of a supplier typically involves a negotiation with one or more bidders with the highest evaluation. The negotiation process provides a legitimate and ethical means for a buyer and a supplier, through give and take, to determine terms and conditions, including cost. The most successful negotiations produce results that satisfy both sides and provide a framework for a long-term, mutually beneficial relationship.

11. Make Purchase/Administer Contract
After the selection of a supplier, both the technical and procurement departments typically handle the contract administration. Progress payments often are used as a way of sharing risk in a buyer/supplier relationship. The buyer releases funds to the supplier at predetermined points of the manufacturing process. This allows the supplier to alleviate some of the risk involved with capital tied up in a product that potentially could be canceled by the buyer. For example, customers typically pay in increments as their products move toward completion in the manufacturing line. This type of payment is typically done with higher dollar value products or products that are unique to the particular customer. Typical purchasing methods include blanket purchase orders, purchase credit card systems, and master schedules.

Blanket Purchase Orders
Blanket purchase orders or blanket ordering agreements (BOAs) allow a buyer and supplier to negotiate the terms and conditions for future contracts, without specific commitment. Then, when the buyer wishes to order equipment or services, only the prenegotiated price and quantity need to be inserted into the final contract. The advantage is that the contracts can be negotiated and finalized on an expedited basis.

Purchasing Credit Card Systems
Another mechanism is to allow certain authorized employees to purchase products and services that are less than a specified dollar amount with a corporate credit card in lieu of the formal procurement process. The advantage of purchasing through credit cards is that it greatly expedites the procurement process. The disadvantage is that there generally is no opportunity to review or negotiate terms or conditions.

Master Schedules
In some instances, products or services are procured in accordance with a master schedule. A master schedule incorporates the manufacturing and delivery schedules for various customers and corporate programs. As a company's or an organization's master schedule is firmed up, major divisions within a company will begin procuring their products and services in accordance with this master schedule.

12. Evaluate Contract Performance
The final step in the purchasing process is to evaluate the contractors, during and after the term of

the contract, against the original bidding criteria. The evaluation process promotes continued attention to the performance requirements and provides input into the next round of contract bidding. The results of the evaluation can lead to any of several outcomes, including project completed/contract expires, development of a strategic alliance, contract extension, or cancellation of contract.

Project Completed/Contract Expires
In this instance, the organization's needs have been fulfilled, the contract expires, and there is no continuing need for the supplier.

Strategic Alliance
After a superior performance evaluation, a company occasionally may develop a strategic alliance with a supplier. A strategic alliance identifies and exploits opportunities to expand business and technical relationships with a few select suppliers.

Contract Extension
If a good or service is still necessary and the contractor performance is acceptable, the contract may be extended. A contract extension can take either of two forms: a straight repurchase or a modified repurchase.

Contract Cancellation
If the supplier fails to deliver an order by the delivery date agreed in the contract, or if it fails to perform in accordance with contract provisions, the supplier may have breached the contract. The breach usually gives the purchaser the right to cancel the order. In addition, the purchaser may be able to sue the supplier for damages. Situations sometimes arise that compel a buyer to cancel an order before the supplier is obligated to supply the material. In making such a cancellation, the buyer may breach the purchase contract. If the cancellation leaves the supplier with semifinished goods, the supplier may suffer injury if the material cannot be resold at the contracted value. The majority of lost business occurs due to lack of attention by the selling company's representative.[3]

ORGANIZATIONAL PURCHASING— INTERNATIONAL
by Snap-on Inc.

Introduction

Globalization has dramatically increased the procurement of goods and services from different countries around the world. *International purchasing*, often called *international procurement* or *contracting*, is the process of selecting, contracting for, and, in some companies, handling the shipping of goods and services in a different country. The need for international procurement is influenced by:

- Better total cost availability (price, quality, delivery, financing) for the company
- The product and service needs of subsidiaries of international companies operating overseas
- Innovative and unique products
- Shorter tooling lead time to launch new products

Marketers should be aware of several issues that can impact the international purchasing process.

International Contract Laws

There are differences in the legal structures of various countries. For example, *Common Law* is based on judicial precedent and is used in many countries such as the United States, China, India, and England. *Civil Law* is based on statutory law, enacted by the legislature, and is used in many countries such as France and Spain. Even though purchasing involves a private contract in which terms and conditions are defined freely between parties, the contract cannot go against basic rules defined in national or local laws.

Contractual clauses commonly used in the United States may not apply or may not be enforceable when used in purchase contracts in other countries. For example:

- **Jurisdictional Claims.** A contract claiming the jurisdiction of the State of New Jersey Courts, with a favorable ruling to an American company, might be difficult to enforce with a supplier or client in another country.

- **Workplace Health and Safety, Human Rights, and Environmental Clauses.** Suppliers have to comply with local regulations, not U.S. regulations.
- **Child Labor Laws.** Suppliers have to comply with all applicable local child labor laws and employ only workers who meet the applicable minimum legal age requirement for their location, not U.S. laws.
- **Intellectual Property, Proprietary, Confidential, and Personal Information.** Suppliers have to comply with all applicable treaties, agreements, laws, and regulations governing the protection, use, and disclosure of intellectual property, proprietary, confidential, and personal information.
- **Language Issues.** A contract may be signed in one language, for example, English, but in case of litigation, a judge will require a translation into the local language performed by a Certified Public Translator, who will translate according to his or her knowledge. Therefore, some wording issues may arise.

Procurement Economic Issues

International procurement also may be affected by international economics. For example, contract cancellations may occur due to economic downturns. Dramatic differences in economic stability may hit various regions or countries around the world at any given time: for example, currencies' appreciation in 2007–2008, commodities' dramatic ups and downs in 2008, the global credit crunch, falling stock markets, and then currencies' depreciation in 2008–2009.

Procurement agents of most major corporations generally develop plans to deal with potential inflation/currency devaluation situations. They track commodity indexes and currency fluctuations. Some tie the price adjustment to an index. Some do currency hedging and/or incorporate provisions in the agreement to adjust prices up and down if the currency is outside the agreed-upon range.

During inflationary years, many countries use an automatic adjustment method for contract pricing. These adjustments are based on the applica-

tions of formulas that include indicators or indexes such as cost of living, wholesale prices, cost of commodities, and devaluation index. These may help contract fulfillment in the short term but also have side effects, such as refueling inflation and eliminating pressure on companies to reduce cost. In some countries today, it is illegal to include such formulas in contracts.

Sourcing Issues

Product and service sourcing decisions may need to consider restrictions based on the creation of regional common markets, such as NAFTA, the European Common Market, and the South American common market, known as Mercosur. The primary benefit of common markets is the reduction of import duties among its members and simplified trading regulations. Thus, commercial exchanges among member countries have increased since the creation of the common markets. For a company in a common market country, procuring products from outside these consortiums may be time-consuming or more costly.

Political Issues

Social and political issues may affect continuity of supply. For example, there are pending changes in labor laws in many countries that may reduce cost and increase competitiveness or increase cost and benefits (for example, China reduced and/or eliminated the VAT rebate for export and increased the minimum wages and benefits in 2008) but are potential causes of social turmoil. However, political stability has dramatically improved in many countries during the last decade.

Delivery Lead Time

Delivery lead time (the time between ordering and receiving) is important for international procurement. This lead time includes not only the manufacturing of the product but all transportation in the country of origin, air or ocean delivery, customs, and internal delivery in the country of final usage. Normally lead time increases cause an increase in work-in-process inventory.

Customs/Import Regulations

The import process is complex due to import restrictions, either economic or political, and customs requirements, including detailed technical descriptions of the product. From time to time, new rules are established. One should be fully aware of these, for example, CTPAT (Customs-Trade Partnership Against Terrorism), ISF (Importer Security Filing 10+2) for ocean imports, TSF for Air Exports, Free Trade Agreements, HTS changes, RLF (remote location filing) expansion, and so forth. Any missed detail may cause the local customs officials to delay the customs clearance process, impose fines, or require additional warehousing payments until customs issues are resolved. It is often helpful to have good public relations between the exporting company and the importing company and country; otherwise, international customs may present frustrating problems. For example, during shipment of mobile telephone equipment, the engineer for the manufacturing company who was helping with packaging decided that a can of special grease would be helpful to install the equipment in the receiving country. The engineer included the can without informing anyone of his action. Consequently, the grease (less than $10) was not listed on the shipping invoice and the shipment was delayed in customs and fines and extra warehousing fees were paid.

Security Issues

Marketers must be aware of the new threats to ports and the need to enhance security for all international shipments. Most countries have enacted new standards to enhance the visibility of the supply chain for targeting purposes by Customs and Border Protection agents. For example, in the United States, the Security and Accountability For Every Port Act (SAFE Port) became effective on January 25, 2009. The new Importer Security Filing (ISF) is focused on those specific data elements that further identify the entities involved in the supply chain, the entities' locations, as well as a corroborating and potentially more precise description of the commodities being shipped to the United States. This data significantly enhances the risk assessment process.

The following 10 data elements are required of the importer and are required to be submitted 24 hours prior to the loading of a U.S.-bound vessel.

1. Manufacturer name and address
2. Seller name and address
3. Container stuffing location
4. Consolidator name and address
5. Buyer name and address
6. Ship-to name and address
7. Importer of record number
8. Consignee number
9. Country of origin of the goods
10. Commodity Harmonized Tariff Schedule number (6-digit number)

An importer should take steps to ensure that the company is complying with all new security rules. A customs/brokerage filer, AMS provider, or a designated agent can transmit this data on the company's behalf.

ORGANIZATIONAL RESPONSIBILITY – CASE STUDY

by IBM

Company: IBM
Case: Qualifying Sources

During the late 1980s and early 1990s IBM's business results deteriorated steadily, reaching nearly disastrous proportions in 1993 when the firm's net loss exceeded $8 billion. There were many reasons for this near debacle, including the company's inability to sense and respond to market and technology changes, bloated and costly departments, fragmented business processes, and an ineffective purchasing process.

A new chief procurement officer (CPO) and his team quickly took steps to address the problems affecting procurement and respond to the corporate strategic imperatives, especially the leveraging of IBM's size, global resources, and scope. They initiated new global procurement policies and strategies, including:

- Segment the purchased goods and services into commodity groups or families
- Create global councils to be fully responsible for each of the commodity groups
- Establish global processes and a virtual global management organization structure
- Develop IT systems and tools to support the reengineered processes

A fundamental concept introduced by the new procurement team was that IBM would embrace a collaborative approach to its suppliers as opposed to its traditional arm's-length, short-term relationships that were based on annual sealed bid requests for quotation. Successful collaborative relationships require careful selection of a limited number of suppliers who operate under long-term agreements based on their ability to consistently meet high performance standards in cost, technology innovation, quality, and service. Another fundamental change the new team introduced was the consolidation of all IBM's global requirements for the various goods and services purchased by the company. Until then, purchases were fragmented by division, geographic region, and IBM site. The combination of a limited number of suppliers engaged in long-term, collaborative relationships and the ability to speak with one voice for IBM was considered essential to leveraging IBM's global scale and scope.

The goods and services purchased by IBM were segmented into 16 commodity groupings of items used in IBM-manufactured products (for example, microprocessors, memory chips, keyboards, cables, and other components used in producing IBM's personal computers), and 12 commodity groupings of items that IBM either consumed internally (such as office supplies and travel services) or used in providing IT solutions for IBM's external customers (such as non-IBM computer equipment or technical professional services). Each of the commodity groupings was set up to be managed by a Global Commodity Council responsible for developing and executing pertinent strategies, selecting and contracting with suppliers, and managing the supplier relationships.

The Technical Professional Services (TPS) Global Commodity Council was given responsibility for annual worldwide purchases of $1.5 billion. TPS typically includes IT programmers, systems analysts, engineers, computer room operators, and other professionals contracted by IBM for a specific, internal project or for direct customer operations. Because there is no truly global supplier, the TPS supply market is made up of several national and multinational companies and thousands of regional or local service providers. Many of the smaller suppliers often specialize in niche or unique skills and have limited resources. In general, there is potential overcapacity of supply; the millennium issue (Year 2000), however, caused shortages on specific programming skills. Average industry wages are widely known and clearly benchmarked. It would be difficult for IBM to control a major portion of any large supplier's business but it would be relatively easy to do with smaller local and niche suppliers. The best suppliers (large and small) aggressively search the marketplace for the best employees and tend to behave opportunistically if allowed to become cozy with the buyer or user.

The TPS global commodity council decided to focus initially on the North American market since it represented the greatest spending by far and thus provided the best opportunity for improvement. Until then, IBM's TPS needs in North America had been serviced by nearly 1,000 suppliers with no

(Continued)

consistent strategy, contract price structure, or terms and conditions. The result was wide variation in service quality, costs, and process management. The TPS commodity council implemented a strategy that ultimately reduced the supplier base to a core of 10 companies capable of servicing the entire North American market. Those national suppliers were expected to subcontract selectively with second-tier suppliers to provide specialized skills they did not have. The selected suppliers also were expected to ensure price competitiveness against industrywide standards, guarantee high-quality service, and offer flexibility in providing the service so that IBM's internal transaction costs could be reduced.

The strategy was implemented in 1995 and led to considerable cost savings from consolidating and leveraging IBM's purchasing volume. Service reliability and consistency in meeting IBM's needs were also improved. There were some difficulties with the strategy deployment, particularly in the area of supplier relations. Many displaced suppliers were naturally unhappy and were unwilling to participate as second-tier subcontractors.

By 1997, TPS purchases had grown to over $3 billion, driven by the rapid growth of IBM's IT services business. TPS had become one of the company's top five spending areas and represented nearly 10 percent of IBM's global purchases. The strategy implemented during the prior two years had delivered significant competitive advantage to IBM by providing considerable cost savings each year. The contracted rates were highly competitive in the industry. The coverage provided by the 10 national providers and their 200 core sub-tier suppliers could meet 85 to 90 percent of all IBM needs under contracts that offered both competitive rates and advantageous terms and conditions in such areas as warranty, overtime premiums, on-call service, and uplift rates.

In mid-1997, this new procurement process was reevaluated, and it was concluded that the national suppliers could not effectively and efficiently meet local demand; thus many purchasers of TPS were bypassing the contracted supplier base. Over time, this led to discretionary pricing, and IBM ended up paying higher rates than those contracted. A newly recommended process shifted from 10 national suppliers that managed over 200 local second-tier subcontractors to a local supplier strategy based on hundreds of local suppliers in some 80 demand locations. IBM pursued aggressive renegotiations of existing contracts with TPS supplier firms and the contracted technical personnel they represent. In addition, the company took a strong stand with internal users to strictly enforce compliance and avoid bypass contracting. This new process has saved IBM hundreds of millions of dollars, which allowed IBM to be more competitive in the marketplace.

ORGANIZATIONAL RESPONSIBILITY – CASE STUDY

by DuPont

Company: DuPont
Case: Purchasing Procedures—2001

DuPont found that the very procedures used in buying essential materials and supplies contribute to a competitive advantage in the marketplace. These purchasing procedures include two major elements: the number of suppliers and total life cycle costs.

In the last two decades, dramatic shifts in the competitive marketing environment required organizations to readdress every aspect of their businesses. One of these shifts, globalization, generated worldwide competition in pricing, quality, service, delivery, and reliability. DuPont now had to compete against lower-cost products manufactured overseas by companies with minimal overhead structures. Shifts in technology have caused radical changes in consumer preferences and business practices because computerizing commerce has resulted in more standardization and lower prices around the world. Successful companies have reduced overhead expenses by streamlining departments, including purchasing, and cutting dollars spent on direct purchases.

In response to changing markets, DuPont studied cost savings opportunities in procurement. The study team found the company was spending more than $250 million per year to purchase maintenance, repair, and operational supplies (MRO). Even for a $25 billion company, an expenditure that large becomes a cost-cutting target.

As a first step, the team tallied the number of MRO transactions, the number of suppliers, and the value of the average purchase. DuPont buyers were processing 2 million transactions each year conducted with 60,000 suppliers, of which 20,000 submitted only one transaction/invoice per year. Further analysis showed that nearly half of these purchases averaged less than $40 each and that purchase order invoices cost DuPont more than $40 apiece in overhead expense to process.

DuPont identified a small number of integrated distributors out of the 60,000 suppliers that could provide nearly all MRO orders. Using a formal process the company selected distributors after evaluating their management, computer capability, prices, logistics, and product coverage. Electronic data interchange capability offered significant potential for cost reductions through streamlining the order/payment paperwork and procedures. A study of logistics determined the geographic proximity of potential distributors to DuPont sites.

Proposing replacement of most local suppliers with a few integrated distributors, however, ended many comfortable buying relationships. At most plants, purchasers had established strong ties with local suppliers. In many company communities, these suppliers were neighbors who depended on DuPont for their livelihood and offered extra services as well as personalized assistance. They were willing to make evening or weekend deliveries. They often introduced new products and materials, explaining how the upgrades could improve DuPont processes. Local suppliers often convinced operating teams to select a particular brand or item before the site buyer was in the loop. In those cases, the buyer had little leverage in negotiating lower prices. When the buyer stepped in and canceled or changed an order, the action reinforced employees' image of red-tape procurement procedures.

For decades, DuPont management has encouraged each internal unit, such as business teams and manufacturing plants, to operate as separate and independent organizations. Each unit developed its own policies and procedures. When it came to purchasing processes in that environment, employees selected their favorite brands for everything from pencils to custom-made prototype manufacturing equipment. Production groups frequently ordered tools and materials with special specifications that required long procurement lead times. One result was that company research and production teams bought several back-ups for every inventoried item to ensure that they did not miss delivery goals because they had to wait for a crucial delivery. Items with similar but not interchangeable specifications also increased inventory costs and presented potential quality problems because damaging or costly errors could occur if someone inadvertently installed the wrong part or used a substitute.

The study team also analyzed total life cycle costs in procurement. Life cycle costs include more than the sticker price of an item whether it is a pump, a valve, or a gallon of paint. In addition to the product price, total life cycle costs encompass the cost of delivery, stocking and restocking the item, maintenance after the warranty period, processing the invoice, obsolescence, duplications of resources,

(Continued)

shortages, downtime, cancellation charges, and modification or customization of an item to ensure that it exactly matches DuPont specifications. The lowest cost calculated across the entire procurement supply chain can differ greatly from the price that appears to be lowest to the requisitioner or buyer.

To change the established system and lower total life cycle costs, the company developed new purchasing strategies that focused on obtaining materials that meet manufacturing specifications and fitness for use from the perspective of total life cycle cost rather than unit price. The new methodology categorizes suppliers based on how critical they are to the success of business operations. In addition, buyers go out periodically to test prices on the open market and compare them to the integrated suppliers' prices to make sure their prices are competitive.

The results proved to be so successful that management implemented the recommended buying procedures across the entire company after just three years instead of the projected five years. The savings DuPont achieved allowed the company to increase research and development efforts for new discoveries. DuPont recognized that strategic buying adds value for the customers through competitive prices and to the shareholders through increased earnings.

CORPORATE PROFILES AND AUTHOR BIOGRAPHIES

THE BOEING COMPANY

The Boeing Company, founded in 1916, is the leading manufacturer of commercial jet transportation aircraft in the world and is at the forefront of military, commercial, and aerospace products. Visit Boeing at www.boeing.com.

Del Hoffman

Del Hoffman was formerly Director of Strategic Planning and Supplier Diversity in Supply Management and Procurement for Boeing Commercial Airplanes. Mr. Hoffman received his BS in aeronautical engineering from California State Polytechnic University.

SNAP-ON INC.

Snap-on, founded in 1920, is one of the largest hand and power tools and diagnostics equipment companies in the world. Visit Snap-on at www.snapon.com.

Govind Arora

Govind Arora is the Vice President of World Wide Strategic Sourcing. Mr. Arora is responsible for working with the Snap-on global businesses to establish best practices and processes for sourcing and procurement; to establish strong business relationships with suppliers around the world; and to formulate strategies to achieve quality, delivery, and cost-savings goals and objectives. Mr. Arora received his BS in Mechanical Engineering from India, his MS in Industrial Engineering from the University of California, Berkeley, and his MBA from Kellogg School of Management, Northwestern University.

IBM

IBM Corporation is a world leader in the design and manufacturing of computers and microelectronic components. Visit IBM at www.ibm.com.

Javier R. Urioste

Javier Urioste was formerly Director of Policy, Strategy, and International Operations for IBM's Global Procurement division. Mr. Urioste received his BS and MS in Mechanical Engineering from Bucknell, his MS in Electrical Engineering from Catholic University in Argentina, and his MBA from James Madison University.

DuPONT COMPANY

The DuPont Company focuses on technology-based life sciences and materials. DuPont researchers discovered nylon, Teflon, fluoropolymer resins, Lycra brand fiber, and Kevlar brand fiber. Charles J. Pederson, a DuPont researcher, was awarded the Nobel Prize for chemistry in 1987. Visit DuPont at www.dupont.com.

Fred Strolle

Fred Strolle was formerly the Global Sourcing Manager for Marketing and Communications. Mr. Strolle was responsible for business agreements covering advertising, public relations, and sponsorships. Mr. Strolle received his BS from Villanova and his MBA from Temple University.

NOTES

1. Institute for Supply Management.
2. *Purchasing Magazine.*
3. According to a study conducted by the Rockefeller Institute.

Part 4
Marketing Communications

MARKETING COMMUNICATIONS MANAGEMENT

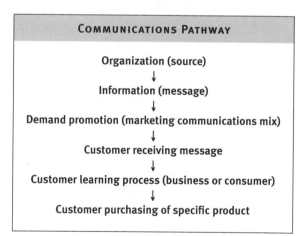

by AT&T

It's always something.

Roseanne Rosanna-Danna (Gilda Radner)
on NBC's *Saturday Night Live*

INTRODUCTION

Whether buying as a consumer or on behalf of an organization, people all have needs and wants...and seek the goods, services, ideas, or people that help fulfill them.

The primary objective of an organization's marketing efforts is to capitalize on those needs and wants by influencing purchasing behavior to promote demand for their goods and services. That influence comes in many shapes and forms, but, most often, organizations use tactics generally referred to as *marketing communications* to deliver messages that increase awareness of offerings, promote demand, and drive preference for their products and services. To be most effective, these messages need to be grounded in how customers learn and buy and be compelling and targeted to the audience the organization is trying to reach.

targeted message, but if you deliver it at the wrong time or at the wrong point in the customer buying cycle, the marketing communications campaign will miss the mark and confuse the audience. See the chart titled "Communications Pathway."

COMMUNICATIONS PATHWAY
Organization (source)
↓
Information (message)
↓
Demand promotion (marketing communications mix)
↓
Customer receiving message
↓
Customer learning process (business or consumer)
↓
Customer purchasing of specific product

COMMUNICATIONS PATHWAY TO CUSTOMERS

Marketers should understand how their customers locate and consume information in the pursuit of the offerings that might satisfy their needs and wants. You might have a really compelling and

MARKETING COMMUNICATIONS TACTICS

Although organizations use many different tactics to promote demand, the two primary categories of marketing communications are personal selling and mass communications.

- **Personal Selling.** Direct personal selling, inside sales/service (inbound telephone sales), telemarketing (outbound telephone sales), and retail sales are all part of personal selling.
- **Mass Communications.** Mass communications includes advertising, public relations, promotional marketing, and direct marketing

These elements can be used individually, or in combination, as part of either business-to-business or business-to-consumer marketing efforts.

DETERMINING THE OPTIMAL MIX

Optimizing customer response is as easy as delivering the right message, at the right time, from the right spokesperson, using the right media, to the right audience. Okay, maybe it's not so easy.

The success of the marketing efforts can be directly correlated to the relevance of the message and the ability to control its communication. Each of the marketing communications tactics needs to:

- Influence customer purchasing behavior.
- Exert control over the message.
- Deliver the message cost effectively.

The capabilities of the various marketing communications elements are ranked in order to select the best mix. Companies select marketing communications tactics based on their corporate objectives and the criteria listed in Table 8.1, and typically use a mix or combination of methods. The goal is to develop a set of tactics that are effective both individually as well as part of an integrated campaign.

A relatively new addition to the marketing communications mix is the concept of *brand ambassadors.* In many instances, the customer chooses a particular company before choosing a specific product. Companies can help customers feel comfortable and secure in their selection of a company. Company employees should be selected and trained for their ability to promote the company's brand (its goals, ideas, and products).

Marketing Communications Goal	Brand Ambassador Capability
Influence customer purchasing	High
Control the message	High
Cost	Medium

TABLE 8.1 MARKETING COMMUNICATIONS MIX RANKED BY SELECTION CRITERIA

	Personal Selling	Mass Advertising	Public Relations	Promotional Marketing	Direct Marketing
Customer Purchasing Influence					
• Attention	Low	High	Medium	Medium	High/Low
• Interest	Medium	Medium	Medium	Medium	High/Low
• Desire	High	Medium	Medium	Medium	High/Low
• Action	High	Medium/Low	Low	Medium	High/Low
Control					
• Control message	High	High	Medium/Low	High	High
• Ability to target specific audience	Medium	Medium	Low	High	High
• Ability to reach large audience	Low	High	High	Medium	Medium
• Timeliness/Adjustability	High	Medium	Medium	Low	Medium
• Feedback	High	Low	Low	Low	High
Costs					
• Absolute costs	High	High	Low	Medium	Medium
• Cost per contact	High	Low	Low	Medium	Medium

Source: A. G. Bennett; AT&T

OVERCOMING COMMUNICATIONS INTERFERENCE

Regardless of the marketing communications mix you choose, the message will need to get from sender to receiver. And no matter how hard you try, those messages sometimes suffer from interference—situations or dynamics that prevent the message from being received clearly.

There are many tools available to help marketers understand the clarity of message delivery: marketing research, sales reports, online visits/clicks, and more. It is important that you develop metrics through which you can measure marketing effectiveness and course correct as necessary. See Table 8.2.

SPECIFIC MARKETING COMMUNICATIONS ELEMENTS

Each of the marketing communications tactics introduced above is detailed in the following chapters:

- Personal Selling and Sales Force Management (Chapter 9)
- Advertising (Chapter 10)
- Public Relations (Chapter 11)
- Promotional Marketing (Chapter 12)
- Direct Marketing (Chapter 13)
- Brand Ambassadors (Chapter 14)

TABLE 8.2 OVERCOMING COMMUNICATIONS INTERFERENCE

Communications Path	Interference Factor	Overcome Interference
Source (company)	Poor knowledge of consumer needs	Additional marketing research, more specific targeting
Message encoding (creative ideas)	Lack of specific appeal, confusing	Better creative team, differentiated message, creative approach, better research/insights
Message channel (communications media)	Competing message clutter	Sufficiency/timeliness of messages, targeted channels
Receiver Decoding (target audience interpretation)	Customer misunderstanding	Simplicity/memorability of message

Source: A. G. Bennett; AT&T

CORPORATE PROFILE AND AUTHOR BIOGRAPHY

AT&T
AT&T is the largest communications holding company in the world by revenue. Visit AT&T at www.att.com.

Stephen E. Block
Stephen Block was formerly Director, Consumer Advertising, and was responsible for brand, local, and Internet advertising. Mr. Block received his BA from Kenyon College.

9 PERSONAL SELLING AND SALES FORCE MANAGEMENT

by Eastman Kodak, Tupperware, 1-800-Flowers.com, American Express, Hilton Hotels, and Coldwell Banker

Everyone lives by selling something.
Robert Louis Stevenson, Scottish Author, 1850–1894

THE ESSENTIALS OF SALES
by Eastman Kodak Company

Introdction

The fundamental unit of measurement for every business venture is sales. At the most basic level, something of value, usually money, must be exchanged for a product or service for a business to be successful. Moving the customer to the point where he or she makes the decision to buy is the objective of every salesperson. Inherent in this objective is the sales organization's focus on customer trust, which promotes an effective sales environment. Personal selling that can properly identify and cultivate a satisfied customer is the basis of a successful marketing process and, ultimately, a successful business.

Personal selling is the element of marketing that creates or enhances demand for a product by discussing the customers' needs on a personal, one-on-one basis and then attempting to solve their problem by selling appropriate goods or services to the customers. Selling works in conjunction with the other demand promotion elements, but is the only method of demand promotion that can instantly respond directly to a customer's concerns. Personal selling is most advantageous when

a customer needs specific handling instructions as with unique or custom items, answers to complex questions as with technical equipment, or confirmation of quality as with an expensive product.

A company's sales force has three main components: sales management, sales representatives (known as reps), and a sales support team. Sales representatives usually are a company's main interface with customers, and customers form an opinion of the company by the actions of a sales rep. The salesperson who interacts well with the customer is extremely important, whether he or she is behind the retail counter or calling on a government customer with a billion-dollar sale on the line. The sales support team, usually comprised of field resources such as Sales Engineers (SEs) is made up of technical people deployed to support complex sales of technology or software, field engineers, break-fix support people who repair equipment at customer locations, and business development managers, who may provide category or vertical expertise to a customer application. Each of these groups affects the relationship your company has with a customer since they are a touch point for that account, and none of them is less valuable than the other. At the end of the day, however, it is the sales representative or account manager who will take responsibility for the success or failure of a particular account.

The interpersonal skill behind the building of customer relationships is very important. Personable, well-trained, and motivated salespeople are an integral part of a successful company. There are several factors that motivate a salesperson to be successful, including recognition, money, the emotional connection with customers, or a belief in what he or she is selling. In many organizations, sales representatives start as sales trainees, and if successful, may become sales managers or join the marketing staff.

Definitions

A *sale* is the exchange of money for a product or service (a transaction). A *salesperson* is a company representative whose contact with a customer hopefully results in an exchange of money for something offered by the company. A *customer* is anyone who is willing to pay for what the salesperson is selling. *Sales management* is the art and science of managing sales people and their transactions. Selling comes in two forms: transactional and relationship sales. *Transactional selling* is based simply on achieving the transaction or sale. *Relationship selling* is based on a long-term series of transactions that meet the customer's requirements. For example, a financial company's advertisement states, "At J.P. Morgan, a relationship with a client is a marathon, not a sprint."

Personal selling, either to consumers or to businesses, is accomplished by the sales rep talking one-on-one with the customer. Businesses sell their products to other businesses in what is known as "business-to-business" sales or to end consumers, in what is known as "business-to-consumer" sales or simply "consumer sales." The salesperson to business-customer relationship is very important because the business in turn resells the product to many end consumers.

There are several formats, or methods, of selling, including direct personal selling, inside selling/sales-service (inbound telephone sales), telemarketing (outbound telephone sales), and retail sales.

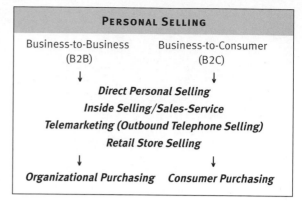

PERSONAL SELLING

Business-to-Business (B2B)   Business-to-Consumer (B2C)

↓   ↓

Direct Personal Selling
Inside Selling/Sales-Service
Telemarketing (Outbound Telephone Selling)
Retail Store Selling

↓   ↓

Organizational Purchasing   *Consumer Purchasing*

SALES FORCE MANAGEMENT

The goal of the sales manager is to secure a revenue stream for the organization by managing the sales force. The best sales managers are those who have had successful sales experience and thus understand the needs of the sales force. A company must determine whether it is better to keep its best salespeople in selling positions or move them into supervisory/management roles. In addition to their sales management tasks, sales managers coordinate their activities with senior management and the marketing staff, including product managers and market researchers.

Sales force managers establish the sales force, coordinate with the sales force, determine sales force strategies, and coordinate with corporate management.

Establishing the Sales Force

In order to establish the sales force, either initially or on an ongoing basis, the sales manager must recruit and select applicants, train the sales force, and determine adequate compensation. The goal of a well-selected sales team is to outperform the competition and to achieve the company's strategic and tactical goals.

Recruiting Applicants

Salespeople usually are recruited through human resource (HR) channels, including classified ads in newspapers and professional publications, referrals from current or former employees, and visits to college campuses. Today, online job sites such as

Monster.com, CareerBuilder.com, and various specialty sites are often used by sales managers and recruiters alike. Industry associations are an effective way to find qualified talent from consumer to the B2B segments. Sources of potential sales reps include the following:

- A rep who has risen through the ranks of a company, affectionately known as "home-grown," knows the company's products, customers, and methods and has the advantage of institutional memory. However, these reps may lack a broader perspective and may have problems with flexibility, because they have worked so long for one organization.
- Hiring a former competitor as a sales rep has several advantages. The outsider can provide a company with a potential source of new market growth by bringing his or her clients along, which is called *buying share*. The outsider knows the market, the competition, and can bring a new perspective to the job. He or she also probably has a sense of the company's products, customers, and methods from studying former competitive intelligence. However, the outsider may have trouble dropping his or her old competitive feelings and may not be accepted in the sales organization.
- A sales rep who is a former customer brings unique perspectives to the job, knows the view from the other side of the desk, is reasonably familiar with the company and its products or services, and knows his or her own customers well.
- A sales rep who is hired from a different business altogether brings a new perspective to the job and a new approach to sales and customer relations, adds to the overall knowledge base, and often can rejuvenate a stagnant workforce.

Selection of Applicants

A successful salesperson requires a combination of selling talent, judgment/adaptability, and training. Companies select the best candidate by using a combination of impartial written tests and subjective questioning by a panel of experts that may include HR consultants, industrial psychologists, and the company's successful sales and management teams.

Sales Training

The goal of sales training is to effectively hone selling skills. The successful salesperson must assimilate both hard and soft skills. The *hard skills*, which include technical and product knowledge, market awareness, and the ability to gather intelligence, are fundamental and can be taught. The *soft skills*, often called *people skills*, tend to be more instinctive. However, there are some soft skills that can be taught or fine-tuned, including listening behaviors, the ability to make things interesting to a specific audience, negotiating skills, and ability to observe the characteristics of customers in an effort to understand them better as individuals (known as reading the room). Management can help by providing training, but the individual salesperson must commit to learning these disciplines.

Often, the company that has the clearest corporate mission, vision, and strategic framework, and that can concisely impart that vision to its sales force will have an advantage in the marketplace. A uniform framework for sales training usually is the best foundation for training and will meet the long-term needs for corporate team building.

Training usually is done when someone is hired, although additional training typically is provided throughout a career. No one method of sales training is inherently superior to another. Initial sales training can be done effectively through manuals, teaching, role-playing, or mentoring. *Mentoring* is the use of seasoned sales personnel to reinforce teaching and to establish positive role models for younger and less experienced sales personnel.

As with any other job category, it is important for salespeople to sharpen and refine their job skills as they progress along their career path with a company. A salesperson's continuing education and training should be done in small increments that are more easily learned and retained. A sales force will stop paying attention to too much information in too short a time span. Sales seminars, sales conferences, conventions, the annual sales meeting, and loaned executive programs with other organizations offer continued training. In recent years, Computer Based Training (CBT) has grown more sophisticated and popular with sales managers as a cost-effective tool for continued training of both the sales force and even the customer's sales force in a two-tiered model. Live webinar types of training are also used, although more expensive and restrictive since they require a live host and everyone to join the webinar at the same time.

Compensation of Sales Force

There are several forms of compensation for salespeople, including salary, commission, bonuses, expense accounts, and car allowances. The compensation of salespeople, unlike that of other employees, usually is tied directly to their success or lack of it. A typical compensatory structure for salespeople is a base salary, with a commission based on the number of sales made, reimbursement for out-of-pocket expenses, and a bonus at the end of the year if they have met or exceeded their quota. The ratio of fixed (salary) to variable (commission or bonuses) compensation ranges from heavily leveraged positions (very small base) such as copier sales to 50/50, and 60/40 in roles where the technical expertise and experience are harder to find. Many plans may also use Management by Objectives (MBOs) or Key Performance Objectives (KPOs) as additional components to the compensation plan, often to complete certain tactical goals that may not be purely revenue based. Most sales plans also include *hurdles* (minimums) and *accelerators* that reward performance once quota is achieved, sometimes at two to three times the normal commission rates to provide exceptional incentives for the top achievers.

Coordination with the Sales Force

The sales manager should spend time with his or her salespeople in order to coordinate the many activities beyond selling. Coordinating with the sales force includes establishing goals, managing sales information, and motivating and evaluating the sales force.

Establish Goals

The sales manager must let the sales force know the intended direction of the company and integrate company goals with sales goals. Sales goals typically are established for the sales force in the form of sales quotas (an agreed-upon quantitative or qualitative amount).

Sales Information Management

In order for the sales force to be well informed, the sales manager must disseminate new product information, updated market data, and client information. The sales manager also must collect competitive information and market information from the sales force in order to update senior management.

Motivation of Sales Force

Sales reps perform better and become top sellers faster when motivated. Sales managers must match their incentive plans to the sales force and to the company goals. Motivation of the sales force should be a continuous process, although pragmatically it often is relegated as an outcome of the evaluation process. A lack of motivation makes people careful, and a lack of risk taking hampers sales growth. The major motivational methods are

- Management respect (closer working relationships, enhanced mentoring)
- Employee recognition (plaques, announcements)
- Rewards (financial, gifts, travel)

Evaluation of the Sales Representatives

It is important for the sales manager to evaluate the performance of each sales rep, just as senior management will evaluate the performance of the sales force in total. Formal evaluation should consist of two-way communication between manager and employee, and be conducted on a regular basis, typically quarterly or twice a year. Informal evaluations can be conducted on an as-needed basis. There are two main methods of sales performance evaluation: quantitative and qualitative. In many cases the evaluation is a blend of both.

- **Quantitative Evaluation.** The quantitative approach is based strictly on the comparison of projected sales (quota) and actual sales figures. The advantages of this type of performance evaluation are that it is easy to administer and is objective. However, it may not take into account subjective skills such as long-term relationship building or the time a salesperson has been on the job.
- **Qualitative Evaluation.** A sales manager should listen carefully to customer comments, both positive and negative, about the sales rep and the company. Areas such as relationship building, team work, new product ideas, and competitive feedback often are not quantifiable. Successful sales managers often spend a lot of time visiting customers with their representatives so that they can observe the salesperson in action.

After the sales evaluations have been completed, sales managers provide rewards or take corrective action.

- **Rewards.** Rewards can be a powerful motivator and can be either monetary or involve recognition. Both are highly desired. *Monetary rewards* include pay raises, promotions, and bonuses in the form of cash, a gift certificate, or incentive travel. *Recognition rewards* can come in the form of trophies or plaques such as those engraved with "Salesperson of the Year/Month"; announcements of success in company newsletters, trade journals, or local newspapers; assigned parking; and so forth.
- **Corrective Action.** *Corrective action* may include additional training, a demotion, or dismissal. Typically a corrective action plan will be a 3- to 6-month program with specific metrics and goals to be met with the consequences for failure clearly defined ahead of time.

Determining Sales Force Strategies

Once the sales force has been established and motivated, the sales manager should determine how the sales force will be directed to interact with the customer base. There are several strategies that must be determined: channel model, sales force structure, selling approaches, and sales force sizing requirements.

Channel Model

There has been a growing trend in recent years to more indirect sales models, especially for technology products. The major criteria that determines the *go to market (GTM) strategy* for any given product is often based on the *average sales price (ASP)*, or typical transaction value. For high-end, complex products such as a Kodak Nexpress, for example, a $500,000 sale is much more suitable for a direct sales organization or model. Low-end consumer products in the $500 or less category obviously work well in either a retail store or Web site environment. Mid-range products, $500 to $20,000, such as Kodak document scanners, fit more logically into the indirect or channel model.

Technology products are mostly sold through a two-tiered distribution model where the manufacturer sells at wholesale to companies such as Ingram Micro or Tech Data, the two largest IT distributors in the world, both with revenues of about $20 billion each. In turn, these distributors sell to the channel of value-added resellers (VARs), integrators (such as IBM Global Services), various online retailers, and Direct Market Resellers (DMRs) (such as CDW). Industry data indicates there are more than 70,000 active resellers just in the U.S. market alone.

According to the Global Technology Distribution Council, more than half of all its goods and services flows through the indirect model, and the trend continues to be in that direction as the average sales prices continue to fall and the products continue to be more user-friendly and easier to implement. Of course, there will always be a place for the direct model where price, complexity, and need for close support by the manufacturer are required.

Sales Force Structure

There are several methods that may be used to effectively structure the sales force. Sales management must decide what strategy will direct their sales force most effectively toward the goal of meeting a sales quota. Many of the sales force strategies may be combined. A sales force should be organized in a way that best understands the customer, obtains quality positioning, and forms a long-term relationship selling approach. If customers fall into groups with common characteristics, then a company can organize its sales force accordingly. More than any other group in an organization, the sales force has a direct impact on top-line revenues, and the pressure on a sales force to perform can be enormous and unrelenting. Many organizations, faced with this pressure, mistakenly fall back to tactical approaches to "get sales done now," rather than taking a longer-term strategic view.

For any company's sales organization, an important issue is deciding how to apply its finite resources to a virtually unlimited universe of possible customers. No company has the financial ability to sell to every conceivable sales prospect. A company has to make decisions about how to narrow the focus of the selling effort. Sales management's mission is to determine the point beyond which the cost of selling outweighs the financial return of a completed sale. The successful sales organization will determine who the best prospects are and how to sell to those prospects in the most cost-effective manner.

The objective of the personal sale is to sell as much as possible while incurring the lowest possible selling costs. Reaching customers always requires a combination of strategies and tactics, such as personal selling, mass advertising, and retail location. It is up to the company to decide what makes the most sense for the budget it has allocated toward making the sale. For example, a company may decide to locate in a shopping mall. This could result in a guaranteed flow of foot traffic, so the company would have some walk-in, self-identified prospects. The company may take dollars that would otherwise have gone to a direct sales force and advertising, and instead put the money into leasing the more expensive mall location.

It generally costs seven times as much to win a new customer as it costs to hold an existing customer. Therefore, retaining an existing customer and building that relationship is critical. Learning the customer's needs and meeting them is essential. Many companies practice Customer Relationship Management by gathering extensive information on the customer, with input from sales reps, management, and marketing researchers. This information is used to allow a more complete dialogue with the customer, making him or her feel more comfortable with the selling company. This customer database may be simple written notes or a comprehensive computer program.

In order to form an effective and efficient sales force, the sales manager must determine sales force structure strategies, which include outside and inside reps, individual versus team selling, and outside sales rep territories.

Outside Reps

Outside reps leave the company premises to call on customers. The main advantage of an outside rep is the ability to personally meet with customers and see their needs firsthand. The main disadvantage is the cost involved in salary, training, and travel. Outside reps include company reps, manufacturer's reps, wholesale reps, and direct-selling reps.

- **Company Reps.** A company's sales reps tend to carry a single company's products and services and sell to other manufacturers, VARs, wholesalers, and retailers. These reps can be sales reps that have general knowledge of products, customers, and finance. Today, many reps are based out of a home office and cover a specific geographic area or group of accounts. They may only visit the corporate office a few times a year, and other than that are totally dedicated to the field. They are usually supported by sales engineers who specialize in a particular technical field and matching territory. Sales engineers are essential to a technology-based company and very often sell products that will be part of a much larger and very complex project. For example, to make a new manufacturing facility work properly, the manufacturer might need to design a production line with each item represented by a sales engineer.

- **Manufacturer's Reps.** These sales rep organizations are often used by new and smaller companies. These are independent sales organizations that contract with various manufacturers to represent their products into a specific territory or group of accounts, and are paid a fee or commission for their services.
- **Wholesale Reps.** Wholesale reps or "route salespeople," represent the wholesaler and resell products or groups of products to the retail level.
- **Direct-Selling Reps.** Most personal selling is business-to-business (in-office), such as with Kodak, IBM, AT&T, and Xerox. These reps are paid a salary and commissions and are trained extensively by the company. However, most business-to-consumer (in-home or door-to-door) sales reps such as with Tupperware, Avon, Fuller Brush, and Encyclopedia Britannica are independent reps. They typically work on their own schedules and may represent multiple product lines.

Inside Reps

Inside reps do not leave the company premises. They typically make and receive sales calls, resolve problems, and provide customer feedback to management. The main advantage to inside reps is the ability to economically talk with many customers in a short period of time. The main disadvantage is the inability to personally visit with the customer to gain a better understanding of his or her needs. Inside reps can be in direct sales, retail sales, or customer service.

- **Direct Sales Reps.** Direct sales reps make sales via the telephone, either by calling customers or by receiving toll-free calls and e-mails from customers. Direct sales reps work for companies, telemarketing firms, or are individuals, such as stockbrokers, who seek out their own clients.
- **Retail Sales Reps.** Retail sales reps sell to customers in retail stores and typically create customer interest by being courteous and quickly locating stock.

- **Customer Service Reps.** Customer service reps work with sales reps and perform initial customer contact or much-needed follow-up with customers.

Individual versus Team Selling

The number of sales reps needed to successfully close a sale may be an individual or a group.

- **Individual Selling.** The advantages of individual selling are that the individual can react quickly to a customer's needs and usually has a better chance of getting to know the customer well. The disadvantage, however, is that individual salespeople can have a short-term, commission-oriented outlook and strive just to complete the transaction.
- **Team Selling.** Team selling requires that the customer's team and the selling team communicate effectively. The advantage of the team selling approach is that it allows for a greater knowledge base of diverse in-house specialists from every aspect of the organization, such as business researchers, technical experts, and financial experts. The disadvantage is the confusion to the customer if there are conflicting messages from the sales team. Another form of team selling is often referred to as "Hunter-Gatherer," where one sales rep specializes in prospecting and the other specializes in making the presentation and closing the sale. The advantage to this approach is that the company has an expert in each aspect of the selling process. The disadvantage again is that the customer may be confused by the change in team players.

Outside Sales Rep Territories

There are three ways to base sales force territories to accommodate the customer: by geography, by industry, and by client size.

- **Geographic-Based Territories.** Sales territories organized geographically is the traditional means of delineating a sales force. The geographic size of a territory is determined by the density of the customer base. Markets tend to organize themselves geographically, either locally, regionally, or nationally. For example, logistical limits based on food distribution have kept the retail food business largely regional. For a small business, the only feasible approach may be local or regional, although the Internet has the potential to make any small business a global marketer. Some mass retailers like Target, Walmart, and Costco, have turned the retail store approach into a national business.

Many industries have geographic concentrations due to common industry needs, such as access to personnel expertise or to raw materials. For example, the automobile industry is located predominantly in Michigan and Ohio, the lumber industry is in the Northwest, and the oil and gas industry is in Texas and the Gulf states. An advantage to organizing the sales force geographically is that they can be stationed near the customers and keep travel time and expenses to a minimum. A disadvantage is the difficulty in controlling and coordinating sales reps from a distance.

- **Industry-Based Territories.** Organizing a sales force around client industries enables familiarization with specific client needs and can result in a closer working relationship and increased sales. For example, every business in the health field (hospitals, doctors' offices, dentists' offices, emergency clinics, etc.) may use the exact same billing software. Hiring experts in key areas allows a sales force to dominate that market. A disadvantage is that the sales force may tend to specialize in one field and not develop additional industry expertise.
- **Client Size–Based Territories.** *Tiering* occurs when a company categorizes its customers based on the size of the account and effectively manages the cost per sale. For companies with many tiers of customers, like Eastman Kodak, at some point the company must make a decision as to which customers buy enough to justify the cost of a sales visit. Every small retail store expects

and deserves good service in the form of a sales call, but it may not make economic sense. Each sales contact costs the same regardless of the size of the sale, and the top 20 percent of customers typically provide 80 percent of sales. Therefore, it makes economic sense to concentrate more of a company's resources on its best customers. The lower 80 percent of customers become a company's second and third tier.

Both retailers' and manufacturers' cost pressures are higher than ever before due to increasing competition. A typical business-to-business sales call can cost hundreds of dollars. Customers expect prices to continue going down while expecting the level of service to remain high. To survive and thrive in this situation requires tiering the customer base.

Major customers typically receive a personal visit from a sales rep. A large customer account team may have a dedicated sales team that services only that client's needs. This close working relationship, or even partnership, usually generates a high level of sales because the sales force typically is familiar with every aspect of the customer's business. The disadvantage of this is that the profits of the dedicated sales force are tied to the business cycle of the client.

Small customers also can be quite valuable for a company. For example, customer turnover is inevitable, so a company needs to keep customers that can potentially move up from the lower tiers to replace higher-tier customers. A small customer account team usually services all the small businesses in a given territory and may be a training ground for new reps. The advantage is flexibility, but the disadvantage is a minimal working relationship. Telesales can be the most cost-effective way of reaching the bottom tier, providing a dialogue with small customers and vendors quickly, easily, and efficiently.

Another option is mailing or e-mailing to small customers. For example, Eastman Kodak sends out a mailing every month to its small retail customers that provides updates on products, pricing, customer policy, and sales opportunities. E-mail has provided the most cost-effective means of touching more customers at a lower cost than traditional direct mail and has the added benefit of allowing instant feedback or action from the customer, either by connecting to the link on a Web site or by placing orders immediately at the company store.

Routine sales account activity can be monitored through the use of a database that measures needs and determines the shipments from a company to its retailers automatically.

As the cost of selling rises and product prices fall, companies may decide it is more cost-effective to sell through third-party agents, dealers, VARs, and Web partners.

Selling Approaches

Sales managers must also determine which approach the sales reps will take with customers prior to the reps calling on a customer. Selling approaches include product selling and solution selling.

Product Selling

Many customers prefer a transaction-based sales approach as they have a thorough knowledge of their own requirements and need only to purchase the needed products. A product-based sales force must have expert knowledge of specific products. For example, a computer company might delineate its sales force by mainframe computers or by personal computers. Advantages of this method are that customers appreciate the expert advice on specific product needs, training is relatively inexpensive, and administration of the sales force is relatively easy. A disadvantage is that sales growth potential may be limited.

Solution Selling

Other customers may require a consultative or relationship-based approach. For example, in technology sales, the customer's requirements may include multiple vendors to solve a particular business problem. During every sales call, there is an opportunity to go beyond taking an order or restocking inventory. As competing products enter the market and competitors achieve near-parity on product quality, a sales force must find new ways to make a sale. The consultative salesperson offers additional solutions to the customer that may result in increased sales and revenues. Consultative sales require a well-trained representative who can assess client needs as they grow and change, and then offer solutions. This strategy may require a support team of experts ready to travel to the customer. Many times the customer appreciates the additional services, such as computer training or software upgrades, of an outside problem-solving consultant, and this translates into additional sales.

In addition, value-added services, such as financing, repair, delivery, and installation can differentiate a company in a crowded marketplace. The challenge to any selling organization is how to add value without losing money on the transaction.

If a salesperson can build upon a relationship with an existing client, the selling process is less expensive. New customer sales are harder and more expensive to get than additional sales from existing customers. Additional follow-on sales (sales that come after the initial sale, such as additional software after the purchase of a computer) usually require incrementally less effort than first sales.

At the retail level this approach is often referred to as "suggestive selling vs. order taking." Order taking only requires that a sales rep, typically an inside rep or retail clerk, wait for the customer to approach and state his or her preference, whether it is for a certain software or a certain shirt. This method is quick, easy, and requires little training. However, it does not maximize sales. Suggestive selling requires that the sales rep take a proactive approach and suggest additional items and upgraded alternatives. For example, at McDonald's, the question "Would you like fries with that?" does generate significant additional sales. The advantage is the additional revenue. The disadvantage is that it requires more employee training, and some customers feel annoyed by this approach.

Location of Sales Meetings

The sales manager, the sales rep, and the customer may all decide the proper location of a sales meeting. Locations include the customer's office, the sales rep's office or factory visit, or a trade show.

New and small business owners often ask where they can have sales meetings (they often erroneously believe they must have a big shiny office to impress the customer).

Sales Force Sizing Requirements

The calculation of the appropriate size of a sales force is determined by the number of potential customers, the number of customers that a sales rep can engage in successful dialogue in a given time period, and the territory's anticipated annual revenue size. This requires a careful balance between the cost of maintaining a sales force and the potential sales determined by the sales forecast.

Coordination with Corporate Management

Sales managers meet routinely with senior management to provide market feedback and sales forecasts.

Market Feedback

The sales manager is responsible for providing sales information from the field sales reps to the marketing staff and senior management. Marketing is responsible for evaluating and applying this data and blending it with ongoing marketing research. The information that the sales force provides includes sales and revenue data, competitive information, new product ideas, new uses for company products, and client information.

Sales Forecasting

The *sales forecast* is the instrument by which a business seeks to predict the future sales of a product. The results are coordinated with other functions of the company in order to determine production levels, staffing, promotion requirements, potential revenue, and the need for capital outlays. The most important purpose of a sales forecast is simply to make sure there is sufficient demand in the market to justify the production of the company's product or service. If the product is new and there is no historical data, then data from a substitute product may be used. An inaccurate sales forecast can have a severely negative impact on the company. For example, if the company makes too much of a product, prices could drop and profits could suffer. If the company does not make enough of a product, there could be lost opportunities to maximize market share and revenues.

Supply chain management is a key driver of better forecast tools and accuracy for any company manufacturing in other countries. Most technology companies have factories or contract production in Asia. With that savings comes very long supply routes and lead times that can affect sales success in a major way. It is very expensive when the manufacturer has to airfreight product due to a poor forecast.

There are several sales forecasting methods available, from qualitative to sophisticated quantitative computer modeling. Typically, companies use a combination. The determining factors in the selection of the appropriate method are financial resources, time, and corporate culture.

Qualitative Forecasting Methods

Qualitative forecasting relies on judgment, experience, and feedback from relatively few but select sources. It is inexpensive, quick, and moderately accurate. Qualitative forecasts can come from sales force estimates, management judgment, customer surveys, or historical projections.

- **Sales Force Estimates.** A corporate sales force, when listening to its customers, can find out a wealth of information about how those customers perceive their needs for the coming year. This field-level information is an important indicator of future trends, but, depending on the organization, it can also result in projections that underestimate or exceed actual performance. Sales managers who are compensated for surpassing quotas tend to underestimate, and sales managers who are provided resources on the basis of projections tend to overestimate. Top management must understand the perspectives of its sales managers.

- **Management Judgment.** Informed management judgment is intuition that comes from long experience in a particular business. These instincts are very important, but they cannot be the sole basis on which to make decisions. Sales managers are fallible, subject to being blindsided by an overly ambitious (or under-ambitious) sales force, and can be prejudiced toward success through wishful thinking. Corporate decision makers should check sales managers' perceptions against objective facts and other subjective opinions.
- **Customer Surveys.** Customer surveys can provide enormous help to a company's sales force. Companies should survey not just their own customers but expand the surveys to the entire marketplace. Third-party research organizations often sell their market assessments for less than it would cost a business to conduct its own customer survey.
- **Historical Projections.** *Historical projections* look at sales or customers over a certain period of time, and then use this data to project the future. For example, a historical projection may examine last year's sales figures and then factor in changes in market size, consumer shifts, competitive thrusts, advances in technology, changes in customer attitudes, and potential losses or gains of important customers. This type of extrapolation is probably the most common methodology used by small service organizations.

Quantitative Forecasting Methods
Quantitative forecasting uses a greater number of inputs than qualitative forecasting. In building statistical models for quantitative forecasting, statisticians find a leading indicator whose performance precedes the behavior of the product sales record on a fairly reliable basis. Examples include an uptick in the sale of desks and related office furniture that could be a leading indicator of an upward trend in the sale of office cleaning services; real estate sales for new factory locations

that may indicate a general trend for the sale of industrial equipment and supplies; or a survey of the intentions of corporate purchasing managers that may show a trend for the sale of office computers. Quantitative methods of forecasting are more expensive to initiate, faster (if done in real time), and more accurate. Because of the expense, small companies may rely on broad-based economic or industrywide quantitative forecasts performed by the government or their industry association. Quantitative forecasting methods include correlation analysis, equation models, end-use analysis, input-output analysis, and trend and cycle analysis.

Customer Relationship Management (CRM) software such as Siebel or Salesforce.com have pipeline management tools that provide some limited forecasting tools. As with all of these systems, the value of the output is directly related to the value of the input. Sales reps are notorious for not entering all of their pipeline data (called *sandbagging*), either for lack of time or sometimes in an effort to underpromise and overachieve. Nonetheless, any system is better than no system at all and if management provides the motivation and oversight to keep these tools up-to-date, the results can be quite positive for forecasting accuracy.

BUSINESS-TO-BUSINESS SELLING

Each customer's needs are different and making a sale depends on the ability of the individual sales rep to discern those needs and match them with the correct product. In order to maximize sales effectiveness, most companies use a proven sales methodology. This process may only take a few moments or a day for a small sale, such as selling a new diagnostic tool to an independent environmental analysis lab. Or, this process may take months or years for a large sale, such as selling an internationally organized construction project to a national government. The business-to-business selling process includes the following steps:

Qualify Prospective Companies
↓
Qualify Prospective Company Individuals
↓
Sales Meeting
- Listening to Needs
- Presentation of Offer
- Overcoming Objections
- Closing
↓
Filling and Delivery of Orders
↓
Follow-up/Customer Service
↓
Record Keeping

Selling Process Steps

1. Qualifying Prospective Companies

After receiving training on a company's products and sales methods, the first step in the sales process is to qualify potential customer companies. This step is often called the *presale preparation*. It is important for a salesperson to research the targeted customer industry base in general and prospective customer companies in particular, prior to calling on individuals within the companies. The goal is to determine a match between company offerings and the potential customer company's needs. There are many sources that can provide lists of potential business customers, including: internal company files, the *Yellow Pages*, government NAICS codes, government census data, and private data banks.

2. Qualifying Prospective Individuals

The next step is to identify and qualify individual *decision makers*, customers within the targeted company who have the need, interest, and financial capacity to buy the product, and then set up an appointment. This step is often called *prospecting*. Getting a lead on prospects may be determined through several methods:

- Referrals through the company's inside tele-sales reps

- Referrals from existing customers, suppliers, or business associates
- Self-identification by calling customer service on a toll-free number or sending in a response card received in a trade publication or at a trade show
- Through an outside sales rep's unsolicited or cold calls
- Through purchased commercial lists

Cold calls and cold lists are typically the least productive means of developing a solid prospect, whereas the best prospects tend to come from a customer referral. Any program that requires the prospect to qualify himself one or more levels (such as some Web programs do), delivers a better qualified candidate for the sale.

The initial sales contact or approach can be made through a variety of channels: telephone call, e-mail, direct mail, personal letter, or an in-person visit. The initial contact must explain why it is in the prospect's best interest to listen to the presentation and grant the salesperson a meeting. The salesperson often has to sell him- or herself before selling the product.

3. Sales Meeting

After determining who the decision maker is and convincing him or her to grant an appointment, the next step is the actual sales visit. The goal of the initial contact is to listen to the potential customer's needs and present the company's products. Making a sale typically takes multiple visits. The sales meetings have several steps: listening to needs, presentation of offer, overcoming objections, and closing.

- **Listening to Needs.** Listening to a prospective customer's comments, whether positive or negative (objections), is extremely important. During a presentation, one objective should be to get the prospective customer to do as much of the talking as possible. As the customer provides more and more information, the discussion becomes increasingly focused on the needs of the prospect.

- **Presentation of Offer.** Effective sales presentations create attention, interest, and a desire to buy on the part of the audience through an emphasis on the product or service's features and benefits. At the core is a connection with the audience and their needs. The salesperson should be aware of who he or she is talking to, the size of the audience, and what the goal is on each side (whether it is a potential sale on the spot or the beginning of a longer-term selling process).
- **Overcoming Objections.** After making the sales presentation, most often there are comments, questions, and objections from the prospective customer. Some objections can be simple, for example, "Your price is too high." This objection could mean that the prospect needs financing, or that the prospect has had a very bad year financially and will not be able to purchase at all, or that the price really is too high and a discount is needed. It is important to overcome each objection by providing solutions to the stated concerns. The implied question is, "If I overcome all of your objections and show you that this is the best solution for satisfying your needs, will you buy?"
- **Closing.** In the end, the customer is the only one who can decide whether to buy. Once the salesperson becomes aware that the customer has arrived at that moment, it is extremely important to close the sale. There are several closing methods that can shift the dialogue away from discussion to the close. They can be serious, "Let me show you where to sign the contract." Or humorous, "Can I wrap that 900 tons of steel for you?" After the close, the departure should not be hasty. The close of a sale should be the beginning of a long-term sales relationship.

4. Filling and Delivery of Orders

After the sale is closed, the next step is filling and delivering sales orders. The customer is depending on the company and the salesperson to fulfill the obligations of the sale. The essence of customer satisfaction is to deliver exactly what the customer wants. Generally, the customer has specific expectations in mind. However, if it is probable that delivery will be in 10 days, it generally is advisable to tell the customer 15 days, allowing a margin for error. If it is objectionable to the customer, he or she will say so. Consider Chief Engineer Scott in *Star Trek* as one of the great underpromisors. He would always complain, "Captain, I can't make her go any faster." But somehow, he always found a way to exceed expectations.

5. Follow-Up/Customer Service

Customer service becomes important after the sale is made and is an integral part of relationship selling. The quality of customer service can make or break the next sale. Any organization can look good until a problem comes up. The customer's feelings must be considered in order to provide adequate sales service.

A basic tenet of marketing is that a customer's awareness of ads for recently purchased products goes up immediately after a sale. Buyers want to be reassured that they have made the right purchasing decision. So, some companies reassure recent customers by calling, sending a note, or sending a gift appropriate to the sale and the product. For example, Mercedes Benz sales reps send service reminders and promotional products (with the MB logo) such as a flashlight for the glove compartment and a silver bookmark for travel books to each of their clients after the sale.

6. Record Keeping

Sales reps should keep thorough records and write everything down (paper and/or computer). Your notepad never crashes and never runs out of batteries. Record keeping is important for several reasons: continued communications with the customer, keeping commitments, and administrative communications with sales management (sales evaluation, sales forecasting, and product/competitive feedback). Fortunately, e-mail and various CRM systems keep track of much of this for the sales rep, automating what used to be a completely manual task.

INSIDE SALES
by 1-800-Flowers.com

The customer experience has a significant impact on a company's bottom line. History indicates that the better the interaction with customers, the more loyal they will become and the more purchases they will make. As sales activities expand beyond face-to-face interaction to telephone, Internet, and mobile applications, the goal of the inside sales rep is to create the same feeling of walking into an intimate storefront and speaking with a friendly, helpful salesperson. Telephones, and especially toll-free numbers, enable customers to always reach a person, either as the first point of contact with a company or as a follow-up to Internet or mobile transactions.

Recruiting, screening, selection, and training for this specialized area of sales have increased in importance as companies grow. Inside sales and service reps must be personable and possess telephone skills as well as computer skills, given the change of many companies' call centers to service centers that support both telephone and online business.

The typical customer contact, whether for sales or service, begins with an offer to help the customer. Depending on whether the customer is placing an order or checking on the status of one already placed, the inside sales associate proceeds to assist the customer in the appropriate manner. In either case, the goal is to have a delighted and satisfied customer by the end of the call. Technology is now available that gives the inside sales rep information about the caller so the conversation can be personalized. Product descriptions may be scripted on a computer for consistency and as an aid to the inside sales rep. The critical relationship building that occurs during a call comes from extensive customer service training and experience.

If the customer's needs are exceeded, you have a call where sales, current and future, and customer service coincide. For example, an elderly woman who wanted to send flowers to her sick sister called 1-800-Flowers.com. The sister lived on a mountain outside a tiny town, and the elderly woman had been unable to find a florist who lived within delivery distance. The 1-800-Flowers.com associate took down all the appropriate information and started to work. There were no easy solutions because, as the inside sales rep reconfirmed, there were no florists in the vicinity. Eventually the associate discovered that there was a police station in the town, and she tracked down the lone officer on duty. As the associate explained the problem, the officer explained that he knew exactly where the sister lived. The associate arranged for a local delivery to the police officer who took the flowers to the sick woman. Two days later, the associate received a return call from the woman who had placed the order. Her sister had been delighted with the flowers, the first special delivery of its kind that had found its way to her distant location. 1–800-Flowers.com had added not one but three new customers (including the police officer).

BUSINESS-TO-CONSUMER SELLING
by Tupperware

Business-to-consumer personal selling, also known as *direct personal selling*, is "the sale of a consumer product or service in a person-to-person manner away from a fixed retail location."[1] Direct selling is strong and growing; nearly 10 million people participate in direct selling in the United States and 73 percent of Americans have purchased goods or services through direct selling.[2] Sales in the United States have gone from $22.21 billion a decade ago to more than $30 billion in 2007, and constitute more than one-quarter of an estimated worldwide market of $110 billion. Two factors generally define and differentiate the direct-selling process and infrastructure from other sales formats: selling methods and the sales management relationship with the sales force.

Selling Methods

The salesperson meets the customer prospect away from a typical retail location. Consumers receive a benefit from the in-person selling process due to personalized customer information and/or demonstrations solving their individual wants and requirements. The product then comes directly to the customer.

Historically, the door-to-door salesman defined the prototype of the direct-selling method: reaching consumers outside the retail store environment in their home. The door-to-door sales method has never disappeared, although other strategies also have become associated with direct personal selling to the consumer.

DIRECT SELLING METHODS

- One-on-one or relationship selling including door-to-door cold calling (64.5%)
- Party plan where groups of consumers are brought together in a party setting, usually in the home (27.7%)
- Customer direct order (6.6%)
- Other (1.2%)

Source: The Direct Selling Association, 2007, Growth & Outlook Survey.

Product demonstrations typify the advantage of direct selling to the consumer. The virtually airtight Tupperware® seal requires that the user learn how to attach and "burp" the flexible top of the plastic container to create a partial vacuum. Even though Stanley Home Products has been credited with originating home demonstrations of its hardware products, it was a former Stanley Home Products distributor named Brownie Wise who was recruited by Earl Tupper and then popularized the Tupperware Party in the 1950s. Usually held at the home of a hostess who invited several of her friends, the Tupperware Party would feature a Tupperware consultant or manager conducting product demonstrations combined with giving tips for the home, ice-breaker games, and activities in which participants (including the hostess) would be awarded prizes. Today, a new Tupperware demonstration is beginning approximately every two seconds somewhere in the world.

DIRECT SELLING LOCATIONS

- Home (70.4%)
- Internet (11.4%)
- Telephone (8.8%)
- Temporary location (3.7%)
- Workplace (2.5%)
- Other (3.2%)

Source: The Direct Selling Association, 2007, Growth & Outlook Survey.

In the past, direct-selling companies attempted diversification into other distribution channels, such as catalogs and retail stores. However, in order to avoid the appearance of competition with, and thus discouragement of, their independent direct sales force, their efforts were constrained. Today, in response to consumer demands, many direct sellers are diversifying into new and complementary customer access venues, including sales force-operated mall kiosks, the Internet, TV infomercials, and TV home shopping programs. Integrating all of these direct access strategies is a planning priority among many companies in the direct-selling industry.

Global opportunities for direct selling have been an important expansion strategy in industrialized countries where work opportunities for women may be limited and in developing countries where the retail infrastructure may be limited. For example, through direct selling, consumers can buy an Avon lipstick in the Amazon jungle, a Tupperware food container in Botswana, or Amway detergents in Russia.

Sales Management/Sales Force Working Relationship

The primary sales force of the direct-selling enterprise is comprised of *independent contractors*, in effect entrepreneurs working for themselves and managing their own businesses. The independent contractor relationship is the cornerstone of the direct-selling industry, whereas the direct-selling company determines the way the sales force is structured, trained, and motivated. The advantages of being an independent contractor are the ability to:

- Pursue income and occupational opportunities that do not require a degree or specific level of education, prior experience, or substantial financial resources
- Work part-time or full-time
- Own, manage, and build a business starting with little or no capital investment
- Receive sales training and continuing support from a successful, established company

Sales Force Structure

At one time, the direct-selling industry consisted entirely of traditional direct sellers such as Avon and Tupperware with relatively flat hierarchical sales force infrastructures. Today, a majority of direct sales companies use a multilevel compensation plan where sellers are compensated both for their own sales as well as for sales made by those they have recruited. Members of the sales force, who may be known as consultants, demonstrators, dealers, distributors, executives, or a variety of other terms, may recruit new sales representatives themselves, build their own business organizations, and advance to higher levels or sales management positions.

Sales Force Training

Successful direct sellers must be good mentors, educating their recruits on the products and selling programs, mentoring prospects, scheduling demonstrations, and teaching sales and recruiting techniques.

Sales Force Motivation

The average individual sales activity and expectations of income varies greatly due to the varied amounts of time dedicated to selling. Therefore, sales force promotions also provide incentives that win loyalties and capture imaginations. Incentives include product discounts, a company car, vacations, and shopping sprees. Annual educational and motivational events produced by the larger direct-selling companies are typically high-energy extravaganzas in resort locations, often showcased with well-known entertainers.

DIRECT-SELLING PRODUCT CATEGORIES

- Personal care products, such as cosmetics and jewelry (32.8%)
- Home and family care products, such as cookware, cutlery, and cleaning products (25.6%)
- Wellness products, such as vitamins and weight loss programs (21.4%)
- Services/Miscellaneous/Other (16.2%)
- Leisure and educational products, such as toys, games, and encyclopedias (4.0%)

Source: The Direct Selling Association, 2007, Growth & Outlook Survey.

SALES — INTERNATIONAL
by American Express

Even though the goal of sales is the same worldwide—to satisfy the needs of the customer—there are many considerations that need to be managed when selling internationally or globally. These issues may require companies to adjust their sales techniques, processes, and methods when entering international markets. They may also require companies to update their expectations, particularly with regard to the time and effort required to penetrate foreign markets.

Language as a Barrier and an Opportunity

Language is the first obvious obstacle when selling internationally, but may not be the primary one. English is a generally accepted language for conducting business throughout the world, and if the sales contact does not speak English, this barrier can be overcome with the use of an interpreter. The danger of language is not actually in the act of translating the words but in conveying the meaning of the words. Use of jargon or slang or even slight variations in meaning due to regional differences (British English versus American English, for example) can cause major delays or misunderstandings. Salespeople should, therefore, choose their words very carefully and use words with universal meanings when communicating even through an interpreter.

Language is also a challenge when considering the manner of one's speech. Different cultures have different tolerance levels when it comes to direct versus passive use of language. Some Asian cultures, for example, tend to be more passive and undemanding. A direct approach can be seen as insulting. Other cultures are suspicious of passive language. If the salesperson is not upfront in his or her approach, the buyer may assume the salesperson is hiding something or, at least, not telling the whole truth. In larger markets, these differences in approach can occur across different regions or provinces.

Use of language can also provide great advantages. If the salesperson has an understanding of the local language and dialect, even if not fluent, it shows that he or she has taken an interest in the market and its culture. In this way, use of language becomes a tool for forming the relationship and bonding with the potential buyer. It is better as a rule to know a bit of the language well than to know a lot of the language and speak it poorly. Learning a language is a great way to be introduced to a culture and their way of thinking.

Humor as a form of language is a good thing. There are important things to remember about the use of humor. Certain types of humor do not translate well. Sarcasm, for example, requires a variation of tone in language and therefore does not translate well. Political, racial, and raunchy humor are best avoided whereas self-deprecating, physical humor (think Japanese game show) is almost universally accepted.

Selling Approach and Cultural Variations

The approach of the sales effort is very important. If international customers get the impression that salespeople consider their market to be just another territory to conquer, they can be very wary. Humility and a show of respect is almost always the best approach.

In markets like China and Japan, the past western approach to business has generally been that of the aggressive conquering nation without regard for the culture or the health and fitness of the people. This approach has led to failure in most cases. In such markets, personal relationships are extremely important. People in international markets want to see that the foreign company is making an investment in the market. Strategies for penetration such as forming a joint venture or hiring a local representative with existing relationships provide confidence that the relationship they are forming is long term.

Forming relationships and partnerships can take time. Naturally companies want to aggressively pursue a market with great potential. Expectations are high, and the sales force is under great pressure to take advantage of the opportunity. Yet, when they enter a sales relationship, they find that the partners in the market are not operating with the same urgency. The first meetings can be frustrating for the salesperson because little business is actually done. Instead, the buyers are sizing up the foreign salesperson to determine if there is a genuine, trusting relationship to be had. Of course, the situation may be just the opposite. The company attempting to enter a market may, according to their own culture, expect to base their sales efforts on forming a deep partnership over time only to find that the buyer just wants to complete the deal and move on. This can leave them insulted and frustrated even though they have won the business.

The propensity to negotiate can be another major cultural variation. Some cultures enjoy the art of negotiation more than others. Some feel that the only way to reach a good deal is by negotiating and not to engage in the process is, once again, insulting. Other cultures look at negotiation as a necessary evil whereas others see the use of negotiation tactics as a way of concealing the truth and assume that they are being manipulated. How the salesperson treats the negotiation process can determine how successful the relationship will be.

A variation on the negotiation theme is the concept of the written contract. Western cultures tend to see the signing of a contract as the completion of the deal. The contract sets the rules of the relationship and is binding. To reopen issues is to say that the partners are not satisfied with the deal and the relationship is therefore at risk. Other cultures don't see it that way. Whereas most have accepted the practice of the written contract, they see it only as a snapshot of the relationship at the time. The contract is an iterative document that not only can be but will be and should be adjusted over the course of the relationship. In these cultures, they ask questions like, "Why let the business environment at a specific point in time determine the nature of the relationship?" or "Things change, the business changes, companies grow or contract, so why shouldn't relationships be flexible to that change?"

One major aspect of a market culture that is often overlooked in the sales approach is religious or nonreligious belief structures. This has less impact in markets with high levels of syncretism, where belief systems have blended or become obscured in a multicultural environment, such as in New York, London, or Singapore. But in cultures with a single belief system or a few dominating belief systems, the influence can be quite significant. Belief systems can influence how and when sales meetings take place, the agenda of meetings (to accommodate prayer times), the pecking order of the attendees, the decision process, and many other aspects of the sales effort. Belief systems certainly influence buying behavior in many cultures. In some Muslim cultures, for example, buyers are required to purchase products at a premium if they have the means. This requirement allows them to fairly distribute wealth to the working population. In other cultures, the belief system acts in a restrictive way, preventing the purchase of certain products that elsewhere would be seen as quite normal. This is true in India where some religious practices prevent the use of animal-based products, Muslim countries where alcohol and pork products are prohibited, and even in parts of the United States where puritan cultures still prevail. When entering a foreign market, it is important that salespeople understand the belief systems of the people. If they do not, it can mean delays or even failure.

Understanding differences in business customs is an important part of presale preparation. Researching the culture of the market is important and accounting for regional or provincial variations can be just as important. Still, for all the research that can be done, success is best driven by experience. Where major cultural variations exist, use local representatives or consultants as guides. Most importantly, be flexible to the environment and be prepared to adjust your approach.

International Sales Management

Managing sales internationally and globally is extremely challenging. The most obvious obstacles are language, logistics (variations in time zone, technology, and distance), and quality of talent (education, product knowledge, sales techniques). Other, more subtle challenges exist as well.

An example of just such a subtle challenge comes from the establishment of a scuba diving franchise business in Borneo. The owner was a banker from England who was very aggressive in his business. He made a change of life decision to develop a tourism business in Kota Kinabalu (KK) and purchased a franchise license. All his training and analysis showed there was a very good opportunity for a western-type scuba business in the rapidly growing city. Working through local authorities, he managed to get all the permits and permissions he needed to do business; he bought a high-quality dive boat and set up a very efficient operation; and, finally, he hired a local sales force to help drive revenue growth. After about six months, the business was doing well but it was not meeting what the owner thought would be very achievable growth numbers. On review, he found that he had not accounted for the local culture in KK. The people in the city were only a generation or two from local fishing village life. Their culture still maintained many elements of the village psyche. In a fishing village, the fishermen would set out to make their catch for the day; when they achieved what they needed to feed themselves and their family, they would return home. This practice had bled over into his sales force for the dive business. The owner found that the sales force would set out to make a single sale a day. Once they achieved this, whether it took three minutes or twelve hours, they would head home or to the local tea shop. Teaching his team that they needed to continue to make additional sales throughout the day proved very difficult, but eventually the team accepted the change.

Sales management challenges can also vary based on the type of sales. Business-to-business selling among large, multinational, and global companies has become fairly standard in the last few decades. This has been enabled by the advancements in global communications and global travel. Yet, there are still considerations, such as infrastructure and talent. For example, sales and service managed through call centers can raise interesting questions. Is it better to manage a call center in the local country and in the local language with the risk that the technologies and talent are of a lower standard? Should there be a centralized call center where the company can be more confident of its capabilities? Will a centralized approach irritate foreign buyers? Or, possibly, is there a hybrid solution to be had? Different companies have developed different solutions based on their needs. How a company deals with these questions can determine the level of success that is achieved.

The greatest challenge in managing international sales may be in the consumer products areas. A definitive consideration when selling consumer products abroad is the economic situation in the market. The availability of disposable income will dictate priorities for buyers, the prices they are willing and able to pay, the type of products that they can purchase, and even where they purchase. To this point, emerging markets are still dominated by small, local establishments that carry locally demanded products at locally acceptable prices. The dominance of small, local stores to meet the demands in developing countries requires sales management to focus on sales efficiency and sales execution. Sales execution must be quick in order to accommodate the number of accounts. Sales force training and incentive systems must be designed to support these activities.

There are, however, other influences that impact consumer sales even when economic, infrastructure, and talent considerations are minor. One such key influence is the people's sense of nationalism or loyalty to local products and services. An interesting example of a product where local branding is surprisingly influential is in the airline business. For example, in Singapore the dominance of the national carrier is apparent wherever one goes in the country. Singapore Airlines has a worldwide reputation and represents not only a quality brand for consumers but is, in itself, the pride of the small nation. Not only has this made penetration of the market by other airlines difficult through the years, but it also influences the sales penetration of other tangentially related products and services. In Singapore, an association with Singapore Airlines through a sales and marketing partnership can mean extreme success in the market. If buyers know about that association, whether it is a retail product or even a credit card, it can positively influence the buying decision. Everyone wants to support the national carrier (even one that is privately owned). This relationship can be seen with other airlines as well, such as Germany's Lufthansa, Australia's Qantas, and UAE's Emirates Airlines. How a sales force works with these local icons can make the process much easier.

International Sales Ethics

When managing sales abroad, there are a number of legal and ethical questions that the salesperson must consider.

One major cultural and ethical variation that a company must deal with, particularly in developing markets, is the question of facilitated payments. In some markets, it is not unusual to pay sums of money to gain access to the market or speed up the sales process. For companies based in the United States, this practice is not only deemed unethical but it is also illegal. This applies not just to facilitated payments made within the United States but to payments made by U.S.-based companies dealing abroad.

By Hilton Hotels Corporation

Company: Hilton Hotels
Case: Team Selling

Maximizing revenues at a large hotel property such as the Hilton San Francisco & Towers (HSF&T) is a big job. With 1,890 bedrooms, 156 suites, 110,000 square feet of state-of-the-art meeting and banquet space and more than a half dozen food and beverage outlets open 365 days a year, the Sales and Marketing team has no shortage of work.

The sales team is comprised of specialists who focus on selling to the different types of businesses that make up the customer market mix for the hotel. The customer mix includes business travel sales, conference center sales, tour and travel sales, and a team of professionals specializing in selling to the large international, national, and regional association markets and to corporations holding large meetings, exhibitions, or product launches.

In April 1993, the HSF&T Sales and Marketing team received a sales lead indicating that the Club Managers Association of America (CMAA) was targeting the West Coast for their 1999 Annual Convention. CMAA is an association of club managers that promotes efficient club operations for a variety of prestigious clubs, including golf, yacht, athletic, city, university, and military. CMAA's 5,000 members hold a variety of meetings, the most important being the annual convention. The convention could be worth in excess of $1.5 million in combined rooms and food and beverage revenue to the Hilton San Francisco & Towers.

The HSF&T team started reviewing the Hilton's research file on the CMAA group and examining the information needed to qualify the account. The first course of action was to turn to the Director of Sales—National Accounts in Hilton's Washington, D.C., National Sales Office to assist with this D.C.-based account. In addition to sales professionals on site at each and every Hilton Hotel, the Hilton Hotels Corporation also has several national sales offices based in key locations. The role of the sales professionals in the national and international sales offices is to establish long-term working relationships with the key contacts in organizations that represent potential for multiple Hilton properties.

A review of CMAA's file indicated that, although Hilton had done some business in the past with them, CMAA had a history of booking with other hotel chains. In fact, two other major competitor chain hotels were strongly preferred by CMAA as both had provided excellent service to their group in the past. In addition, CMAA had particular concerns over the Hilton San Francisco & Towers' location (4 blocks away from the Moscone Convention Center), the quality of food and beverage, and the service levels at the hotel.

The HSF&T team continued its research and was able to establish CMAA's convention objectives and personal needs. It also determined that the CMAA board would vote on a site within a week of its site inspection trip to San Francisco.

The first and most immediate challenge was to get a chance to make a presentation to the CMAA Board of Directors. The Board and CMAA executives (15 people altogether) were going to be staying at a competitor's hotel for a site review for two days in July 1993. Hilton's Washington, D.C., office was able to persuade CMAA to give Hilton a chance to make a presentation. It was clearly going to be an uphill battle to change some of the perceptions of the CMAA Board in less than two hours over a breakfast when one of Hilton's competitors was going to have their attention for almost two days.

After getting answers to all the questions needed to qualify the account, the HSF&T team put together the "Hilton Solution." The customer's unique business, event, and personal needs were set out in order of priority. The corresponding features and services of the Hilton that met each of the needs were identified. The benefits of buying Hilton were listed and the competitive spin (how Hilton is bigger, better, different, or uniquely qualified to handle this business) was highlighted. The HSF&T team put together a strategy that would present the Hilton Solution to the CMAA Board over breakfast and then give a tour of the hotel. The entire presentation was scheduled to be less than two hours. A pivotal decision was made that Hilton would do a team sell, pulling together the key Hilton players at the Corporate, National Sales Office, and Hotel level to impress CMAA. It would later be revealed that the other competitors used a single-salesperson approach.

The Hilton team was given from 7 A.M. to 8:45 A.M. to show their hotel and serve breakfast. It was decided that the entire Executive Committee of the hotel, headed by the General Manager, would host the breakfast. The key requirements for CMAA, identified earlier by the HSF&T team, were printed on presentation boards and placed on easels around Cityscape, the hotel's spectacular rooftop restaurant.

The CMAA requirements included:

Requirement #1: 1,600 rooms on the peak nights of the convention, all within close proximity of each other and the Moscone Convention Center. They wanted a first-class facility and a hotel dedicated to "keeping up appearances" to create an environment conducive to education, networking, and recognition of individual achievement.

The Hilton Solution: Hilton proposed committing 1,300 rooms per night (100 more than the competition), with overflow into four-star properties directly across the street. Hilton noted that the attendees would be able to network better because the Hilton Solution saved time and effort in covering shorter distances between colleagues' accommodations. The fact that Hilton also was spending $7 to $9 million a year in upkeep and maintenance of its San Francisco hotel also was highlighted.

Requirement #2: Top-quality, creative food and beverage concepts.

The Hilton Solution: The Sous Chef and the food and beverage team created a spectacular breakfast, including blintzes and caviar, exotic fruits, and lox and bagels. The room was decorated with beautiful flowers, fresh vegetables, polished fruit, and ice sculptures. A variety of different creative ideas were put forward, with emphasis on Hilton's commitment to buy fresh foods from local farms around the San Francisco Bay area. Hilton also demonstrated credibility by revealing that the Hilton San Francisco & Towers had just accommodated a high-profile culinary group, a group of demanding food and beverage professionals with 1,000 chefs in attendance.

Requirement #3: Flawless and attentive service, and involvement from top management in executing the events.

The Hilton Solution: In addition to showing the support and enthusiasm of the entire HSF&T team by having them all present to host the breakfast, Hilton demonstrated that the San Francisco hotel had one of the lowest turnover rates in the company. Many of the service staff had been with the hotel since 1964, when the hotel first opened its doors. Hilton advised CMAA that the convention servicing and catering management would move into the hotel when the group was in-house, giving them 24-hour coverage. The benefit to CMAA would be peace of mind that there would be immediate assistance for any unexpected eventuality. This would give CMAA time to focus on the reasons for having their annual convention: "education, camaraderie, and successful advancement of its members." This quote, from their mission statement (researched by the HSF&T team), was woven into the Hilton presentation boards around the restaurant.

Forethought and planning also was demonstrated prior to the arrival of CMAA in San Francisco. Hilton had prepared a customer-focused sales proposal for each site inspection attendee, along with a personalized letter from Barron Hilton. Each package was expressed overnight to each CMAA site inspection attendee.

(Continued)

At the appointed time, Hilton escorted a minivan over to the competitor's hotel to pick up the CMAA Board and on the way back to the Hilton showed them how easy it was to get from the Moscone Convention Center to the Hilton Hotel. As the minivan pulled up to the front entrance, members of the Hilton Sales Management Team were curbside to welcome them with a red carpet and a welcome banner.

The CMAA group then proceeded to the breakfast where they met the rest of the hotel's executive committee. Each executive committee member talked about what they do, in casual conversation rather than in a formal presentation. The flow of conversation was well orchestrated by the Hilton team, and the breakfast ended at 8 A.M., giving 45 minutes to conduct the tour of the hotel.

When the CMAA Board decision was made, it was unanimous; they booked its 1999 Annual Meeting at the Hilton San Francisco & Towers. Solid research; good qualification work; a smooth, customer-focused presentation; creativity; and a team sell made the difference and landed a very lucrative signed contract.

SALES – CASE STUDY

By Coldwell Banker

Company: Coldwell Banker
Case: 10-Day Sales Event

Background/Business Challenge

During 2008 the residential real estate industry made headlines as a sector in trouble. In an effort to bring home buyers and sellers together and help jump-start the U.S. real estate market, Coldwell Banker, the nation's oldest residential real estate brand, devised a bold initiative to help move home buyers off the sidelines and into homes.

The Coldwell Banker "10-Day Sales Event" kicked off on October 10, 2008, with immense enthusiasm and support. During this time, participating home sellers from across the United States agreed to reduce the listing price on their homes. The goal of the national "10-Day Sales Event" was to bring participating sellers and interested buyers together—and to help Americans recognize that *now* truly is a smart time to buy.

Further demonstrating the need for a leader in real estate to take a stand, a survey of 3,379 Coldwell Banker real estate professionals in markets across the United States found that 56 percent said that listing prices in their market remain above where they need to be to attract qualified buyers. Additional findings from the survey included:

- 77 percent agreed that the majority of sellers in their market still had unrealistic expectations regarding the initial listing price for their homes.
- 79 percent agreed that homes in their market that were priced appropriately were attracting more buyers and moving more quickly.
- 76 percent felt that a 10 percent or less reduction in listing prices in their area is all it would take to help push these homes over the tipping point to a sale.

Jim Gillespie, president and chief executive officer, Coldwell Banker Real Estate LLC, was quoted in the event kick-off press release stating:

Despite the difficult headlines regarding our overall economy, the residential real estate market has been showing several positive signs over recent months that could be signaling a tipping point. Because of higher inventory, buyers have more homes to choose from and they can take advantage of near historically low interest rates and affordability levels that are the best they have been in years. The recent housing and economic recovery legislation also provides first-time homebuyers with the added incentive of a $7,500 tax credit.

PR Strategy

To generate buzz about this event, a focused public relations effort was implemented including a detailed "communications blueprint" for the Coldwell Banker affiliate and company-owned offices with messaging, Q&A, fill-in-the-blank press releases, and so on. In addition, two media training sessions were conducted to provide tips and tools for offices speaking with the media during the 10-Day Sales Event.

Because of this intensive preevent coordination, local media coverage for the 10-Day Sales Event was impressive. Coldwell Banker CEO Jim Gillespie kicked off the media buzz with national interviews and the affiliate and Coldwell Banker–owned offices continued this media attention on a local level throughout the event.

As part of the integrated communications platform, sellers who participated in the 10-Day Sales Event also had added promotional power from the Coldwell Banker brand behind their listing. Those sellers' listings were specially promoted through national and local radio and print advertising as well as being featured prominently on the coldwellbanker.com Web site.

Results

The 10-Day Sales Event was particularly successful generating media attention both nationally and locally. Below are highlights of the media coverage and business highlights to date for the 10-Day Sales Event.

Media Coverage

- Media Impressions (to date): 28 million
- Ad Equivalency: $6.7 million
- 101 national and local broadcast segments, including CNBC Power Lunch, FOX—Opening Bell, FOX—Cavuto on Business, NPR, Reuters TV, Bloomberg TV, and more
- 15 Satellite Media Tour and radio interviews with Jim Gillespie
- More than 300 print and online hits including *Los Angeles Times, Chicago Tribune, Denver Post, Boston Globe, Atlanta Journal-Constitution,* and others
- Stories in 10 of the top 30 newspapers

Sales

Across the country, more than 32,000 homes listed with Coldwell Banker participated in the sale. The average price reduction was around 9 percent. The number of sales varied from market to market with an average of 6 percent of sale properties going under contract during the sale. These results were exceptional considering the financial and credit collapse that occurred just days before which further eroded consumer confidence.

The sales strategy proved effective in a variety of markets:

- Markets that have been historically stable in terms of price such as Ohio, Pittsburgh, Dallas/Fort Worth
- Markets with a high level of inventory such as Chicago
- Markets affected by high levels of speculation such as Utah
- Many entry- and mid-level markets across New England

(Continued)

In addition, close to 70 percent of participating properties maintained the reduced price after the sale, indicating support for the event's main goal of bringing buyers and seller together on the issue of price.

Web traffic to coldwellbanker.com during the 10-Day Sales Event saw an 11 percent increase in property searches during the event with a total of 2.5 million searches executed.

Many Coldwell Banker offices also reported significant increases in phone inquiries and Open House visits related to the reduced price listings. In some cases, properties that had been on the market for months, now reduced in price, received offers within the first few days of the 10-Day Sales Event.

CORPORATE PROFILES AND AUTHOR BIOGRAPHIES

AMERICAN EXPRESS

American Express, founded in 1850 and headquartered in New York City, is one of the best known brands in the world for quality service, personal security, and personal recognition. Visit American Express at www.americanexpress.com.

David Lee

David Lee is Director, Advisory Services. Prior to this, Mr. Lee was Director, Product Development. He received his MBA in International Management from Thunderbird School for Global Management.

COLDWELL BANKER

Since 1906, the Coldwell Banker organization has been a premier full-service real estate provider. It is a pioneer in consumer services with its Coldwell Banker Concierge® Service Program and award-winning Web site. Visit Coldwell Banker at www.coldwellbanker.com.

David Siroty

David Siroty is in his fifth year as Senior Director of Public Relations for Coldwell Banker. He is responsible for all U.S. and Canadian external and internal communications, along with franchise marketing and cause marketing activities, which promote the Coldwell Banker brand and initiatives to media, staff, and affiliated companies.

HILTON HOTELS CORPORATION

Hilton Hotels Corporation is the leading global hospitality company. For more information about Hilton Hotels Corporation, visit www.hiltonworldwide.com. To learn more about their "be hospitable" philosophy, visit www.behospitable.com.

Martin C. Lowery

Martin Lowery was the Senior Vice President—Organizational Development & Chief Learning Officer for Hilton Hotels Corporation. Mr. Lowery earned received his BS with Honors in Hotel Administration from the University of Surrey in England.

EASTMAN KODAK COMPANY

Kodak, as the world's foremost imaging innovator, helps consumers, businesses, and creative professionals unleash the power of pictures and printing to enrich their lives. Visit Kodak at www.kodak.com. Visit blog sites at 1000words.kodak.com, PluggedIn. kodak.com, and GrowYourBiz. kodak.com.

Don McMahan

Don McMahan is Vice President of Sales and Regional Business Manager for the Document Imaging business of Eastman Kodak Company for the United States and Canada. Mr. McMahan received his BA in Communications from California State University at Fullerton.

1-800-FLOWERS.COM

1-800-FLOWERS.COM Inc.—"Your Florist of Choice"—has been providing customers around the world with the freshest flowers and finest selection of plants, gift baskets, gourmet foods, confections, and plush stuffed animals perfect for every occasion for more than 30 years. Visit 1-800-FLOWERS.COM at www.1800flowers.com.

James F. McCann

Jim McCann, founder and CEO of 1-800-FLOWERS.COM, INC., opened his first retail store in 1976 and successfully built his own chain of 14 flower shops in the New York metropolitan area. In 1986, he acquired the 1-800-FLOWERS phone number and continued to grow his business under the 1-800-FLOWERS name.

TUPPERWARE CORP.

Tupperware, headquartered in Orlando, Florida, is the world's leading supplier of microwave oven products and one of the world's leaders in direct selling with sales reps in over 100 countries. Visit Tupperware at www.tupperware.com.

Lawrie P. Hall

Lawrie Hall was formerly Director of External Affairs and was responsible for exposure management on a global basis and administration of the Tupperware Foundation. Ms. Hall received her BA in Fine Arts from Goucher College and management certificates from the Crummer Graduate School of Business at Rollins College and the Simmons Graduate School of Business.

NOTES

1. Direct Selling Association Growth & Outlook Survey, 2007.   2. Ibid.

10 ADVERTISING

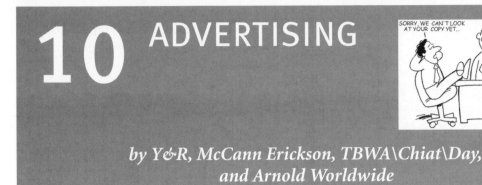

by Y&R, McCann Erickson, TBWA\Chiat\Day, and Arnold Worldwide

As an employee in an [ad] agency creative department, you will spend most of your time with your feet up on a desk working on an ad. Across the desk, also with his feet up, will be your partner. And he will want to talk about movies. In fact, if the truth be known, you will spend fully one-fourth of your career with your feet up talking about movies.

Luke Sullivan, *Hey Whipple, Squeeze This*[1]

THE ESSENTIALS OF ADVERTISING
by Y&R

Introduction

Advertising is the element of marketing that involves communicating a message from a sponsor, through a purchased communication channel, to a particular audience. To influence decisions about purchases, marketers present consumers and organizations (target audiences) with rational, factual information as well as emotional appeals. Advertising has both long-term and short-term goals as it attempts to drive both sale and brand relationships. For most marketers, the short-term goal of business-to-consumer advertising is to stimulate demand (predispose a customer to make a purchase), or to influence an opinion or behavior. The short-term goal of business-to-business advertising is to stimulate demand and promote awareness of the brand to organizational purchasers in order to assist the company's sales force. Longer term, marketers seek to build relationships with their consumers or customers that help drive loy-

alty and commitment. Recently, the relationship between marketers and consumers in advertising has become more interactive. With the Internet and social networking, marketers are able to engage consumers in new domains that allow for more communication. This has shifted the consumers' decision process to be more emotionally and behaviorally driven.

In order to achieve their goals and make their appeals relevant, marketers and their agencies try to understand the consumers' values, needs, and wants. For example, Swatch does not just sell watches, it sells style. Perrier does not just sell water, it sells status. In today's new, digital world there are all sorts of forms of advertising. Traditional television advertising is most advantageous and cost-effective as a promotional element when there are larger numbers of customers that need to be reached and the product or service can be easily understood in a brief time period. Because television advertising reaches large numbers of people, it is considered a mass communications vehicle. Other forms of advertising, such as online activities, are highly targeted and are an increasingly large part of the media mix.

Definitions

Advertising is "the placement of announcements and persuasive messages in a time or space purchase in any of the mass media by business firms, nonprofit organizations, government agencies, and individuals who seek to inform and/or persuade members of a particular target market or audience about their products, services, organizations, or ideas."[2]

THE ADVERTISING PROCESS

THE ADVERTISING PROCESS

The Advertiser's Needs
↓
Selecting an Ad Agency
↓
Advertising Planning/Communications Planning
↓
Media Planning
↓
Creative Development
↓
Production
↓
Execution
↓
Results Research

Although the advertising process appears very linear, in actual practice it is much more fluid. For example, many clients have retained ongoing relationships with their agency so a selection process is not necessary. Further, depending on the timeline for the project, steps like media planning and creative development may happen simultaneously.

1. The Advertiser's Needs

The advertising process stems from the advertiser's business goals. The advertiser often determines their goals during their internal planning process, before reaching out to their ad agency or involving an in-house agency. It is critical that those respon-

sible for the development of advertising understand and embrace the business goals. Typical goals are to increase sales, increase awareness, or introduce a new concept or product.

2. Selecting an Ad Agency

An organization usually assigns a person or team to be responsible to carry out their marketing communications goals. In small organizations, the owner or the president typically will be involved in advertising goals and strategies. In larger firms, chief marketing officers, product/brand managers, marketing managers, or sales managers often make these decisions. Some companies have in-house advertising capabilities. Most companies rely on outside agencies to perform advertising services for them. Clients look for an agency with the baseline level of services desired but may make the selection based on the actual people they meet.

Types of Agencies

Typically there are three types of agencies that make up the advertising industry: the larger full-service agencies, general agencies, and the smaller specialty agencies.

- **Full-Service Agencies.** These agencies offer their clients integrated and global communications options. Several of the largest agencies offer direct marketing, public relations, promotions, and even corporate logo design. These agencies are usually large or midsize.
- **General Agencies.** These agencies typically offer general advertising services only, such as creative services and sometimes media buying. They may charge slightly lower fees and provide more direct access to senior staff. These agencies range in size from midsize to small.
- **Specialty Agencies.** These agencies offer specialized services depending on the need. For example, there are several advertising agencies that specialize in areas such as Internet advertising, ethical advertising, promotional advertising, and direct response advertising. These agencies are typically small in size.

Agency Structure

The majority of full-service agencies are organized in a similar manner, and usually consist of the following departments: account management, account planning, creative, production, delivery organization, and financial. Even though at one time media was integral to advertising agencies, today many media companies are independent from creative agencies.

- **Account Management.** This department is responsible for maintaining and building the relationship between the client and the advertising agency. Account managers are the key contact/liaisons who manage the scope of work between the client and the advertising agency. The *account manager* manages every facet of a client's account, from strategic direction and briefing creative teams, to media, production, and billing.
- **Account Planning.** Account planning brings the consumer into the advertising process and, at the same time, envisions a powerful future for the brand. *Account planners* (or *brand planners*) help to develop advertising that is both distinct and relevant by considering the context, the brand, and the consumer. Successful planning depends on creativity to acquire and leverage research insights and client information to drive relevant and distinctive creative strategies and advertising ideas.
- **Creative.** The creative department consists of the *copywriters* and *art directors* who are responsible for the development and the execution of all advertising. Whereas account management determines the campaign's strategy, with the client and account planning, the creative department determines the most effective way to communicate this message to the target audience.
- **Production.** Modern production departments have been integrated to include all aspects of production: television, radio, print, digital, and new media. Any project that has components that need to be shot or produced can be considered content for use in various media outlets.
- **Delivery Organization.** This group helps enable the production and execution of work. It can consist of traffic, production, project management, and so forth. This team helps manage the production timeline and delivery of materials.
- **Financial.** The financial department is responsible for the accounting and financial management of the advertising agency.
- **Media.** Similar to the creative/advertising agency, the media agency has multiple departments as well. The core team tends to consist of media planners and media buyers. *Media planners* are responsible for developing media strategies and objectives for a brand, for setting a brand's communication goals, and for developing a media plan based on this criteria. *Media buyers* take a client's media plan and purchase different types of media, such as television and radio time, magazine and outdoor space, at the best possible price.
- **Project Management.** *Project management* is the flow of creative assignments and timetables going in and out of an agency. Project managers act as the internal liaison between the account team and the creative team.

3. Initial Advertising Planning

Initial advertising planning consists of ad planning research, ad strategy development and selection, competitive assessment, and budgeting.

Ad Planning Research

In order to start the advertising process, an ad agency first determines the client company's business objectives, marketing goals, and target markets.

Company Goals Research

The ad agency generally works with the client to determine what the client seeks to accomplish through advertising: for example, a certain level of sales or consumer awareness (specific percentages), what message it wants to convey to the public (such as high quality or low prices), and what budget is appropriate. Having specific goals allows the company to measure the results and provides direction for the various strategies. This aspect is sometimes referred to as *DAGMAR*, for *Define Advertising Goals for Measurable Results.*

Target Audience Research

Identifying the correct target audience is a result of marketing research and market segmentation. Marketing research helps to define the prime market segments; product research can identify the needs of those segments; and creative research explores the most appropriate messages necessary for the success of the brand (product or service) in its competitive environment. Demographics, psychographics, and behavioral trends play key roles in identifying the designated group. A target audience can consist of individuals or organizations (large or small, for-profit or not-for-profit, and governments). Audiences can be end users, purchasers, or even purchase influencers. Good target identification enables successful advertising.

Ad Strategy Selection

In developing advertising, it is best to have a formal strategy or plan before any creative work begins. Creative strategy is developed by the advertiser and the agency. The more involvement from the different disciplines earlier on, the more robust the strategy will be. There are several options that make up part of the advertising plan: types of advertising, types of messages, and various other strategies.

Types of Advertising

Types of advertising include product/services/brand, institutional, and cause marketing.

- **Product/Services/Brand Advertising.** Product advertising can attempt to persuade the members of a target audience to change their behavior in order to use or purchase particular goods or services. For example, the GAP clothing store ads try to sell clothing and Hilton Hotel ads try to promote use of their lodging services.
- **Institutional Advertising.** Institutional advertising, also known as industry advertising, promotes an entire industry and its members' products or services that consumers do not

typically associate with a particular brand. For example, the milk industry attempts to persuade consumers that milk (any brand) is worth considering as a beverage through their "Got Milk?" campaign.
- **Cause Marketing.** Cause Marketing promotes ideas. For example, the World Wildlife Fund tries to get consumers and government officials to understand issues concerning loss of habitat and then do something about the cause, such as donate money or vote a certain way.

Message Components

Advertisements can be designed to communicate many different ways. They can be informative, persuasive, based on rational or emotional appeals, or simply offer a reminder. They can also use a combination of these elements.

- **Informative Advertisements.** Informative advertisements primarily provide information to a target audience. Usually these ads are simple and announcement-oriented. For example, "Blood pressure testing will be conducted free this weekend at Costco."
- **Persuasive Advertisements.** Persuasive advertisements try to provide the consumer with an emotional or rational reason to purchase their brand over the competitive brand. For example, "Body Shop products are not tested on animals," appeals to the emotions of a target audience but from a rational perspective. Persuasive ads may have high information content especially in more involved marketing categories or when they are introducing new products or concepts.
- **Reminder Advertisements.** Reminder advertisements provide a quick message, such as "Vote on Tuesday" or "Drink Coke." These ads usually do not require as much time to get their message across as do persuasive ads and therefore are less expensive. These ads are often used when the brand name is well known, usually late in the product life cycle after a series of informative or persuasive ads.

Additional Strategies

- **One-Time ad vs. Campaign.** One-time (also called one-off) ads (or a short series) may be all that is necessary, such as before an election or for the introduction of a new product. However, a campaign, or long-term themed approach, running the duration of a brand's life cycle can help brands present a consistent and recognizable brand image.

- **B-to-B Push and B-to-C Pull.** A push approach may be used in the introductory stage of the product life cycle in order to promote a product to business. Business-to-business advertising stimulates the wholesalers and retailers to push the product through the supply chain pipeline. Typically this information is technical and informative. Pull advertising to consumers urges them to request a new product from their retailer or salesperson and thus pull the product through the supply chain pipeline. The pull and push approaches are often used in conjunction.

- **Client Product Only vs. Comparative Ads.** Some advertising emphasizes the features and benefits of one product, and does not address competitive brands at all. Comparative ads display information about the competition, and can be more informative and perhaps more persuasive. However, it may be confusing to consumers when one company gives publicity to its competition. Comparative ads are considered aggressive by some consumers and are illegal in some countries.

- **Reputation Management.** When a product is endorsed by a third party, such as a celebrity or a consumer, this is called reputation management. For some brands, the quickest and most effective way to resonate with consumers is to have someone else speak for your brand, whether it is a celebrity that consumers aspire to be like or a company that people admire and trust. For example, when Xerox faced trouble in early 2000, their credibility was challenged with some customers and prospects. They recruited some of their tried-and-true customers to be spokespeople for their advertising campaign. Alternatively, many fashion, luxury, and cosmetic brands use celebrities to help attract customers.

- **Single Company vs. Cobranding.** Advertising only one client's product allows the customer to concentrate on one message or brand image. For example, "Go Greyhound." Cobranded advertisements feature two products delivering a unique combination of benefits, which may be appealing to the customer, and provides a shared ad cost to the two advertisers. For example, Hershey's chocolate and Keebler cookie crumbs combined for a chocolate pie crust.

Brand Planning

A brand makes a promise of an experience the consumer is going to have. Often the brand experience is described as a mirror, that is, a reflection of how the brand is seen by the consumer. It is the sum of all emotions, thoughts, and images that consumers associate with a certain product. Brand image is what makes it acceptable to wear a particular item of clothing to a party or give a particular product as a gift. Brands are assets. To be valuable they must deliver competitive insulation as well as margin and pricing power. An advertising idea must not detract from brand equity. It should help define it and make it stronger.

Brand planning is critical to generating ideas and creating successful advertising communications to the targeted consumer. Advertising communication is not effective unless it has a positive impact on the brand, and ultimately contributes to the business objectives. The goal of the brand planning process is to help create a powerful vision for the brand that can be expressed in marketing communications and use all elements of the communication mix to help the brand realize its full potential.

Brand planning is involved in three fundamental aspects: research, insights, and communications platform.

Research

As the first step in the brand planning process, planners should immerse themselves in information about the brand and its consumers as well as the historical marketing and advertising information. Planners study a target consumer's everyday experiences, from the practical demands of their target's lives to their hopes, aspirations, and wishes. Planners seek to understand the relevance of a particular brand and its pricing, packaging, and distribution in the consumer's life. During this immersion process, planners look for pieces of information that provide insights into consumer reactions to the brand and its competitors. The research process typically involves the following steps:

- Conduct a wide initial consumer inquiry about the brand and its competitors.
- Review all of the research, business information, and client concerns.
- Personally identify and talk to the appropriate people.
- Fill in identified knowledge gaps with primary research.
- Identify specific information about the brand and its connection to its consumers.

Insights

The value of the immersion process is to synthesize research in order to derive insights that can positively transform consumer perceptions about a brand. Transforming information and data to the level of insight requires sorting the relevant from the irrelevant, bridging data gaps, and extrapolating new ideas. Data collection and information reporting are about what happened in the past, whereas insights lend themselves to future predictions.

Brand planning is the ability to recognize an insight and then use the insight as the foundation of a story that can inspire communications that influence consumers. Brand planners use a combination of intuition, knowledge, and experience in developing and acting on insights. Brand planners generate ideas about the brand's potential and the kinds of relationships that consumers could have with the brand.

Communications Platform

An insight is only significant if it can develop a powerful communications platform that evokes successful advertising communications that positively impact a client's business. A *communications platform* is defined as the overarching idea that builds the relationship between the brand and the consumer. It is a platform that encompasses how the consumer should think about the brand in the future, in a way that is relevant and distinct. A communications platform typically serves as a guide for all advertising efforts on behalf of the brand. It is the responsibility of the brand planner to generate a future strategy for the brand and plot the execution of this strategy over time.

Because brand planners must continually analyze both the target consumer and the future strategy of the brand, it is desirable for them to:

- Have a continuous presence in agency and client meetings.
- Represent the target consumer and his or her relationship with the brand throughout the entire advertising process.
- Act as the direct link between the consumer and the creative function.
- Nurture creative ideas and help improve their consumer authenticity.
- Develop a relevant and distinct advertising strategy, together with the agency team.
- Be held accountable for advertising that is relevant to both the brand strategy and the execution of this strategy.
- Support the effectiveness of the platform by monitoring the in-market performance of the creative work that it fosters.

Advertising Budgets

Companies should determine an advertising budget in order to allocate appropriate funding to successfully accomplish their marketing goals. Budgets can be set on a local, regional, national, or international level. Budgets can be set for the company alone, in conjunction with supply chain partners, or as part of an overall industry approach.

There are several methods of determining budgets, including percentage-of-sales, competitive-parity, objective-and-task, and affordable-level method.

- **Percentage-of-Sales Method.** Uses a percentage of the total sales revenue to determine how much to spend on advertising. This method is simple to administer and relates advertising to sales.
- **Competitive-Parity Method.** Compares one company's advertising budget to another company's. This allows a company to adjust its budget to meet any threats (or opportunities) posed by expanded (or contracted) competitive advertising campaigns.
- **Objective-and-Task Method.** Also known as "according to need method," establishes a budget by (1) determining marketing goals/objectives, (2) determining the tasks that will accomplish these goals, and (3) determining the cost of accomplishing the tasks. This method typically requires the most
- **Affordable-Level Method.** Also known as the "available funds method", allows a company to spend on advertising only what management thinks it can afford.

4. Media Planning

Media planning is the selection of the appropriate media mix for an advertising campaign in order to maximize audience exposure in relation to the budget. This process results in the formation of what is called the *media plan.* Media plans should properly reflect the client's business needs; marketing goals; and the creative direction of the products, services, and brands that are being advertised. Once the initial plan has been analyzed and approved by the account manager and client, it becomes the final media plan that then can be implemented.

There are four basic stages to the media planning process: determining objectives, media selection, media scheduling, and media buying.

Determining Media Objectives

The company's objectives and strategies define the advertising objectives, such as increase trial, expand market share, or source business from a specific brand. Determining objectives begins with a full analysis of the client's business, an understanding of the target audience, and a competitive spending analysis.

Analysis of Client's Business

First, the media planner must immerse him- or herself in the client's business and attempt to understand it from every vantage point. The media planner performs a SWOT analysis (strengths, weaknesses, opportunities, and threats) on the client's brands, and determine the brand's market drivers.

Target Audience

A complete understanding of the client's target audience or prospective consumers is key, in both demographic and psychographic terms. This helps to understand why these consumers make particular media choices, how the various media fit into their lifestyles, and what frame of mind they are in while spending time with these media. Having a complete understanding of the consumer as a person gives the agency a better perspective from which to evaluate the most effective media in which to communicate the message.

Target audiences typically are analyzed from several perspectives. Demographics include factors like age, gender, income, occupation, education, and household size. Psychographics include lifestyles, personalities, traits, and attitudes. The analysis of a product's use by a target audience can be categorized by brand, category, and/or degree of product usage. There are several sources available for target audience analysis; they can include database analyses, both from media companies and client proprietary data. They also can include extensive qualitative research from focus groups to one-on-one interviews, as well as specialized companies such as Nielsen and Arbitron, often used for television and radio audience measurement statistics.

Competitive Spending Analysis

A competitive spending analysis compares a client's media presence to its competitor's. This media analysis looks at areas such as share of voice, brand/category media usage patterns, media mix, daypart usage, magazine types, and programming formats (television and radio). This knowledge enables the advertising agency to understand the competitor's media strategies.

Communication Goals

Communication goals should be set to determine the required media weight levels, the percentage of an ad budget spent on the various media, and to ensure that the media activity reaches the targeted consumers. Each media plan has trade-offs, such as accomplishing objectives with fewer weeks of advertising in order to have higher activity per week or eliminating primetime in order to afford activity in all four seasonal quarters. These goals can be expressed by reach, frequency, effective reach, or gross rating points.

- **Reach.** Is the number of different individuals or homes exposed to advertising one or more times, expressed as a percentage of the population base.
- **Frequency.** Quantifies the number of people exposed to a media schedule, based on the exact number of times that they have seen the specific media.
- **Effective reach.** Is the percentage of the target audience that is exposed to an ad schedule a sufficient number of times to produce a positive change in awareness, attitude, or purchasing action.
- **Gross Rating Points (GRPs).** Are the aggregate number of rating points in a given ad campaign, derived by multiplying reach times frequency.

Media Selection

Media is anything on which a message can be placed. The selection of specific media to convey the advertising message is based on an analysis of their cost, coverage, usage by a target audience, and their advantages and limitations. For example, skywriting at the beach for suntan lotion and an ad wrapped around the safety bar of a ski lift showing resort property may be appropriate. The *media plan* is the recommendation of the total package of media alternatives. The *media mix* is composed of elements such as broadcast, print, out-of-home, interactive, Internet, social marketing, user-generated content, and more.

Broadcast Media

Broadcast media is divided into two major subcategories: television and radio. The television subcategory includes network and local television, cable television, direct broadcast satellite television, and syndicated television. The radio subcategory includes local and nationally syndicated radio shows. Advertising time can be purchased on both television and radio on a national or individual (local) market basis.

- **Television.** Approximately 98 percent of U.S. households have at least one television set, as of 1999. There are 98 million television households in the United States. The average home views over seven hours of television per week and watches an average of 10 to 11 different channels. The average U.S. household receives 45 different channels. Over the years, television has moved from a single-set family-viewing environment to a multiset environment with each viewer in charge of what he or she watches. Multiset homes account for almost 75 percent of U.S. households.
  - *Network.* Network television is the broad distribution of programming, generally via satellite, from one source to a group of local stations (affiliates). The current U.S. broadcast networks are ABC, CBS, NBC, FOX, UPN, WB, and PBS. PBS (public broadcasting) does not accept commercials, but rather makes announcements of corporate underwriters. Also, DVR and digital TV have introduced an alternative way to advertise on television. Rather than commercials that DVRs can skip over, embedded content has become more prevalent in programming. This embedded content comes in different forms, such as a ticker at the bottom of a screen or an icon in the corner of the screen.
  - *Cable.* Cable television is programming distributed via cable (fiber optic or copper wire) directly to homes. Cable is a more targeted medium, and many cable networks have niche programming, such as MTV, Discovery, ESPN, Nickelodeon, and Syfy.

Therefore, advertisers are better able to select networks that closely parallel their product's user profile. Cable penetration of U.S. television households (including DBS homes, described below), is estimated to be well over 60 percent by the year 2000, making its distribution close to that of the broadcast networks.

○ *Direct Broadcast Satellite.* DBS service uses digital satellite technology for direct delivery to homes. DBS offers more channels than cable or over-the-air broadcasting (especially for pay-per-view and sports), and better picture and sound quality. DBS is able to reach areas that are not wired for cable; therefore, advertisers may reach additional households. Currently, DBS services, such as DirecTV and Dish Network, are in 6 million U.S. households.

○ *Syndicated.* Syndicated television is the distribution of programming directly to individual stations by a supplier or studio, and varies from market to market. This collection of unaffiliated stations provides another source of programming for consumers. Syndicated programs can either air on network affiliates during times not filled by network programming or at any time on independent, or nonnetwork-affiliated stations. These shows can be originally produced (*Star Trek, Jeopardy,* and *Oprah*), or off-network reruns (*Seinfeld* and *Home Improvement*).

• **Radio.** Radio reaches over 90 percent of all consumers and is considered a mass communications vehicle. Studies have shown that consumer recall of radio ads can be close to that of television, yet radio ads are generally much less expensive. Radio is used primarily as a frequency medium, sending many messages over a relatively short period of time. Radio also allows for targeting of messages by selection of station formats that match listener profiles.

Print Media

Print media is divided into four major categories: newspapers, magazines, directories, and direct mail.

• **Newspapers.** Newspapers are a good medium for targeting individuals at or near the purchase decision. Newspapers may be national (*USA Today*), regional (*Los Angeles Times*), or local (*Herndon Times*). They also may be general in scope (*Washington Post*), have a specific content (*Wall Street Journal*), and be circulated daily or weekly. Advantages of newspapers as a medium include a sense of immediacy, ample space for detailed messages, geographic flexibility, and a short lead time between creative development and ad placement. Disadvantages include cluttered ad environment, high initial expenses, poor reproduction quality, and limited targeting capabilities.

• **Magazines.** Magazines, through their editorial features and pictures, forge relationships with their readers that often last over time. There are several types of magazines: consumer or business and vertical or horizontal. There are hundreds of consumer magazines targeting every demographic and psychographic segment. A *vertical publication* addresses a particular interest or industry (it is very singular in its editorial coverage). For example, a magazine such as *Barron's* is considered a vertical publication because it only deals with the subject of finance and is targeted to financial specialists. A publication such as *Fortune* is considered a *horizontal publication* because it deals with the general subject of business and its readership can be comprised of executives in any variety of industries or professions.

Magazines provide advertisers with the ability to target audiences and use copy-intensive creative messages not suited for television or radio.

Numerous studies have assessed the effectiveness (impact on the reader's recall) of: magazine size, coloration versus black and white ads, spread units (multiple pages) versus single-page ads, and the ad's location within the magazine. For example, an ad placed on the Table of Contents page has a 25 percent higher consumer recall than ads placed in the middle of the magazine, according to a Roper Starch study. Creative execution ultimately has the greatest impact on recall.

- **Directories.** Directories play a vital role in consumer and business-to-business marketing communications as well as in attracting new customers to an established business. They can be a national listing of businesses by industry, such as the *Thomas Guide*, or a more local version such as the telephone *Yellow Pages*. The advantage is the low cost; the disadvantage is the advertising clutter.
- **Direct Mail.** Direct mail is a growing method of advertising. Direct mail, either catalogs or letters, targets specific audiences through the use of databases and mailing lists. The advantage of direct mail is its cost-effectiveness. The disadvantage is the lingering perception of the medium as junk mail. Direct mail is covered in detail in Chapter 13, "Direct Marketing."

Out-of-Home Media

Outdoor media reaches consumers in every place that they can be exposed to a selling message outside the home. The name of this medium has changed from outdoor advertising to out-of-home media (OOH). OOH is used primarily to promote awareness and as reminder advertising. Out-of-home media usually is the most cost-efficient of all media forms, despite the high up-front production costs. These costs should be balanced against the reach of out-of-home media, which is often in excess of 85 or 90 percent of a market's population. Another key advantage is that the advertiser can specifically target desired groups. For example, recent out-of-home advertising formats have been developed to reach consumers where they work, travel, shop, and spend their leisure time. The key disadvantages to out-of-home media are its lack of ability to communicate detailed information and no audio capabilities with which to attract its audience. Outdoor media represents a mix of billboards/building murals, stadiums, transit stations, transit signs, and aerial advertising.

- **Billboards/Building Murals.** Unlike other media where ad pages or the number of tele-vision spots can simply be increased, outdoor advertising has a finite universe, where supply and demand for the best billboard sites makes for an active and volatile marketplace. For example, billboards for gas stations are strategically placed before major freeway exits, and major movie releases show their celebrities on huge billboards in Hollywood. The new digital billboards allow a campaign to be initiated within a few days. Murals typically are located on the sides of buildings in metropolitan areas such as Los Angeles and New York where they are seen by large audiences.

  A key advantage of billboards is size. Billboards can exceed 1,000 square feet on a single sign. Signs of this size attract consumer attention. However, a disadvantage is that messages must be brief and simple in order to maximize the impact on the audience (who may be passing by at 65 mph). Another key disadvantage is the regulatory limitations. State and local anti-billboard legislation has created certain limitations on the outdoor advertising market, and there are a relatively fixed number of outdoor signs available to marketers. Some states have banned traditional outdoor billboards, and other states have limitations on size and location.

- **Stadiums.** Stadium advertising can be located on scoreboards and placards/banners surrounding the stadium complex. These signs provide promotional messages to the large crowds at sporting events or concerts, the television audience, and subsequent print photos of the event.

- **Transit Stations.** Transit stations include airport, subway, train and bus stations, and bus stops. Messages at these locations target the relatively captive audience of commuters and business/leisure travelers.

- **Transit Signs.** Transit signs include truck siding, taxi signs, bus signs, and mobile billboards also known as street blimps. Messages on these mobile media target the millions of people who are in transit each day.

- **Aerial Advertising.** Aerial advertising includes blimps (such as the Goodyear airships' coverage of sporting events), airplane banners (such as for Coppertone suntan lotion at the beach), and skywriting. The advantages of these media are that they are highly visible, create attention, are memorable, and are fun for the consumer to watch. The disadvantages are the vagaries of the weather, short duration of visibility, and lack of editorial content.

Internet

The primary interactive medium is the Internet. The Internet's infrastructure allows for the two-way transmission of text, high-resolution and 3-D graphics, video, and audio signals. For marketers, the Internet offers six key advantages: one-to-one communications, globality, cost efficiency, convenient purchasing capabilities, product demonstration quality, and a short lead time.

1. The Internet's greatest potential lies in its ability to create one-to-one communications that are tailored to the needs of a specific individual viewing a marketer's Internet site. Programming technology allows advertisers to customize Internet pages to a particular user. This can be based on a user's answer to a question, the user's previous Web site, or from information stored in a cookie in the user's computer (a *cookie* is a special file that records relevant information about the user).

2. The Internet is a global medium. A site may be viewed by anyone having access to the Internet. The Internet can create a global marketer out of even the smallest retail store or enterprise.

3. The relatively low cost of using the Internet. The initial production costs will vary depending on the complexity of the site. The ongoing maintenance costs are minimal and consist of updating the material and the hosting cost.

4. The Internet's ability to conduct electronic commerce. Banks and credit card companies are leading the way in making the Internet safe for electronic commerce. Software is now available that enables secure transactions, through encryption and digital signature authentication.

5. It is ideal for demonstrating products in use due to the high quality of its video.

6. The extremely short lead time. Ads on Web sites can be seen by customers the day they are completed, not weeks or months later as is often the case for television or magazines.

Social Marketing

With the accessibility of the Internet, consumers have learned to use this platform as a way to engage and network with others. Sites like MySpace, Twitter, and Facebook have become a catalyst for individual expression. Marketers are starting to leverage these social platforms and others as a means for engaging in two-way dialogue with their customers, gaining feedback on products and services that often help inform product development.

Search Engine Marketing and Optimization

In the late 1990s, early 2000s, as the Internet grew in popularity, so did the need to navigate the Web. Search engines like Google, Yahoo, and MSN emerged as the dominant players in this business. Today, they sell advertising space on their search engines in the form of actual ads, as well as pay-per-word key words. For advertisers, when a consumer uses a search engine and types in the words *hair spray* or *sneakers* or *post office,* much of the search response and hierarchy of that response is controlled by advertisers who pay through key word searches and various search engine optimization techniques. As of 2009, this continues to be an emerging area of marketing that many brands are still researching.

Other Media

Other interactive media such as CD-ROMS, interactive television, and interactive kiosks in shopping malls hold significant promise for marketers. Other media that can provide advertising opportunities include the time preceding movies and videos. Both movies and videos are excellent at showing the product and are widely viewed. However, target audience receptivity to the intrusiveness in an otherwise relaxing experience is still in question.

Media Scheduling

The goal of media scheduling is to maximize advertising exposure among the target audience within the assigned budget. The greater the frequency of exposure, the greater the awareness and potential purchase of the product. Media scheduling consists of geographic, timing, and format strategies.

Geographic Strategies

Geographic or regional strategies help determine where to place the advertising nearest the target audience, therefore making the media scheduling more cost-effective. The advertising budget is usually invested where sales are strongest in order to counter inroads by competitors or to develop weaker sales areas—on a broad national scale, low-impact approach, or a local high-impact schedule. Often, geographic spending options can be analyzed by the relationship between brand sales or category sales and the population distribution, on a market-by-market basis. For example, the four-wheel-drive market is particularly strong in Colorado and the New England states.

Timing/Scheduling Strategies

In media planning there are four basic scheduling strategies: continuity, flighting, pulsing, and dayparts.

- **Continuity.** Provides a consistent advertising presence at all times. This strategy is used if there is strong competition or the customer can enter the market at any time, such as a need for a new mattress.
- **Flighting.** Creates waves of alternating intervals of advertising activity and hiatus periods. This strategy is used for seasonally specific products, for low budgets, and when the customer is likely to remember the product or brand for at least some time period. Seasonal strategies, normally measured in quarter years (fall, winter, spring, summer), can be used to determine how best to allocate advertising budgets by time of year, based on sales data and product usage. Media costs should be evaluated by season, since media costs can vary for each quarter. For example, allergy

medication is needed primarily in the spring and fall; therefore, advertising is purchased for those periods.

- **Pulsing.** Occurs when there is a continuous basic level of advertising with bursts of superimposed additional spending. This strategy is used during key selling periods, such as the beginning of the fall television season and sweeps weeks.
- **Dayparts.** Are specific segments of a broadcast day, specifically early morning, daytime, early fringe, prime access, primetime, late night, late news, early evening news, weekend, kids, sports. Each daypart has a specific audience that can be analyzed and quantified, and then a cost is assigned. A primetime show, such as *Two and a Half Men* will have a larger audience than an early morning show and thus command a higher advertising fee.

Advertising research with consumer purchase panels (Information Resources Inc., 1991, and John Philip Jones, 1995) has demonstrated that advertising can have a short-term impact on sales. Jones' analyses demonstrated the largest effect was in the first week of a consumer's exposure to a commercial. This finding refuted an advertising conventional wisdom that a product needs at least three marketing communications exposures to gain consumer acceptance. Further, Jones determined that the quality of the advertising message is key, as the strongest advertising campaign generated six times the amount of immediate sales as the weakest campaign. Jones determined that brands often lose sales in weeks not advertised and thus recommends that a brand advertise on a continuous basis. Both IRI and Jones determined that an advertising campaign can have a long-term (year two and three) impact on sales, but only if the advertising campaign has a short-term sales effect first. Only a series of short-term gains builds into long-term gains.

Format Strategies

Creative messages may be tailored to suit the specific audience demographics or psychographics for specific programming types or formats. Radio, television, magazine, and newspaper formats are each targeted to specific audiences.

- Radio program formats include news/talk, sports, business, rock, urban contemporary, classic, and jazz.
- Television formats include sitcoms, dramas, news, talk, sports, and news magazines.
- Magazine formats include women's interest, men's interest, hobbies, outdoors, and profession specific.
- Newspaper formats (sections) include main, sports, business, and style.

Media Buying

The goal of media buying is to purchase time or space with the greatest reach or exposure at the most advantageous cost to the client. Media buying consists of determining media costs and purchasing methods.

Media Costs

Media cost is the price paid for the media and is determined by the number of people the particular medium reaches or is exposed to, the value of the target audience, and the prestige of the medium. An *exposure*, also known as an *impression*, takes place when a member of the target audience views, hears, reads, or clicks on a message one time. Reach, or *coverage*, is the percentage of a given population base that reads a particular print vehicle or the percentage of homes that can receive a broadcast signal in a given geographic area. For example, a television show with a large audience, such as the Superbowl or the final episode of *Seinfeld,* can charge more than a show with a smaller audience. Costs can be quantified and compared as costs-per-thousand exposures or CPMs (M is the Roman numeral for thousand).

Purchasing Methods

Advertisers purchase both broadcast time and print space in two basic ways: long-term and short-term. Long-term (up-front) requires commitment of funds for at least three-quarters of the time of the activity, January to September, for example. In exchange, a long-term commitment usually earns concessions from the media sellers, usually in terms of protection of audience delivery. For example,

television advertising during the Olympics requires a long-term commitment with a large up-front payment; however, this payment is tied to a certain guaranteed audience level. If these levels are not met due to lower than expected viewership of the Olympics, then the advertiser usually receives a rebate.

Short-term (flighted) purchases allow for greater flexibility of advertiser budgets but may result in higher pricing or lack of desirable programming. The decision of which method to use is an important one and is decided by advertisers with their agencies.

5. Creative Process

After the advertising strategies and the media have been determined, the creative department takes the strategy and crafts a compelling message that will be presented to the public. The creative process determines what language and which visuals will inspire the audience to accept the product, service, or idea.

Most creative departments at advertising agencies are staffed by teams of copywriters (or verbalists) and art directors (or visualists). These individuals, collectively known as creatives, develop the ideas that become print ads, posters, radio commercials, digital experiences, and television spots. They write the headlines, design the visuals, and go to the selected location to help organize the photo shoot or filming of the commercial. The creative process includes idea generation, creative format/tone, and message delivery.

The following steps are processes that creative departments go through, but they tend to happen in a less linear fashion. The processes are more organic and do not always follow a regimented protocol.

Idea Generation

Advertising creatives come up with selling ideas by several methods:

- Keeping in touch with a variety of current aspects of society
- Brainstorming with colleagues
- Long hours of concentrated thinking

> *In the 1940s, a copy writer named James Young at the J. Walter Thompson advertising agency published a methodical albeit somewhat tongue-in-cheek five-step process for idea generation:*
> *An idea is a new combination of old elements. How do you get ideas? The mind follows five steps.*
>
> 1. *Gather [information]…specific…and general.*
> 2. *Take one fact, turn it this way and that. Bring two facts together and see how they fit. Partial ideas will come to you.*
> 3. *By and by, you will get very tired of trying your puzzle together. Drop the whole subject. Turn the problem over to your subconscious mind. Go to the theatre or movies.*
> 4. *Out of nowhere the Idea will appear. Eureka! I have it!*
> 5. *The final shaping and development of the idea to practical usefulness.*
>
> *Source:* James Webb Young, *A Technique for Producing Ideas,* NTC Business Books, 1994.
> Reprinted with permission, McGraw-Hill.

One copywriter reports that the "Eureka!" moment usually comes while he is walking his dog or taking a shower. Therefore, he keeps notepads and pens in every room of his house.

Creative Format/Tone

There are no formulas for the creative process; however, there are some historical practices that creative teams have used to create effective advertising. One of the most familiar steers the customers' thought processes using a four-step communication model known as AIDA (create Attention, create Interest, create a Desire to buy, and create a stimulus to Action).

The tone of the ad (humor, drama, informative) can evoke an emotion that sparks the target audience's response to the ad and ultimately to action. Formats may be shortened for reminder advertising or expanded for persuasive advertising without changing the tone.

Once the creative team hits upon an idea that brings the strategy and brand to life, they typically develop the details of the idea in a rough form. This could be simple sketches for a print ad, a script for a radio commercial, or a storyboard for a television commercial.

Most creative departments have creative directors who operate much like the editors of a newspaper. It is their job to make sure that the creative output maintains the agency's standards. After an agency develops the creative work and internally approves this work, the work is presented to the client. The client presentation typically consists of a meeting where storyboards are presented and scripts are read and acted out by the agency creatives. After input from the client (and sometimes the client's lawyers), many ideas are reworked and then re-presented to the client. In some cases, the storyboards are then shown to consumers in qualitative work to see how they receive the idea.

Once all of the reviews have been cleared, the storyboard is ready to become a television commercial, the script a radio spot, or the layout a print ad. These elements are then taken to the production department.

COMMUNICATION MODEL (AIDA)	
1. Attention	Make people pay attention to an ad often through humorous/dramatic/informative statements, visuals, or music.
2. Interest	Make people feel "I'm interested" in hearing more about the product's features and benefits.
3. Desire	Make people feel "I need or want that" by relating the features and benefits to the target audience.
4. Action	Make people feel "I must get that now" by indicating a short time of offering.

EXAMPLE OF BROADCAST PRESENTATION	
Attention:	"Attention hay fever sufferers."
Interest:	"There is a new therapy for your allergy."
Desire:	"All doctors agree, this works every time."
Action:	"Try your free sample this week only at your local pharmacy."
Brand ID:	Company/Product name

EXAMPLE OF PRINT PRESENTATION	
Attention:	Headline copy and visual
Interest:	Subhead copy and visual
Desire:	Body copy (writing that tells what the product/service does)
	Tagline (a few words or short phrase typically used to describe the essence of an advertiser's business)
Action:	Coupon, listing of sale days
Brand ID:	Company name/logo

Message Delivery

A key creative decision is determining how the message will be delivered. A product may be presented by itself, with a voice-over, or by a spokesperson, also known as the testimonial. A testimonial is a method used to attract attention to ads and may be delivered by persons viewed by consumers as attention-getting or credible. Spokespersons may be individuals, to allow concentration on the message, or a group, to indicate a group belongingness or bandwagon effect. It is important to fit the spokesperson with the product, brand, and target audience.

- **Celebrity Spokesperson.** Using a retired movie star reflecting on the fact that even celebrities get hay fever and this product can provide relief for him or her is a good way to use a celebrity spokesperson. Some companies have moved from isolating only one celebrity endorser for their products because of the public problems of so many celebrities (drug use, messy divorces) as well as the high cost of hiring them on an exclusive basis. Today, many advertisers are willing to share celebrities in order to keep costs down. Consumers, however, sometimes feel skeptical about celebrities,

knowing that these spokespersons are paid very well for their time.

- **Everyday Spokesperson.** A spokesperson can be an everyday real person, or noncelebrity endorser, who also can be very effective. For example, a jogger who talks believably about her hay fever suffering.
- **Expert Spokesperson.** A spokesperson can be an expert on a particular subject. For example, using a leading university researcher providing a compelling testimonial on lab results regarding the new hay fever medication.
- **Fictional Spokesperson.** A spokesperson also can be a fictional character. For example, an animated box of medicine might humor the hay fever sufferer. Advantages of using a fictional character include creative control and the low cost.
- **Product with Voice-over.** An advertisement may show only the product and have a voice from off-screen, known as a voice-over, describe the product attributes. This method is simple, inexpensive, and focuses attention on the product.
- **Product without Voice-ove.r** This method focuses on the product and may be silent or have music. This unusual approach is used as an attention-getting device; however, it lacks the ability to describe the product.
- **Consumer Only.** This method shows the consumer's reaction to the product, its use, or its results. It is helpful in suggesting an image or connection to the target audience. However, it does not allow the viewer to remember the look of the product or its packaging. This method may be best for advertising of services, such as insurance.

6. Advertising Production Process

Each broadcast, digital, new media, and print advertisement is a unique production, with many unpredictable elements, such as the weather, personnel, equipment, props, and animals. The approaches outlined below are commonly used by most advertising agencies.

Content Production Process

The approval of a script or storyboard for production initiates a complicated, risky, and possibly expensive process. Any type of content is a custom-built creative work that can be plain or elaborate. Views on how the content should look or sound will be as varied as the people reviewing it. It is the advertising agency's job to meld these divergent points of view into a cohesive, concrete, and systematic approach.

Producer/Director

As a first step, the agency will assign a producer, who manages the entire production process, including:

- **Scheduling (Establishing and Meeting a Schedule).** Scheduling and budgeting should be discussed in advance of storyboard development. Content production can take anywhere from a few days to 6 to 8 weeks for simple film and video projects to 12 to 16 weeks for more complex projects with heavy special effects and computer graphics. Projects that include Web site design and creation can take 4 to 6 months.
- **Budgeting (Establishing and Controlling the Budget).** The cost of a production is determined by the number of locations, number of actors, and other variables that are written into the script. The overall look and feel desired determines the production value required, whether it should be shot on film or video, high def or standard def, and so on.
- **Creative (Effectively Translating the Script or Storyboard into Film).** Advertising agencies usually do not handle production in-house. Instead, they contract with a production company to take the job from script through delivery of dailies or data files if shot in a digital format. Agencies also contract with an editorial service, a visual effects company, and music composers to edit the dailies into a finished commercial.

The production process is a collaborative effort. The agency producer's first step is to meet with the authors of the storyboard and the account manager to discuss the assignment in detail. Out of these discussions, the agency producer will write specifications to be provided to the production companies and editorial services that will be asked to bid on the job.

The director is an important influence on how a commercial will look and feel and how much it will cost. Usually, an advertising agency will spend a lot of time and effort on the selection of the director. In many cases, clients will take an active role in the prebid discussion and specification review, either directly or through an outside television production consultant.

Cost Estimation

The production company and subcontracting suppliers will estimate their costs to produce a job, after receipt of the bid specifications from the agency, and submit standard industry bid forms to the advertising agency. The agency evaluates and aggressively negotiates the bids. The agency then prepares a cost estimate based on these bids. A typical cost estimate will include the following major categories: production, editing, talent, casting service, music, color correction, on-screen typeset, and other (taxes, agency travel, and so forth).

Preproduction

Upon award of the production contract(s), the preproduction process starts. This is an intensive development period. The advertising agency's team of producer, writer, and art director work closely with the production company producer, the director, and various specialists to work out production details. Casting is initiated, potential locations are scouted, and/or set sketches are developed. The production company will hire a crew for shooting the commercial or content.

The Shoot

The shoot, or actual filming, will move smoothly if preparation has been meticulous, although unexpected events often arise. For example, problems often occur when shooting external locations with uncooperative weather or when working with temperamental children and pets.

A set is a crowded place. The film crew may number up to 25 people or more, plus the cast, plus the agency team consisting of the producer, writer, art director, and account manager. There also are attendees from the client. If the shoot is to proceed efficiently, it is essential that a strict protocol be followed on the set. The director controls the shooting day while communicating with his or her crew, the talent, and the agency producer.

Postproduction

Once shooting is completed, the producer will have the dailies sent to the editor. Typically the agency team will sit through the first viewing of the dailies as they are being loaded into the computer. At this stage, selected takes are marked.

The editor will then assemble the footage into a rough-cut of the final commercial. Once the rough-cut has been approved by the client, then the agency will add final music, sound effects, and if called for in the script, a voice-over talent (announcer). Both the advertising agency and the client then screen the commercial for the final time, prior to airing the commercial or uploading the content.

DIGITAL PRODUCTION PROCESS

Digital encompasses many different types of productions, and each has their own unique challenges. Developing Web sites for clients can often be a very different process than developing a Web site on your own. Typically, clients will have an infrastructure built out by an Information Technology (IT) team that has measures in place to account for security and compatibility of hardware and software used throughout the organization. Typical types of projects include:

- **Web site Development.** Large-scale site builds and campaign microsites
- **Online Advertising.** Standard banner campaigns, rich media banner campaigns, e-mail, and search

Most agencies follow the standard steps below.

Kick-Off

During the Project Kick-Off phase, the producer assigns a team to the project and starts to develop some initial project plans to get a rough idea of timing and costs.

- Present draft project plan to team.
- Assign project team: roles, communication, expectations.
- Brief team: supply research, materials.

Discovery and Planning

The purpose of the discovery phase is really to understand exactly what the client is trying to accomplish. There are often many different solutions available to achieve any given goal. The agency partners with the client to validate what the best solution is and digs deeper into the business drivers, context, and risks. Additionally, the discovery process opens the lines of communication and enables teams to establish relationships.

- Conduct interviews.
- Perform research and analysis.
- Develop creative brief.
- Create visual explorations/mood boards.

Concept/Creative Development

The creative development phase is much like any other ideation phase in other groups within the agency. The creative teams attempt to pull together concepts that help deliver the overall message of the campaign. During the concepting phase, it is important for the producer to act as the voice of reason and make sure that the ideas being developed can be producible within the limitations of technology and costs.

- Have brainstorming session.
- Refine ideas.
- Prepare logistics checkpoint.
- Prepare presentation of ideas with any visual support.
- Develop creative guidelines.
- Develop high-level information architecture.
- Finalize project plan (scope, timeline, task delegation, client team, communications plan).
- Present ideas and plan to client.
- Obtain client approval of idea and plan.

Design

This is the phase when ideas are transformed into reality. Through the discovery phase and then concept development, the agency finally arrives at the primary idea. This phase informs how the online experience will take shape. The project scope for construction/production is finalized, the site architecture is drafted, final design elements are developed, and the groundwork for the technical and information design is laid out. The goal of this phase is to draft the road map that will be used in production/construction.

- Develop initial design directions.
- Develop interaction design.
- Develop copy.
- Develop prototype.
- Test.
- Obtain creative lock (design direction and copy is approved).
- Perform photo shoot.

Production

After planning exactly what needs to be developed, this is the phase when it actually gets built.

All creative assets and flash modules needed for final coding are developed and optimized. In addition to all of the html container pages, the agency will move into final production of all applications associated with the Web site, banner, or e-mail campaign. Quality Assurance (QA) test plans are developed to check the stability of the application, and usability test plans will be produced and distributed to the team for testing.

- Brief the production teams (internal and external).
- Purchase/negotiate stock photography.
- Develop flash/html.
- Develop data tier.
- Proofread QA.
- Integrate final pieces from vendors (metrics, rich media, software).

Delivery/Execution

- Deliver to client.
- Monitor research.
- Track results.
- Document site/event (video and photos/testimonials).

Art Production and Print Production Processes

Most large advertising agencies have specialized art and print production departments. These departments are responsible for maintaining the highest standards of quality at a reasonable cost in the conversion of creative works into final printed advertisements.

After a client approves a print ad concept, the account manager notifies the art production and print production departments that there is an ad scheduled to be produced. At this point a production team (consisting of an art producer, project manager, and a print producer) is assigned the task of producing the ad. Production is moved forward in two phases. The first phase is the art production phase in which the art is produced with a photographer or illustrator. The print producer handles the second phase, in which the printed materials are produced.

Art Production Process

The art producer acts in a similar capacity to a broadcast producer, managing the production schedule, budgeting, photographer/illustrator search, cost estimating, and any postproduction digital work the photographer may do. The art producer works with the creative team to determine what photography or illustrations will be appropriate for the execution of the ad, taking into account the schedule and the budget. The art producer also will discuss usage rights that pertain to how long a selected piece of art will be used and in what publication(s) the ad will be seen. Usage rights are a key element in determining how much a photographer or illustrator will charge for his or her work. The art producer is responsible for the following steps in the process:

- **Production Schedule.** Once an art producer is assigned to the project, he or she will evaluate the creative and determine a schedule. The schedule will include time for a photographer or illustrator search, bidding the job, preproduction, shoot, and postproduction.
- **Photographer or Illustrator Search.** Like a director on a commercial shoot, the photographer or illustrator is an important influence on how a print ad will look and feel and how much it will cost. The art producer works with the creative team to determine the best photographer and illustrator to fulfill the creative vision and bring the ad to life. Portfolios and Web sites are referenced, and a short list is drawn up for client approval.
- **Cost Estimation.** The art producer will determine the usage rights needed by the client and pair that with all the creative needs to bid the job. As a rule, most jobs are triple bid with three photographers or illustrator to ensure that the client is getting a fair price for the scope of work required. It is the responsibility of the art producer to evaluate and negotiate the bids.
- **Pre-Production.** Upon award of the job, the preproduction process starts. The creative team writes specs for casting, locations, and styling. The photographer hires a crew to handle the casting, location scouting, set building, prop styling, wardrobe styling, and hair/make-up styling. Prior to the shoot a formal preproduction meeting will be held with the creatives, art producer, account management, client, and photographer to review the overall creative goals; get formal approval on casting, locations, scouting, styling; and review the shoot and postproduction schedule.
- **The Shoot.** The shoot is fairly straightforward, if the preproduction process has gone well. The creatives, art producer, account team, and client attend the shoot. The art producer is responsible for getting legal clearance on any trademarked props and obtaining talent releases from the models. As with a commercial shoot, there is a communication protocol to follow on set. The photographer and creatives work closely to ensure that the vision is fulfilled. The art producer acts as a liaison between the photographer/creatives and the account team/client.
- **Post-Production.** After the shoot, the art director makes selects from all images shot. Those selects are presented to the client for approval. Once the client has approved the images, the photographer's retoucher will bring all the selects together to create the final images. Most photographers work in a digital medium and partner with a retoucher to ensure that all final images have the photographer's signature look and feel. The art producer works with the creatives, photographer, and retoucher to ensure that the overall creative goals are met on time and within budget. Once the photographer's retoucher is finished, the art producer gives the image to the print producer, who will take the image into the studio for final retouching and prep for printing.

Print Media Schedules and Requirements

The print producer is responsible for verifying the print media schedule that has been approved, the creative work, and the sizes and any special requirements that the publication(s) may need when the ad(s) are completed and shipped for insertion in publications. This process can be easy when there are only one or two publications involved. However, in some circumstances, the sizing and scheduling process can become very complex. For example, if there is an ad that is approved to run in a variety of publications each with different sizes, such as a magazine, a newspaper, and an out-of-home poster that may be printed as large as $16'' \times 48''$, then it will be necessary to prepare separate layouts and designs to accommodate the additional sizes.

Most publications require that agencies deliver the finished ad to the publication as early as four to six weeks before they are on newsstands. Daily newspapers will accept black and white ads as late as one day before printing; however, full color ads for newspapers require much longer lead times. In the future, with the advent of digital technology, many magazines and newspapers will accept ads for both black and white and color much later than they have in the past.

Building the Final Page Layout

The print producer will work with the creative group and review the ad sizes and schedules so that the art director can start to produce the final page layouts. The term most commonly used to refer to the final page layout is mechanical. Mechanicals are produced with a computer program that indicates the ad size with crop marks to the outside of the page area, plus all sized and positioned graphic elements such as photos and illustrations.

After all of the advertising agency's personnel (the print producer, creative team, art buyer, account executive, and legal staff) are satisfied that all of the elements are correct in an ad, it is presented to the client for approval. Once the client approves the ad, the print production process moves into its final stage, and the approved ads and materials are sent to the publications for printing.

7. Execution
After production is completed, the broadcast spot is aired, the print ad is run, or the banner ad on a Web site is posted.

8. Results Research
Marketing research, typically called tracking research, is often conducted to assess the impact of an advertising campaign, which will assist in the formulation of the next campaign. The best tracking research informs marketers about the return-on-investment (ROI) of the campaign and provides recommendations about channel mix and media level as well as advertising response.

ADVERTISING—INTERNATIONAL
by McCann Erickson

International advertising has expanded dramatically over the last 20 years. This growth is a direct result of increasing globalization of business and standardization of products and brands. Coupled with the growth of media availability, especially digital, across all markets and the growing sophistication of consumers, it is now possible to standardize campaigns to achieve strategic control over brand development and achieve financial savings.

Advantages/Disadvantages

The primary advantages for international campaigns are that they develop a consistent brand image on a multicountry basis; provide a greater management control of the brand; reach a large, selected audience; and can be very cost-efficient in terms of production and media expenditures. Multinational advertising can promote a consistent brand image so that a brand achieves increased awareness and a positive profile that can maximize sales opportunities in many countries. Multinational advertising can be cost-efficient in production terms. For example, if television is being employed, frequently only one basic commercial is used with common music, a common logo, and only the voice-over is produced in the local language.

The primary disadvantage of international advertising is that, despite movements toward what is often called the Global Village where local differences are reduced, markets can still differ dramatically in terms of consumer behavior, demographics, and economic conditions. These differences limit the effectiveness of global advertising and its ability to promote products and services. In addition, legislation can exist at a national level that constrains advertising content. For example, Scandinavians have strict legislation about advertising targeted at children, and Germans allow no directly comparative advertising, or below-cost sales promotion.

Use of humor is also very different across countries, and definitions of taste and decency can vary widely. Recognition of personalities differs and perceptions of the advantages and disadvantages of countries of origins can vary widely.

International Advertising Development

Products or services that are used and recognized similarly across cultures, such as high-tech goods, petroleum, and business-to-business products benefit from common consumer role and usage, aspirations and desires, and should adapt well to a global approach to international advertising. Luxury goods and products with designer names, or personal care products that reflect the worldwide human desire for status and acceptability also usually work successfully in a multicountry campaign. However, products or services that evoke a personal or cultural response, or taste preference (such as food, drink, and household products) usually favor a local domestic approach.

It is also important to consider the culture of the company when deciding whether an international approach is appropriate. Some companies have a very centralized culture where leadership from the center is accepted, but others are used to a high level of local autonomy, and indeed this might be reflected in the kinds of people joining those companies and the way they are remunerated.

Historically companies aimed for a "One Sight, One Sound, One Sell" model of advertising, usually associated with Coca-Cola in the 1970s and 1980s. Now they are usually more ready to "Glocalise" campaigns with varying degrees of local adaptation, transliteration, or reexecution to a common theme.

This results in five distinct levels of creative consistency, which might vary for the same product within regions or for different products within a brand range. (See Figure 10.1.)

International Advertising Development Strategy Model

- **Level 1.** Appropriate where there is a high level of uniformity between the structure of the product category from country to country, where the role and usage of the product are essentially the same, and where consumers are similar in attitudes and socioeconomic factors. It requires a similar level of media literacy, that is, the ability to understand the language of advertising. The culture of the company is conducive to strong central leadership.
- **Level 2.** Implies the need for more extensive editing of the material to accommodate local

Figure 10.1 Five Levels of Creative Consistency

Source: McCann Erickson

differences in the market, and/or "transliteration" of the verbal proposition, due to having no direct local equivalent. Expensive video footage or photography would remain essentially unchanged.

- **Level 3.** Means that commercials are reshot using the same idea, but using local actors or showing local scenes. It can also show significantly different product usage or target consumers. It is the level most associated with the world's most extensive campaign: MasterCard's "Priceless." The core global selling idea of responsible spending resonates everywhere, but how people use money and what they value most differs greatly.
- **Level 4.** Means that conditions are very different locally and perhaps the culture of the company only extends to people agreeing to a common positioning for the product. It can also mean that a maximum fit with local cultures is needed, as is often the case with highly cultural categories like beer, where any foreign scenarios would simply be ignored by consumers.
- **Level 5.** Becoming rare for international companies, except those that are structured so that each market is totally independent and requires top-level people who would not agree to handing over control of a large part of their marketing responsibility. It can also apply to companies that have grown by acquisition of strong local brands that cannot easily be amalgamated into regional or global brands. The health-care category has many examples of this.

International Client Relations

Simplistic Model

The flow of client/agency contact, known as client relations, underpins the development of multicountry advertising. In the development of a multicountry campaign, the client must determine how much scope is given to the local management and the local agencies. Also how much input from the countries needs to be fed back to the center and how central decisions and policies are to be dissem-

inated and overall progress is to be coordinated and monitored.

The simplest level of coordination lines is shown as a box and assumes that there is contact between client and agency at more than just the HQ level. (See Figure 10.2.)

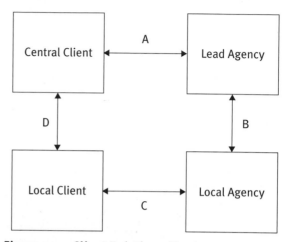

Figure 10.2 Client Relations Chart

The central client and lead advertising agency (Interface A in Client Relations Chart in Figure 10.2) need to be in regular dialogue and work together as a cohesive team. They should determine the overall strategy, the creative message brief, media choice, allocation of budget, and the production methods to be employed. Then each communicates this down to the local level on their own sides (Interfaces B and D) and collects any feedback, or solves any problems. The importance of the local agency and client increases in relation to the level of standardization shown in the pyramid in Figure 10.1 that they are working toward. Finally, the local client and local agency (Interface C) must work together to ensure the optimal cooperation and adaptation and media placement of the communications.

A fundamental principle is that information should flow vertically and horizontally, but never diagonally, which leads to confusion and waste: "Never cross the box."

Hub and Spokes System Model

Since several of the conditions described in relation to the pyramid in Figure 10.1 might apply to a single client across their product ranges and across markets, it is becoming more usual to adopt a "Hub and Spokes" system, where there is a global center (Interface A) in Figure 10.2, and a series of regional or product group-related centers of excellence or hubs.

These typically will be places where the particular product is well understood, where there is expertise in dealing with a particular regional culture (such as Southeast Asia, Latin America, Francophone Africa), or where there are strong subheadquarters that have a high level of control over all marketing aspects.

Local clients and agencies may then report in to these hubs, rather than to the center. There might also be further subhubs to control a multitude of small markets that are essentially treated as one, like the Baltic states or Central America.

ADVERTISING—CASE STUDY

by TBWA\Chiat\Day

Company: Mars Petcare U.S.— PEDIGREE Food for Dogs
Case: The Pedigree Adoption Drive 2008

The Approach: Disruption (TBWA Speak for "changing the rules of the marketplace")

Context
In 2004, TBWA\Chiat\Day and The PEDIGREE Brand worked together to define the brand's core essence. This disruptive brand belief transformed Pedigree from a rational dog food manufacturer *"We make great dog food,"* into an emotionally driven company passionate about dogs *"Everything we do is for the love of dogs."* But to convince dog lovers that they truly love dogs, the company had to do more than just say so. They had to prove it by doing something good for dogs. Pedigree's cause became shelter dogs.

For the last three years, we have helped Pedigree achieve record-breaking business results by tapping into people's desire to give back. Each year Pedigree ups the ante, and we are challenged to outdo past success. But rather than reinvent for the sake of change, we left the original disruptive idea of "help us help dogs" intact, and used the practice of media arts (all the elements of marketing communications) to give it deeper meaning and uncover new ways to engage dog lovers in the cause of dog adoption.

Conventions
The conventional wisdom in the category is that selling dog food is a rational business. Whether listing ingredients or using gimmicks to highlight product benefits, dog food manufacturers have lost sight of what really matters: the dogs themselves. Instead of celebrating people's love for man's best friend, dog food brands relegate dogs to props in the feeding moment.

Insight
All over the world, people love their dogs like their own children and yet dog food manufacturers missed this seemingly universal truth about owning dogs. The opportunity for Pedigree was to stop selling to its customers as "dog owners" and start connecting with them as "dog lovers." By recasting the target through their love for dogs, the key to success was the audience insight that "if you convince me that you truly love dogs, then I'll let you feed mine." This set the course for how Pedigree needed to behave to earn a powerful place in dog lovers' hearts.

(Continued)

The Vision

The PEDIGREE Brand's vision was to own the emotional high ground: to rise above the rational conventions of the category and be the first brand to epitomize loving dogs. This vision would transform Pedigree from a dog food company into a dog loving company.

The Disruption

The brand's heritage as a company founded on a passion for dogs can be shared through the disruption that "everything we do is for the love of dogs." This credo is more than just an advertising platform; it serves as a principle that guides the way the brand behaves at all levels: from internal culture to business practices, from product development to marketing. It positions the PEDIGREE brand's role in culture as an advocate for all dogs and all things canine. And it inspires a system of brand beliefs, which leads to media arts ideas that help PEDIGREE more meaningfully connect with their audience.

The Delivery Tool: Media Arts (How We Engage the Audience in the Idea/Brand)

Championing the dog adoption cause was a game-changing idea that was inspired from the brand belief that "every dog deserves a loving home." This initiative was not only a clear demonstration of the PEDIGREE brand's love for dogs, but also a way for the brand to become something dog lovers were interested in. It marked the first time we were able to translate people's love for dogs into love for a dog food brand. The success of the Adoption Drive not only manifested in record-breaking sales results and positive brand perceptions, but from a media arts perspective, this initiative inspired our audience to want to interact with the brand.

As we approached year three of this campaign, the task was to leverage new insights on how people show they care about causes.

By exploring the landscape of cause marketing, we discovered that causes that make the problem personal succeed in getting people to act. These organizations recognize that in today's society, there are too many causes for people to care about. So whether it is breast cancer, access to clean water, the environment, or even saving dogs, a person's motivation to act is strongly influenced by how close to home the issue is. In other words, the more connected you are to the problem, the more likely you are to help.

Thus, our media arts strategy was to make the problem of shelter dogs more personal and close to home. The creative expression of this was "one dog at a time."

"One dog at a time" was a way to turn an incredibly overwhelming and complicated problem of 4 million dogs that are abandoned every year into a heartbreaking story about Echo, a loving shelter dog who just wanted to go home. This sentiment was our way to reframe the problem. Pedigree's challenge was to make as much of an impact on a local level as we did nationally, and to remind dog lovers that participating, even in a small way, can make a real difference.

The PEDIGREE Adoption Drive kicked off with a pop-up dog adoption center in Times Square in the heart of New York. For two weeks, when America's most enthusiastic dog lovers congregate to attend the Westminster Kennel Club Dog Show, PEDIGREE created a place where you could learn about dog adoption, purchase cause-related merchandise that we designed, and donate to the PEDIGREE Foundation. Most importantly, people could personally spend time with actual shelter dogs and discover for themselves that they are really good dogs caught in unfortunate circumstances.

To promote the PEDIGREE Dogstore, we created special guerrilla installations of individually cut-out dog signs in Central Park and tennis ball drops at other city dog parks directing people to the store. We also created a commercial that ran exclusively on Taxi TV, when cabs were within 10 blocks of the store. PEDIGREE street teams were strategically placed around Times Square and Madison Square Garden, where Westminster was held, to drive additional store traffic. We also invited American television celebrities, such as Kate Walsh, to help out with store press events.

Beyond the PEDIGREE Dogstore, "One dog at a time" inspired a very honest approach to our storytelling. While we chose mass media as a way to tackle this widespread problem, we were careful not to lose the sentiment of making this problem personal. Our creative executions told stories about each dog's journey, from shelter to loving home. To produce this work, we met over 165 wonderful dogs at three local shelters, which we later helped all get adopted. We also visited nine breed rescue groups across the country to document stories about how saving dogs has changed people's lives.

In the end, we produced a collection of 18 documentary-style films and print ads that told the individual stories of Echo, King, Sid, Bailey, Otis, Mary Grace, and many others. We broadcast these stories on television, published them in magazines and newspapers, shared them with bloggers on YouTube, showed them to visitors at the PEDIGREE Dogstore and at other Westminster-related events, and featured them on the PEDIGREE Web site and on our Adoption Drive Facebook community. Our goal was to put as many faces to the problem as we could. Because we knew from our own experiences visiting these shelters, that as soon as you meet these wonderful dogs it becomes impossible not to feel compelled to help.

We also used partnerships to reach consumers in new ways and different places. Led by Pedigree's public relations agency, Weber Shandwick Worldwide, Pedigree partnered with big names such as Martha Stewart and the Celebrity Apprentice in order to generate additional impressions among consumers. Martha Stewart featured the Adoption Drive during her talk show and did a special PEDIGREE insert in *Martha Stewart Living* magazine. *The Celebrity Apprentice* challenged contestants to create a commercial for PEDIGREE, and the winning commercial was featured during the Westminster broadcast.

Pedigree recognized that another important element of the campaign would be to create an online community behind the cause. The PEDIGREE Web site was used as a hub for all things adoption: a donation tracker, adoption guide, and shelter dog stories. A Facebook fan page was created, allowing users to become fans of the Adoption Drive and invite their friends to do the same—over 2,000 people joined within two weeks. PEDIGREE's digital agency, Catapult Marketing, also set up the Million Dog Mosaic, asking dog lovers to upload photos of their dogs to create the largest photo mosaic ever built. Over 25,000 photos were uploaded in the first month alone, and the mosaic now contains more photos than any other online photo mosaic.

The last major piece of our campaign was expanding the numerous ways people get involved in the cause. "One dog at a time" acted as our challenge to give people more ways to help—whether it was donating money through the Westminster Telethon (on-air ads placed during the television presentation), buying cause-related Dogs Rule merchandise, donating through Pedigree food sales, donating money online to the foundation, buying food directly for a local shelter of your choice, searching for adoptable dogs in your neighborhood, or volunteering at a local shelter or animal rescue groups. We created more ways to participate because of the response we had received from dog lovers in years past. And of course all of this information remains accessible to our audience throughout the year on Pedigree.com.

(Continued)

Results

- **PEDIGREE ® Dogstore.** We attracted 50,000 visitors in just two weeks and helped 25 local New York shelter dogs get adopted from the store. In addition, we received another 100 adoption applications, which we gave to Animal Haven, a local animal rescue group we worked with.
- **PR impressions.** Press events held at the PEDIGREE Dog Store helped generate over 91 million branded media impressions in more than 2,100 media outlets and 30 dedicated TV interviews.
- **Fundraising.** To date, we have raised over $600,000 and we are on track to reach the brand's $1,000,000 goal. This brings PEDIGREE total donations over the past three years to over $4 million.
- **Web Traffic.** *Views:* 2.8 million page views (up 27 percent from 2007); average time spent on the site 6 minutes. *Participation:* 300,000 dogs searches were made on our adopt-a-shelter dog search engine; 181,000 drives to dogsrulegear.com; $350,000 donated to the PEDIGREE Foundation online; 2,200 bags of dog food donated to local shelters through the buy-a-bag program; 1,200 people have registered with 449 nonprofit animal rescue organizations to be a volunteer.
- **Adopted Dogs.** Due to the decentralized nature of shelters, it is nearly impossible to estimate the number of dogs saved as a direct result of this campaign. However, during this year's Adoption Drive we distributed 325,000 adoption kits to thank people for adopting a dog from the 4,000 shelters we work with. This brings the grand total to more than 2 million adoption kits since the PEDIGREE Adoption Drive campaign began in 2006.

The remarkable, consistent success of the PEDIGREE Adoption Drive in the United States has inspired Pedigree offices around the world to also champion the dog adoption cause. This year will mark the first time that the brand will launch dog adoption initiatives in five markets across three continents. All this goes to show how the practice of disruption and media arts can help a brand find its soul and connect meaningfully with its audience.

ADVERTISING—CASE STUDY

by Arnold Worldwide

Company: Choice Hostels International—Comfort Inn
Case: Attracting a new target market

The Strategic Communications Challenge

By most standards, Comfort Inn, a midscale hotel, has achieved success. At 98 percent[3], it has the total brand awareness others would envy. It is seen as a good brand for families with children and a good value for the money.[4] Not bad for a brand in a category with 32 well-known competing brands.

But in the hotel industry, awareness alone does not put heads in beds. And family values and good prices arc not terribly sexy. Although the brand was strong overall, it had noticeable chinks in its armor when it came to younger audiences. In fact, among all guests, only 20 percent were under 35.[5] It just was not showing much traction among this elusive younger consumer, who saw the brand as a little stale. Comfort Inn had to secure its position with younger travelers or risk its own long-term security.

Travelers under the age of 35 are more spontaneous in their travel habits and are not always traveling with families. But that is not the only thing they do differently. They also consume products and media in less traditional ways—they are online more. They socialize and connect with friends online, they shop online (69 percent)[6] and bank online (65 percent)[7]. They also play games and watch TV on their computers.

But they are also notoriously cynical about advertising. And they do not think a whole lot of Comfort Inn. So the challenge was to get them to connect with the brand on their own terms, in their world. We needed to bring our message to them and get them to interact with it.

The Objectives

The main objective was to engage online consumers with Comfort Inn to create an emotional connection with the brand and drive revenue. Comfort Inn was already doing a lot to get its message out there—seasonal promotions with value-added offers, a national television buy (cable and broadcast), national print (national magazines and newspapers), in-hotel point-of-sale (POS) materials, and online marketing including microsites and outbound e-mails. But to reach this target, we could not just rely on the approach already taken. We had to get them to think differently about the brand.

The Big Idea

The big idea was to depict a series of awkward or uncomfortable moments playing off of the brand's name as a way to engage this target, using a customized and highly interactive environment—Full Episode Player (FEP) via broadband advertising.

Why Full Episode Players? Why broadband at all? Three reasons: Engagement! Engagement! Engagement! We found distinct differences in the way people consume television versus the way they engage online. The online environment is, by nature, participatory. These consumers are making a conscious decision to consume media by logging on to a specific site. As such, they are more engaged from the start. The attitude toward commercial breaks is also different. Instead of seeing an opportunity to raid the fridge in the traditional two-minute break, the 15- and 30-second breaks for online television are seen as part of the deal. Consumers watch the commercials just as they watch their shows. There can be a downside to all of this wonderful engagement. Burnout. With online viewers, 28 percent grew "tired" of seeing ads compared to 15 percent of television and 19 percent of DVR viewers.[8] Astute advertisers account for this in their online approach.

The key is creating ads that are better suited to the Internet rather than repackaging television spots.[9] The big idea was born. The Full Episode Player offered the perfect platform for engaging this younger target audience in an entertaining environment. FEP is an online video environment housed on a network's Web site where users can watch episodes of their favorite shows. FEPs, as on NBC's Web site, offer multiple points of interaction; viewers can stream shows, view online-only content, play games, and share stories. For advertisers, FEPs offer various opportunities to reach consumers including a branded canvas to house the video, video ad breaks, billboards, active logos, and so forth. FEP viewers accept that in order to view television content, advertisements are part of the package.

(Continued)

Bringing the Idea to Life

To encourage brand engagement with this new audience, we needed to reevaluate the message. Wholesome family fun was not enough to break through to this consumer. We prepared to entertain and engage in a way that was unfamiliar to Comfort Inn. With a series of amusingly "awkward moment" videos that depicted those uncomfortable encounters we can all relate to or sympathize with, we entertained viewers while delivering a simple, memorable message about Comfort Inn. We invited viewers to avoid discomfort in their own lives while finding their "Comfort Zone" at Comfort Inn. The result was a video that made a relevant connection between the brand and the real world the viewers live in. And the videos were just the beginning.

Marrying the "Awkward Moments" campaign to Full Episode Players was the perfect fit. Who is more awkward than the character of Michael Scott on *The Office*? Buying a spot or two in *The Office* on network television would be the simple fix but would not include engagement. This gave us the opportunity to participate in primetime content without the premium. Even better, because we were not limited to 30-second spots alone, we were able to engage and interact with viewers in a way that traditional television does not allow. With multiple executions, the viewers experienced several "awkward moments" while viewing their favorite television programs online, avoiding burnout, and increasing engagement.

Working with NBC, we negotiated ownership of a first-ever customized content sponsorship inclusive of a sweepstakes and user-generated content. Playing on the synergies of the "Awkward Moments" campaign, content from hit shows like *The Office, My Name Is Earl,* and *30 Rock* were available with Comfort Inn as the exclusive sponsor. Viewers were invited to stream "Hilarious Awkward Moments" from the home page of the Full Episode Player. The content consisted of a combination of Comfort Inn "awkward moments" and similar uncomfortable scenes from the hottest NBC shows such as Michael kissing Oscar on *The Office* or Jack advising Liz Lemon on *30 Rock*.

To add further interest and engagement, NBC added a sweepstakes layer. Viewers were invited to enter to win a $5,000 cash prize sweepstakes during two separate sweepstakes time periods. Both the sweepstakes and content sponsorship were heavily promoted on the NBC FEP and included on-air primetime mentions on *My Name Is Earl* during highly rated sweeps weeks (February and May 2008). Additionally, a user-generated component was included in the program that invited viewers to share their own "awkward moments" through online submission.

Results

Engagement of Online Customers

Many industry professionals measure the success of their online execution against the reputed click-thru-rate standard of .03 percent.[10] Based on this, the "Awkward Moments" campaign more than tripled the industry average on NBC.com and completely destroyed it on ABC.com. Consumers online for the sole purpose of watching an episode of *Ugly Betty* noticed our ads and intentionally clicked on them to find out more. This engagement also resulted in Comfort Inn's aided and unaided awareness on both ABC.com and NBC.com to be better than the overall advertiser average on these sites.[11]

Create a Connection with Online Consumers

Customers were not only engaging with the ads, they were laughing at them, identifying with them, and enjoying them. On ABC.com the overall ad rating for Comfort Inn was 53 percent, which was 6 percent higher than the advertiser average.[12] Also, 59 percent rated the ads as entertaining.[13]

The entertainment numbers were also impressive on NBC.com. Of those surveyed, 47 percent rated the Comfort Inn ads as entertaining, 20 percent higher than the average advertiser.[14] In addition, the campaign avoided the burnout trap and was even more well-liked over time. After two quarters of air time, NBC.com viewers increased its "entertaining" score by 10 percent and its "attention-getting" score by 13 percent.[15]

Drive Revenue

The foundation of this campaign was designed to engage visitors and get them to spend some quality time with our brand. But the campaign did more than that. It delivered bookings, too. People who had logged on specifically to catch their favorite television shows actually stopped what they were doing to click on our link and make a reservation. When you add in all the viewers who visited later to make a reservation, the campaign exceeded all expectations.

CORPORATE PROFILES AND AUTHOR BIOGRAPHIES

ARNOLD WORLDWIDE

Arnold Worldwide is an international advertising agency with numerous elite clients, including VW, McDonald's, truth, Royal Caribbean "Great Work Works." Visit Arnold at www.Arnolddc.com.

Karen Riordan

Karen Riordan is President of Arnold, D.C. Ms. Riordan received her BA in English and Speech Communications from Boston College.

McCANN ERICKSON

McCann Erickson is the world's largest advertising network with operations in over 120 countries. Visit McCann at www.mccann.com.

Mike Longhurst

Mike Longhurst is Senior Vice President, Business Development EMEA, and also heads the agency's Global Planet McCann Sustainability consultancy. Mr. Longhurst received his degree in Advertising and Marketing from the University of CDT (now the University of the South Bank, London).

TBWA\CHIAT\DAY

TBWA\Chiat\Day is part of TBWA Worldwide and was recently recognized second on *Advertising Age* magazine's exclusive A-List of top U.S. agencies. TBWA Worldwide is part of Omnicom

Group Inc. (NYSE: OMC) (www.omnicomgroup.com), and creates Disruptive Ideas for global clients. Visit TBWA at www.tbwa.com.

Margaret Keene

Margaret Keene is Group Creative Director TBWA\Chiat\Day L.A. As a child, Ms. Keene was obsessed with commercials. In 1993, she found Chiat\Day and has been a creative force there ever since. Her passion and talent have helped create some of the best work in the agency for Apple, Kinko's, Taco Bell, ABC, EarthLink, Mark Levinson, Nissan, Infiniti, Singapore Airlines, The LA Tap Project, and PUR.

Chris Adams

Chris Adams is the Group Creative Director at TBWA\Chiat\Day L.A. and has been with Chiat\Day since 1994. Mr. Adams has helped sell cars for Nissan and Infiniti, helped Steve Jobs introduce iMacs and iPods, and, most recently, helped turn Pedigree from a dog food company into a dog-loving company.

Suzanne Powers

Suzanne Powers is the Global Strategy Director for TBWA\Worldwide, working across the network's global brands to drive the TBWA\ strategic philosophies and practices of Disruption and Media Arts. Ms. Powers focuses on crafting

global ideas that can help TBWA's brands move at the speed of culture, and is passionately dedicated to nurturing the conversations between brands and their audiences the world over.

Y&R

Y&R, founded in 1923, is headquartered in New York City. Y&R has developed memorable commercial spots for many clients, including Dr Pepper, Virgin, Xerox, Schweppes, and Land Rover. Y&R has 186 offices and 7,000 employees in 80 countries, and was acquired by WPP in 2000. Visit Y&R at www.yr.com.

Belle Frank

Belle Frank is Executive Vice President, Director of Strategy & Research, Y&R. Ms. Frank's awards include Advertising Women of New York, Trailblazing Working Mother of the Year award in 2007. She is on the Board of Directors, Advertising Research Foundation. Ms. Frank received her BA in French from Tufts University and her Ed.M from Harvard University School of Education.

Lora Schulson

Lora Schulson is Executive Director of Content Production, Y&R. Ms. Schulson's awards include Cannes Lions, D&AD, and One Show. Ms. Schulson received her BA from New York University.

Nathy Aviram
Nathy Aviram is Executive Director of Content Production, Y&R. Ms. Aviram's awards include Cannes Lions, D&AD, One Show, and Emmy. Ms. Aviram received her BS from the University of Maryland.

Lara Griggs
Lara Griggs is Senior Vice President at Y&R Brands. Ms. Griggs received her BA in Communications from California State University, at Fullerton.

Megan Sutcliffe
Megan Sutcliffe is Communications Coordinator, Y&R. Ms. Sutcliffe received her BA in Psychology from College of the Holy Cross.

NOTES

1. Luke Sullivan, *Hey Whipple, Squeeze This*, p. 15, John Wiley & Sons, 1998. Reprinted with permission, John Wiley & Sons, Inc.
2. Peter D. Bennett, *Dictionary of Marketing Terms* (Chicago, IL: American Marketing Association, 1995), p. 6. Reprinted with permission.
3. Millward Brown Midscale Advertising Tracking Study, Spring 2008.
4. Ibid.
5. Choice Hotels Guest Tracking Study, 2005, prepared by Market Research and Information Systems.
6. eMarketer.com, ComScore Networks survey, Sept. 18, 2009.
7. Ibid.
8. Millward Brown, 2007.
9. Forbes.com, 2008.
10. Reported by Media Industry Professionals.
11. ABC Exploring the Success of Ad Supported Videos on ABC.com Q2 2008 Report; Q4 2007 and Q1 2008 NBC Rewind Intercept Study.
12. ABC Exploring the Success of Ad Supported Videos on ABC.com Q2 2008 Report.
13. Ibid.
14. Q4 2007, Q1 2008, and Q2 2008 NBC Rewind Intercept Studies.
15. Ibid.

11 PUBLIC RELATIONS

*by Burson-Marsteller, Porter Novelli, and Edelman
Public Relations Worldwide*

Reputation, reputation, reputation! O, I have lost my reputation! I have lost the immortal part of myself and what remains is bestial.

Cassio in Shakespeare's *Othello*

THE ESSENTIALS OF PUBLIC RELATIONS
by Burson-Marsteller

Introduction

Public relations, also known as PR, is the element of marketing that builds and promotes the awareness or reputation of an organization, such as Starbucks or the Red Cross; an individual, such as a movie star or a politician; or an idea, such as improving reading skills or proper health maintenance. Reputation is the most important thing that an organization or individual has. If an organization or individual does not manage its reputation, no one else will. In today's competitive, cluttered, and fast-moving business environment, success boils down to one thing: perceptions. Reputations are colored by what the public perceives, thinks, interprets, or believes. Perceptions create or diminish value, generate or solve problems, influence stock prices, differentiate a product, make it relevant to consumers, and create a value that allows pricing for high profit margins.

Everything communicated must be grounded in the ultimate realities of product and price. False perceptions cannot be sustained, at least not for long. No amount of hype will keep a bad movie or a lousy band high on the charts. There must always be a reinforcing interaction between perceptions and quality output, especially in the minds of the target audiences and clients.

A time-honored example of excellent public relations is Johnson & Johnson's exemplary crisis management effort in the face of the horrific contamination of their Tylenol product in 1982. Tylenol capsules were tampered with on a store shelf resulting in the death of an individual. That day the company announced that it would pull every bottle off of every store shelf, reimburse every consumer for unused portions, and develop a safer tablet and tamper-evident packaging. The public appreciated the company's candor and quick response. When the improved product returned to the shelves some months later, Tylenol's market share actually increased.

Large organizations typically have extensive, in-house public-relations departments, with media-relations personnel, speechwriters, and event managers. For smaller companies, or larger firms that prefer to keep staffs small, all of these services are available through a wide variety of outside agencies.

Definitions

Public relations is "that form of communications management that seeks to make use of publicity and other non-paid forms of promotion and information to influence the feelings, opinions, or beliefs about the company, its products or services or the value of that product or service or about the activity of the organization to buyers, prospects, or other stakeholders."[1]

Public relations is "the planned and sustained effort to establish and maintain goodwill and mutual understanding between an organization and its publics."[2]

Public relations also may be defined as *perception management.* Public relations or perception management uses communications tactics (described later) to create and change a target audience's perceptions to motivate behavior in order to achieve specific business results. The critical issue is for communications activities to motivate the target audience. This is done, in part, through the use of third-party endorsements such as the news media. Third-party endorsements add credibility to the information needed in the consumer learning process.

Public relations is not advertising. The advertiser pays for the use of the space or airtime, and the announcement appears as contracted. Most of the time, it is absolutely clear to the audience that what they are exposed to is an advertisement. It is clear which company is footing the bill for a Nike shoe commercial. However, like advertising, PR is considered a mass communications vehicle.

It is always preferable to take a proactive approach and formulate these steps under normal circumstances. However, in a reactive time environment, such as a natural disaster or other crisis, several steps may be coordinated concurrently.

PUBLIC RELATIONS

Communications → Perceptions → Behavior → Business Results

Public Relations Process

Define Business Objective
↓
Develop Situation Analysis
↓
Identify Target Audience
↓
Develop Messages
↓
Determine Strategy
↓
Create Strategic Programming
↓
Determine Media Selection
↓
Execute Campaign
↓
Measure Impact

---

1. Define Company's Needs/Objectives

An organization may need to reverse declining sales, overcome increased competitors' activities, defeat a proposed law that could deter business, or promote a new product. Public relations activities should have clear and measurable goals in order to achieve the desired business objectives for the company. The goal is usually expressed as a measurable perceptual or behavioral change that will be achieved within a specific time frame. A well-written goal would be "(1) To raise enough funds for the new endangered species breeding facility and (2) Attendance at this year's fund raiser should be 15 percent higher than last year's event." A PR objective that says, "To obtain publicity for the project" is not specific enough.

2. Develop Situation Analysis

The starting point in public relations is having a clear understanding of the current situation or context. The two main elements are the company background assessment and the problem/opportunity definition.

Company Background Assessment

When defining a situation, it is important to use as many different assessment criteria for the company as possible, which may include the following:

- Analyze secondary research or other available information that may include reports; competitive analysis; and economic, regulatory, political, and market conditions.
- Conduct primary research among key stakeholders, which could include employees, the media, analysts, competitors, customers, and consumers.
- Assess the current landscape, taking into consideration geographic location, industry sectors, and cultural and environmental aspects.
- Determine time parameters and constraints.
- Assess competitive conditions—both direct and indirect competitors.
- Assess financial situation/budget capabilities.
- Determine available human and technical resources.
- Assess online health and reputation.

Problem/Opportunity Definition

The key problems, challenges, or critical issues that an organization faces (and that a program will need to address) should surface in defining the current situation. There should be no more than three or four critical issues, and they must be addressable using communications tools and techniques. In addition, they should be clearly defined so that the business result and campaign strategy can evolve. In order to identify critical issues, it is important to define a clear understanding of the real problems and challenges. One way to facilitate this is through a SWOT analysis (Strengths, Weaknesses, Opportunities, and Threats). Examples of a problem or issue can range from the threat of decreased government research and development funding for the solar energy industry to a new, well-funded competitor coming into an existing market.

3. Determine Publics/Target Audience

A major objective of public relations is to reach audiences and identify ways to make them allies—or at least "verifiers" of what the company is working to do. The more specific the identity of the public, or target audience, the easier it will be to design an effective public relations program.

Some publics also are known as stakeholders. Stakeholders are people who have a stake or vested interest in the outcome or success of whatever a company or organization is involved in. Anything a company or organization does in the way of public relations should acknowledge the impact of the activity on stakeholders. For example, variations on a corporate theme could be tailored to the stakeholders' needs. Perhaps they should get advance notice of activities. Corporations do not want key people finding out about things from the newspaper, radio, or television, when they should have been told directly. Stakeholders can be powerful allies. Corporations and organizations should consider not only telling them about activities but also getting them involved in planning and execution.

The general public, also known as the community at large, encompasses all the specifically identified publics that an organization targets. Organizations typically do not reach out to the general public due to message specificity and budgetary constraints. However, it is important that an organization be mindful of the potential for segments of the general public to be included in any future endeavors and be responsive to inquiries by the community. Companies may focus on one or all target publics. Target audiences or publics include customers, opinion leaders, employees, nongovernmental organizations (NGOs), the financial community, suppliers, distributors, and governments.

Customers

Customer focus is the most important aspect of marketing activity. Companies have to make customers into believers. A goal of PR is to encourage customers to interact with the brand and further involve them with the company and its products through communications activities.

If products or services are good, customers will be happy and probably will not object to helping companies or organizations tell their story. For example, in some corporate videos, they *vox-pop* customers (capture informal and spontaneous comments on camera) and then edit them together to make the message stand out. Hard copy and online fan mail can be used in promotional material and some companies frame satisfied-customer letters in their lobby. If a journalist is doing a story about a company, he or she also may be willing to interview a customer or two. Customers also can be invited to speak at corporate seminars.

Influencers/Opinion Formers

Consumers listen to those with well-informed opinions as part of their research before purchasing products or services. Reaching these influencers or opinion formers who provide third-party endorsements is extremely valuable because word-of-mouth is one of the most powerful and inexpensive forms of communication. It also is important to determine and monitor the press activities both on- and offline of key opposition opinion leaders in order to react appropriately.

Employees

Employees are a very important part of the stakeholder audience. Employees influence product quality, customers, and investors. Employees most often are proud of where they work and will tell friends, neighbors, and relatives of positive experiences. However, occasionally, televison news items will feature interviews with disgruntled employees bad-mouthing their company because of some painful problem. Therefore, listening to and including employees in the organizational dialogue is an important part of the process that identifies a company as a caring organization, a good place to work, and thus a good place to patronize.

Many companies have employee-recognition programs, involving nominations, presentations, pictures in lobbies, and engravings on plaques. Companies often frame pictures of the "Employee of the Month" in corporate offices. Some people get their names and pictures in the local newspaper, the annual report, or the in-house magazine.

Nongovernmental Organizations

Nongovernmental organizations, or NGOs, have emerged as a critical set of stakeholders for compa-

nies over the past decade. Such groups today span a broad spectrum of issues arising with respect to companies' activities and approaches on environmental, labor, and human rights; supply chain; diversity and inclusion; and governance issues.

The Financial Community

The audiences within the financial community include shareholders, bankers, stockbrokers, analysts, financial reporters including broadcast media and Web sites, and bloggers and online chat rooms.

Maximizing shareholder value is a critical, objective measurement of the success of a company and its management team. How well a corporation understands and manages perceptions can influence investor confidence. Investor relations is simply another form of marketing—not a product, but a stock.

Suppliers/Vendors

Suppliers and vendors often are part of the "quality" story of a company. If they feel that they are part of the team and understand how important excellence is to an organization, they may be inspired to do better. Companies often highlight how a supplier or vendor worked in partnership to develop a corporate solution in company newsletters or trade publications. Another popular way of involving suppliers/vendors is to give an award of recognition.

Distributors

A corporation needs a distributor's (wholesaler or retailer) support of its activities because in many cases they represent the corporation to the customer. Therefore, it is important that distributors understand and buy into a company's or client's strategies, message points, and mind-set.

Governments

Politicians and officials (federal, state, local, and foreign) make daily decisions that can affect any organization. Legislation, regulations, and other government decisions, such as environmental regulations, tax code changes, and laws restricting cell phone usage in automobiles can change market conditions and make a significant difference in a company's competitiveness or an organization's objectives. Public affairs experts implement political strategies for businesses and organizations designed to achieve objectives by influencing the public policy decision-making process.

4. Develop Message/Theme

A message is what an organization wants its audience to think about its product, service, individual, or idea. Messages and themes are the campaign idea(s) that bring the underlying emotional and rational elements to life for the target audience. A clear objective statement facilitates the creation of messages to achieve it. In developing messages, an organization usually listens to its targeted public to identify the most specific theme.

Once an organization knows what its audiences are currently thinking, the company can focus on what they want them to think. Key messages or program themes should be clear, simple, sincere, factual, beneficial, consistent, memorable, and relate to the target audiences' needs in order to move them from their current behavioral process to the desired one.

For example:

- To encourage Americans to consume more milk, the dairy industry developed the slogan, "Got Milk?"
- U.S. government spending is allotted in part by where people live. To overcome consumers' natural tendency not to disclose personal information, the U.S. Census Bureau developed the message, "It's your future. Don't leave it blank."
- To let people with depression know that there is medical relief, the makers of Prozac developed the message, "Depression is an illness, not a weakness."

Messages can be developed through research, such as:

- Talking with the target audience informally
- Conducting marketing research
- Talking with the salespeople or trade outlets
- Talking with the media
- Scanning Internet chat rooms

5. Determine Strategies

Well-thought-out strategies provide the road map for the overall communications approach to a campaign and usually are determined early in the process by the company and the PR firm. These strategies can help determine the budget, the message, and the tactics, and are based on a variety of factors including target audiences and those issues identified through the situation analysis. Communications strategy and ultimate tactical execution can include independent programs versus coalition campaigns, proactive versus reactive response, immediate versus delayed response, centralized versus decentralized response, and high profile versus low profile budget options.

Independent Programs vs. Coalition Campaigns

Many companies have independent PR campaigns. The advantages of working independently include control over the campaign message and shortened response time. The disadvantages, particularly for a small company or start-up, is that they may lack clout in the marketplace and may not have the resources required to execute a robust program.

A coalition campaign is typically employed to affect the outcome of an issue in front of the public, Congress, or a state legislature, which is significantly helped by the addition of allies. To build coalitions of like-minded interests, it is necessary to identify and work with partners and political allies. This may mean facilitating existing relationships, forging new alliances, or belonging to several coalitions. The advantages of developing a coalition of like-minded groups are that it can provide more resources (people and money), save time and money, and have greater overall impact. The disadvantages of operating through a coalition are that coordination can be time-consuming; the message may deviate slightly from the company's specific goals; and there is little or no opportunity for the company to build its own brand recognition, as the coalition takes center stage.

Proactive vs. Reactive Response

A preventive, or proactive, strategy seeks to identify problems or threats in advance, through continuous research and monitoring of issues. The advantages of a proactive approach are that issues are anticipated in advance and managed. From a budget perspective, a proactive approach may cost more at the outset but will be less expensive in the long run.

Prevention is not always possible when an unanticipated event puts an organization, its program, and its messages at the mercy of others. For example, who would have thought that millions of consumer identities could have been stolen over the Internet from seemingly secure institutions? In such circumstances, the reactive approach should be the company communicating information in a timely matter. Whereas a reactive response of "No comment' is preferable to a response that is not carefully and thoroughly constructed, the best course of action is to communicate what is known at the time and get back to the media and other key stakeholders with a full answer, once additional facts and information are assembled.

Immediate vs. Delayed Response

Generally, the faster a problem can be contained, the better. As news and information races around the globe instantaneously via the Internet, it is growing increasingly difficult to contract an issue. Local news can take on global proportions in a matter of seconds or minutes. However, the advantages of a quick response are the rapid dissemination of information to parties that need the information, such as during a product recall, and the promotion of the public's perception that the company has nothing to hide.

Reasons for a delayed response, however, might be lack of necessary information, or waiting for something else to happen that would affect a response, such as an announcement of a merger or a new plant opening. Some actions may be controlled by such things as stock exchange disclosure rules, which might impose delaying an announcement until after the market has closed. Delaying a response in the hope that a problem will go away does not work.

Centralized vs. Decentralized Response

Centralized responses are answers (generally to media inquiries) that come from or through one person or entity; they are the result of a centralized program. Even though such responses may be more controlled and add assurance from the highest level, they often lack spontaneity and local color, and may take longer to be delivered. For example, the central response from the corporate president of an oil company regarding an oil refinery fire in one state could assure the public that all aspects of the problem on a national basis have been resolved.

A decentralized response is designed to allow a customized local response that keeps a local perspective on an issue and prevents unnecessary tainting of the larger corporation. A decentralized program needs central guidelines to ensure consistent delivery of key messages by different sources within a regionally diverse organization. For example, the strategy to use a decentralized response from the local oil refinery manager could assure the public at the local level that the fire has been contained and that it is a local problem that has been resolved and not a corporatewide problem.

High Profile Budget vs. Low Profile Budget

Budgeting is an important part of program development and implementation and will depend on the company's goals and capabilities. Since cost can impact decisions concerning campaign activities, program reach, and staffing, it is important to have a clear idea of profile and project budget options before starting. A low profile/low budget may call only for general activities. For example, a smaller budget may dictate using an internal spokesperson to speak on behalf of a product, issue, or opportunity. A larger budget may allow a team of experts to direct a high profile media and communications campaign around the clock and around the globe.

6. Determine Programs/Campaigns

In order to achieve the business results or objectives, there are various campaigns that a company may undertake.

Image Enhancement/Community Relations

Public relations is often employed to enhance a company's or product's image, to make it appear better, brighter, bigger, safer, or cleaner in the eyes of key audiences. In order to do so, it is important to understand what differentiates the company or product from its competitors and what defines its distinctive character. It is critical to find out how the corporation or product is currently perceived by its various audiences and develop strategies that will improve these perceptions and/or bridge the gap between the current and desired perceptions. In doing so, it is helpful to find a point of differentiation that resonates with the public, and then advance that position with a campaign of strategic communications.

The practice of community relations has evolved over the years into a more encompassing effort termed *Corporate Social Responsibility*. Companies worldwide face growing scrutiny on issues ranging from climate change to labor standards, their supply chains to reporting on their various activities and operations. Corporate policies and practices are under review by governments, investors, nongovernmental organizations (NGOs), and customers—and their own employees.

Smart businesses are finding new ways to embrace such challenges and turn them into opportunities. They recognize that corporate responsibility can be good for their bottom line. They want to find ways to engage with outside stakeholders, produce in a responsible way, be recognized as good employers, and partner with the communities in which they invest and operate. In short, more and more companies are seeing that it's good business to be good corporate citizens—and to make these efforts part of their core business strategy.

A company may want to raise its image by focusing on community relations issues such as corporate citizenship or corporate philanthropy. Corporate responsibility may turn neutral or negative impressions into positive ones.

- **Corporate Citizenship.** This is part of an overall positioning program. A survey by Wirthlin Worldwide shows that the public defines a good corporate citizen as a "company that is involved in its communities, cares for its employees, safeguards the environment, contributes to charities, supports education, and acts ethically."[3]

- **Corporate Philanthropy.** A philanthropy program, or corporate financial donations, can tie directly to a company's business mission, and improve its standing with its constituencies. Examples of local corporate giving programs include sponsorship of a food bank, scholarships, a library, or a cultural institution. With corporate philanthropy programs, companies should look for ways to leverage their charitable giving, either through media relations, events, promotions, or employee participation.

Crisis Management

Any company, organization, or institution is vulnerable to crisis. As was clear in the Tylenol case, although it is usually the action a company takes to address the crisis that will ultimately resolve it, very often the effectiveness of its communications is an enormously influential factor in determining success versus failure.

Crisis management can be thought of in three phases:

- **Crisis Readiness.** Companies should prepare ahead of time to avert or handle crises, including product recalls, product contamination, government investigations, litigation, strikes, or natural disasters. This is particularly important since the rise of the Internet, because information (and misinformation) can travel instantaneously around the globe. If the organization is not fully prepared when the crisis hits, events can quickly spiral out of control. Basic crisis preparedness activities include:
  - *Vulnerability Audit or Assessment.* This a process in which the company defines current and future areas of vulnerability and identifies the highest-level threats in order to develop specific plans against them.
  - *Crisis Plan.* A good crisis plan designates a Crisis Management Team to develop and direct the crisis response, lays out basic procedures that should be followed (such as how to address media inquiries or to activate a "dark" standby Web site), identifies all of the audience groups with whom the company will

need to communicate, and contains various checklists and lists of important contacts. It should also have more detailed instructions for handling a few high-risk scenarios, such as a plant-site explosion/fire or a product recall. For example, after the high profile recalls of pet food and toys made in China in 2007–2008, many companies added crisis-plan scenarios involving adulterated products or ingredients imported from overseas.

  ◦ *Crisis Simulation.* The crisis plan and crisis management structure should be tested regularly by running crisis drills that put the Crisis Team through a hypothetical crisis situation.

• **Crisis Response.** The response to a crisis situation must be swift and clear. Communication with all key audiences must be immediate and continuous—regardless of how much is actually known about the situation at any given time. The goal is first and foremost to protect public health and safety. From the standpoint of the organization and its reputation, the objective is to maintain public confidence by demonstrating that the company is aware of, and concerned about, the situation; is taking action to contain and address it; and intends to live up to its stakeholders' expectations.

  The U.S. beef industry applied these principles successfully when the first U.S. case of bovine spongiform encephalopathy (BSE or "mad cow disease") was diagnosed. Based on a comprehensive crisis plan already in place, the National Cattlemen's Beef Association launched an immediate and aggressive communications effort to drive accurate information through the media, counter misinformation, and maintain consumer trust. Polling conducted a week after the news broke showed that while an astounding 96 percent of Americans had heard or read about it, the public's high level of confidence in the safety of beef remained unchanged.

• **Crisis Recovery.** The ultimate goal of successful crisis management is a swift, genuine, and sustainable recovery. The path to recovery is unique to each situation and must be calibrated very carefully. Just because a situation is no longer front-page news does not mean it is no longer on stakeholders' minds or affecting their perceptions and behavior.

  If the organization has promised some type of reform or change, media and others will be watching closely to make sure it follows through. Trying to force recovery with a too-hasty return to "business as usual" may alienate some audiences who feel the company is trying to gloss over the crisis or is not taking its commitments seriously. On the other hand, if closure truly has occurred, a company does not want to prolong discussion of the past crisis and inadvertently reinforce negative impressions.

  Opinion research, which is extremely useful in every phase of crisis management, is helpful during this period to track the awareness and attitudes of key audiences and help determine how the organization should be communicating about past events.

  Virginia Tech in Blacksburg, Virginia, is a case study in effective crisis recovery. In the months after the 2007 shooting rampage on campus that left 32 people dead and many more injured, the university was determined to fulfill what had become its rallying cry through the tragedy, "We are Virginia Tech. We will prevail." The administration remained highly sensitive to the attitudes of students, faculty, alumni, and others to balance the need for remembrance with the desire to return to a normal college environment. Also, leadership consistently kept its actions and communications consistent with the school's values and the "Hokie Spirit." As a result, just over a year after the tragedy, public support for the university had never been stronger, and the school was experiencing the highest application levels in its history.

  Effective crisis preparation and management is about acting and communicating effectively in order to protect or reinstill reputation, brand equity, and financial performance. The perception that a company has mismanaged a crisis can badly strain customer loyalty, investor confidence, and employee morale. Conversely, the belief that the organization has faced adversity with integrity can enable it to emerge as strong as before, or even stronger.

Issues Management

Organizations must pay careful attention to issues of public concern. Public relations programs and activities are frequently developed to help identify, monitor, and manage issues of concern in an effort to develop and maintain strategic relationships with key audiences. In addition, they must maintain consistent policies no matter where in the world they operate.

Today, people are immensely well informed about almost everything. For example, even the purchase of a bar of soap may evoke thoughtful consideration rather than an impulse decision. Some concerns that might go into a buyer's decision, and are therefore issues that would need to be anticipated and managed by a soap manufacturer's PR department, include animal testing and recyclable packaging.

Government Relations

Organizations should have a very specific need and message when lobbying in either Congress or the state legislatures. The number of people, organizations, and issues vying for the attention of legislators and elected officials make the lobbying process difficult. Political action is usually sought to enhance an organization's strengths. Political action can be effectively motivated by using key contacts with legislators and pointing out the benefit or harm of certain legislation and the number of employees and location of facilities within the legislator's district.

Examining the bigger picture is critical in government relations. Issues have moved to the states at an accelerating rate, and state legislators and regulators have become increasingly active and sophisticated, frequently leading rather than following the federal government. Likewise, the methods by which those involved in state issues, from legislators to public interest groups, communicate to their constituencies also have become more sophisticated and immediate. Public opinion on an issue may become solidified, almost overnight, creating a communications crisis for those on the opposing side. Increasingly, the key to success is a strong communications campaign.

Product Publicity

A complete understanding of the product's features and benefits and consumer attitudes is essential to the implementation of programs designed to raise awareness and increase market share. Communications messages that will be compelling to specific audiences can be crafted to personalize the product, differentiate it from the rest of the pack, and support sales. Product publicity uses events, product placements in movies, in-store sampling, sponsorship activities, and demonstrations in appropriate venues to promote the uniqueness of the product and imply a third-party endorsement. For example, Revlon supports breast cancer awareness and has used top-tier models to serve as spokespeople to generate media attention to their good deeds.

Internal Communications

Companies need to build and maintain cohesiveness and trust among employees, also known as internal audiences, to encourage loyalty and productivity. Employee endorsement of both large and small changes is critical for long-term business success. For example, when a company rolls out a revised benefits plan, the company should include internal audiences in the process. This is accomplished through newsletters, memos, e-mail, company bulletin boards, and speeches at all-hands meetings. Creating an effective organizational communications program depends on three factors: mission and strategy clarification, internal communications assessment, and change management.

- **Mission and Strategy Clarification.** A well-defined expression of an organization's central goals and values is needed. It is important that a company's senior management develop clear strategic visions and plan cultural changes to support them. Then employees are actively involved in programs designed to bring the corporate vision to life in the day-to-day work of the organization.

- **Internal Communications Assessment.** A company's management should evaluate the strengths and weaknesses of current internal communications and then build and use effective programs to reach and involve all employees. Research can be used to identify employee perceptions of their organization and the communications practices affecting them. Companies can analyze what is, and is not, being communicated in the organization and then assist management in designing programs to more effectively manage employee perceptions and interpretations to make them consistent with corporate strategies.
- **Change Management.** Companies should manage corporate changes such as mergers or acquisitions, downsizing, strategic shifts, or labor negotiations that require discreet, sensitive handling of internal communications in order to gain the widest possible support within the organization.

Executive Training

Senior executives are often required to be spokespeople for their organizations, and their roles often require media training and international cultural training.

- **Media Training.** Executives should be trained to handle a variety of interview situations. During this media training, they go through a structured process designed to develop their interview experience and raise their comfort level. The objectives are to help the participants develop and deliver key message points effectively that can "tell their story."
- **Intercultural Training.** As the globalization of organizations expands, another aspect of executive training is assisting executives in understanding their new or potential international clients. Familiarization with appropriate behavior and cultural perceptions in different parts of the world will greatly assist an international marketing effort. Business etiquette, social customs, body language, and other areas can vary significantly.

7. Determine Media Selection

Media tactics are the approaches, activities, and mass media used to deliver the messages to targeted audiences. The tactics may be written, verbal, or visual. Media selection emanates from an organization's strategies, understanding of target audiences, and message development. For example, younger people tend to be more comfortable with digital media and social networks than older audiences. Tactics can include engaging the news media, using formal corporate communications, and organizing various events.

News Media

Journalists gather, write, edit, or direct news for presentation through the media channels, including newspapers, magazines, radio and television programs, press agencies and wire services, newsletters, Web sites, bloggers and vloggers, and freelance writers who may work with any of these outlet categories. Journalists gather their information from various sources. Sports reporters go to games and interview the players, the coaches, and the fans. Political reporters hang around Capitol Hill or the state or county equivalent and call their reliable sources to confirm or deny rumors.

Journalists attend industry events, track down knowledgeable sources, and ultimately get most of their information from people who want something to be known and therefore are willing and able to talk. Also, many journalists rely heavily on public relations professionals for information and access to key sources. Journalists can be a conduit through which companies and individuals can get their messages into print or over the airwaves. The disadvantage to using journalists for information dissemination is that there is no control over the final product; specifics of the message may be diluted or left out and errors are possible.

Any program designed to change opinions, perceptions, and attitudes must consider the news media. It is often the most influential channel available for delivery of key messages to targeted audiences. In most cases, one of the main objectives of public relations is to get journalists to report on what companies are doing in such a way as to reflect desired messages and achieve desired business results. In practicing media relations, it is important to know how to catch journalists' attention, provide them with complete, useful information, and generate interest on their part to tell a story in a particular way.

Setting a media selection strategy and determining which outlets to communicate messages through involves a number of things, including identifying what media target audiences use. Most people watch television, but not everybody reads. The main followers of trade press are those involved or vested in specific industries. Hence, if an organization's goal is to reach homemakers, it may consider focusing on television, parenting Web sites, online recipe sites, parenting-oriented and home-decorating magazines, and mass market publications like newspapers, rather than trade press.

Targeting audiences extends beyond just identifying who they are to understanding effective ways to communicate with them. For example, some people are very busy, such as doctors or executives. Messages aimed at them within the realm of their day-to-day activities may get very little attention, but reaching these same people during a relaxed setting can be an entirely different proposition. They may be reached through their interests or hobbies, such as placing a message about arthritis and its remedies aimed at doctors in a golf magazine.

Just as important as selecting the right publication or broadcast outlet is the targeting of specific journalists. Determine which writers or producers are most likely to cover the story you have in mind. Read the newspapers and watch or listen to the programs you have targeted. Get a feel for what they usually cover, see what elements they routinely include in stories, and craft your pitch appropriately.

Media relations is at the heart of many public relations programs. Media relations specialists tend to get to know the journalists in a particular field and are in daily contact with representatives of important consumer, business, and trade media. These relationships are considered key in the battle for news space and positioning. Being accessible as a source of information is very helpful to these journalists.

WHAT INTERESTS A JOURNALIST

- A story that will interest the medium's key audiences.
- An unusual or provocative angle.
- Accurate, verified facts.
- Ability to meet the deadline. Deadlines are all-important in publishing. Therefore, to a journalist, a completed story by a certain date and time is very important.
- An exclusive. But "hot news" may be only mildly interesting to someone who has news items pouring in all the time. Stories have to stand out among stiff competition.

News media tactics include media kits, press/video/audio news releases, press conferences, press interviews, bylined article placements, and Web-based events.

- **Media Kit.** Journalists usually create their own version of a story, but are happy to use public relations materials as background. A *media kit* is usually a folder or some other container providing a selection of material for the press to use in reporting a story. Often an online version of the media kit is developed that can be posted to a corporate Web site or e-mailed to reporters. A typical media kit contains:
  - The latest press releases
  - A fact sheet of the product or service
  - Photos with captions
  - Reprints of news stories that have already appeared
  - An annual report or brochure of the company
  - A sample of the product, if feasible
  - "Collateral materials"—devices designed to make the kit memorable and to encourage its use, such as posters, audio files, and promotional products
  - Imagery representing the company and/or products
- **Press Release.** One of the main features of a media kit is a press release. A *press release* is a written document describing the focus of public relations activities. It is generally presented as news and usually has a sense of urgency. The objective of a press release is to encourage the

publishing of a story, or at least a mention. This release also may prompt a call from a media outlet asking for more information, thereby resulting in a more detailed story. A press release delivers a solid, relevant punch, and quickly answers the journalists' immediate questions: Who? What? When? Where? Why? How?

Journalists may receive dozens of press releases a day. Consequently, most are not read all the way through, if at all. The first step is to get a journalist's attention: The headline and the opening paragraph are the most important words on the page. The release typically is no more than two or three pages of double-spaced typing, with a compelling headline and introduction (or lead). It includes contact information (name, e-mail, phone, fax), and if the news is time-sensitive, an embargo or hold date ("Not for release until after 2 P.M. EDT Tuesday, June 24").

Given that reporters use the Internet to research story ideas and stories, and since bloggers can be as influential as the mainstream media, it is often advisable to create a social media press release. This is based on a traditional press release but breaks up the information in a way more conducive to online publishing. A social media release should include images and rich-media assets to support the story as well as links to additional information.

• **Video News Release.** A *video news release* (*VNR*) is a video press release that is provided to television program producers with the objective of their using it in their show. It gives them pictures and sound without their having to go to the trouble and expense of creating them. A VNR is news-oriented, and is usually scripted and produced to resemble a news clip on a typical news program. There are no guarantees that the footage will be used. The more interesting and compelling it can be, the better the chance of getting it aired. VNRs are sent primarily to news program producers or general interest producers. However, if they have a special-interest application, their distribution can be more tightly focused. For example, a VNR about a new type of contact lenses would be sent to a health or a fashion program.

• **Audio News Release.** An *audio news release* (*ANR*) is a press release on audiotape and is typically a 30-, 60-, or 90-second tape produced for distribution to radio stations. ANRs might include a narrator interviewing a person-on-the-street or a spokesperson, or it could be structured so that the spokesperson provides answers and the local radio station is provided with a script of the questions giving the impression that a live interview is taking place.

• **Press Conference.** When an organization has something important and newsworthy to communicate, and wants to reach a lot of people at once, it can hold a *press conference*. These are events that generally run up to an hour in length and are staged to present some statement of significance. They usually end with questions from the floor. The very nature of the press conference technique can promote a sense of immediacy and perceived importance.

A typical press conference will have several presenters, led and moderated by a senior person or perhaps the PR advisor. It may also feature a separate spokesperson, such as a celebrity who is endorsing the cause or product. Each presenter or spokesperson might speak for a few minutes, addressing a particular issue or area of expertise.

Press conferences can be held almost anywhere. Typical venues include hotel meeting rooms, client or agency meeting rooms or facilities, clubs, and restaurants. Others can be at the site where news is happening or at a location that is visually engaging, such as the location for a new building that is being announced, a school where a new program is being introduced, or the steps of city hall where important legislation is being debated. Sometimes it is helpful to select a location that is easy for the media to reach. For instance, if most of the media being targeted is based in the downtown area of a city, it may be helpful to hold the event close by. The prospect of a long drive may dissuade some journalists from attending an event. To this end, online press events are sometimes employed where journalists can join an event via computer or press conferences can be conducted over the phone with media participating through a dial-in number.

The start time of a press conference should be carefully considered. The rule is to use the most appropriate time for the key media because journalists work to deadlines and must be provided time to write up the story. For print media, that usually means staging events in the morning. Invitations to a press conference should be sent out a couple of weeks in advance, if possible. They should state the purpose of the press conference; identify the presenters; and give obvious details like time, date, and location. The press conference should be scripted to ensure that each presenter knows what to say and when, and that the messages are communicated clearly and succinctly. Rehearsal (preferably on-site) is absolutely essential.

- **Press Interview.** Many times information may be given to individual reporters. The company spokesperson may travel to the interview or an event where he or she is interviewed. Or a reporter may travel to the company spokesperson to get an interview. Discussing issues one-on-one allows for a greater dissemination of details and tailoring of the message to the reporter's audience. However, this process can be time-consuming. Spokespersons should prepare for an interview by considering the many questions a journalist may ask, especially the tough ones, and practicing ways to answer them.
- **Article Placement.** An *article placement* is a prewritten article designed to build credibility or provide background for a cause, an activity, a product, or that can help establish the author as an authority on a subject. An article can be more effective than an advertisement because

people tend to believe more what they read in an article than what they see in a paid ad. The more an article promotes a particular brand or company, the less credibility it will have and the harder it will be to have it published. The substance, style, and tone of the article should be tailored to the publication and its audience.

Corporate Communications

When business media is allowed greater control over the message, the costs are greater. Business media includes annual reports, speeches, newsletters, corporate Web sites, and trade shows.

- **Annual Report.** All companies that issue shares to the general public are required to publish an annual financial report. It is read by shareholders, the financial community, employees, supply chain partners, and the public. Beyond the financial requirements is the opportunity to present the company's message, including comments about the company's management strategy, business results, prospects, special activities, and new product development.
- **Speeches.** There are many opportunities to give speeches to present an organization's message, such as conventions, trade shows, exhibitions, seminars, after-dinner speeches, symposia, ocean cruises, and congressional testimony. It is a matter of finding the right medium for the message. Speeches should be heavy on content and light on promotion.

  To pursue speaking opportunities, designating a senior executive of the company as the company spokesperson is helpful. In many cases, especially those involving technical content, the spokesperson may be an outsider, usually a professional with acknowledged expertise.
- **Newsletters.** If a company develops a mailing list of clients, prospects, and the media, a newsletter is a good way of building relationships and letting important audiences know what is going on. It is a controlled method of keeping people informed of new developments, refinements in product lines, new customers, new ways of using products, or special

offers. Often newsletters are developed in both an online and offline format.

- **Corporate Web Site.** All of America's Fortune 1000 companies[4] and 61 percent of small companies[5] now have a presence on the World Wide Web.

  Corporate Web sites should provide basic company information, expose key audiences to messages, and provide a forum for announcing new products and posting press releases.

  Many corporate Web sites are supplemented by a corporate blog. A *blog* is an online diary of sorts with entries posted by an individual or group of people in reverse chronological order. Blogs often contain pictures and video, and usually allow readers to post comments. Blogs provide an excellent opportunity for executives to connect with their stakeholders in a meaningful way as they facilitate one-on-one communication.

- **Social Media.** Social media is comprised of various Web sites that allow and encourage participants to congregate online based on vocation, hobbies, political views, or other interests. People share information, imagery, video, and points of view. Social media is highly influential in that the general public has had to find a new way to evaluate what they trust. There is so much information available all the time that today's consumer tends to trust other consumers—people like them. Therefore, corporations need to find a way to participate in order to remain relevant.

  Companies that do so well are often rewarded with deep loyalty, positive word of mouth, and increased credibility for other communications programs. The most popular social media Web sites include Facebook, YouTube, Flickr, LinkedIn, and MySpace.

- **Trade Shows.** Most special-interest groups sponsor an annual trade show or exhibition. Industry influencers, experts, competitors, consumers, and media flock to them. An organization that wants to be known as active in its field should attend, exhibit, and create publicity at trade shows. A well-organized trade show will also have its own press office and provide the opportunity to offer media materials or a press conference.

Various Events

Media tours, product placement, and other special events are tactics that allow for a significant degree of control while building and attracting interest from the news media and other audiences.

- **Media Tour.** During a media tour, a spokesperson travels around the country or the world and meets with interviewers in key markets giving a series of interviews. A media tour can have significant impact because it saturates the media with interviews and helps deliver a concentration of communications in a very short time. Examples include Jane Seymour highlighting her jewelry line on a national morning show, Stephen King promoting his latest novel at bookstore signings with local media invited to attend, an oil company executive addressing a community group on why gas prices are so high, or George Clooney discussing his latest movie on late-night television.

  A media tour should be planned well in advance, with an appropriate time frame coinciding with the release of the news item (the product, event, book, or movie), and with a relevant local angle predetermined for each location. For instance, if a tour is organized to promote a new book, then the books should actually be in the shops when the author is in town. Once the dates have been identified, locations should be selected considering the size of the market, the impact a spokesperson will have in the market, local events that may preempt media coverage, and the most important media to hit (local television talk show, a popular radio show, an influential blogger, or the local paper).

  A satellite media tour allows for a rapid response and allows use of a spokesperson who may not be able to take the time necessary to participate in a standard media tour. In a satellite media tour, the spokesperson goes to a local television studio (with television uplink facilities where a segment of satellite time has been reserved). Other stations are advised of the availability of the spokesperson and invited to reserve interview slots within the scheduled time segment. Then two-way live interviews can be conducted. A satellite media tour is less expensive than a standard media tour.

- **Product Placement/Cross Marketing.** Product placement is an excellent way of promoting a brand because of the implied endorsement by the protagonist. To take maximum advantage, the placement should be linked to a strategic copromotion. In the case of movies, this would include tie-ins with the film, theater lobby displays, advertising, and contests. In addition, successful placement is enhanced when the placed product is shown in the promotional clips of the movie screened on the various television programs previewing the show. A meaningful connection and subtlety are important to enhance credibility and status. For example, an expensive car or watch featured in a James Bond movie is very appropriate, while lower-priced merchandise would not fit the image of his character.

- **Special Events.** Special events are noteworthy happenings that are capable of generating a high level of warmth or positive response toward the company. Events include symposiums, seminars, screenings, parties, concerts, fashion shows, and charity runs. It is important that a company choose an event and event location that is relevant to it and/or its products. For example, holding a symposium or seminar is a technique often used by pharmaceutical companies that want to reach doctors. A company may sponsor ancillary meetings during a main event that might be running under the aegis of the relevant professional association. Many special events have celebrity spokespersons intended to generate additional publicity.

8. Implement Program/Campaign

After all strategies and tactics have been decided upon, the public relations programs, or campaigns, are implemented by the PR staff or agency. All elements of the program are integrated at this time. This process may take weeks, months, or years.

9. Measure Impact

Measuring the impact of communication programs has become increasingly important in recent years as public relations, like other organizational functions, has seen additional pressure to demonstrate the value it provides. One consequence of this is that measurement has become more refined, more specific, and, importantly, more closely tied to program objectives.

The approaches to measurement selected should align as closely as possible with the objectives of the campaign, and should be determined at the outset of the project as the objectives are being identified, answering the question, "How will success be defined?" Bearing in mind the adage that "what gets measured gets done," setting the measurements to closely reflect the objectives helps keep the entire program focused on these goals.

There are a range of measurement techniques available, and those selected may look at different levels of accomplishment toward the campaign goals, from very specific things that measure elements of the process used, to measures of whether the specific target audiences were reached and affected, to whether the ultimate business-related goals were achieved.

As discussed earlier, the strategies and tactics developed to implement the program should align with the program objectives. At the tactical level, the specific campaign elements are chosen because they are expected to contribute in some way to achieving the larger objective. Each tactic of the campaign can be examined and evaluated in some way to determine how successful it was at contributing toward the program goal.

Earned Media Coverage

Much of traditional public relations is geared toward obtaining *earned media coverage*. For such programs, a standard and important component of measurement is analysis of that coverage. Although an impressive stack of media clips may help make the case for success, a systematic analysis of the content is important to demonstrate in detail that the coverage did what it was intended to do, including appearing in publications that reach the target audience and contain key messages. For example, if the objective was to communicate with the broad public, but the media clips were exclusively from trade publications, or if they were either simply passing references or worse, negative stories, this suggests that the effort may have fallen short.

Consequently, a more specific analysis of content is necessary to evaluate the effort. This typically includes an analysis of the topics covered, where the stories appeared, how extensive they were, whether they were positive, negative, or neutral, and, importantly, whether the specific messages intended to be communicated were actually included in the stories. Again, the extent to which the message(s) are conveyed is an indicator of success. Often, other elements also are included in the analysis such as whether spokespersons or third-party supporters are quoted. Metrics used can be expressed as the number or percentage of stories that included various pieces of information or percentages of targeted publications that covered the story. To give a broad picture of coverage, one measure sometimes used is the total number of impressions or "opportunities to see," which represents the total number of individuals who may have been exposed to a message through the media. This is calculated by adding the circulation figures for publications in which the message has appeared.

Some practitioners try to place a dollar value on earned media coverage by estimating a comparable cost for advertising that would occupy the same amount of space in the same publications. Unfortunately, this process has many problems and may be misleading. One essential difference is that advertising allows you to precisely control the message disseminated, including the use of powerful imagery, whereas earned media does not. Other limitations that complicate this process include the fact that some publications do not permit front page advertising and there is no way to estimate this cost. Another issue is the contention that earned media has greater credibility than advertising, and therefore should use some multiplier to take this fact into account in these calculations. Unfortunately, determining whether earned media is more credible than advertising, by how much and in what circumstances, remains muddy, and there is currently no solid rationale for using any specific multiplier number.

Online Media Coverage

In addition to traditional media, online media is now an integral part of the communications mix, and if it is used as a vehicle in a public relations program, it should be measured as well. Measures in the online world include the extent to which one's own Web site is tapped, as well as relevant discussion on other sites, blogs, chat rooms, and so forth. For one's own Web site, a variety of metrics can be tracked, such as Web site and Web page hits, unique Web site and Web page visitors, as well as time spent on the site. To the extent that specific target audiences of interest can be evaluated separately, more value is added to the analysis.

As with other media, relevant online discussion on Web sites, forums, blogs, and so forth, can be monitored and measured to determine how much discussion there is and what is being said. As with analysis of print and broadcast media, some outlets may be considered more important than others with respect to the program goals. Sites or discussions that are disproportionately influential should receive greater attention than others.

Other PR Activities

Although media coverage and now online presence are core functions of public relations, a program may involve other types of campaign elements as well. These may include activities such as speaking opportunities, forming alliances, trade show exhibits, and event sponsorships. Whatever the tactics, one or more metrics can be developed to help capture the extent to which goals were achieved. If an objective was to form alliances with nonprofit groups to help carry the message, ways to measure success could include the number of groups that joined; their outreach efforts through internal or external publications, including how many people they may have reached and whether they conveyed all key messages; Web site links provided; participation in events; or an assessment of the quality of the relationship.

The shortcoming of many of the tools just described is that while they measure what communications were sent out to audiences, they do not capture whether target audiences received, understood, remembered, were influenced by, or acted upon them. Conducting survey research with members of the target audience helps measure these dimensions.

Survey Research

To determine any awareness, attitude, or behavior changes as a result of a communication program, it is essential to establish a *baseline*, an initial set of measurements on the key questions that will be the basis for measuring success. This means conducting an initial survey before the communication effort begins, as well as identifying what the key questions for measuring success will be, and exactly how they will be measured. For example, if a key measure is to improve favorability, will it be measured using a 10-point scale? If so, will the measure itself be the percentage that gives a favorability score of 8, 9, or 10, or will we use the average score, or something else? Or, if the goal of the program is to improve a company's reputation, will that be its reputation in specific areas, such as corporate citizenship or innovation, and how exactly will that be measured?

After these questions have been decided, an initial survey is conducted before the communication effort begins. Either during the course of the program or at its end, a follow-up survey using the identical questions can be conducted to determine whether things have changed. Measures tracked may include awareness, recall of messages, attitudes, level of interest, intention to do something, and whether they have actually taken some action.

Although it would be ideal to identify targets for change, such as a "10 percentage point improvement in favorability" (as measured by scores of 8, 9, or 10 on a scale from 1 to 10), it is extremely difficult to make a reasonable estimate at the outset of a program, especially before the baseline data has been collected and the starting point is known. Increasing awareness, for example, from 10 to 20 percent is likely to be easier than increasing it from 90 to 100 percent. Without knowing the starting point, it is hard to know what might be achievable. And, unlike advertising, where exposure is directly related to cost, and we can predict how many people a given media buy is likely to reach, each public relations program and the circumstances surrounding it are complex and unique; there are no simple algorithms available that allow us to predict how much change can be expected from, say, a $1 million program.

Finally, to return to the beginning, the ultimate objective of the program is generally a business-related result, although this is sometimes not stated: an increase in sales or stock price, better recruitment, higher productivity, and so forth. The communication program is designed to make a contribution toward this goal, although it may be somewhat indirect. Of course, there are many factors that go into achieving these larger objectives. Among them are advertising and other marketing activities, but also many other factors besides communications: the quality of products, activities of competitors, broader economic conditions, government legislative or regulatory activity, and so forth. These also need to be taken into account in assessing the campaign's success.

Measures at the level of program objectives should be looked at along with the other measures that are more specifically focused on communications. Tying business results directly to public relations activity is not simple, but the evaluation should look at this relationship along with the consideration of other factors. Looking at the overall program objectives in combination with more specific communication metrics helps ensure that goals, strategies, and tactics remain aligned and are likely to produce maximum effectiveness.

PUBLIC RELATIONS—INTERNATIONAL
by Porter Novelli

With a single keystroke, a message can travel the world instantly. This rapid acceleration of information distribution is shaping global markets, which can thrive without borders. Technology has revolutionized our participation in the global community and its economy, challenging traditional boundaries of language, culture, custom, and regulation. However, even though evolving technologies continue to facilitate new methods of communication, best practices still hold for what is said, whose voice is used, and who is spoken to. In other words, more than ever, global communicators need to ensure consistency of messages, incorporate knowledge of their markets, speak to stakeholders as individuals, and encourage intelligent dialogue.

Ensure Consistency of Messages

With the emergence of global news channels, many audiences, whether they are targeted stakeholders, can consume and respond to messages immediately from anywhere in the world. To make sure their story is understood clearly, companies must plan to deliver consistent messages to everyone from customers to suppliers, regulators to investors, via diverse activities in each market including direct communications, media relations, and corporate social responsibility. Vehicles can range from the corporate Web site to YouTube, from community meetings to professional society activities. But even before vehicles are identified, companies must develop a strategic communications plan focusing on what they wish to communicate and how various audiences may interpret the delivery. It is no longer possible to lay a discrete pathway for channeling information to a particular audience. Everyone has access, so consistency is key.

For example, Porter Novelli (PN) provides public relations for international technology company HP (Hewlett-Packard), developing strategy and implementing many worldwide activities targeting consumers and business, including product reviews, event management, executive positioning, intranet development, and crisis management. PN must ensure close coordination among diverse product lines, global programs, and worldwide teams spanning 13 countries and 21 cities while working closely with teams from two other PR agency partners.

Understand the Market

In the global market, the eye of the local beholder is an important element in communications success. The same story will resonate differently with different international audiences. Therefore, the delivery of messages should take attitudes and cultures of individual markets into account, which requires local market knowledge, an understanding of language, symbols, humor, politics, and socioeconomic norms. Because no one person can understand the nuances of every culture, the counsel of nationally based public relations professionals who have experience with local audiences can help ensure the content and intent of corporate messages.

Media relations tactics may frequently differ by market in pursuit of the same goal. For example, instead of simply providing press releases for translation, global public relations teams may disseminate key messages and quotes to national offices for use as a framework. A standard press release written for the U.S. market cannot simply be translated into Italian, because it may not be relevant to the Italian market. Instead, a local team should tailor the release to reflect how products are perceived in the Italian region they target, as well as be cognizant of how the company is viewed locally and key societal concerns.

Press conference styles also vary from country to country. For example, a press conference in the AsiaPac should be organized to include only very senior officials, in a formal atmosphere over a long meeting. In the United Kingdom, busy journalists who do not have time to attend many events may prefer one-on-one interviews. And globally, Webcasting allows information sharing around the world 24/7.

Most global brands must compete on a local level, building a consumer connection that transcends core product features and benefits. Public relations can promote an international company through a consistent message that is perceived as credible by local audiences. It may deliver information to a number of audiences using local third-party objective sources such as journalists, industry experts, and celebrities.

Until recently, tech giant HP's marketing efforts in the United Kingdom were driven by individual product specifications. However, after 360° research into consumers' attitudes toward technology, Porter Novelli realized that the British public is less interested in tech specs than in how technology can affect their everyday lives. Porter Novelli saw that HP needed to reposition its U.K. approach to something more human, focusing on broader benefits to consumers. The solution was Smile, based on the universally understood expression of happiness, unity, and joy. Also, a smile is our natural response to having a photo taken. The multiphase program incorporated photography and printing while allying the HP brand with the word *smile* and the benefits of smiling. It activated the British public by encouraging them to send in smiling photos as part of a major exhibition at London's Royal College of Art, with HP adding incentive by donating to a well-known children's charity based on the number of participants. A famed sports figure (ex-captain of England's World Cup–winning rugby squad Martin Johnson) worked with children to demonstrate how powerful a simple smile can be to brighten kids' lives. Launched with national and regional angles, the campaign resulted in lifestyle and celebrity-focused smile coverage in major media outlets, and garnered positive consumer associations and momentum for the HP brand. While Porter Novelli's idea was originally intended for British PR only, Smile was so compelling and successful that HP decided it should sit at the heart of all strands of its consumer marketing, including advertising, direct marketing, Web marketing, and point-of-sale.

Speak to the Consumer as an Individual

Public relations can provide consumers with detailed information that helps them understand a new company, product, or product category. When a major pharmaceutical and health-care company developed a new vaccine for children, it recognized that private practice pediatricians in many countries rarely saw young children with the targeted disease, as it generally requires emergency treatment in a hospital. For this reason, many pediatricians believed the illness was rare, and they were underestimating the importance of vaccination.

Porter Novelli developed a global PR program for the vaccine maker in order to create international consumer awareness among parents about the disease, and about vaccination as a solution. The program has helped humanize the illness by providing real-life, local examples of its consequences. The parent-focused programs have been implemented in a number of European and Latin American countries. In one country, sales of the vaccine increased 47 percent in institutions that conducted the program.

By speaking to consumers in the context of their beliefs, interests, and lifestyles, public relations can build an emotional connection between the individual and the company. Though consumers may be different in each locality, they share products and brands more than ever before. The emergence of international brands such as Apple, McDonald's, and Gap, as well as the use of the Web to acquire products from just about any country, has allowed consumers from Beijing to Berlin to Buenos Aires to speak a common language through their lifestyle connection. Today, individuals may be targeted more by lifestyle choices than by their country of origin.

Even though a feeling of cross-cultural lifestyle has developed, individuals often see themselves as deeply rooted in their communities and connected by religious beliefs, single-issue politics, and environmental concerns. Technology and political change may bring people closer together, but they also give them a greater desire to assert distinctiveness, which brings enormous opportunity for specialization. As niches develop and mature, they fragment into subniches. This further fragmentation is driven by a response to individual consumer interests, but in turn it also drives media consumers' expectations for tightly customized offerings. One downside of this fragmentation is that although media consumers can seek out channels that reflect their own interests and opinions, they can avoid those that don't, which minimizes the opportunity to challenge them with new ideas.

Facilitate Intelligent Dialogue

In further marketing of the pharmaceutical leader's new children's vaccine, Porter Novelli developed a peer-to-peer educational program in order to facilitate an international dialogue among pediatricians about the disease and the vaccine. The global program was led in each market by a local ER pediatrician who has witnessed cases and their consequences on a child's life firsthand. The program educated doctors about the benefits of an effective vaccine. Developed as a template initiative for use by client offices worldwide, it has been utilized globally. Porter Novelli partnered with a prominent opinion leader to lead the program at a major international medical meeting with pediatricians from around the world. The program opened a forum for discussion among important prescribers. Of those physicians who completed program evaluation forms, more than 98 percent stated that the information will be useful in their practice and 98 percent agreed that there is proven benefit in vaccinating children against the disease.

As yesterday's national mass media morph into today's global interactive media, people expect to take part and talk back to opinion leaders. Yesterday's way was set-piece monologues broadcast to passive audiences by powerful brands and media owners. Today's way is fluid, evolving dialogues conducted across multiple, linked channels. Ongoing dialogue is now possible and is truly the best basis of dynamic long-term relationships. Public relations professionals need to cultivate open, questioning minds that ask smart, creative questions.

PUBLIC RELATIONS—CASE STUDY

by Edelman Public Relations Worldwide

Company: Liz Claiborne/Claiborne for Men
Case: Special Event—National Campaign for Men's Casual Clothing

Background

When IBM relaxed its notoriously strict dress code in 1994, it signaled a change in corporate culture that was nothing short of miraculous. Companies across the country began allowing their employees to dress casually and the phrase "Casual Friday" was here to stay. Gone were the days of the traditional uniform of a blue suit and white shirt. Instead, both men and women were reaching into their closets for khakis, sport shirts, and sweaters. Although the loosening of dress codes improved productivity and morale among the workforce, it also created confusion about what to wear to the office, especially among men. Men understand how to wear a suit and tie to work and their jeans and T-shirts on the weekends, but anything in between was cause for anxiety. Very few companies provided guidelines or offered men any direction of what "dressy casual" or "corporate casual" actually meant.

The Goal

To address this confusion and seize the opportunity presented, Claiborne for Men launched *The Claiborne Changing Room Tour*, a grassroots mobile marketing program designed to educate men on how to dress and position Claiborne as the authority on office casual wear.

Claiborne for Men is a division of the women's apparel giant Liz Claiborne, Inc. Sold in department stores, the sportswear line is comprised of updated and modern suits, slacks, sport coats, sport shirts, sweaters, and casual shirts. The men's division has been in business since 1986, but up until this point, had virtually no brand recognition in the marketplace. Claiborne's attempt to capture the corporate casual market was met with several challenges:

- How to overcome consumers' perception of Claiborne as a designer of women's clothes.
- How to increase brand awareness while competing against the millions of advertising dollars spent by Tommy Hilfiger, Levi Strauss & Co.'s Dockers, Ralph Lauren's Polo, and Nautica.
- A Yankelovich survey found that 71 percent of men ages 30–49 stated that shopping for clothes is often a frustrating and time-consuming experience.

Thus, the goals for Claiborne's campaign were to:

- Establish an image that puts Claiborne in front of the corporate casual category.
- Generate national, regional, and local media coverage for the brand.
- Increase brand awareness among the target audience and stimulate sales.

The Approach

The overall strategic approach was to set out across the country to talk to men who were confused about what to wear on casual days.

Several options were considered including a humorous approach centering on a "Comedy Night" at local retail stores where invited men would be subjected to lighthearted barbs aimed at their outmoded clothes. They would then be shown new and appropriate alternatives. This plan was rejected, because the risk of alienating potential customers was considered too high. Another option was selected.

The Claiborne Changing Room was created to hit the road to tell men that Claiborne is the appropriate wardrobe for casual days. The theme emphasizes that the line is

- Easy to mix and match, which means creating many looks with several basic garments
- Easy to care for, which means less money spent on dry cleaning
- Versatile, which means that customers can go from the office to any social occasion

The Changing Room was a 35-foot tractor-trailer outfitted as a mobile Claiborne showroom that visited department stores and downtown, high-traffic locations in cities across the country. The trailer folded out to an all-inclusive event site that featured a deck with a canopy and awning, a sound system, and café. The interior of the truck simulated a Claiborne shop with fixtures, mirrors, and clothing displays.

Consumers were invited aboard to preview the latest fashions from Claiborne and to receive a one-on-one consultation from Claiborne style consultants and fashion editors from leading magazines. Attendees received a free style booklet, a gift of a briefcase, and a 25-percent-off coupon to purchase Claiborne clothing. After their consultation, Claiborne sales associates accompanied men to a local department store to help coordinate a wardrobe appropriate for their specific line of work. The events were promoted with local radio and newspaper advertising, in addition to in-store signage prior to *The Changing Room* arriving in a particular city. The sheer size and visibility of *the Changing Room* often drew much attention from passers-by, and coupled with media outreach, the events attracted 500-plus visitors at each tour stop.

Results

Sales increases of 100 percent or more were realized at every event in comparison to same-day sales from the previous year. The media embraced the story enthusiastically, featuring Claiborne and *The Changing Room* on *Good Morning America,* the *Today* show, and *CNN* as well as in the *New York Times, the Associated Press,* and other outlets. Media impressions totaled 300 million for 1997.

by Burson-Marsteller

Company: The Bureau of Engraving and Printing and the Federal Reserve System
Case: Introducing the New Color of Money

Situation Analysis

In a preemptive move against counterfeiting, the Bureau of Engraving and Printing (BEP) and the Federal Reserve Board (FRB) began introducing a new series of redesigned notes into circulation in 2003. The new notes—including the $5, $10, $20, and $50 notes—each included enhanced security features and the subtle addition of color. The BEP and FRB understood that changing the world's most trusted brand involved risks: confusion in commerce, millions of retail cashiers and other cash handlers unaware of how to authenticate the new notes, and international concern over recalls and devaluation.

Because U.S. currency is a product used by every American and by hundreds of millions of people around the world, the launch of the new notes became the largest new product introduction in history. And it required a global communications program to control the risks, to allow for a smooth launch, and to build quick confidence in the new notes.

The BEP set clear goals: gain near universal public awareness of the new design, increase recognition of the note's security features, and train tens of millions of cash handlers how to use the new features.

Implementation

The BEP, FRB, and Burson-Marsteller designed a fully integrated public education program that relied on virtually every communications discipline. Burson-Marsteller took on the role of integrator, program manager, and strategic counselor—bringing together all of the program's elements to markets around the world, including materials development, media outreach, paid media, graphic design, product placement, direct outreach, minority outreach, and research.

Training on how to use the security features to detect counterfeit notes was central to the public education effort, with particular emphasis on cash handlers, who are the front line of defense against counterfeiting. The improved security features, coupled with cash handlers and consumers who are well informed about the security features, help ensure that counterfeit U.S. currency remains low. Tactics to achieve a high level of awareness are detailed below.

- **Research.** Qualitative and quantitative research—including focus groups, individual interviews, and telephone and Internet surveys—to formulate messages and track awareness and authentication behavior among domestic and international audiences. Initial research was used to develop messages to reassure the public that the new designs would stay ahead of counterfeiting and protect individuals from fraud. Measurement surveys were done throughout the program to track progress.
- **Communications Plan Development.** Based on research findings and existing best practices, B-M worked closely with the BEP and FRB to develop a communications plan for each denomination that served as a road map for all outreach activities.
- **Materials Development.** Materials that were engaging and informative and usable in a number of applications were designed to educate cash handlers and consumers about the new design. Materials—including brochures, posters, take-one cards, tent cards, training videos,

and CD-ROMs—are available free of charge, with some materials available in 24 languages, through Internet, telephone, and fax order forms. For the $5, $10, $20, and $50 notes, more than 78 million pieces of material have been distributed to 120 countries worldwide.

- **Media Relations.** A direct and aggressive media relations effort at the national and local levels, coupled with press releases, fact sheets, satellite/radio media tours, and special events, generated more than 1 billion impressions worldwide over the course of the program. The public was also reached through mentions in pop culture like David Letterman, Jay Leno, and Jon Stewart.
- **International Outreach.** With 60 percent of U.S. currency circulating overseas, international outreach has been integral to the program. Burson-Marsteller has leveraged dozens of its offices around the world to assist with outreach at various times.
- **Direct Outreach.** A database of more than 50,000 businesses was developed to reach grassroots contacts in each targeted sector. As a result of outreach to this group to date, training materials reached more than 100,000 business locations around the country.
- **Stakeholder Outreach.** Outreach to key stakeholder groups—such as the AARP, National Consumers League, and the National Federation of Independent Business—and local and civic groups—such as the Southeastern Pennsylvania Transit Authority—ensured that campaign messages reached audiences through existing communications vehicles like newsletters and Web sites. In total, more than 30,000 companies have placed orders for educational materials.
- **Integrated Partnerships.** Partnerships were developed with a number of high profile companies including Wal-Mart, Ace Hardware, Circuit City, Pepperidge Farm, and Harrah's Entertainment, to educate more than 1 million cash handlers and millions more consumers that visit partner companies each day.
- **Interactive Elements.** A comprehensive Web site was developed to include an interactive press room with materials in 24 languages, children's games, order forms for free materials, a section where anyone can download educational materials, and "interactive notes" that highlight new and enhanced features of the new notes.
- **Paid Media.** Because U.S. currency had not changed significantly in more than 70 years, advertising became an essential element in the introduction of the first denomination to be redesigned—the $20 bill. Penetration of the program's message had to reach near-saturation, so that this significant change to everyday life would not be disruptive or cause panic.
- **Product Placement.** Also for the $20 program, images of the new note and campaign messages were seen on *Wheel of Fortune, America's Funniest Home Videos,* Pepsi's *Play for a Billion Challenge,* and *Who Wants to Be a Millionaire.* Placements and script integration also appeared on dramas like *Law and Order, CSI, The District,* and *The Shield.*
- **Team Management.** The Burson-Marsteller team, led by its core team of senior leadership in Washington, D.C., was responsible for the implementation and monitoring of the expenditures against the contract price along with general management of the program and team members. The firm also managed 6 domestic and 11 international Burson-Marsteller offices as well as 10 subcontractors that worked on the worldwide integrated communications plan.

Results

In the first year of the program, public awareness of changes to the currency jumped from 30 to 82 percent.

(*Continued*)

To date, more than 1 billion domestic media impressions and more than 1.5 billion international media impressions have been generated. More than 30,000 companies have ordered materials—educating more than 4 million cash handlers worldwide about the currency change and more than 78 million pieces of educational materials have been distributed to more than 120 countries.

The overall program blended and sequenced many communications tools seamlessly into a cost-effective and cost-efficient program. Public relations and direct outreach demonstrated their value at delivering big impressions and awareness at a modest cost, while paid media and product placement reinforced awareness and recognition of new currency design features.

CORPORATE PROFILES AND AUTHOR BIOGRAPHIES

BURSON-MARSTELLER

Burson-Marsteller, founded by Harold Burson and Bill Marsteller in 1953, is a leading global public relations and public affairs firm. Visit Burson-Marsteller at www.bm.com.

Harold Burson

Harold Burson, in a survey conducted by *PRWeek,* was described as "the century's most influential PR figure." He cofounded Burson-Marsteller and was CEO of the agency for 35 years.

PORTER NOVELLI

Porter Novelli today is one of the world's top public relations firms, helping clients in 60 countries achieve their business goals in the commercial, government, and not-for-profit sectors. Visit Porter Novelli at porternovelli.com.

Gary Stockman

Gary Stockman is a partner and the chief executive officer of Porter Novelli, with responsibility for the agency's overall growth and development in the Americas, Europe, the Middle East and Africa (EMEA), and the Asia Pacific region. He is based in Porter Novelli's New York office.

EDELMAN PUBLIC RELATIONS WORLDWIDE

Edelman is the world's leading independent public relations firm, with over 3,200 employees in 54 offices worldwide. Visit Edelman at www.edelman.com.

Andrew Silver

Andrew Silver was formerly the General Manager of the Shanghai office at Edelman. Mr. Silver received his BFA from Long Island University.

NOTES

1. American Marketing Association.
2. United Kingdom Institute of Public Relations.
3. Wirthlin Worldwide.
4. Fortune, 2008.
5. Small Business Administration, 2002.
6. Ibid.

12 PROMOTIONAL MARKETING

WOW! NOW I CAN GET 12 CDs, WITH NO OBLIGATION TO PURCHASE MORE – AND I CAN CANCEL AT ANY TIME!

by VISA, OgilvyAction, Mars, New York Times, and PepsiCo

THE ESSENTIALS OF PROMOTIONAL MARKETING
by VISA

Introduction

Promotional marketing is the element of marketing that encourages people to ACT NOW, such as purchase or try a product, by providing a short-term added benefit to consumers, distributors, or retailers. The goal is to move people to action, and get past their natural hesitancy. Promotional marketing can provide a short-term boost to supplement the impact of advertising and other marketing activities and also can have long-term effects both on attitudes and behavior. Historically, promotional marketing has not been used to build long-term brand image or equity. Today, however, promotional marketing is an integral part of the long-term branding process.

For example, in the credit card industry VISA uses advertising to make people feel good about the brand and promotion to give consumers a reason to use their card now. The brand's advertising campaign focuses on VISA's acceptance, security, and convenience. VISA uses promotion to give consumers extra reasons to obtain a card and to use it, to build market share in key merchant categories and at specific merchants. These promotions include sweepstakes offers to win trips, merchandise, or cash prizes, coupon offers that save the customer money when VISA is used for payment, and cause-related promotions linking card use to non-profit donations, such as the Olympics.

Advertising alone does not maximize a brand's total marketing potential. Promotion can speed the product adoption process by inducing product awareness, trial, repurchase, and loyalty more quickly than advertising alone. Speeding up this process means that sales volume and profits can be achieved faster, and a company can start getting paid back for its investment to develop and market a product or service.

Sometimes, promotions are so successful that they become a permanent component of the product. The airline frequent flyer promotions initially started as short-term promotional programs. Similarly, McDonald's "Happy Meals" started as a series of short-term premium promotions to appeal to families with children.

Another aspect of marketing is obtaining the support and loyalty of product distributors, retailers, or service providers. Promotional marketing can help gain distribution for a product, encourage distributors to have adequate stock on hand, convince retailers to display or showcase the product or service to their customers, encourage extra effort and attention from sales personnel, or help obtain additional advertising and promotional support from retailers or others.

Definition

Promotional marketing is "the strategic and tactical marketing planning and execution for a brand using the full mix of business and consumer communications designed to work in concert to influence behavior in a way that builds sales and reinforces brand image."[1]

PROMOTIONAL MARKETING PROCESS

Determine Business Objectives
↓
Perform Creative Process
↓
Determine Promotional Marketing Tactics
↓
Determine Media Appropriate for Tactics
↓
Evaluate Outcome

PROMOTION OBJECTIVES

The primary objectives of promotional marketing are to get consumers to act or purchase now, and to gain brand acceptance over time. In addition there are several specific objectives that include product trials by potential customers, increased usage by existing customers, higher average purchase amount, loyalty of purchases over time or customer retention, and brand image enhancement. Promotion can also be used to defend a brand from short-term competitive marketing activities.

Trials by Potential Customers

Most consumers are hesitant to try a new product. Consumers, either consciously or unconsciously, make a risk assessment before trying a new product or service. Consumers are concerned with the loss of benefits by switching from a favorite brand, the money it would take to buy the new product, and the time that might have to be expended to obtain the new product or learn how to use it. Promotion is used to temporarily reduce this risk. Companies should be willing to look at the long-term profit from a potential customer (lifetime value), and be willing to forfeit short-term profits in order to encourage consumer trial. If a product has clear functional superiority over competitive offerings, then trial-generating activities are a must.

When Burger King introduced new French fries that were being touted as better than its competitor's, Burger King encouraged consumers to try the new fries by having a "Free Fry-day" event. Every customer on a specified Friday received free fries. Literally millions of people came that day, overcoming their hesitancy and providing the potential for additional future sales.

Increased Product/Service Usage by Existing Customers

Most products get 80 percent of their business from 20 percent of their customer base. Similarly, they get an even higher percentage of their profits from this same 20 percent. The more a marketer can increase the number of loyal customers, the more sales and profits can be made. Trial-generating activities that place a product or service into the consumers' considered set of products will at least encourage occasional purchases.

Once a marketer obtains consumer trial of a product and that product is then included in the consumers' considered brand set, the marketer's priority is to build a product's share of consumer usage. Generally, it is much less expensive to increase the frequency of product purchase among existing customers than it is to recruit a totally new customer. For example, in the credit card industry, it currently costs from $50 to $100 to persuade a customer to open a new account. In comparison, there are many successful promotions to increase usage that cost less than $10 per account. In this situation, it makes better economic sense to spend more on usage promotions among existing customers than to find new ones.

In another example, many companies, such as Coca-Cola and M&M/Mars, have long maintained that every consumer is in the market to buy another product as soon as the current product is finished. Much of both companies' success stems from their ability to gain greater visibility in stores and thus encourage more frequent purchases. Other companies increase the frequency of purchase by suggesting additional uses for a product. Other food products accomplish this by developing and distributing recipes or by conducting recipe contests.

Retention of Customers

Retention is more than just continued use of a product. Retention primarily applies to products and services that require an active renewal of an agreement for such things as insurance policies, credit cards, subscriptions, or leases. Promotion can be used to increase the probability that the company will get a renewal.

Enhancement of Brand Image

Promotions that reinforce key product benefits or relate to other marketing communications efforts can positively influence consumer perceptions. For example, many television and radio shows use on-air contests or sweepstakes that appeal to their audience. The goal of these is to add excitement to the viewing experience, get involvement from viewers, provide an incentive to listen or watch more often, and enhance the image of the television channel or radio station.

Defend Against Competitive Activities

When a competitor's new product enters a product category, a "loading" promotion can be used to prevent or delay trial of the new product. If a customer can be motivated to buy more of a product at one time, such as buying the larger size or agreeing to an extended subscription, then a marketer virtually has eliminated the chance that a competitive product will be bought until the customer's supply is gone. Well-timed promotions can preempt competitive programs by locking up retail advertising, display, and shelf space to the detriment of competitors.

Another way promotion can be used to defend against a competitor is by temporarily improving the value of a product relative to the competition. By offering a discount on the product, or adding a gift with purchase at the normal price, the value proposition to the consumer improves. That makes it more difficult for competitors to obtain trial of their product.

Some product categories have a disproportionate share of sales during specific time periods. During peak periods, it is most likely that competitors will hold special promotions. So sometimes, a company is forced to promote its product during these time frames to offset the activities of competitors. For example, snowblowers sell best at the start of winter (or after the first major snowstorm), specialty candy sells best during the Halloween season, and credit card transactions peak during the holidays.

PROMOTION CREATIVE

Promotion creative includes the words, visuals, and overall design of promotional materials that the consumer sees on point-of-purchase materials, advertising, direct mail, or other promotional media. If a promotional concept cannot be explained in a single sentence on a point-of-sale sign or advertisement, then the promotional program is probably too complicated. The most important aspect of promotion creative is to explain the offer (the reward) and to make a call to action (what is required to earn the reward).

Point-of-sale signs generally are limited to a blunt statement of the offer and a call to action because of the cluttered retail environment in which they exist. A key to clear communication on signage is limiting the number of graphic elements The most effective signs are those that are clear and simple, such as: "Save," "Buy," "Free," and "Use."

Few companies maintain full-service in-house staffs to create and develop promotional programs and communication materials. Generally, a limited number of in-house marketing personnel are responsible for guiding the development of promotional plans and programs. The marketing staff hires and manages outside agencies to actually implement promotional programs. For example, the promotion group might conceive of a promotion, work with the company's research department to confirm the concept's consumer appeal, and guide the development work of a promotional marketing agency.

PROMOTION TACTICS TO CONSUMERS

The ideal promotion tactic holds real and perceived value to the consumer, costs the marketer virtually nothing extra, requires little or no extra administration, is simple to communicate to consumers, requires little effort from consumers other than purchasing the product, and has universal customer appeal or at least appeal among the product's customer base.

Consumer promotional marketing also is known as pull marketing because it urges the consumer to request or pull products and services from the distribution channels. Each promotion tactic can apply regardless of the industry, product, or target audience. The promotional techniques of companies such as M&M/Mars, NBC Television, and AT&T are very similar.

The promotion tactic that works best for a given product or service category depends on the amount of the consumer's involvement in the purchasing decision, the amount of risk the consumer takes in buying the product (financial, social, and personal esteem risk), and the competitiveness of the product category. Selecting the right approach in the right situation for the right product or service is the art within the discipline of promotional marketing.

Promotional techniques include premium offers, trade shows, point-of-purchase displays, promotional products, coupons, cause-related promotions/sponsorships, samples, contests/sweepstakes/games, loyalty/frequency promotions, and rebates/refunds.[2]

Premium Offers

Premiums are merchandise offered for free or at a special price in order to generate sales, loyalty, and repeat business. Fast-food companies such as McDonald's, Burger King, and Taco Bell seem to always have a toy as a premium available with the purchase of a child's menu selection. At one time, banks were famous for offering free toasters to consumers who opened new checking accounts. Premiums work most efficiently when the consumer's perceived value of the premium is greater than the cost of the premium to the marketer.

When perceived value exceeds cost, a premium will be more effective and profitable than an equivalent price reduction, coupon, rebate, or other financial incentive.

Premiums can be offered to the consumer free at company expense, partially subsidized, or self-liquidated (fully paid for by the customer). Premiums use a marketer's buying power and economies of scale to bring a great price to the consumer at minimum or no cost to the marketer. For example, Chevron has offered toy cars at a reduced rate to customers who purchase a minimum of 12 gallons of gasoline.

Many companies will offer premiums thematically linked to a major event such as a motion picture or sports event. The thematic link is a way to take a mundane or inexpensive item and give it extra appeal by associating it with a "hot" property. For example, Disney and McDonald's had a 10-year joint sponsorship relationship that ensured that every major Disney movie release would result in some kind of special McDonald's promotion.

Projecting consumer demand can be very difficult. Buying too many premiums before knowing the response rate is costly; therefore, companies may buy a set amount of premiums and state in promotional communications that the offer is available "while supplies last." Or, companies may desire to fulfill all responses to a promotion by ordering the item from the manufacturer after responses are in, and announce that consumers should "allow up to 6 to 8 weeks for delivery."

Premium offers made by manufacturers can be included in packaging (in-pack), attached to a product (on-pack), displayed near a product (near-packs), bonus packs, or delivered to consumers by mail.

- **In-packs.** Cracker Jacks brand caramel corn made in-packs a permanent feature of the product. Now, cereal makers are probably the most frequent users of in-packs. At any given time there are many "Free Toy Inside" offers announced on the face of cereal boxes. Another common in-pack is a set of coupons for other products. Supplemental film footage included with a DVD release or special software included with a new personal computer are examples of in-packs.
- **On-packs.** On-packs are premiums (merchandise or other products) that are attached to a product's package at no additional cost to the consumer. On-packs generally provide a high perceived value to consumers at a low absolute cost to the carrying company. An on-pack can lure new customers, increase sales to existing customers, or gain trial of a new product by attaching the premium to an existing brand. The on-pack might not cost the carrying brand anything except packaging and administration fees, which are compensated by increased sales. For example, an on-pack might include a free toothbrush with purchase of toothpaste or a free contact lens case with the purchase of lens solution.
- **Near-packs.** Near-packs are used when it would be too costly, require too much lead time, or cause manufacturing problems to try to attach the premium to the product. Near-packs are often used as a way to motivate retailers to purchase prepacked displays. The near-pack included in the prepacked display could be a cookbook, a sports team schedule, a CD/ROM with software for a game, or any other premium. The best near-packs are ones that directly relate to the sponsoring product. Some credit card issuers use near-packs at events or on college campuses to sign up new cardholders. At special tables or booths, consumers are often offered free T-shirts when they fill out an application for a credit card.
- **Bonus-packs.** Bonus packs are special offerings of a product that contain an extra quantity of product at no additional cost to the consumer. Examples of bonus packs can be found in the product industry ("super-sized" fries when you order a hamburger) and the service industry (an extra lane when you bowl three lanes or an extra movie rental when you rent two). Bonus packs can provide a brand with a temporary price/value advantage over competitive products, provide consumers with a reason to stock up, increase usage simply by increasing the supply in a customer's home, and preempt purchases of competitive products by increasing the amount of time between purchases. Bonus packs take advantage of the fact that the perceived value of the extra quantity is higher than the cost of the materials.

Some retailers prefer this type of premium as it results in higher sales. However, other retailers are unwilling to accept the extra administrative expense of using a different package configuration or stock keeping unit (SKU). Extra costs might include reconfiguring warehouse or on-shelf space, changing computer codes at check out, or changing cost per ounce labels that might appear on shelves.

- **Mail-ins.** The most common approach to distributing a premium offer is via the mail. Consumers can be made aware of the premium offer by advertising, in-store point-of-purchase material, on-packaging, or on Web sites. To obtain the premium, consumers simply send in proof of purchase, and the premium is delivered by a postal delivery service. Many marketers use mail-in offers to avoid the cost and logistical issues of the other premium delivery methods. Costs also are lower, because the consumer must take action to actually get the premium. This slippage reduces costs, but also reduces the impact of the premium offer.

Trade Shows

Trade shows exist to build awareness for companies, to generate sales leads, or to sell products. They offer a company an opportunity to meet hundreds of potential and current customers face-to-face. This would not be possible by traveling to meet these people individually, from either a cost or time perspective. To attract visitors to a specific exhibit or booth, many exhibitors will conduct sweepstakes, give free gifts to visitors, or have special entertainment. These promotional activities usually are tied to soliciting business cards from visitors for follow-up sales efforts.

TRADE SHOWS

Over 100 million people visited the 1.5 million exhibitors at over 14,000 trade shows held in 2008, according to the Center for Exhibition Industry Research. The largest annual trade show is the International Consumer Electronics Show, the most fun is the American International Toy Fair, and the tastiest is the International Baking Industry Exposition.

Point-of-Purchase Displays

Point-of-purchase (POP) refers to the usage of a promotional product signage at the physical point where the product or service is purchased in order to remind customers of a product and generate impulse purchases. For many inexpensive products, especially packaged goods, consumers do not specifically plan in advance to purchase them when shopping. The decision to purchase often can be made at the point of purchase. The incidence of this happening can be greatly increased with extra visibility for the product in the retail store, such as freestanding displays, end-of-aisle displays, or shelf talkers on the supermarket shelf. POP also can be in the form of a display where the purchase is made at an Internet site.

Shelf talkers are printed cards or signs designed to mount on or under a grocery store or drug store shelf and display the product name, company logo, and a promotional message such as "Buy one, get one free."

The keys to a successful POP presence are providing an extra economic incentive to the retailer in exchange for displaying materials, taking extra effort to ensure that the materials are delivered and placed in the store correctly, and making sure that there is a compelling call to action for the consumer. (Point-of-purchase was formerly referred to as point-of-sale, but the name was changed to better reflect the perspective of the consumer.)

Promotional Products

A *promotional product* is any product that has been imprinted with a company name, logo, or message. These are given to consumers free in order to promote the company or organization by building name recognition and increasing goodwill. The most prevalent products used are T-shirts, pens, and mugs. In general, consumers love receiving items for free, and most promotional products are appreciated and used for some time. The requirements for a good promotional product are that it be useful, of high quality, allow multiple uses, fit the audience needs, and be imprintable. Their advantages are that they usually are in continuous use, relatively inexpensive, and are highly effective. Promotional products also are used as employee or executive gifts (clocks, watches, trophies) to build loyalty and motivation, and to remind the recipient of the product as he or she uses the product at a later date. (Promotional products were formerly known as ad specialties.)

Coupons

Coupons permit the consumer to buy a product at a reduced price at the place the product is normally sold. To be effective, coupons must generate enough new sales revenue to offset their use by consumers who would have bought the product anyway. When the coupon is created by a retailer or merchant, the cost of the coupon is paid by the merchant. For coupons distributed by manufacturers, the retailer sends the coupon back to the manufacturer or a coupon clearinghouse and is then reimbursed for the face value of the coupon plus a handling fee.

In the travel and entertainment industry, coupons are used to motivate product or service usage during nonpeak periods. A hotel room or an airplane seat is a perishable product. If not used each night or flight, potential revenue is lost forever. Coupons with restrictions are used to strategically limit use of the coupon to times when business is most needed.

Coupons permit companies to use different customers' elasticity of demand to maximize revenue and profits. Some customers are very price sensitive, whereas others are not and do not use coupons at all. The net effect is that companies are able to reduce prices to consumers who care about price, and maintain a higher price for those who do not care enough about price to use a coupon.

The percentage of consumers who redeem coupons varies according to several factors. These factors include the medium by which the coupon is delivered (such as newspaper, newspaper supplements, magazines, direct mail, online, on-package, in-package, and in-store distribution); the degree to which the coupon is distributed to specific targeted customers; the value of the coupon; the product being supported; the quantity or size of the required purchase; and the advertising creative (headline, copy, and visuals) used with the coupon. Depending on these factors, response rates range from a tenth of a percent to 20 percent.

Cause-Related Promotions/Sponsorships

During cause-related promotions (CRPs), a contribution is made to a charity every time a consumer purchase is made. One of the first CRPs was conducted by Clark Gum during the early 1970s. For every pack of gum purchased during the Halloween period, one penny would be contributed to UNICEF. Since then, many national charitable groups have linked to marketers and vice versa. Campbell's soup started their "Labels for Education" program in 1973 and students, parents, and teachers still collect soup labels and turn them in for school-related equipment.

Cause-related promotions work best when there is an obvious or logical connection between the cause and the marketer and when the cause is relevant to the customers of the sponsoring brand. The organization should be well known, financially responsible, and have a high percentage of its revenue going to the cause rather than administrative expenses. The timing of the promotion should coincide with when the charity gets the greatest visibility.

For example, BMW used cause-related marketing in 1997 to motivate women to test-drive a new automobile model. For every test mile driven, BMW made a $1 contribution to breast cancer research organizations. Thousands of women came to BMW dealers to test-drive the vehicles, resulting in hundreds of sales. The benefits of cause-related marketing to the sponsor include increased sales, the positive image impact from becoming associated with a nonprofit organization or charity, and improved employee morale.

Celebrities often can be solicited to become spokespersons for companies that are sponsoring a cause-related promotion. The fees for the celebrity for a cause-related promotion often are less than the fees charged without the cause. The celebrity often opens the door to publicity and attention that would otherwise not be gained.

Samples

Manufacturers use sampling to encourage potential new customers to try new or existing products and services. Sampling speeds the process of new product adoption by condensing the process of product awareness, intent to purchase, and actual trial. Samples can be offered to consumers either in-home or in-store. Examples of sampling techniques include a free taste test at the local grocery store or an event, a free product coupon distributed in a newspaper or magazine, a special small package sold at low prices through normal sales outlets, a free product sent in the mail to households, or a vehicle test-drive.

With sampling, the consumers do not have to trust the product's advertising in order to become buyers because they can experience the product firsthand and evaluate the claims for themselves.

Sampling also can be used in conjunction with a reduced price, which reduces or eliminates the cost risk that a consumer must take to find out if a new product is acceptable. For example, fast-food companies often price new products at a special price point to encourage sampling, such as an "Introductory price of 99 cents."

Although it is very effective, sampling is generally the most expensive promotion technique. The marketer must pay for the product, packaging, and distribution to consumers. Typically, the payout period (how long it will take for the new users to buy enough product to pay for the initial sample) for a sampling program is 6 to 18 months. Promotional sampling is most cost-effective for low-cost products that are purchased frequently, because the cost of the free sample can be recouped quickly by future purchases.

In evaluating the value or worth of sampling from the perspective of the marketer, the key variables are the absolute cost of the product, the percentage of potential customers who actually try the sample, the number of consumers who try a sample and then eventually buy the product at the regular price, and the frequency of purchases.

Contests/Sweepstakes/Games

The goals of these techniques are to increase product awareness, encourage repeat purchases, encourage retailer point-of-purchase displays, drive traffic into stores, and involve consumers with the product. A *contest* is a promotional program that asks consumers to complete activities, such as writing an essay, drawing a picture, creating a recipe, or sending a proof of purchase to win a prize. A *sweepstakes* is similar, but no skill or purchase is necessary. A *game* is a variation of a sweepstakes that usually incorporates game pieces ("each one is a separate way to win," or "collect the set and win").

These types of promotional programs provide themes and creative flexibility. A brand can construct a program to connect with the advertising campaign, image, product features, product benefits, or the target audience's special interests. A marketer can often "borrow interest" from an exciting promotion partner to come up with a compelling promotion (for example, win a trip to the Olympics or the Super Bowl). This can be a very useful way to build awareness of an event sponsorship program.

For example, a company whose product appeals to teens might have a prize package that includes appearing on MTV, a trip to a Florida beach during spring break, or a college scholarship.

The cost for a contest or sweepstakes can be very predictable. The marketer can set the number of winners and the value of prizes at the start of the program. This contrasts with most other promotional techniques where consumer response rates significantly affect promotion budgets.

It is slightly more difficult to project the cost of games than it is for contests or sweepstakes. Although it is generally easy to estimate the number of game pieces needed for a specific time-based program, it is more difficult to predict what percentage of winning consumers will actually redeem their prizes. A surprising percentage of winners never come forward, perhaps because the consumer with the winning game piece never really looked at the piece. This percentage of unknown and unclaimed winners is known as *slippage*. Key influences on slippage include the type of game piece, the prize value, the intrusiveness of the game piece (a soft drink winning symbol inside the can versus a fast-food coupon that reveals the words "You Win!"), the product category being promoted, whether the winners need to collect a set of game pieces, and the total number of winners or the consumer's perceived chance of winning.

The goal of lotteries is to increase revenue, and they are limited in their use only to governments. However, exceptions may be made for charity raffles for nonprofit organizations.

Loyalty/Frequency Promotions

The goal of loyalty or frequency promotions is to encourage consumers to buy the same product brand numerous times. They also build a psychological bond to the product or service in the mind of the consumer. For example, the best-known loyalty programs are run by airlines. One of the main reasons airlines adopted frequent-flyer programs, which have evolved into a standard product feature, was to reward business travelers who, since they were not paying for the ticket, were not price sensitive. The free miles give a reason to concentrate travel with a specific carrier. In addition to the free miles, these programs also incorporate recognition and status to the airline's most frequent fliers. Designations such as "Premier," "Gold," and "Platinum" tell the customer they are important.

The airline mileage programs have been so successful that other companies such as credit cards, telephone companies, restaurants, and retailers now tie into the airline programs and also reward customers with "miles." Many consumers do not spend enough at any one place to earn a free trip. If purchases at several places are combined, trips become possible in a much shorter period of time.

The original frequency programs used stamps to track purchases. Stamps were given to customers to reward purchases. The stamps were collected and redeemed for merchandise. S&H Green Stamps, Blue Chip Stamps, and Gold Bond Stamps were ubiquitous. Because of the stamps' ubiquity, customers were no longer loyal to just one store; thus stores abandoned stamps and took the money previously spent on stamps to lower prices, advertise more, or conduct other promotional activities.

Many grocery stores and other retailers issue *loyalty cards* to customers. These cards provide savings to customers and allow retailers to track customer buying patterns. In addition, many retailers today use mainframe computers to track consumer purchases. In the near future, smart cards (credit cards with computer chips built in) will track consumer purchase histories and provide security protection to prevent fraud.

The key to evaluating frequency programs is to determine whether the product's margins will be sufficient to provide a meaningful reward to consumers in a reasonable amount of time, and generate enough incremental business to pay for the reward. For example, a credit card that gives a 1 percent rebate at the end of the year to a regular $1,500 per year spender would pay out approximately $15 per year. Most consumers are not impressed by this reward level. But, if the consumer consolidates all credit card spending on one card, the spending can easily become $8,000 and yield a payout of $80. Now the consumer payout has value, and the incremental volume to the credit card issuer is meaningful.

Major cost elements in frequency promotions are database and communication costs. Each mailing to a program participant costs at least 50 cents (printing, postage, letter shop fees). Database costs can vary widely based on the method of tracking purchases. The annual cost per customer typically is $5 to $10, depending on the frequency of statement mailings and the cost of tracking sales data. These costs need to be taken into account when calculating the payout of any program.

One of the most important factors that affects the value offered to the consumer is *slippage* or *breakage*. These are credits earned but not used by the consumer. For example, some airline programs have expiration dates for earned miles, and the traveler must use the miles within three or four years, or the miles expire. Sometimes mileage credits are claimed, but the tickets are never used. Slippage can significantly reduce the cost of a program, or be used to enhance the value of the reward. For example, a 10 percent slippage rate could reduce the actual cost of an $80 reward to $72. Or the slippage could be used to increase the value of the reward to $88.

An important consideration in developing frequency programs is whether to require *enrollment*, which is the aspect of agreeing to be in a program and is often a necessity in order to track transactions. It encourages participation among consumers who want the reward and promotes slippage among those who do not care or those who do not wish to divulge personal information. Enrollment also helps the consumer make a psychological commitment to the brand and the program. The major drawback to requiring enrollment is that the program will probably only influence the purchase behavior of those consumers who enroll. If only a small percentage of customers enroll, then only a small percentage will have their purchase behavior changed. The fixed cost of setting up the program might not be recouped.

Frequency programs also must determine what the reward or recognition element will be. Most companies try to use rewards whose perceived value is higher than the cost to the company.

When creating a loyalty program, the marketer should have definite plans about how to end the program. Every program should have a formal end date, even if the program is planned to be permanent. At a minimum, a program end date will allow adjustments to the program rules. In case the loyalty program is not cost-efficient or cost-effective, the end date provides a way to avoid unnecessary losses.

Rebates/Refunds

Rebates spur sales by offering after-the-fact cash (check or credit) rewards for purchasing a product or service. Rebates ensure that the discount is given to consumers who submit a proof-of-purchase, and is not absorbed by the distributor or retailer, which can sometimes be the case with other price discount programs.

A rebate is a form of temporary price reduction that appeals to price-sensitive consumers who are willing to do extra work to get the rebate, and who are willing to purchase a larger than ordinary amount of product to get the money back. Rebates, when merchandised to retailers, can often help motivate special display features, help gain special in-store promotional support, or get extra visibility in retailer advertising. Motor oil marketers often use rebates to gain retailer support. These oil retailers often will display the cost per quart of the oil less the manufacturer's rebate. This advertising approach makes the cost per quart look exceedingly low. Computer retailers for hardware and software increasingly use this same tactic.

Chrysler, Ford, General Motors, and other automobile companies have used rebates to overcome imbalances of supply and demand for specific vehicles. Often consumers are offered $500 back if a certain model of car is bought by a certain date. Most times the rebate can be applied to the down payment of the vehicle or lease, thereby enabling a greater percentage of people to make a suitable down payment. Sometimes the rebate can be exchanged to obtain a lower interest rate, which results in lower monthly payments.

During the late 1980s, rebates were an effective marketing tool for the automobile companies. However, during the early 1990s, they became overused and predictable. Once consumers could safely predict when rebates would be used by the manufacturer, the consumers would delay purchases. Since consumers held back purchases, the need for rebates grew. This became a vicious cycle that severely impaired profits. It took many years for automobile companies to extricate themselves from this cycle.

New forms of rebating are currently appearing. For example, credit card companies such as VISA are now introducing systems that will allow retailers to reward customers with rebate credits on their VISA account if the customer spends a specified amount at a specific merchant within a particular time frame.

A form of rebate that is not temporary bases its consumer value on a rebate for all purchases at the end of the year. For example, the Discover Card provides a 1 percent rebate to consumers.

Sometimes a consumer can receive a rebate in the form of free service. For example, some cellular phone companies offer free minutes of air time if a customer signs an annual agreement.

Slippage from customers makes many rebates financially desirable to the marketer. Only a small percentage of consumers who buy a product will go to the trouble of mailing in a rebate form or calling a toll-free telephone number to claim a credit. For packaged goods, response rates can vary from a fraction of a percent up to 20 percent. It is possible that a $5 rebate could actually cost a manufacturer less than a 50-cent coupon depending on redemption and slippage rates.

PROMOTIONAL MARKETING TO THE TRADE

Trade promotions attempt to build relationships with and motivate wholesalers and retailers to actively sell a company's products or services. The retailer hopes to increase its percentage of category sales relative to other retailers, while the manufacturer hopes to increase its share of the category compared to other brands in the category and to balance supply and demand. Another purpose of trade promotions is to get a temporary price advantage or greater retail visibility over the competition. Extra product displays, inclusion in a retailer's advertisement, or special prices can significantly increase sales. Promotional marketing to the trade also is known as *push promotion* because it helps to push products and services through the distribution channels to the consumer.

Trade promotions include:

- Temporary price reductions to retailers
- Special payments to distributors or retailers for the display and advertising of the featured product
- Slotting allowances (payments) to retailers to stock the product
- In-store coupons
- Free samples
- End-aisle displays
- Pay for performance bonuses
- Special product packs
- Frequent shopper bonuses
- Window banners or other in-store signage
- Check-out coupons to encourage repeat store visits
- Circulars
- Freestanding newspaper inserts
- Local cause-related promotions
- Mail-in offers
- Special events including celebrity appearances

Trade promotions can prevent the need to permanently reduce prices and lower profit margins, while yielding incremental sales. However, when overused, trade promotions become expected and consumers and retailers adjust their purchasing behavior with no benefit to the company sponsoring the promotion. For example, some packaged goods were supported with trade promotions on a predictable, quarterly schedule. Retailers of these products would order months of inventory at the trade promotion price so they would never have to buy the product at the regular selling price. The retailer would feature a special deal for a week to qualify for the discount. Then, the retailer would sell the remaining months of discounted merchandise at the regular price until the next trade deal occurred or the supply was sold off. As long as warehousing costs were less than the extra margin, the retailer would add extra profit.

Trade promotions are typically linked to concurrent consumer promotions such as couponing, sampling, sweepstakes, or a combination of these. The marketing objective is to concentrate all activity at once so that the likelihood of getting the attention of retailers and consumers is maximized.

Coupons can be useful in enlisting special retailer or distributor support for a product, because a major coupon drop (major distribution to millions of homes) is a reason for grocers and retailers to order an extra supply of product to avoid being out of stock. Retailers are willing to pass on price discounts to consumers in order to generate additional volume created by the promotion. Retailers often give the product being couponed a special display, feature the product prominently in retail advertisements, and give the product better shelf placement.

PROMOTIONAL MARKETING MEDIA

All advertising media can be used for promotional marketing programs: television, radio, print, Internet, or out-of-home. In addition, promotional marketing media can include in-store media, product packages, and direct mail. The keys to proper media planning and buying are virtually the same for promotional marketing as for brand advertising. The main differences are that promotional programs generally need to build awareness more quickly than brand advetising, and therefore occur within a limited time frame and use the media closest to the point of transaction.

Broadcast Media

Television and radio are best suited to build awareness quickly, can be both national and regional, and are viewed by distributors and retailers more favorably than most other media for their impact on consumers. The absolute cost of broadcast advertising support is generally affordable only by major brands in such industries as automotive, retailing, travel and entertainment, credit cards, fast food, broadcast, motion pictures, and soft drinks. Broadcast media provides a better opportunity to creatively use approaches that combine the rational appeal of a promotional offer with humor, emotion, or brand imagery. Also, more information can be included in broadcast media such as product descriptions.

Print Media

Print media is most often used to support promotional programs. Print usually can be better targeted to prospects than broadcast media. Print usually costs less on an absolute basis than a broadcast advertising schedule, although the cost per thousand impressions usually is higher than television or radio. Newspapers and freestanding inserts (FSI), usually found in the Sunday section of newspapers, can build awareness for a promotional program quickly, whereas magazines build awareness more slowly. Print advertising, given its brief visual appeal, requires an approach that is very straightforward. Attempts to incorporate emotion, humor, or brand imagery can obscure the promotional message.

Direct Mail

Direct mail is another medium used to support promotions. Stand-alone direct mail can be extremely effective, but is one of the most expensive media. Syndicated direct-mail programs, such as "Carol Wright" or Valassis mailings, provide marketers with a relatively cost-effective way to get information about a promotion or an actual product sample into a prospect's home.

Many frequency promotion programs, such as airline and grocery clubs, are now offsetting the cost of sending participant communications by selling space in envelopes. In general, direct mail should be considered only if the target buyer universe is small, highly targetable, or if it is used as a means for delivering a product sample which has high profitability or a frequent repurchase rate, and is noticeably better than competitive products. An example of a highly targeted direct-mail effort would be a mailing from VISA to Chief Financial Officers (CFOs) of Fortune 500 companies to introduce them to the VISA Purchasing Card. Because there are only 500 CFOs for the Fortune 500, the most efficient way to reach them is via mail.

Internet

The Internet and the growth of e-commerce have radically changed the sales process by offering a convenient and efficient communications and sales distribution channel.

Pay per click (PPC) advertising on search engines such as Google, Yahoo, or MSN has become an incredibly powerful way to attract prospects to a marketer's Web site. Search terms (such as "credit cards") are bought on a search engine, and then an ad for the sponsor appears in the search results when someone uses the term. In addition, banner ads and other forms of online advertising are placed in sites with content appealing to a specific target audience. The special offer could be a price special, a sweepstakes, gift with purchase offer, or any number of other promotional tactics. All PPC and most online ads contain links to take interested consumers to the ad sponsor's Web site, a special landing page within a Web site, or the Web site of an authorized retailer.

Once a consumer enters a marketer's Web site, the Web becomes a sales distribution channel. The challenge is to motivate the consumer to explore the site, and to lead the consumer to make a purchase. Promotional marketing can help keep consumers interested in a site, motivate an immediate purchase, and encourage consumers to visit the site again.

Most e-commerce sites now include a "promo code" area on check out pages. This is the way a consumer redeems special offers they may have found on the Internet when making a purchase.

Most Web sites now ask site visitors if they would like future information from the site regarding new products or other news. This type of "permission marketing" can provide a real service to consumers and businesses by using inexpensive e-mails to keep the two parties in touch, something prohibitively costly in the brick-and-mortar world. The key is judicious use of the communication channel so as not to offend the customer with spam or junk e-mail. The most successful Web sites clearly state their privacy policy, security standards, and post "trust marks" such as VeriSign, McAfee SECURE, HackerProof, and BBB Accredited Business.

In-Store Media

In-store media is probably the most common element of any promotional program. For example, many fast-food outlets display a menu board that is surrounded by signs that tout the current promotion. Department stores frequently have ceiling banners, door posters, and freestanding signs announcing the current promotion. Warehouse stores, such as Costco, have become well-known for the variety of free samples they provide to customers who are shopping. The key to point-of-purchase signage is its distribution and placement. Some companies do so with their own sales force, while others rely on third-party vendors to distribute and place these types of material.

FINANCIAL ANALYSIS OF PROMOTIONAL PROGRAMS

Every promotional program budget should be analyzed in advance to ensure that it will be profitable. Most times, a simple break-even and payout analysis can be conducted to economically justify a promotional program. The following analysis is a quick way to evaluate the cost-efficiency and likelihood for success with any promotion.

FINANCIAL ANALYSIS

Total cost of promotion ÷ Average profit on an incremental sale = Incremental sales volume needed to break even or pay for the promotion

Once this evaluation is done, it is easy to assess the feasibility that the promotion can break even by looking at the incremental volume relative to actual volume.

Incremental volume to break even ÷ Normal volume during the promotion time period = Sales increase needed to break even

---

A promotion that would require a 5 to 10 percent increase in volume to break even is probably well worth pursuing. One that would require a 50 percent increase in sales is clearly not very feasible, and should be drastically modified or dropped from consideration before time and effort are devoted to it.

Every company should create a research system that leads to an understanding of what works and what does not work. Consumer research should be used to select from among various promotion concepts for implementation, to refine the ideas to better meet the needs and wants of targeted consumers, and to evaluate the impact of the promotion. Research allows standard comparisons of promotion results over time and captures this knowledge for the benefit of future marketing employees.

Every promotion should be evaluated after the fact. A simple analysis of the promotion results versus the prior period often can yield information that is incomplete or inaccurate. The challenge of postpromotion evaluation is to determine the incremental volume gained from the promotion. The depth of the analysis should depend in part on how much was spent on the promotion or the sum of similar promotions being done by the company. The ideal approach to determining incremental volume from a promotion would be to leave some markets as controls where the promotion is not conducted.

For example, VISA adopted a technique that simulates a formal "test versus control group" research approach. A telephone follow-up survey is conducted during and after a major national program among a minimum of 500 to 1,000 consumers. The telephone survey includes questions about aided and unaided promotion awareness for VISA, MasterCard, American Express, Discover, or other card promotions; perceived payment card usage during the past month(s); perceived value of the different promotions the consumer is aware of; how the consumer heard about the promotions; attitudes toward the different card companies; and demographic questions.

These research respondents were separated into those aware of the promotion and those not aware. The rationale is that if a consumer was not aware of a promotion, the promotion could not have influenced his or her behavior. If a consumer is aware, then the promotion could have affected behavior. A comparison of the two groups on the different questions and on actual card behavior (the prior year's promotion period versus this year's promotion period) shows how the promotion affected the two groups. The differences should primarily be due to the promotion, since economic, competitive, and other conditions should have influenced the two groups equally.

PROMOTIONAL MARKETING— INTERNATIONAL
by OgilvyAction

With the growth of global brand and portfolio management, the role of international promotional marketing is increasing. International promotional marketing takes into account local market conditions, brand development, and local regulations as they create specific local needs. It also creates complementary brand messages with other elements of the communications mix.

Goals

The goals of international promotional marketing are twofold:

1. Change or influence consumer behavior in the near term

2. Change or influence consumer perception of a product or service over time

Strategy and Tactics

The international message approach that combines strategy and tactics is relatively new, because global brand development is relatively new. It is increasingly viewed as a useful way to build global brands. Promotional strategy (global image, promotional methods) is developed on a global basis for global brands. Promotional tactics usually are local because they are selected based on particular local objectives at specified times. These include product trial at the time of a launch, increased usage during the summer, and loyalty building in a hotly competitive environment.

The international approach is the only way to add an element of consistency to promotions around the world because local conditions vary greatly. For example, a World Cup theme may be strategically correct from a brand communication standpoint. However, a themed tactic that worked well in the United States might be offensive or illegal in another country. A new local tactic should be used rather than abandoning the strategy or concept.

For example, every Coca-Cola promotion must be built on the strategic foundation of authenticity, fun, and refreshment. Local Coca-Cola bottlers around the world, addressing specific local sales objectives, must coordinate tactical promotions with the strategic platform. For instance, they may elect to sponsor community sports teams or dance competitions, both of which embody fun.

Global Promotional Marketing Cost-Effectiveness

Promotional marketing tends to be one of the largest marketing expenditures for consumer product companies. As products such as Kodak film are offered in multiple markets around the world, the company might be developing up to 100 different ideas in different countries to promote the same product.

The costs of manpower, agency fees, merchandise, printing, talent fees, creative, and all the other elements that go into developing a successful idea are significant for one promotion in one market. These costs are multiplied significantly when applied to developing hundreds of ideas. For this reason, companies try to use big global events, like the World Cup or the Olympics, as strategic platforms for promotions. The companies then develop promotional concepts and merchandise that can be used to satisfy a wide range of objectives that any given market might be trying to meet. The ideas are then distributed to all the country marketing directors or brand managers. These ideas give them a head start on developing strategically relevant, tactically appropriate promotions for their market. This type of global promotion planning can save millions of dollars for a global brand, while allowing managers in smaller countries a chance to use big events that they could never afford with their local budgets alone.

For companies that do not have a global event to build around, compiling an idea book of the best 10 or 20 promotions for a brand around the world and distributing it to every market can still create enormous efficiency and brand consistency across the globe.

PROMOTIONAL MARKETING—CASE STUDY

by Mars Inc.

Company: Mars Inc.
Case: Seasonal Product Reinvention—Green is the "New Color of Love"

Legend has it that green M&M'S® Brand Chocolate Candies, otherwise known as *The Green Ones*®, are an aphrodisiac, and rumors of their special powers have been circulating since the 1970s. These rumors presented a unique opportunity in the United States for Mars Inc., which is known for its creative, fun, and innovative marketing campaigns.

To celebrate the myths, rumors, and innuendo surrounding green M&M's in the United States, Mars proclaimed green as the new color of love during the Valentine's Day 2008 season and supported the declaration with an unexpected and completely integrated "New Color of Love" promotion.

To bring the program to life, the company used its most flirtatious and romantically inclined spokescandy, the illustrious Ms. Green.

The goals of the promotion were to:

1. Create positive consumer awareness for the brand.
2. Drive incremental sales during the Valentine's Day season by introducing a new purchase occasion.
3. Celebrate the myths, rumors, and innuendo surrounding green M&M's.
4. Position M&M's as the fun and suggestive candy for Valentine's Day.

The New Color of Love program was brought to life with an integrated marketing campaign that surrounded consumers in-store, on air, in print, and online.

In-Store

Retailers across the country displayed limited-edition packages of all-green M&M's which immediately stood out among the sea of red and pink products. Ms. Green, the first (and only) female spokescandy,

(Continued)

appeared on the all-green packages along with a disclaimer that stated: "Consumption of *The Green Ones®* may result in elevated Romance Levels. If you experience this effect, contact your Significant Other immediately." The all-green M&M's packages were available from January 2008 through the Valentine's holiday.

On Air and in Print

The New Color of Love program was also brought to life with public relations activities that strategically elevated—and validated—the rumors surrounding green M&M's and reached consumers, using the media to provide a third-party endorsement. Live-animation technology brought the flirtatious, alluring, and confident Ms. Green to life via local and national television interviews. During the interviews, Ms. Green, the "star" of the product packaging and the New Color of Love campaign, bantered with celebrity love guru Chris Harrison, host of ABC's hit show *The Bachelor.*

Top-tier journalists at magazines, newspapers, and Web sites around the country received press materials housed in a teaser press kit emblazoned with the message "*What is it about the Green Ones®*" which contained a product sample, a love letter from Ms. Green, and a fact sheet with "historical" perspective on the myths of *The Green Ones®,* including the following juicy factoids:

- A certain perm-bearing early 1980s rock star had it in his contract for three pounds of Green M&M's backstage for, uh, "inspiration."
- *The Green Ones®* have even made it into outer space. Green M&M's Chocolate Candies have been requested on 31 space shuttle flights. According to unofficial reports, the astronauts wanted to keep that lovin' feeling when traveling so far away from home.
- The color green has a strong place in history, long associated with love and fertility. Green is also associated with energy, youth, growth, hope, and new life.
- In the fifteenth century, green was the preferred color for wedding attire and the Celtic symbol of fertility was The Green Man.
- Today, green is considered an emotional stabilizer and pituitary stimulant.

Online

Media articles encouraged consumers to engage directly with an interactive Web site which allowed Americans to show their support for Ms. Green in her quest to make green the new color of love. By visiting www.mms.com, consumers and fans were able to demonstrate their love for green and learn more about the lady behind the legend.

Consumers and retailers alike engaged with Ms. Green, resulting in the following:

- Fully integrated marketing communications plan that reached 40 percent of Americans and further cemented the nontraditional marketing model.
- The interactive site received nearly 2.2 million Web site visits, with more than 1,000 users submitting content. An additional 600 Ms. Green e-cards were sent by consumers through the site.
- Ms. Green enticed close to 350 members of the Twitter community to follow her on her own page which delivered a steady stream of saucy chatter through the Valentine's Day season.
- The media relations program resulted in nearly 44 million media impressions across national media outlets including *Maxim, Redbook, Star*, NPR, Fox Business Network, and 26 television placements nationwide.

The end result of the integrated campaign, which successfully brought the animated Ms. Green to life and engaged consumers and media with the lore surrounding *The Green Ones*® successfully spellbound retailers who were on board to expand distribution and their participation in the campaign for year two.

PROMOTIONAL MARKETING—CASE STUDY

by The *New York Times*

Company: The *New York Times*
Case: Contest—"Challenge of a Country"

In the fall of 1996, the *New York Times* celebrated the 100th anniversary of the purchase of the newspaper by Adolph S. Ochs. The *Times* marked this milestone for the newspaper by creating a promotional contest called "The Challenge of a Century." The goals of the Challenge were to:

1. Celebrate this momentous anniversary and inform readers of its significance.
2. Engage readers in an intellectually challenging, interactive, and entertaining *Times*-related contest.
3. Promote the content of the *New York Times* as well as its unique role in documenting history in the making.
4. Encourage sampling of sections readers might not be familiar with.
5. Increase sales of the newspaper.

For this promotion, the *Times* chose to use a combination of contest and sweepstakes, a game of skill as well as a game of chance. The reason for this dual approach was to narrow down the tens of thousands of entries to a few winners, a task that would have been overwhelming just by choosing correct entries.

The *Times* could not require purchase of the newspaper in order to win, since by definition that would be an illegal lottery. This called for an alternative means of entry. In this case, the paper offered copies of the clues and entry forms to anyone who mailed a self-addressed, stamped envelope (SASE) to our fulfillment company. This address was listed in the rules in the Sunday ads. In order to sell more copies of the paper, the paper did not allow photocopied entries. (A large percentage of many sweepstakes' entries are multiple entries, duplicates, and photocopies.) Readers would be chosen at random from correct entries.

To stress the significance of 100 years, the paper decided to offer a list of 100 prizes, each consisting of 100 things, such as 100 hours of a chauffeured car, 100 hours of Broadway theater, 100 tropical fish and a tank, and 100 tickets to the Yankees' games. The contest asked questions regarding content of the *New York Times* over the past 100 years.

Each day, four clues to the answers to that day's question were placed in different sections throughout the paper. The questions were easy at first and became harder throughout the contest in order to draw in more people and then keep them interested. In order to allow people who learned about

(Continued)

the Challenge in mid-week to play, the paper divided the three-week contest into three one-week challenges. The contest provided a dedicated phone number with a recording of the rules and entry requirements for readers who called in.

Promotion was very important in getting the word out and in establishing a large base of participants. The *Times* ran full-page ads and one-quarter–page ads, posted signs promoting the Challenge on vending machines and at newsstands, and ran radio spots. The promotion ads began with a "teaser" ad on Tuesday, a full-page ad on Sunday the week before the launch of the contest (Sunday is the day of highest circulation and readership), and another ad on the following Sunday, the day before the contest began.

It is the nature of most businesses that the goal of increasing sales can rarely be directly attributed to one specific promotion. Some of the reasons that preclude newspapers from directly attributing results to specific promotions, both year-over-year and month-over-month, include price increases (there was a price increase during this particular period), marketing dollars spent, the news environment (for example, more papers are sold in wartime than in times of peace), production and distribution delays, and the weather.

The *Times* received approximately 40,000 entries, by far the most the paper had ever received for any contest or sweepstakes at that time. An impressive response, considering that each entry represented at least a week's worth of buying and reading the *Times* and answering questions, as opposed to just filling out an entry form. The 40,000 entries assured the paper of its success in both its short-term and long-term goals of reader enjoyment and loyalty.

The answer to the first Challenge question was, of course: *Gone with the Wind.* The Grand Prize winner chose the following prizes from the list of 100 potential prizes: 100 Gourmet Meals Delivered, and 100 CDs, and 100 paperback books from Barnes & Noble.

PROMOTIONAL MARKETING—CASE STUDY

by PepsiCo

Company: PepsiCo
Case: Premium Offers and Promotional Products—"Pepsi Stuff"

In the summer of 1996, Pepsi faced a formidable challenge. The Summer Olympics had turned the world's attention to Atlanta, the corporate and spiritual home of Coca-Cola.

Coca-Cola was determined that everyone who attended the Games, tuned in on television, or followed Olympic coverage in their local newspaper, would come away feeling good, and perhaps even passionate, about its brand of soft drink. Coke had set itself an objective of nothing less than to "own" Olympic fever, and, by extension, to brand the summer of 1996. Coca-Cola reportedly had invested $500 million in sponsorship rights and Olympic-themed tie-ins to do exactly that.

The question for Pepsi was, How to respond? And not just respond, but how to preempt its competition? More than holding its own, Pepsi wanted to claim the Summer of 1996 for Pepsi, at a fraction of the Olympic-sponsorship cost, and through a program that could live beyond the summer. Therefore, in time for the summer of 1996, Pepsi launched Pepsi Stuff, the single-largest consumer promotion in Pepsi-Cola history. The Pepsi Stuff program was mechanically simple: Consumers would drink Pepsi, collect Pepsi Points, and redeem them for Pepsi Stuff, a wide array of high-quality T-shirts, hats, sweatshirts, denim and leather jackets, sunglasses, mountain bikes, beach chairs, duffel bags, and other summer stuff for active people.

Pepsi launched its promotional program in April to embed Pepsi Stuff in the market before the Olympics. The program was aimed at a target market of 18- to 24-year-olds. Pepsi distributed more than 170 million Pepsi Stuff catalogs; at least one for every other person in the United States. The catalogs featured cameo shots of famous sports stars and models, including Cindy Crawford, Andre Agassi, and Deion Sanders wearing Pepsi Stuff. Pepsi affixed a total of 7 billion points on more than 4 billion packages of Pepsi, Diet Pepsi, Caffeine Free Pepsi, Caffeine Free Diet Pepsi, Wild Cherry Pepsi, and Diet Wild Cherry Pepsi.

In addition to the Pepsi Stuff catalog, Pepsi supported the program with television, radio, and print advertising; outdoor advertising; and links with Pepsi's Web site. The theme line running through all Pepsi's consumer communications was intended to be simple but compelling: "Drink Pepsi. Get Stuff." In breadth, scale, and intensity, Pepsi's massive consumer outreach campaign dwarfed all previous company marketing efforts. Pepsi's projections were equally ambitious: Pepsi estimated that by the close of the campaign, consumers would redeem 4.5 million items valued at $125 million retail.

Their response exceeded its wildest expectations. Nearly 30 million consumers participated in the program by actively collecting points. They redeemed their points for some 12 million items, nearly tripling Pepsi's estimate. In prompted awareness tests, 65 percent of U.S. consumers surveyed between July 22 and August 18, 1996, were aware of Pepsi Stuff, while just 46 percent of those same consumers indicated that they knew that Coke was sponsoring the Olympics.

More importantly, Pepsi Stuff reversed declines in consumers' preference for Pepsi. Before the summer, consumers who were asked to choose between Coke and Pepsi (in forced-choice marketing research tests), regardless of price, chose Coke 57 percent to Pepsi's 43 percent. By the end of the summer, preference had swung Pepsi's way, 51 percent to Coke's 49 percent.

The effect on Pepsi's sales was dramatic. In the four weeks bracketing the Summer Olympic Games, the sales of Pepsi-Cola's soft-drink brands grew six times faster than the total industry, and more than twice as fast as Coca-Cola's soft-drink brands, in the vast and highly competitive supermarket channel. Market-share momentum swung dramatically in Pepsi's favor. Brand Pepsi emerged with a 16 share, Coke Classic with 15.5.

On the last day of Pepsi's promotion, 30,000 consumers phoned Pepsi's fulfillment company, to inquire when Pepsi would bring the Pepsi Stuff program back. On May 14th, 1997, Pepsi unveiled Pepsi Stuff 1997. This time the program offered hipper, edgier merchandise, as well as the opportunity to enjoy sports-related fantasy experiences with famous sports personalities. The *"Shaquille O-Neal Fantasy,"* for example, offered an opportunity to meet Shaq at the Los Angeles Great Western Forum, and to pass a ball to Shaq for a $25,000 slam dunk. In response to overwhelming demand from millions of Mountain Dew drinkers, Pepsi added Pepsi Points to popular Mountain Dew packaging, and augmented its promotion catalog with specially designed "Dew Stuff."

Pepsi learned that contrary to its fears that promotions tend to erode brand imagery, Pepsi Stuff worked exactly in reverse. The program actually built Pepsi's equity by connecting with realistic aspirations to the Pepsi lifestyle. The Pepsi Stuff catalog was more than a parade of merchandise and

(Continued)

more than a printed warehouse of point-of-purchase materials. The Pepsi Stuff catalog was successful because it "popped" with images of top-quality merchandise in the hands, on the heads, and around the shoulders of handsome, high-energy young people and edgy celebrities. Every item in the catalog was emblazoned with unique iterations of the Pepsi logo.

Pepsi succeeded in eclipsing the sales of Coca-Cola in the summer of 1996 by leveraging the equity inherent in its own brand. Rather than relying on an event such as the Olympics that has many corporate sponsors, Pepsi harvested its own strengths in its promotional program by incorporating the aspirational and emotional appeal of the Pepsi brand.

CORPORATE PROFILES AND AUTHOR BIOGRAPHIES

VISA

VISA operates the world's largest retail electronic payments network providing processing services and payment product platforms. Visit VISA at www.corporate.visa.com.

Robert C. Pifke

Bob Pifke was Senior Vice President of Marketing Services. Mr. Pifke was responsible for all VISA promotions and for developing marketing communication programs directed toward Visa member financial institutions, merchants, and consumers. Mr. Pifke received his BA in Communications and his MBA from the University of Illinois.

OGILVYACTION

OgilvyAction is the brand activation arm of the Ogilvy Group. Visit OgilvyAction at www.OgilvyAction.com.

Robert Mazzucchelli

Robert Mazzucchelli was President of 141's Americas Division (now Ogilvy Action). Mr. Mazzucchelli received his BA in Communications and Economics from the University of Richmond.

MARS, INC.

Mars, Incorporated, is a privately held company that produces some of the world's leading confectionery, snackfood, frozen snacks, main meals, side dishes, organic foods, drinks, petfood, and now with the acquisition of Wrigley, gum and sugar products. Please visit Mars, Inc. at www.mars.com.

Ryan Bowling

Ryan Bowling is the Public Relations Manager at Mars, Inc., where he manages external relations for the multibillion-dollar North American snack division. Mr. Bowling received his BA in Communications from the University of the Pacific.

NEW YORK TIMES

The New York Times is considered the nation's newspaper of record. Visit the Times at www.nytimes.com.

J. Jeffery Honea

Jeff Honea was the Times' Creative Director, and his responsibilities included the content and quality of NYT ads and promotions. Mr. Honea received his BS in Marketing from the University of Arkansas.

PEPSICO (NYSE: PEP)

PepsiCo is one of the world's largest food and beverage companies. Please visit PepsiCo at www.pepsico.com.

Brian Swette

Brian Swette was the former Executive Vice President and Chief Marketing Officer for Pepsi-Cola Company. In this capacity, he was responsible for the worldwide marketing and advertising for all of the company's brands. He also directed new product activity and package innovation. Mr. Swette received his BA in Economics from Arizona State University.

NOTES

1. Association of Promotional Marketing Agencies Worldwide.

2. Veronis Suhler Stevenson Communication Industry, Forecast. "Less Is More" PROMO, April 20.

13 DIRECT MARKETING

by RAPP, L.L. Bean, Draftfcb, and Wunderman

THE ESSENTIALS OF DIRECT MARKETING
by RAPP

Introduction

Direct marketing began with a simple, revolutionary thought: What if marketers could put their messages directly in front of an individual consumer? All other marketing communications practices focus on consumers as parts of an aggregated whole—a sum audience communicated to as a single entity. Direct marketing lets the brand connect with individuals on a personal level, shifting the paradigm in extraordinary ways.

Definition

Direct marketing allows brands to have targeted, measurable conversations with consumers that create growing relationships and act as catalysts for desired changes in consumer behavior.

Direct vs. Traditional Marketing

Direct marketing began with an extremely tactical focus: to leverage a broader group of strategies focused on consumer action, measurement, and accountability. Today, these qualities have made a direct approach increasingly appealing to marketers and their clients, as both continually seek to be more effective as well as being more efficient.

- **Proliferation of Sophisticated, Yet Affordable Databases and Analytics Technologies.** There is much more data available to a marketer than ever before—both from the client's business and its customers. Almost every consumer touchpoint has become an opportunity to gather data and the information technology landscape has evolved to the point where all of it can be efficiently captured and analyzed.
- **Rapidly Declining Production Costs.** Enormous leaps in the technology for producing content (both online and offline) have driven the cost to publish ever closer to zero, enabling almost anyone to speak to the world—instantly and with a production value rivaling that of any professional.
- **Increasing Market Penetration of Efficient, Quick-Response Channels.** Entirely new channels of reaching consumers have been made available to marketers as new personal technologies are adopted by a growing majority of audiences. E-mail, short message service (SMS)/multimedia messaging service (MMS) messages, outbound voice messaging (OBVM), and even online social media all have allowed marketers to reach individuals with more speed and targeting than ever before.
- **Growing Cultural Filter Screening Marketing Messages.** As marketing messages have become cheaper to produce and easier to distribute, the consumer culture as a whole has begun to

strictly screen incoming information, often ignoring messages that would have been very effective not long ago. Consumers have evolved an advanced filter for identifying what is from a real person and what is from a brand.

Ironically, the same trends that have hampered the abilities of traditional marketing communications have made the approach and tenets of direct marketing more attractive. In the hands of a skilled marketer, the same methods that allow for the individual to have a megaphone to the world also can allow a company to have a dialogue with the individual. As publication costs decrease, it becomes easier for direct marketing to segment, focus, and target—reaching fewer customers with more messages at a higher degree of customization.

Direct marketing accomplishes this by combining creative messages with customer data and constantly refining the marketing experience as the data changes. As such, it is often referred to as relationship marketing, one-to-one marketing, or data-based marketing. This synergy between data and creativity is what allows marketing communications to truly become a dialogue, because each new message is based upon and reflects a growing understanding of the consumer's needs, behaviors, and receptiveness.

Direct Marketing Principles

A well-built direct marketing campaign will adhere to seven key principles:

1. Direct marketing messages are based on a relationship with the customer—whether initiating the relationship, broadening the data about that consumer, or responding to recent changes in behavior.
2. Direct marketing seeks to change customer behavior. Each message sent to a consumer will have calls to take action, although these will not always be toward a purchase.
3. Direct marketing focuses on individuals or segments of an audience. The most brilliant message sent to the wrong individual or group of individuals will never outperform average messages sent to the right people at the right time.
4. Direct marketing uses both the left and right brain. Decisions are made based on the data, but the messages used to affect that data are creatively enticing and feel increasingly authentic.
5. Direct marketing has a measurable tie to a return on investment (ROI). That return may not always be measured in revenue, but each dollar is spent to achieve predetermined goals.
6. Direct marketers fully embrace every testing opportunity possible. Testing yields more data, increased insight, and, ultimately, higher response rates. Direct marketers always are on a path of continuous improvement, even within a campaign already under way.
7. Direct marketers base their insights on a database of customer knowledge and continually update the database to refine the picture of the customer.

Opportunities for Direct Marketing

Direct marketing provides many advantages for targeting customers, driving behavior changes, and producing a measurable ROI. Using these strengths on an existing customer base can identify and retain best customers, intercept customers trending away from a desired pattern of behavior, and "place your best bets" on the customers who will easily change.

Direct marketing communications can be triggered by life cycle events or customer actions, so there is a better chance to reach people with the information they want when they want it. Depending on the medium used, marketers can act quickly in response to changes in the marketplace or changes in customer behavior. Direct marketing also allows companies to test everything from products, offers, and creative approaches to media plans or marketing methodologies. Each time, clients can measure effectiveness through clearly defined changes or responses.

Privacy Considerations

Although the use of personal data can be extremely helpful in determining a target audience and creating targeted communications, marketers must act responsibly with this data. Many consumers feel there is too much personal information available to marketers and are reluctant to respond to certain direct offers. Marketers must respect consumers' privacy concerns by disclosing list rental policies, allowing customers to opt out of list exchanges, and withholding the names of concerned consumers from future contact.

CONSUMER DATA GATHERING

Direct marketing is completely intertwined with the one version of the truth—a singular database containing all the information collected on each consumer or marketing contact. Having this in place is crucial to beginning a direct campaign, because it is in the intersections of these data points that skilled analysts can find insights and trends, yielding more motivating, creative, and relevant communications. Moreover, every communication will capture more data—through behavior, response, or action—and all this captured data has to be fed back into the same database, continually refining it.

Most organizations do not have this kind of data collection and storage system in place—their consumer information landscape is inaccurate, fragmented, or absent. This is a key challenge in direct marketing. Campaigns have to focus on generating effective and relevant marketing messages and managing (or creating) this backbone of data infrastructure. For this reason, direct marketers often will have close ties with other business organizations, including information technology, business analysis, e-commerce, and customer service.

Data Sources

Actionable consumer data can come from almost any point within the organization; any moment when the customer and business meet generates reactions for both parties which, ideally, are recorded and learned from. When beginning a direct campaign, it is best to start by gathering as much of this free data as possible, then augmenting it with information requested from consumers. Working in this order keeps marketers from bombarding contacts with requests for information they should already know, and allows marketers to ask smart questions about the things they need. Some direct campaigns will focus entirely on gathering more information, often giving an offer to consumers in exchange for providing their personal information.

Transactional Data

At any moment when a consumer purchases a product, a wealth of information has to be exchanged to complete the sale. Direct marketers often focus on the RFM analysis, referring to three elements:

- How *recent* was the last transaction?
- How *frequent* are the transactions?
- How much *money* is spent each time?

In most cases (especially when there is a credit card involved), organizations can capture the consumer's name and home address. Many retailers will ask for additional information at the point-of-sale, such as a phone number or e-mail address.

Web Site Analytics

New applications for tracking and interpreting consumer behavior online have broadened the view marketers have on how consumers interact with brands and approach purchases. Even sites that do not have an e-commerce function can provide a powerful story about the consumer through metrics like page affinity, page view times, search keywords, clickstreams, bounce rates, and many more. Many direct marketers also have leveraged the customer profile, not just for displaying customized content and marketing messages, but also for tying online behavior to online actions through merges with transactional data and other sources.

Loyalty Programs

In the past, this generally has been relegated to a retail-specific strategy for gathering consumer data.

Many grocers still practice a more classic loyalty strategy by providing consumers with cards or key fobs that can be scanned or swiped at the point-of-sale. In exchange, consumers receive special pricing discounts or program points redeemable for future benefits. Today, industries such as consumer packaged goods, dining and hospitality, automotive, and even companies focused on a business-to-business (B2B) market have started incorporating loyalty program tactics into their overall marketing strategies. Any instance when the consumer is given preferential treatment or pricing in exchange for data insight could be considered a loyalty program, and all of these strategies can provide a growing relationship that benefits both the business and the consumer. Marketers can use these programs to gather more than just transactional data, simply by placing rewards on other key consumer actions such as referring a friend, reviewing a product, or taking a survey.

Call Center/Customer Care

Many organizations see these areas as pure cost centers; an element that is part and parcel with any consumer interaction and a piece that does not return any direct value back to the organization. However, when these interactions are captured in a database and held next to existing data, a direct marketer can capitalize on the stories that emerge. For example, direct marketers can follow up on calls regarding a negative product experience with targeted offers designed to win back those consumers. Using direct marketing as a tool to change consumer behavior, campaigns can even address frequently asked questions by informing relevant individuals about an important product insight before they ever pick up the telephone.

Purchased Third-Party Data

Numerous data brokers work with direct marketers to add to consumer lists or append additional data to an existing list. These organizations can provide a data overlay by taking an existing customer list and using algorithms to match each individual to records in their data warehouses. This process is known as *fuzzy matching*, as the algorithms attempt

to compensate for variations in name spelling, typos, or address changes. Data returned by these processes often has a degree of confidence percentage associated with each match, so marketers can decide whether to accept that information into their master consumer databases.

Data Hygiene

Once the sources of customer information have been identified, they need to be integrated into a single master consumer marketing database, a source of truth, for each consumer profile. Regardless of the source, every bit of data needs to go through a complete screening and error-correction process before it can be integrated with the master database. This art of seamlessly incorporating new sources of data while maintaining an accurate and up-to-the-minute database is known as *data hygiene*.

In most organizations, data hygiene is defined as an information technology function, but since the success of this function is so central to direct marketing, marketers have to take this just as seriously as a piece of creative or a line of copy. Poor data hygiene quickly can lead to wasteful marketing as messages are sent to the wrong customers, duplicate customers, or incorrect contacts altogether. Since the power of direct marketing is in its personalization and targeting, it is easy to see how bad data can make for a bad direct campaign—even if everything else is executed perfectly.

When evaluating the health of a customer database (another expression for determining its data hygiene), some common issues to check for include:

- **Duplicates.** Marketers want to ensure the same customer is not listed in the database twice—this creates waste, and will impact any cost estimates on production.
- **Text Formatting and Typos.** Many databases are set up only to accept text in all uppercase letters. Naturally, this can be a problem when marketers want to personalize messages with this data (such as "Dear [first name]"), as they

would want these variables to flow seamlessly with the rest of the copy.

- **Physical Address Validation.** It is estimated that approximately 20 percent of Americans change addresses each year, so mailers of any size will generally check their lists periodically against the National Change of Address (NCOA) file. This list is compiled by the U.S. Postal Service and includes address corrections for people who have moved and wish to have their mail forwarded. Another file that mailers match their mailing lists against is the Direct Marketing Association's Mail Preference Service, which lists consumers who do not want to receive direct mail of any kind.
- **E-mail Address Validation.** It is estimated that as many as 31 percent of e-mail users change their primary e-mail addresses every year and more than half of those have lost touch with Web sites (and, by association, marketers) because of it. Keeping these addresses active and updated with consumers is as much a marketer's job as it is to get the consumers' information in the first place. Many e-mail service providers (ESPs) and data management firms can help in this process by identifying e-mail addresses coming from expired domains or by inferring the new address from the known physical address or telephone number data.

List Selection Criteria

Once a direct marketer has compiled a reasonable customer database, the marketer will start to define groups of customers who can be impacted by similar messages—a process called *segmentation*. Well-constructed customer segments can exponentially affect a campaign by gaining the greatest impact for the lowest costs. Segments also can improve creative by narrowing the focus on a few defined personas, rather than attempting to address a client's customer database all at once.

A direct marketer will define a set of selection criteria for each segment. Segments can be based on a number of different criteria at once, but there has

to be a balance between the number of segments and the costs involved in marketing to each. Not all customers need to fall into a segment; in fact, some marketers will use segmentation as a way to define which customers might not be responsive to marketing or which groups do not provide a good ROI.

Purchasing Behavior

Marketers often can infer future purchasing behavior based on past history in ways that do not just look at an overall revenue trend:

- **Recency.** Customers who purchased recently or have a trend of recent purchases within the recent past often are more likely to purchase again. Customers who have not had a transaction in a long time may be no longer worth a marketing investment.
- **Dollar Value of Purchase.** Marketers often use this statistic to infer a client's "share of wallet"—the amount this customer purchases from the client versus other companies in the same industry. For example, if studies show that typical customers generally spend $100 per week on groceries and a marketer knows an individual already spends $90 with the grocery client, they may not be able to spend much more with the client.
- **Item Affinity.** Customers often buy similar sets of items together, especially as they move through different life stages. For example, if customers are buying lots of diapers and formula, they may be open to an offer on baby bottles.

Demographics

Customers in various demographics often respond very differently to different types of direct media, so a marketer may want to tailor his or her marketing mix based on these factors. Demographic data is usually the easiest to get on a given customer.

- **Geography.** Lists can target different geographic areas by ZIP code, city, region, and many other options. Some segmentations also can target customers within a specific radius of store locations or other landmarks.

- **Gender.** Marketers often will segment messages by gender, even within the same campaign. For example, a jewelry store might send a totally different message about Valentine's Day to a male than a female.
- **Age.** Age is usually selected in ranges (such as 23–34, 35–49, etc.).
- **Children.** Lists can be targeted based on number of children in a household or just the presence of children.
- **Job Title.** With business lists, it might be possible to select names by job title to help target offers to the most appropriate audience.
- **Sales Volume or Employee Size.** These options often help B2B marketers sort out prospects that may need a certain product.
- **Business Type.** Every business is classified by the North American Industry Classification System (NAICS) (formerly Standard Industrial Classification). A qualified business audience can be chosen from a compiled list by selecting appropriate NAICS codes.

DIRECT MARKETING TACTICS

Successful direct marketing campaigns start with a strategy that is completely platform neutral. By keeping the message completely separate from the medium, marketers can reach out to consumers through the channels that make the most sense, rather than interrupting a consumer with what potentially could be the right message at the wrong moment.

Also, it is important to note that not all marketing problems can be solved with a single solution, and that a campaign may have to cross multiple media to find the right mix that works with the target audience.

The direct marketer has a broad range of tactics available for a complete campaign.

Direct Mail

Direct mail is any printed material (letters, postcards, catalogs, etc.) delivered to individuals at their physical addresses. By this definition, many communications pieces that are not generated by a marketing function can become an opportunity for consumer messages. These might include statements, bills, welcome packets, or reminders. Most likely, most businesses are doing some kind of direct mail already, even though they may not be aware of it.

Since direct mail is delivered to an individual, generated pieces can be customized for and targeted to each person on a mailing list. However, this level of targeting is not significantly scalable—individually targeted pieces become increasingly more expensive as the size of the mailing list increases. Bringing the targeting up to a broader level (such as by ZIP code or city) decreases the cost, but at the expense of effectiveness and impact.

Each contact with a direct-mail piece is an advertising impression that allows for deeper, more extensive brand exposure than most other forms of advertising. Only direct mail can put a tactile experience directly in a customer's hand—an experience that could be tailored specifically for that individual. Direct-mail pieces also can be carried outside the home, as in the case of coupons or gift certificates. These types of pieces can drive customers to stores, act as a point of reference to gain mindshare or even create a pass-along opportunity to expand the message to the recipient's social network. Marketers of commodity products such as laundry detergent and bar soap have used direct mail to send a product sample for trial, highlight product advantages, and distinguish their brands as superior to competitors.

Advantages

Direct mail has a number of unique advantages over most advertising media. Individually targeted mailings mean that marketers can contact just those people most likely to be interested in their offers—eliminating the opportunities for wasteful circulation found in mass media and allowing them to invest more heavily on better-qualified prospects. Marketers can personalize copy based on given variables, such as incorporating a customer's name, address, past sales activity, or transactions into a personalized message. For example, frequent-flyer statement mailers based on airline loyalty programs oftentimes reflect and are even triggered by customers' flight history.

Leveraging external sources of data, marketers also can target consumers based on demographics, life stages, or household information. For example, a publisher of children's books can tailor a mailing list to reach only households with young children. B2B marketers can offer different message versions to different prospects, depending on the size and inferred needs of their businesses. Advanced direct mail campaigns can follow consumers through a life stage cycle, such as a series of informational mailings and coupons targeting households with a new baby and following the growth of that child with relevant marketing messages through kindergarten.

Marketers also can segment mail campaigns into any number of test groups, allowing for the evaluation of mailing formats, creative approaches, offers, mailing lists, or other variables. This often is referred to as a multivariate test, or MVT. Each test group can be tracked using distinct codes on reply forms, phone numbers, or Web site addresses. Reliable response results can be determined fairly quickly, typically projected within weeks of the drop date.

Another advantage of direct mail is that it offers greater flexibility than most other media. Advertisers can schedule mailings to reach specific audience segments at specific times. For example, advertisers can reach people with relevant messages at the time their subscriptions or contracts are nearing expiration. Or a company can take advantage of trigger events, like a move to a new home, to reach people with timely offers.

Disadvantages

The biggest disadvantage to using direct mail is cost—both in setup expenses and cost per piece. Working in this medium with any level of scale simply requires specialized people, equipment, and materials.

Other disadvantages include:

- Marketers are required to have an address for each contact—something they may not have when dealing with consumers' concerns about their privacy.
- Development and production times can be longer than other media.
- Response requires a consumer to complete an attached form and take it to the post office or a store—these could be barriers to response rates for certain audiences.
- Large mailings can be seen as an excessive use of paper and other natural resources, which can appear environmentally irresponsible.

Mail Formats

Marketers have a number of formats available for delivering direct mail, each with varying creative limitations and costs. The most common formats include:

- **Postcards.** Inexpensive mailers that allow for brief copy. Best used for creating general awareness or providing a single offer.
- **Self-Mailers.** Nonpostcard mailings that do not use envelopes. Usually a single sheet that has been folded one or more times and gummed closed for mailing.
- **Catalogs.** Present a variety of products at once, available either for purchase by mail or at a retail location. Expensive to produce but spreads the cost across all products and/or offers presented.
- **Package Mail.** Parcels can be mailed to consumers, usually containing a product sample or giveaway item. These are very expensive but can provide a unique tactile experience with a product.
- **Multimailers (or Shared Mail).** Programs like Valassis (formerly ADVO) and Valpak allow multiple marketers to share the cost of a single mailing. These usually allow each participant to have a stand-alone insert, and programs usually limit one participant per industry, per mailing.
- **Classic Mail.** Exactly what most people get in their mailboxes every day—a letter in an envelope that usually contains a brochure and a reply form.

Financial Analysis

Direct-mail costs usually are described in terms of cost per thousand (CPM), which is determined by totaling the production, printing, paper, letter shop, addressing, and mailing costs and dividing the sum by the quantity mailed in thousands. Typically, the costs for creative development are not included in CPM calculations because these costs are a one-time fee—once a direct-mail effort has been designed and written, it can be mailed repeatedly.

E-Mail

The new contrast to the direct-mail piece has been e-mail, which has increasingly taken a more equal seat at the table with its print relatives. E-mail's strengths neatly dovetail with direct marketing priorities.

Consider the following:

- In 2007, 91 percent of U.S. Internet users went online and sent or read e-mail.[1]
- Approximately 56 percent did this as part of a typical day.[2]
- There were approximately 1.2 billion e-mail users in 2007, expected to rise to 1.6 billion by 2011.[3]
- 183 billion e-mails were sent each day in 2006 and it is predicted that wireless e-mail users will grow "from 14 million in 2006, to 228 million in 2010."[4]
- In 2007 the number of business e-mail users was approximately 780 million.[5]

Advantages

E-mail's greatest advantage always will be its cost. The total cost of designing, executing, testing, and sending an e-mail campaign of 5,000 can cost 78 percent less than an equivalent campaign in direct mail. E-mails also can be infinitely personalized, allowing marketers to create an extremely unique experience for each contact. Not only can marketers insert data variables directly into an e-mail (such as a customer's name), but they can use these to alter copy or even the complete look and feel of an e-mail.

E-mail offers a channel that can work for the direct marketer on any day or at any time. Consumer actions can be recorded and an automated response can be sent based on a set of business rules and templates. Since these e-mails already are in a Web medium, responses can be collected and acted upon at any time by linking the consumer to a Web form.

Finally, e-mail results are extremely measurable, and each campaign can provide marketers with a wealth of actionable data. An e-mail service provider can provide metrics describing behaviors leading up to and including responses. Evaluating these can provide insights to improve response rates on future campaigns—something that cannot be learned immediately from direct mail.

Another advantage is the practice of *dayparting* where the direct marketer can deliver e-mails to different addresses within a list at different times of the day. Many e-mail marketers prefer to send to personal e-mail addresses later in the day, since these are usually checked once consumers get home from work.

Disadvantages

E-mail messages rely on technology to develop, send, and display correctly for a consumer. Since it is impossible to know exactly what operating system, Web browser, and e-mail client each contact will use, e-mail construction requires a developer to take all of these into account when coding a marketing message. Even when following all of the best practices, an e-mail will look slightly different on every consumer's computer—an inconsistency not experienced with the printed page.

E-mail marketing also requires a significant investment in database management. Basic blasts can be sent to a simple mailing list, but a database has to tie an e-mail address to a customer profile before a message can be completely personalized.

E-mail marketing also does require some legal diligence, mostly due to the CAN-SPAM act of 2003. These laws apply to any commercial e-mail message, regardless of the size of a mailing. One major element is the "clear and visible unsubscribe mechanism" in all e-mails—meaning that e-mail marketers must have the necessary channels built and tied into their marketing databases to let consumers opt out from each e-mail. The costs involved in constructing or outsourcing this mechanism must be factored into marketing budgets and may be prohibitive.

Finally, e-mail marketing does lack the tactile experience of a direct-mail piece. Consumers can easily carry a piece of mail to a store for a discount but they will have to print out the same offer if it comes in an e-mail. E-mail cannot provide the consumer with a product sample, and it is always a click away from being deleted.

E-mail Analysis

- **Bounces.** Number of e-mails returned to the e-mail service provider due to inactive or blocked addresses.
- **Open Rate.** Percentage of total e-mails that are opened by a user. This is checked by tracking which users' e-mail clients download the images for an e-mail, so it cannot be measured on text-only e-mails.
- **Clickthrough Rate.** Percentage of total e-mails where a user clicked on a link within the e-mail. Most e-mail service providers can tell marketers which links were the most popular for each mailing.

Direct Print

Direct marketers have used print or space advertising in magazines and newspapers for more than a century, offering everything from patent medicines to home construction plans. These direct print ads combine the response mechanisms of direct mail with the broad reach of mass print media.

Advantages

Print is one of the most commonly used media for direct-response marketing because it is widely distributed, relatively inexpensive, and has a response mechanism clearly associated with the advertisement. Print advertisements may include more than one response mechanism, such as a coupon, telephone number, and a Web site. This allows consumers to use response channels of their choice. To track performance, direct marketers can use coupons and reply cards that include codes or department numbers associated with the publication or offer, unique telephone numbers, and personalized Web addresses.

Direct marketers also can customize their mix of publications to best fit their targeted audiences and ideal response environments. *Woman's Day* and *Popular Science,* for example, generally perform well for direct response. *Architectural Digest* and *Scientific American* (so-called coffee table magazines) are generally designed for prestige and readers are less likely to tear out coupons or response cards from their pages. Some publications even offer a mail-order section or special direct-response rates at a discount.

Disadvantages

Finding the right mix of publications can be a difficult process, as readers evolve and marketing media needs change. Some direct print campaigns can take a longer time to ramp up, as marketers want to avoid response fatigue from bombarding a publication's reader base too often or too quickly. Marketers also may need time to test message or publication seasonality, ad position, and multiple publication categories before the ideal mix is found. Print advertising rates also are aggressively negotiated, as costs are dependent on a number of factors: ad position (placement within the publication), size, timing, and print requirements (color versus. black and white). Discounted rates or direct-response sections usually offer less-than-optimal placement or timing.

Direct Print Components

- **Headline.** Strong, attention-grabbing copy used to attract consumers and lead them into the body copy of the ad. Headlines may promote the major benefit of the product, ask a question, present an offer, lead the reader into a story, or use any other eye-catching method.
- **Body Copy.** Words that are printed in the central part or body of the ad is where the main sales pitch is made. In the body copy it is important to tell the readers exactly what they will receive for taking the action requested.

- **Graphics.** Photos or illustrations used in an ad. Graphics in direct-response advertising should complement the text of the ad, giving it more stopping power. Graphics typically feature the product being sold or in use. They may show the end benefit (such as in "before" and "after" pictures) to make a compelling case for a product.

Direct Print Formats

- **Bind-in Cards.** Response cards bound within the spine of a magazine, placed near an accompanying ad. This is often a postage-paid business reply card that consumers have to pull out of the publication. Bind-in cards are costly, including expenses for printing, shipping, and inserting.

- **Magazines.** Offer the widest variety of consumer segments, as well as the best color reproduction in print (important for fashion or jewelry marketing). Generally offers fractional-page ads, full-page ads, multipage ads, gatefolds, and inserts. People save magazines for longer periods of time, giving the ads a longer life cycle. Magazines also can offer the chance to test multiple concepts, spreading each across different geographic regions.

- **Newspapers.** Offer broad coverage to a diverse population of readers in a local market. Marketers can place ads in relevant sections, targeting specific audiences. Newspapers allow marketers to include timely messages in ads, as space can be purchased within days of publication. Complex images or dense copy will not work well in this medium.

- **Freestanding Inserts (FSIs).** Preprinted inserts allow for almost all the reproduction quality of magazines, so they come at a high cost. Printing and space costs are much greater than the cost per thousand for on-page ads. Because insert space availability is limited in many papers and because inserts must be printed in advance, advertisers do not have the advantage of short closing dates.

Direct Response Broadcast Media

Direct Response Television (DRTV) and Direct Response Radio allow marketers to promote offers direct to consumers using the most widely available media in the United States. The creative positioning of a direct broadcast commercial has one purpose: to generate a call to action. This differs dramatically from the creative imperative of general advertising, that of brand recall. The direct marketer is not so much interested in creating images as she is in driving a direct sale through a telephone number or Web site.

Advantages

Successful direct-response ads construct a compelling offer that drives response. Expressions such as "only available through this television offer," "free trial—no obligation," or "call for free information" are used to increase urgency or reduce a sense of commitment or obligation. Orders can be completed on the Web site or over the telephone, so direct broadcast ads can refer to these for program details. With this media, it is possible to adjust the schedule over the course of a campaign by continually measuring the responses and sales. Marketers can then concentrate their spending on the strongest performing stations, dayparts, or response messages.

Direct broadcast ads can be used effectively to support direct marketing efforts in other media. For example, radio spots often direct listeners to look for more information about a product or take advantage of special offers on Internet sites, in the mail, in a magazine, or in a newspaper.

Disadvantages

Television spots with the largest viewing audience usually are aired during shows with a strong following. Although there has been some success with driving these viewers to a Web site during their favorite shows, it is difficult to engage them in response that requires a telephone call or lengthy time commitment. Longer television ad formats, such as infomercials, often air during slots that have a much lower viewership.

Radio tends to be consumed by people outside the home, often in cars or at the workplace. This makes it difficult for listeners to stop and jot down a telephone number or Web address. The lack of visuals to show or demonstrate a product also could impede the success of a marketer's message.

With both media, it can be hard to measure granular results if all direct broadcast ads are pointing to the same telephone number or Web address. Although this strategy gives consistent messaging to the consumer across channels, it means marketers cannot use response rates to determine which message had the highest ROI.

Broadcast Formats

As with direct mail, marketers have a number of format options to choose from, each with its own costs and benefits:

- **Spots.** DRTV spots are typically purchased at a discounted rate, sometimes less than half of a normal spot rate. Direct marketers get these rates because DRTV spots are preemptible, meaning they run within a certain block of several hours (called a daypart), rather than airing during a specific show. This gives the station flexibility to fill in its unsold airtime in ways that benefit it the most.
- **Infomercials.** Feature program–length segments on one particular product or service generally run for 30 minutes, and are broken up into three or four distinct segments. These provide more time to display and sell products in a direct-response context.
- **Home Shopping.** Home-shopping channels became the ultimate extension of infomercials because they are accessible 24 hours a day, 7 days a week, to the consumer and are low cost to the advertiser.

Response

- **Response Mechanisms.** Direct broadcast messages drive customers to a toll-free telephone number or Web site for more information and to complete orders.
- **Response Analysis.** After the messages air, marketers can compare response volumes to

the times when a commercial was broadcast to indicate the campaign's success.

- **Radio Response Hooks.** Since listeners often cannot write down a telephone number or Web address, marketers often will use an easy-to-remember hook such as 1–800-DENTIST or FixMyCredit.com. These often become part of the overall brand so that remembering the site or telephone number is like remembering the brand name.

Telemarketing

Outbound telephone selling, known as telemarketing, is one of the most effective ways to speak to an audience on a one-to-one basis, while still producing large-scale results quickly and effectively. The price point of the product or service is not always a factor in its success, as consumers regularly take advantage of offers to refinance their homes and even open large credit card accounts. Even though automobile manufacturers may not use telemarketing to sell their latest models, some do use it as follow-up after a service experience to gauge customer satisfaction and build loyalty.

Advantages

Outbound (versus inbound) telemarketing is a flexible, multifaceted, proactive sales medium. Programs can be initiated at any point in a product's or service's life cycle, both to build awareness and generate sales. It enhances direct mail and other advertising efforts and builds lists of potential customers.

Telemarketing is well suited for many specific applications, including commercial sales, grassroots lobbying, membership acquisition and retention, fund-raising, research, lead generation, appointment setting, continuity marketing programs, subscriptions, and renewals.

Telemarketing also is a beneficial marketing tool because it can test advertising, messages, and offers instantly, with low cost and a broad reach. The immediate consumer feedback afforded by telemarketing often can lead to as many as a dozen versions of a script and offers in a single day.

Disadvantages

Telemarketing is less effective in situations that require the consumer to see or touch the product or in cases where a great deal of explanation and message reinforcement is needed (as with products sold in 30-minute infomercials).

Telemarketing Components

- **Telemarketing Strategy.** Before creating a telemarketing program, a teleservices firm will generally create a strategic approach defining the most appropriate offer and pitch for each target segment, depending on program goals and objectives.
- **Telemarketing Sales Representatives (TSRs).** These individuals play a key role in the campaign's success as they handle actual customer and prospect interaction. Different call centers may specialize with TSRs best suited to a particular industry or offer style.
- **Script Development.** Scripts provide a framework for TSRs that reflects the overall brand promise to the consumer and continues other marketing efforts. Several versions of a script will be developed for different segments altering offers, tone, and positioning. Scripts often include the following elements:
  - *Introduction.* Short, to the point about company/service. Builds some rapport without too much small talk.
  - *Body.* Focused on generating interest, not necessarily explaining everything about the product/service. Sells the benefits, not just features.
  - *Close.* Successful scripts get to this quickly, always asking for the sale. Assumptive, positive language is always used. May include a second close (reclose) after objections are answered.
- **Frequently Asked Questions (FAQs).** In telemarketing, this refers to a list provided to TSRs that is used to handle the most common refusal reasons or program questions. This list also will evolve during the campaign as new questions or issues arise.

- **Inbound Telemarketing.** As e-commerce and e-marketing proliferate, consumers are turning to the telephone as a customer support or order-fulfillment opportunity. Great programs provide excellent cross-sell and up-sell opportunities, while answering consumer questions or issues thoroughly. A representative often will pull up the caller's record with any previous information such as purchase history, frequency of past calls, and personal data to provide a customized cross-sell pitch.
- **Business-to-Business (B2B) Telemarketing.** Many B2B purchases, such as office phone systems and photocopiers, are of significant dollar value and require a higher level of technical expertise and more sophisticated level of conversation and approach. These telemarketing programs often focus on a longer buying cycle for a narrower list of target customers.

Online and Mobile Media

As the technology for capturing consumer data and tracking Web behavior continues to evolve, nearly every online or mobile medium is becoming an opportunity for direct marketers to target marketing messages to segmented audiences. Even with a minimal amount of information, direct tactics can use the Web to leapfrog traditional mass advertising strategies by reaching consumers where and when they often make purchase decisions.

Display Advertisements

The concept of reserving space on a Web page for advertising (also known as *banner advertising*) is almost as old as the medium itself. However, the content in these areas has become increasingly tailored to users, even without their direct request.

Custom Site Content

Many enterprise-level Web sites are based on content management systems (CMSs) that already manage broad libraries of copy and images, serving these up on user interaction. Advanced CMSs can tailor that content based on business rules triggered by customer profiles, browsing patterns, or search requests.

Search Engine Marketing/Optimization

An entire industry has sprung up around managing how sites present themselves to major search engines. Search engine optimization (SEO) best practices allow Web sites to tailor their content and code to rank higher in search engine results for selected key words. Search engine marketing (SEM) firms manage advertisements within these search results, usually focusing around the Google AdWords program.

Mobile Marketing

Early mobile marketing campaigns focused around text messages, also known as short message service (SMS) and multimedia message service (MMS). Direct marketers often can embed custom coupon codes in these messages, allowing them to both drive customers to a store and track interaction with these campaigns. As mobile devices have become increasingly sophisticated, entire mobile Web experiences have been developed by direct marketers to serve up tailored content, much like what is being done with standard Web sites.

Social Media

Social media represents the next generation of online communication and often is referred to under the broad umbrella of Web 2.0. At its core, social media simply represents opportunities for content readers to transform into content publishers—a paradigm shift that radically changes how people discover new products or news, gather information, and trust marketing messages. Social media changes the relationship between brand and consumer from monologue (one to many) to a dialogue (many to many).

Social Direct Marketing

The landscape of social media continues to expand at a tremendous rate, and many brands are flocking to the Web in an attempt to harness and capitalize on the billions of consumer conversations happening every day. Direct marketers have a unique role to play in this space since their practice always has focused on brands talking directly with consumers.

Social media simply brings a new twist. Now, as brands talk with consumers, consumers also will talk with each other and back to the brand.

Selecting the right social media strategy for a particular brand is a complicated process, since the landscapes of these media already are extremely complex. All media and actions taken in this space by a brand should deliver on four business objectives:

1. Build the brand.
2. Engender loyalty.
3. Drive sales.
4. Gain customer insights.

Owned, Paid, and Earned Media

Brands have the opportunity to leverage three types of media to fulfill these goals:

- **Owned Media.** *Owned media* refers to the digital properties and content a brand already controls and uses to communicate with its consumers. These can include a company Web site, product sites, partnerships, podcasts, SEOs, and even offline experiences. All these elements create and distribute messages that are the origin of consumer conversations. An active social strategy can leverage owned media to support or influence specific conversations by providing tailored content or custom applications. For example, a fashion boutique may provide a discussion forum on its site highlighting new items for sale, giving consumers a chance to get insider information and talk about the products.
- **Paid Media.** *Paid media* is purchased content placements that goes beyond a brand's owned properties to reach consumers at key conversation points throughout the Web. Banner ads are included here, as well as video ads, sponsorships/partnerships, SEM, mobile marketing, and affiliate marketing. A marketer can consider any campaign, online or offline, as part of this paid media since they are all seeds for consumer conversation.
- **Earned Media.** Ultimately, the goal of a social media strategy is to use the right mix of the owned and paid types of media to influence a

third type: earned media. *Earned media* is where the consumer conversations happen and is often the most trusted and influential sources of information for consumers. Earned media is also referred to as *word of mouth (WOM) marketing* or *user-generated content (UGC)*. When the earned media positively reflects a client's brand and acts as a catalyst for more favorable consumer conversations, a marketer knows that the social media strategy has been successful.

DIRECT MARKETING— INTERNATIONAL
by L.L. Bean

Selling products internationally using direct marketing is similar in many ways to marketing domestically. However, globalization brings about a degree of complexity. There are several international factors that must be considered before selecting the best direct marketing option.

Product

In designing a direct marketing campaign, a company should recognize the unique customer needs within the target market. Marketing research will determine if the product and service offering is something the international customer wants.

Price

It is important to examine the pricing structures in the targeted country (including exchange rates, duties, tariffs, and taxes) to determine what products and services a company can provide through direct marketing. Since it is usually more expensive to ship an order overseas, international customers must feel a compelling reason to seek out products, such as the product not being available in the customer's market, or the price/quality relationship of the product being very competitive. It must be determined in what currency the price will be marked. If it is in the foreign currency, then hedging against monetary fluctuations may be advisable.

Copy and Language Differences

The country's language must be clearly understood. It is not enough to simply translate from English. The creative copy must put forth a message that is familiar to prospective international customers, thereby creating for them a level of comfort with what they are seeing and reading.

Shipping and Order Fulfillment

Logistics arrangements with package delivery agents and freight forwarders must ensure quick delivery and accurate customs compliance to compensate for the long distances covered in overseas deliveries.

Guarantees

A strong guarantee program is important to assuage fears of customers who are not used to ordering through direct means or who are not satisfied with the product. The return process should be simple and quick.

Legal

Diligence is paid to trademark infringement and counterfeiting in foreign countries. Many foreign governments now are willing to cooperate with companies to stop these illegal practices.

Marketing Research

Before entering a new overseas market, it is important to know the demographics and psychographics of the potential customer base. In order to determine the state of the market in a foreign country, companies may seek professional marketing research advice from consulting firms that specialize in the target country or tap into an advertising or public relations agency within the new market.

Infrastructure Capabilities

When marketing internationally, a direct marketer should determine if it is more desirable to do business from the home country or operate in a foreign country. This can be determined by the level of sophistication of the direct marketing infrastructure:

- Postal system (speed and reliability).
- Telephone (availability and reliability).
- Credit cards/payment methods (availability).
- Lists and databases (availability and reliability). Some countries' lists are becoming increasingly difficult to access as data privacy laws are implemented and enforced.

Direct Marketing Options

Once the international factors have been considered, the marketer has the same direct marketing options that are available in the home country, but with some differences.

Television

Television as a direct-response medium is becoming increasingly popular throughout the world, but not to the same extent as in the United States and Japan. In some countries, regulations limit the amount of commercial time stations can devote to advertising in general and to infomercials specifically.

Internet

Internet marketing is exploding in most developed countries; however, the dollar value of consumer purchases on the Internet in the developing world remains minuscule for both demographic reasons and reasons unique to the medium. Low volumes reflect lack of access to computers, high Internet connection fees, and the upscale demographics of computer ownership. Some major impediments to consumer acceptance of Internet ordering are the same as for offline: fulfillment difficulties, payment mechanisms (lack of credit card usage in many countries), and the inability to touch and feel the goods. Two problems are unique to the Internet: consumer concerns about security of credit card details and concern about privacy of information.

Telemarketing

Outbound telemarketing is widely used in the United States, Europe, and parts of Latin America, but rarely used elsewhere. This is due both to the high cost of calling and the difficulty of finding trained telemarketers fluent in the nuances and customs of other languages and countries. However, service bureaus that serve clients across multiple borders are increasing in number dramatically. Inbound telemarketing is used almost exclusively as a customer service function or in response to direct mail and television advertising.

Catalog

The typical approach to international catalog marketing has been to develop a market base in the home country, then to expand by mailing catalogs from the home country, printing in the same language, pricing in the home country currency, and shipping customer order packages from the home country base of operations.

DIRECT MARKETING – CASE STUDY

by Draftfcb

Company: MilkPEP (Milk Processor Education Program)
Case: Community Building/Loyalty — Integrated Media

The Milk Processor Education Program, MilkPEP, is the marketing entity that promotes milk as a beverage. In 2004, the marketing situation was daunting. Sales of white milk had been declining for years, and a significant price hike was on its way. Retailers viewed milk as an unexciting commodity product that was purchased without much thought by moms for their kids. These women were procurers, but not consumers of milk. They considered it a fatty food high in calories and out of sync with a healthy adult diet. However, as a market segment, women represented strong upside potential for increased sales. They were already buying the product for their families. The challenge was to get them to consume it.

(Continued)

A recently discovered product benefit provided an opportunity; the calcium in milk burns fat and enhances a weight loss diet's effectiveness. As little as 24 ounces of milk as part of a daily regimen helps burn more calories. This should be welcome news to American women 18 to 50, 42 percent of whom, according to research, claim to be on a weight loss diet at any given time. Now, a product already in their homes can make a sensible, easy-to-implement addition to their weight management plans.

MilkPEP's team of agencies—representing such marketing disciplines as direct marketing, advertising, promotional marketing, public relations, and event marketing—joined forces to build a seamless, integrated campaign platform: "Milk Your Diet. Lose Weight. 24 ounces in 24 hours." Every element of the campaign worked together to give moms a relevant reason to buy and drink milk regularly. Market research showed that the target audience needed strong reasons to believe they should drink milk in order to change their attitudes and habits. So the campaign not only had to generate awareness of milk's weight loss benefit, it had to convince consumers that the claims were true.

The campaign launched in spring, when women start planning to get in shape for warmer weather. The popular celebrity "milk mustache" branding campaign was evolved to introduce milk's weight loss benefits. Print executions featured the actress Kelly Preston and television's Dr. Phil (a trusted source for no-nonsense practical advice) and included a Web address for more information. In addition, television advertising was created specific to the "24/24" proposition, including executions designed to drive Web site traffic.

The www.2424milk Web site was created to back up the product claims and activate the target audience. Concurrently, a retail support campaign was launched, turning the grocery dairy aisle into a promotional venue with dairy case window clings, shelf strips, and floor displays offering a free 24/24 Weight Loss Guide. The guide, featuring editorial copy from *Shape* magazine for credibility, also included $200 in partner coupons and easy-to-prepare low-calorie recipes. Distributed at retail and available for direct order through newspaper insert ads, the guide explained the science behind milk's weight loss claim.

To further stimulate sales, a "24/24 Starter Kit" was developed that featured a unique curvy white plastic bottle that holds 24 ounces of milk. This was promoted in the Weight Loss Guide, online, and at events. Those who ordered the starter kit formed the foundation of a customer base to receive occasional personalized e-mail messages and offers that encouraged milk consumption and healthy eating.

Public relations was another key discipline in this integrated campaign, beginning with a launch event that took over an entire block in New York City and featured female celebrity athletes and the cooperation of the American Dietetic Association and the American Osteoporosis Foundation. A Milk Bar mobile tour cruised the United States, and key cities were targeted for in-store sampling and events with nutrition experts. News stories were placed in top broadcast and print media. MilkPEP also sponsored a national conference on obesity attended by 400 health-care leaders.

As the campaign progressed, active consumers were rewarded through a summer sweepstakes. Consumers could register online with a UPC code from a milk purchase for a chance to win one of 24 white Volkswagen Beetle convertibles given away daily for 24 days. Registrants also could opt in for the e-mail customer relationship program. The sweepstakes was supported by in-store signage, promotional tags on television spots, and rich media banner ads on Web sites frequented by the target audience.

The results of this integrated campaign were nothing short of remarkable. Within six months, 40 percent of American women 18 to 49 were aware of the milk and weight loss connection. Four million Weight Loss Guides were distributed in a two-month period. Roughly 350,000 people visited the Web site in the first months of the campaign, and that number nearly doubled during the sweepstakes month. More than 127,000 opted in for the direct e-mail customer relationship program. Best of all, the decline of fluid milk sales was reversed. Sales for the second quarter of 2004 were 1.5 percent above forecasts, despite unprecedented, raw material–induced price increases during that time.

Year-on-year sales continued to show improvement as the campaign extended into the following years with new promotions, new partnerships (including Curves health clubs), and new online opportunities to interact with MilkPEP's weight loss message. Four years after launch, online communications—especially the Web site—remain a central part of MilkPEP's community building efforts, helping turn moms who once bought milk only for their kids into loyal, regular milk consumers.

DIRECT MARKETING – CASE STUDY

by Wunderman

Company: **American Institute of CPAs**
Case: **Changing the Perceptions of a Generation (2008)**

Talking to young people, especially teens, about serious stuff like career choices and preparing for their future can be daunting, even for their parents. But together, Wunderman and the American Institute of Certified Public Accountants (AICPA) did exactly that. Eight years after creating the "Start Here. Go Places." student recruitment program, the AICPA team is able to point to results like improved regard for the profession, more students pursuing accounting, and a shelf full of awards from the experts.

The Problem

In the spring of 2000, the AICPA conducted a major study and discovered a drop in the number of students majoring or planning to major in accounting.

- In 1990, 4 percent of college students majored in accounting and 4 percent of high school students were planning to major in accounting.
- By 2000, college numbers had dropped to 2 percent and high school to 1 percent.

These troubling survey results were confirmed by the fact that accounting firms were reporting a shortage of graduates to fill positions. Subsequent research performed by the AICPA among high school seniors and college students revealed lack of knowledge, misinformation, and negative perceptions toward the accounting profession. Possibly reinforcing these misconceptions and negative perceptions were the high profile business scandals at the start of the twenty-first century (such as the Enron scandal), which not only focused attention on the critical role that CPAs play but also sparked renewed interest in the profession.

The Goal

Challenges do not come much tougher than this: trying to fill the pipeline for future CPAs by influencing a notoriously skeptical, marketing-averse audience in a tumultuous, scandalous climate, with a limited budget.

(Continued)

From the beginning, we set three specific objectives:

1. Improve perceptions of the accounting profession among high school and college students.
2. Attract college students to major in accounting and to pursue CPA certification.
   Increase the number of accounting majors above the 2000 level of 2 percent.
   Increase the number of high school students intending to major in accounting to above 1 percent.
3. Engage 50,000 new students yearly throughout the life of the program.

Direct Marketing Practices

Wunderman defined the discipline of direct marketing and practices in the book *19 Things All Successful Direct Marketing Companies Should Know*. In creating the AICPA program, we focused on two practices in particular:

1. **Build the Brand Experience.** Customers need to feel the brand as an experience that serves their individual needs at each stage in the relationship.
2. **You Are What You Know.** Collect data that can become information to help build on success and minimize failure.

The Audience

Students today are faced with many options relating to their future, and they want to be as prepared as possible. Agency marketing research showed that students are looking to develop substantial knowledge and skills that can help them make a difference in the real world; they like to be challenged, and they want experiences that will let them test their skills to find that special edge that will set them apart from others.

We knew we needed to provide students with the chance to experience the world of accounting as an exciting, interesting, and rewarding career path. We also knew we were dealing with Millennials, the first generation to learn about their world, to express themselves, to gauge themselves against their peers, and to entertain themselves—digitally. So, the obvious place to connect was to satisfy their innate expectation of an online experience and to do it in a way that would give them a taste of the surprising things they might do if they were working as a CPA.

The Big Idea

Every really cool, interesting job in life from sports to music to fashion to volunteerism is supported by accounting, so the idea was to give students a hands-on chance to discover that you do not have to be P Diddy to live in P Diddy's world; accounting can get you there, too.

Multimedia with a Digital Hub

The campaign had to show efficiencies in media selection and across channels to gain maximum impact at campuses in all 50 states. We went to media that went to students where they live (direct mail and e-mail), where they learn (on-campus, place-based media and posters), and where they play (interactive banners, online games, and sponsorships). And we extended our student lifestyle penetration through guerrilla and viral marketing and by incorporating key influencers (professors and teachers) to reinforce the messages.

All of this drove students to StartHereGoPlaces.com, the program name we developed to telegraph the benefit we were offering. This Web site is the hub of the campaign with practical career information, interactive elements like polls, quizzes, and online business simulation games where students have the ability to learn more about the CPA profession and test their CPA skills.

- Students can explore their inner entrepreneur as they learn how to create, build, and successfully market their product through 10 levels of the *MoneyMeansBusiness Workshop.*
- Developing a solid plan to turn around a struggling record label in the *Turnaround Game* allows students to experience CPA consultant challenges through video simulation.
- Working as a forensic accountant is fun when students actively track down and stop fraudsters in *Catch Me If You Can.*
- Students can put their financial management skills to the test in the entertainment, sports, or fashion industry by playing *BizzFun.* They play individually and compete in leagues against other students to feed their competitive spirit.

Content within contests has been proven to maintain ongoing interest and student involvement in StartHereGoPlaces.com. Through the *Trivia Challenge,* students have the chance to win hip prizes in exchange for their willingness to explore the site content for answers to trivia questions relating to the Accounting Profession. Each answer is one submission into the contest; the "tell-a-friend" feature is another way to gain additional entries into the challenge.

Other elements of the campaign include search engine optimization to drive qualified traffic to the Web site, as well as a custom-published magazine for additional awareness and lead generation.

The Results

At the heart of direct marketing efforts has always been the ability to test and learn as you go to optimize your results. For AICPA, our primary measurement tools were:

- **The Student Recruitment Database.** A program-tracking database that captures and tracks response to individual media channels and promotions as well as the migration of students along the CPA continuum.
- **The Annual Tracking Study.** An online, self-administered gauge of student attitudes and behaviors conducted by an independent third-party vendor.

Over time, we have used results from these databases for targeting and media adjustments and creative guidance. But, from its inception, this program more than lived up to the goals we set, and after seven years in the market, results continue to confirm success against all objectives.

OBJECTIVE 1 RESULTS: SIGNIFICANTLY IMPROVED PERCEPTIONS OF THE ACCOUNTING PROFESSION*		
Perception	**2001**	**2008**
Profession for intelligent people	9%	16%
Profession that requires problem solving	14%	30%
Profession that others respect	6%	18%
Profession that requires leadership	3%	12%
Profession that has career choices	5%	23%

Source: Annual Tracking Study conducted by third-party vendor.

OBJECTIVE 2 RESULTS: SIGNIFICANT LIFT IN THE NUMBER OF STUDENTS ON AN ACCOUNTING CAREER TRACK*

Career Track	2001	2008
Interest in accounting major	4%	39%
Interest in accounting career	5%	39%

*Source: Annual Tracking Study conducted by third-party vendor.

OBJECTIVE 3 RESULTS: A RELIABLE MAGNET FOR STUDENT ENGAGEMENT AND CONSISTENTLY ABOVE GOAL*

- More than 512,000 students have registered with the Start Here. Go Places. Program (about 73,000 new students per year).
- The vast majority of campaign participants represent incremental value to the AICPA and the profession, that is, students who were not already on an accounting path.

*Source: The program's Student Recruitment Database.

CORPORATE PROFILES AND AUTHOR BIOGRAPHIES

DRAFTfcb
Draftfcb is a modern agency model for clients seeking creative, accountable marketing programs that build business and deliver a high Return on Ideas™. Visit Draftfcb at www.draftfcb.com.

Sid Liebenson
Sid Liebenson is Executive Vice President, Director of Marketing for Draftfcb. In this position, he works with all of the agency's worldwide offices, assisting them with marketing counsel and information. Mr. Liebenson received his BS and MS from Northwestern University.

L.L. BEAN
L.L. Bean is one of the world's leading international mail-order concerns. Visit L.L. Bean at www.llbean.com.

Thomas Harden
Thomas Harden is Executive Vice President for L.L. Bean. Mr. Harden received his BS from Indiana University and his MBA from Ohio State University.

MaryRose McKinnon provided additional information.

RAPP
RAPP, founded in 1965, is the world's largest multichannel CRM agency, with more than 50 offices in 30 countries and 2,000 employees worldwide. Visit RAPP at www.rapp.com.

Loren Grossman
Loren Grossman is the Global Chief Strategy Officer. Mr. Grossman oversees strategic planning at the global, regional, and local levels to develop solutions that are equally grounded in data and creative insight. Mr. Grossman received his BA from the University of Pennsylvania. He received his MA from New York University in both comparative literature and marketing.

Eric Swayne
Eric Swayne is the Digital Strategist for RAPP Retail. Mr. Swayne brings his background as an award-winning Web designer, developer, and writer to his role. A National Merit Scholar, he received his BA in 2002 from Harding University.

WUNDERMAN
In 2008, *Advertising Age* ranked Wunderman the #1 marketing services network in the world. Visit Wunderman at www.wunderman.com.

Kris Slocum
Kris Slocum is Senior Vice President, Group Planning Director. Ms. Slocum's work involves exploring the secret lives of consumers to understand their link to client brands, and developing insights and briefs, and working closely with creatives to bring the work to life. Ms. Slocum studied Commercial Art at Memphis State University and music composition at the Manhattan School of Music/Composition.

NOTES

1. Pew Internet & American Life Project data, March 2007.
2. Ibid.
3. October 2007 report by technology marketing research firm The Radicati Group.
4. Ibid.
5. Ferris Research.

14 BRAND AMBASSADORS

I LIKE YOUR SPIRIT, BOYS - BUT I HAVE A FEELING H.R. WILL KICK UP A FUSS...

by BzzAgent, Zappos.com, Nordstrom, and Washington Nationals Baseball Club

BRAND AMBASSADORS—CONSUMER ADVOCATES
by BzzAgent, Inc.

Marshaling influential, gregarious brand ambassadors—or advocates—to recommend a product throughout their extensive social circles is the ultimate goal of every marketer. After all, marketing can be heavy work, and the load is lightened considerably when thousands of consumers help with the lifting.

Historically, brand advocacy has been thought to occur by happenstance. A particularly memorable advertising campaign, a surprise pleasantry at point-of-sale, a product that performed just a little better than expected ... such moments have always contributed to brand advocacy. But until recently, consumer endorsement was considered to be a chance output of success elsewhere in a product's value chain. This thinking has recently changed, thanks in large part to marketing's ability to trigger and track the spread of product-related opinions on the Internet as well as in social interactions.

Marketing-friendly behaviors such as positive word of mouth and customer evangelism are now recognized as the natural by-products of a person feeling connected to a company. The more a company can engage with its customers in new and meaningful ways, the more ambassadors it is apt to create.

Johnnie Walker is a prime example of a company that understands how to nurture advocacy. Throughout the year, its marketing department hosts Johnnie Walker Journey events in which fans of the brand can learn about the history of the company, sample its scotch whiskey blends, socialize with attendees, and, of course, interact with official brand ambassadors.

Like any relationship, brand-consumer rapport is built over time. A singular interaction, no matter how invigorating, is only a starting point in the road to advocacy. Johnnie Walker's decision to name its event series "Journey" suggests a keen awareness of this easily overlooked fact. To ensure that the carefully orchestrated experience is not an isolated event, the company built an online community where attendees can upload pictures, post testimonials, and invite friends to register future events. Johnnie Walker understands that as fans build relationships with each other, they are also strengthening ties to the brand itself. To that end, the marketing team created a self-perpetuating machine that converts customers to insiders, insiders to ambassadors, and ambassadors to recruiters.

Organizing customer appreciation days and building virtual communities can be effective advocacy-building techniques, but they are not prerequisites. Many companies have enjoyed similar success through much less sophisticated means. For example, Pabst Blue Ribbon, an antiestablishment icon, is discussed in the book *Buying In* by best-selling author and *New York Times* columnist Rob Walker. He theorizes that the beer's fan base surged "not despite the lack of marketing support, but because of it." Of course, Walker doesn't claim Pabst avoids marketing entirely, but rather points out that the company zigs when the rest of the beer industry does a billion-dollar zag.

Pabst, or P.B.R. to friends, built advocacy not through tireless broadcast advertising or celebrity endorsements but rather by listening to its zealots and marketing *with* them—not *at* them. While other brewers might sponsor a high profile concert series, Pabst donates prizes to counterculture events, such as bike messenger polo competitions. It earns advocacy in the simplest ways imaginable: through mutual respect and dialogue.

Johnnie Walker and Pabst Blue Ribbon represent two ends of the advocacy spectrum. The former has executed an intricate, multitouch customer intimacy program; the latter has committed to looking at itself through its ambassadors' lens. Most companies operate somewhere in the middle. Premium denim label True Religion, for example, won instant confidence by supplying $300 jeans to an image-conscious, most-trusted source: hair stylists. Hilton Hotels reversed one of the most popular customer complaints when it eliminated black-out dates from its rewards program. Health and beauty upstart Carol's Daughter corralled the support of the blogosphere to gain immediate visibility in a crowded market. These unconventional campaigns not only contributed to the brands' success, but they also captured the attention of the traditional media. In fact, the industry's most recognized publication, *Advertising Age,* applauded several of these ambassador programs.

Because technology changes nearly as quickly as online mores, many brands have turned to outside specialists for activating consumer advocacy and measuring its impact on sales. New media companies like BzzAgent and VocalPoint have assembled vast networks of consumer volunteers, eager to spread the word about goods and services. Product-centric parties made famous in the 1950s by home goods brand Tupperware have achieved massive scale with the introduction of marketing company House Party. And regardless of how much buzz a brand can generate, analytics organizations like Nielsen Online and Cymfony can measure it.

BRAND AMBASSADORS—EMPLOYEE ADVOCATES
by Zappos.com

Building a brand today is very different from building a brand 50 years ago. It used to be that a few people got together in a room, decided what the brand positioning was going to be, and then spent a lot of money buying advertising telling people what their brand was. And if you were able to spend enough money, then you were able to build your brand.

It is a very different world today. With the Internet connecting everyone together, companies are becoming more and more transparent whether they like it or not. An unhappy customer or a disgruntled employee can blog about a bad experience with a company, and the story can spread like wildfire by e-mail or with tools like Twitter.

The good news is that the reverse is true as well. A great experience with a company can be read by millions of people almost instantaneously.

The fundamental problem is that you cannot possibly anticipate every touchpoint that could influence the perception of your company's brand.

For example, if you happen to meet an employee of Company X at a bar, even if the employee is not working, how you perceive your interaction with that employee will affect how you perceive Company X, and therefore Company X's brand. It can be a positive or a negative influence. Every employee can affect your company's brand, not just the front-line employees who are paid to talk to your customers.

Advertising can only get your brand so far. If you ask most people what the brand of the airline industry as a whole is (not any specific airline, but the entire industry), they will usually say something about bad customer service or bad customer experience. If you ask people what their perception of the U.S. auto industry is today, chances are the responses you get won't be in line with what the automakers project in their advertising.

So what is a company to do if they cannot just buy their way into building the brand they want? What is the best way to build a brand for the long term?

In a word: culture.

At Zappos, our belief is that if you get the culture right, most of the other stuff—like great customer service, or building a great long-term brand, or passionate employees and customers—will happen naturally on its own.

We believe that your company's culture and your company's brand are really just two sides of the same coin. The brand may lag the culture at first, but eventually it will catch up.

Your culture is your brand.

So how do you build and maintain the culture that you want?

It starts with the hiring process. At Zappos, we actually do two different sets of interviews. The hiring manager and his or her team will do the standard set of interviews looking for relevant experience, technical ability, fit within the team, and so forth. But then our HR department does a separate set of interviews, looking purely for culture fit. Candidates have to pass both sets of interviews in order to be hired.

We have actually said no to a lot of very talented people that we know can make an immediate impact on our top or bottom line. But because we felt they weren't culture fits, we were willing to sacrifice the short-term benefits in order to protect our culture (and therefore our brand) for the long term.

After hiring, the next step to building the culture is training. Everyone who is hired at our headquarters goes through the same training that our Customer Loyalty Team (call center) reps go through, regardless of department or title. You might be an accountant, or a lawyer, or a software developer—you go through the exact same training program.

It is a four-week training program, in which we go over company history, the importance of cus-tomer service, the long-term vision of the company, our philosophy about company culture—and then you are actually on the telephone for two weeks, taking calls from customers. Again, this goes back to our belief that customer service should not be just a department; it should be the entire company.

At the end of the first week of training, we make an offer to the entire class. We offer everyone $2,000 to quit (in addition to paying them for the time they have already worked), and it is a standing offer until the end of the fourth week of training. We want to make sure that employees are here for more than just a paycheck. We want employees who believe in our long-term vision and want to be a part of our culture. As it turns out, on average, less than 3 percent of people end up taking the offer.

One of the great advantages of focusing on culture is when reporters come and visit our offices. Unlike most companies, we do not give reporters a short list of people they are allowed to talk to. Instead, we encourage them to wander around and talk to whoever they want. It is our way of being as transparent as possible, which is part of our culture.

We have formally defined the Zappos culture in terms of 10 core values:

1. Deliver WOW Through Service.
2. Embrace and Drive Change.
3. Create Fun and a Little Weirdness.
4. Be Adventurous, Creative, and Open-Minded
5. Pursue Growth and Learning.
6. Build Open and Honest Relationships with Communication.
7. Build a Positive Team and Family Spirit.
8. Do More with Less.
9. Be Passionate and Determined.
10. Be Humble.

We believe that it is really important to come up with core values that you can commit to. And by *commit*, we mean that you are willing to hire and fire based on them. If you are willing to do that, then you are well on your way to building a company culture that is in line with the brand you want to build. You can let all of your employees be your brand ambassadors, not just the marketing or PR department. And they can be brand ambassadors both inside and outside the office.

At the end of the day, just remember that if you get the culture right, most of the other stuff—including building a great brand—will fall into place on its own.

BRAND AMBASSADOR—CASE STUDY

by Nordstorm

Company: Nordstorm
Case: Building Customer Loyalty through Word of Mouth

Founded by John W. Nordstrom in Seattle in 1901, Nordstrom is a fashion specialty retailer offering clothing, shoes, and accessories for the entire family. For more than 100 years, Nordstrom has been guided by its founder's philosophy: offer the customer the best service, selection, quality, and value.

The company's approach to marketing starts with the belief that the best representatives of the Nordstrom brand are the frontline employees who are closest to the customer. The philosophy is that if you take care of your customers, then they become your emissaries, your best advertising. Nordstrom does very little conventional advertising, believing that the best publicity is word of mouth.

At Nordstrom, reputation is everything and depends on having salespeople who will take ownership for the customers' experience. Salespeople are empowered to do whatever it takes to take care of the customer. When this doesn't happen, unhappy customers will probably share their experience with others. Conversely, when their service expectations are exceeded, they become loyal customers and brand ambassadors, sharing their story with family and friends, who in turn visit Nordstrom.

Nordstrom is grateful for the positive reputation it has managed to earn over the years. The company is fortunate to receive regular feedback from customers that send letters and e-mails or make telephone calls to salespeople, store managers, and the Nordstrom family. Customer feedback is a direct way for the company and its employees to learn about what they are doing well or how they can improve.

The following are excerpts from customer letters, showing how the Nordstrom reputation lives on through salespeople's actions, which create superior service experiences that customers share with family and friends.

A salesperson at the Mall of America store in Bloomington, Minnesota, wowed her customers by taking the time to complete all their shopping needs throughout the entire store, creating a lasting impression.

I'm writing this letter to share the experience my father and I had at your Mall of America store. My father has difficulty walking so he does not go shopping much, but has always made it a point to go to Nordstrom. When shopping, we happened upon a wonderful salesperson who could tell we were having a hard time shopping. She got the earrings my dad wanted and asked if she could help us with anything else. … She took the time to pull everything he needed from departments throughout the whole store. Men's, Women's, Jewelry, Handbags, and even got some other items shipped to us from another store. Recently, it is the only story my father tells everyone—our shopping experience. And my mother can't stop talking about the amazing jewelry and handbag my father picked out for her, which was really all the salesperson's doing. She has made one of the best memories for my parents.

A salesperson at the North County Fair store in Escondido, California, has built strong relationships with three generations of women from one family, so much so, that they continue to shop with her even though some of them are hundreds of miles away.

I am writing this letter to bring to your attention the wonderful customer service that I, as well as my family, have received from one of your salespeople. She has helped us through the holidays, graduations, vacations, as well as coping with the consequences of serious illness. The amazing part is that she has helped many of my family members who live hundreds of miles away. I have relied on her for many years to help me find clothing for everything from special events to everyday life. In a day where customer service has seemed to disappear, it is so refreshing to shop at your Nordstrom store and be treated with such respect and kindness. This salesperson has made, and will continue to make, shopping for me, as well as my family, a great and successful experience.

Nordstrom offers to split shoe sizes for customers with a size and a half or larger difference in their feet; selling the split shoe pair for the same price as the original pair. In Men's Shoes at the Providence Place store in Rhode Island, a salesperson's actions to split shoe sizes to meet his customer's needs created a Nordstrom customer for life.

I went to the Nordstrom in Providence and was fortunate enough to meet a great salesperson as I was browsing in the shoe department. … I happened to mention to him a situation that I am always embarrassed about and that is the fact that I always needed to buy two pairs of shoes in order to accommodate my need for different sized shoes. … The salesperson assured me that this was nothing to be embarrassed about and mentioned to me a service that Nordstrom offers that would certainly take care of my shoe sizing need. I asked him why he would take the time to accommodate me and he said quite confident and proud that he hoped I would become a "Nordstrom customer for life." Whenever I return to the store, he always greets me by name and is ready to help me. When I travel I always seek out a Nordstrom and it really doesn't matter if it is a pair of socks or a suit, I am a Nordstrom customer for life, thanks to him. I have passed along my Nordstrom experience to my family, colleagues, and friends and only hope they too become Nordstrom customers for life. I thought you might like to know my experience with Nordstrom and that it started with one extraordinary employee. Thank you.

A salesperson at the Twelve Oaks Mall store in Novi, Michigan, created such a service impression that went beyond expectations that the customer has continued to fulfill other shopping needs with her.

Today to my surprise, I received a Thank You card from one of your salespeople. I say "surprised" because I feel like I should be the one doing the thanking. When I visited your store for the first time this past week, I was showered with the utmost excellent service. … I came in looking for an outfit for an upcoming event and for a few new casual outfits for the fall/winter season. The salesperson I met was energetic and tireless when selecting many outfits for me to try on. Any time one size would not fit, out she went to find the right one. … When I had mentioned that I needed to buy some new make-up, she went down to gather it for me while I was trying on clothes. Now that's taking care of

(Continued)

the customer! Since I had such a positive first visit, I came back for a second visit. Of course I went to see the same salesperson. From my first visit, I brought back a pair of pants that just didn't quite match what I had. With no problem or hassle, she willingly returned the pants and helped me select a better pair. I'd like to thank Nordstrom for the service that went beyond my expectations. As a result of it, I am now certain to choose Nordstrom over other retailers and I'm going to spread the news to all of my family and friends. Thank you again for such a wonderful experience, and I look forward to my next visit.

BRAND AMBASSADOR—CASE STUDY

by the Washington Nationals Baseball Club

Company: Washington Nationals Baseball Club
Case: Connecting with the Local Community

When baseball returned to Washington, D.C., in 2005 in the form of the Washington Nationals, it was the first time in 34 years that Major League Baseball was played in the nation's capital. Baseball had left the District for good in 1971, and local fans were forced to accept nonlocal teams as their own. The Nationals were faced with the challenge of connecting to an audience that, for many years, had no hometown team for which to root. The National Pastime was once again going to be played in the nation's capital, but would the needed support exist to sustain a Major League ball club?

In 2004, the year before the Montreal Expos moved to Washington, D.C., to become the Washington Nationals, over 70 million people attended Major League Baseball games.[1] The excitement in the District was palpable about the team relocating to Washington, and the organization needed to find a way to build upon that excitement before the novelty wore off. The team had to create a brand, and one that would resonate with the Greater Washington, D.C., community. Even though the Nationals are not an expansion franchise, the team and its players and coaches were new to Washington. The organization faced significant challenges, including:

- How to garner the hometown fan support that comes natural to other cities
- How to create a genuine connection between the organization and the surrounding community
- How to solidify and publicize a brand that tens of thousands of people would identify with and support

Ownership of the team was transferred from Major League Baseball to the Washington, D.C.–based Lerner Family in July 2006. The family and team executives identified three pillars as the focal points for the organization:

- Scouting and Player Development
- Community Relations
- Fan Experience

Each pillar provides an opportunity for an ambassador from the Nationals organization to be used to bridge the connection to the community. Nationals players, coaches, mascots, and front office staff all represent the ball club's brand and could act as ambassadors in the community to harness fan support and loyalty necessary to solidify the Nationals brand.

Players, Managers, and Coaches

The Nationals have 25 players on their major league roster during the regular season and a coaching staff of seven, including their manager. The team plays 81 regular-season games in Washington, D.C., and 81 on the road. Most baseball games are played in the evening, freeing up team personnel to take part in community events during the late morning and early afternoon hours. Players visit local schools, libraries, and hospitals, and participate in autograph sessions, meet and greets, and charity fund-raisers throughout the year. Since the Nationals relocated in 2005, players have made 445 appearances in the Greater Washington, D.C., community.

Coordinated by the Nationals' Community Relations Department, the appearances by Nationals players, managers, and coaches help to create young fans. Often, the team will donate tickets during an appearance so kids and other participants can attend a game and see firsthand what a great experience baseball at Nationals Park can be.

Mascots

Players, coaches, and managers may change, but the mascot is the constant throughout all the wins and losses. The Nationals Mascot Screech, a baby bald eagle, was hatched on April 17, 2005, at RFK Stadium. Even though Nationals players cannot make every appearance due to the rigorous schedule of baseball, Screech is available to attend community events all year long. A mascot appearance can go a long way in building goodwill in the community. During games Screech can be found dancing around Nationals Park, visiting with his fans, and rooting for the Nationals.

Four new faces were introduced to the mascot family in June 2006, The Racing Presidents. What began as an animated race on the scoreboard became a live race on the field during the fourth inning break each game. George Washington, Tom Jefferson, Abe Lincoln, and Teddy Roosevelt were an instant hit with Nationals fans, who soon developed a favorite in Teddy. Though he tried valiantly, Teddy did not win a race during the 2006 season and his streak of losses continues in 2009. The team's marketing department realized the opportunity to capitalize on Teddy's popularity through viral marketing, creating a Facebook page and MySpace account to give fans access to their favorite Racing President. Teddy, Abe, Tom, and George make various appearances throughout the community, furthering both their popularity and that of the team.

Front Office Staff

Each Washington Nationals employee is considered an ambassador for the team. When accepting a job with the team, an employee is expected to take pride in the team and its brand. Nationals employees are often asked to speak to groups about the team and their roles and responsibilities within the organization. All staff may also take part in the team's Employee Volunteer Program. The organization will launch a Speakers Bureau during 2009 to create additional opportunities to meet the community.

Nationals Park is the "Official Home of the National Pastime in the Nation's Capital." By reaching out to fans through the various types of brand ambassadors, the team strives to be a source of pride and brand loyalty in the Greater Washington, D.C., Metropolitan Area.

(Continued)

CORPORATE PROFILES AND AUTHOR BIOGRAPHIES

BzzAgent

BzzAgent has an international network of over 500,000 consumer volunteers who have generated more than 120 million conversations about its clients' products and services. Visit BzzAgent at www.bzzagent.com.

Joe Chernov

Joe Chernov, Vice President of Communications and Associate VP of Marketing for BzzAgent, is a frequent lecturer on word-of-mouth marketing at universities, international conferences, and Fortune 500 companies.

NORDSTROM, INC.

Nordstrom (NYSE–JWN), founded in 1901 as a shoe store, is one of the nation's leading fashion specialty retailers. Visit Nordstrom at www.nordstrom.com.

Linda Finn

Linda Finn is the Executive Vice President Marketing for Nordstrom. Ms. Finn received her BA in English from Stanford University.

WASHINGTON NATIONALS BASEBALL CLUB

The Washington Nationals Baseball Club, owned by the Washington, D.C.–based Lerner Family, was relocated to the District in 2005 from Montreal. Visit the Nationals at www.nationals.com.

Lisa Pagano

Lisa Pagano is currently the Communications Manager for the Washington Nationals. As the publicist for the team's off-field events, she is responsible for promoting the team's Community Relations, Foundation, and Marketing and Business activities. Ms Pagano received her BA in Psychology from George Washington University in 2003. She is originally from Mineola, New York.

ZAPPOS.COM

Zappos is an online retailer that has grown from $0 in 1999 to around $1 billion in gross merchandise sales in 2008 by focusing on customer service. Visit Zappos at www.zappos.com and www.zapposinsights.com.

Tony Hsieh

Tony Hsieh is the CEO. Prior to founding Zappos, Mr. Hsieh was Co-Founder of Link Exchange, and General Manager of Venture Frogs, LLC. Mr. Hsieh received his BA in Computer Science from Harvard University in 1995.

NOTES

1. ESPN: MLB Attendance Report-–2004.

Part 5

Supply (Goods and Services)

15 PRODUCT MANAGEMENT

by PepsiCo

THE ESSENTIALS OF PRODUCT MANAGEMENT

Introduction

A product is the element of marketing that provides utility in assisting customers to satisfy their needs. Businesses provide these products, either goods or services, to both consumers and other businesses. Many products seamlessly integrate goods and services. A good or a service becomes immensely more valuable when it becomes a sought-after brand. Therefore, the goal of marketing a product is to shift it from being a commodity to being a brand experience. While the distinctions between goods and services are blurring, the same basic elements of marketing may be used to successfully market both.

Definition

A *product* is "a bundle of attributes (features, functions, benefits, and uses) capable of exchange or use. A product usually is a mix of tangible and intangible forms such as an idea, a physical entity (a good), a service, or any combination of the three. It exists for the purpose of exchange in order to satisfy individuals and organizational objectives."[1]

PRODUCT CLASSIFICATIONS SERVE CUSTOMER NEEDS

Customers have specific needs, and various product classifications serve these needs. Companies tradi-tionally organize around product categories. It is important to understand the categories and sub-categories because they can determine marketing planning strategies for both demand promotion and the supply chain.

Traditional product classification lines are blur-ring. This is evident in the definition of products, in the product mix, and in the ways that products are being classified. For example, Dell Computer was founded on a business-to-business model, but today includes a large consumer component that sells the same product line. The two broadest clas-sifications are consumer and industrial.

Consumer Products

Traditional consumer product and service classifica-tions include convenience, shopping, and specialty.

- **Convenience Goods and Services.** Conve-nience products and services are those that consumers need quickly and easily. Consumers usually know the brands they desire but will readily substitute others for the sake of time and location. For convenience products, price is a minor consideration. These are not com-modities but are reasonably similar to each other. Examples include milk, gasoline, diapers, film, and dry cleaning. For these products, marketers should try to establish a strong differentiating image to encourage consumers to seek out their brand to move the product into a higher category. In addition, marketers should place these products in as many retail locations as possible. Subcategories include impulse items (candy, magazines), staple items (eggs, butter, car wash), and emergency items (radiator repair, first-aid kit).

- **Shopping Goods and Services.** Shopping products and services include those that consumers feel are important but purchase infrequently. The consumer knowledge level required to make such a purchase with any degree of confidence is relatively low. Therefore, the consumer is likely to spend time shopping around and researching comparative product attributes and price levels. Examples include universities, cars, computer systems, and health care. For these products, marketers should provide high amounts of information through advertising and a well-trained sales force. Pricing should be competitive. Marketing research should provide the product development team with feedback to make product upgrades as rapidly as possible.

- **Specialty Goods and Services.** Specialty products and services are defined as those that consumers feel have special attributes that they will seek out and remain loyal to, regardless of price or location. Examples include a Tiffany diamond ring, a particular surgeon, and a Harley-Davidson motorcycle. Marketers should maintain and emphasize the unique qualities that set these products apart.

Industrial Products

Industrial products and services have several classifications: capital items, raw materials, parts and components, supplies, and services. They must meet specific manufacturer or consumers' quality standards and feature requirements.

- **Capital Items.** Capital items are products used in the production process or operations of a business. They require a major cash or capital expense and last for years or decades. These items include installations (factories, warehouses, office buildings) and fixed/accessory equipment (office equipment, steel presses, delivery trucks). To promote these products, marketers should provide information and technical and financial support.

- **Raw Materials.** Raw materials are consumed in the production process, are usually purchased by grade, and have a commodity price structure. Raw materials are comprised of unprocessed products (vegetables, meat, ore) and processed products (steel, lumber, leather, chemicals). Marketers should differentiate raw materials based on quality and ease of delivery.

- **Parts and Components.** Parts and components become part of the finished product. They can be manufactured in-house or supplied by another company. Examples include computer chips, tires, and electric motors. Marketers should differentiate parts and components based on quality and price.

- **Supplies.** Supplies assist in the production or operation of the business but are not consumed in the actual production process. They usually meet a minimum quality threshold and are price sensitive. The supply category has three subcategories: maintenance supplies (light bulbs, cleaning fluids, air-conditioning filters) repair supplies (paint, nuts and bolts, asphalt) and operating supplies (electricity, industrial lubricants, pens). Marketers should differentiate supplies based on quality and price.

- **Services.** Services facilitate the production and operation of a business. Services may be provided in-house or by an external firm. Services usually are bid on quality of reputation and price, and have a fixed contract duration. Examples include accounting, legal, insurance, security, and cleaning. Marketers should differentiate services based on price, quality, and image.

Durable and Nondurable Goods

In addition, there are two main product classifications: durable and nondurable goods. *Durable goods* are principally items that can be used repeatedly because they are not consumed, or are consumed very slowly. Examples include furniture and heating equipment. These purchases typically are expensive and require thorough research before purchasing. *Nondurable goods* are principally items that are consumed as they are used. Examples include printing paper, groceries, and chemicals. Nondurables typically are inexpensive and require less research prior to purchase.

PRODUCT MIX

A *product mix* is the combination of products that a company offers. The greater the number of offerings, the greater the chance of satisfying a customer. Many companies offer only one product. The company may have expertise in this one product and completely satisfy the needs of its customer base. If customers' needs warrant and the company capabilities are available, the original product, or master brand, may be expanded into additional offerings.

Companies can evolve and grow by enhancing their product mix to meet additional needs of the customer or needs of different customers. However, when companies offer more products, a larger marketing budget is required and may lead to some overlap of marketing efforts and same company product competition in the marketplace. For example, the Dodge Challenger and the Ford Mustang each fill a consumer need yet compete directly against each other. Most companies have grown up behind a single product concept: the Nike running shoe, Pepsi Cola, and State Farm Insurance.

The success of the organization depends on the scope and speed with which the product definition evolves. If the company moves too far or too fast, it will likely end up without marketing focus, and probably with declining revenues. If the company

moves too narrowly or too slowly, growth opportunities will be limited. Nike evolved successfully into an athletic apparel company. State Farm Insurance expanded from providing auto insurance to farmers into all types of insurance.

In order to plan the proper product mix, a company should determine customers' needs; the competitions' product offerings; and internal manufacturing, financial, and marketing capabilities. For example, even though State Farm Insurance provides a wide product mix to consumers it does not provide insurance coverage for commercial risk (airlines, ocean freight, factories, etc.). PepsiCo added a snack food line and shed its restaurant line as advertising and distribution ties were more closely linked.

The product mix is typically discussed in terms of product line depth, breadth, and width.

Product Line

A *product line* is a group of related products that a company offers. The products may be related by customer usage, price, or distribution.

Product Line Depth
The number of products within the line determines the line depth. For example, PepsiCo's product line for beverages includes Pepsi, Mountain Dew, and Slice.

Product Line Breadth
The variation of each product within the product line determines the breadth. Variations may include size, color, and formulation. For example, Pepsi's cola beverage line's breadth of offerings includes Pepsi, Caffeine Free Pepsi, Diet Pepsi, and Caffeine Free Diet Pepsi. Each type of beverage comes in multiple sizes, cans and bottles, and is sold individually, in 6- or 12-packs.

Product Line Width
The number of lines in the mix determines the mix's width. The product lines may or may not be related. For example, PepsiCo's product mix consists of their beverage line and snack food line. Estée Lauder's

product mix consists of their make-up line, treatment line, and fragrance line. Disney's product mix consists of its movies, theme parks, retail stores, cruise line, and community development.

Associated Products

Marketers may expand product sales with associated products. *Associated products* are those that are used in conjunction with the primary product. For example, tennis rackets have several associated products such as tennis balls, racket covers, new strings, and new grips. Associated products also may be services. For example, a new automobile may have warranties, extended repair contracts, and financing. These products may be sold separately or as a package. See Figure 15.1.

PRODUCT COMPETITION AND DIFFERENTIATION

Company products and product lines compete with other companies' products in a variety of ways. Consumers often substitute a competitor's product in lieu of their original choice when motivated by price,

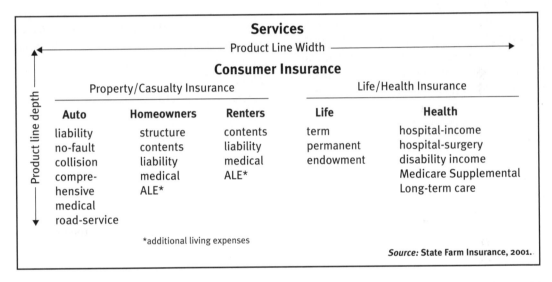

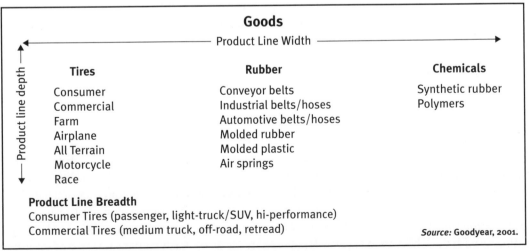

Figure 15.1 Product Line Mix (Width/Depth/Breadth)

convenience, or superior quality. Proper product differentiation, or delineation of features and benefits, will motivate the consumer to seek out his or her preferred choice. Product competition includes general, indirect, and direct.

General Competition

In *general competition*, a product competes for the consumer's attention against all other offerings in the marketplace. For example, a consumer will not buy a new sofa if other needs come first, such as rent, dinner, a must-have CD, or vacation. Marketers should understand the relative importance of their product to the consumer in order to form a realistic promotional approach. Overstating a product's importance loses credibility in the marketplace. Marketers should understand how to differentiate their product category in order to elevate its general importance, such as stressing how a product solves a particular problem for the consumer. This is done through informative advertising and public relations.

Indirect Competition

In *indirect competition*, one company's offering competes with several other offerings within the same general product category. For example, when consumers are interested in entertainment they have several options, all in indirect competition with each other, including movies, television, live sporting events, and video rentals. Marketers should differentiate their offering based on the needs of the consumer. For example, cable companies provide entertainment but stress the convenience of staying home.

Direct Competition

In *direct competition*, one company's product or service specifically competes against a similar product or service from another company. For example, a McDonald's hamburger competes directly with a Wendy's hamburger. The NBC evening news competes directly with the CBS evening news. Marketers should learn the specific features and benefits and subtle consumer nuances that can differentiate their

product from the competitor's often very similar product. Differentiation is promoted through comparison ads.

PRODUCT LIFE CYCLE

Life cycles occur when products, services, and ideas, like people, move from one stage to the next as they evolve across their life spans. The life cycle spans the product's economic viability in the marketplace from conception to obsolescence. The life cycle usually is referred to as the product life cycle. The product life cycle concept is important because a life cycle may last only a few months or years or can be extended and made profitable indefinitely by using various strategies designed to enhance sales. Although each product is unique, a typical product life cycle has the following stages: product development, branding strategies, product (market) introduction, growth, maturity, sales extension/expansion, decline, and discontinuance. See Figure 15.2.

Goals of Product Management

Two major goals of marketing are to reduce the time between the product development stage and the product introduction stage, and extend the time between the introduction stage and the decline stage.

1. Product Development
Product development is explained in detail in Chapter 16, "Product Development."

2. Branding
Branding is explained in detail in Chapter 4. "Branding."

3. Brand Legal Protection
There are legal protections for a company's brand, which is very important because of the immense budgets that can be spent promoting a company or product to achieve brand recognition and other marketing goals. Different types of legal protection are available for brand names, phrases, logos, written material, product function and design, and trade dress. Each confers a degree of exclusivity on the owner. Brand legal protection includes trademarks, service marks, domain names, copyrights,

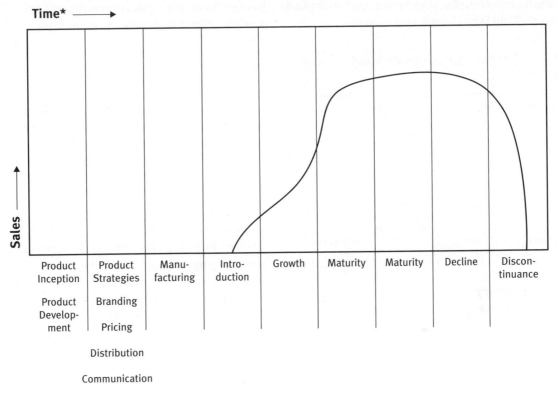

Time* ⟶

Sales ⟶

| Product Inception | Product Strategies | Manu-facturing | Intro-duction | Growth | Maturity | Maturity | Decline | Discon-tinuance |

Product Development

Branding

Pricing

Distribution

Communication

*Timeline not to scale.

Figure 15.2 Typical Product Life Cycle

patents, and trade secrets. The purpose of securing such legal protection is to prevent the brand from being mistaken for, confused with, copied, or diluted by some other brand or company in the eyes of relevant consumers (actual or potential customers). *Trade dress* is the distinctive look and feel of the collective aspects of a brand's communication, such as package design, logo, advertising look, motifs, and themes, and may be protected as a trademark. For product and package shapes to become distinctive trade dress, the chosen look need not be primarily functional but must serve as an identifier of the brand. The shift of marketers from simple brand naming to aesthetics and experiential marketing has dramatically increased the number of trade dress cases in the courts over the last decade.

Aside from the risk to a brand posed by competitors and other outsiders, a brand may lose its trademark protection, ironically, as a result of successful promotion. Sometimes the public over time will come to identify the company's well-known product name as the common or generic name for that particular type of product. Unless the brand owner strictly follows the rules of good trademark usage and actively polices its trademark rights, the widespread use of a brand name as the generic name of a product can eventually lead to a loss of valuable trademark rights. In some cases, brands that became household words could no longer be distinguished from the generic product name and ceased to function as trademarks, even after substantial sums had been spent promoting the product name by the originating company. Nylon, aspirin, and zipper were once brand-specific names. This danger can be largely avoided by making the trademark stand out visually in any advertising and always using a separate generic identifier for the product. For example, Chesebrough-Pond's uses the phrase "Q-tip brand cotton swabs," not just "Q-tips." Xerox works diligently to educate industry, the news media, and individuals that its XEROX trademark is not a verb.

BRAND LEGAL PROTECTION

Brand Message	Legal Protection	Symbol	Example
Names	Trademark	®(registered w/Patent Office) ™(not registered)	Pepsi, Mountain Dew
Names/ Web site	Domain name	Internet registry	pepsi.com
Phrases	Trademark	®(registered w/Patent Office) ™(not registered)	Joy of Cola, Do the Dew
Logos	Trademark	®(registered w/Patent Office) ™(not registered)	Pepsi globe
Trade dress	Trademark		Label design
Written/ artistic material	Copyright	©	Ads, text in Web site
Product equipment function	Patent	Patent Number Patent Pending	Fountain dispenser improvement
Product/ package design	Patent	Patent Number Patent Pending	Bottle design
Product Formulation	Trade secret		Pepsi Formula

Source: PepsiCo.

4. Marketing Strategies

Marketers develop pricing, marketing communications, and distribution strategies concurrently with product strategies.

5. Manufacturing

After the product and other marketing mix strategies have been finalized, the manufacturing phase is started. Through proper marketing research and product development, the marketer can aim for the largest potential market, thus creating a greater opportunity for manufacturing economies of scale and a lower product price. However, a new marketing-based approach to manufacturing products is called *mass customization* or "a market of one." This approach will allow marketers to reach a mass market with a product that can be customized or made to order for individuals of the target audience. For example, a new laser device allows a shoe store to scan a customer's foot and produce a shoe (within a week) that matches the foot exactly. This approach satisfies the customer and lowers the cost of product marketing by reducing inventory to zero.

6. Product Introduction

The product (market) introduction stage occurs when a product is first manufactured and then launched (or rolled out) in the marketplace. At this stage companies will use a pricing option depending on the competition, usually a high price if there is no competition and a low price if there is competition. Advertising, public relations, and promotional marketing efforts, typically informative, are initially aimed at the opinion leaders, innovators, and early adopters. Sales training is given to the wholesalers and retailers. Introductory promotion budgets may be small, relying on word of mouth, or they may be large, such as the $20 million spent for the introduction of Mentadent toothpaste. At this stage some products have already been distributed to wholesalers and retailers. Expenses are still greater than sales.

There are two main timing strategies for introducing new products to the marketplace: first-to-market and second-to-market.

First-to-Market

Being the first-to-market (also known as the early mover) with a new product offers many advantages. The consumer is aware of the first product for a longer period of time and associates the brand with innovation. If the consumer is grateful for the convenience and usefulness of the new product, then he or she may remain loyal to the company, even as newer and better products come to market. Distribution channels may be inclined, for convenience, to partner with only one company for a particular product category. Government patents and copyrights may assist a company that is first-to-market by precluding direct competition for a period of time. A company culture that promotes quick management decision processes, accelerated test marketing, and extensive research and development (R&D) will assist in providing first-to-market products or services. For example, in 1997, Intel spent 33.8 percent of its net income on research and development as a methodology to motivate innovation and provide new products to the marketplace faster than its rivals.

Second-to-Market

The second-to-market (also known as me-too) entry strategy has several advantages. By waiting until a competitor's product has successfully entered the market, the second company can provide a similar product and make inroads with consumers by offering the product or service at a lower price. This strategy saves substantially on R&D costs. Sometimes the initial product, in its rush to be first, still has flaws. Therefore, a slower but more precise approach allows the second company to enter the market with a superior product.

7. Growth

The growth stage occurs when many consumers (early adopters and early majority) become aware of the product and the product starts selling well. Profits are achieved for the first time. Competitors may see the value in this market and begin to enter their products. Price may be adjusted for this competition. Promotional efforts, typically persuasive, are aimed primarily at early and late majority. Distribution begins to be widespread.

8. Maturity

The maturity or plateau stage occurs when product or service sales reach a mass market and stabilize. This happens as the customer market and distribution base become saturated and/or competition increases. Typically pricing drops and competitive promotions increase usually touting pricing. Due to low prices and competitive promotions, profitability is reduced. As profits drop, companies will consider either discontinuing the product or making efforts to expand sales.

9. Life Cycle Extension/Product Sales Expansion

Life cycles and sales can be extended if marketers innovate and keep their products, services, and ideas tied to the changing needs of consumers. Choosing the appropriate sales expansion strategy is critical because it can lead to life cycle extension rather than discontinuance. Marketers continually attempt to expand the sales of existing brands in general by altering the marketing mix of pricing levels, distribution, product offering, and promotional levels. In addition, marketers may use several specific strategies to connect their products with potential customers, such as expanding the sales territory, cultivating new users, creating new usage occasions, boosting loyalty, and establishing new uses.

- **New Territory.** If the brand's premise is universal, then expanding its sales territories (and ultimately taking it around the world) may provide the best opportunity for sales expansion. For example, the explosive growth of Coca-Cola occurred after the brand was positioned within reach of the entire world. Many firms, such as banks, cellular phone companies, and cable companies have acquired other companies in order to expand their customer base into new territories.

- **New Users.** Increased promotional efforts may be needed to achieve sales to the late majority and laggards. Many brand premises are identified with a highly defined user group. Breaking that mindset can open up additional avenues to growth. For example, Gap for Kids moved the Gap brand into a new demographic consumer group. Starbucks coffee now is also sold in supermarkets, Kellogg's has been promoting their Corn Flakes to adults, and Columbia Women's Hospital in Washington, D.C., is expanding its services for men.

- **New Usage Occasions.** Finding new opportunities for using a brand is always fertile ground for growth. For example, Starbucks cold coffee and iced tea drinks have moved the Starbucks brand of products into warm weather and refreshment occasions. The use of English muffins for lunch sandwiches, traditionally consumed only at breakfast, doubles the opportunities for sales. Also, the orange juice industry's ads touted "Orange juice isn't just for breakfast."

- **Increased Usage from Existing Customers (Loyalty).** Marketers try to secure a greater proportion of category usage through repeat or loyalty business. It costs less to keep customers than to find new ones. The marketer's goal is to keep consumers in the franchise and to discourage them from trying a competitor's offering. There are several methods to accomplish this goal, including enhanced or additional product or service offerings for the frequent user, or cash discounts. For example, the airline frequent-flyer loyalty programs reward repeat customers. Restaurants print punch cards allowing a free meal after a set number of dinners are purchased.

- **New Product Uses (New Platforms).** Finding new uses for the product is known as creating a new platform. Although this has potential payoffs, it is a risky approach since a company can dilute or even destroy a brand's essence. For example, Arm & Hammer baking soda traditionally had been used only for baking. Arm & Hammer expanded sales of its product by promoting new uses for its product, including household cleaning, household deodorizing, and use in toothpaste.

Product Extensions (Line Extensions)

Product extensions are additional product offerings under the same brand name that expand on the original or existing product's (parent or master brand) features. These new, modified offerings are designed to suit additional consumers' tastes or needs and can provide new flavors, new sizes, new ingredients, new colors, or new styles. Line extension can extend the length or depth of the product line. For example, Frosted Flakes was extended from Corn Flakes, *Travel & Leisure Golf* was extended from *Travel & Leisure,* and Diet Pepsi was extended from Pepsi. Sales of the original product may be diminished or cannibalized by the new product; however, the goal is to have total sales be larger than sales of the original product alone.

PRODUCT EXTENSION			
1898 Pepsi	1963 Diet Pepsi	1998 Pepsi One	2007 Pepsi Max

Brand Extension (Name Extension)

A product can expand sales through brand extensions. Brand extension occurs when the brand name is used to add awareness to a range of unrelated products, product lines, and product categories. For brands to be extendible, the corporate image must stand for something that is greater than their original products. For example, Nike expanded sales by extending its brand from running shoes to athletic shoes to sports apparel. Calvin Klein added its name to eyewear, and The Gap line now includes perfume.

Licensing

A *license* is a legal contract where a licensor grants a licensee permission to use its company trademark name, symbol, recipe, manufacturing process, or characters. A license usually is offered for a fee or a royalty (a percentage of sales). The licensee often can achieve instant brand recognition and, hopefully, increased sales. The licensor receives additional revenue from products or distribution that they cannot achieve on their own. For example, a clothing brand owner, such as Calvin Klein, may license a manufacturer to make, distribute, and sell a line of its products, such as sunglasses. Similarly, an entertainment brand owner, such as Disney, licenses Disney characters to adorn an ice cream package. The licensor should constantly monitor the quality level of the various licensees in order to maintain a uniform appeal in the marketplace.

Franchising is a form of licensing that is used throughout the service industry. A company that has developed a successful name, strategy, or operational technique may expand its sales by allowing others to license or franchise their business methods. For example, McDonald's, Subway Sandwiches, H&R Block, TrueServe Hardware stores (TrueValue and ServiStar), and Hallmark Cards are all successful franchise operations. The franchise system allows an owner-operator to feel independent, yet use a proven business approach. The licensor offers expertise and retains control over business operations and marketing.

Cobranding/Joint Ventures

Cobranding provides additional incremental sales when two companies, each with successful brand names in different categories, jointly offer a product. Consumers are assured that the new addition to their favorite product is the best available. For example, Post Raisin Bran offers Sun-Maid raisins in its cereal; United Airlines offers Starbucks coffee on its flights;

and Betty Crocker Premium Brownie Mix offers a Hershey's chocolate syrup pouch in its package.

Joint ventures provide additional sales when two companies jointly provide unique expertise to upgrade an existing product line. For example, Microsoft and Hasbro have teamed up to put several classic games on the Web in an interactive format.

10. Decline

The decline stage occurs when a product or service has diminishing sales due to obsolescence, which can be driven by a new technology, and/or a change in consumer habits. Profits decline and a decision should be made as to whether to discontinue the product or to improve sales by spending money on additional R&D to improve the product or additional promotions to shift public perception. Shifting to a low-price strategy may entice additional laggard customers or only result in less profitability. The competition may be in the same stage and may drop their product offering providing only a short monopoly period and thus revived sales from a diminishing client base. As sales decline, distributors may abandon the product, hastening its ultimate discontinuance. For example, sales of vinyl records have declined precipitously and many stores no longer carry them.

11. Retro

Occasionally, after the decline stage, the product may enter a retro or revival stage where it has a brief return to prominence in the marketplace. This stage may come about through consumer fad, such as the occasional reincarnation of a particular fashion, or astute promotions, such as with Hush Puppies. The product may command a higher price than normal, as it typically will be in a monopoly status and have an eager customer base. Distributors that understand the short-term nature of the retro stage and can react quickly will participate in the product's distribution.

12. Discontinuance

The discontinuance stage occurs when product or service sales have declined below profitability and is ultimately taken off the market. A product that has been discontinued may still have some value, as it may be donated to a charity for the tax value or may be given away with another product as part of a promotional marketing program. This step allows the company to allocate resources to other more productive products.

EXAMPLES OF PRODUCTS IN LIFE CYCLE STAGES (2008)	
Life Cycle Stage	**Products**
INTRO	Blu-ray DVD players, Large LCD TVs
GROWTH	Flat panel TVs, iPods
MATURITY	Desktop computers, digital cameras, cell phones
DECLINE	Audio cassette players, VCRs
DISCONTINUED	8-track players, analog TVs

Source: Consumer Electronics Association, 2008.

ADDITIONAL LIFE CYCLE SCENARIOS

There are several product life cycle scenarios that differ from the aforementioned traditional life cycle, including sales extension, seasonal, retro, fad, failure, and continuous R&D.

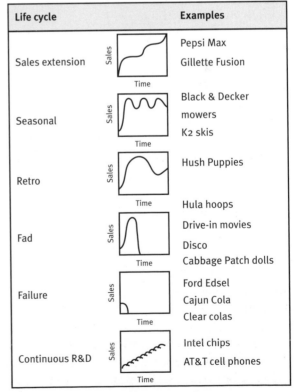

Life cycle	Examples
Sales extension	Pepsi Max / Gillette Fusion
Seasonal	Black & Decker mowers / K2 skis
Retro	Hush Puppies
Fad	Hula hoops / Drive-in movies / Disco / Cabbage Patch dolls
Failure	Ford Edsel / Cajun Cola / Clear colas
Continuous R&D	Intel chips / AT&T cell phones

CORPORATE PROFILE AND AUTHOR BIOGRAPHY

PEPSICO

PepsiCo (NYSE–PEP) is one of the world's largest food and beverage companies. Visit PepsiCo at www.pepsico.com.

Brian Swette

Brian Swette was the former Executive Vice President and Chief Marketing Officer for Pepsi-Cola Company. Mr. Swette received his BA in Economics from Arizona State University.

NOTES

1. *Dictionary of Marketing Terms*, Peter D. Bennett (Chicago, IL: American Marketing Association, 1995).

16 PRODUCT DEVELOPMENT

by AntiMicrobial Technologies Group, Ford, Wilson Sporting Goods, Gillette, Hair Cuttery

Everything that can be invented has been invented.
Charles H. Duell, Commissioner, U.S. Office of Patents, 1899

ESSENTIALS OF PRODUCT DEVELOPMENT
by Antimicrobial Technologies Group

Introduction

In business and engineering, product development is the term used to describe the complete process of bringing a new product or service to market. Companies typically see product development as the first stage in generating and commercializing new products within their overall product life cycle management to create, maintain, or grow their market share.

The product life cycle begins with the development of the product based on customer needs and wants as determined by marketing research. Development also is known as research and development (R&D). In order for a company to stay viable, it must continuously introduce new products as old ones decline.

Significant dollars may be spent in development with the hope of achieving a quality product and subsequent sales and profits. Product development and innovation requires companies to encourage creativity in staffing, planning, branding, developing new business processes and new ideas, defining risk, and even tolerating failure.

Product development also includes service development. For example, Mirage Resorts became a leader in the gaming industry through a simple but creative idea: give people great service, great food, and entertainment they cannot find elsewhere, and they will pay for it. The Mirage Resort's $475 million Treasure Island casino hotel in Las Vegas was the first casino designed to generate more revenue from nongaming sources than from gaming.

Not all products need to change. Uniformity or consistency may be used as a differentiating factor. For example, product consistency has helped McDonald's build the most successful fast-service brand in the world. In recent years, salads and more healthy options for children have been added to its menu to respond to changing tastes of its customers but hamburgers, fries, and sodas remain its core business.

To successfully and efficiently develop ideas, companies need to channel creativity through a structured process. There are two parallel paths involved in the product development process: one involves idea generation, product design, and engineering; the other involves marketing research and marketing analysis.

Because the product development process typically requires both engineering and marketing expertise, cross-functional teams are a common way of organizing projects. The team is responsible for all aspects of the project, from initial idea generation to final commercialization, and it usually reports to senior management. In those industries where products are technically complex, development research is typically expensive, and product life cycles are relatively short, strategic alliances among several organizations help to spread the costs, provide access to wider skill sets, and speed the overall process.

Products can be characterized by their newness to the market and to the company. At one end of the spectrum, companies release new products with minor improvements. This may be done quickly to address a product deficiency (for example, a software update) or in product areas where there is limited opportunity to make changes (for example, scented soap). At the other extreme, new innovative products are introduced to a predefined market. For example, MP3 players changed the portable music market in the late 1990s by taking advantage of new widely available digital music and low-cost memory storage. See Figure 16.1.

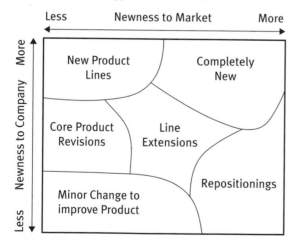

Figure 16.1 Types of New Products

Definition

In business and engineering, *product development* is the term used to describe the complete process of bringing a new product or service to market. Compa-nies typically see product development as the first stage in generating and commercializing new products within their overall product life cycle management to create, maintain, or grow their market share.

PRODUCT DEVELOPMENT PROCESS

1. Idea Generation

Every product begins with an idea. The idea may be simple or complex, but the marketing professional's critical contribution is to identify opportunities and validate them during each step of the product development process from initial concept through the final product release.

Ideas for new products can come from many sources, including:

- **Demand-driven Pull.** Results from consumer research. For example, Mattel's reconfiguration of Barbie arose from consumer suggestions. Business customer feedback may be achieved through field sales reps given their proximity to the customer. Direct feedback and recommendations may also be solicited via the company's telephone customer support centers and online Web presence. Having early customer involvement in a new idea is essential to success.

- **Product Push.** Comes from engineering and manufacturing research, either basic research (generic research that hopes to find new products and new ideas) or applied research (directed at specific improvement in products and their uses). For example, polymers developed in research labs became lightweight plastic used in automobile bumpers.

- **Competitor's Products.** Are purchased and analyzed to find strengths and weaknesses that may spur new ideas.

- **Products That Are Popular in Other Countries.** May be duplicated. For example, Häagen-Dazs introduced its dulce de leche flavor ice cream to the United States after being developed by its Argentinean franchise.

- **Cross-functional Company Experts.** Brainstorm with marketing consultants, inventors, and independent engineers.

- **New Regulations.** Require innovation. Auto companies had to modify their engine designs to meet or exceed minimum gas mileage and air quality standards in states such as California where the standards are stricter than the federal standards.
- **Failed Products.** Present new business opportunities. For example, Pfizer originally created Viagra to treat angina. The U.K. clinical trials did not show the treatment helped, but a side-effect of Viagra led to its being tested as an anti-impotence pill.
- **Simple Creativity**.

2. Evaluating Ideas

Ideas must be evaluated by prioritizing and financially analyzing the product mix. Only a few ideas will turn out to be economically feasible when considered in the context of risk and reward, time taken to develop them into a sales stream, and overall resource level required. The object is to eliminate unsound ideas before devoting resources to them. Areas for evaluation include:

- Customer needs—product and pricing
- Company capabilities—marketing, financial, R&D, manufacturing
- Balanced risk perspective (both high-risk/high reward and low-risk projects)
- Time perspective (need new applications tomorrow as well as five years in the future)
- Product mix perspective (all product lines need the appropriate level of support)
- Competitive offerings
- Company requirements (profit potential, strategic importance)
- Additional company opportunities (service offerings, add-ons, future line extensions)

These evaluations are set up as projects with a formal quality analysis (described in Chapter 19, "Product Quality") to ensure the necessary comparability between different opportunities. At the end of the evaluation, a decision is made about whether this opportunity should become an active development project. One of the outputs of this process is a clear statement of expected results in terms of sales and customer base. This provides a means of measurement and accountability during the marketing process.

A major aspect of this step of the development process is enlisting the support of a company's own senior management. The support of senior management can provide a mandate to move quickly, together with valuable input from people with extensive industry experience.

3. Concept Development and Testing

Marketing and engineering details are developed once an idea has been approved (or may be done in conjunction with the product idea approval process). The initial product idea is further defined in this phase, and critical resources are identified. A sample of prospective customers is asked what they think of the idea. The purpose of this step is to understand:

- Target market and decision maker in the purchasing process
- Product features that must be included
- Potential obstacles to product acceptance
- Benefits the product will provide
- Likely reaction by customers to introduction and availability of product

4. Technical Definition

After an idea has been approved (perhaps in conjunction with the product idea approval process), research must be conducted to determine the product's technical needs. The product's technical definition, or specification, describes the product's features in great detail and is the road map for development. Throughout the process, as feedback is obtained and the product is tested, the specification will be further refined until it becomes the blueprint of the final product.

Technical specifications are often shared with strategic partners or other company divisions who create products that will work with the new product; the tighter the product integration, the earlier the involvement by the other group. For example, a company creates a new GPS device that must be able to run certain software. The hardware and software teams will review each others' specifications to make sure that both product sets will be able to work together and that the overall goals can be met (price points, time lines, etc.)

5. Product Design

Designers (either outside design studios or in-house staff) with feedback from marketing research and manufacturing make the initial and subsequent product designs. Design elements include color, ergonomics, product feel, materials selection, technical interface, and so forth. The design should balance customers' needs and wants, manufacturing capabilities and budgets, and quality and environmental requirements.

6. Test, Test, Test

Throughout product development, the R&D and product design teams will perform functional testing. For example, clinical trials are run in the pharmaceutical industry as new medications are developed. In the software industry, potential users are brought into usability labs to try interface designs. For every product or service, testing and the resulting feedback are critical to ensure that the best product for the target customer can be offered.

Testing not only improves the product, it also helps to clearly define the product from the point of view of the target customer. Testing helps:

- Prioritize product features.
- Identify missing features.
- Evaluate different implementations of the same feature.

7. Manufacturing Options

Once a product has been conceptualized and development is initiated, many factors affect what can actually be delivered. In any development process, trade-offs are made. A company may look to outside resources or other companies if the development capabilities are not available inside the company, a product must be delivered to the market quicker than can be developed in-house, or a better implementation is available elsewhere. This is known as a *make versus buy decision*.

8. Prototype or Alpha Product

It can be very useful to assemble a *prototype*, an original model often built by hand, from which later models may be based. They can be used for in-house testing, refinement, test marketing, and budgeting analysis. The prototype may only represent the vision for the product and may not be fully functional. Prototypes or alpha products can, however, help identify early problems before they lead to costly mistakes.

9. Beta Testing

A beta product has more functionality than a prototype and is much closer to the finished product. There is still an opportunity for product refinement, and the beta release will be tested more broadly. The purpose of the beta release is (1) to ensure that there are not any detrimental product design issues, (2) to further validate that the product is meeting customer needs, and (3) to allow a broader range of strategic partners to interact with the product so that they may be ready with add-on products and services at product release.

Beta testing may be restricted to individuals who agree not to share product details publicly so that product features are kept confidential and not shared with competitors.

10. Limited Release

Limited release test marketing evaluates both the product and the product's positioning and messaging. The product at this stage is close to final. Full-scale test marketing may be conducted by putting products into many uses in many geographic areas. The advantage of this approach is that it provides the largest amount of consumer contact and response. Depending on the means of distribution and the cost to manufacture the product, the disadvantages of this approach are that it may take a long period of time, be expensive, and may provide information to competitors.

As a substitute, many companies use a quicker, more cost-effective version, which involves hands-on placement of new products in real-world selling environments. For example, PepsiCo has tested new soft drinks in settings such as pizza parlors, company cafeterias, and convenience stores. This approach provides companies with a direct observation of such key indicators as consumer acceptance, sales rates, and repeat purchases (as determined by store club card data analysis).

PRODUCT DEVELOPMENT— INTERNATIONAL

by Ford Motor Company

In international product development, companies face three key challenges.

- **Increasingly Global Scope of Competition.** New competitors arise from growing economies (China, India) who want to develop a domestic industrial base and from regional competitors who drive into new markets to satisfy their need for growth (driven in part by a desire to utilize the overcapacity that exists).
- **Increasingly High Consumer Expectations.** These expectations go beyond the basic requirements for products. As competitors seek to differentiate themselves, they introduce, collectively, new levels of product attributes (safety, design appeal, performance, technologies, service, comfort, and convenience). As soon as one competitor has raised the bar in their area of focus, a new level is set that all competitors seek to match.
- **Increasingly High Pressure on Profits and Margins.** Global competitiveness requires increased needs for R&D, process innovation, and globally competitive resources while simultaneously putting downward pressure on pricing and margins.

In order to meet these challenges, companies should develop products for the broader international market.

Consumer Needs

To remain competitive in the global marketplace, companies focus on the customer—both the individual consumer and the aggregate segmentation insights that focus on group evolution and macro trends. This is called *listening to the voice of the customer.* Customer needs usually are categorized in three ways:

- **Points of Parity.** *Points of parity* are the basic functionality that all consumers require, meaning the product is reliable in ways that we do not even perceive—we just expect it to be there. This criterion is perhaps the most important attribute of all. For example, a car should start every time the ignition key is turned.
- **Points of Differentiation.** *Differentiation* is defined as the product's level of ability to perform its basic functions in such a way that it becomes a reason to love the product, because you do it better than your competitors do. For example, a car should have good fuel economy—which you must deliver to be considered—but when you can offer significantly better fuel economy than your competitor, you start to differentiate yourself.
- **Points of Brand Signature.** *Points of brand signature* are innovative attributes your product offers that others cannot easily duplicate—the attributes that deliver the passion and excitement that define your brand. Passion and excitement can be described as a response to a collection of features that surprise and delight customers and generate an emotional connection between the owner and his or her product. For example, a car may have a unique design and exciting driving performance.

International product marketers employ a number of critical tools to help understand global consumer needs, macro segmentation trends, and competitive trends.

- **Marketing Research.** Is a primary tool that contributes to a company's ability to understand consumer needs on both rational and emotional levels.
- **Scenario Planning and Consumer/Market Segmentation Analyses.** Allow companies to identify likely future states and unmet

consumer needs, that they can focus their resources on addressing.

- **Competitive Benchmarking.** Allows a company to assess whether its planned products will continue to be differentiated and/or win the consumer's purchase versus focusing on attributes that can be forecasted as moving to the basic functionality realm (for example, airbags at first were differentiators, but now they are basic requirements).

It is equally important to manage the product design process to succeed in the ultimate balancing act: leveraging the totality of disparate global resources (people, processes, plants, etc.) for efficiency and scale, while delivering world-class products that are true to a core global brand position and that satisfy the different rational and emotional needs of a diverse global consumer base. For example, Ford developed its new world-class small car, the Ford Fiesta, to meet global consumer needs, using global resources spread across Europe, Asia, and the United States. A pure one-size-fits-all approach is not feasible due to different market factors (government regulations, road conditions, traffic patterns) as well as consumer preference factors (social and personal priorities are different by market). Likewise, engineers in the various locations contributing to the product's development need to be linked to each other and to common goals and metrics to ensure that regional differences in process, attitudes, and experiences do not compromise the global product targets.

Product Development

Fulfilling customer expectations is the challenge of the design process. In an international company, the design process may occur simultaneously in different design studios located throughout the world. Each studio may be linked electronically so that designs and data can be shared simultaneously with other designers in the next room or on the next continent. Utilizing this technology, companies can fulfill the expectations of global customers with the creativity of designers who live and work in different parts of the world. For example, Ford employs computer design and simulation that provides images of "finished-looking" vehicles that are then shown to customers.

In order to achieve its international product development goals, companies should focus on three interrelated fundamentals: quality, cost, and time.

- **Quality.** To improve product quality, a company should employ best practices in everything from a process or subsystem to an entire product. Best practices should be derived from research on companies in as many countries as possible, not just the home country.
- **Cost.** To reduce cost, companies employ the affordable business structure, which puts customer needs at the focus of how costs are planned. Under the affordable business structure, company revenue goals are stated conservatively for each product in each country, then profit targets are subtracted. The remainder is the amount that can be invested in the product.
- **Time.** To reduce the time needed for product development, companies utilize proven systems developed in one country and only make alterations for specific needs in another country. Also, setting time requirements for product design elements eliminates cultural differences and concentrates on achieving goals.

Usually, an international company has a number of different products. Each product is supported by a product team made up of a product manager, engineers, purchasing agents, and marketing and finance personnel who may be from different countries and are responsible for running the product line as a business. Cooperation and teamwork are essential, as is the global alignment on core brand attributes that all products in the company's portfolio are expected to deliver. The end result is an independent, entrepreneurial business unit that is responsible for its own objectives and fulfills them with available resources generated by the selling of their products.

by Wilson Sporting Goods

Company: Wilson
Case: Consumer Goods — Tennis Racket R&D

Wilson Sporting Goods has earned its reputation as the leader (45 percent market share) in racket sports technology with the introduction of many breakthrough technologies such as those used in the Sledge Hammer® and Hammer® head heavy tennis rackets.

In the tennis industry, wood was used in rackets pre–1970, steel and aluminum were the material used in the late 1960s and early 1970s, and graphite and fiberglass in the late 1970s. Each was introduced because it provided more stiffness, greater strength, increased lightness, or any combination thereof. In 1997, racket materials continued to evolve as Titanium swept through the entire sporting goods industry. Titanium was well-received by consumers and dealers, and as a result, one of Wilson's competitors, considered the first to exploit the Titanium phenomenon, grew their market share 12 points. Wilson realized its reputation was threatened as the technological leader in racket sports.

One of Wilson's core strategies as a company is to produce game improvement products for the average player. While Wilson was concentrating on developing a product with improved weight and balance to increase the size of a racket's sweet spot (area of the racket face that provides maximum hitting power and minimum vibration), its competition focused on Titanium. Titanium has been used successfully in many sporting goods products such as golf clubs and golf balls; however, its application in tennis rackets provides little enhanced performance. Wilson knew that if the Titanium momentum continued, its leadership and market share would be threatened. There were two options to consider:

1. Follow the Titanium hype, even though that would offer no specific product differentiation.
2. Regain the position of industry leader by focusing on a new material that offers true game enhancement for the average player and offers a point of differentiation.

The acceptance of Titanium by consumers proved they were aware of the benefits of different tennis racket materials. Wilson knew that if it could find a material that was better than Titanium, could be incorporated into high-performance tennis rackets, was truly game improving, and was exclusive to Wilson, it would be on the verge of something much bigger than the Titanium craze. Wilson went to Toray, its 15-year partner in Japan (the world's number one supplier of high-stiffness composite materials with 70 percent market share and over $9 billion in sales) with its materials request. Wilson needed a new, revolutionary material that is stiffer, stronger, and lighter than anything ever used in tennis rackets. The second challenge was timing. Typical development time cycles are 18 months. Wilson needed to act fast, as Titanium was gaining momentum and posing a real threat to Wilson's technological leadership.

Toray presented a material to Wilson used mainly in the aerospace industry for satellites and state-of-the-art airplanes. The material, a carbon fiber, is four times stiffer, four times stronger, and 65 percent lighter than Titanium, and could be produced in an extremely pure form exclusively for Wilson. In only nine months, Toray and the Wilson technology department were able to strategically apply what Wilson named "Hyper Carbon" to a racket for ultimate power, lightness, and strength.

(Continued)

The launch of Hyper Carbon in November 1998 was Wilson's largest and most comprehensive publicity campaign. Special ads were produced to communicate the features and benefits of Hyper Carbon, all created around a space theme to tie into its origin in the aerospace industry. A direct-mail card was sent to consumers and retail outlets. Key Wilson dealers worldwide were invited to a special Hyper Carbon launch at the U.S. Open where Wilson serves as the official ball and sponsor. A press conference at the U.S. Open included all tennis publications as well as other reputable consumer magazines. At the grassroots level, dealers were given dynamic point-of-sale items to display in their pro shops. Aggressive pricing to purchase demo rackets was extended to dealers to encourage racket trial. Hyper Carbon was the focus of Wilson's Web site in 1998.

The positive outcome of the introduction of Hyper Carbon in the marketplace has been overwhelming. Total dollar sales of the new racket were the highest ever for Wilson Racquet Sports for a new product launch. Market share grew from 41 to over 50 points in the over $100 wholesale category after the introduction of the *Hyper Sledge Hammer 2.0*.[1]

PRODUCT DEVELOPMENT – CASE STUDY

by Gillette

Company: Gillette
Case: **Consumer Goods — MACH3 Product Launch 1998**

When The Gillette Company, the leader in the worldwide shaving market, goes to market with a new shaving system such as the MACH3, it is a critical event in the life of the company. The development and launch of the new product is tremendously costly, nearly a billion dollars in the case of MACH3, and the future of the company rides on the product's success. The launch of a new shaving product, therefore, is vital to the company's health and continued success. Every aspect of the launch, from product design through to in-store display, is meticulously planned and executed.

The planning of such an important launch is a collaborative effort that involves many people and disciplines within the company. Gillette is the worldwide leader in male shaving, and, as of 1998, the company held more than a 50 percent blade unit share in North America and a 70 percent dollar share worldwide. Senior executives established the overall business objective: "category leadership." This means that Gillette intends to be #1 in every product category in which it chooses to compete.

To achieve the business objective of continued market leadership set by corporate executives, it is up to the business management executives and marketing staff to establish specific objectives for the product itself. For MACH3, the marketing objectives were to achieve #1 value share in all markets, accelerate consumer trade-up, attract new users, and contribute to sales and profit growth in the double digits: 10 percent or more annually.

MACH3 faced a difficult challenge because it would have to achieve its objectives in a mature market. Most men of shaving age already own a razor. The bulk of MACH3 sales, therefore, would have to come by convincing users of competitive brands to switch to MACH3, or by trading up users of current Gillette brands (including disposables) to MACH3, and, of course, by appealing to the young, first-time shaver.

Because male shaving is a mature market, it is difficult to increase the product unit sale year after year. To increase dollar sales volume, therefore, Gillette seeks to build *value share*, that is, to generate a higher profit with each sale. To do this, MACH3 would have to deliver a significantly better shave than Gillette's current market leading brand, the Sensor family. MACH3, therefore, would have to be a breakthrough product, a next-generation shaving system, rather than simply an improved version of the SensorExcel.

Gillette, through corporate senior executives, marketing managers, and manufacturing and technical managers, plans its businesses five years ahead. In 1993, it was determined that the next generation male shaving system would be launched in 1998, just nine years after the previous major system, Sensor. Once a new product launch date is defined, work begins in earnest to plan the elements of the new system, those elements that will deliver the required perceptible and meaningful differences. For years, the designers and engineers had been working on the development of a three-bladed system, but tests had proved that it caused an unacceptable amount of skin irritation. Now, Gillette decided that if the three-blade cartridge could be perfected, it would be the best candidate for true product breakthrough. Over the next three years, engineers developed two key improvements: a progressive blade alignment that significantly reduced skin irritation and a new, extremely hard blade coating called Diamond-Like Carbon Coating (DLC). This coating enabled Gillette to make a thinner, sharper blade that cut more effectively and with less irritation. The more innovative the product, the more difficult it is for competitors to match the innovation. MACH3 would be granted a total of 35 patents.

A critical part of the Gillette planning process is consumer testing, which begins early in product development and continues through to launch. The most important testing is called Consumer Use Testing (CUT), and it is designed to gauge two key aspects of the new product: performance and appearance. The first tests for MACH3 involved a small number of consumers who were asked to shave with a MACH3 prototype, SensorExcel, and two competitive products from a competitor. The test group included men of diverse cultures and all ages, who possessed a variety of beard and skin types. After shaving, the men were asked to rate the razors on a number of attributes, including closeness, comfort, freedom from nicks and cuts, as well as ergonomics and aesthetics. The tests showed that men preferred the MACH3 two to one over SensorExcel, and by much more of a margin over competitive systems.

Once the product design for MACH3 had been finalized, marketing managers then worked with their communication partner, the New York–based advertising firm BBDO, to create the product name identity and plan the marketing communications program for the MACH3 launch. They focused their attention on answering the question: "How will we convince the consumer to trade up to this system?" The answer becomes the core consumer proposition, a simple and succinct statement of MACH3's key features and benefits:

Introducing a remarkable new triple-blade shaving system that will give you the closest shave ever in fewer strokes—with less irritation.

The statement serves as the basis for planning the communications campaign and positioning the product against the competition. It emphasizes the most obvious product feature—the three blades—and links them to the major consumer benefit, a close shave. The naming process is a rigorous one, involving careful definition of the requirements for the name. The name had to be distinctive, memorable, and convey the attributes of the new system, suggestive of breakthrough technological innovation. It also had to be easy to understand and pronounce in all of Gillette's market countries, and available for

(Continued)

trademark ownership worldwide. MACH3, which means three times the speed of sound, was selected from the hundreds of names that were considered, because it suggests high technology, the breaking of performance barriers, and offered rich opportunities for creating appealing and memorable imagery. The MACH3 name and concept were tested with consumers in several countries. Gillette found that men made a positive connection between the MACH3 name and high-speed flight. With the name and concept in place, brand imagery for advertising, packaging, and retail displays was developed that focused on flight and aerodynamics. For example, television advertisements incorporated imagery of ultra-modern aircraft with the associated sound of a sonic boom. As communication and pricing strategies were being developed, a manufacturing strategy plan was put in place. With the Sensor razor, Gillette had failed to anticipate the enthusiasm of the consumer response and did not have sufficient inventory to meet demand. Consumers came into stores with the intention to buy and found the racks empty, a situation every manufacturer wants to avoid. For MACH3, marketing research indicated that production should begin early. A pilot manufacturing line was installed where the production process was tested and perfected.

The core objective of Gillette's marketing communications plan was to create an explosion of public attention for MACH3 through the integrated use of advertising, public relations, and retail displays. The launch had several key audiences in addition to the consumer.

The first public announcement of the MACH3 was to the sales force, in April 1998. It was imperative that the members of the sales force appreciate the importance of the new product, understand its features and benefits, and be excited about the product in order to generate sales. Gillette's salespeople work closely with retailers to develop shelf-stocking strategies called "plan-o-grams" and place in-store displays and ads, all of which make a new product more visible and help promote sales.

The next audience was the press; some 100 editors and journalists attended a press event in May 1998. Attendees received samples and press kits that contained detailed information and stories about every aspect of the new system. Gillette also mailed press kits to hundreds of media contacts around the country, and a restricted-access press Web site published MACH3 information.

As a result of the press campaign, which continued through the summer of 1998, MACH3 received a tremendous amount of coverage in all media, including television, radio, newspapers, and on the Internet.

Then came the launch to the consumer, which would be marked with a variety of events, including the breaking of the advertising campaign. The launch began with the unannounced appearance of the product in retail outlets, during late June and early July 1998. The intention was to capitalize on the press coverage and pique the consumers' interest. Two weeks before the official launch date, a series of teaser ads appeared in print, on radio, and on television that alerted the audience that "a breakthrough shaving system was coming," without showing the product itself.

On the advertising launch day, advertisements appeared everywhere, on television, radio, Internet, and billboards, in print, in sports stadiums, and stores. The Gillette NASCAR racing team wore MACH3 race suits. In major retailers, MACH3 stickers and ads appeared in such unexpected places as the motor oil aisle and on the parking lot asphalt. In-store POP, or point-of-purchase, displays drew attention to MACH3 at the cash register where it is easy for customers to buy.

By August 1998, two months after its release in stores, MACH3 had achieved #1 status among blades and razors. MACH3 sold 30 percent more units than any other brand. It sold more units in two months than any other razor has ever sold in the same time period. MACH3 boosted Gillette's total Blades &

Razor sales by 20 percent. The major competitor countered by offering $2-off coupons for their razors. MACH3 still sold three times as many units as the *combined* sales of the competitors' razors.

PRODUCT DEVELOPMENT – CASE STUDY

by Hair Cuttery

Company: Hair Cuttery (Division of Ratner Companies)
Case: Services — Service Packages

Hair Cuttery is the largest family-owned and -operated chain of hair salons in the nation. For 34 years the company has maintained a reputation for being a "people company," boasting an industry-leading 70+ percent retention rate among its stylists. This accomplishment is due largely to the company's efforts to implement ways to help stylists increase their earnings potential.

Packages are prevalent in fast-food, travel, hospitality, and other service-oriented businesses. It is not necessarily a new concept; however, it was new to a chain whose pricing structure strategy has been based solely on a la carte offerings.

The service packages were derived from a Chicago salon chain acquisition in the late 1990s. The acquired chain already had service packages as part of its menu. Hair Cuttery decided to incorporate the packages into its service menu for all markets. Existing packages included style, hair color, and partial and full highlights. Three additional packages were created, incorporating waxing, curl, and relaxer services.

All in-salon promotion and sales materials were developed by Hair Cuttery's in-house marketing and graphics team. It was decided that the existing team had a better understanding of the "Stylist-centric" aspect of the company culture (Happy Stylists = Happy Clients) and could, therefore, design the materials in a manner that was consistent with other promotions and easier for stylists to understand. The company assigned great value to the idea that its stylists needed to sell the packages to their clients.

Even though not promoted in any Hair Cuttery market prior to 2008, the Chicago region alone turned in half of the entire company's service package revenue—likely due to the fact that the packages originated in this market. Hair Cuttery realized it was missing opportunities to further develop this category of the business in other markets.

In 2008, service packages were integrated into the in-salon experience. This included in-salon client communication materials, in-salon promotions, stylist education, and field- and salon-level goal setting. Technical training was unnecessary since the services included in the packages were already part of the Hair Cuttery's menu.

First, a new, larger menu board was installed where customers check in for their services. Not only could customers view the services packages offered, but stylists could use this menu as a tool for educating their clients.

Each monthly salon promotion featured a service package as part of the promotion deals. For example, if color was the focus for the promotion, both color services and color service packages were highlighted on in-salon client communication materials. Mirror clings at each station communicated to a captive audience in the salon chair.

(Continued)

Stylists were instructed to educate their clients about the current salon promotion and discuss how the promotional offer might fit their hair needs.

Lastly, monthly promotional goals were created for each salon. By converting the revenue goals into service package units, it made it very easy for salon leaders to divide the goal among their stylists. Accountability to reach goal was shared by the salon staff.

At the end of 2008 the Service Package program resulted in an increase of 91.2 percent in package revenue over 2007. Hair Cuttery is currently evaluating the service package program to determine effectiveness and growth potential.

CORPORATE PROFILES AND AUTHOR BIOGRAPHIES

ANTIMICROBIAL TECHNOLOGIES GROUP

Antimicrobial Technologies Group produces commercial finishes and additives for products ranging from diabetic socks and protective face masks to wall paint that provide infection protection, odor control, and biofilm remediation to safely kill germs and ultimately improve people's lives. Visit Antimicrobial Technologies Group at www.antimicrobial.us.

Pamela Goldschmidt

Pamela Goldschmidt is Executive Vice President of Antimicrobial Technologies Group. Previously at Microsoft, Ms. Goldschmidt was responsible for product planning, business development, and product introductions for specific versions of the Microsoft Wndows operating system on mobile devices, desktops, and services. Ms. Goldschmidt received her BA in Political Economy from the University of California, Berkeley.

FORD MOTOR COMPANY

Ford Motor Company designs, develops, manufactures, and services cars and trucks worldwide. Visit Ford at www.ford.com.

Jack Palazzolo

Jack Palazzolo, Ford's Senior Manager, Advanced Product Marketing and Innovation, is a 16-year Ford veteran who has held leadership positions in Product Marketing, Advertising, Brand Management, Regional Marketing, Strategy, and International Operations. Mr. Palazzolo received his BSME and his MBA from the University of Michigan.

WILSON SPORTING GOODS CO.

Wilson, headquartered in Chicago, is one of the world's leading manufacturers of sports equipment. Wilson is the official racket of the U.S. Professional Tennis Association. Visit Wilson at www.wilsonsports.com.

John R. Embree

John Embree is formerly the vice president/general manager for the Racquet Sports Division of Wilson and had global responsibility for P&L and all marketing aspects. Mr. Embree received his BA from Washington & Lee University.

Jeffrey S. Karp

Jeffrey Karp is formerly Marketing Director, Racquet Sports Division, and also contributed to the case study.

THE GILLETTE COMPANY

The Gillette Company is the world leader in male grooming, a category that includes blades, razors, and shaving preparations. Visit Procter & Gamble at www.pg.com.

Eric A. Kraus

Eric Kraus was Vice President, Corporate Communications of The Gillette Company, and was responsible for overseeing the company's worldwide strategic internal and external communications effort. Mr. Kraus received his BS in Journalism from Boston University.

HAIR CUTTERY

Hair Cuttery is the largest family-owned chain of salons in the country, with more than 800 company-owned locations on the East Coast, in New England, and the Midwest. Hair Cuttery is a division of Ratner Companies, based in Vienna, Virginia. Visit Hair Cuttery at www.haircuttery.com.

Susan Gustafson

Susan Gustafson is the President of Ratner Companies, the parent company of Hair Cuttery. In this role, Susan works closely with founder and CEO Dennis Ratner to lead the company's growth and develop strategic initiatives to drive the continued success of the business. Ms. Gustafson received her BA in Communications from the University of Wisconsin.

Kerry Storey

Kerry Storey is Marketing Director for Hair Cuttery. Ms. Storey is responsible for driving brand awareness, customer traffic, and sales through marketing programs both in-salon and externally. Ms. Storey received her BBA with a concentration in Marketing from George Washington University.

NOTES

1. Tennis Industry of America, Fourth Quarter Results, 1998.

17 PRODUCT PACKAGING

by O-I, Caraustar, Alcoa, Silgan, Sealed Air, Fabri-Kal, MCC, Sara Lee, Tanimura & Antle, and Dean Foods

The best things come in small packages.

Nineteenth-century proverb

THE ESSENTIALS OF PACKAGING
by O-I (Owens-Illinois)

Introduction

In marketing it is always important to consider your target audience. Because the packaging industry is usually B-to-B (Business-to-Business), there is an important distinction between customers and consumers. *Customers* are the brands or companies that buy the packaging from manufacturers. For example, Coca-Cola is a customer of packaging manufacturers. *Consumers*, on the other hand, are the ones buying the end product in the stores.

Consumer studies show that 70 percent of purchase decisions are made in-store. For example, a consumer may have tomato sauce on the shopping list, but the specific brand decision is delayed until reaching the store aisle. In the vital three feet between product and consumer, one of the most important things influencing the consumer to buy is usually the appearance of the product on the shelf. Therefore, packaging has become important in product differentiation. Packaging can communicate the value of a product, reinforce national and regional advertising, and produce the extra allure that can result in a sale.

The types of packaging materials—glass, paperboard, plastic, steel, and aluminum—are all detailed below.

Definition

Packaging is comprised of a product's physical container and its labeling. Packaging serves four purposes: it provides protection capabilities, usage capabilities, it helps establish the brand's identity, and it offers information.

PACKAGING ASPECTS

Physical Protection

Consumers' regard for a brand often is determined by the consistent state of quality with which the product is delivered. The product packaging, or container, must provide protection during shipping and storage. There are several different materials that can be used for product packaging. Each material should be considered in terms of cost, product protection, ease of use, and attractiveness.

Packaging industries compete for market share by providing more value than competing packaging materials. For example, the coated paperboard industry touted a report that indicated milk stored in see-through plastic was susceptible to light degradation of vitamin D. The plastic industry responded by promoting the convenience of a built-in handle and a no-leak container.

A protection requirement for many product packages is that they be tamper-evident to indicate improper usage by someone before the consumer purchases the product. This process has added an additional cost to products, but is considered worthwhile by the public. Pepsi experienced the importance of having tamper-free products and a tamper-free production line when a consumer claimed to have found a syringe in a Pepsi product. The company was so sure of its production process that they created the "Pepsi is pleased to announce nothing" campaign supporting the impossibility of tampering. The syringe story was later found to be a hoax.

Usage

How the consumer uses the product should be considered when designing the product's packaging. The package should be easy to open and provide easy access to the goods inside. Companies have spent considerable sums on research and development to improve the convenience of packaging. For example, Procter & Gamble promoted their new cap on Tide liquid laundry detergent that allows excess drips from inside the cap to drain back into the plastic jug and not down the side. Dean Foods, one of the largest milk processors, introduced the "Milk Chug," round plastic milk bottles in half-pint, pint, and quart sizes, to accommodate the round opening in automobile drink holders. Sales increased over 50 percent (packaged milk sales had been flat prior to this packaging development).

Design/Brand Identification

Whereas some consumers are brand loyal for specific food products—maybe ones they had growing up or ones that evoke emotional responses—the majority of purchase decisions are made in-store. Consumers are influenced by the look of the entire product: the size, color, packaging material, and label.

Although once seen as nothing more than a container, the physical attributes of packaging are increasingly being redesigned to pull in consumers. For example, Pringles, a brand of potato chips, is packaged in a cylindrical container, a departure from the traditional snack-chip bag. Toothpaste now comes in pumps, in addition to tubes. Soft drinks come in sports bottles. The physical dimensions of a package, and its materials and contours, once engineered for utility alone, now can be used as marketing tools.

Packaging manufacturers make many shapes of packaging, depending on the individual preferences of brands. O-I, the world's largest glass packaging manufacturer offers two production options. Companies can purchase stock bottles that come in predetermined shapes, sizes, and colors that are usually cost-effective and can be available without much advance notice. However, many brands that want to ensure consumer recognition of the product based on the design and shape of the packaging will opt to have a customized mold. Any glass jar or bottle that has a brand name or logo embossed on it requires a customized mold. One of the best known examples of glass packaging that can be recognized due to its size, shape, and customization is the iconic Coca-Cola bottle. This bottle can be recognized without a label due to the consistency of the glass packaging design.

In addition to the look and feel of the packaging, some consumers buy products based on the material in which it is packaged. Consumers' purchase decisions can be based on the safety, convenience, sustainability, or image provided by the material.

Package redesigns can come infrequently, such as Wheatena, International Home Product's hot cereal, which changed only after several decades, or frequently, such as Procter & Gamble's Clearasil acne medication, which gets a package change every three to four years. However, package redesigns should not be taken lightly, and not all brands lend themselves to packaging changes. The last thing a company wants is for a consumer to think the company has changed the formula when only the package was changed. Because of that fear, packaging redesigns at some companies are few and far between. For example, Campbell's Soup continues to use the familiar red-and-white color scheme for its cans.

Informational (Labeling)

To create a strong marketing edge, many graphic and creative capabilities are now available for labeling, such as applied ceramic, clear pressure-sensitive shrink sleeve, thermal-transfer labels, and photographic-quality imaging. Package labels can give a mature brand a much-needed facelift, target niche brands to their appropriate markets, and tie brands to current events, such as new movies and the use of a national sports celebrity. Labels can even create a collectible package that promotes the brand not only on the store shelf, but long after it has been taken home.

Environmental

Another factor in packaging material choice is determining the environmental friendliness of each material. As consumers become more green-focused, they are more cognizant of how packaging materials impact the environment. *Sustainability*, a relatively new term, describes a product's ability to be maintained indefinitely so that fewer resources are depleted. This is becoming increasingly necessary as we continue to consume more resources than can be naturally replenished.

The sustainability of products involves the big picture: extraction of raw materials, shipping, production, use, recyclability, and disposal. The entire life cycle of a packaging material must be considered to tell its sustainability story. The health impact as well as safety of the product for humans and the environment must also be calculated into the sustainability of a packaging material. Packaging will continue to evolve as more and more consumers begin to consider sustainability in their purchasing decisions.

PACKAGING—GLASS
by O-I (Owens-Illinois)

Applications

Glass can be used to package virtually any product, and it is one of the only packaging materials that can be reused safely. Glass packaging can be used for foods, juices, nonalcoholic beverages, wines, beers, spirits, specialty markets, and baby bottles.

Benefits

Glass packaging is competitively priced and is attractive to consumers, because it delivers a premium image while providing the ultimate protection for the products it holds.

Protection

Because glass is *chemically inert* (not composed of any chemicals), it does not leach or impart any odors, tastes, or chemicals into the product it holds. Glass is also extremely long-lasting as it does not deteriorate, corrode, stain, or fade over time. Therefore, glass not only provides physical protection from outside contaminants but it ensures that the packaging itself will not mar the purity of the product.

Usage

An extremely user-friendly product, glass is microwave and dishwasher safe, will not melt under heat, and is able to keep chilled products cold longer.

Environmental

Glass is also the only type of packaging that is safe to reuse and is endorsed by the Food and Drug Administration (FDA) as the only packaging material that is "generally recognized as safe."[1] Glass packaging is truly a *cradle-to-cradle packaging material.* This means that it can be recycled infinitely to be remade into bottles, jars, or containers that are equally as pure as the original. The recycled product is so pure it can touch food or beverages, which is not true for other recycled packaging materials. Many materials claim to be recyclable, yet they can only be downcycled into products different from their initial form, for example, a plastic bottle might be turned into a plastic bag.

Although glass is heavier than other packaging materials and can be broken, glass manufacturers have started to lightweight their products to reduce the weight. This lightweighting process works to distribute the glass uniformly throughout the bottle or jar so that less glass is used.

Branding

A 2008 consumer research study spanning nine countries found that when glass was compared to its competitors, it was the closest to what consumers considered to be the ideal packaging material.[2] In a 2007 study, 1,002 consumers rated their packaging choices for nonalcoholic beverage products based on packaging qualities.[3] Glass was the preferred choice for creating an impression of prestige and premium branding, making a minimal impact on the flavor of a beverage, safely protecting products from contamination, and being good for the environment.

PACKAGING—PAPERBOARD
by Caraustar Industries, Inc.

Applications

Paperboard packaging is the preferred form of packaging for delivering products of all types, shapes, and sizes to market. Even those products that may be packaged in other substrates (for example, aluminum cans, glass bottles, or plastics) usually go to market in a corrugated box or in a paperboard overwrap. In many cases paperboard packaging, such as folding cartons, will be conveyed to a filling line on a paperboard pad in a corrugated tray. In many cases the support packaging (that is, the packaging that does not go on to market) is reused and eventually recycled.

Benefits

The many benefits of paperboard packaging include its design versatility, printability, heat resistance, and positive environmental attributes.

Design Versatility

Paperboard can be formed to fit all products whether round or rectangular or specially formed to best show off the product. Paperboard packaging can be made with windows so the buyer has direct visibility of the product or fully paneled to create a billboard for displaying the brand. Paperboard is often formed into a sleeve to hold beverage pouches or a handheld tray for aluminum or plastic packed beverages. It can be made with a resealable lid—such as P&G's Pringles—or with a gable-top pour spout used for milk or juice cartons. For hardware applications, it can be made into a cartridge to fit adhesive or sealant guns. Paperboard can be combined with foils or plastics to enhance either the form or function of the package.

Printability

Due to its graphic design properties and flexible forms, paperboard creates a primary sales tool for the packaged product.

Heat Resistance

Paperboard packaging can be made ovenable or microwaveable for cooking ease and flexibility.

Environmental Attributes

Paperboard packaging is the most recovered and recycled packaging product in the world by percentage and by volume. The United States is the largest consumer of paperboard packaging and the largest collector of recovered fiber in the world. Paperboard has the lowest life cycle impact of all packaging materials, with 40 percent of paperboard packaging made from recycled fiber. Even the original virgin material is made from replanted tree farms, grown sustainably and primarily harvested for the purpose of dimensional lumber and paper manufacturing.

PACKAGING—ALUMINUM CONTAINERS
by Alcoa, Inc.

Introduction

The aluminum beverage can is probably the most often used package in the world—100 billion are sold each year in the United States alone. That is almost a can a day for every man, woman, and child in the United States. Markets for aluminum cans outside the United States are growing at double-digit rates. Two-piece aluminum cans emerged in the late 1950s as an alternative to three-piece steel cans. The amazing success and widespread use of this package are the result of several important packaging attributes. Some attributes are based on the metallurgical characteristics of the aluminum substrate, and others are related to brand marketing benefits that this ubiquitous container offers packaged goods companies.

Applications

Rigid aluminum cans are the predominant packaging for soft drink and beer products. New applications include milk- and coffee-based drinks, juice-based drinks, and flavored waters. Aluminum bottles are being introduced in the beer market and other sectors of the beverage industry. Aluminum cans also retain a significant share of the shallow food can market, predominantly in the pet food sector. Easy open ends, recyclability, and colored coatings have led to growth in this market segment.

Benefits

Technical Performance
Technically, the lightweight aluminum can literally is a modern marvel. The sheet metal-forming technology behind aluminum cans enables a container as thin as a couple of sheets of paper to withstand more than 90 pounds per square inch of pressure. Alloy development over the last 30 years provides can makers with a very formable, yet incredibly strong, array of alloys used to manufacture cans. Today's cans feature new shapes and sizes, and lids with large-mouthed, vented, and even resealable openings that hold products with varying degrees of carbonation. Special coatings can withstand the high temperatures involved in retort processing, opening new coffee- and milk-based drink markets to aluminum cans.

Supply Chain/Logistics
The aluminum can's efficient, cylindrical aspect ratio; its "cube efficiency" in multipacks; its extreme light weight; and its durability all contribute to provide marketers with a transportable, low-cost package with the added supply chain benefit of relatively long shelf life compared to other packaging. Shelf life is derived not only from the impermeable metal substrate and coatings, but also from the material's opacity (cans keep both air and light from reaching the contents of the package).

Sustainability
No other package in the world is as universally recyclable as the aluminum can. Recycling rates in markets around the world generally range from 50 to more than 90 percent. Aluminum cans are not only infinitely recyclable, but roughly 50 percent of today's aluminum can is made of previously recycled containers. The enormous energy savings created through recycling is what drives the aluminum can's intrinsic value. By recycling used cans, rather than producing aluminum from ore, aluminum producers save 95 percent of the energy needed for the manufacture of the base material.

Marketing and Brand Image
Marketers use the highly reflective, printable surface of aluminum cans to support brand image, differentiate brand extensions, and run promotions. The can is used as a mini-billboard by some marketers who use multicolor lithography, textured, glow-in-the-dark, or thermo-chromatic inks to grab consumer attention and to reinforce brand image.

PACKAGING—STEEL
by Silgan Containers

Applications

Steel cans are popular for foods and beverages, as well as for aerosol products, paint, chemicals, and decorative tins. Shoppers have many selections of easy-to-use and convenient steel packages, including twist-top, resealable lids; easy-open pull-tab lids; and distinct, easy-to-grasp cans shaped like bowls, kettles, and even squares.

Benefits

Nutrition

The canning process delivers long-term food quality and product shelf life. Processing conditions must be approved by the U.S. Food and Drug Administration. Once sealed and heat-processed, canned food maintains its high quality for more than two years. To ensure that foods are packed at their peak of freshness, most canning facilities are located within a few miles of the point of harvest; fruit and vegetable canneries are just miles from the fields; seafood canneries are within minutes of the docks; meats, soups, and stews are canned within the facilities in which they are prepared.

Safety

Once packed, canned food is heated to a temperature that kills all microorganisms. Foods are closely monitored using a Hazard Analysis and Critical Control Point (HACCP) system that identifies areas of potential contamination and builds checkpoints to ensure the highest possible safety standards. Steel cans offer protection from dirt, parasites, and bacteria as well as protection from moisture, oxygen, and light, all of which can impair food quality. Additionally, cans are tamper-resistant and tamper-evident, which helps ensure that food stays safe.

Cost-Effective

Partly due to their stackability, cans are easy to transport and efficient to store. This ability also allows for easy palletization, therefore making for easy loading and unloading, saving time and handling costs. Due to lower costs for manufacturers to produce, ship, and store, canned food products are also some of the most economical choices for consumers.

Environmental

Steel cans are 100 percent recyclable and can be infinitely recycled without losing strength or quality. Steel packaging has a recycling rate over 60 percent in the United States and is the most recycled packaging material in the world.

PACKAGING—FLEXIBLE PACKAGING
by Sealed Air Corporation

Introduction

Flexible packaging refers to any package whose shape can be readily changed. It includes a range of packaging formats that utilize plastic films, paper, or thin metal foils. Flexible packaging can take many forms, including bags, pouches, liners, shrink sleeves, shrink and stretch wrap, and bulk shipping sacks. Almost 80 percent of flexible packaging is printed. In the United States, it is estimated to be a $26 billion market segment, which represents approximately 18 percent of the total U.S. packaging industry. Flexible packaging is the second largest packaging segment, exceeded only by the corrugated box packaging segment.

Applications

Flexible packaging is used for a wide variety of food and nonfood applications. Applications include retail and institutional food (54 percent), retail and institutional nonfood segments (12 percent), consumer products (10 percent), pharmaceutical and medical segments (7 percent), and industrial and other (16 percent).

Within the food segment, the largest applications for flexible packaging are refrigerated meats, salty snacks, confectionary, and produce. Nonfood segments include pet food, lawn and garden supplies, and photographic products. The consumer products segment includes household bags and wraps.

Benefits

The key benefit of flexible packaging compared to other packaging formats is its low cost and economy of materials. Flexible packaging, by its very nature, makes very efficient use of raw materials to provide essential packaging functions. Flexible packages are typically much thinner and lighter in weight than rigid or semirigid alternatives. In addition, flexible packaging makes efficient use of space, during both storage and distribution.

Other benefits of flexible packaging include:

- Preserving freshness and quality and extending shelf life of perishable products by protecting them from oxygen, moisture, microorganisms, odors, and light.
- Ensuring safety before, during, and after use. Flexible packages do not have sharp or dangerous edges and are resistant to breakage and damage.
- Enhancing product quality and image with consumers through eye-catching graphics and product design. Flexible packages are easily printed and formed into almost any shape.
- Providing convenience and portability to consumers through easy opening features, portion control, and minimal storage space.

Materials

Flexible packaging uses a wide range of materials to deliver features and benefits. Flexible packaging primarily consists of plastic packaging, but also includes paper, metal foil, and blends.

The most common flexible packaging material is polyethylene, which accounts for 62 percent of all plastics, followed by polypropylene at 17 percent.

Environment

The use of mixed materials to create thin, lightweight packaging can create challenges for end-of-life disposal. Currently, most flexible packaging is disposed of as waste. An active area for the flexible packaging industry is the development of economically viable means to collect and sort flexible packaging for recycling, energy recovery, or composting. Flexible packaging of the future will continue to reduce the amount of packaging materials needed to provide functionality while minimizing waste throughout its life cycle.

PACKAGING — RIGID PLASTICS
by Fabri-Kal Corp.

Introduction

Plastic is the general term for a wide range of synthetic or semisynthetic, organic, solid materials suitable for the manufacture of industrial products. Plastics are typically polymers of high molecular weight and may contain other substances to improve performance and/or reduce costs.

The word *plastic* derives from the Greek *plastikos*, "fit for molding," from *plastos* "molded." It refers to their malleability or plasticity during manufacture that allows them to be cast, pressed, or extruded into a variety of shapes, such as films, fibers, plates, tubes, bottles, boxes, cups, and much more. Plastic products typically are either heavy-gauge or thin-gauge. Heavy-gauge products typically are of a permanent end use nature, while thin-gauge parts are more often designed to be disposable or recyclable and are primarily used to package or contain a food item or product.

Applications

Resins most common for rigid plastic packaging are:

- **Polypropylene (PP).** Food containers, appliances, car fenders (bumpers)
- **Polystyrene (PS).** Packaging foam, food containers, disposable cups, plates, cutlery, CD and cassette boxes
- **High-impact polystyrene (HIPS).** Refrigerator liners, food packaging, vend cups
- **Polyethylene terephthalate (PETE).** Carbonated drink bottles, jars, plastic film, microwavable packaging

Benefits

As a packaging material, rigid plastic has many benefits. It can be formed to almost any shape imaginable, is lightweight and high-strength. Rigid plastic is also waterproof, airtight, and chemical resistant. Finally, it is inexpensive, reusable, and recyclable.

PACKAGING—LABELING
by MMC

Introduction

Customers seek out information in order to make better choices. Labeling is one method that provides information to the customer and is often the last source of information seen before a customer makes a purchase decision. Therefore, marketers should make every effort to provide as much information in as clear a fashion as possible on the product label. Marketers have several options as to the types of label application and label printing technologies they can use.

Informational Aspects

Labeling provides four types of information: product identification, safety and warning, consumer information, and retail information.

Product Identification

The primary purpose of a product's label is to identify the product for the consumer. The product name should be prominent and assist in distinguishing the product from competitive products. Any marketing claims (such as "new and improved" or "gets clothes cleaner") also should be prominent.

Safety and Warning

Product labels serve as conduits for health, safety, and product content information. The governments of most countries take an active approach to ensure that all brands provide accurate, adequate, and uniform information. For example, the U.S. Food and Drug Administration mandates that manufacturers print a principal display panel on all food product packaging that includes the following information: product name, contents, company identity, grading (Grade A eggs), quantity or weight, flavor (cherry-flavored cola), and a flavor qualifier

("with other natural flavors"). The back panel of a food product is just as important as the front panel. On food products, the back panel contains the following information: nutrition information, the ingredient legend, and the manufacturer's contact information.

Labels now must indicate product expiration dates for product categories such as food and pharmaceuticals, show the age appropriateness for children's toys regarding choking hazards for children younger than three years of age, and provide affirmation of third-party safety testing. For example, an Underwriters Laboratories (UL) label indicates that an electronic device has been tested by the UL and certified as safe. Many products now carry an industry seal of approval, verifying that the product meets industry standards of approval. For example, flooring materials are tested and certified for grading, moisture content, and shape, and the findings are labeled in a seal bearing the imprint of the National Oak Flooring Manufacturers Association.

In addition, warning labels for certain products that may pose a risk when used follow a voluntary labeling process set forth by the American National Standards Institute (ANSI) that indicates the extent of the risk. The choice for the appropriate word or signal word to appear on the safety sign, label, or tag should be based on two components: (1) the seriousness of the injury and (2) probability of occurrence. As Figure 17.1 illustrates, the component of probability has two factors: (1) the probability of the accident occurring and (2) the probability of an injury if the accident occurs. In practice, the decision on choosing the right signal word begins with asking how serious the possible injury can be (serious injury/death or minor/moderate). That decision leads the company to use *either* chart A or chart B to determine the right signal word. Then the company must assess the probability of the accident occurring and match it with the probability of the injury occurring; the end result is the correct signal word. The only place where this method does not work is when your hazard falls into the category in between Charts A and

B that contains both WARNING and CAUTION for a signal word. If this is the case, exposure frequency and accident history may assist the company in determining which of the two signal words to choose.

Figure 17.1 illustrates the signal words from the 2008 ANSI Z535 standards.

Consumer Information

Labeling also can provide differentiating information on consumer issues, such as:

- Food or drug contents (including government requirements)
- Country of origin

The following matrices show the signal words, colors, and presence or absence of a safety alert symbol that are assigned for each combination of accident probability, worst credible harm, and probability of worst credible harm.

CHART A

If Worst Credible Severity of Harm is Death or Serious Injury

		Probability of Accident if Hazardous Situation is not Avoided	
		Will	Could
Probability of Death or Serious Injury if Accident Occurs	Will	⚠ DANGER	⚠ WARNING
	Could	⚠ WARNING	⚠ WARNING

CHART B

If Worst Credible Severity of Harm is Moderate or Minor Injury

For all probabilities:	⚠ CAUTION

CHART C

If Worst Credible Severity of Harm is Property Damage

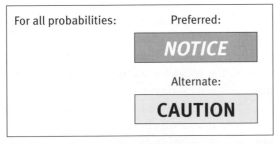

For all probabilities:	Preferred: *NOTICE* Alternate: CAUTION

Source: National Electrical Manufacturers Association —Secretariat ANSI Z535.

Figure 17.1 Signal Word Selection Matrices

- Union affiliation
- Environmental/sustainability efforts
- Animal testing

Retail Information

Product labels contain another piece of vital information called the Universal Product Classification Code (UPC). UPCs are the "social security numbers" of products. These codes are placed on packages in number and bar form. They can then be scanned electronically to identify packages by brands and size, and automatically note their prices at checkout. These codes were developed along with laser scanning equipment to expedite retail checkout and keep track of what is sold and inventory control. UPC codes are administered by the Uniform Code Counsel (UCC). UPCs consist of 12 digits. The first is assigned by the UCC; the next six digits, called the "company prefix," identify the company or manufacturer; and the next five digits track the product and are called the item ID number. Affixing UPC codes to products is a voluntary process and not mandated by federal or state governments. However, it is virtually impossible to penetrate retail shelves today without them.

Label Application Technologies

There are five technologies used in the application of labels: pressure sensitive, cut and stack, in-mold, heat transfer, and shrink sleeve.

- **Pressure Sensitive.** *Pressure sensitive* is a label application technology in which printed labels are peeled from their liner and transferred to the container with pressure. They are virtually self-adhesive stickers.
  - Primary market segments: home and personal care, food and beverage
  - Allows sharp, bright colors and shimmering metallic inks
  - Wide versatility and low application costs
  - Application typically in-line with filling operations
  - Wide range of face stocks and adhesives
    Pressure-sensitive labels are the dominant technology in the industry, encompassing two-thirds of the market.

- **Cut and Stack.** *Cut and stack labels* are adhered to containers and products using an adhesive applied during the labeling process.
  - Primary market segment: food and beverage
  - Wide range of looks from paper stock to high gloss metallized film
  - Excellent graphics reproduction and on-product durability
  - Dependable high-speed application
  - Cost-effective choice for high-volume applications
  - Performance characteristics from standard paper to full wet strength paper
    Cut and stack labels will continue to be the low-cost option for the food and beverage industry.

- **In-Mold.** *In-mold* is a labeling application technology in which a label is adhered to the container during the bottle molding process.
  - Primary market segments: home and personal care, food and beverage
  - Ability to handle unique container shapes
  - Provides a high degree of product security
  - Eliminates delamination issues
  - No post-mold labeling costs
  - Potential for lightweighting of the bottle as the label becomes a part of it

- **Heat Transfer.** *Heat transfer* is a labeling technology in which reverse printed labels are transferred off of a special release liner onto the container using heat and pressure.
  - Primary market segments: home and personal care, food and beverage
  - Brings out sharp, bright colors and can use metallic and/or pearlescent inks to provide differentiation on shelf
  - The ultimate "no-label look" as there is no facestock applied, only ink
  - Ideal for a variety of shapes and sizes of containers

- **Shrink Sleeve.** *Shrink sleeve* is a label technology in which labels are shrunk over containers for maximum label area and contour.
  - Primary market segments: home and personal care, food and beverage

- 360° graphics
- Bright metallic and pearlescent effects
- Scuff resistance by reverse printing
- Contour fit can be applied to virtually any size or shape container
- Multipack presentation

Shrink sleeve labels are the fastest-growing segment of the industry. Consumer products, food and beverage, personal care, and many other markets are moving to shrink sleeve labels for their complete container decoration capability.

Label Printing Technologies

There is a wide range of print applications that can be used with labels.

- **Rotogravure.** In the *rotogravure* process, an image is engraved into a cylinder. Its outstanding density range and fine vignettes facilitate top quality. Durable gravure cylinders are conducive for large-volume printing using a range of substrates.
- **Flexographic.** In the *flexographic* process, graphics are imaged onto a polymer plate, creating raised surfaces. Flexo quality has been dramatically improved recently with the use of digital plates and technology advances. Newer flexo presses can be combined with in-line processes such as gravure, rotary screen, and foil, allowing for highly customizable, cost-effective solutions.
- **Lithographic.** *Litho technology* is based on the principle that oil and water do not mix. An image is engraved on a printing plate, creating an area receptive to oil-based inks. The technology is exceptional for reproducing high-definition images and extremely fine vignettes. It is ideal for medium to large size runs and allows utilization of a wide range of substrates.
- **Rotary Screen.** In the *rotary screen* process, the image is incorporated into a finely meshed screen where the nonimage areas become nonpermeable, forming a stencil. Ink is pumped into the center of the screen, and a squeegee forces it through the open image areas and onto the substrate. Screen printing delivers a high volume and thick layer of ink creating superb opacity and tactile surfaces for graphics that require these enhancements and special effects.
- **Digital.** *Digital printing* is a process by which digital images are printed directly to the substrate, eliminating the need for printing cylinders and plates. Digital offers a cost-effective solution, especially for lower-quantity runs. Its quick changeover capability and the elimination of print tools makes it ideal for customization. Digital can be combined with other offline processes, such as foil stamping and screen printing to obtain special effects on a variety of substrates.
- **Hot and Cold Foil Stamp.** *Foil stamping* is a process in which a sheet of metallic foil is stamped onto a substrate using a tool or die in the shape of the desired image.
- **Ultraviolet (UV) and Electron Beam (EB).** *UV* and *EB* are processes in which coatings or inks are cured using energy from these sources rather than heat. The ultraviolet light spectrum in a UV lamp and the focused electrons in EB interact with specially formulated chemicals to cure materials—typically faster and using less energy than other methods. UV and EB are considered to be environmentally friendly since most of the solvents in inks and coatings can be eliminated during curing.

PACKAGING — INTERNATIONAL
by Sara Lee Corp.

Introduction

In the United States most marketers typically do not advertise the package, but concentrate on the product's features and benefits. However, in many countries the package plays an important role in marketing. To be successful in packaging on an international level, marketers should understand several key areas: consumer needs, functionality, differentiation, cost, counterfeiting, and environmental issues.

Consumer Needs

The success of any package is based upon its being intuitive. For consumers who do not read directions, the package must be easy to open, use, and store. The package is also a badge that you are happy to show others; it is an extension of who you are. For example, Wrigley launched a new product in Taiwan and the team came up with a commercial that did not talk about the product but emphasized the new package in the three situations where it could be used: the car, the office, and at home. The commercial was so successful it created double-digit growth.

It is also important to understand the similarities and differences in customer needs and wants among countries within a region. For example, in Europe Wrigley developed a new hard candy and needed to understand in each country who the market leaders were, the ranking of popular candies by flavor, and the preferred package type (single packs or multipacks). Consumer needs in Germany and Austria were very similar, England and Central Europe were similar, the Mediterranean countries were similar, and the Scandinavian countries were similar. Grouping country needs will lead to economies of scale in packaging.

Functionality

Marketers should understand that the most important aspect of packaging, in every country, is functionality—the need to indicate freshness and security. Quality is essential in selecting materials and packaging suppliers.

Differentiation

Packaging is another way to differentiate the product for the consumer and can add significant marketing value. It is helpful to incorporate the senses when the consumer interacts with your package. A truly differentiated package will include as many of the senses as possible. If you accomplish the connection with the senses, you may have made an emotional connection and secured the consumer with your product.

We often focus on the sense of sight, which is how the consumer sees your product on the shelf. For example, in China we developed a different package based on consumer testing showing that since we were making breath-freshening claims, Chinese consumers felt the package should be more medicinal looking. The package we came up with looked very similar to a pill bottle. The package was so well received by consumers that there was little cannibalization of our existing products, and sales grew by taking share from the competition.

Cost

Consumers in some Asian countries, such as Japan, Hong Kong, Taiwan, South Korea, and in recent years China, are willing to pay more for sophisticated or attractive packaging and expect it to change with some frequency. In most developed countries, consumers concentrate on the product and bristle at the cost of excessive packaging.

Counterfeiting

Counterfeiting is a big issue in international packaging. Patent and copyright laws are not strictly enforced in every country. It is important to always be on the lookout for counterfeit products so as not to lose customers. In many cases the counterfeit packaging can look as good as the original; however, the product inside is typically far below the quality of the branded product. For example, the Wrigley product manager was shown a box of (counterfeit) chewing gum by the country manager and asked what he thought. He replied that it looked like they must have changed suppliers since the quality of the wrapper had improved. When counterfeits are found, the company should work quickly with the local government or hire private investigators to find the counterfeiters and shut them down.

Research and Development

A major goal of marketing is to bring products from concept to finished package to shelf as quickly as possible. Speed to market is important to keep costs low and achieve first to market advantage. Thus, it is important to get quick alignment on packaging needs from the marketers in all the targeted countries. For example, for one product, Wrigley was able to get Hong Kong, Taiwan, and Korea to agree on a single package with different numbers of pieces of gum in the different countries to hit the needed price points.

Shipping

For international shipping, the packaging material should be lightweight and break resistant. However, more often, the product and packaging are made locally to service the local country's needs. Many times, the needs of the consumer supercede those of the shipping manager.

International Sizes

Most countries use the metric system. The United States still uses the imperial system, but U.S. consumers have been very accepting of metric packaging. Using one measurement system for packaging is far more cost-effective than accommodating two systems.

Environmental Issues

In every country it is important, and in many it is mandated, to make packaging recyclable, so the marketer must specify that the recycling number be clearly visible on the package.

PACKAGING – CASE STUDY

by Tanimura & Antle

Company: Tanimura & Antle
Case: Fresh Salad and a Packaging (R)evolution

Today's consumers are increasingly concerned about nutrition and are more willing than ever to consume healthy, minimally processed foods. As workdays lengthen and more meals are consumed on the go, portability has also become a key requirement in meal selection. Add to these trends the fact that more families consist of working mothers and single parents, and the result is an eager public demanding more choice in fresh, nutritious, ready-to-eat meals.

Tanimura & Antle, the nation's largest independent lettuce grower, provides a broad range of premium vegetables to the retail and commercial (restaurant and cafeteria food service) markets. It is completely vertically integrated managing seed development, crop and land optimization, efficient harvesting practices, and ultimately packaging or processing of the product, and thus is well positioned to understand and respond to changing consumer needs.

The produce section of the grocery store had always been an assured profit center in the retail arena. Consequently, the section had not been one that experienced major product innovation or strategic marketing. For decades, grocery shoppers approached the produce department the same way. A shopper would visit the produce area with a few upcoming meals in mind, select ingredients arranged in a staid, generic fashion on the grocer's shelves, take them home, and diligently wash and chop prior to consumption. The consumer's expectation was easily met by the grocer, whose primary function was to ensure that fresh, crisp vegetables were made available on a daily basis. Little else was done to progressively market vegetables, and there were few, if any, perceived areas of growth in this very traditional supermarket category.

(Continued)

In the mid-1970s, however, growers of lettuce began packaging prechopped lettuces for their commercial customers. Placed in plastic bags with a content weight of as much as five pounds, the lettuce blends were easily handled by restaurant operators who wanted the convenience of a premade salad, thereby eliminating labor cost and maximizing their raw material yield.

This packaging milestone had been achieved due to the work done by food scientists, who for decades had experimented with putting chopped lettuce into plastic bags to understand how long the vegetable could remain without spoiling. The respiration of the lettuce leaves was the primary focus. The greens, like all plants, breathe, emitting carbon dioxide as they respire. The carbon dioxide that is released during a plant's breathing process ordinarily mixes with other gases and poses no threat of product damage. However, in a closed environment, a high level of carbon dioxide causes cellular breakdown of organic material. In the case of lettuce, this would result in either rust spotting or decay.

It was identified that different blends of vegetables require a precise amount of carbon dioxide and oxygen as they respire. Breathable packaging films with different oxygen transmission rates (OTRs) were developed to ensure a desirable level of both carbon dioxide and oxygen in the bag containing the particular lettuce blend. For certain blends, nitrogen was injected into the bag so that the optimum concentration of oxygen and carbon dioxide would be maintained. This modified atmosphere packaging (MAP) technology helped maintain the freshness and quality of salad blends for a relatively long period of time (approximately two weeks).

The Antles had led the produce industry with a strong history of innovation since its vacuum-cooling success story of the 1950s. Until that decade, lettuce and other vegetables had been packed and shipped in ice, a messy and wasteful approach that used large blocks of ice surrounding lettuce in wooden boxes (hence the term "iceberg lettuce"). The lettuce was then usually shipped across the country by rail. Often, the rail cars would be opened to reveal a soggy, unusable product. The Antles devised a system of cooling the produce immediately after it was harvested. The vacuum-cooling technology converts vegetables' moisture (water) content into a vapor form, thereby reducing the temperature of the plant tissue.

Because of the ability to control the environments in which these vegetables were packaged, Tanimura & Antle, among others in their industry, was able to successfully package and market chopped lettuces, lettuce blends, precut vegetables, and, most recently, whole heads of lettuce. The result is a revolution in how consumers plan, shop for, and prepare their meals.

The highly competitive packaged salad category now boasts over $2 billion in annual sales, with a household penetration of 71 percent. The category continues to grow at a healthy pace, and is constantly responding to consumers' tastes and preferences with new product introductions. In an era of highly targeted marketing, packaged salads and vegetables have led an otherwise complacent grocery section into a new era by creating a category with mass appeal, broad application, and an extremely high level of convenience.

by Dean Foods

Company: Dean Foods
Case: Innovative Packaging—Milk Chug

In 1996, Dean Foods found itself facing a tough decision. And, over the next two years, the outcome of this particular decision would revolutionize the milk industry.

Like other U.S. dairy processors, Dean Foods produced its quarts and other smaller-sized containers of milk in paper, gable-top cartons. These paper cartons were certainly not ideal from a consumer standpoint. They were difficult to open, even harder to close, often leaked, and the cartons sometimes picked up ambient refrigerator odors. Like its competitors, Dean Foods received major consumer complaints about the paper cartons. However, from a manufacturing standpoint, the paper containers were highly cost-efficient to produce.

In 1996, the equipment that the dairy processor used for filling paper cartons had worn out. Thus, Dean could either purchase new paper carton filling equipment, or they could listen to years of consumer comments and create a better single-serve milk container.

After a great deal of debate, the Dean Foods team decided to listen to their consumers. They realized that consumer needs were not being met by the company's current offerings. Dean Foods saw consistency among the consumer complaints and developed a strategy to meet those particular consumer needs. Consumers asked for a plastic bottle. They also wanted it to be resealable. And they wanted convenient size offerings. To Dean Foods, this meant that consumers wanted milk to be portable. Consumers had readily accepted the benefits of plastic, resealable soda bottles, while milk remained a drink-at-home beverage. Dean Foods realized that by placing milk in a single-serve, plastic, resealable bottle, they would be bringing this same degree of convenience and portability to the milk category.

Based on this strategy, Dean Foods designed and patented three sizes of single-serve, resealable milk bottles (quart, pint, and half-pint). The bottles were developed in an old-fashioned shape similar to the original glass milk bottles to convey feelings of nostalgia and quality. And the bottle was designed to fit in standard car cup holders in order to make Dean milk even more portable.

Originally, the bottles were made of clear plastic; however, they were quickly changed to white opaque plastic as consumers became aware of the benefits of protecting milk from light. The white plastic bottle also lent itself to high-quality labels. Four-color process labels were used with bold colors in order to make the new product stand out in the dairy case. It is important to note that all design decisions were made based on consumer research, not on cost or operational issues.

Once the design was complete and new single-serve filling equipment was installed, an 18-month product test was run in the Athens, Tennessee, area, home of Mayfield Dairy, a division of Dean Foods. For this test, the product was branded as Mayfield milk. However, it was determined that the single-serve product needed a more fanciful name to inform consumers that the product was an immediate consumption beverage. The name "Milk Chug" was selected. The Milk Chug was branded with a combination of the local dairy name and the Milk Chug name (such as Dean's Milk Chug, T. G. Lee Milk Chug, McArthur Milk Chug, and Mayfield Milk Chug).

(Continued)

Based on the strategic platform of convenience and portability, a marketing plan was developed that revolved around the tagline, "Milk where you want it." The campaign focused on the concept of making Milk Chug products available to consumers wherever single-serve beverages are sold. The program used several advertising media including television, radio, and billboards. All creative elements of the marketing plan were tested in focus groups.

Consumer research also helped to determine the size offerings for the Milk Chug products. Based on the needs for convenience and portability, quart, pint, and half-pint sizes were developed. The half-pints come in a six-bottle multipack and are primarily used for refrigerator loading.

Milk Chug products were priced relative to other single-serve beverages rather than to milk. This practice allowed for substantially higher margins than the norm in the milk industry. It also allowed Dean Foods to influence Milk Chug sales with special promotions, and it provided enough margin to fund heavy marketing and advertising in the launch years.

The initial target for Milk Chug was moms as they were the primary supermarket shopper. Children ages 9 to 17 were the largest milk consumption segment, and men ages 18 to 24 were secondary targets for the product. At the time of the product launch, Dean Foods' primary distribution channel was supermarkets. However, the single-serve Milk Chug gave the company the opportunity to further penetrate the convenience store, gas station, and food service channels. Since the launch of Milk Chug, these new channels have been such a source of dramatic sales growth for Dean Foods that the Milk Chug marketing efforts were changed to focus not on the moms but the children ages 9 to 17 and men ages 18 to 24, the primary convenience store demographic.

In addition to the successful launch of the new Milk Chug product, there have been other positive residual effects that are attributed to Milk Chug. First, the Milk Chug product transformed many local dairy brands. By using a combination of the local dairy name and the Milk Chug brand, the local dairy brands received a halo effect that increased their brand equity among consumers. Secondly, consumers began to purchase dairy-branded gallons and half gallons of milk once they had tried Milk Chug.

When full Milk Chug distribution was gained in 1998, chocolate milk sales increased 2.5 to 3 times. Even though pint and half-pint white milk sales increased by 25 to 30 percent, chocolate milk drove the most volume. Upon the product launch, Dean Foods' consumer hotline was inundated by women who asked for a fat-free version of the Milk Chug product. As a result of a continued consumer focus, Dean's developed a fat-free white Milk Chug in 1999, which helped to bring women back to the dairy category. Dean Foods has experienced success on many levels from its Milk Chug product, meeting the consumer needs of convenient and portable fresh milk.

by O-I (Owens-Illinois)

Company: O-I (Owens-Illinois)
Case: Packaging and Rebranding

Making the decision to redesign a product is a big step and can sometimes be risky. However, when done correctly, the redesign can breathe new life into a struggling or overlooked brand. Brown-Forman, an O-I customer that sells a variety of liquors, has had great success in redesigning glass packaging for some of its products. The secret to this success is the integration of the redesign with a rebranding promotional campaign. By changing consumers' perceptions of the liquors through packaging, pricing, and promotions, Brown-Forman was able to project the upscale image it desired for its products.

One of Brown-Forman's most recent and successful redesigns was with Gentleman Jack Rare Tennessee whiskey. This type of whiskey, known for being exceptionally smooth and having a rich taste, belongs in the high-end premium segment for bourbon and Tennessee whiskey. However, the company did not feel the old bottle portrayed the refined image that should accompany this mature liquor. With a long neck, rounded body and large label, the old bottle blended in with other whiskey bottles and didn't show off the liquor inside. The new bottle features a slimmer profile, with a shorter neck, a more rectangular base and broad sloping shoulders. The clear glass and smaller, dignified embossed label also allow consumers to see the appealing amber color of the whiskey.

This bottle redesign was launched in concert with a redesigned Web site, national magazine, outdoor advertising, and point-of-sale displays. Since the redesign, sales of the Gentleman Jack Rare Tennessee whiskey have increased approximately 40 percent.

Another liquor brand owned by Brown-Forman is Finlandia Vodka. Finlandia has been through a few package redesigns, as it strives to keep the brand dynamic and ensure consumer excitement. Finlandia was first introduced in 1972 and became an overlooked brand of vodka due to the marketing campaigns that touted Absolut, Stoli, and Skyy vodkas as "top-of-the-line." After doing brand research to determine what qualities of Finlandia could stay and which needed to change, Finlandia Vodka embarked on a $72 million rebranding effort. Dubbed Finlandia's renaissance, this program included a bottle redesign and an advertising campaign focusing on the geographic roots of the vodka, playing up its glacial tie.

By tying the glacial theme into the appearance of the redesigned bottle manufactured by O-I, and by connecting the brand with high fashion via runway appearances and top fashion designers, Finlandia was able to transform into a premium accessory. This put it in line to finally compete with the other top vodka brands. According to Lori Tieszan, Vice President of Sales and Marketing for Finlandia, "If the brand needs to evolve and you only change the advertising, it doesn't work. For us, the bottle design has been the linchpin that has held all the other elements together." The Finlandia bottle redesign and the promotions tied to it led to a sales increase of nearly 49 percent.

O-I (OWENS-ILLINOIS)

Millions of times a day, O-I glass containers deliver many of the world's best-known consumer products to people all around the world. Visit www.o-i.com.

Carol R. Gee

Carol Gee is Chief Communications Officer for Owens-Illinois, Inc., and is based at the company's worldwide headquarters in Perrysburg, Ohio. Ms. Gee received her BA in Journalism from the University of Missouri.

CARAUSTAR INDUSTRIES, INC.

Caraustar (NASDAQ—CSAR) founded in 1938, is one of North America's largest integrated manufacturers of 100 percent recycled paperboard and converted paperboard products. Visit Caraustar at www.caraustar.com.

Thomas V. Brown

Thomas Brown is the retired President and CEO of Caraustar and was a member of the board of directors. Mr. Brown received his Bachelor's degree from Cornell University.

ALCOA, INC.

Alcoa, Inc. is the world leader in the production and management of primary aluminum, fabricated aluminum, and alumina, and is actively participating and growing in all major aspects of the industry. Visit Alcoa at www.alcoa.com.

Elizabeth Schmitt

Elizabeth Schmitt is Commercial Director for Alcoa's Rigid Packaging Division in Alcoa, Tennessee. Ms. Schmitt received her BA in Communications with a major in journalism/PR, from the University of Tennessee. She also graduated from the University of Tennessee's Executive Development Business Program.

DEAN FOODS

Dean Foods, founded in 1926, is one of the leading food and beverage companies in the United States. Visit Dean Foods at www.deanfoods.com.

Dave Rotunno

Dave Rotunno was formerly the Director of Marketing for the Midwest region of Dean Foods. Mr. Rotunno has spent the last 23 years with the company in various departments and roles.

Sarah Cheek

Sarah Cheek was formerly Marketing Manager for milk and ice cream brands in the Midwest region.

FABRI-KAL CORP.

Fabri-Kal, founded in 1950, was named second in the 2006 Packaging Innovation Processor of the Year contest by the Foodservice Packaging Institute, and has also developed 100 percent corn-based plastic drink cups named Greenware. Visit Fabri-Kal at www.f-k.com.

John Kittredge

John Kittredge is the Vice President of Marketing. Prior to joining Fabri-Kal, John was a Master Brewer. John received his BA from Lewis and Clark College in Oregon.

MCC

MCC produces primary decorative labels for the home and personal care, food and beverage, wine and spirits, and specialty markets around the globe. MCC is recognized as the market leader in in-mold labeling and heat transfer labeling technologies. Visit MCC at www.multicolor-corp.com.

Dirk Edwards

Dirk Edwards is Director of Marketing for MCC. Dirk received his BA and MBA from the University of North Carolina.

SARA LEE CORP.

Sara Lee, founded in 1939, sells food products in over 180 countries worldwide. Sara Lee, headquartered in Downers Grove, Illinois, has annual sales of $13 billion and has over 50,000 employees. Visit Sara Lee at www.saralee.com.

Glenn A. Ventrell

Glenn Ventrell is Director of Packaging and Development and has worked in international business in the fields of procurement, supply chain, new business locations, hiring local talent, and regional business reviews. Mr. Ventrell received his BA in Psychology from Newark State College in New Jersey.

SEALED AIR CORPORATION

Sealed Air, founded in 1960, is a leading global innovator and manufacturer of a wide range of packaging and performance-based materials and equipment systems that serve an array of food, industrial, medical, and consumer applications. Visit Sealed Air at www.sealedair.com.

Dr. Ronald L. Cotterman

Ronald Cotterman, Executive Director of Sustainability, is responsible for Sealed Air's companywide strategy in sustainable business practices across Sealed Air's global business units. Dr. Cotterman received his BS in Chemical Engineering from the University of Florida and a Ph.D. in chemical engineering from the University of California, Berkeley.

Market data provided by:

The Flexible Packaging Association.

SILGAN CONTAINERS

Silgan Containers, founded in 1987, is the largest manufacturer of metal food containers in North America. Visit Silgan at www.silgancontainers.com.

Brian Ksicinski

Brian Ksicinski is the Marketing Manager. Brian received his BA from the University of Minnesota-Twin Cities and Certificate of Market Research from the University of Georgia.

TANIMURA & ANTLE INC.

Tanimura & Antle, headquartered in Salinas, California, is the largest independent lettuce grower and distributor in the United States. Visit Tanimura & Antle at www.taproduce.com.

Dr. Gurmail Mudahar

Gurmail Mudahar, Vice President, has been responsible for Research and Development for Tanimura & Antle Inc. Dr. Mudahar received his Ph.D. in Food Science from the University of Georgia.

Lara Grossman

Lara Grossman was formerly the Value Added Product Manager for Tanimura & Antle, Inc. Ms. Grossman received her BBA in Business Administration from the University of Arizona, and her MBA from Golden Gate University, Monterey, California.

18 PRODUCT PRICING

HOW MUCH IS THAT DOGGIE IN THE WINDOW? THE ONE WITH THE WAGGLEY TAIL?

Bob Merrill, American Songwriter, 1921–1998

by International Paper, NCR, Papa John's, and United Airlines

THE ESSENTIALS OF PRICING
by United Airlines

Introduction

Pricing is the element of marketing that helps determine the value of a product or service for the customer. Price is the most flexible component of the marketing mix because it can be modified quickly in response to changes in the market. For example, the airline industry, one of the most competitive industries in the world, often changes fares up to three times per day. It is important to know how companies determine the proper pricing strategies for their products and what factors affect these pricing strategies.

Consumers and businesses need to know the price of a product or service before they commit to a purchase. In free market economies, it is considered essential that firms have the freedom to set and change prices, and that the consumer has the freedom to determine how much to buy in order to ensure that resources are put to the best use. For example, if consumers value a new product very highly, a seller can capitalize on that demand by setting a higher price. Pricing is a more efficient method than waiting lists and lotteries in deciding who gets the limited supply. The higher price also signals producers to increase supply, which may then drive prices downward.

There are many strategies to determine the prices of goods and services, and there are many factors that determine which of these strategies are most appropriate. The goal of any pricing strategy is to allow the customer to feel that it is a fair price for the item, and thus make the sale.

The trends for factors that may affect pricing strategies in the future can be separated into two areas: those that are likely to cause prices to go higher and those that are likely to cause prices to go lower. Examples of factors favoring higher prices include greater consumer demand brought on by the ever-increasing population and an increase in raw material prices due to overconsumption of finite resources. Examples of factors favoring lower prices include greater competition among businesses, greater demand from consumers for value, product improvements, and product/service innovations.

Many people in the organization are responsible for determining the price of the company's products or services. For example, the company president, chief financial officer, vice president revenue management, and comptroller may be involved in setting overall pricing goals and companywide pricing strategies. The brand manager, product manager, and store manager may determine specific product prices. The salesperson, in certain situations, may alter the price within a specific range to accommodate the customer.

Definition

Pricing is "the formal ratio that includes the quantities of goods or services needed to acquire a given quantity of goods or services."[1]

FACTORS AFFECTING PRICING STRATEGIES

Pricing decisions are influenced by numerous factors, including costs, product demand, product supply, legal requirements, a company's strategic goals, and consumer perception. Pricing decisions should be supported by marketing research that determines competitors' actions and the target market's reaction to prices. Companies must strive to understand each of these factors in order to develop pricing strategies that support the company's objectives.

Cost

The cost of the product or service is one of the most important factors in determining the price. Cost factors include fixed and variable costs, avoidable costs, and opportunity costs.

Fixed and Variable Costs

Understanding costs as they relate to pricing decisions is challenging because there are many different ways to measure costs. From accounting data, managers can determine production costs already incurred by the company. These costs can be broken down into fixed and variable costs. *Fixed costs* typically include plant, equipment, and other costs that are ongoing and do not depend on the company's short-term changes in production levels. *Variable costs* are those costs that vary depending on how much is produced, and typically include such items as raw materials, labor costs, and product distribution costs (warehousing, transportation, and sales commissions). The balance between fixed and variable cost components can influence a company's pricing objectives. In manufacturing, the variable costs of producing and distributing the product are typically larger than the fixed costs associated with running the company. When variable costs considerably outweigh fixed cost components, the company will strive to achieve the highest average price and the lowest average cost. The profit margin can be maximized by producing and selling at the level where the difference between the average price and the average cost is greatest.

In other industries, however, fixed costs predominate over variable costs, making it more difficult to achieve enough sales volume to cover fixed costs. Airlines, for example, incur large fixed costs such as aircraft cost, jet fuel, labor, and airport fees. These costs do not vary depending upon the number of seats sold. In a business with such high fixed costs, one basic objective in pricing is to achieve enough sales volume to reach a breakeven level of utilization. The variable costs for each passenger are quite low, namely the cost of a meal (or other passenger amenities) and travel agent commissions. Because so much of the expense is fixed regardless of the number of seats sold, the airline has a certain level of capacity utilization that must be achieved in order to avoid a loss. After the breakeven level of utilization is achieved, any additional sales volumes contribute to profits because of the very low variable cost of additional passengers. For example, once an aircraft is approximately two-thirds full with paying passengers, the airline is at the breakeven point, and each additional passenger contributes to profits. This cost structure explains the business logic behind the low fares that airlines offer from time to time.

Marginal Costs

Marginal costs consider the cost associated with making one additional sale, such as serving one additional passenger or filling one more hotel room, while *unit cost* measures only costs that already have been incurred. The forward-looking marginal costs concept leads to better pricing decisions because costs from the past are considered sunken costs. For example, airlines offer deeply discounted special fares that induce additional customers to fly and generate incremental revenue for the company.

Life Cycle Costs

Life cycle costs, also known as *total cost of ownership*, account for all costs involved with ownership of the product throughout its useful ownership period. These costs include all costs involved with the purchase, operation, maintenance, and disposal of the product. For example, one product that is designed better than its competition may have a higher initial cost but a lower life cycle cost.

Supply Chain Costs

Pricing should be high enough to provide the members of the supply chain (wholesalers and retailers) with a profit level that will encourage them to carry and promote a company's products. Profit margins should not be so high that the end price is higher than the competition's price. This leads to potential conflicts with supply chain partners.

Opportunity Costs

When a company employs assets toward production activities that generate a certain amount of revenue, the company is forgoing other uses or opportunities for these assets that may have generated other revenue. Over time, the cost of keeping working capital tied up in inventory that is not moving off the shelves gets very expensive. For example, the cereal company's production plant could be used to produce a different brand of cereal, perhaps one made from wheat, which may have lower raw material costs than the currently produced cereal made from corn.

The opportunity costs of holding products in inventory become important in pricing decisions. When a store stocks merchandise, it appropriately uses capital to finance that inventory that is essential to serving customers. However, managers should keep in mind that the funds used in acquiring and keeping inventory could be used for other business purposes if the merchandise does not sell as well as predicted. The cost of capital involved in maintaining inventories is a cost that could be avoided if the inventories were reduced by having a sale.

For example, suppose a record store manager bought 10,000 CDs that cost $6 per CD and sold only 9,000 units. The remaining units are not moving off the shelves very quickly. The manager wants to recover his cost so he tries pricing the CDs just above cost. Even at $7, they are still selling slowly and will not be sold for several months. For all of that time, the store has working capital tied up in financing $6,000 worth of inventory that could have been used to finance other opportunities.

Product Demand

Although cost plays an integral role in establishing prices, the demand for a good or service is also an important consideration. *Product demand* is "the quantity of a good which consumers are able and willing to buy at a given price, in a given market, during a given period of time."[2] A number of factors can cause a shift in product demand, including:

- Price of the good or service
- Price of related goods
- Level of consumer income (often a reflection of the state of the economy)
- Size of the potential market
- Customer preferences
- Product quality
- Availability of product substitutes
- Time sensitivity (perishable, seasonal, emergency)

The consumer demand for most normal goods is inversely proportional to the price charged as illustrated by the classic economic demand curve. As the price for a product is increased, demand for the product falls; similarly, as price is reduced, demand increases.

Product substitution can occur when the prices of related goods fluctuate or when consumers' preferences change. Substitution is one of the biggest factors affecting product demand, and therefore its price. There are other products that may meet the buyer's needs, and beyond a certain price the consumer may substitute a different product for the one in question. In the airline industry, airlines not only compete with each other for customers, but also with other modes of transportation that serve as product substitutes for air travel.

Producers typically utilize demand forecasting whether they are selling toothpaste or airplanes. Pricing assumptions usually are built into these demand forecasts. In fact, most firms have a reasonable idea of the demand for their product at the current market price, but have very limited understanding of what will happen to the demand if they alter the price. Consumer behavior or competitors' actions can cause demand to behave quite differently from expectation or from the forecast. This leads to one of the most fundamental concepts of pricing, called price sensitivity or demand elasticity. Customers respond differently to changes in products price. *Price sensitivity* or *elasticity of demand* is the responsiveness of demand to a change in price. Mathematically, demand elasticity is measured as % change in demand divided by % change in price.

$$\text{Demand elasticity} = \frac{\% \text{ change in demand}}{\% \text{ change in price}}$$

If an elasticity is greater than 1, then demand for the product is referred to as *price elastic* or *price sensitive*, meaning that the quantity demanded is very responsive to price. Alternatively, if elasticity is less than 1, then the demand for the product is referred to as *price inelastic* or that it is *not price sensitive*, meaning that the quantity demanded is less sensitive to price changes.

Product Supply

Product supply is the quantity of a good which producers are able and willing to offer for sale at a given price in a given market at a given time.[3] There are two main factors in supply: amount and competition.

Amount
As the price of a commodity increases, there are economic incentives for producers to increase production and, in the long term, increase production capacity. As the supply of a product or service increases, demand is satiated and falls, causing prices to fall. Individual companies can offer different prices for varying amounts. Individual products require more packaging and sales effort, therefore bringing a higher price than the same product sold in bulk.

Competition
Buyers evaluate a product's or service's pricing in comparison to the competitor's pricing. There always is an alternative, be it direct or indirect. If a number of producers leave the market, the supply of the goodwill diminish, and, if more producers enter the market, the supply of the product will increase. A firm with the goal to maximize profits will raise prices in a situation of diminishing supply. When product supply increases, firms tend to cut prices in order to maintain market share or cover fixed costs.

Organizational Objectives Factors

Senior management usually incorporates organizational goals when setting pricing strategies. Corporate goals include:

- Profit maximization (may suggest high price strategy)
- Target return on investment (may suggest high price strategies)
- Volume objectives/sales maximization (may suggest a low price, especially during an economic downturn when it is important just to keep employees working)
- Corporate image (may suggest high or low prices depending on the image of the company)

Product Life Cycle Factors

The price of a good or service often depends on its relative age in the marketplace and will fluctuate as the product matures during its life cycle. The life cycle of a product can vary tremendously, depending on many factors including the quality of the product, levels of government regulation or patent protection, the ability to effectively market the product, cost containment, and the presence of competition. The life cycles of products generally have four stages where there is pricing interaction with customers: product introduction, product growth, product maturation, and product decline.

Introduction Stage
The first stage of the product life cycle is the introduction stage. The product may represent new

technology, such as the television, or the enhancement of an existing product, such as the color television. Despite the competitive advantage the new product may have, this stage is filled with uncertainty for the manufacturer. The new product may face difficulties, including the high cost or low reliability of production, defensive marketing from producers of existing products, or protectionist foreign government policies. During this stage, the pricing of the new product must reflect these factors. If necessary to become established in the marketplace, the product may be priced near cost, or, if there is no competition, then a higher price may be needed to recapture R&D costs.

Growth Stage

The second stage of the product life cycle is the growth stage. During this stage, the product has established itself in the marketplace and sales grow. As the demand for the product grows, and the cost efficiencies of production are realized, the margins will increase as long as a competitive advantage remains, and therefore pricing may remain stable. However, at the same time, the competitive advantage of the product may diminish due to new competition from other companies, such as other television manufacturers, and therefore prices may need to be cut.

Mature Stage

The third stage of the product life cycle is the mature stage. During this stage, the demand for the product may level out and become very price sensitive, or the competitive advantage may disappear. Economies of scale now apply. For example, the market for televisions is saturated with 99 percent of households already owning a set. The price for the product may decrease and only those able to make a profit at this price will continue production.

Decline Stage

The fourth stage is the decline stage where demand for the product falls or a new innovation renders the product obsolete, for example, analog TV has now been supplanted with the introduction of high definition television (HDTV). In the decline stage, as competitors drop out, the company with the last remaining product may be able to increase the price of the product as it is now in a monopolistic setting once again.

Customer Behavior Factors

Customers often form strong opinions about appropriate price levels for products. Consumers have several different behavior patterns that are factors in pricing.

- Consumers want to feel they have been smart with their purchasing and have received the lowest price.
- Consumers aspire to be better than their peers and feel a sense of prestige or achievement.
- Consumers desire simplicity and do not like to waste time shopping. They want to feel that they can research a price level that they are comfortable with, and shop at that level. In addition, they may prefer flat and/or bundled rates and usage-based rates.
- Consumers feel that prices will fall into an expected range and/or an acceptable range.

Legal Considerations

Pricing strategies work well as long as the marketplace is truly a competitive one in which sellers compete against each other and buyers act independently. Laws intervene in order to ensure that the free market is truly competitive. There are several kinds of pricing practices prohibited by U.S. law because they are believed to reduce competition. They include price fixing, price discrimination, predatory pricing, and tying contracts.

Price Fixing

Price fixing is prohibited by law in order to protect competition. It occurs when a company agrees with one or more of its competitors to modify or stabilize prices or limit supply. Price fixing agreements interfere with the free function of markets and reduce competition. The federal government has successfully prosecuted cases in which, although there was no direct contact among competing companies, they were found to be signaling one another as a tacit form of negotiation. Furthermore, a company's attempt to fix prices does not have to be successful in order to be illegal because the law prohibits any attempt to reach an agreement with competitors regarding price changes or stabilization.

Price Discrimination

In the United States, another antitrust regulation known as the Robinson-Patman Act prohibits charging different prices to different similarly situated buyers for the same product. However, there are several important exceptions that cover many situations. First, different prices may be charged where there is a discernible difference in the grade or quality of the products. Secondly, different prices may be charged where there are differences in the costs of manufacturing or distributing the products. Thirdly, quantity discounts are also permitted, but these types of discounts may sometimes be subject to government regulation. Lastly, the law recognizes that different buyers may pay different prices at different times simply because the competitive market pricing has changed in the meantime. Businesses are always permitted to change their prices to match a competitive price change, and the Robinson-Patman Act is not violated when a company changes prices to match a competitor's prices.

Predatory Pricing

Predatory pricing occurs only when a competitor takes the initiative to lower price below marginal cost for the purpose of driving another out of business, only to later recoup losses by raising the price. Of course, competitors must always be allowed to match another competitor's price.

Tying Contracts

Bundling prices can be beneficial to the consumer. The vast majority of price bundling arrangements are entirely legal, but certain kinds of price bundling and other kinds of tying arrangements have been found illegal under the antitrust laws. The Clayton Act prohibits "tying contracts" in which the sale of one product is conditioned on the purchase of a different product. A tying contract insulates the tied product from competition. The typical package price bundle arrangement involves complementary products, each of which is sold separately in entirely competitive markets. For example, package vacation offers (air + hotel + car) are legal because the market for each component of the package is freely competitive.

Tying or bundling arrangements may not be permitted, however, where they involve the extension of a market share advantage in the market for one product to the market for another tied product. For example, one landmark case (U.S. vs. International Salt Co.) involved a company that leased industrial salt machines and required customers to purchase the salt products (used in the machines) from the machine manufacturer. The manufacturer had a patent on the machine, but no similar position in the market for salt. The Supreme Court determined that the tying condition (requiring that salt be bought from the machine manufacturer) lessened competition in the market for salt products. However, certain kinds of price bundling arrangements have been determined to be anti-competitive when a company uses bundle pricing of several goods to leverage its market power (where it has large market share) over the marketing of a competitor's goods or services.

Government-Imposed Price Restraints

The U.S. government typically uses monetary and fiscal policy to manage the economy. However, very rarely, it imposes price restraints to limit the movement of prices, typically in a time of crisis. For example, during the OPEC oil crisis of the early 1970s, the federal government enacted wage and price controls in an effort to control inflation. Local governments also can impose price restrictions. For example, both New York City and Santa Monica, California, have strict apartment building rent control regulations.

Regulated Industries

There are a number of industries where the prices charged are regulated by some government entity and rate changes require an approval process. This usually occurs because the industry has high fixed costs and other factors which create a situation called a natural monopoly. In a natural monopoly, such as utilities, it is more efficient for one company to invest in the infrastructure required to offer the product. In industries like these, the government typically establishes one company (or several) as the provider and then regulates the rates charged to prevent the company from driving up prices. Regulated industries typically are governed by a form of cost-plus pricing known as rate-of-return regulation. The regulators determine what costs the company incurs in providing the service (and that these costs are reasonable) and then determine what a fair or reasonable rate of return is on this investment, considering the level of risk undertaken. Prices are then set or approved by regulators to permit this fair rate of return, but no more.

PRICING STRATEGIES

Many factors can affect a company's pricing strategies, as discussed earlier; therefore, no single pricing strategy is appropriate for all situations or companies. Successful companies often use several pricing strategies, and each may be different than other successful companies' strategies within the same industry. Pricing strategies usually are based on one of four major principles that include product/corporate–based pricing, market-based pricing, low-price–based pricing, and high-price–based pricing.

Product/Corporate–Based Pricing Strategies

Product/corporate–based pricing strategies are based on financial requirements and corporate image. The advantage of product/corporate–based pricing strategies is the ease of administration. The disadvantage is the lack of customer input. Product/corporate–based pricing strategies include cost-plus, transportation, leadership, and list price.

Cost-Plus Pricing

Cost-plus pricing is perhaps the most common and easiest pricing methodology. The company determines what specific cost it bears to produce and distribute a product. Then the company determines how much beyond that cost it should charge in order

to achieve the strategic objective, perhaps a 10 percent net profit margin or a 4 percent increase in market share, and so on. The apparent simplicity of cost-plus pricing makes it appealing, but that simplicity can become illusory in practice. Pricing the product to cover costs plus an estimated return does not always maximize profits, as there may be additional profit potential allowances from customers.

For many products, the average unit cost can be expressed in terms of the fixed costs associated with developing the product, divided by the quantity of product to be sold, plus the variable costs for producing each unit. To produce a profit, the price of the product must be sufficient to cover the variable costs of the product, as well as cover the fixed costs until the entire quantity of the product is sold.

$$\text{Average unit cost} = \frac{\text{Fixed costs}}{\text{Quantity to be sold}} + \frac{\text{Variable cost}}{\text{Unit}}$$

An example of using average unit cost may be seen in pricing T-shirts for a fund-raising sale. The sellers want to be certain that the price for which the T-shirt sells is enough to at least cover all of their costs. So, if 100 T-shirts cost $7 each, and there are fixed costs of $300 for design and delivery, then the average unit price would be $300 ÷ 100 + $7 = $10. If 200 T-shirts can be sold, then the average cost would drop to $8.50. If the fund-raiser is estimated to sell 100 to 200 of the shirts, then it would be wise to price them after taking the higher cost estimate into account.

In some regulated industries, companies may not have a choice of pricing methodologies because prices for the product may be subject to regulatory approval. In industries such as these, target rate-of-return pricing, a variation on cost-plus pricing, often is employed. In target rate-of-return pricing, a government regulatory authority will determine what costs the regulated company bears and also will determine a reasonable target return on the company's capital investment. Prices are set or approved to permit recovery of costs, plus an additional fair or reasonable target return on investment. The target rate of return approved by the regulatory authorities is below the return the company would earn if it priced without regulatory intervention. In these industries, the regulatory process involved in changing rates can be lengthy and cumbersome. Examples of the rate-of-return method include many public utilities (especially electric power), although there are clear trends toward deregulation and greater market competition.

The major disadvantage of cost-plus pricing is the lack of concern with how customers perceive or value the product. In any transaction, price is an expression of the value of the transaction to both parties. In order for a sale to occur, the buyer must believe that the value of the product is equal to or greater than the price being charged. Similarly, the seller must believe that the price is enough to induce the seller to part with the good. Cost-plus pricing fails to recognize when customers are willing to pay more than cost for a product. Companies therefore might miss opportunities for additional revenue.

Transportation/Delivery Pricing

In transportation/delivery pricing there are two common pricing methodologies (assuming the same weight of the products to be delivered): uniform delivered pricing and geographic zone pricing. *Uniform delivered pricing* is one set price for a package or product to be delivered anywhere within a designated delivery zone. It is easy to administer and is easy for the customer to understand and budget. One example is a $3.95 shipping and handling fee attached to a shirt ordered from a catalog that ships anywhere in the United States. Another example is the 42-cent stamp that the U.S. Postal Service sells to deliver a letter to any state. Yet, customers who are paying for expensive flat rate delivery of heavy or bulky items to go only a short distance will probably not want to subsidize those who are paying the same fee for longer distance delivery. Hence, a *geographic zone delivery pricing* structure will be beneficial to customers by allowing them to pay for only the distance needed.

Price Leadership

In a variety of industries, one competitor typically initiates pricing actions, and then others make independent decisions to follow. For years, General Motors has led the domestic automobile industry in announcing annual price increases, and other competitors typically would follow with a comparable increase. In this situation, as is often the case, the biggest competitor led the pricing actions. Pricing leaders should anticipate how their competitors will react to pricing changes: whether the competitors will leave prices unchanged, match the price change, or perhaps charge even more. Anticipating competitive response is particularly important in markets where prices change frequently and are easily monitored by competitors, such as the paper and steel industries. The fact that a pricing leader must anticipate market response does not suggest an agreement with its competitors. Indeed, each competitor will use its own independent judgment as to whether to match a pricing action.

List Pricing

List pricing is the exact offered price suggested by the manufacturer. List prices are referred to by a number of different names in different industries, including manufacturers suggested retail prices, rack rates in the hotel industry, sticker prices, and structure fares in the airline industry. In many cases the list price is the selling price for a large number of customers. However, even when they do not reflect the final selling price for many companies, list prices can serve a useful function. A list price may be an establishing price from which other strategies may evolve. List prices can serve as a basis of comparison and provide a gauge of relative value among products to the consumer. Although few customers pay sticker price for a car, they know that they will pay more for a car with a $40,000 sticker price than a $20,000 sticker price. List prices also serve as a consistent basis for the supplier when applying discounts, particularly when there are many prices that require adjusting. For example, department stores may apply a 10 percent discount off the tagged price on all merchandise.

Market-Based Pricing Strategies

Market-based pricing strategies are based on what the customer is willing to pay. The advantage of market-based pricing strategies is that they are accepted by the consumer. The disadvantage is the time and cost of marketing research to determine the customers' desired prices. Market-based pricing strategies include competitive pricing, customer-derived pricing, price point pricing, auction pricing, barter pricing, and trial and error pricing.

Competitive Pricing

A popular pricing methodology is to simply maintain a competitive pricing strategy. In *competitive pricing*, companies follow the market and price their product equal to or competitive with the prices charged by their competitors (provided there is no agreement to do so as specified by the Sherman Antitrust Act). Pure competitive pricing is typical in markets for commodity goods and other items in which there is little, if any, brand or product differentiation. Gasoline is a good example of a commodity product where competitive pricing is commonplace.

Competitive pricing behavior can vary depending on the number of sellers in a market. Where the number of sellers is plentiful and there are few buyers, sellers have little option but to base their prices on the prevailing market price. This is the case for many types of bulk commodities, such as wheat, sugar, and crude oil. For example, although there are many thousands of farmers who have wheat to sell, nearly all wheat is purchased by a small number of food product companies through established commodity markets. Therefore, the farmer has little choice but to accept the market price.

Customer-Derived Pricing

Customer-derived pricing means determining how valued the product is by the customer and subsequently pricing the product as close to that value as possible. Customer-derived pricing allows the company to determine the price customers will pay and then engineer the product to a quality level that will satisfy both the customers' needs and the company's profit level. The challenge then becomes determining with some precision how potential buyers value your product and how that value compares to the price of competing products.

The way to determine how customers value a product is to ask them through marketing research or some form of sales bargaining. Companies that choose some form of customer-based pricing often turn the job of pricing over to the sales and marketing departments. These departments naturally have the most extensive customer knowledge and contact. However, they also typically have sales volume goals of their own. Discounting can always be used to keep customers happy and to achieve sales goals.

Price Point/Reference Pricing

Usually, consumers consider whether to make a purchase by comparing the value of the product or service to their income; then this perceived acceptable price becomes their *reference price*. Marketing research shows several points along a continuum of prices to be fairly consistent for many buyers. For example, there are several price points considered by consumers when searching for an automobile: $10,000 to $15,000, $15,000 to $20,000, $20,000 to $25,000, and over $25,000. The same thought process is used when buying a man's suit: $200, $300, $400, and over $400. Consumers will not stray too far from the price point where they are most comfortable.

Reference prices are generally based on past purchase behavior, pricing for similar or alternative products, and advertising. An example of reference pricing is Value Meals at McDonald's. People have become accustomed to paying $2.99 or $3.99 for a sandwich, French fries, and a drink. If customers were to walk in and see that same combination for $5.00, they would believe they were overpaying for the meal because of the reference price in their mind, despite the fact that $5.00 is still a fairly inexpensive lunch bill.

Auction Pricing

Another market-based pricing strategy is auction pricing. The goal of *auction pricing* is to achieve the highest price possible from one of the people or groups of people who have assembled at a particular location or via the Internet for the purpose of bidding on a particular item. The advantages of auction pricing are that it is quick and usually achieves a fair market value (the owner may establish a minimum bid). A disadvantage is that the final price achieved is the highest bid from an extremely limited market.

Barter Pricing

Bartering (also known as *countertrade*) is the exchange of goods or services for other goods or services without the use of money. Bartering also may be conducted for trade credits if done through a barter exchange. There are several reasons why people engage in barter activity, including a shortage of money, a lack of convertible currency (for international transactions), a surplus of product, a profitable alternative to liquidation, and the attempt to reduce the tax burden although most countries collect taxes on bartered transactions. The advantages of bartering are that it is easy to manage and can be implemented when the parties have product but not cash. The disadvantage is that barter relies on the negotiating skill level, and the amount "paid" by one side potentially can be inequitable. Barter was commonly used in the former Soviet republics in the early 1990s when they exchanged commodities such as oil for Western products such as wheat.

Trial-and-Error Pricing

Trial and error can be used effectively to determine the optimal price of a product in industries with frequent transactions, relatively low transaction costs, and timely data measuring the success of a pricing action. For example, the trading in a stock market or exchange reflects repeated attempts to raise or lower prices. The share price of a company or commodity is offered at a price and is adjusted regularly based on subsequent transactions.

Low-Price–Based Pricing Strategies

Low-price–based pricing strategies are based on the thought that there must be customers for whom price is the primary motivation for selecting a product or service. The advantages of low prices are typically a higher unit sales volume and repeat customer business. The disadvantages are the low margins and lower profitability. Low-price–based pricing strategies include penetration pricing, discount pricing, everyday low pricing, periodic sales pricing, bundling, and odd-number pricing.

Penetration Pricing

In *penetration pricing*, the seller sets a price low enough to quickly generate a large sales volume. Penetration pricing often is employed by manufacturers with large economies of scale. By pricing a product attractively, sales volume grows very quickly and variable cost economies of scale are realized. The success of this strategy depends on finding a price that achieves a sales volume where marginal costs decline dramatically (because of economies of scale), thereby improving the margin with lower unit costs.

Of course, all firms are subject to competitive pressures and may see their market share change depending on how competitive their prices are with other products. Penetration pricing works best when a company is the first in that particular market. Due to customer loyalty for the original product, the penetration strategy may prevent competitors from ever reaching the sales volumes necessary to achieve competitive costs or even attempting to enter the market.

Discount Pricing

List pricing is, in many instances, a starting point for discount strategies. Discount strategies may be used when companies want to continue to promote a suggested list price or when competition dictates a need to lower prices. There are many discount strategies employed, including:

- **Stimulating Trial.** Discounts are targeted at nonusers in the hopes of generating future loyal customers.
- **Price-Sensitive Customers.** Discounts are targeted at price-sensitive market segments (for example, seniors, families, students) while charging list price to less price-sensitive customers.
- **Competitive Matching.** Discount levels are adjusted by market/product line to meet competitive price offerings.
- **Supply-Demand Matching.** In industries with seasonal or other supply-demand imbalances, discounts are offered to stimulate demand and sales during typically low demand periods.

Everyday Low Pricing/Value Pricing

Frequent customers generally like the predictability and the reduced search costs of the low and stable everyday low pricing (ELP), also known as value pricing. Several major retailers have tried everyday low pricing with varying results. For example, in the fall of 1997, the major airlines experimented with a shift toward everyday low fares with excellent results.

Periodic Sales

Occasionally, retailers reduce prices, usually on a seasonal basis, in order to lure customers away from the competition. For example, retailers hold back-to-school or winter clearance sales. The deepest of the periodic sales typically offers a lower price than everyday low prices. Sales also could be fine-tuned to match supply and demand, whereas everyday low prices are typically adjusted on a less frequent basis. It also appears that Internet sales, or targeted promotions such as direct mail, may be taking the place of periodic sales from traditional retailers.

Bundling Pricing/Package Pricing

Price bundling, also known as *package pricing*, consists of offering several different goods or services combined at a single price that is lower than the prices of the items purchased separately. Typically, the goods and services are complementary to one another. Price bundling is offered to increase sales to buyers who may have reservations about purchasing products because the total price of the separate items is higher than they would like to spend.

Odd-Number Pricing

If a consumer can save on a number of small purchases, then it will eventually add up somewhere down the line as a worthwhile savings. If a company prices an item at $3.99 instead of $4.00, usually the $3 is emphasized and the consumer pays little attention to the 99 cents. A $9.99 lunch can have the perception of being far less than a $10.00 meal, psychologically almost a dollar less. Odd-number pricing recently was used in the luxury or high end of the pricing scale with great success. For example, Mercedes Benz introduced their C-class automobile at $29,900. The ads trumpeted "A Mercedes for under $30,000."

High-Price–Based Pricing Strategies

High-price–based pricing strategies are based on the thought that there must be enough customers who can afford a high price and for whom the product is in extremely high demand. The advantages of high-price–based pricing strategies are the higher profit margins and the perceived prestige. The disadvantage is the preclusion of a large percentage of the buying public. High-price–based pricing strategies include premium/prestige pricing, skimming pricing, and even-number pricing.

Premium/Prestige Pricing

Product or brand differentiation has a major impact on pricing decisions. Commodity products typically are priced at a market price because of the lack of differentiation between products. *Premium pricing* is the practice of pricing a product higher than competing products. The premium price differentiates higher-quality products or additional features, and capitalizes on those buyers who are willing to pay more for higher value. Not surprisingly, premium pricing is most often associated with luxury items and products having additional value. When premium pricing a product, the seller is making a trade-off between higher sales volumes with lower margins and lower sales volumes with higher margins. The seller tries to find the right point in that trade-off to maximize profits.

Consumers often equate high price with high quality under the assumption that only the best materials could drive the price of a product past its competition. This is true most of the time. For example, granite is a superior and more expensive alternative to laminates for kitchen countertops. Some prestige products, such as a designer tie or designer perfume, may have ingredients that cost roughly the same as a lower-priced product, but are worth the price to the buyer based on limited supply or an exclusive brand name.

Skimming Pricing

When a product is completely new or has many new features, sellers may adopt a skimming strategy. *Skimming* is the practice of initially pricing a product very high to capture the value that some buyers put on the new features or innovations. The price eventually is lowered once the seller is convinced that all of the consumers willing to pay the skim price have been reached. At the lower price, the potential market for the product grows, and additional sales are made as the price makes it attractive to a new segment of consumers. Many innovative products, such as calculators, computers, and patented medicines are introduced with a skimming pricing strategy.

Even-Number Pricing

Many customers are aware that the difference in odd-number pricing is, in many instances, only a penny or a dollar. These customers do not want to be bothered with the small numbers at the end of the main price number. Therefore, some companies catering to upscale clientele will use a less visually intrusive, simpler, and less manipulative even-number pricing. For example, upscale restaurants will price menu items in even numbers, such as Crab Soup $7 (instead of $6.99).

REVENUE MANAGEMENT

The art and science of selling the right product to the right customer at the right time for the right price is known as *revenue management* or *yield management*. The goal of revenue management is to manage demand forecasts and product supply and thus set pricing in order to generate optimal revenues.

Originally started in the airline industry, this practice subsequently has found uses in many industries including car rentals, hotels, railroads, and entertainment. Revenue management works best in industries displaying the following three characteristics:

- There are significant differences in price sensitivity among the different customer segments, and certain market segments are willing to buy early at a low price.
- The products being offered are of a perishable nature such as hotel rooms, airline seats, television advertising time, and even electrical power–generating capacity.

- Mechanisms exist to forecast demand for the various segments as well as mechanisms for controlling the availability of products under each segment.

Revenue management begins with forecasting demand for a product at a segment level. Users of revenue management segment their products based on the customers' demands. For example, car rental companies and hotel chains segment into weekday/weekends, length of stay, or peak/off-peak seasons. Radio stations segment their market for advertising time based on the time of day and the program popularity. Based on the demand forecast for each of these segments, a certain number of units of the product (for example, seats on a flight) are made available to each of these segments in order to maximize overall revenue.

PRICING—INTERNATIONAL
by NCR

The goal of multinational pricing is to provide competitive and profitable pricing strategies for a company's products and services. Multinational pricing generally does not require a unique pricing methodology. Companies still analyze competition, set a strategy, quantify cost, quantify the value provided, and set a price based on this information. However, in setting pricing strategies for many countries, there are numerous complexities. The primary considerations when developing a global pricing methodology are access to local market information, swings in country cost structure, currency management, and success measurement.

Access to Local Market Information

Competitive environments and cost structures change rapidly, and a company must be able to quickly assess these changes. A key component of global pricing is having a quick way to obtain local market information. This can be accomplished through a worldwide price database; a company's own intercompany infrastructure; or a global network of business experts to provide local market, cost, and regulatory information as needed.

Wide Cost Swings

There is a wide disparity in the cost structure of goods and services from country to country. This disparity is created by several factors, including labor rates, infrastructure, resource availability, and other overhead costs. The cost of labor is impacted by supply and demand and employment laws in each country. Infrastructure costs vary due to transportation availability and communication capability. In addition, marketing factors such as operation size and density of customer base also could affect cost.

The price of products and parts that must be exported will be impacted by export transfer pricing, value-added tax (VAT), freight, insurance, and duty. Many countries assess a value-added tax on goods or services sold within the country. Global pricing must be structured to ensure reclamation of VAT, freight, insurance, and duty.

The lowest infrastructure and labor rates generally are in emerging markets and the highest rates usually are in the Pacific Rim and Western Europe. For example, NCR's (formerly National Cash Register) facilities costs can vary by a factor of 10 from a low-cost to a high-cost country.

Currency Management

Traditionally, U.S. companies have priced products and services in U.S. dollars because this was considered to be the safest pricing practice. However, companies may miss opportunities for better profit margins through pricing in stronger local currencies. They also may lose sales if they insist on dollar-based pricing when competing against weaker currencies. A company may be able to avoid foreign exchange risk when pricing in any currency by purchasing currency futures at a designated exchange rate, but a company may have to pay a percentage of profit to do so.

Profitability/Success Measurement

The desired results of pricing structures must be determined before a company can analyze whether it has made appropriate pricing decisions. In global markets, some of the traditional financial measurements are not valid. For example, profit or loss can be more indicative of foreign exchange rates than management skill. Return on investment, return on assets, market share, employee productivity, and inventory measures can be misunderstood when taken out of the U.S. context. Local laws vary on profit repatriation (profits returned to the home country). Some countries may allow total repatriation of profits and others may require a large percentage to be reinvested in the local economy.

Global Pricing Methodology

The preferred pricing strategy for many companies is to provide pricing on a per country basis. This allows the company to appropriately align costs and revenues. However, setting prices regionally or on a worldwide basis also may be appropriate. Ideally, a company may be able to gather local pricing information from its network of contacts and then make central decisions such as what profit margin is acceptable for a given customer or a given volume of business. A company then can discount or apply a premium to the local prices and provide per country pricing unique to each customer.

Some customers may require flat pricing (one set international price) and be willing to pay an overall premium, in order to simplify their central budgeting and allocation processes. However, flat pricing does not allow companies to accurately match expenses to revenues, and can impact profit for a company's local operations. Also, a flat price should be set so that a profit is generated in the highest cost country, as many governments prohibit loss-generating pricing. They may view it as dumping or as a tax avoidance strategy. Setting a flat price to generate a profit in the highest cost country could inflate overall pricing.

Regional pricing often can be a good pricing compromise, because it allows countries to be grouped by cost structure and prices set per region. This could increase overall pricing at a slight premium compared with per country pricing, but can be much easier to administer.

by Papa John's International

Company: Papa John's Pizza
Case: Factors Affecting Pricing

Developing an effective pricing strategy is extremely important in order to achieve successful levels of sales and profits. In industries such as the pizza category, effective pricing is one of the most important elements of the marketing mix and key to overall performance. Marketers in the food service industry are faced with a number of factors in determining the price of their products.

Determining which pricing strategy to use at Papa John's can be a very delicate balancing act due to operating in a variety of markets with unique characteristics and a competitive landscape. In markets that are highly elastic or price sensitive, lowering prices can bring about an increase in sales and transactions. On the other hand, raising prices in our price-sensitive markets can result in decreased sales and transactions. Further, we've experienced sales growth in tandem with price increases in some markets. We have a mixture of markets that are marked by price inelasticity whereby increasing price adds to total sales, yet in some markets it has the opposite effect.

To help determine the elasticity in each market, we rely on a few basic ways to help us estimate the elasticity in pricing:

1. Run analytics on how sales and transactions have responded to price changes from a historical perspective.
2. Test different price scenarios in several markets.
3. Survey consumers on their perception of price scenarios.
4. Survey competitor's prices.

Cost Structure

Menu prices must be sufficient to cover fixed and variable costs and provide adequate profit. In the pizza delivery industry, we have food cost targets (includes the cost of food and packaging), and this enables us to target profit as a percentage of sales. Accordingly, our menu prices reflect this component, but we realize that this does not include the value that a consumer places on our products.

Value Pricing

With promotional value pricing, marketers attempt to drive sales by pricing products lower at the expense of realizing a higher food cost, in hopes of generating more profit by increasing transactions. Marketers at Papa John's, as in most industries, are often challenged to inject value into promotional offers while protecting margins. Occupying a high-quality position in the pizza industry, Papa John's is careful not to be overly aggressive in discounting our products. We have a long track record of being rewarded by our customers who are willing to pay reasonable prices for our great tasting, quality products. Realizing the need to offer value-pricing periodically, however, we recently tested the bundling of multiple pizzas for a special price such as 3 medium 3 topping pizzas for $7.00 each. This offer met consumers' needs, not only on value, but also variety. As a result, we increased sales, increased gross margin per transaction, increased traffic, and increased the average check spent by customers, all while providing value.

Competitive Pricing

Another factor that Papa John's considers in determining prices is the competitors' prices. Often companies set their prices to maintain a predetermined relationship with key competitors. Usually the category leader in an industry is regarded as the price leader. However, as the world's third largest pizza chain and a quality provider, Papa John's has been careful not to price below our primary competitors. Price is important in maintaining our quality position. Further, we look for ways to leverage our pricing due to our quality position with signature products that the competition cannot copy easily or quickly.

Summary

As Papa John's contemplates price changes, we examine the store sales volume in elastic and inelastic markets, the impact on margins, competitive considerations, and legal issues. We then construct a timetable for incorporating the changes to the advertising materials and communicating to our employees, and, ultimately to our customers.

PRICING – CASE STUDY

by International Paper

Company: International Paper
Case: Factors Affecting Pricing for Recycled Copier Paper

In 1962, Rachel Carson's book *Silent Spring* set off an alarm resulting in an effort to save the environment. The conservation of trees was brought to the forefront of environmental consciousness, thereby increasing demand among consumers for recycled paper. At that time there was no infrastructure to support recycling of office papers. Recycling drives focused on newspapers, magazines, and telephone books, but none of these materials are suitable for making copier paper. The available recycled paper fiber that was suitable for copier paper did not work well in the paper mills, nor did the finished goods made from it perform very well in office copiers. Consumers were unwilling to buy inferior products. The poor product performance of recycled copier paper lowered interest in the product category.

In the late 1980s, though, the claim that the number of landfills was decreasing was true in absolute numbers. However, actual landfill capacity provided by large, regional landfills was growing. Due to the cost of seeking alternative arrangements for trash disposal, recycling of paper products again made both financial and civic sense.

High-volume paper producers had to find equipment that would work in a very high speed and delicately balanced operation. Small changes in chemistry and paper fiber are enough to bring a large mill to a screeching halt. Processing machinery in the paper industry (washing tubs, agitators, ink

(Continued)

removal systems) is custom made, and the designs are usually proprietary. Therefore, the lead time to prepare to use a different fiber source (postconsumer waste) was between 18 and 24 months. Another mill design variable was the source of postconsumer fiber the mill would use. These were important considerations for any company that was looking at capital expenditures ranging from $5 million to as much as $100 million for companywide integration. These expenditures would affect the price of the recycled paper.

Paper manufacturers were caught between public policy interests and good business. Large consumer products and service companies wanted to print promotional materials and sales brochures on recycled paper and were willing to pay a small premium for that privilege. However, usage for this type of application was very small compared to overall consumption. Price and performance were and still are the driving factors on the majority of paper purchased and consumed by businesses. Companies said they were willing to pay a small (about 5 percent) premium for recycled products. Business consumers in the late 1980s believed that their purchases would shift to recycled products either voluntarily or through government mandate.

Paper manufacturers did not want to be perceived as being nonresponsive to this issue. Further, both governmental and private purchasers wanted to be seen as supporting the public agenda of being green. Mills proceeded with their engineering design firms to build additional equipment based on this premise despite the uncertainties of sources of raw materials and a known market. Investment decisions were based on the presumption of a sustained pricing premium of 5 to 10 percent above the standard virgin product. Since copier paper is treated like a marginally differentiated commodity, the industry did not create a new product category in the consumers' minds. Missing the opportunity to develop a new category was costly to the manufacturers.

The pricing strategy was a form of cost-plus, although the incremental cost was initially more than the market would bear. Manufacturers accepted this as a cost of entry into the recycled market, expecting that in the long term the incremental cost would be less than the premium associated with the product. Projections of the size of the recycled market varied from 25 to 50 percent of the entire copier paper market.

In the years 1991 to 1993 as manufacturing firms were in the design phase or the construction phase, end users were becoming stymied by a barrage of local laws concerning what was or was not recycled and what was or was not recyclable. Average firms did not want to become embroiled in a legal tangle, and, therefore, many decided being green carried unknown risks and decided to forgo such marketing concepts. This cold feet syndrome came at a point when paper manufacturers had already spent large sums on engineering and design fees.

Then, in 1990, an executive order issued by the first President Bush mandated use of recycled paper by federal governmental agencies, the largest purchaser of paper. This created a large enough demand for the paper industry to invest in a serious effort to provide recycled paper as a standard product. As the price differential declined, private industry soon followed. Some of the strongest pockets of demand in the commercial market are from companies in industries with perceived public images as spoilers of the environment, such as petroleum producers, who want to improve their image. Schools and universities typically are very aware of environmental issues and are major users of recycled products.[4]

CORPORATE PROFILES AND AUTHOR BIOGRAPHIES

UNITED AIRLINES

United Airlines is the largest air carrier in the world. Visit United Airlines at www.ual.com.

Greg Taylor

Greg Taylor, Vice President Revenue Management, is responsible for setting United's worldwide passenger fare levels and seat allocations and participates in setting the overall direction of various marketing and planning efforts. Mr. Taylor received his bachelors in Mathematics and MBA from the University of Chicago.

Additional contributing authors include:

Daryl Hultquist, Amit Khandelwal, Bob Merz, Todd McClusky, John Morrey, Diane Nachazel, and Jeffrey Erlich.

NCR CORPORATION

NCR Corporation (NYSE—NCR) is a global technology company leading how the world connects, interacts, and transacts with business. Visit NCR at www.ncr.com.

Roxanne Batterman

Roxanne Batterman was formerly the Marketing Director for NCR's Worldwide Retail Store Support Services responsible for managing NCR's portfolio of Retail Store support services, including the development and deployment of new service products. Ms. Batterman received her BA in International Studies from the University of Arkansas. She received her masters in International Business from the University of South Carolina.

PAPA JOHN'S

Papa John's (NASDAQ—PZZA) is now the world's third largest pizza company. Visit Papa John's at www.papajohns.com.

Mark Olive

Mark Olive is Vice President, Field Marketing. Mr. Olive received his BS from the University of Kentucky, Lexington.

INTERNATIONAL PAPER

International Paper is the world's largest paper and forest products company. Visit International Paper at www.internationalpaper.com.

David H. Easley

David Easley is Marketing Manager for Hammermill Brand Imaging Papers. Mr. Easley received his BA in Economics and Speech Communication from the University of Richmond.

NOTES

1. *Dictionary of Marketing Terms*, Peter D. Bennett (Chicago, IL: American Marketing Association, 1995).
2. Roger Maille, *Core Business Studies—Economics*, UK: Mitchell Beazely Publishers.
3. Ibid.
4. American Forest and Paper Association, RISI.

19 PRODUCT QUALITY

by Cargill, Ritz-Carlton, 3M, and Stoner Solutions

Several years ago, a U.S. company, seeking the promise of lower costs and higher quality, decided for the first time to purchase parts from a Japanese manufacturer. At the end of their negotiations, the company sent one of their standard purchase orders containing the provision that they would accept no more than 3 percent defective parts within any shipment. When the first shipment arrived, there were two boxes. A large one labeled PERFECT PARTS and a small one labeled DEFECTIVE PARTS. Also enclosed was a letter that stated:

"Gentlemen: Pursuant to our contract we are hereby delivering 97 percent perfect parts, as ordered, and 3 percent defective parts. We do not understand, however, why you want any defective parts. Producing defective parts increases our costs. Therefore, we propose shipping only perfect parts in the future and trust this will not unduly interfere with your normal policy."

American Folk Tale

THE ESSENTIALS OF QUALITY AND PERFORMANCE EXCELLENCE
by Cargill

Definitions

There are many definitions of quality. Casual use of the word frequently equates quality with terms such as expensive or good. According to Dr. Juran, author of the *Quality Control Handbook* in 1951 and awardee of The Order of the Sacred Treasure by Emperor Hirohito for the development of quality management in Japan, *quality* is defined as fitness for use, or how well the product or service accomplishes the desired goal. Dr. W. Edwards Deming, professor of physics and statistical studies at New York University and namesake of the Japanese Union of Scientists and Engineers annual corporate quality award, often observed that words

have little meaning unless they are used in context. An example of this point centers on cleaning a table. The definition of *clean* depends on the proposed use of the table. One degree of cleanliness would be suitable for repairing an engine, but would not be clean at all if the table were to be used for dining. Philip Crosby defined *quality* as "conformance to requirements" and counseled executives that "quality is free" if you account for the cost of doing things wrong and doing things over as the "price of nonconformance." Crosby spoke the executive language of money.

U.S. Congress Establishes National Criteria for Quality and Performance Excellence

In 1987, the U.S. Congress passed legislation authorizing a national award for quality and performance excellence. The idea at the time was to bring together the best minds on the subject of quality and write a set of criteria that would be used to evaluate organizations and to identify role models from whom other American companies could benchmark and learn. President Ronald Reagan was initially reluctant to sign the legislation as he opposed any actions that appeared to increase the size of government or its role in the economy. However, when his good friend and Commerce Secretary Malcolm Baldrige was killed in a rodeo accident, the sponsors of the bill went back to the President asking if he would sign the bill into law if it was named after his good friend. He agreed and since then, the United States has had a standard for organizations to use to assess and improve overall performance in key areas, including quality without being limited to that dimension. The Baldrige criteria provide a more holistic and strategic view of quality and have evolved significantly from the first set of criteria. Initially, processes to measure and improve product and service quality and to involve employees in the process were the primary focus areas. Today, challenges such as innovation, management, improvement of the entire supply chain, and customer engagement in the process are emphasized.

The Baldrige Criteria for Performance Excellence provide a systems perspective for understanding performance management. They reflect validated, leading-edge management practices against which an organization can measure itself. With their acceptance nationally and internationally as the model for performance excellence, the Criteria represent a common language for communication among organizations for sharing best practices. The Criteria are also the basis for the Malcolm Baldrige National Quality Award process.

Cargill has used the Baldrige Criteria to assess and improve the performance of its business units since 1991. Cargill has found this approach to quality far more strategic and impactful on overall performance than the more limited focus on product and service quality. Cargill calls this systematic approach to assessment and performance improvement Business Excellence. See Figure 19.1.

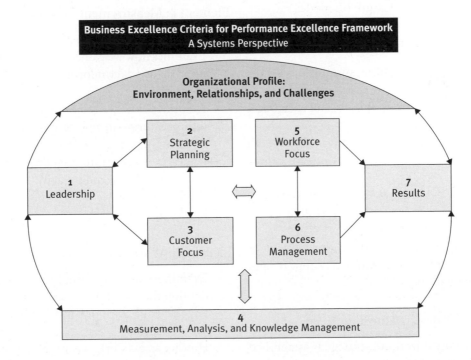

Source: Cargill.

Figure 19.1 Business Excellence Criteria for Performance Excellence Framework

BUSINESS EXCELLENCE CRITERIA

The Business Excellence Criteria provide a set of questions against which organizations can evaluate their management system. This evaluation provides transparency to the organization about areas where they have relative strengths and areas where they have gaps or opportunities for improvement. In the Cargill system, the decision as to which strengths to leverage or gaps to close is left to the leaders of the organization since they are closest to their strategic challenges and opportunities.

The Cargill BE Criteria, like the Baldrige Criteria, are divided into six areas that focus on process (or how the organization operates) and one section that focuses on the outcomes (or the results of the process work). In scoring in the BE process, half of the points are linked to process and half are linked to results. This balance puts a slightly heavier weight on results than the Baldrige process because we want to send the message that both are equally important.

Below is a short summary of each of the seven process elements in the Cargill BE model.

Element 1: Leadership

- How leadership's actions sustain the organization
- How leadership communicates and encourages high performance
- How talent management is advanced through connectivity and collaboration by senior leaders
- Examines the organization's governance system, approach to leadership, and fulfillment of corporate responsibilities
- How we identify key communities and areas of emphasis for organizational support and involvement

Element 2: Strategic Planning

- How the organization's strategy is established to address strategic challenges and leverage its strategic advantages
- Examines the organization's most important goals and strategic objectives and how these will address long-term sustainability and core competencies
- How the organization aligns its action plans with its strategic objectives
- How the organization identifies and compares key benchmarks, goals, past performance, and addresses current or projected gaps

Element 3: Customer Focus

- How we engage our customers for long-term marketplace success
- How we build a customer-focused culture
- How we leverage connectivity and collaboration in building customer relationships
- How we listen to the voice of our customer and use this information to improve and identify opportunities for innovation
- Examines how customer information is used to improve marketplace success

Element 4: Measurement, Analysis, and Knowledge Management

- Examines how we gather, analyze, manage, and improve our data, information, and knowledge assets
- Examines how we review and use reviews to improve our performance and respond rapidly to changing organizational needs and challenges in the operating environment, workforce capabilities, and capacity
- Examines how we build and manage our knowledge assets

Element 5: Workforce Focus

- Examines how we engage, manage, and develop the workforce to utilize its full potential and align with our mission, strategy, and action plans
- How we assess workforce capability and capacity needed to build a workforce of high performance

- How a safe, secure, and supportive work climate is maintained

Element 6: Process Management

- How our work systems are designed
- How our key processes are designed, managed, and improved in order to successfully implement work systems that deliver customer value, success, and sustainability
- Examines how our work system design prepares for potential emergencies

Element 7: Business Results

- Examines performance against Cargill's four key performance measures of engaged employees, satisfied customers, enriched communities, and profitable growth
- Examines performance and improvement in all key Baldrige Criteria areas: product outcomes, customer-focused outcomes, financial and market outcomes, workforce-focused outcomes, process effectiveness outcomes, and leadership outcomes
- Performance levels examined relative to those of competitors and other organizations with similar product offerings

CUSTOMER SATISFACTION

Customer Needs

Customer needs are determined by identifying customers, determining their expectations, determining their satisfaction levels, and forming engaged relationships. Customer engagement is a strategic action aimed at achieving such a degree of loyalty that the customer will advocate for your brand and product offerings. Achieving such loyalty requires a customer-focused culture in your workforce based on a thorough understanding of your business strategy and the behaviors and preferences of your customers. A relationship strategy may be possible with some customers but not with others. The relationship strategies you do have may need to be distinctly different for each customer, customer group, and market segment. They also may need to be distinctly different during various stages of the customer life cycle.

Identifying Customers

Customers can be defined as anyone who is touched by or touches the product or service. This implies that each product or service has many customers ranging from those who purchase and/or use the product to those who are affected by its use (such as the government purchase of a traffic light and the resulting general public's enhanced traffic safety). For a food company like Cargill, farmers are technically suppliers because we pay them for their grain, oilseeds, or livestock, but are referred to as customers and are treated as such because of their importance to the food supply chain.

Determining Customer Expectations

It often is thought that the key to the survival of any organization is its focus on its customers. Understanding their requirements, or knowing the voice of the customer, is perhaps the most vital step in producing quality goods and services. Customers' use of a product or service and their spoken and unspoken expectations and requirements are the ultimate determination of the value of a product or service.

Selection of voice-of-the-customer strategies depends on your organization's key business factors. Increasingly, organizations listen to the voice of the customer via multiple modes. Some frequently used modes include focus groups with key customers, close integration with key customers on project teams, interviews with lost and potential customers about their purchasing or relationship decisions, use of the customer complaint process to understand key product attributes, win-lose analysis relative to competitors and other organizations providing similar products, and survey or feedback information. These methods are used to systematically obtain actionable information from customers. Information that is actionable can be tied to key product offerings and business processes and can be used to determine cost and revenue implications for setting improvement goals and priorities for change.

In a rapidly changing technological, competitive, economic, and social environment, many factors may affect customer expectations and loyalty and your interface with customers in the marketplace. This makes it important to continually listen and learn. Customer quality expectations can be identified by three levels: basic quality, expected quality, and exciting quality. Quality expectations rise over time with product experience or usage. These levels of expectations were first described by Dr. Noriaki Kano, a professor of Management Science at the Science University of Tokyo, Japan, in what is now described as *the Kano Model*.

- **Basic Quality.** *Basic quality* is defined as the minimum set of expectations that the customer absolutely requires. Any lack in basic quality assures customer dissatisfaction. However, note that basic quality alone does not create customer satisfaction. An example of basic quality expectation in the grain industry in the 1980s and 1990s was to deliver corn that was within the specifications of "number 2 yellow corn" as defined by the industry. Grain that was not within this specification would be immediately discounted by the seller. Discounting of off-spec grain was a standard practice.
- **Expected Quality.** *Expected quality* is defined as expectations of quality that the customer knows and wants, but at a higher or improved level than is received in basic expectations. Expected quality provides a path toward customer satisfaction. The greater the amount of expected quality that is met by a particular product or service, the greater the degree of customer satisfaction. An example of expected quality in the grain industry was the improvement in segregation of grain to help reduce the amount of discounting (and subsequent formula adjustments) that were needed due to off-spec grain.
- **Exciting Quality.** *Exciting quality* is reserved for features that go well beyond a customer's expectations, to new and different features that provide an exciting experience. True customer satisfaction requires two or three exciting quality features in each product. An example of an

exciting quality in the grain industry was the ability to trace grain directly to the farm that produced it to ensure it was the precise quality of standard, organic, or genetically modified grain. Another exciting quality feature was the ability to improve the upside price potential for a farmer selling grain while reducing the downside risk. Risk management has become an increasingly important service relative to the purchase or sale of all food commodities as food has begun to compete with fuel in the world market creating substantial market price changes in short periods of time.

The difficult part about determining customer expectations is that they are constantly changing. What is an exciting quality level today can become expected quality tomorrow, and basic quality soon after. Thus, the Kano Model implies the necessity for continuously providing new and exciting product ideas and features in order to attain customer satisfaction. See Figure 19.2.

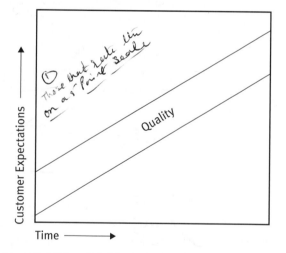

Source: Noriaki Kano, Nobuhiko Seraku, Fumio Takahashi, and Shinichi Tsuji. (1984). "Attractive Quality and Must-Be Quality." Translated by Glenn Mazur. *Hinshitsu 14*, no. 2. (February): 39–48. Tokyo: Japan Society for Quality Control.

Figure 19.2 Kano Model of Quality

Determining Customer Satisfaction

In determining customer satisfaction and dissatisfaction, a key aspect is their comparative satisfaction with competitors, competing or alternative offerings, and/or organizations providing similar products. Such information might be derived from your own comparative studies or from independent studies. The factors that lead to customer preference are important to the understanding of factors that drive markets and potentially affect longer-term competitiveness and organizational sustainability.

It is important to connect what customers say with their actions. Customer surveys have traditionally been used to collect information of this nature. The types of questions that should be asked to determine customer expectations include:

- What does the customer expect?
- How important is this expectation?
- How does the company's performance meet expectations?
- How does a competitor's performance meet the customer's expectations?

The results of these questions can be compared to an organization's own internal performance results, and actual customer repeat business can be measured to determine the accuracy of the survey results and to forecast future performance results.

Customer Relationships

Highly satisfied customers (those that rate the relationship as a 5 on a 5-point scale) are most likely to be loyal and engaged customers. Customer satisfaction, therefore, is closely tied to business success when the satisfaction is at the highest level. Even though many companies seek customer satisfaction data, few seem equipped to respond in ways that truly satisfy customers. A product or service problem followed by what the customer perceives as an "I don't care" attitude can cause the customer to seek a quick path to a competing company. To counteract this, many companies are focusing on methods by which their employees can provide greater customer satisfaction. For example, at Ritz-Carlton Hotels, all employees are instructed to immediately and personally take responsibility for providing guests with satisfaction for their concerns. Instructing guests to discuss a problem with the front desk is not an option.

MANAGING QUALITY WITHIN THE COMPANY

A major step in most quality improvement processes is involving management and employees across an organization. If a broad quality focus fails to exist, any quality gains will be difficult or even impossible to sustain. The key to sustaining a quality effort is to ensure it is not something extra or a "bolt on" to the organization's management approach. Quality or Business Excellence must be fully aligned and integrated with the management system of the organization in order for it to be sustained.

Leadership and Company Culture

Quality leadership must start at the top and be instilled in each successive layer of management. Leaders set the direction for the organization, what level of employee performance is expected, and what level of quality is expected. Successful leaders typically initiate through their words and follow through with their actions.

In recent employee surveys,[1] it was shown that the most common issue employees have with employers is not how much money they make, but rather a lack of communication within the firm. Management should promote a quality focus with their employees. For example, after senior leaders conduct their strategic planning, they must explain the plan to all employees—in person, and in small enough groups to encourage Q&A interaction whenever practical. In this way, all employees will be able to articulate how they fit and why they matter to the success of the organization. This is key to high employee engagement, which leads to high customer satisfaction and a sense of ownership of the reputation of the brand in the local community.

There are several things that make up the culture of an organization and impact quality and performance excellence, none of which may be overly important by themselves, but together, if done well and consistently, will allow an organization to excel.

Some internal components that influence the culture of an organization that management has the ability to change include:

- Vision, mission, and/or values statement (customer focus, a strong work and moral ethic)
- Clear strategy that every employee can understand
- Senior leaders' face-to-face communication with employees
- Senior leaders' active role in customer relationships
- Ethics discussions as a regular part of employee communications
- Assuring that employees have the training, education, and resources needed to do their job

There are external factors that management usually does not have the ability to change, but the following factors should be monitored for potential influence on the culture of the organization:

- Government regulations
- Competition
- Technology innovations
- Culture of the community

Positive customer reactions are signs that leadership has developed a culture of trust, respect, and responsibility among employees who are comfortable with each other. This company culture touches all customers who come in contact with the organization.

ESTABLISH QUALITY GUIDELINES

There are many well-respected quality methodologies to enhance an organization's quality program, including: Deming's Fourteen Points, Crosby's guidelines, Continuous Improvement, Six Sigma, Lean Manufacturing, and Benchmarking.

Deming's Fourteen Points for Managing Quality

Central to the quality improvement philosophy of Dr. W. Edwards Deming is the concept that it is management's duty to give employees meaningful work that provides them with a sense of pride and self-esteem. Attributing 85 percent of workplace problems, including quality problems, to conditions over which only management has control, Deming's Fourteen Points for Management charge organizational leadership with specific responsibilities that must be assumed if improvement is to follow.

DEMING'S FOURTEEN POINTS FOR MANAGING QUALITY

1. Create constancy of purpose toward improvement of product and service, with the aim of becoming competitive and staying in business, and providing jobs.
2. Adopt the new philosophy. We are in a new economic age. Western management must awaken to the challenge, must learn their responsibilities, and take on leadership for change.
3. Cease dependence on inspection to achieve quality. Eliminate the need for inspection on a mass basis by building quality into the product in the first place.
4. End the practice of awarding business on the basis of price tag. Instead, minimize total cost. Move toward a single supplier for any one item, and develop a long-term relationship of loyalty and trust.
5. Improve constantly and forever the system of production and service, to improve quality and productivity, and thus constantly improve costs.
6. Institute training on the job.
7. Institute leadership. The aim of supervision should be to help people and machines and gadgets do a better job. Supervision of management is in need of overhaul, as well as supervision of production workers.
8. Drive out fear, so that everyone may work effectively for the company.
9. Break down barriers between departments. People in research, design, sales, and production must work as a team, to foresee problems of production and use that may be encountered with the product or service.
10. Eliminate slogans, exhortations, and targets for the workforce asking for zero defects and new levels of productivity. Such exhortations only create adversarial relationships, because the bulk of the causes of low quality and low productivity usually are part of the system and thus lie beyond the power of the workforce.
11. Eliminate work standards (quotas) on the factory floor. Substitute leadership. Eliminate management by objective. Eliminate management by numbers and by numerical goals.

---

12. Remove barriers that rob the hourly worker of his or her right to pride of workmanship. The responsibility of supervisors must be changed from sheer numbers to quality. Remove barriers that rob people in management and in engineering of their right to pride of workmanship. This means abolishment of the annual or merit rating and of management by objective.
13. Institute a vigorous program of education and self-improvement.
14. Put everybody in the company to work to accomplish the transformation. The transformation is everybody's job.

Source: Dr. W. Edwards Deming, *Out of the Crisis,* MIT Press, 1986. Reprinted with permission of MIT Press.

Crosby's Quality Is Free

The "quality is free" concept, initiated by Philip Crosby, former Vice President of Worldwide Quality Operations for IT&T, contributed to a widespread awareness of quality principles and activities in the 1970s and 1980s. Crosby's premise was that, although quality was not actually free, it was usually less costly to an organization than a lack of quality in goods and services. The Crosby quality program focuses on preventing defects through individual employees conforming to certain requirements. Crosby asks management to transform the quality culture of the organization by creating an understanding by management and employees of the Four Absolutes of Quality.

CROSBY'S FOUR ABSOLUTES OF QUALITY

1. **Definition—(What is quality?)**
   Quality can be defined as conformance to specific requirements. This definition can be applied to any job, since all jobs must have requirements.
2. **System—(What prevention system will ensure quality?)**
   Prevention means eliminating the potential for error. It involves identifying opportunities for error and taking actions to eliminate those opportunities before a problem occurs. Prevention is different from appraisal. Appraisal requires that errors be found, evaluated, dispositioned, and corrected. Appraisal activities are not necessary with an effective prevention system in place.
3. **Performance Standard—(What performance standard will ensure quality?)**
   The standard that should be communicated to customers is that the product or service has "Zero Defects," the symbolic expression of "right the first time." When employees believe they have the option of not doing things right the first time, they do not take the necessary actions to improve.
4. **Measurement—(What measurement of quality is meaningful?)**
   The best way to measure quality is to calculate what it costs to do things wrong. This becomes a clearly understood measure: the money wasted due to rework, repair, reprocessing, and reconciliation. A method of measuring quality is the "Cost of Quality," which is made up of two parts: the price of nonconformance, which is the price paid for not doing the job right; plus the price of conformance, which is the price paid for making certain that requirements are met the first time.

Source: Philip B. Crosby, *Quality Is Free,* New York, McGraw-Hill, 1979. Reprinted with permission of McGraw-Hill Companies.

Continuous Improvement

Continuous improvement (CI) recognizes the philosophy that everything can be and should be improved. This concept is fundamental to quality and performance excellence. It is a process of ongoing improvement involving both management and employees and focuses on process and strives for total involvement as well as specific immediate results.

Continuous improvement can be integrated into the behaviors and eventually into the culture of an organization by systematically integrating CI tools within an overall assessment and improvement framework such as Business Excellence or Baldrige. Two tools that have been widely deployed over the past 15 years in the United States include Six Sigma and Lean Manufacturing.

Six Sigma

Six Sigma seeks to improve the quality of process outputs by identifying and removing the causes of defects (errors) and variation in manufacturing and business processes. It uses a set of quality tools including statistical methods, and creates a special infrastructure of people within the organization ("Black Belts," etc.) who are experts in these methods. Each Six Sigma project carried out within an organization follows a defined sequence of steps and has quantified financial targets (cost reduction or profit increase).

• *Sigma Levels*

Short-term sigma levels correspond to the following long-term DPMO (defects per million opportunities) values:

1 sigma =	690,000 DPMO =	31.0% efficiency
2 sigma =	308,000 DPMO =	69.2% efficiency
3 sigma =	66,800 DPMO =	93.32% efficiency
4 sigma =	6,210 DPMO =	99.379% efficiency
5 sigma =	230 DPMO =	99.977% efficiency
6 sigma =	3.4 DPMO =	99.9997% efficiency

These figures assume that the process mean will shift by 1.5 sigma toward the side with the critical specification limit some time after the initial study that determines the short-term sigma level. The figure given for 1 sigma, for example, assumes that the long-term process mean will be 0.5 sigma *beyond* the specification limit, rather than 1 sigma *within* it, as it was in the short-term study.

• *Six Sigma Methodology*

The basic method consists of the following five steps:

1. *Define* high-level project goals and the current process.
2. *Measure* key aspects of the current process and collect relevant data.
3. *Analyze* the data to verify cause-and-effect relationships. Determine what the relationships are and attempt to ensure that all factors have been considered.
4. *Improve* or optimize the process based on data analysis using techniques like design of experiments.
5. *Control* to ensure that any deviations from target are corrected before they result in defects. Set up pilot runs to establish process capability, move on to production, set up control mechanisms, and continuously monitor the process.

Lean Manufacturing

Lean manufacturing or lean production, which is often known simply as "Lean," is a production practice that considers the expenditure of resources for any goal—other than the creation of value for the end customer—to be wasteful, and thus a target for elimination. Working from the perspective of the customer who consumes a product or service, *value* is defined as any action or process that a customer would be willing to pay for. Basically, Lean is centered around creating more value with less work. Lean manufacturing is a generic process management philosophy derived mostly from the Toyota Production System (TPS) and identified as Lean only in the 1990s. It is renowned for its focus on reduction of the original Toyota seven wastes (delays, excess inventory, etc.) in order to improve overall customer value, but there are varying perspectives on how this is best achieved. The steady growth of Toyota, from a small company to the world's largest automaker, has focused attention on how it has achieved this.

Benchmarking

Benchmarking involves comparing a company's processes, products, and services against similar processes, products, and services of the world's best companies. Benchmarking is an attempt to discover the best practices used by any company. Benchmarking was popularized in the 1980s when U.S. companies, especially Xerox, found that Japanese competitors could sell a product in the United States for a profitable price below what the same product would cost to manufacture in the United States. The benchmarking process revealed that the advantage lay in more efficient designs, better processes, higher productivity, and less waste.

Benchmarking is not simply trying to copy a competitor's methods. It is comparing one company's processes, goals, and results against the similar processes, goals, and results of a world leader or best in class, and improving a company's process by adapting those ideas that make sense. Benchmarking also can be used to look outside a company's industry in order to identify and adapt breakthrough performances from other industries. Going outside an industry is usually easier, since proprietary information is less likely to be an issue.

1. Identify the goal.
2. Define internal company process and relative measures.
3. Determine what would like to be known about another company's similar process.
4. Identify other high-performing organizations to benchmark.
5. Solicit their cooperation for benchmarking and be willing to share internal processes and measures with the benchmark partner.
6. Conduct the benchmark study (by telephone, paper, or site visit survey).
7. Review and analyze the study results.
8. Incorporate what has been learned into process improvements.
9. Evaluate and improve the benchmark process itself.

QUALITY — INTERNATIONAL
by The Ritz-Carlton

International quality, like domestic quality, involves understanding the customers' requirements, executing them consistently, and constantly striving to improve and exceed customer expectations. As the world continues to flatten, most companies are operating as a global business, or at a minimum relying on services and products being provided from other countries. In the fast-growing business arena, leading companies commonly maintain core quality beliefs that unify their quality approach. The use of a framework to develop a system that drives performance excellence is also a great tool for an organization to assess its deployment internationally, as well as domestically. Many countries offer a performance excellence model. One framework that is available is the Baldrige Criteria for Performance Excellence (see Figure 19.3). The guardians of the excellence models from around the globe make up a group called GEM (Global Excellence Model), where they share best practices and work to align common principles. Each site, domestic and international, should follow the same criteria to establish the framework of the system. This process serves the purposes of keeping senior staff aware of how each site is doing with a common framework, allows

benchmarking between sites, and stresses the need for a common set of goals among the sites.

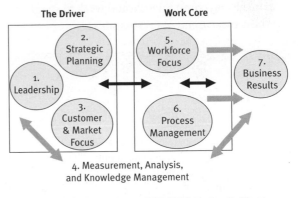

Source: NIST, U.S. Department of Commerce.

Figure 19.3 Baldrige Criteria for Performance Excellence Framework: A System Perspective

Although the core quality criteria remain the same, it is important that organizations understand and recognize that the driving forces of each part of the framework may vary based on geographic locations. Three primary drivers that will differ based on location are customers' requirements, process management ("how work gets done"), and local workforce culture.

Customer Requirement

The research of Dr. G. Clotaire Rapaille, the French researcher who developed techniques for applying cultural archetypes to product development, indicates that the meaning of quality varies with our cultural background. Companies should gather research on requirements and expectations before moving into a new market. Coca-Cola is an example of a company that studied its markets throughout the world, to identify the correct formulas for its Coke beverage that would satisfy the local customers in those markets.

Process Management

As industries have crossed international boundaries, there is a greater need for product and service consistency and a means of comparison. The ISO 9000 standard defines the framework for a basic quality process system. This approach originated in Europe and has spread throughout the world. Certain processes and measurements have been established as critical, and companies should work to standardize these measurements across sites.

ISO 9000 PRINCIPLES

1. Customer focus
2. Leadership
3. Involvement of people
4. Process approach to business activities
5. Systems approach to management
6. Continual improvement
7. Factual approach
8. Mutually beneficial supplier relationships

Source: ISO.

Workforce Culture

Although it is important that a company keep its overall culture that drives the success of its vision, it is equally important that senior leadership understand and embrace the local culture so that it can be incorporated into the greater company culture.

When The Ritz-Carlton opens a new hotel, a team of leaders is brought in from around the world to train on The Ritz-Carlton philosophy, as well as to train on processes. After the first international hotel opening, The Ritz-Carlton realized the need to train the opening trainers on the local culture of the new hotel site. The trainers were then able to effectively translate how to bring to life the company's philosophy including the motto of "ladies and gentlemen serving ladies and gentlemen."

Quality's fundamental principles are based on understanding the needs of both internal and external customers to drive performance excellence. By ensuring these requirements are understood, and by ensuring processes ("how work gets done") are designed to meet the requirements, an organization will build the foundation for success. As companies continue to expand globally, so too does the opportunity for benchmarking best practice, within one's own company. It is through the sharing and implementation of these best practices that a corporation can increase the global teamwork and achieve greater performance excellence.

QUALITY – CASE STUDY

by 3M Dental Products Division

Company: 3M Dental Products (3M ESPE)
Case: Quality Service and Customer Loyalty

3M is known throughout the world as a leader in innovation. Entry opportunities to new markets often present themselves by applying product solutions found in unrelated industries. 3M Dental was formed to service the dental market after combining two 3M technologies—polymers and ceramics—for use in the restoration of teeth using tooth-colored filling materials.

Manufacturers in the dental industry are faced with increasing competition from large and small competitors. This market turbulence caused 3M to reexamine its approach to marketing products to the dental profession.

The traditional market approach in the dental industry involves interaction among three groups: manufacturer, distributor, and dental professional. Manufacturers rely on distributors (dealers) for delivery of the products to the doctor/customer. In this approach the manufacturers' sales representatives have very little interaction with the dental professional, the end user of their product offering. 3M Dental felt that this detachment caused a reduced sense of service quality by the customer and a lack of feedback to the company that was needed for the development of new product solutions.

A customer focus approach to the marketplace is new to the dental industry. The shift toward enhancing the relationship with the end user involves total commitment within the organization. If improved sales strategies were developed within the organization to increase overall customer satisfaction and brand loyalty, customers would be likely to pay higher prices, use more products, and provide more detailed feedback.

Because previous sales were produced through a network of authorized distributors, 3M lacked the transactional data needed to determine which sales method would improve the quality of customer service. Four customer contact methods were tried: remote (customers serviced by inside reps), shared (customers serviced by field and inside reps), interactive (customers serviced through the Internet), and a control group (customers serviced by the existing distribution channels).

Field implementation of baseline and follow-up tests were applied by sales representatives. The Customer Program was divided into four phases:

Phase 1: Define customer/sales method segments.
Phase 2: Test the market to generate baseline measurements.
Phase 3: Execute sales activities.
Phase 4: Conduct postprogram measurements.

A database was developed to house all information on pre- and posttest data as well as the accumulated notes from field reports. Measurements were taken from the same participants to accurately measure movement over time. To determine customer satisfaction, dentists were asked questions for every product they used.

3M CUSTOMER QUESTIONNAIRE

1. Think of the last time you used (PRODUCT A). Overall, how satisfied are you with (PRODUCT A)?
   Would you say you are...
   5—Very satisfied
   4—Satisfied
   3—Neither satisfied nor dissatisfied
   2—Dissatisfied
   1—Very dissatisfied
2. How likely are you to recommend (PRODUCT A) to friends or associates?
   Would you say you would...
   5—Definitely recommend
   4—Probably recommend
   3—Undecided
   2—Probably not recommend
   1—Definitely not recommend
3. The next time you purchase (category of Product A), how likely are you to repurchase (PRODUCT A)?
   Would you say you are...
   5—Very likely
   4—Somewhat likely
   3—Undecided
   2—Somewhat unlikely
   1—Very unlikely

(Continued)

The satisfaction loyalty index survey provided information on product use, satisfaction, and the likelihood to recommend products. This information allowed the pilot program sales participants to determine which segments were most satisfied and therefore which selling methods worked best.

The overall hypothesis of using an integrated internal/external sales effort to increase satisfaction and loyalty was proven in this test program. There was significant movement in the shared versus control accounts. The change to a new sales method impacted overall satisfaction and loyalty as well as revenue generated for 3M.

QUALITY – CASE STUDY

by Stoner Solutions, Inc.

Company: Stoner
Case: Companywide Quality Program

Background

Stoner is a small family-owned business, located in Lancaster County, the heart of Pennsylvania Amish country. The company was founded more than 60 years ago by Paul Stoner, an orphan, chemist, and entrepreneur who started the business by making printing inks. In 1986, the company was purchased by Paul Stoner's grandson, Rob Ecklin, who repositioned the company for growth, and evolved the product line to several hundred specialized cleaners, lubricants, coatings, and car care products. Today, Stoner is the largest supplier in the United States of aerosol and bulk release agents for plastics and other molded materials. In other market segments, which include automotive, car care, and electronics cleaning, Stoner is a niche player, and highly competitive with much larger companies.

In 2003, Stoner was the smallest business ever to receive the Malcolm Baldrige National Quality Award. The award acknowledges the results of the combination of a highly effective business structure and a far-reaching corporate vision (to enjoy exceptional business results and personal fulfillment with a highly effective team that provides high value to lifetime customers).

Problem

Stoner needed to adopt the Baldrige principles to (1) effectively and efficiently transition the business from a family-run business to a professionally managed corporation, (2) continuously improve the organization, and (3) grow the business. Stoner's commitment to business excellence began in 1992.

A New Approach

Stoner president Rob Ecklin personally managed the company throughout the 1980s. Whereas Ecklin is still sole owner, in 1990, he empowered a six-member senior leadership team to manage the business. These hands-on leaders facilitate strategic planning, develop team processes, and mentor team members to implement the company's strategy. The company's core values are to exceed customer expectations; foster and develop a motivated team; be safety, health, and environmentally responsible; innovate new and better solutions; and continuously improve. These core values guide all aspects of Stoner's business culture.

- **Quality System.** At the heart of Stoner's success is the Stoner Excellence System, visualized as a pyramid with leadership at the top, supported by strategy and process. Stakeholder value has a prominent place in the center of the system and is surrounded by Assess, Improve, Implement—the company's simple but effective three-step process for continuous improvement. All Stoner employees, known as "team members," understand that continuous improvement is the key to sustaining competitive success, and all are focused on finding and implementing ways to remove waste and add value for customers.
- **Advisory Board.** Stoner's advisory board, which includes people outside the company, is another resource to help provide direction and focus to the strategic planning process and advice on high-priority improvements. The board helps evaluate risk, assess leadership effectiveness, and oversee financial and ethical governance.
- **Leadership Team.** The leadership team uses a scorecard called "Stoner 60" to set goals and measure business initiatives. This scorecard identifies 60 key measurements, linked goals, and strategic milestones for a five-year period. Senior leaders regularly monitor and discuss business results, compare them to the Stoner 60 goals, and develop improvement action items at weekly, monthly, and quarterly meetings. Stoner also uses an integrated key indicator database known as "Key 1" to collect, analyze, and deploy data to help in weekly decision making. The database helps to spot emerging trends that require corrective action or reallocation of resources.
- **Employee Investment.** New team members receive a multiweek orientation before starting their jobs. In addition to ethics and safety training, new team members spend one day shadowing every job in the company and have a personal meeting with the company president.
- **Customer Feedback.** Product managers meet with more than 100 customers per year and the sales team speaks by telephone with more than 1,000 customers each week to help define the company's direction, based on what the customers want or need.

Results

By focusing on quality, and through clearly articulated goals, missions, objectives, values, and beliefs, Stoner has achieved remarkable results. Results from a national industry survey showed that Stoner ranks first in satisfaction on four of the five factors most important to its customers: quality, delivery, service, and value. It is in the top quartile for the fifth factor: price.

- **Delivery.** 100 percent of orders are shipped on the same day they are received and shipping errors are less than 0.05 percent of all orders shipped.
- **Service.** Since 2000, Stoner has increased sales substantially, has won three times as many customers as it has lost, and over the past five years has retained more than 98 percent of its top customers. The company's detailed approach to continuous improvement also has led to a significant increase in Stoner's automotive market share for its glass cleaner, Invisible Glass®, gaining more than 15,000 retail outlets.

(Continued)

- **Environment.** As a chemical specialty company, Stoner is well aware of the impact its products can have on the environment. Moreover, one of the more attractive aspects of Stoner to consumers is its commitment to developing environmentally friendly products. Stoner has reduced the amount of hazardous chemicals used since 2000 by over 30 percent and its use of more environmentally friendly, water-based formulations has increased by over 70 percent.
- **Employee Satisfaction.** According to a survey conducted by the Hogan Center for Performance Excellence, Stoner scored in the top 10 percent of companies surveyed. Stoner team members are very satisfied with the content and quality of training they receive (83 percent vs. 72 percent for the survey average), believe that their company provides high-quality products and services (98 percent vs. 91 percent), and believe that management views quality as being at least as important as getting the work out (94 percent vs. 71 percent).
- **Financial.** Stoner has sustained consistent profitability that has grown along with its sales, fueling the company's improvement initiatives and growth. Manufacturing productivity has increased 150 percent. Stoner's 39 percent return on assets exceeds the industry average by 29 percent and its best competitor by 14 percent.

CORPORATE PROFILES AND AUTHOR BIOGRAPHIES

CARGILL

Cargill, founded in 1865, is an international producer and marketer of food, agricultural, financial, and industrial products and services. Visit Cargill at www.cargill.com.

Philip Forve

Philip Forve is Assistant Vice President, Cargill Business Excellence. He is responsible for leading the Business Excellence Team whose mission is to identify the strengths and opportunities for improvement of Cargill's various business units. Mr. Forve received his BA in International Economics from the University of California, Davis.

THE RITZ-CARLTON

The Ritz-Carlton Hotel Company, L.L.C., of Chevy Chase, Maryland, currently operates 72 hotels in the Americas, Europe, Asia, the Middle East, Africa, and the Caribbean. Visit The Ritz-Carlton at www.ritzcarlton.com.

Janet Crutchfield

Janet Crutchfield is Senior Director of Quality for The Ritz-Carlton Hotel Company, L.L.C. Ms. Crutchfield received her BS in Hospitality Administration from Florida State University.

STONER SOLUTIONS, INC.

Stoner, Inc., founded in 1942, is headquartered in Quarryville, Pennsylvania. In 2003, Stoner was the smallest business ever to receive the Malcolm Baldrige National Quality Award. Visit Stoner at www.StonerSolutions.com.

Rob Marchalonis

Rob Marchalonis is Chief Executive Officer of Stoner. Mr. Marchalonis received his BS in Electrical Engineering from Penn State. He joined Stoner in 1985 after employment with General Electric.

Harry Zechman

Harry Zechman is Chief Operating Officer of Stoner. Mr. Zechman received his BS in Chemical Engineering from the Pennsylvania State University. He received his MS in Agricultural Engineering from Michigan State University.

3M

3M is known throughout the world as a leader in innovation. The 3M Dental Division was created in 1964 with the introduction of a single product, and today manufactures and markets more than 1,300 products. Visit 3M at www.3M.com.

Timothy R. Kinsky

Timothy Kinsky is currently the Marketing Manager for 3M Dyneon. Mr. Kinsky received his BA in Environmental Science from State University of New York at Plattsburgh, New York.

NOTE

1. Standard and Associates of Chicago, Illinois.

Part 6
Supply Chain

20 SUPPLY CHAIN MANAGEMENT

by Procter & Gamble and McDonald's

THE ESSENTIALS OF THE SUPPLY CHAIN MANAGEMENT
by Procter & Gamble

Introduction

Supply chain management, also known as supply chain synchronization, supply network management, or channels of distribution coordination, is the element of marketing that takes an end-to-end perspective. Customers provide the essential demand signals and suppliers, manufacturers, wholesalers, and retailers respond. Customers determine their needs, then purchase accordingly, and the supply chain responds by determining which supply chain configuration best facilitates these needs. By improving the product flow to the customer and thus creating value for the customer, the supply chain is also often referred to as the value chain.

POTENTIAL SUPPLY CHAIN CONFIGURATION				
Supplier →	Manufacturer →	Wholesaler →	Retailer →	Customers
International Paper	Procter & Gamble	McKesson	Safeway	

Definition

Supply chain synchronization is defined as all activities involved in getting a product to market in order to efficiently match supply with demand. At every step, from raw materials to finished goods, the supply chain must ensure that the product meets the requirements of various customers and ultimate consumers as cost-effectively as possible. Consumers are the most critical part of a supply chain because they are the ultimate decision makers of consumption. The supply chain coordinates all of the participants, processes, materials, and information involved in getting a product to market.

SUPPLY CHAIN COMPONENTS

The supply chain has several components, including the participating companies, supply and demand processes, materials, infrastructure, and information.

Participating Companies

There are many participants in the supply chain. Each has particular service requirements, such as on-time delivery to the warehouse or product availability at the retail shelf.

Typical participants include:

- Suppliers of materials (International Paper for cardboard packaging and, more frequently today, global companies from Asia)
- Manufacturers of finished goods (Procter & Gamble for toothpaste)
- Wholesalers or distributors (McKesson, Supervalu)
- Retailers (Kmart, Safeway)
- Transportation providers (Schneider, UPS)

- Warehousing (EXEL, DSC)
- Other service companies (financing, computer services, backroom operations)

Supply and Demand Processes

There are two primary categories of processes: demand processes and supply processes. Each consists of numerous subprocesses.

Demand Processes

Demand promotion activities, category management, and tracking of customer demand must be coordinated with the supply chain in order for the supply chain members to be flexible and provide an adequate supply of products and services to meet the demand.

Supply Processes

Supply processes are aimed at fulfilling demand and include purchasing raw materials and components, forecasting inventory levels and materials planning, manufacturing, warehousing and distribution of finished goods, retail store operations, and reverse logistics. For example, in the supply process, one distributor may work closely with its suppliers to make sure that the supplier's cartons are not too big to handle or too heavy to stack. The distributor's planning also may take the retailers into account by placing labels on the cartons to match the retailers' scanning devices and packaging together stock keeping units (SKUs) that would be located near each other in the stores.

Materials

The manufacturing of any product requires raw materials. For example, toothpaste requires calcium carbonate, fluoride, and flavorings. The toothpaste also must be packaged, which requires tubes, caps, and boxes, and the tubes must be shipped in cartons to retailers who use pallets to move the cartons.

Infrastructure

Infrastructure includes all of the assets involved in moving products across the supply chain. Supply chain infrastructure consists of manufacturing, distribution assets, information technology, cash management, and support functions.

Manufacturing

Manufacturing utilizes an extended supply chain and a strategic selection of sites to manage costs. World-class manufacturing recognizes that costs can be lowered by carefully integrating with suppliers; utilizing third-party manufacturers; forging strategic alliances, including alliances with competitors; and leveraging best-in-class short cycle manufacturing capability to provide the desired supply network agility. Many companies operate their plants independently to serve local markets, and thus lose out on inherent economies of scale (sourcing leverage, tax burden minimization, and labor optimization). However, because of global demand, global branding, and harmonization of product formulas (such as toothpaste), many manufacturers may operate more effectively and efficiently from fewer strategic sites.

Distribution Assets

Distribution assets are the facilities in a supply chain that manage and move products, and can include warehousing, distribution centers, and transportation capabilities. An optimized supply infrastructure examines all of the distribution assets or facilities in a supply chain and determines which are the most effective in terms of time and cost. Optimizing supply infrastructure requires examining all of the distribution assets in the supply chain, not just those owned or managed by a single company.

As a result of this examination of cost/cash/service tradeoff, many companies have made drastic changes. For example, some consumer packaged goods companies have cut their network of distribution centers (DCs) from approximately 15 down to 3 or 4. Some progressive firms routinely share distribution infrastructure capacity and outsource selectively to third-party logistics providers in order to reduce costs. Other companies have begun to use the infrastructure assets of partners, such as wholesale distributors, or they are partnering with indirect noncompete companies. Thus, some companies are making infrastructure asset decisions based on supply chain synchronization.

Many firms will align their distribution asset level with their customer service objective. For example, a manufacturer that wants to provide customers in all major markets with next-day product delivery may have distribution centers in every major market or clustered in a way that enable them to reach the market within the service objective. This number of distribution centers may be more than the optimal number of warehouses required for minimizing transportation and distribution costs.

Information Technology

Information technology (IT) is a company's electronic data computing and voice communications system. IT can improve supply chain synchronization by enhancing the speed and accuracy of information flow. By automating and standardizing routine transactions across the supply chain, IT can dramatically improve efficiency through delivering information at the right time for optimal decision making and trade-off analysis in the supply system. This information is important because it can provide insight into key performance indicators needed for strategic decision making. IT facilitates the rapid sharing and analyzing of planning, production, purchasing, and sales information.

Three IT applications are the foundation of supply chain synchronization: Electronic Data Interchange (EDI), the data warehouse, and collaboration via Web-based models. Without these, more sophisticated supply chain integration and operating cost reductions are not normally possible.

Many transactional activities, such as mail, telephone, or fax, are routinely and instantaneously sent electronically throughout the supply chain via EDI or Extensible Markup Language (XML) with minimal human intervention on either end. EDI is a computer-to-computer exchange of business documents in a standard electronic format that can be sent, received, and processed quickly. For most supply chain participants, EDI has become a standard. Suppliers, manufacturers, distributors, and customers use transaction sets (standardized sets of information) to share demand information such as purchase orders and advance shipment notices.

Historically, companies utilized mainframe-based computer systems that were appropriate for individual functions, such as accounting or manufacturing, but did not facilitate sharing information. As a result, each business function had its own repository of data and was not coordinated with other functions across the organization. Now, data warehousing is the norm. Many companies are replacing these stand-alone and redundant systems with a single system used in all transactional and decision-making activities and supported by a common store of information. This intracompany data warehouse also is becoming intercompany, so that it is now accessible to supplier and/or partners and key customers to allow them to respond more quickly to disruptions in the supply chain and work on systemic improvement projects.

The Internet has allowed a greater opportunity for deeper and broader collaboration across the supply chain. For example, Collaborative Planning, Forecasting, and Replenishment (CPFR) is a joint business process enabled by the Internet that provides greater access to forecasts by all members of a supply chain. A manufacturer and a retailer can communicate a joint promotional plan to all interested departments, such as sales, marketing research, transportation, and finance, and update the plan regularly as the promotion unfolds, improving customer service and reducing total supply chain costs. It is also possible to link the electronic management or materials, formula cards, and operating plans with suppliers.

Support Functions

Supply chain synchronization requires an infrastructure of administrative support functions that stand outside the supply and demand processes. This infrastructure consists of finance, human resources, legal, and communications.

Information

All people and processes involved in the supply chain require information concerning demand, service, cost, and inventory.

- **Demand Information**. Includes consumer demand at the cash register, the retail store's demand for replenishment of finished goods, and the retail DC's demand for replenishment by the manufacturer or wholesaler.
- **Service Information**. Includes the speed with which a retailer requires a manufacturer to service an order. Service speed is measured from the time of order placement to the receipt of orders at the retailer's DC.
- **Cost Information**. Includes the fixed and variable costs of manufacturing, raw materials, infrastructure components, and inventory.
- **Inventory and Capacity Information**. Includes the amount of inventory at any point in the supply chain at any time and the available capacity to meet inventory and demand requirements.

FACTORS INFLUENCING SUPPLY CHAIN CONFIGURATION

The traditional business practice of manufacturing products and then aggressively marketing them to stimulate consumer demand no longer suffices. The business environment is becoming more competitive as technological changes, excess capacity, and market fragmentation escalate. There has also been a significant decline in the cost of capital to replicate efficient manufacturing processes while the life cycle for product innovation has continued to shrink, placing a premium on the efficient use of cash. The factors that affect supply chain configuration are customer demands, market forces, the balance of power within industries (supply chain leadership), and the timing of configuration needs.

Customer Demands

As consumers' demographics, economics, and lifestyles change, so do their needs and preferences. For example, slow population growth means slow growth in consumer demand and a more diverse population requires more diverse products. The supply chain must respond to these demands as efficiently as possible by offering a diverse selection to meet the value sweet spot of these consumer segments while still delivering a cost- and cash-efficient supply system.

Market Forces

Companies are, and will remain, buffeted by external market forces. Market forces impact decisions on infrastructure investment, outsourcing, and partnership choices. Market forces include volatile activity in capital markets that can make financing uncertain and risky. A few of these volatile activities are technology such as the Internet that reshapes ways to reach consumers, cultural movements such as environmental concerns, and international trade barriers that are being lifted and/or harmonized through initiatives such as the North American Free Trade Agreement (NAFTA) or the World Trade Organization (WTO).

Supply Chain Leadership

The balance of power, also known as supply chain leadership, among industries within the supply chain has shifted from manufacturers to retailers. Manufacturers formerly dictated pricing and distribution based on manufacturing needs. Today, retailers are best positioned to understand consumers and local markets, some products have become less differentiated, and competitive sourcing has increased with global trade. Retailers, or trade customers, have become more demanding in terms of lower cost; cash and/or service requirements, such as orders being delivered to their facilities on-time and complete; or replenishing their systems well within payment terms. Retailers, such as Wal-Mart, also have become more sophisticated in terms of business processes and technology, and require that their consumer product suppliers have a similar level of operating sophistication. Trade customers also look for value-added services, such as suppliers that place bar codes or radio frequency identification (RFID) tags on pallets and cases to facilitate material tracking in the retailer distribution network.

Timing Configuration Needs

In today's environment of constant change, the lead times for strategic implementation of new programs are shrinking. The companies that are able to implement first usually stand to gain strategic advantages over competitors. Thus, companies should grow and learn while implementing new supply chain strategies, rather than deferring implementation until a perfect strategy emerges.

SUPPLY CHAIN CONFIGURATIONS

A company has several options in determining a supply chain configuration, also known as a distribution channel, that its products will take to reach the end consumer. A company may choose any of the configurations discussed below based on the performance measurements and selection of partners.

Companies should assess the potential benefits and costs of forming specific supply chain configurations. The costs that should be evaluated include business processes, assets, technology, and human resources. *Business process costs* are the actual operating costs required to support the initiative (i.e., the costs for manufacturing, distribution, inventory, and overhead). *Asset costs* include both inventory and fixed assets, such as plants and distribution centers. *Technology costs* cover software, hardware, and implementation. *Human resources costs* are for training and meeting other people-related implementation requirements. Customer segmentation strategies also provide direction for decisions about which distribution channel a company should choose. For example, a manufacturer may change the mix of its retail versus wholesale sales based on costs and the strategic importance of one customer segment over another. A manufacturer may also seek to expand distribution through unique business channels not previously serviced, thus requiring new supply network configurations.

All of these options should be assessed against the consumer value equation—what system will deliver upon the value expectations of the product/service for the target audience. Doing so will keep positive tension on finding creative supply system solutions for how best to configure and design the supply network to meet these needs.

SUPPLY CHAIN CONFIGURATION OPTIONS

Business-to-Consumer

Suppliers → Manufacturer →   Consumer
Suppliers → Manufacturer → Wholesale → Consumer
Suppliers → Manufacturer → Retail → Consumer
Suppliers → Manufacturer → Wholesale → Retail → Consumer
Suppliers → Manufacturer → Intermediary/Broker → Wholesale → Retail → Consumers

Business-to-Business

Suppliers → Manufacturer →   Business
Suppliers → Manufacturer → Retail → Business
Suppliers → Manufacturer → Wholesale → Business
Suppliers → Manufacturer → Wholesale → Retail → Business
Suppliers → Manufacturer → Intermediary/Broker → Business
Suppliers → Manufacturer → Intermediary/Broker → Wholesale → Business

---

Advantages/Disadvantages of Supply Chain Configuration Options

Marketers may choose a supply chain configuration that requires synchronizing with partners or choose a direct to customer chain. The more partners the longer the chain; the fewer partners the shorter the chain.

Advantages of a Long Supply Chain

Supply chain synchronization with distribution partners provides important benefits to all participants including:

- Increased sales by delivering better customer service, such as the service expertise provided by a specialized team member, shortening lead times, and improving fill rates (orders completed) for customers' orders
- Operational cost savings from lowering costs for procurement, plant operations, transportation, and inventory
- Improved asset utilization and capital deployment from optimizing manufacturing capacity, reducing inventory, and making manufacturing more efficient

For example, Procter & Gamble (P&G) implemented a vendor-managed inventory program with the Kroger grocery chain for Pampers™, Luvs™, and Always™. P&G offered net pricing, which reflected a lowered price by netting out promotional allowances. In return, Kroger offered everyday low pricing below its competitors' prices rather than periodic promotional sales. Kroger provided P&G with daily information on product withdrawals (shipments) from the Kroger distribution centers (DCs). P&G used this information from Kroger to provide DC replenishment. As a result, Kroger's inventory levels fell from 12 weeks to under 1 week, and P&G's sales volume increased because of low pricing. Overall customer savings amounted to over $1 per case, which is a significant amount given the thin profit margins of grocery retail. More importantly, the supply chain was configured to deliver a better value equation to the consumer.

Disadvantages of a Long Supply Chain

The disadvantages of a long supply chain with distribution partners include:

- Less competition for the consumer in the marketplace overall
- Organizational reliance on other companies
- Management time spent on coordinating efforts
- Need to share sensitive information
- Less potential profit through price concessions
- Conflicts with dual or multiple distribution partners
- Issues with bringing innovation to market efficiently and quickly to meet consumer expectations
- Inability to meet the demand signal resulting in out of stocks at the retail store

Advantages of a Short Supply Chain

The advantages of a direct-to-customer supply chain include:

- Maintenance of organizational control over marketing mix
- Direct contact with customers
- Possible enhanced profitability by not lowering prices
- Exclusivity of company information

- Revenue enhancement from bringing new products to market faster
- Opportunity to exploit upside growth potential through supply network agility

Disadvantages of a Short Supply Chain

The disadvantages of a direct-to-customer supply chain include:

- No economies of scale in marketing communications
- Management time diluted on noncore competencies

SUPPLY CHAIN SYNCHRONIZING STRATEGIES

If a long supply chain is selected, then delivering value to end consumers requires close collaborative management or synchronization of both the core supply processes and the demand processes across the supply chain. This helps optimize each supply chain partners' combined effectiveness.

The supply processes include product, inventory, transportation, and sales planning. An example of supply process synchronizing is how Kraft Foods studied the demographics of each neighborhood where its products are sold to predict sales in each supply chain partners' stores. This demographic information provided critical input to Kraft's planning process and enabled Kraft to ensure that its products were available so consumers could buy them.

The demand processes include category management, promotional elements, and services such as credit, order entry, billing and collection, dispute resolution, promotion management, and coordination of special promotional shipments. An example of demand process synchronization is how a manufacturer of diet food products worked closely with retailers to develop demand promotions and then arranged special shipments of the promoted products to ensure their availability throughout the promotion.

Effective management of supply chain synchronization requires a comprehensive approach focused on understanding and mapping shared processes to look for improvement opportunities, selecting the correct supply chain partners, and integrating the new partners.

Shared Processes

In supply chain synchronization, a company should be internally prepared for the changes brought on by the supply chain integration process. Shared processes include planning and services.

Shared Planning

Historically, companies have utilized supply and demand planning methods that examine individual business functions (manufacturing, finance, marketing, sales, etc.), each with its own forecast and all usually having different outcomes. Today, many companies are eager to follow one plan, such as that produced by CPFR, and eliminate the inherent conflict created by multiple predictions of the same event. By adopting a combined supply and demand, or sales and operations planning process, only one business function administers the forecasting process, with all functions having input into the final product. This cross-organizational approach produces a one-number forecast that is then shared with all external members of the supply chain.

In addition, shared planning (through the use of the Internet, CPFR, and EDI) helps to eliminate large swings in the variability of demand known as the bullwhip effect. For example, the normal demand for toothpaste is relatively steady and nonseasonal. Replenishment of toothpaste stocks in retail stores traditionally has been triggered by periodic sale pricing or discounts for bulk purchases. Then, orders from the warehousing or distribution centers to the manufacturers would be based on a similar format and thus exacerbate the need for large inventories at the manufacturer (creating a bullwhip effect at the end of the procurement chain). By reading demand signals at the consumer end and sharing the plans for constant replenishment, expensive inventory levels are decreased.

Shared Services

In the optimal supply chain configuration, companies eliminate supply chain redundancies by consolidating and sharing support functions, such as distribution and customer service, across product lines. For example, one health-care supply company created an internally centralized service division to handle several supply chain activities.

Supply Chain Partner Selection

Most of the risks associated with supply chain synchronization are difficult to assess because initiatives require a continuous process of reshaping relationships with both customers and suppliers. Companies should select their synchronization partners carefully because not every supply chain partner is suited to the demands of synchronization. Supply chain synchronization often requires shifting from transactional relationships to interactive or interdependent relationships. *Transactional relationships* involve little sharing of information or decision making whereas *interactive relationships* require information sharing, some joint planning, and some asset sharing. Retailers can only effectively partner with a limited number of manufacturers, so it is critical for the manufacturer to offer intellectual capital to the retailer that is not available from others.

Performance measurements are an important element in the selection of, and the continuous monitoring of, supply chain partners. An example is the implementation of a vendor-managed inventory (VMI) program in which the manufacturer monitors the inventory level of its product at a retailer's DC. When the inventory falls to a certain level, the manufacturer must generate a replenishment order on behalf of the retailer and ship products to the retailer's DC before inventory dips below the safety level. For this synchronization program to work well, the manufacturer and retailer must agree on service performance measurements or requirements, This synchronization program now extends to the suppliers of raw materials and packaging components for the manufacturers' products, by sharing data on actual demand and production schedules.

Integrating Supply Chain Partners

Strategic alliances, also called partnering or teaming, can take many forms. Partnering strategies enable a company to maintain their focus on critical process areas and to obtain price and product sales advantages. In addition, a strategic alliance can leverage others' economies of scale, capture comparative advantage, free up capital, and unburden resources. For example, Apple Computers outsourced all product delivery and order fulfillment activities to Skyway (a logistics company), thereby freeing up Apple to focus on its core competencies of computer development while taking advantage of Skyway's logistics expertise.

In another example, Procter & Gamble employs teaming extensively in its sales organization to ensure market penetration and to increase its market share in the highly competitive grocery industry, such as P&G's teaming strategy with Kroger, and mass merchant channels, such as P&G's teaming strategy with Wal-Mart. At P&G, account teams represent several product lines and develop and execute selling strategies targeted at the key account level. P&G account teams also include resources in finance, logistics, marketing, and analytics to partner with the same function at the retailer.

Effective supply chain synchronization should balance supply chain partner requirements with individual company growth and profitability targets. Success depends on thoroughly understanding partner needs and segmentation strategies so that supply chain partners can be grouped by similar service requirements. Each supply chain partner has a unique merchandising orientation that requires tailored service strategies and operational capabilities.

A company's approach to strategic sourcing should provide for a predictable supply of materials and a reduction in the total cost of materials and services. The approach should be dictated by what is being purchased and the competitiveness of the market. The lack of a sourcing strategy can lead a company to focus on price alone. For a growing number of unique or differentiated product components, protecting supply, not obtaining the lowest price, is of paramount concern.

After selecting a supplier source/partner, a company must successfully integrate the supplier into its own operations in order to create a true end-to-end supply chain enterprise. The most prevalent integration method is information sharing, including real-time forecasts; raw materials and work-in-progress inventories; production schedules; and certified, preinspected shipments. Some manufacturers have established *gain-sharing initiatives*. This means the benefits of collaborative efforts to reduce overall costs and improve service and quality are shared equitably between the manufacturer and supplier.

EVOLUTION OF SUPPLY CHAIN MANAGEMENT

Over the past several decades, supply chain management has grown in sophistication. In the 1970s, management sought to maximize the performance of individual functions, such as manufacturing and sales, with little attention to functional interdependencies. In the 1980s, the walls between functions began to erode, as cross-functional integration increased within the organization combining sales, manufacturing, and distribution. By the 1990s, integration across companies produced tangible results. For example, in 1992, manufacturers, distributors, and retailers launched an initiative to improve the efficiency of the supply chain. This initiative was called efficient consumer response (ECR) and included:

- Continuous replenishment of retailer distribution centers (DCs) through vendor-managed inventory
- Automated handling of item maintenance, price changes, promotion announcements, invoices, and payments through Electronic Data Interchange (EDI)
- The use of standard bar coding to facilitate tracking of materials and goods across the supply chain

- Automatic reordering at the store level based on accurate scan data collected by the cash register at point of sale (POS)
- Efficient assortment, promotion, and new product introduction

In the 2000s, the industry is focusing on an initiative called "New Ways of Working Together." This initiative is being led by Wegmans, P&G, Oracle, and Smuckers and has recruited numerous other retailers and manufacturers to participate. The objective of the initiative is to eliminate supply chain disruptions and enable growth through four key planks:

- **Focus on the Consumer.** Strategy alignment, joint long-term planning, innovation
- **Connect Business Information.** Common goals and measures, information sharing, ePC (electronic product code via RFID technology), and data synchronization
- **Prepare People for the New World.** Build knowledge, skills and capabilities, create incentives and rewards, revamp organization design
- **Share Our Supply Chain.** Sustainability efforts, cross-industry integration, and development of an integrated supply chain

REVERSE LOGISTICS

Reverse logistics (often referred to simplistically as *recycling*) is an organization's retrieval and management of material resources obtained from customers, retailers, or waste collectors. Reverse logistics includes the coordination of processes to ensure effective utilization of products and materials throughout their entire life cycle. These resources can include materials, packaging, or out-of-date or damaged products (known as unsalables by retailers). Companies are beginning to develop the appropriate systems designed to gain maximum value from the returned products and materials at minimum cost.

Reverse logistics encompasses any of six different processes. Upon receipt of the returned product, the product may be

1. Refurbished
2. Repaired
3. Reused
4. Resold
5. Recycled
6. Scrapped to a landfill or incinerator

REVERSE LOGISTICS

Suppliers ← Manufacturer ← Wholesale ← Retail ← Customers

Companies should configure a physical network to facilitate these processes. Two main systems are available to manage reverse logistics: closed loop and open loop. Many companies will use both to maximize the life and value of their assets.

- **Closed Loop System**. Occurs when used materials are returned and processed by the producer. The closed loop system makes use of the returned product, any of its elements, or any reusable parts of the product. A traditional use of a closed loop system is the refurbishment of spare parts for machines or other capital items.
- **Open Loop System**. Occurs when used materials and products are collected by the originator, but processed by other parties. A traditional use of an open loop system is the processing of secondary packaging via paper and plastic recyclers.

Companies are incorporating the concept of reverse logistics into their strategic agenda due to: government legislation/environmental issues, shortening product life cycles, new channels of distribution, shifting power in the supply chain, and economics. Currently, many manufacturers provide retailers with an adjustable rate allowance for unsaleables, and the retailer is responsible for disposing of the product.

Government Legislation

Government legislation (particularly legislation on environmental issues) throughout the industrialized world is effectively forcing companies to take lifelong responsibility for the products they create. The increasing trend of consumer concerns over environmental issues, such as global warming and increased pollution, will advance this trend. Initial legislative efforts may be just the beginning, as governments continue to force companies to change the way they develop and manage their products through waste disposal. Many firms are not waiting for legislative initiatives. Instead, they are proactively preparing for the next generation of environmental legislation by reexamining their responsibilities and opportunities in relation to the products they make.

Shortening Product Life Cycles

This phenomenon is evident everywhere in industry, and is most visible in the personal computer industry. Shorter product life cycles provide consumer benefits such as greater choice and performance. However, this trend also results in obsolete but still usable products, such as an unwanted computer, which results in more packaging, more returns, and more waste. Shortened product life cycles have increased the volume of waste entering reverse logistics systems, as well as the costs of managing this waste.

New Channels of Distribution

New distribution channels are being developed to provide consumers with easier and quicker ways to buy. For example, consumer direct channels (such as catalog and Internet sales) facilitate the delivery of goods directly to consumers. However, direct channels increase the likelihood of returned products when items are damaged in transit, or they simply do not appeal to the consumer in a real (rather than virtual) state. Where the average retailer can expect returns between 5 and 10 percent of product sales, those selling through catalogs and directly to consumers can expect up to 35 percent of the products purchased to be sent back.

Shifting Power through the Supply Chain

Increased competition and a larger supply base mean buyers now have more power in the supply chain. Retailers can, and do, refuse responsibility for the burden of disposing of unsold products and unnecessary packaging. Most product returns to retailers are taken back by the original suppliers for rework or disposal.

Economics

As the above factors become more commonplace, and the cost of raw materials continues to increase, it will become more economical to reuse and recycle than to use virgin materials.

SUPPLY CHAIN MANAGEMENT— INTERNATIONAL
by McDonald's

Many companies' objectives in international marketing are to provide customers with quality, consistency, and value. It is a lot more difficult than it sounds. In order to support this effort, companies build and manage an international supply chain. For example, McDonald's manages a supply chain that provides products such as hamburger meat, shake machines, and outdoor signs to 31,000 restaurants in 118 countries. In order to meet these objectives, not the least of which for McDonald's is serving 56 million customers every day, the management of supply chains in international countries must assure that products are delivered on time, established quality standards are consistently met, and mutually agreeable pricing and payment arrangements are in place. These objectives are achieved in different countries whatever the language, culture, infrastructure, legal system, financial capabilities, and supply chain partner business capabilities.

Language

Different languages will affect how supply chain management is conducted. It is important to use common business terms or the least complicated expressions in describing business requirements rather than vernacular from either the home or host country. The local markets know their cultures, customs, and customers far better than a corporate headquarters can. For example, one of the true strengths of McDonald's is our teams of local men and women adroitly managing their businesses in their own countries.

Culture

Understanding the culture of a different country is a key to success in supply chain management. For example, in certain cultures, such as the Middle East and Asia, it is an accepted practice to continually keep negotiating a deal, such as a payment arrangement, even though an agreement already has been reached, in the spirit of ensuring that it is the best deal possible. This is a tremendous contrast to practices in the United States where striking a deal means it is considered final and both parties agree to satisfy their requirements. In another example concerning product selection and supplier capabilities, McDonald's adopted beef-free menus in the Indian market, Halal menus in Muslim countries, and kosher menus in Israel. It is important to find suppliers that can conform to each separate product requirement.

Infrastructure

A company's supply chain relies upon a country's infrastructure to carry out its requirements to the company. This infrastructure, including the banking system, public mail, and transportation networks (road, rail, ports, and airports), allows the smooth transportation of goods and information from supplier to consumer. A reliable infrastructure is only now being developed in a number of countries. A company that is considering conducting business and establishing a supply chain should first determine the quality of the infrastructure in any country. This is best done through research and evaluation on-site.

For example, one of the major infrastructure issues considered before McDonald's enters a new country is the quality of its agricultural industry. In many cases McDonald's helps introduce new strains of potatoes or assists in making cattle husbandry improvements within the country long before the company is ready to build its first restaurant. When McDonald's entered the Russian market more than 17 years ago, it built a $50 million food processing center called the "McKomplex" to make certain that quality control, product distribution, and food management were under one high-standards roof.

As technology races ahead and the pace of change quickens for global brands, companies should leverage new efficiencies to enhance savings and continued competitive advantages. For example, McDonald's benefits from longtime, proven suppliers who are nimble, highly trusted, and deeply experienced to keep us ready for changing customer trends. McDonald's now serves more chicken than any other brand in the world. This kind of consumer demand and the ability to meet it requires an aligned system of suppliers, operators, and both local and corporate management functions working together to meet these consumer needs.

Legal and Financial Systems

The legal requirements for conducting business among the many partners in the supply chain are extremely important and vary considerably by country. Despite handshake agreements between partners, many countries require an extraordinarily large number of minor documents in order to conduct business. Legal research on these requirements is imperative. Multigovernmental agreements (EU, NAFTA, etc.) make this process more accommodating.

When selecting supply chain partners, where the potential suppliers, manufacturers, wholesalers, and retailers might each be located in a different country, the method of payment, currency convertibility and fluctuations, tariffs, and the ability to take profits out of a country are important considerations.

Supply Chain Partners

Each of the supply chain partners should be researched for product quality, service dependability, and financial capabilities. Once this is completed, an approved list can be finalized and business can be conducted. Having several partners for each need is important due to potential shortages and disruptions that occur on a global basis because of weather, insurgency, political changes, and altering business practices.

Companies should select supply chain partners large and flexible enough to have capabilities to meet current and future supply needs. Therefore, a company can quickly expand into new countries if demand warrants. A recommended strategy to shorten the supply chain development cycle is to use existing partners. Selection of local partners should be through trusted contacts, such as banks, business associations, and government agencies.

CORPORATE PROFILES AND AUTHOR BIOGRAPHIES

PROCTER & GAMBLE
Procter & Gamble markets more than 300 brands to consumers in over 180 countries, and is consistently recognized as one of the top manufacturers with an excellent supply chain by various industry entities. Visit Procter & Gamble at www.pg.com.

Ralph Drayer
Ralph Drayer was previously Chief Logistics Officer, Procter & Gamble. During his 32 years with P&G, Mr. Drayer held a number of distribution, logistics, customer service, and customer business develop-

ment responsibilities, both domestically and internationally. He received his BSBA from the University of Richmond. He is currently Chairman of Supply Chain Insights in Cincinnati, Ohio.

McDONALD'S
McDonald's is the leading food organization in the world. Visit McDonalds at www.mcdonalds.com.

Doug Goare
Doug Goare is the Corporate Senior Vice President of Worldwide Supply Chain for McDonald's Corporation. Mr. Goare is

responsible for McDonald's $20 billon purchasing spend and worldwide purchasing strategy. He received his BBA in Business Administration from Ohio State University and is a nonpracticing CPA registered in the state of Ohio.

21 WHOLESALING

by McKesson Corporation, Ingram Micro, SUPERVALU, and United Stationers

THE ESSENTIALS OF WHOLESALING
by McKesson Corporation

Introduction

The wholesale industry has become an extremely diversified industry, selling virtually every type of product, from potato chips to computer chips. Large manufacturing and retailing companies require that wholesaler-distributors provide them with the necessary products, financial resources, and sophisticated information technology to address the needs of their larger, more demanding customers. This necessitated consolidation among wholesaler-distributors and has transformed their overall profile from small, regional, specialized companies into large, national networks. Technology and process innovation have helped manage these changes and have created opportunities for wholesaler-distributors to provide more than the traditional sorting and sales capabilities. In addition to selling products, wholesaler-distributors now provide value-added services and technologies that improve the efficiencies of moving products through the supply chain, from manufacturer to wholesaler to retailer and ultimately to the end user.

SUPPLY CHAIN CONFIGURATION

Manufacturer → Wholesaler → Retailer → Customers

Definition

A *wholesaler* is "a merchant establishment operated by a concern that is primarily engaged in buying, taking title to, usually storing, and physically handling goods in large quantities and reselling the goods usually in smaller quantities to retailers or to industrial or business users."[1] *Wholesaling* is the element of marketing that simplifies the buying and selling process for both manufacturers and retailers by serving as an intermediate single point of contact. Wholesalers also are known as *wholesaler-distributors*. For manufacturers, wholesalers act as a conduit through which products reach a broad base of retailers quickly, efficiently, and cost-effectively. For retailers, wholesalers serve as an immediate, centralized supplier of competitively priced products, and eliminate the need to invest in inventory and warehouse management processes.

GOALS OF WHOLESALING

Wholesalers reduce the number of transactions and associated costs and achieve economies of scale by buying, selling, warehousing, and transporting products in volume. The advantage of economies of scale is the lowered per unit cost derived from spreading fixed costs over a larger number of units. The larger the wholesaler, the greater its ability to buy and sell in volume at lower prices (this is known as leverage). Wholesaler-distributors leverage their high-volume buying power to acquire goods from manufacturers at a significant discount. Wholesaler-distributors pass this discount on to retailers typically after imposing a markup. Retailers buy products from wholesaler-distributors in large quantities at a low unit price, and then sell the goods to consumers in smaller units at a higher unit price.

Unlike companies that manufacture raw materials into finished goods, wholesalers typically yield smaller profit margins than manufacturers or retailers. Large-scale wholesaler-distributors usually have operating expense margins of 2 percent or less. Therefore, they rely on selling a high volume of products and tight operational controls to make a profit. As wholesaler-distributors increase the volume of sales, they leverage their sales volume to receive lower pricing from manufacturers and therefore decrease their operating expenses.

Economies of scale provided by wholesalers save consumers billions of dollars each year. For example, drug wholesaler-distributors reduce the number of direct distribution transactions between manufacturers and pharmacies by more than 91 percent annually, resulting in cost savings of more than $17 billion to the health-care system.[2] See Figure 21.1.

Full-line or general wholesalers have low costs due to volume economies of scale. Specialty wholesalers and self-distributing companies have low costs due to simplicity of operations (complexity reduction due to fewer SKUs).

FUNCTIONS OF WHOLESALING

Wholesaler functional responsibilities are the same despite differences in industry, business size, and the scope of goods and services provided. Wholesale functions include purchasing/selling, picking/packing, warehousing, shipping, providing market information, transferring title, and financing.

Purchasing and Selling Function

Wholesalers provide manufacturers access to a broad base of customers and act as a centralized resource

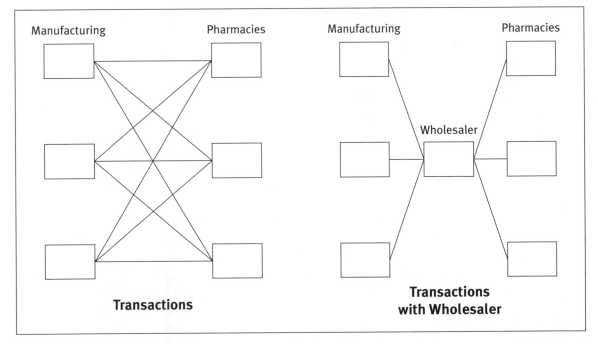

Source: NWDA

Figure 21.1 Wholesaler Economies of Scale

for retailers. For the typical wholesaler-distributor, the purchasing department maintains relationships with manufacturers, vendors, brokers, and retail customers and determines how many items retailers need, when they need it, and where the items must be delivered. Optimal purchase time and quantities are based on a number of variables, including past consumption patterns, product price, and expected contract wins. The goal in purchasing is to balance on-hand inventory with on-order quantities, and to minimize safety stock. This balance is pursued on both a national and a regional basis.

Wholesaler-distributors have a sales force that contacts retail stores and secures orders for product distribution. For many large wholesaler-distributors, such as those in the drug distribution business, sales are based on long-term, contractual relationships with institutional providers and chains.

Warehouse clubs, discount chains, mass marketers, and convenience stores have emerged to meet consumer demands for value and convenience. As a result, the traditional patterns of the manufacturers and wholesalers setting prices have changed in that wholesaler-distributors and retailers now negotiate price. In some industries, large retailers bypass wholesaler-distributors altogether. For example, mass merchants such as Walmart, category-dominant superstores such as Toys "R"Us, and national supermarket chains such as Safeway use merchant-owned low-cost distribution systems that simplify or compress the distribution channel. These new self-distributing mass merchants increase pressure on wholesaler-distributors to differentiate themselves with lower costs and value-added services that enhance the supply chain process.

This movement toward interactive partnerships between wholesaler-distributors and retailers has been driven by the consolidation of retailers; the need for them to be more competitive in their particular niches; and the increased need for small retailers to have reliable, cost-efficient sources of wholesale consulting services. Wholesaler-distributors have identified and responded to these needs and now offer retailers customized services that meet their financial, technological, and customer-service needs.

Picking and Packing Function

Wholesaler-distributors stock products purchased in bulk in large warehouses; pick or select the products from inventory based on customer request; pack the products into smaller, customized orders; and then ship the products to retailers in economic quantities, which are customized, smaller, and more economically suited to the size of the retailer. New technology, such as computers and laser scanners, continually improves communication and service to customers, increases efficiency in managing inventory, and reduces costs in warehouse systems by reducing error rates in packaging and shipping.

Warehousing Function

Warehousing is a storage, inventory, and distribution function that allows the wholesaler to aggregate demand from a large number of retailers and supply from a large number of manufacturers. The goal of this storage and distribution function is to turn inventory in the warehouse over more quickly. *Inventory turns* are the number of items that are picked, packed, shipped, and sold through a single warehouse in a given year. The more inventory turns, the lower the unit cost, the more efficient the use of capital, and, therefore, the greater the profitability.

To improve accuracy and speed of processing in the warehousing function, wholesaler-distributors have adopted electronic ordering and barcode and scanner technology. Online ordering helps speed order picking by enabling product orders to be sorted by the slot location of items in a warehouse. This is made possible because every item in a warehouse is stocked by its unique stock keeping unit (SKU). Each SKU has a universal product code (UPC) associated with it that identifies manufacturer and item description. Manufacturers, wholesaler-distributors, and retailers track each item by this code to determine product fill rates and to more efficiently manage inventory. *Fill rate* is the percentage of products ordered by a retail customer that is in current stock. Lowering the SKU, or product, count means less handling of fewer products and aids in inventory turns. However, this specialization strategy provides fewer product choices for the retailer.

Barcodes applied to product labels have improved the effectiveness of a picking technique called batch picking, or picking large quantities of a particular product at one time, and have reduced shipment errors. Scanners read barcodes and receive information about item sorting, inventory monitoring, and record keeping. These barcoding and radio frequency (RF) systems for warehouse automation also track the historical data that reveals customer ordering patterns. These patterns provide useful information that helps the wholesaler and provides asset management information to customers.

Inventory management in the warehouse, as well as at the distribution and retail levels, is essential to ensure the accurate and timely flow of products and to maximize the wholesaler-distributor's investment. Inventory management is one of the biggest challenges for wholesaler-distributors, because hundreds of thousands of items may be stocked in a warehouse at any given time. Economics and the limited shelf life of many products mandate close inventory management. The wholesaler-distributor is continually challenged to reduce inventory, decrease total safety stock, turn over items as quickly as possible, while still meeting the service requirements of its customers. *Safety stock* is defined as the amount of product that wholesaler-distributors keep on hand to ensure maximum fill rates.

Shipping and Transportation Function

Fast, efficient, and reliable transportation is a major element of the wholesale operation. Transportation enables wholesalers to deliver a product within a given time frame to its customers. The mode of transportation for product shipments depends on a number of factors, including product cost per cubic foot, volume of shipment, distance, and time frame for delivery. It also is a source of significant expense to the wholesaler, and is constantly evaluated for efficiency and effectiveness. Wholesalers continually seek alternative modes of transportation to reduce the cost of delivery or to increase the load value.

Market Information Function

It is important for wholesaler-distributors to monitor and evaluate the national and regional market trends as well as the performance, price, and services provided by competitors. By understanding these conditions, wholesaler-distributors can evolve their role in the supply chain and create services in anticipation of customer needs. For example, in the health-care industry, wholesalers routinely monitor the number of new products used in clinical trials or undergoing the review and approval process by regulatory agencies such as the U.S. Food and Drug Administration. Market information helps companies determine the timing of introducing new products and assessing potential demand from consumers that could impact the amount of on-hand inventory required to fill orders.

Understanding the competition to wholesalers is another important area within marketing information. For example, the consolidation among retail customers such as pharmacy and grocery stores is a trend that will permanently change the product and service needs of these groups. To compete effectively, small independent pharmacies and supermarkets now are being represented by buying groups that join together for better leverage on prices directly from the manufacturer.

Title Transfer Function

There are essentially two times when title or ownership of a product transfers from one party to another. Title transfer occurs when the wholesaler-distributor takes possession of a product from the manufacturer, and again, when the retailer takes possession of a product from the wholesaler-distributor. Title transfers directly from the manufacturer to the retailer during direct-store-delivery (DSD) when the wholesaler acts as a broker. The process begins when the wholesaler-distributor creates a purchase order for an item or group of items from the manufacturer. When the items are received at the warehouse, the wholesaler-distributor takes title of the product. This means that the wholesaler-distributor owns the goods and they become a payable in the wholesaler-distributor's accounting system and a receivable in the manufacturer's accounting system. This is fundamentally the same practice that occurs with the retail customer. When the customer acknowledges receipt of an item or group of items from the wholesaler-distributor, then the customer takes title or ownership of the goods and carries the payable, or inventory expense.

Financing Function

A number of alternatives exist for wholesaler-distributors in funding the acquisition of inventory. The prudent management of working capital, or the dollars required to run the business, determines the financial stability of the wholesaler-distributor. The financial stability impacts the wholesaler's ability to borrow money, if necessary, to finance inventory or investments in technology. Given the narrow net profit margins in the wholesale business and the need to have credit available as a financing vehicle, wholesaler-distributors must be adroit in managing finances.

Large wholesaler-distributors have finance groups focused on monitoring the performance of their retail customers to assess their capital management practices and thus risks. For retailers with low risk, wholesaler-distributors often provide financing for their inventory purchases.

Wholesaler-distributors also develop and provide information systems that can have a financial impact on independent members of their networks. For example, in health care, these information systems interface with existing pharmacy software and can improve efficiency and profitability by reviewing third-party and cash transactions. Other services accelerate funding of reimbursement from insurers and provide complete financial reconciliation.

WHOLESALE TYPES

The U.S. Department of Commerce identifies three categories of wholesale trade: merchant wholesaler-distributors; manufacturers' sales branches and offices; and agents, brokers, and commission agents.

Merchant Wholesaler-Distributors

Merchant wholesaler-distributors are establishments primarily engaged in buying and selling merchandise produced by other firms. Wholesaler-distributors sell this merchandise for their own account, through their own sales force.

The advantages of independent wholesaler-distributors are that they have market flexibility and can attempt to service many manufacturers and many clients. An additional advantage is that they have the products on hand, which allows them to supply the customer quickly and carry an assortment of merchandise. Merchant wholesaler-distributors also may provide additional services, such as research and development of products for certain customers, labeling, repackaging, financing, and delivery.

Disadvantages include the expense of carrying a broad line of merchandise. In addition, independent wholesaler-distributors do not have the financial backing of a manufacturer or the same level of consumer recognition as a retailer-owned wholesaler.

There are two types of merchant wholesaler-distributors: full line and specialty.

Merchant Wholesaler-Distributor (Full-Line)

A full-line wholesaler-distributor carries a full range of merchandise and delivers merchandise at retail establishments or business sites. Carrying a complete line allows the wholesaler to satisfy most retail needs. Examples of product lines include grocery, pharmaceuticals, automobile parts, health and beauty aids, and stationery.

Merchant Wholesaler-Distributor (Specialty)

A wholesaler-distributor may specialize in a product line and develop an expertise in a particular line. The product line usually is deeper than with a full-line distributor, which provides the retailer with greater choice. Examples include meat, seafood, and dairy.

Route Salesperson/Outside Merchandiser

A *route salesperson*, also known as an *outside merchandiser* or a *rack jobber*, supplies on a regular basis racks and shelves with a narrow range of merchandise. The products typically are found by the cash register at grocery stores, drug stores, hardware stores, and gas stations. Products usually are on consignment, and unsold products are taken back. Rack jobbers are responsible for stocking, pricing, display management, and invoicing. Product examples include magazines, toys, hardware, and baked goods. One advantage of this method is that the wholesaler is assured of prominent retail space. A disadvantage is the additional operating expense of extra personnel to maintain the products at the retail location.

Drop Shippers

The *drop shipper* takes orders from customers, places orders with the manufacturer, takes title to the merchandise, and then has the product shipped to the customer. This usually is done with heavy products where it is more cost-effective to ship directly to the consumer rather than route the product through the wholesaler. Product examples include coal, lumber, and building materials.

Truck Wholesalers

Truck wholesalers, also known as *truck jobbers*, deliver perishable merchandise to local retailers on a cash-on-delivery basis. Examples include gasoline, heating oil, fresh bread, pastries, and snack foods.

Mail-Order and Internet Wholesalers

Mail-order and Internet wholesalers use catalogs or Web sites as selling tools, and usually have no sales force. The main advantage to the company is the reduced cost of operations (typically 90 percent lower than human interaction), the ability to coordinate electronically with suppliers, and the collection of additional data such as cost per order or cost per customer. The main advantage to the customer is the ability to order at any time, input orders quickly, receive in-stock and shipping details instantly, and participate in online auction pricing. However, the disadvantage is the reduced ability to provide specific sales information. Examples include industrial supplies, school supplies, shoe repair industry, automobile parts, specialty foods, and office supplies.

Producer-Owned Cooperatives

Cooperatives are owned by groups of farmers who pool their commodity-type products to gain economies of scale in the marketing functions. Profits are divided among members based on a percentage share of their input. The advantage for the farmer is ease of marketing operations. The disadvantage is a fixed commodity pricing structure that does not account for potential product differentiation. Examples include Sunkist fruit, Blue Diamond nuts, and Sun Maid raisins.

Manufacturer-Owned Wholesalers

A *manufacturer-owned wholesaler* is an establishment or distribution outlet selling goods manufactured by either the same or an affiliated company. The advantages are that the outlets allow direct interaction with customers and may be less expensive than other sales channels as prices are controlled by the manufacturer. Sales strategies also are controlled by the manufacturer, and major customer accounts may be given special attention. A disadvantage is that the line of merchandise is limited to one manufacturer. Manufacturer-owned wholesalers fall into two categories: manufacturers' sales branches and manufacturers' sales offices.

Manufacturers' Sales Branch
A *manufacturers' sales branch* is a facility with an inventory of merchandise for sale. Examples include petroleum refinery bulk stations, computers and computer equipment, and specialty groceries such as meats and frozen foods.

Manufacturers' Sales Office
A *manufacturers' sales office* is an office without stocks of merchandise on hand. Examples include automobiles and trucks, chemicals and allied products, and specialty groceries.

Other Wholesalers

There are many additional types of wholesalers, including cash and carry, grain elevators, and farm-products assemblers.

- **Cash and Carry.** *Cash and carry wholesalers* have products on hand for quick pickup by local retailers and businesses. The advantages include immediate access to products and low prices. The disadvantages include no delivery or other services. Examples include construction materials, bakery and deli food service, and office supplies. Recently, many cash and carry wholesalers are becoming retailers to expand their business to consumers.
- **Grain Elevators.** *Grain elevator wholesalers* receive grain either directly from farmers or from other intermediaries and sell to manufacturers. Many customers of grain elevator wholesalers are international.
- **Farm Products Assemblers.** *Farm products assemblers* market farm products, except grain, purchased directly from farmers and sell to manufacturers or retail stores.

Agents, Brokers, Commission Merchants, and Auction Companies

Agents, brokers, commission merchants, and auction companies are organizations primarily engaged in buying or selling merchandise for other businesses, rather than dealing on their own account. They are paid a predetermined percentage of the sale. They may carry noncompeting product lines or lines from a limited number of manufacturers or wholesalers, and may provide storage capabilities. The advantages of using this type of wholesaler are that a company can expand its sales without hiring additional sales staff. Also, agents and brokers tend to know their customer base well. The disadvantages are that management has less control over independent personnel than over employees, and they offer no credit capabilities.

- **Manufacturers' Agents or Representatives.** *Manufacturers' agents or representatives* sell merchandise on a commission basis on a continuing agency basis. "An *agent* is a person appointed by another person or company, called the principal, to carry out certain duties. The agent may be given limited or complete authority to make agreements and close transactions on behalf of the principal."[3] An advantage is the variety of offerings and the expertise of the agent. Products include automobile parts, shoes, clothing, forest products, and furniture. Import agents sell foreign merchandise for delivery inside the host country and collect a commission for the sale of goods. Export agents represent manufacturers or firms selling host country merchandise for delivery outside the host country.
- **Brokers.** *Brokers* buy and sell merchandise as a representative for a company, but do not receive goods. Brokers usually represent a few manufacturers and specialize in a specific product line, such as coal, food, or lumber. Brokers represent either the seller or the buyer, but not both. The advantages of this method are that the broker can develop customer expertise and it may be less expensive than other channels due to low overhead selling costs. A disadvantage is that the broker does not have product on hand and may not provide a long-term channel partnership.
- **Commission Merchants.** *Commission merchants* receive goods on consignment, such as industrial supplies, industrial machinery, agricultural products, and food, and then sell them in a central market for the highest price possible. They are paid a predetermined percentage commission of the sale price. Commission merchants provide storage and delivery.
- **Auction Company.** A *wholesale auction company or auction house* sells merchandise on behalf of other sellers from a permanent location using the auction method, where merchandise is sold to the highest bidder. Auction companies are paid a specified percentage of the sale price. The advantages of this wholesale method include quick turnaround of merchandise and the highest possible price at the time. The disadvantages

are that there is no price guarantee and the auctioneer provides no delivery service. Examples of products sold at auction include used automobiles, furs, and livestock.

WHOLESALING—INTERNATIONAL
by Ingram Micro

International wholesaler-distributors buy in bulk from product manufacturers or suppliers in any country and sell to resellers and retailers in any country. The objective of international wholesaler-distributors is to create time-to-market savings for manufacturers and suppliers and one-stop shopping for retailers and resellers.

Different wholesale-distribution models have evolved in different countries and regions, depending on the characteristics of the local resellers and business environment. International wholesale-distribution channels are more fragmented than those in the United States. Therefore, suppliers and resellers pursuing global growth seek wholesaler-distributors with international sales and support capabilities. Support capabilities include marketing reseller programs and logistics networking capabilities.

International wholesalers use bar coding on all products and secure multiple sources of international cargo carriers in order to assure highly accurate and timely transportation performance. Worldwide regional wholesale-distribution centers tend to keep a broad product inventory in order to facilitate order execution and maintain high order fill rates. Purchasing associates usually become experts on the product lines they manage and regional parts of the world they serve in order to forecast product demand in various world markets. The sales organization (field, telesales, and customer service groups) should be fluent in the language of the country they serve to ensure customers' needs are met and orders are executed quickly. International wholesaler-distributors typically source the lowest cost of financing worldwide in order to expand the selling capability of suppliers and increase the purchasing capacity of resellers.

Role of Cultures and Governments

International wholesalers observe the unique cultural traditions, governmental regulations, and business practices of each country. The main elements of wholesaling—picking, packing, and shipping—are culturally transparent and cross international borders seamlessly. However, other elements of wholesaling—sales, marketing, human resources, accounting, and administration—usually adopt the cultural characteristics of the regions being served, and therefore differ from country to country.

International Supply Chain

International channel management involves wholesaler-distributors working closely with manufacturers and retailers on a global basis. For example, PC manufacturers authorize distributors to stock computer components and assemble them into completed computer systems that are ordered by resellers. The distributor ships the configured product to reseller customers.

Internet

The Internet facilitates the wholesale-distribution of products by allowing retailers and resellers in every region of the world to research products, manufacturers, and publishers online. Customers can shop in a virtual marketplace of products, then place orders online. Customers also can check on order status and communicate with distributors through e-commerce. This allows wholesalers to expand their business without additional cost.

by United Stationers

Company: United Stationers
Case: Office Products Wholesaling

Historically, independent office products dealers (servicing local small businesses) had priced their products at a 10 to 30 percent discount from the manufacturer's suggested list price. This resulted in gross margins for the reseller that approached 40 percent and also allowed for operating expenses that would be considered high today. However, in the fall of 1986 Staples and Office Depot opened the first retail superstores. The first consequence was increased price awareness on the part of the consumer as the superstores promoted loss leaders and low prices.

Even if a superstore was not in the immediate trading area of a local dealer, the dealer suffered a margin impact since their customers still saw newspaper ads or heard radio commercials and demanded lower prices. As independent dealers experienced lower margins and loss of revenue, they started to buy more products directly from manufacturers to compete on price with the superstores. Buying groups for dealers had existed for some time but had few members. Over the next few years, the increase in buying group participation resulted in lost sales and lower margins for wholesalers.

The next wave of change began when the national contract stationers (larger dealers) decided that in order to have the volume to compete with the superstores for the best manufacturer pricing, they would grow by buying up independent dealers. Thus began the rapid consolidation that did as much to decrease the number of independents from 13,000 to 6,000 as did business closures due to eroding margins. In the late 1980s and early 1990s, the demise of wholesaling was predicted to be imminent as the independent dealer base rapidly declined, and the large national distributors were expected to build their own distribution infrastructure.

The office products channel has long had a high service orientation. In the late 1970s and early 1980s, the typical end user business office moved away from maintaining an on-site inventory of supplies to next-day delivery from their supplier. The just-in-time supply strategy was used in these offices generally before it became popular in manufacturing. As a reseller takes orders from the end user, the resellers' computer is determining what they have in their own inventory and what they will need to buy from the wholesaler. Up until as late as 6 P.M., the reseller will transmit orders to the wholesaler's computer, which the wholesaler acknowledges with fill rate information within minutes.

As a wholesaler, United Stationers fills an individual order from any of their 30 distribution centers across the country, packaging the order for the reseller's individual end user customer. The product is then brought during the night to one of United Stationers' facilities in order to provide a single next morning delivery to the reseller or drop shipment to their end user. This results in fill rates in excess of 98 percent. Deliveries are frequently made to resellers who are hundreds of miles away from a United Stationers distribution center at 2 and 3 A.M. for orders that were received only hours before.

Of the approximately 500,000 line items of product processed at United Stationers distribution centers each night, 95 percent of them are for reseller orders that have been preordered by the end user rather than for the reseller's inventory. As a result, average product lines per order are 2.5. The wholesaler no longer ships just pallets and full cases.

United Stationers realized that the competition was not so much the other wholesalers but rather the ability of the customers to perform the same distribution functions that United Stationers provided.

United Stationers was determined to be the lowest-cost alternative for these services. They knew that if they did not, it would only make sense for the large national players (Staples, Office Depot, Office Max) to invest even more in their own infrastructure or for a dealer-buying group to build distribution centers. Through a series of mergers and acquisitions as well as significant investments in technology and infrastructure, United Stationers continued to reduce operating expenses. Dealers and contract stationers actually started buying more from the wholesaler again as they worked to take costs out of their own operations.

With more and more of the dealer's order being packaged for delivery to the end user, it became the end consumer that was the judge of the service quality. United Stationers determined that accuracy, quality of packaging, and timely delivery were the most important service factors. As these service quality expectations continued to be met, United Stationers saw a dramatic increase in the number of requests for orders to be drop shipped directly to the dealer's customers. In the past few years it has grown from less than 5 percent of orders to approaching 30 percent.

As offices look for ways to take costs out of nonessential processes, they are continually combining categories of consumable supplies and looking for single sources of supply. Thus, whereas an office products dealer, computer supplies reseller, janitorial supply distributor, and industrial supply reseller all feel that they sell very distinct categories of products to the end user, these are all items that are used in a business environment. United Stationers has expanded its product offering to include an even wider range of products used by business. Today across all business units and customer groups, almost 100,000 products are available to nearly 30,000 resellers from 67 distribution centers with next-day delivery to over 90 percent of the United States.

United Stationers must be a critical element in all facets of their customers' business in order to be successful in the distribution channels they serve.

WHOLESALING—CASE STUDY

by SUPERVALU INC.

Company: SUPERVALU
Case: Grocery Wholesaling

Background

Historically, the grocery retailing/wholesaling industry is one of the most competitive in the United States and the world. In the past few years, mass merchandisers' entry into the traditional grocery channel has significantly increased the industry's retail square footage and created an even greater emphasis on competitive pricing. Vertically integrated efficiencies of retail grocery chains and mass merchants put the wholesale/independent retail channel at a cost disadvantage. Each year the national chains captured increasing amounts of market share from the wholesaler/independent retailer channel.

Independent grocery retailers (defined as owning less than 10 stores) have been the grocery industry's traditional mainstay, and through local ownership pay close attention to both their customers and markets.

Before 1970, independent retailers held a dominant share of grocery industry sales. From 1970 to 1990, the grocery supermarket chain—especially the larger combination stores featuring a much

(Continued)

wider assortment of goods across more product departments, resulting in much higher sales per store—became the growth vehicle. The smaller size and volume of the independent retailers created a retail price/gross margin challenge.

During this same time, there were significant periods of high inflation across most goods and services including the grocery industry. Grocery wholesalers had historically charged very low fees for warehousing and transporting products to independent retailers. During this 20-year period of high inflation, grocery wholesalers in general, and SUPERVALU in particular, developed sophisticated methods to calculate how to buy goods at lower promotional prices (on deal) from the manufacturer. The wholesaler would then hold additional inventory of the same product to sell at regular list price after the deal period ended (a forward buy). This technique accounted for more than 50 percent of wholesale profits by 1990.

Problem

The cost of goods and the cost of service became so entangled that there was little clarity between the two costs. The result was a very inefficient channel that had four "silos" of operation: the manufacturer, the wholesaler, the retailer, and the consumer. These silos were only loosely connected, a fact that resulted in higher costs when compared with the chains.

By the early 1990s, the independent retailer/wholesaler channel faced two growing challenges:

- Inflation was minimal, thus wholesalers' profit garnered from holding inventory was quickly disappearing. It appeared that low inflation would be the long-term business environment.
- Mass merchants' rapid growth in the grocery business through the introduction of supercenters was a serious and growing threat.

By 1990, SUPERVALU had grown to a leadership position within the retailer/wholesaler channel. However, the ability to achieve profit was becoming more difficult.

Possible Solutions

The first, most popular, and easiest option was *to do nothing strategic*. This option included: cutting all unnecessary costs, especially any investments for the future; spending most of the company's time and resources toward affiliating or attracting other wholesalers' retailers, as current retail customers closed their stores due to their inability to compete; and hoping that something would change.

The second, and less obvious option, was *to cure the cause of the problem*: the convoluted pricing of goods and services that created the inefficiencies within the channel. Service fees were a very small part of the wholesalers gross profit. Forward buy and other methods to reflect service costs and profit for the wholesaler were included within the sell price of goods to the retailer. Retailers, under pressure from chains and mass merchants, were very unreceptive to any changes in dealing with their wholesalers since it required their time and energy at the same time they were competing with the chains.

SUPERVALU's Solution

SUPERVALU had the strongest balance sheet in the industry, and although sales were flat, margins were good and profit was satisfactory. This allowed SUPERVALU to look forward and *change the structure of how goods and services were charged to the independent retailer*. The focus of this new pricing system was to:

- Create real business incentives for all parties: the retailer, manufacturer, and SUPERVALU, to deliver the lowest cost of goods to the retail store.

- Separate cost of goods from cost of service.
- Separate cost of goods from fees paid to SUPERVALU to warehouse and deliver product.

Results

In 1995, SUPERVALU began its new pricing structure, Activity Based Sell (ABS). The first implementations were challenging for both retailers and SUPERVALU. SUPERVALU changed from a buying focus to a retail selling focus. This change in focus helped lower the cost of goods and aligned SUPERVALU with the retailers to drive retail sales. Under the new pricing system, buyers were no longer responsible for wholesale gross profit. The gross profit for wholesale was achieved through the ABS fees, all calculated by computer programs. Now there was a significant amount of time for buyers to get involved in category management and focus on consumers and retail store needs. Buyers focused on bringing every promotional dollar possible to the retailers, finding methods to lower the retailers' cost of goods delivered to the retail store, and implementing category management in retail stores.

Retailers did make many important changes, including: ensuring full-truck deliveries; placing larger orders; changing delivery schedules; ordering seasonal/promotional product in full pallets; providing SUPERVALU with the authority to negotiate deals and promotions on their behalf; and using SUPERVALU'S Category Management program.

ABS implementation is a dynamic process. The entire channel is now focused on removing unnecessary expenses and delivering the lowest cost of goods.

CORPORATE PROFILES AND AUTHOR BIOGRAPHIES

McKESSON CORPORATION
McKesson is the world's leading healthcare services company. Visit McKesson at www.mckesson.com.

Kimberly Kraemer
Kim Kraemer was formerly director of public relations and was responsible for external communications with the news media and key constituents. Ms. Kraemer received her BA in English/Writing Communications from the University of Massachusetts.

INGRAM MICRO
Ingram Micro Inc., headquartered in Santa Ana, California, is the world's leading wholesale distributor of technology products and services. Visit Ingram at www.ingrammicro.com.

Jerre L. Stead
Jerre Stead, now retired, was Chairman and CEO of Ingram Micro. Mr. Stead received his BBA in Business Administration from the University of Iowa and attended Harvard's Advanced Management Program in Switzerland.

SUPERVALU INC.
SUPERVALU holds leading market share positions across the UnitedStates with approximately 2,500 retail grocery locations. For more information about SUPERVALU, visit www.supervalu.com.

O'Neill McDonald
At the time of the first publication, O'Neill McDonald was the senior vice president for wholesale foods and was responsible for marketing, merchandising, buying, military, and SUPERVALU International. Mr. McDonald received his bachelors in Marketing, graduating with honors, and his MBA from Indiana University.

UNITED STATIONERS INC.
United Stationers is the largest wholesale distributor of business products in North America. Visit United Stationers at www.unitedstationers.com.

Larry Miller
Larry Miller is the Vice President Channel Management for United Stationers. Mr. Miller received his BBA from the University of Notre Dame and received his MBA from the Kellogg School of Northwestern University.

Additional information was provided by:
National Association of Wholesale-Distributors, Ron Schreibman, President.

Adam Fein, Ph.D. "Wholesaling," in 1999 *US Industry and Trade Outlook*.

NOTES

1. *Dictionary of Marketing Terms*, Peter D. Bennett (Chicago, IL: American Marketing Association, 1995).
2. National Wholesale Druggists' Association, 1999.
3. American Purchasing Society.

22 WAREHOUSING/ DISTRIBUTION CENTERS

by OHL, APL Logistics, SAFEWAY, and DSC Logistics

George Carlin, American Comedian, 1937–2008

THE ESSENTIALS OF WAREHOUSING
by OHL

Introduction

Warehousing and distribution centers are the elements of marketing that store and distribute goods, provide value-added service at strategic points within the supply chain, and lower the total cost of product distribution. Warehousing services help to create the essential time and place utilities. Warehousing, along with wholesaling and transportation, is also referred to as physical distribution.

Warehousing activities represent a main element in the supply chain processes. There is considerable pressure to reduce inventories and improve cycle times and responsiveness throughout the entire supply chain. As companies refine their abilities to move products and information smoothly throughout the supply chain, these warehouses have evolved into distribution centers.

This capability is highly marketable, and progressive firms are using warehousing and distribution as a cornerstone of a complete corporate marketing effort to establish and grow a competitive advantage in the marketplace.

As firms continue to move toward the adoption of inventory and supply chain techniques such as just-in-time (JIT), efficient consumer response (ECR), direct store delivery (DSD), continuous replenishment (CRP), and vendor-managed inventory (VMI), the demands on warehouses and distribution centers will increase. Distribution managers will be asked to improve their abilities to move products quickly and effectively into, through, and out of their facilities. As a result, distribution centers will continue to add services to become product transformation centers.

SUPPLY CHAIN CONFIGURATION			
Manufacturing → Wholesaling → Retailing and E-tailing → Customers			
⇕	⇕	⇕	⇕
Warehouse	Warehouse	Warehouse	Shed, basement, garage, attic, closet, etc.

Definitions

A *distribution center* (distribution warehouse) is a "facility for the receipt, storage, and redistribution of goods to company stores or consumers. A distribution center may be operated by a retailer, a manufacturer, or distribution specialist known as a third party logistics provider (3PL) and is used to facilitate rapid distribution to resellers."[1]

A *crossdock* is a facility designed to rapidly mix product for redistribution. In a crossdock, receiving and shipping activities are typically performed on opposite sides of the facility with mixing facilitated by using temporary storage locations called *staging lanes* located between the inbound and outbound sides of the facility. Goods usually pass through a crossdock in a matter of hours and no more than a few days.

Hybrid facilities called *flow-through centers* have emerged that combine the capabilities of the crossdock and distribution center to meet the wide range of product distribution requirements that may span the product line of a manufacturer, wholesaler, or retailer.

Nearly all modern distribution centers, crossdocks, and flow-through centers are operated using computerized systems called *warehouse management systems (WMS)* that direct and control all activity in and around the facility and are heavily integrated with the entire supply chain.

Warehousing and transportation together are commonly referred to as *logistics* (from the Greek *logistikos* meaning calculation).

PRODUCT STORAGE FACTORS

Each product category has its own storage needs. There are several major types of public and contract warehousing operations that can accommodate these unique needs.

General Merchandise

The *general merchandise warehouse* is the most common type of warehouse. It is used by manufacturers, distributors, and retailers for storage and distribution of a wide range of products. This type of facility is one which serves as a point of storage and/or transfer for general merchandise such as consumer products, wholesale and retail products awaiting shipment to final destinations, and parts and materials pending further shipment to manufacturing and/or assembly points. Products in a general warehouse typically do not have special requirements with regard to temperature control, security, or other unique circumstances.

Special Commodity

The *special commodity facility* is dedicated to a single type of product or commodity with special warehousing needs. The unique facilities requirements typically cost more than general merchandise warehousing. Special commodity warehouses store raw materials, work-in-process, finished goods, food products, high-value goods, temperature-sensitive products, hazardous materials, and controlled pharmaceuticals.

Raw Materials
This type of facility holds materials prior to their use in a manufacturing, processing, or assembly operation. These facilities usually are owned by the manufacturer or the 3PL and are specifically built for the products being stored. Examples include automotive parts awaiting replenishment requests from the plant floor, chemicals stored in bulk prior to use in a manufacturing process, and lumber awaiting finishing assembly into furniture.

Work-in-Process
In the manufacturing process, between raw materials and finished goods, are semifinished goods known as work-in-process (WIP). Work-in-process moves continuously through the assembly process. However, it may reach a stage where separate and further treatment is needed before the final product is achieved that will have its own specific storage requirements. For example, partially assembled television sets awaiting installation of cabinets prior to packaging and shipping may have assembly areas or may be kept ultraclean to assure product assembly quality.

Finished Goods
Typically, the finished goods warehouse is one that accommodates products that are ready for market, or for final use. Sometimes finished goods themselves move into further stages of manufacturing or production, such as tires and windshields into automotive plants. These facilities must be spacious enough to avoid overcrowding and therefore prevent damaging the finished goods.

Temperature Sensitive

The temperature-sensitive facility helps to maintain conditions, including temperature and humidity, that are acceptable for specific product types. There are numerous products that require this type of facility prior to arrival at their intended destination, including produce, dairy, meat or fish products, certain chemicals, and flowers. For example, Safeway, a national grocery store chain, uses a temperature-controlled warehouse to better control the ripening process of bananas.

Hazardous Materials

Very special safety precautions are taken at a hazardous materials (HAZMAT) or chemicals facility. Typically, the chemicals or other products being stored have certain characteristics that require continuous monitoring. Steps are taken not to disturb their physical state, and systems are in place to mitigate problems such as spills or explosions. Facilities of this type are usually higher-cost operations, in order to account for the many different types of safety needs.

Controlled Pharmaceuticals

Facilities that contain controlled products such as pharmaceuticals must be equipped with security measures to prevent theft. Detailed inventory control procedures are taken to make sure that these products are accounted for at all steps in the logistics process through close monitoring of production and lot control numbers.

WAREHOUSING TYPES

There are five main types of warehousing: private, contract, public, foreign trade zones, bonded, and field warehousing.

Private

Proprietary use of resources for the warehousing function is referred to as private warehousing. Large companies, such as Nestle, use many proprietary warehouses. The advantages of in-house operations include economies of scale in ownership of multiple warehouses when levels of usage are high and control over all aspects of a company's storage needs is required. The disadvantages include tying up capital and management time for warehouse operations. For this reason, there is an established trend away from private warehousing toward contract warehousing.

Contract

Contract warehousing, or leased facilities, refers to a "long-term mutually beneficial arrangement which provides unique and specially tailored warehousing and logistics services exclusively to one client."[2] Justified by the longer-term commitment made by the client (typically 3 to 5 years), providers of contract warehousing services (3PLs) are able to customize capabilities to specifically meet the needs of individual clients. These capabilities include custom storage space, dedicated labor, and advanced information systems that are needed to serve an individual client. Contract warehousing may be dedicated to one customer or a shared-use facility with multiple customers taking advantage of shared resources.

The advantages of contract warehousing include higher levels of customer service, focused management expertise, increased geographic coverage, flexibility to increase or decrease warehouse space quickly, and minimization of labor issues. The disadvantages include a slightly higher expense of paying fees to another company to manage the operations.

Public

Public warehouses are commercial services that are available to any company on a first-come first-served basis. The advantages include conservation of capital, flexibility of products served, the ability to rapidly increase or decrease warehouse space to cover peak requirements, tax advantages of expense versus debt, up-front knowledge of costs for storage and handling, and minimization of labor disputes. The disadvantages include the higher cost, the potential of inadequate availability, and the lack of management control. Typically, public warehousing contracts are for 30-day periods of time with no specified termination date.

Foreign Trade Zones

Foreign trade zones are enclosed areas, operated as public utilities, under control of U.S. Customs with facilities for handling, storing, manipulating, manufacturing, and exhibiting goods. The merchandise may be exported, destroyed, or sent into Customs Territory from the zone, in the original package or otherwise. It is subject to Customs duties if sent into Customs Territory, but not if reshipped to foreign points.

Bonded Storage

Bonded storage is a service in which goods are held until applicable federal taxes and fees are collected. This form of storage applies to certain alcoholic beverages, tobacco, and agricultural products over which the government retains control until they are distributed to the marketplace.

Field Warehousing

Field warehousing is used when a firm requests a receipt for goods stored in a public or contract warehouse that are under the control and supervision of the warehouse operator. Typically, the firm uses the receipt, which is a negotiable instrument, as collateral for a loan against the value of the goods.

WAREHOUSE/DISTRIBUTION CENTER PROCESS

Many warehouse facilities today place greater emphasis on the timely movement and distribution of product and the availability of needed information than they place on the long-term storage of the product. To help meet customer demands in a just-in-time business environment, many warehouse managers are looking at a wide range of alternatives and types of innovation that will lead to improved service, seamless product flow, and reduced cost. Warehousing operations include a wide range of standard functions and value-added services. See the diagram in Figure 22.1.

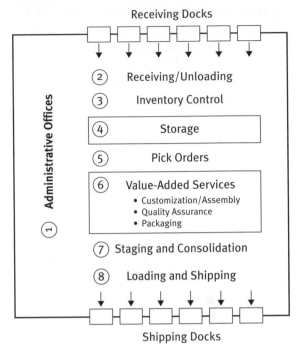

Figure 22.1 Typical Distribution Center Layout

1. Customer Order Receiving/Administrative

Customer orders are received at the administrative office (either at the warehousing facility or off-site). The activities that then take place in a warehouse require that for each physical change in the form or location of a product there is a parallel information transaction. Increasingly, all activities within a distribution facility are controlled by a sophisticated information system typically referred to as a warehouse management system (WMS). The WMS relies on timely and accurate information flows, and it is becoming very common for firms to emphasize the availability of effective information capabilities at its warehouses and distribution centers. Whereas the use of Electronic Data Interchange (EDI) has become the standard of communications at many of these facilities today, there is a growing emphasis on the utilization of Internet systems for information transfer.

2. Receiving/Unloading

Products are received from vendors or other suppliers at the receiving dock where they are unloaded from the trailers, trains, ocean containers, or cargo containers. This step in the process is known as making bulk or collecting a wide assortment of goods from a variety of suppliers. The timely receipt and unloading of incoming shipments is a critical step in the effective utilization of warehouses and distribution centers as each delivery is timed ultimately to outbound shipments.

3. Placement in Inventory/Inventory Control

As products are received, warehouse accountability begins, and each product is assigned a location in the warehouse or distribution center. Accurate inventory and record keeping, typically done now in real time through a cycle counting process, provides warehouse management and customers with the ability to locate their products at all times.

4. Storage

Storage allows products to be available when and where they are needed by customers. Storage permits companies to protect against uncertainties such as transportation delays, vendor stockouts, and significant fluctuations in demand, which may disrupt inventory availability and distribution effectiveness. Inventories are placed in strategic locations in warehouses or distribution centers to be close to other functions as needed.

5. Pick Orders

Picking orders (selecting products or breaking bulk), as required by customers, is when small assortments of products are picked mechanically or by hand from the larger bulk of available merchandise in the warehouse. Product mixing allows companies to efficiently create assortments of products that may have been manufactured at different locations. For example, the automotive industry routinely does this through the use of regionally located mixing, or consolidation centers.

6. Value-Added Services

- **Customizing/Product Assembly.** At this stage, products may be customized or additional assembly performed to meet customer requirements.
- **Quality Assurance.** Warehouses and distribution centers play a valuable role in the continual pursuit of quality assurance. Through activities such as grading, inspection, and product testing, the warehouse or distribution center has an enhanced ability to fill customer orders accurately.
- **Packaging and Marking.** Traditionally value-added activities, such as pricing or subassembly, have been accomplished at other points in the distribution channel. The warehouse or distribution center is quickly becoming a key location for the conduct of these important activities, due to EDI capabilities, strategic site locations, and the desire to perform these tasks. For example, today it is common practice for the consumer goods manufacturers like Procter & Gamble to outsource value-added activities such as packaging, pricing, repricing, bar coding, and repackaging.

7. Staging and Consolidation

Staging is the initial placement of products in a particular area of the warehouse in preparation for shipment and possibly consolidation. *Consolidation* is the combining of smaller shipments into larger shipments to common destinations, which reduces the cost of transportation services. This activity facilitates the process of subsequently moving volume-sized shipments through to their final destination or to other intermediate points in the distribution process.

8. Loading and Shipping

Once the products have been consolidated, they must be physically loaded onto the transport vehicles. Loading is accomplished with human labor, forklifts, mechanized rollers, and conveyor belts.

It is critical to match customer product orders with outbound shipping.

WAREHOUSE/DISTRIBUTION CENTER LOCATION FACTORS

The issue of where to locate manufacturing, distribution, and retail facilities has never been more complex or critical as firms search for new and innovative ways to lower costs and improve service to customers. The overall design or configuration of a firm's distribution or logistics network is a critical component of its competitive strength.

The facility location decision has two factors. The first step determines required service levels to indicate how many facilities are needed and where they should be located generally to within a 25-mile radius. The second step involves site-specific capabilities and cost factors.

Service Levels

Service levels are determined by proximity to customers and suppliers.

- **Proximity to Markets/Customers.** Historically, a greater emphasis had been placed on *decentralized warehousing*, having a large number of warehouses located near major markets of consumption. The advantages of an expanded, decentralized network of distribution facilities include lower transportation costs and less risk in reliance on a few warehouses.

  Today, the trend is toward *centralized warehousing*, a smaller number of strategically located distribution centers. The availability of centrally located computers and logistics services that provide timely and accurate information has justified the move to a more centralized network of distribution facilities by improving the levels of service experienced by warehouse customers.

  The advantages of strategically placed distribution centers include lowered overhead costs and the ability to provide a more timely flow of goods. Through a consolidation of facilities,

inventory carrying cost savings exceed any added transportation costs involved with moving product to the customer from a more limited number of facilities. By consolidating distribution centers and improving computer information and order processing systems capabilities, customers experience an improved overall responsiveness and enhanced levels of service.

- **Proximity to Supplier Networks.** In the case of a warehousing or distribution center, it is important to know how proposed facility sites fit with the geographic locations of key supplier facilities. The relative location impacts the cost of inbound transportation and the timing of deliveries.

Infrastructure Capabilities and Costs

Infrastructure capabilities and costs include land costs, labor availability and cost, the availability of transportation services, and taxes.

- **Land Costs.** Land costs will vary widely as various geographic locations are considered for distribution facilities. In addition to the cost of land for the facility itself, additional acreage may be needed for parking or future expansion. Typically considered in conjunction with land costs, the availability and cost of utilities such as electrical power, sewerage, and industrial waste disposal need to be factored into the decision-making process.
- **Labor Availability and Cost.** Regarded in many instances as the most important location factor, the availability of a skilled labor force is a key criterion for many companies. In addition to locally prevailing wage rates, other factors relating to the labor climate include overall work ethic, the extent to which additional training and education will be needed for new employees, and general stability of the workforce.
- **Transportation Availability.** Effective access to transportation is necessary to ensure the efficient flow of materials into the warehouse or distribution center, and of products outbound

to customers. Features needed are proximity to a major highway network, or access to rail, water, and/or air facilities. In addition, it is important to determine whether there is an acceptable choice of firms offering the desired range of modal services.

- **Taxes.** It is important to have knowledge of state and local taxes that apply to both businesses and individuals. Prevailing business, inventory, and property taxes will significantly impact the cost of operating a facility in an area of interest. Personal taxes that may affect the ability to attract labor and management include income, property, and sales taxes.
- **Quality of Life.** Although quality of life is difficult to quantify, it does affect the well-being of employees and the quality of the work. Criteria include climate, housing costs, health care and environment, crime, education, recreation, and the arts.

INVENTORY CONTROL

The goal of inventory control is to maximize service to the customer (by increasing product and information availability as described in this chapter) and minimize costs (by decreasing the amount of inventory and the length of time that it is held). Inventory carrying costs include storage, handling, inventory risk, services, and capital costs.

INVENTORY CARRYING COSTS

Storage Space Costs
Taxes on land and building
Insurance on building
Depreciation on building (if owned) or rent (if leased)
Maintenance and repairs of buildings
Utility costs (heat, light, water, etc.)
Janitorial, security, and maintenance salaries

Handling Equipment Costs
Depreciation on equipment
Fuel for equipment
Maintenance and repair of equipment
Insurance on equipment
Taxes on equipment
Pallet rack
Conveyor
Radio frequency (RF) infrastructure

Inventory Risk Costs
Insurance on inventory
Losses resulting from obsolescence of inventory
Physical deterioration of inventory
Pilferage of inventory
Security alarms and closed-circuit television systems (CCTV)

Service Costs
Taxes on inventory
Labor costs of handling and maintaining stocks
Clerical costs of record keeping
Employer contributions: taxes, insurance

Capital Costs
Interest on money invested in inventory, handling equipment, and land and building (if owned)

Source: National Association of Wholesaler-Distributors.

Warehouse operations increasingly are turning into distribution centers (DC) in order to save on inventory costs. Examples of companies that have shifted to a distribution center-type warehouse format include IKEA and Starbucks Coffee Company.

WAREHOUSING DESIGN FACTORS

There are several warehouse design requirements to facilitate the management of distribution needs, inventories, and information flows.[3] Marketers should follow these guidelines:

- Warehouses should be designed in modular form to allow for future growth of product storage and new product lines. This provides for flexibility, expandability, and construction cost economies.
- Warehouses should store high-volume items close to picking, packing, and shipping areas to make the most efficient and effective use of available storage and distribution capacity.
- Warehouses should incorporate a range of high-tech automation, semiautomation, low-cost automation, and manual storage for the range of high-, medium-, and low-demand items. These include robotic retrieval systems, floor-to-ceiling shelves, and conveyor belts.

- Warehouses should examine inventory usage patterns on an item-by-item basis to consolidate inventories to most desirable quantities, and to smoothly flow items into, through, and out of the warehouse or distribution facility.
- Warehouses should be prewired for radio frequency (RF) type WMS and have fiber optic infrastructure for voice and data communications.

Advanced warehouse operations systems have helped to shorten, and improve the quality of, the distribution process at many companies. For example, the Boeing Commercial Airline Group, the world's largest manufacturer of commercial jet airplanes, operates two warehouses from which parts and supplies are shuttled daily to the company's manufacturing facilities. These warehouses use state-of-the-art, computerized voice-recognition systems to improve warehouse labor efficiency and inventory accuracy. The automated system includes a voice/data collection terminal using software that can be programmed to recognize more than 1,000 words. The system's capability enables the operator to speak into a headset microphone that is connected by radio frequency (RF) to a central computer. When the operator speaks into the microphone, the computer verifies the correctness of the activity being performed.

LOGISTICS SERVICE PROVIDERS

Companies use *logistics service providers (LSPs)*—defined as external suppliers that perform all or part of a company's logistics functions, including transportation, warehousing, distribution, and financial services—in order to reduce costs and enhance customer service by extending their logistics capabilities. LSPs are also known as third-party logistics firms (3PL), contract logistics, or outsourced logistics. Activities outsourced most frequently by corporations include warehousing, outbound transportation, freight bill auditing and payment, inbound transportation, and freight consolidation/distribution.[4] The primary factors used in evaluating third parties include service capabilities, cost, service quality, and responsiveness. Information technology is viewed as a key to the success of third-party operations.

WAREHOUSING—INTERNATIONAL
by APL Logistics

With the spread of globalization in the twenty-first century, few business functions have become more directly tied to marketing success than supply chain management.

Most of today's consumers fully understand that billions of dollars' worth of manufacturing has shifted from the Americas to Asia. However, they are less aware of the logistical repercussions: longer transit times, higher transportation costs, international congestion, and delivery volatility. As a result, many continue to expect the same aggressive turnaround times that they enjoyed in the late 1990s—even though many of their purchases now have to travel thousands more miles to reach them.

In light of these developments, international warehousing has emerged as one of this era's most effective marketing tools.

Placing and Configuring International Warehousing Networks

There are several end markets to consider when configuring an outbound international warehouse network. And each presents a distinct set of challenges.

In the United States, which continues to be the world's largest consumer market, a robust warehousing presence is both essential and relatively easy to attain. However port and airport access have become especially critical (and thus more hotly competed for) because these locations—rather than domestic factories—are now the manufacturing gateways for many products.

Asia, particularly China, is a major market of its own, thanks to the infusion of new production jobs. But few countries in Asia have the infrastructure needed to move products quickly from warehouse to end user. Thus Asian warehouses must be located closer to their customers than warehouses in the United States.

Information Systems vs. Inventory Levels

During the late 1980s and 1990s, companies placed a huge emphasis on achieving razor-thin inventory levels with the help of sophisticated information systems. That mindset is still alive and well in many circles. However, thanks to the volatility of many international supply chains, higher inventory levels are becoming more common and, in some cases, imperative—again. By bringing more products into the United States (or other countries of final consumption) ahead of time and then staging them at warehouses until they are needed, companies can help offset much of the delivery volatility associated with international sourcing.

On a different note, there are some countries where it is still not possible for companies to even consider substituting information for inventory, because state-of-the-art logistics information systems are not available. Companies will usually have to carry more inventory within these countries' warehouses, unless they happen to be working with a global logistics provider that has imported its inventory management systems.

Company Management vs. Contract Management

When establishing a warehouse outside the United States, companies have three primary options: (1) They can manage it themselves (usually with the help of local expertise), (2) work with one of the many local operators in their country of choice, or (3) go with a global third-party logistics provider. The latter option has changed the most over the past few years, thanks to the ongoing geographic and service expansion efforts of many 3PLs. A viable option in countries where there is a lack of internal management expertise or international third-party logistics companies is to ally with some other reputable company or consultant in the area; each could provide the knowledge and connections needed to get started.

Warehousing Layout

Throughout the world, the key requirements for warehouse space are the availability of dock doors, basic utilities, adequate lighting, and adequate column spacing for storage and warehouse vehicle maneuverability. Finding such space does not pose much of a challenge in highly developed countries such as the United States or in cities such as Shanghai, where global third-party logistics providers and local developers have begun constructing new facilities. However, it is a different story in developing countries or places where developable land is at a premium.

Additionally many overseas facilities do not have the quality of construction, cleanliness, or security that U.S. and European companies enjoy. In these cases, companies may have to rethink their rigorous facility selection standards, choosing the best available in a given market at that given time.

Equipping Your Warehouse: Labor vs. Capital

Whether your company chooses to use more machine power or manpower for its various international warehouses will often depend on prevailing wage and real estate rates. In places such as Japan and Europe, where the price of real estate and labor is extremely high, it will probably be more economical to substitute mechanization and information systems for hands-on material. By contrast, in places such as South America, Mexico, or India, where the comparable price of labor and real estate is relatively inexpensive, it will often make more sense to have employees do more of the actual logistics work like picking and packing.

Cultural Differences

Although the basic practices of warehousing may be similar from country to country, the mindset of the people performing these functions varies significantly from country to country. No matter how Americanized or European an international facility's processes and systems are, those in charge of managing these facilities must never lose sight of each facility's context. Among other things, they should observe the local or national holidays (such as the Chinese New Year), accommodate varying work schedules, and honor preferred communications parameters. How well each country's warehousing employees are respected for who they are culturally could have a huge impact on international logistics success.

Free Trade Zones

Although the relevance of foreign or free trade zones (FTZs) has been partially diminished by the creation of new international trading territories, these facilities still exist, in the United States and in many other parts of the world. Their potential advantages remain unchanged: international merchandise may be brought in for assembly, storage, or shipping, but companies delay payment of duties until the product is completed and shipped to customers. In recent years, many companies doing business in China have begun expressing more interest in using logistics facilities within FTZs, a phenomenon that may be associated with the current trend toward performing more value-added services overseas. FTZs may also become more attractive to U.S. companies that wish to significantly increase their domestic inventory levels for foreign-sourced goods.

WAREHOUSING—CASE STUDY

by Safeway Inc.

Company: Safeway Inc., Eastern Division Distribution Center
Case: Perishables Warehousing—Banana Ripening Rooms

As one of the major retailers in the highly competitive grocery industry, Safeway is continually looking for ways to improve on their consistent offering of high-quality foods. Produce is one of the many areas with which Safeway has distinguished itself from the competition. Fresh produce provides a great opportunity for sales success as well as a great challenge. A customer's perception of a store's quality and freshness is often directly related to the visual appeal of the product on hand.

Bananas are one of the most popular produce items in any grocery store, and their purchase depends a lot on how they look. Considering the fruit's popularity and the volume at which bananas are sold, it is very important that Safeway has consistently appealing bananas available at all times. Bananas are harvested in a far less edible state (very firm and dark green) to allow for transport from farm to outlet, a process that can take five to seven days.

Upon arrival at the warehouse, the product needs to be ready for distribution and sale within as few days as possible. In order to maintain consistent quality in the ripening process and therefore achieve customer satisfaction, the Safeway distribution center is equipped with electronically operated banana-ripening rooms. The warehouse was designed to accommodate peak demand periods, such as holidays and marketing promotions, during which the number of boxes can dramatically increase.

The bananas arrive in the warehouse not fully ripened and must be prepared for sale. The bananas are placed in the room for ripening shortly after being received. Ripening involves exposure to an even distribution of heat and ethylene gas, which is naturally secreted by bananas and many other fruits as they ripen. (At home, green bananas will ripen more quickly if they are kept in a brown paper bag as the ethylene gas produced is trapped near the banana.) Utilizing this principle in a more sophisticated fashion, the rooms are filled with this natural gas for one full day. At the same time, the temperature is raised from 40 degrees to between 62 and 65 degrees. The gas is then evacuated from the

(Continued)

room leaving the bananas there for three to four additional days to complete the ripening process. They are then removed and entered into the selection queue where they will ultimately be transported to retail stores.

The opening of the new center has allowed Safeway to change the way the company receives banana shipments. In the past, Safeway ordered bulk loads of bananas that required the product to be handled numerous times prior to shipping, which increased the possibility for bruising. Now, the bananas are received in containers from the point of origin, significantly reducing the amount of times the product is handled. Although containerized shipping is costly, the reduction in losses due to product damage outweighs the cost.

Due to improved warehousing strategies, Safeway now provides more consistent quality bananas deriving additional consumer sales.

WAREHOUSING—CASE STUDY

by DSC Logistics

Company: DSC Logistics
Case: Supply Chain Management/Warehousing—Customer Partnership

DSC Logistics, one of the largest privately held logistics and supply chain management companies in the United States, has built their business on transforming conventional working relationships with their customers into strategic partnerships that use the supply chain to achieve overall business goals.

The first such relationship to be transformed was with DowBrands, a nationwide manufacturer of consumer goods that was acquired by S.C. Johnson in 1998. For nearly a decade prior to the sale, DSC provided third-party logistics for Dow's well-known line of household products, which DSC stored and distributed. The working relationship was a straightforward exchange of fees for services, in which neither company crossed the functional boundaries defined by the different roles in the supply chain.

However, the relationship began to change when Dow decided to create a new production facility. They recognized the decision as an opportunity to review their total system performance and expense, how well and how cost-effectively material moved from source to point of sale, and to look for improvements.

DSC met with Dow to discuss new possibilities. An agreement emerged to try a totally new kind of partnership between the companies, based on shared information, collaborative processes, and a joint vision.

Dow was looking at the proposed production site as a possible new logistics hub. Through acquisitions, they had cobbled together a sizable network for manufacturing and distribution. It was not very efficient, though, and they wanted to lower costs. DSC offered to do a network study evaluating the new site's potential as a distribution hub and how the two companies might function together at the new site. One option was to place the manufacturing operation in one building, putting the

DSC-run distribution facility next door. It was a conventional way of organizing such work. However, it would also accrue unnecessary transportation costs, since it required constantly moving material between buildings.

It was agreed that a better option was to locate the manufacturing and distribution efforts under one roof, in the same building. Material could flow from loading dock to production line and back to loading dock or into storage. The employees of both organizations would work together as one team.

The companies shared access to each other's operations, systems, business objectives, and information. Such an open arrangement challenged a lot of assumptions about the way businesses should work together regarding risk and trust. Yet it made profound sense. At the highest level, a supply chain is a complex system, constantly influenced by shifts in consumer behavior, the availability of materials, and production capacity. To succeed, businesses should use their supply chains as tools to identify, respond to, and leverage ongoing change. Yet that is impossible as long as the business views its logistics effort as a series of discrete functions instead of a continuous flow of information and material.

Once DSC's network study confirmed that Dow could cost-effectively consolidate manufacturing and distribution efforts at the proposed site, work began to prepare the location for this collaborative effort.

As the operation progressed from start-up to steady-state manufacturing, the partnership provided:

- A jointly designed facility that would tightly integrate manufacturing, warehousing, and distribution.
- A jointly drafted vision statement that spelled out what both sides wanted from the relationship.
- A jointly created Partnership Committee that met once a month to discuss any issues at the facility.
  As the partnership evolved, Dow also began engaging DSC's expertise in additional ways.
- DSC created hundreds of custom pallet designs for Dow's distribution effort, which was then shared with all their other distribution centers nationwide.
- DSC responded to Dow's changing marketing requirements by creating many customized displays and packaging options to support different promotions.
- DSC was incorporated into more aspects of production, such as scheduling and carrying out deliveries of raw material to the production line on a just-in-time basis, as well as managing the flow of corrugated boxing supplies into the facility and to the production line as needed.
- DSC used an automated storage and retrieval system, which decreased cycle times, reduced labor hours, and improved inventory accuracy for both companies.

The partnership was profoundly satisfying and cost-effective for both companies. Over four years, DSC saved DowBrands $3.7 million annually by reducing operating costs. By locating under one roof, Dow was able to cut the costs of transporting material, limit the amount of product damage, and reduce shrinkage. Further savings accrued from shared services and programs such as training, security, and maintenance. Other savings accrued from more efficient manufacturing. DSC's willingness to take on various support roles as the needs of the production line evolved allowed Dow to generate more material with fewer people.

DSC also enjoyed financial benefits from the collaboration. DSC demonstrated to Dow that they could be their partner and invited Dow to engage in more processes than just transporting boxes. Creating and delivering such responsive, value-added services for Dow meant strong profitability for DSC.

(Continued)

DSC also embarked upon a new marketing strategy. In the past, the logistics industry was focused on managing buildings and boxes. Customers tended to base buying decisions on the number of square feet a warehouse had in a particular city or on the transportation services there. Therefore, it made sense to sell on the basis of a list of locations, a menu of services, and the number of trucks at hand. The new view of logistics emphasizes people, processes, and ideas. This view encourages successful long-term partnerships that result in a well-designed, well-executed, and highly adaptable supply chain.

CORPORATE PROFILES AND AUTHOR BIOGRAPHIES

APL LOGISTICS, INC.

APL Logistics is one of the world's largest global logistics providers. It employs approximately 4,500 professionals and operates more than 26 million square feet of warehousing space in more than 60 countries on six continents. Visit APL Logistics at www.apllogistics.com.

John Hurst

John Hurst is Vice President of Warehouse Management Services in the Americas for APL Logistics. He is responsible for 65 facilities spanning five countries. Mr. Hurst received his BA in Materials and Logistics Management from Michigan State University and his MBA from Pepperdine University

DSC LOGISTICS

DSC Logistics, an integrated logistics and supply chain management company, focuses on supply chain capabilities that are based on changing customer needs. Visit DSC Logistics at www.dsc-logistics.com.

Ann M. Drake

Since becoming CEO of DSC Logistics in 1994, MS. Drake has guided DSC through a transformation from an extended family of 22 separate companies to a dynamic network of integrated logistics and supply chain management operations. She received her bachelors from the University of Iowa and her MBA from the Kellogg School at Northwestern University.

OHL

OHL is one of the largest 3PLs in the world, providing global supply chain management solutions including transportation, warehousing, customs brokerage, freight forwarding, and import and export consulting services. Visit OHL at www.ohl.com.

Scott McWilliams

Scott McWilliams has served as CEO of OHL since May 2001. Mr. McWilliams received his BS in Logistics from the University of Tennessee.

SAFEWAY

Safeway is the third largest company in the food and drug industry based on sales. Visit Safeway at www.safeway.com.

Roger J. Herding

Roger Herding is Director of Supply Chain for Safeway's Eastern Division. Mr. Herding previously worked for Red Owl, National Tea, and A&P.

Craig M. Muckle

Craig Muckle, Public Affairs Manager for Safeway's Eastern Division, is responsible for media, government, community, and consumer relations. Mr. Muckle received his BA in Communications from the University of Dayton.

NOTES

1. *Dictionary of Marketing Terms*, Peter D. Bennett (Chicago, IL: Marketing Association, 1995).
2. The Warehousing Research Center at Miami University.
3. Roy L. Harmon, *Reinventing the Warehouse*: *world class Distribution Logistics*, New York: Siman & Schuster Adult, 1993.
4. University of Tennessee's Center for Logistics Research.

23 TRANSPORTATION

by FedEx Trade Networks, Con-way Freight, BNSF, Atlas Air Worldwide Holdings, Overseas Shipholding Group, Ingram Barge, Colonial Pipeline, Southwest Airlines, Greyhound, MTA Long Island Rail Road, Carnival Cruise Lines, John Deere, SkyHook, and Amtrak

Segment of an 1829, pro-canal, anti-railroad letter to President Andrew Jackson:
As you may well know, Mr. President, "railroad" carriages are pulled at the enormous speed of 15 miles per hour by "engines," which in addition to endangering life and limb of passengers, roar and snort their way through the countryside, setting fire to the crops, scaring the livestock and frightening women and children. The Almighty certainly never intended that people should travel at such breakneck speed.

Martin Van Buren, Governor, New York

THE ESSENTIALS OF TRANSPORTATION
by FedEx Trade Networks

Introduction

Definition

Transportation is the element of marketing that focuses on delivering a product to the customer and is an essential link in the supply chain. Transportation's goal is to deliver the product to the customer where he or she wants it, at the time it is needed, with no damage, and at the lowest cost. The extent to which these goals are met may allow a company to differentiate itself from competitors. The product transported may be cargo or passenger. Transportation, along with warehousing, often is referred to as physical distribution or logistics. "Transportation is a marketing function that adds time and place utility to the product by moving it from where it is made to where it is purchased and used."[1]

SUPPLY CHAIN CONFIGURATION		
Manufacturer → Transportation → Wholesaler →		
Transportation → Retailer →		
Transportation → Customers		

TRANSPORTATION MARKETING EVOLUTION

The transport of production or finished goods has been in the background of everyday business transactions for centuries, but a revolutionary transformation in the business of moving goods has been taking place that will balance speed to market and cost.

The evolution of a merchant class in fourteenth-century Europe was a blend of ownership of the merchandise, limited competition, and owning the means to transport, whether that meant moving barges up the Rhine River system or later in the seventeenth century moving a company's own finished products on its own ship to the Americas and returning with raw materials.

Every mode of transport today can trace its beginnings to the time when the first group of merchants did something unique. One revolutionary idea was when a few entrepreneurs decided that rather than transport only their own goods, they would move for hire the finished and raw materials of other traders.

In Europe these middlemen provided a wide range of transportation arrangement services that also included the payment of duties and taxes. In the nineteenth century, middlemen became increasingly important with the beginnings of rail transport.

In the first half of the twentieth century, the business of moving goods to market took place on waterfront piers, in warehouses, and on loading docks. Transportation was not managed by someone in the executive suite but was relegated to a warehouse or production manager. In some organizations, traffic managers routed truck and rail transport and maneuvered a maze of transport pricing tariffs that were federally regulated until a period of deregulation of air, motor, and rail that started in the 1970s and lasted through the early 1980s. Ocean was later partially deregulated, but there are still vestiges of federal rate regulation for international ocean transportation in the United States.

With rate deregulation, carriers could establish their own pricing and in many instances sign individual contracts with shippers.

Product, pricing, place, and promotion, the four *P*s of marketing, meant little to a consumer in the 1920s looking for a new carpet sweeper when choices were few and outlets even fewer, depending on the size of the town. Sears, Roebuck and Co. introduced its first catalog in 1894 to compete with an earlier entrant into the business of mail-order catalogs—Montgomery Ward. By the 1920s across the United States, mail-order and national retail stores were displacing general stores. Consumers now had choices and could purchase at a retail outlet in a city or through a catalog with postal delivery.

Consumers of larger products such as automobiles had a large assortment of companies to purchase from in the 1920s. What Sears and Montgomery Ward did for retail, Ford Motor Co. did for automobile production, not only through mass production but through control of its supply chain.

Production and retail demands elevated the lowly role of the traffic manager to that of a logistician. Logistics became the buzzword of the industry. A national organization of transportation professionals founded in 1963 called the National Council of Physical Distribution Management (NCPDM) even changed its name in 1985 to the Council of Logistics Management. The value of bringing products to market and the higher demand for a variety of transport services became a key driver.

Japanese transplant factories were moving into new markets all over the world bringing in new sourcing and delivery techniques like Kanban and Just-in-Time (JIT) inventory. The collision of longer international supply chains along with the information age forced a change in both manufacturing and retail techniques that became dependent on efficient and timely transportation.

Today, transportation is purchased in terms of supply chain demand. The distribution channel has become a critical component whether it is sourced domestically or internationally. The market drives the speed. If the product is a new introduction of a higher-priced consumer electronic, then speed becomes the norm, preferably via express air. As the product moves down its life cycle, conventional air is an appropriate second stage until the product approaches near market saturation. At that point it is moved down another mode to ocean or motor carrier depending on its origin. The process is repeated as new versions of the product are subsequently introduced.

The Council of Logistics Management changed its name again——to Council of Supply Chain Management Professionals (CSCMP). The simple movement of a railcar load of carpet sweepers and then final delivery to hundreds of catalog buyers in the 1920s by a traffic manager evolved to the multiple truckload shipment to the retailer that the logistician was coordinating in the 1980s, to the supply chain manager who sourced product anywhere in the world and provided his or her organization with a variety of speeds to any destination in the world as well as up-to-the-minute information on the individual parts, components, color, or size characteristics of the shipment. The shipment can be viewed from the time the purchase order is issued to the time it is delivered to the end consumer or the retail location where it will be sold—live via the Internet. Manufacturers and retailers alike have become dependent on information about the entire supply chain process.

In order to adapt to today's fast-changing demand, a manufacturer or retailer may require an internal broad-based, decision-making tool such as an enterprise resource planning (ERP) application that incorporates components of a company's manufacturing, financial, customer relationship management (CRM), distribution, supply chain, and other systems. They also rely on transportation and related trade services suppliers that can update their system with both carrier and trade-related data.

Information is a key component of every transportation transaction because of changes in product demand, economic conditions, sourcing and manufacturing issues, customs and tax requirements, and new cargo security initiatives.

Today's customers do not depend on the cargo of one ship to make their buying decisions. When today's customers call, they want the seller to confirm immediate availability or to have their size and color by the end of the week. And even more so, customers want the options to have the order shipped by standard delivery, two-day, or overnight.

Ownership Options

Companies from retailers to manufacturers have to decide whether to own their own transportation or to buy transportation services from a service provider.

- **Contract/For-Hire Carriers.** Contract carriers, also known as for-hire carriers, will provide services to any company or the general public. Contract carriers will provide services to companies on a one-time or regular basis. The advantages of using a contract carrier are the competitive rates and company management can then focus on core competencies.
- **Private Carriers.** Private carriers are fleets owned by individual companies. The advantages are the control of costs, travel routes, pickup and delivery times, and the ability to advertise the company brand on company-owned vehicles.

TRANSPORTATION PLANNING AND ADMINISTRATION

Proper transportation administration allows a company to lower costs and speed product delivery—both powerful marketing claims. Extreme weather conditions and unpredictable changes in business requirements, day-to-day or even hour-to-hour, require quick decisions to avoid, or recover from, service failures. Transportation administration includes choosing the correct information technology, mode of transportation, transportation support services, materials-handling equipment, transaction documentation, and payment options. It also includes understanding the appropriate mode selection factors.

Information Technology

Information technology improves transportation planning capabilities by allowing managers to optimize the selection of transportation service between modes and then within a group of carriers within a specific mode. Technology enables buyers of transportation services to respond quickly to changing markets and adjust the volume and speed of freight as well as identify shipments that are at risk of failing to meet service requirements. Technology, such as databases, Web sites, toll-free-telephone numbers, Electronic Data Interchange (EDI), and tracking information delivered to a mobile device provides the capability to deliver freight and information faster. This information gives customers advance notice of deliveries, confirms deliveries, and provides more flexibility to plan their manufacturing and distribution programs. This planning capability reduces the risk of overproducing products, having to divert excess products to warehouses, or pay for premium transportation to avoid stock-outs. For example, FedEx has always used the latest technology and thus is able to tout their excellent delivery record in their marketing communications: "When it absolutely, positively has to be there overnight." Customers heard the message and responded; FedEx became the first U.S. company to reach $1 billion in sales within 10 years of start-up.

Asset Carriers

Carriers, commonly referred to as asset carriers, include a variety of transportation mode operators that offer transportation services such as ocean, motor carrier, air, rail, barge, and pipeline for hire to the general public. They operate the equipment or conveyance that moves freight from origin to destination under general tariff rates or contract rates for volume shippers. In some instances carriers may offer transportation services to a parent company or affiliate only. Many retail operations manage their own motor carrier truck fleets for set delivery runs from their distribution centers to their retail operations. Most pipelines that transport coal slurry or petroleum products operate for the exclusive use of a parent company.

Transportation assets include trucks, ocean vessels, railroad cars, river or ocean barges and tugs, aircraft, and pipelines.

New international transportation conglomerates, called integrators, offer multimodal transportation solutions—both asset and nonasset-based. Both FedEx and UPS are examples of integrators that are multimodal and provide asset and nonasset-based transportation on a global basis.

Transportation Services Options

Third-party suppliers of transportation services do not own their own transportation assets, but instead contract with asset owners for transportation services for their customers. Third-party suppliers often will use combinations of carriers and modes to provide their customers with the best cost and service attributes of each transportation service required. They can leverage their greater volume of business with the carriers to get a lower price than their individual customers might be able to obtain on their own. Third-party suppliers include domestic and international freight forwarders, contract logistics companies, intermodal companies, and domestic transportation motor carrier brokers.

Freight Forwarders

There are several kinds of freight forwarders; some are exclusively domestic or international, and others are both. Additionally some freight forwarders concentrate exclusively on airfreight, ocean freight, truck freight, or may handle any combination. Still others focus on specific commodities such as perishables. Some freight forwarders will contract with local less-than-truckload motor carriers (LTL) to pick up LTL in surrounding states.

When freight is destined for surrounding states outside the destination of the truckload, a domestic freight forwarder may consolidate freight from multiple shippers, arrange for transport of the freight in a truckload to a particular region, and then hand off the shipment to LTL carriers for delivery.

A great deal of air cargo revenue is forwarded to the airlines for transit by third-party airfreight forwarders. Airfreight forwarders usually do not own their own aircraft, but instead contract for cargo space on passenger and cargo air carriers. These contracts usually include an agreed-upon price to move a set volume of freight within a set period of time, months or annual, on specific scheduled flights. Some airfreight forwarders may own local delivery trucks or may contract with local delivery motor carriers or dedicated contract motor carriers.

Since most commercial passenger carriers do not advertise the fact that they also carry freight, they rely on airfreight forwarders to provide freight volumes. Airfreight forwarders offer flexibility of service through the use of multiple flights from a variety of air carriers. The end product is packaged as a seamless service to the customer by one responsible transportation provider from origin to destination. The entry barriers are low because capital investment is low. However, depending on the market and geographic scope of the service, a variety of skilled professionals are involved. Knowledge of the freight delivery industry and the customer base being served are the requirements for entry. Hence the industry contains many small suppliers as well as large global providers. Domestic freight forwarders in the United States are licensed by the Surface Transportation Board. Ocean international freight forwarders, commonly known as Non-Vessel Operating Common Carriers (NVOCC), are licensed by the Federal Maritime Commission and are required to file independent tariffs or provide transport through contracts for ocean cargo moving into and out of the United States. Airfreight forwarders, both domestic and international, comply with the guidelines of the International Air Transport Association (IATA) as well as the U.S. Transportation Security Administration or other international security guidelines.

Shippers Associations

Shippers associations may set up operations called consolidations or distributions to achieve economies of scale for their members. Shippers or receivers use methods similar to freight forwarders to contract with asset owners or dedicated warehouses for assembly and distribution services.

Contract Logistics Companies/Third-Party Logistics

Logistics (transportation, wholesale, and/or warehousing) companies handle the agreed portions of a shipper's or receiver's transportation functions. Often the services are tailored to meet the specific customer's needs, which might include parcels, packages, LTL, truckload, warehousing, along with some or all components of freight forwarding. Some logistics companies also provide subassembly operations, kitting, inventory control, auditing and payment of freight bills, as well as route optimization of traffic among the carriers. Some logistics companies are subsidiaries of asset owners, but others are stand-alone entities. They operate on long-term contracts and manage the carrier relationship for the customer.

Intermodal Companies

Intermodal companies serve the occasional user of rail TOFC (trailer on flat car) or COFC (container on flat car) rail service. These companies buy space wholesale from railroads and resell it at their own rates. Intermodal companies will arrange the movement of trailers or containers from origin to rail and rail to destination by contracting with local and long-haul truckers. Intermodal companies provide other customer services in addition to the movement of freight, including expediting shipments, tracking, and auditing freight bills. Similar to most nonasset carriers, they make their profit on the spread between their contract prices and the retail charges to their customers. The rate charge is generally less than the shipper could secure on its own by contracting directly with the carrier.

Transportation Brokers

Transportation motor carrier brokers contract with shippers or receivers and arrange for motor carriers to meet their service needs on specific movements of freight. In the United States, motor carrier brokers are licensed by the Federal Motor Carrier Safety Administration.

Materials-Handling Equipment

Materials handling is the process of moving bulk or packaged freight while in transit. It also includes the movement of components, raw materials, or finished products in manufacturing plants or warehouses. The use of automated and mechanized materials handling can reduce costs through reduced handling time, reduced breakage, reduced theft, increased load capacity, and improved worker handling conditions. Elements of materials handling include the following:

- **Air/Ocean Containers.** *Air/ocean containers* are large metal containers used to hold assorted small pieces of freight. These containers can be locked for inventory or security purposes and sealed against salt air. Standardized container sizes for air transport are dictated by aircraft model. Ocean containers come in a variety of configurations: 45-foot, 40-foot, and 20-foot. In addition, ocean containers can be enclosed boxes similar to a truck trailer without wheels, a flat rack similar to a flatbed truck without wheels, refrigerated, or even a tank version.

- **Pallets.** *Pallets* are either wood or plastic bases used to hold stacks of products and have slots for convenient movement by forklifts. Pallets come in several configurations, some dependent on industry and regulatory requirements.
- **Other.** Additional equipment is also used in moving materials from one mode of transportation to another, including conveyor belts, forklifts, and cranes.

Transport Transaction Documentation

Transaction documentation is the recording of information relative to a particular shipment or transportation movement. The major documents include:

- **Bill of Lading.** A *bill of lading* is the principal document in the transaction between the shipper and carrier. It acts as a receipt, as routing instructions, as evidence of ownership of the goods, and as a contract for carriage.
- **Air Waybill.** This is similar to a bill of lading but for airfreight.
- **Freight Bill.** A freight bill contains a detailed description of the shipment and the charges due for transportation and other services performed by the carriers.
- **Packing List.** A packing list may accompany a shipment and contains quantity of freight and general description for a specific shipment but no information about charges.
- **Delivery Receipt.** A *delivery receipt* is a record and description of each shipment that is signed by the consignee or agent at the time of delivery. It is proof that the shipment was delivered in good order (or with shortage or damage notations) on the date of delivery.
- **Claim Form.** A claim form is filed with the carrier when freight is damaged or missing. Liability rules vary by mode and type of carrier.

Payment Options

Freight traffic typically has several contractual options for payment of shipping charges. Examples include:

- **FOB—Origin.** Free on Board—Origin indicates that the buyer (consignee) pays for the freight charges when they receive the goods (collect). When the carrier signs the Bill of Lading on an FOB—Origin shipment, the title passes to the consignee.
- **FOB—Destination.** Free on Board—Destination indicates that the shipper pays for the freight charges (prepaid). Title does not pass on the FOB—Destination until the consignee signs the delivery receipt.
- **ExW (Ex Works).** Ex Works obligates the shipper to provide necessary packing and make the freight available at the inland point of origin only.
- **CIF (Cost, Insurance, and Freight).** CIF obligates the shipper to pay all of the charges to the named port of destination. The exporter/shipper will be responsible for making all arrangements for the shipment and will bear all costs for inland freight, ocean or airfreight, packing, container stuffing, port fees, loading on board, unloading, and any drayage (local delivery) fees.

TRANSPORTATION MODE SELECTION FACTORS

Several factors should be considered when determining the *mode*, or method, of transportation needed for a product. Selection influences include the market location, the product, timing, cost, shipment integrity, and inventory control.

Market Location

The resources needed to create a transportation distribution network are determined by the location of the manufacturer, or shipper, and the markets or customers to be served. Transportation may be influenced by markets that are geographically dispersed (local, national, or international) or seasonal (snowblowers or bathing suits). Customer dispersion may require a wide range of wholesale or retail receiving points. Distribution may be to a warehouse or distribution center or directly to the end user, saving both cost and time, through a process called distribution bypass.

Product Characteristics

The selection of the transportation mode is determined by the following product factors: physical characteristics, quantity, value, perishability, and hazardous characteristics. Products may be easily packaged and handled, or they may be large and bulky and require special handling equipment to load, transport, and deliver to the customer. For example, perishable and temperature-sensitive items, such as ice cream and hothouse flowers, require specialized carriers that have refrigerated or heated transport units. Liquid items, such as vegetable oil, require rail tank cars, tank trucks, or ocean container tanks, or pipelines. Other features of the product also may limit the distribution options, such as susceptibility to damage (automobiles or glassware), or the potential to damage other freight while en route (steel beams or chemicals).

Shipping Time

Some products can be time-sensitive because of their high cost, such as computer chips, or because of their perishability, such as flowers or fresh food. Thus, neither the shipper nor receiver of these goods wants to keep a large inventory on hand and will select faster transportation options. At the same time, not having these items when needed can cause a retailer to miss sales and lose customers. For example, a shortage of computer chips can cause a computer manufacturer to shut down an assembly line and fail to make timely shipments to its customers. Some products on market launch will use faster transport such as air yet as the product moves down in demand may end up toward the end of its life cycle in rail, truck, or ocean modes.

Shipping Cost

Shipping prices can be based on several factors, including product weight, container size, length of haul (the number of railroad boxcars or truck containers), and distance and speed of delivery. Carriers desire to be profitable and thus must create economies of scale by hauling loads as full as possible. Lower per-unit rates are charged for a truckload rather than less-than-truckload (LTL), and ocean container-load rather than less-than-container-load (LCL).

Some products are price-sensitive and will not support a large transportation cost. For example, the value of a ton of coal or ore is so low that it must be shipped by the lowest cost method. The transportation cost will determine what geographic markets can be served from a producing location, as well as the mode of transportation. For example, coal or iron ore usually are shipped in bulk by rail or water. Both rail and water are relatively low-cost, slow modes when compared to alternative transportation modes.

For some products, the transportation costs are small in relation to the value of the product, or when compared with the alternative costs of large inventories or lost sales and unhappy customers. Therefore, the shipper or receiver will accept larger transportation costs for these products. These products usually are transported by faster and more expensive modes, such as air or truck rather than rail. The costs of transporting a product of high value that is lightweight, low-bulk, and easily packaged (clothing, computer chips) usually will be an insignificant part of the cost to both the consumer and manufacturer.

Shipment Integrity

Customers expect their shipments to arrive intact. Shipment integrity may be compromised due to damages or cargo theft. Damages may be derived from accidents due to weather or driver fatigue or poor packaging. Losses of items with motor carriers, such as consumer electronics, jewelry, and appliances, amount to over $10 billion a year.[2]

Inventory Control

Controlling inventory costs is an important goal of most companies. This goal can be aided significantly by the reliable and timely delivery of parts to the manufacturer and then timely delivery of product to the customer. The savings derived through decreasing inventory and safety stocks (minimum inventory) should be balanced with the cost of using faster transportation and potential stock-outs from late Just-in-Time deliveries. Keeping a low inventory can be a marketing advantage.

CARGO TRANSPORTATION COMPARATIVE FACTORS

Mode	Cost per Ton-Mile	Average Speed	Commercial Market Points Served
Train (1)	2.34 cents	19 mph	31,500 rail stations
Ship (2)	5.0 cents	12 mph	185 ports
Barge (3)	<1.0 cents	10 mph	5,426 ports
Truck (4)	12.5 cents	45 mph	Millions of retailers
Air (5)	58.8 cents	420 mph	124 major cargo airports
Pipeline: (6)			
Gas	NA cents	15 mph	1,000+ cities/towns
Oil	NA cents	5 mph	1,000+ cities/towns

Source: (1) Association of American Railroads; (2) Port Association, Chamber of Shipping; (3) U.S. Corps of Engineers; (4) Air Transport Association, Air Transport Association of America; (5) Federal Aviation Administration; (6) INGA, Association of Oil Pipe Lines, U.S. Department of Transportation, 2000.

FREIGHT TRANSPORTATION MODES
Freight Trucking
by Con-way

During the 1960s, trucking replaced rail as the dominant form of freight transport in the United States. Trucking companies (also referred to as motor carriers or common carriers) remain the principal method of transporting freight, collecting 84 percent of all revenue spent moving freight. The industry was effectively deregulated in 1980 when President Jimmy Carter signed the Motor Carrier Deregulation Act when there were fewer than 20,000 trucking companies in business. Today there are over 500,000 trucking companies in operation. Most of these companies (87 percent) are small businesses and operate six or fewer trucks; 96 percent operate with fewer than 20 trucks. Trucking is not competitive with rail and water transport for the movement of low-value, high-density commodities such as coal, some agricultural products, and international intermodal containers.

The trucking industry relies on a strong national system of highways and state roads to move goods. In 2007 commercial trucks drove 114 billion miles. Trucks are the only mode of freight transport that services 100 percent of the communities in America, with 80 percent of the country served exclusively by trucks delivering and picking up freight.

Trucking's major advantage is that it serves 100 percent of the country and can move almost any type of freight, sometimes on specifically designed vehicles. Quick transit times are also an advantage, especially for short-distance deliveries. As distances increase, this advantage decreases to some extent but is replaced by the ability to pick up and deliver freight without changing transport mode, thereby minimizing cargo handling to avoid possible cargo damage.

Some freight requires special handling and has regulatory requirements that are sometimes more restrictive for transport by truck than by other modes. This is particularly true for moving hazardous materials, chemicals, and explosives. Trucks are far more restricted by their size and weight than other modes.

Classifications of Trucking

To understand how the different segments of the trucking industry serve the country's varied freight transportation needs, it is helpful to separate the industry into categories. There are three basic ways to classify trucking: by ownership of goods, by volume of goods, and by type of truck moving the goods.

Ownership of Goods

When classifying the industry by ownership of goods, there are two components: private carriers and for-hire carriers. Private carrier companies such as PepsiCo, Walmart, and Giant Foods own their own truck fleets and haul much of their own freight. In contrast, for-hire carriers such as Schneider National, J. B. Hunt, Con-way, U.S. Xpress, and UPS haul goods for other owners. Today, the industry splits around 50 percent private and 50 percent for-hire carriers.

Volume of Goods

The trucking industry also is classified by volume: truckload (TL), less-than-truckload (LTL), small package delivery, intermodal, and specialized.

- **Truckload Carrier (TL).** A truckload carrier transports a trailer full of a single commodity, generally for a single shipper to a single destination. For example, a truckload of computers is moved from a manufacturer to a distribution center or a truckload of lumber is moved from the mill to the lumber yard. Approximately 80 percent of truck freight is moved by the truckload.

  Truckload carriers have few maintenance and terminal facilities. Each tractor semitrailer is assigned a driver or a driver team and moves when the freight is loaded at the shipper's point of origin to be transported directly to the receiver destination. Truckload carrier companies often focus their operations on commodity markets, geographic areas, certain lanes of traffic, or common routes (such as New York to Chicago).

  Truckload service is fast, reliable, and cost-competitive with rail on short and medium distances (less than 750 miles) but less competitive as distance increases and delivery time is of less importance.

- **Less-Than-Truckload (LTL).** LTL shipments are smaller-sized shipments of freight that require transport, often just a pallet or two. An LTL carrier will move many shipments to many destinations on one truck. For national LTL carriers, that is generally a tractor with twin pup trailers. National LTL companies—like Con-way, YRC, ABF, FedEx Freight, and UPS—use a network of distribution centers, known as terminals or service centers, with cross-docking capabilities. These facilities function as either local pickup and delivery centers or as sorting centers. Sorting centers, often called break-bulk, hubs, or freight assembly centers (FACs), serve to combine shipments from several pickup/delivery facilities and combine common destination shipments in a full truck. The double trailer trucks move between hubs on regular schedules and routes. When the shipment reaches its final hub, it may be moved to a local delivery trailer for its final move to the receiver.

  The national LTL network and infrastructure of terminals uses a business model similar to that of the major airlines—a hub and spoke strategy for moving LTL freight around the country. The advantage when serving the small shipment market is that the LTL carrier can provide the benefits of flexibility and proximity to the customer not available in the truckload market. The disadvantages are the high overhead costs of terminal facilities and the need for employees to staff them.

- **Small Package Delivery.** Individual consumers, utilizing Internet and catalog retail services, require transport service for small packages. Companies such as United Parcel Service, FedEx, and the U.S. Postal Service deliver hundreds of millions of these small packages each year.

- **Intermodal.** There are some transportation relationships between truckload, less-than-truckload, small package carriers, and railroads. Transcontinental traffic takes advantage of the flexibility of trucks and the cost advantage of rail on long-distance moves. These relationships can offer the customer a combination of reduced cost and, at times, faster service.

- **Specialized.** Many trucking companies cannot be easily classified as either truckload or less-than-truckload. These companies are specialized carriers, and their emphasis is on serving a specific market or type of operation. They may even provide services in several different categories. They are best described by the size or type of truck they use to serve their customer base. Sizes and shapes vary widely within the industry and largely depend on the type of freight that needs to be moved. Specialized truck companies can serve nationwide or in only one metropolitan area.

Types of Trucks

Trucking size is generally divided into three weight categories:

- **Light Trucks.** Small straight trucks mostly used in city operations move local merchandise (flowers, grocery delivery, etc) from point to point within a metropolitan area.
- **Medium-Weight Trucks.** Larger but still comfortable on a city street; used by utility companies and for food and parts delivery, and so on.
- **Heavy-Duty Trucks.** Used in construction and interstate commerce.

The amount of freight needing transport has steadily increased over the years and can be expected to increase further as economies grow and become more global by nature. The number of trucks and the highway networks they use will have to increase in order to keep up with the demand for transport.

FREIGHT—TRAINS
by BNSF

Among all modes of land transportation, railroads are best suited to moving large volumes over long distances quickly and at low cost. Railroads account for 43 percent of U.S. intercity freight volume (in ton-miles), more than any other mode of transportation. Increasingly, railroads form a key link in multimodal supply chains that may stretch literally halfway around the world; that includes ships and trucks as well as trains.

Railroads are unique from other forms of transportation in North America in that they own and maintain (and pay taxes on) their own infrastructure. From 1980 to 2007, railroads reinvested $420 billion into their systems.[3] On the other hand, infrastructure used by motor, water, and air carriers is provided by the public in exchange for user fees, which may or may not cover the total cost—including maintenance—of the infrastructure used by those modes of transportation.

The key advantage of railroads is the relatively low friction encountered by a steel wheel rolling on a steel rail. That inherent advantage makes railroads more fuel- and emissions-efficient than other modes of overland transportation. Freight trains can move one ton of freight 436 miles on just one gallon of fuel. If just 10 percent of the long-haul freight that currently moves by truck were diverted to rail, fuel savings would be more than 1 billion gallons per year.

Greenhouse gas emissions are directly related to fuel consumption. That means that moving freight by rail instead of truck reduces greenhouse gas emissions by two-thirds or more. And unlike the trucking industry, railroad companies have increased their fuel efficiency more than 85 percent since 1980. Today, one train can take nearly 300 long-haul trucks off the highway—and that means fewer emissions, cleaner air, and less congestion on our highways.

Increasingly, railroad and trucking companies are working as supply chain partners to provide customers with the flexibility of trucking and the long-haul efficiency of rail. Shipments—from small packages to truckloads—are picked up at a customer's facility by a trucking company, which then hauls the loaded trailers or containers to a railroad intermodal hub center, where they are loaded aboard a train for the long haul. Unloaded at a similar intermodal hub center, shipments are delivered to their final destination by a trucking company.

Using rail for the long haul allows trucking companies to retain their customers, while managing issues such as driver availability, insurance, volatile fuel prices, and highway congestion. Depending on the markets served, intermodal service can be competitive at origin-destination distances from 700 miles on up. Intermodal service also provides a key link for imports and exports, which are moved directly from ship to railcar, or vice versa, at ports. Where port capacity is inadequate for on-dock loading and unloading, containers are moved a short distance by highway.

Intermodal trains typically run from an origin hub center to a destination hub center with little or no intermediate switching, and railroads are at their most efficient when moving whole trains from a single origin to a single destination. Traditionally, railroads gathered individual freight cars, or small groups of cars, and combined cars for similar destinations into trains in a nearby switchyard. Today, many railroads are moving toward a logistics park concept, where warehousing and distribution centers are combined with rail and highway access to make the freight-car gathering and distribution process more consistent, reliable, and efficient.

The ultimate in train efficiency is the *unit train*—a whole train that moves a single commodity from a single origin to a single destination. Most coal moves in unit trains, and more and more grain is moved in unit trains and shuttle trains, which load and unload within a specified time period and move from origin to destination with no intermediate switching. They then cycle back to the originating elevator for another load. Along with double-stacking containers on railcars, the advent of the unit train dramatically altered the economics of railroading.

In the future, railroads may play an even greater role in surface transportation. National transportation policy needs to adopt a multimodal approach that seeks to leverage the inherent advantages of each mode of transportation from a total global supply chain perspective, rather than viewing each mode in isolation. Under that approach, America's rail network can be used to lower greenhouse gas emissions, improve overall fuel efficiency, and reduce highway congestion, while providing the transportation our economy needs to function and to be competitive in the global marketplace.

FREIGHT—AIR
by Atlas Air Worldwide Holdings, Inc.

Airfreight is a dynamic global industry, linking producers, manufacturers, and shippers on different continents with business customers and end use consumers around the world.

High-value, time-sensitive-to-market products, produce and express packages, and Just-in-Time intermediate goods rely on airfreight for timely delivery and effective supply chain management over great distances.

Airfreight plays a vital role in the increasing pace of international trade, whether flying semiconductors and consumer electronics and apparel from Asia, fresh seafood and fresh-cut flowers from South America, fresh fruits and vegetables from Africa, pharmaceuticals from Europe, or capital goods and equipment from North America, among many other uses.

IATA (International Air Transport Association), estimates that airfreight carriage generates approximately $55 billion in total annual revenues for the airline industry, or roughly 11 percent of the industry's total revenue. This revenue is predicted to reach new highs in the years ahead. Commercial airfreight carriers include cargo-only operators, carriers whose fleets provide both passenger belly-cargo and pure-cargo service, passenger airlines offering only belly-cargo capacity, and outsource providers of freighter-aircraft assets and services such as Atlas Air Worldwide Holdings, which enable carriers without the necessary scale or in-house capability to optimize their presence in the airfreight market.

Commercial airfreight providers generally operate airport-to-airport routes on a specific schedule, and customers—primarily international freight forwarders and shippers—pay to have their freight carried on those routes and schedules.

More than half of the world's airfreight is currently transported in the belly space of passenger aircraft, but airfreight and airline passengers frequently do not travel to the same destinations on the same schedules. Cargo-only scheduled service operations seek to address this issue and are designed to provide prime-time arrivals and departures on key days of consolidation for freight forwarders and shippers, coordinating various departure and arrival combination points in order to offset directional imbalances of traffic, and arranging global connecting or through-service networks between economic regions to achieve higher overall yields and aircraft load factors.

Airfreight traffic, however, is highly seasonal in nature. Peak activity in global trade flows typically occurs during the retail holiday season, which traditionally begins in September and lasts through mid-December. This usually results in a significant decline in demand for airfreight services in the first quarter of the year.

Global airfreight activity is characterized by substantial east-west trade flows between Asia, North America, and Europe; strong intra-Asia development; and growing economic ties between the northern and southern hemispheres. With exports from Asia, especially China, usually outweighing imports from North America and Europe, airfreight operators must be especially mindful about managing the economics of front-haul (more fully loaded) and back-haul (less fully loaded) routes.

Industry studies forecast that global air cargo traffic will triple over the next two decades, driven mainly by demand in Asian markets but also benefiting from improved links between Latin America and Africa and more advanced markets in the northern hemisphere.

As airfreight demand continues to increase, the world's freighter fleet is forecast to double in number over the next 20 years, with a preference in long-haul, international trade lanes for new, wide-body freighters; increased revenue payloads; more fuel-efficient and emission-friendly engines; and other modern design technology. Given the expected improvement in wide-body operating dynamics, industry observers expect that freighters will begin to carry a greater share of airfreight than passenger-aircraft.

Aircraft utilization and the ability to obtain favorable rates can be affected by many factors, including global demand for airfreight, global economic conditions, and fuel costs, which have been both high and volatile over the past few years.

The market for air cargo services is highly competitive and fragmented. Competitors vary by both geographic market and type of service. Primary competitive factors include access to desired airports at commercially viable times, flight frequency, reliability, geographic coverage, payload capacity, and price.

Freight transportation is generally a choice between several means of movement: road, rail, ocean, air, or some combination of each. Long-haul, intercontinental freight transportation, however, is generally a choice between ocean and air transport, and the most important factors in making that decision are volume and weight, cost, value, speed to market, and security.

Measured on a per-kilo basis, airfreight can be approximately 10 times more expensive than ocean transport. As a result, bulk commodities and more widely available, less time-sensitive-to-market consumer and capital goods generally are shipped by lower-cost ocean transport. Meanwhile, higher-value, lower-density products with relatively short shelf lives, urgent delivery requirements, or more significant security considerations benefit from the speed, reliability, and tighter monitoring of items shipped by airfreight.

FREIGHT—OCEAN SHIPPING
by Overseas Shipholding Group Inc. (OSG)

Introduction

The contribution of shipping has been vital to the growth and prosperity of the global economy. Shipping has been, is, and will remain an integral part of the world's economic growth for the simple reason that it represents the most cost-efficient means of moving freight from major producing centers to major consuming centers.

There are two primary types of ocean carriers: liner and tramp. Liners provide regular service over fixed routes on an arrival and departure schedule. Tramp carriers operate on a contractual basis and go where the traffic leads them on a nonscheduled basis.

International cargo moves via ocean lines between ports over repetitive ocean routes known as trades. Ocean shipping handles bulk commodities (primarily oil) and containers (packed with products from shirts to cars). Commodities account for 91 percent of all ocean shipping (by tonnage); cargo containers account for 9 percent.[4]

Advantages

The primary advantage of water transport for most cargoes is that it is very cost-efficient. Water transportation can move large quantities of freight with no limits other than the size of the ship and the ability of the ports to accommodate the vessel. The financial advantages of water transport for commodities, where speed is not a decisive factor, are significant. However, freight rates are highly cyclical and variable, a market factor that can minimize the cost-effectiveness of waterborne transportation. The major costs of water transport for water transportation companies tend to be fixed. This is a result of the large investment in capital required to build the ships, the cost of fuel, and costs associated with crewing and shoreside support. Thus, the variable expense to move the cargo is generally lower than all other transportation modes except pipeline.

Disadvantages

The major disadvantage of water transportation is transit time, which is slow relative to other modes and freight rate volatility. In addition, water transportation lacks market service flexibility so must involve other transportation modes and additional costs for final delivery to customers not directly located on water.

Shipping Rates

Strong competition exists among container shipping lines. In order to offer more sailings, without actually increasing capacity, many ocean carriers have formed partnerships. These partners agree to move containers on each other's ships allowing for ocean carriers to avoid partial-load sailings. Cost savings occur when less-than-container-load (LCL) shipments are combined to create full containers for the ocean carriers or third-party suppliers who contract with shipping lines for lower full-container rates.

The delicate balance between vessel demand and vessel supply drives day rates in the unregulated freight transportation market. Charterers seek to get the lowest freight rate price while ship owners seek the highest. In the tanker industry, for example, the supply of oil, not price, predominantly drives rates. Market psychology factors that impact tanker freight rates can cause the market to move 50 percent or more within a few days. Such factors include geopolitical events that impact oil supply sources and transportation availability, war, weather, and, most recently, piracy in the Gulf of Aden. Additionally, some nations have sought to diversify their sources of oil. China, for example, has reduced its dependence on imported oil from the Arabian Gulf and increased imports from South America, a long-haul route that impacts the supply of tankers available to trade in the market at any one time.

Global Regulations and Standards

As a result of shipping's inherently international nature, regulations concerning the industry are developed at a global level. It is vital that companies worldwide be subject to uniform regulations on matters such as construction standards, navigational rules, and standards of crew competence. In the shipping industry, the principal regulator is the International Maritime Organization (IMO), which is the United Nations agency responsible for the safety of life at sea and the protection of the environment.

FREIGHT—INLAND BARGE
by Ingram Barge

The inland barge industry annually transports about 620 million tons of dry and liquid cargo to ports along the Mississippi River and major tributaries such as the Ohio, Illinois, Tennessee, Cumberland, and Arkansas rivers. Operations also occur on the Gulf intercoastal waterway from Brownsville, Texas, to the Florida Panhandle.

Carriers operate about 22,000 barges and 4,000 towboats. The towboats push a group of individual barges secured together by steel cables into an integrated tow. The number of barges within each tow depends on river geography, barge type, and the towboats' horsepower.

Most dry and liquid cargoes move as heavy bulk. About 20,000 hopper barges transport products such as coal, grain, fertilizer, aggregates, and cement. Tank barges move petroleum, chemicals, asphalt, and liquid fertilizers. The industry's largest tows operate on the Mississippi River between St. Louis and New Orleans where sufficient channel depth is maintained without lock and dam structures. On this stretch of river a single towboat of up to 10,000 hp can push 30 to 60 hopper barges, or up to 70,000 tons, depending on the mix of empties and loads. Most barge lines operate a hub and spoke distribution network.

The advantages of inland barge transportation include low operating costs and relatively low environmental impacts vis-à-vis traffic congestion, noise, and emissions. Barge operations are able to carry additional volume without significantly higher unit costs due in part to the U.S. inland waterways infrastructure capacity. The disadvantages include slower transits and seasonal, weather-related navigational disruptions.

FREIGHT—PIPELINES
by Colonial Pipeline Co.

Over one-half of the total energy consumed in the United States is delivered to consumers through pipeline networks that transport oil, refined petroleum products, and natural gas. Together, oil and natural gas satisfy almost two-thirds of the U.S. energy demand. Pipelines make up the entirety of the domestic natural gas transportation system and are responsible for 67 percent of the domestic deliveries of oil. These pipelines are a safe, efficient, reliable, and irreplaceable link in the U.S. energy infrastructure.

There are several distinct energy pipeline networks in the United States that depend on the energy product being transported. There are approximately 300,000 miles of large-diameter, high-pressure transmission pipelines that move natural gas from processing plants in producing regions or liquefied natural gas import terminals to local distribution utilities, industrial consumers, and electric power plants. There are approximately 168,000 miles of crude oil and refined product trunk lines and delivery lines. These include distinct networks for delivering crude oil from producing regions and import terminals to refineries; refined products; highly volatile liquids; and carbon dioxide. In addition, there are gathering lines for both natural gas and crude oil that move energy from producing wells to the long-haul highway pipelines, as well as smaller diameter distribution or delivery pipelines that transport energy from the transmission pipelines to the consumer (or in the case of refined petroleum products to the point of transfer to trucks or other delivery systems).

Energy pipelines often span multiple states and, in some cases, multiple regions. This is because, both globally and within the United States, the regions that supply energy frequently are far removed from the regions with the most demand for energy. As a result, these long-haul pipelines are engaged in interstate commerce and are regulated by the federal government. In addition to the federal regulations that apply to all types of businesses, energy pipelines are subject to safety and rate regulations under federal laws written specifically for the pipeline industry.

Natural gas pipeline rates are regulated under laws premised on the assumption that the pipeline operators are natural monopolists that do not have competition. As a result, rates are set on a cost-of-service basis, much like the rates for a local electric or natural gas utility. Oil pipeline regulations require that transportation rates be just and reasonable as well as nondiscriminatory. Pipeline companies compete to construct new pipelines to attach new supplies or serve growing consuming markets.

In most cases, energy pipeline companies do not own the energy products that they transport. In this sense, pipeline companies are like a trucking company, a railroad, or an airfreight company (i.e., the business model is based on the service of transporting goods on behalf of third parties rather than on the sale of the good that is being transported).

Energy pipelines are capital intensive, long-lived assets. Also, unlike other modes of transportation where assets can be redeployed to other markets (i.e., trucks, airplanes, railroad cars), pipelines cannot be moved. This fact, together with the fact that energy pipelines are subject to rate regulation, means that a pipeline owner is unlikely to commit its capital to a new project unless there are shippers (i.e., customers) that are willing to sign long-term contracts to take pipeline capacity on a firm basis.

Pipeline operations are increasingly automated, run from control centers where specialized communication systems monitor the pipeline and control equipment used to power the pipelines. The Supervisory Control and Data Acquisition (SCADA) system transmits operating status, flow volumes, pressure, and temperature information. Regular maintenance, pipeline coating, and efforts to prevent corrosion can extend the life of pipelines indefinitely. Government regulation and outreach efforts such as the national "811—Call Before You Dig" campaign help protect the public in areas where pipelines are buried as well as help prevent disruptions in supply.

PASSENGER TRANSPORTATION MODES

Passengers' predominant concerns for transportation are time, cost, and safety. Passenger transportation modes include, in order of number of passengers served: airlines, bus lines, trains, and cruise lines.

PASSENGER MODE COMPARISON			
Mode	U.S. Destinations Served	Cost of Cross-Country Trip	Speed of Cross-Country Trip
		(Miami, FL, to San Diego, CA, one-way)	
Air (1)	3,364	$ 394	6 hours
Bus (2)	3,066	$ 242	2 days 15 hours
Train (3)	515	$ 502	4 days
Ship (4)	150	$1,800	14 days

Source: (1) Airports Council International—North America, Southwest Airlines; (2) American Bus Association, Greyhound; (3) Amtrak; (4) American Association of Port Authorities, Holland America Line, 2009.

PASSENGER—AIRLINES
by Southwest Airlines

Introduction

On December 17, 1903, the world was forever changed with the first successful flight of an airplane by the Wright Brothers. Ten years later on New Year's Day, 1914, the world's first airline flight was operated over a distance of 18 miles from St. Petersburg to Tampa, Florida—and the flight took 23 minutes. In the ensuing century of airline history, airlines grew from flimsy flying boats to massive jet-powered airplanes that can fly halfway around the world nonstop with a payload of hundreds of passengers. However, the airlines' path to success has been an arduous one. In the 1920s and 1930s, airmail paid the way, and passengers were an afterthought, often sitting atop mailbags. Familiar names such as United, TWA, Eastern, and American were born during this period. Modern metal airplanes like the Douglas DC–3 ensured that passengers, not mail, were the airlines' focus. Aircraft size continued to grow leading to today's efficient designs such as the Boeing 737 and Airbus A–320 families.

Location

Until 1978, the Civil Aeronautics Board (CAB) determined which routes airlines could fly and how much they could charge. The CAB also restricted entry by new carriers into the marketplace. To circumvent this, intrastate carriers were formed inside those states with large populations and distances, and their fares were much lower than the bigger, regulated carriers.

Pricing

By the mid–1970s, the intrastate carriers were the primary airlines for travel within California and Texas, and they created large markets of new travelers. The Airline Deregulation Act of 1978 eliminated all regulations on routes and fares, along with the CAB itself by 1985. Consumers at all economic levels benefited from lower fares. In 1971, only 15 percent of adult Americans had flown; today that figure is close to 85 percent. Air travel has become mass transportation for intercity travel, and because of the rise of the low-cost carriers, legacy carriers have had to reduce fares in order to compete.

Service

There are two basic kinds of airlines today. Low-cost carriers like Southwest, JetBlue, and AirTran serve key markets with high frequency, low fares, and in Southwest's case, point-to-point service. Legacy carriers like United and American operate large hubs and rely primarily on connecting traffic through hubs. Legacy carriers belong to alliances with foreign airlines to provide seamless travel from domestic to international points. In many ways the distinction between the types of service these two categories of airlines offer (especially on domestic flights) has blurred over the years, and it is not unusual for the low-cost carriers to offer more free amenities than the older airlines.

Safety

Safety is the primary duty of the airline industry. Pilots go through a stringent frequent evaluation process that includes medical exams. Flight attendants are responsible for safety in the cabin, and they too have a strict recurrent evaluation training/examination process. Aircraft undergo regular and thorough inspections.

Environment

The airline industry has set a goal to aggressively reduce fuel consumption and greenhouse gas emissions. To meet this objective, airlines operate more efficient aircraft, have reduced airport emissions with electric-powered ground vehicles, and some, like Southwest, have purchased route optimization software to find the most fuel-efficient routing between airports.

PASSENGER—BUSES
by Greyhound

Introduction

Bus lines provide regularly scheduled passenger service within cities and between cities. There are hundreds of intermodal transportation centers (a transportation building encompassing multiple transportation modes including bus lines) across the country. Intermodal centers can improve the quality of life in a town or city. Cities with good public transportation systems have a larger, more educated workforce, stronger economic growth, and a better environment. Cities with intermodal facilities also see increases in jobs, household income, property values, and property taxes collected. They become anchors for development and revitalization efforts, attracting other development—both retail and residential.

Environment

Bus travel is inherently environmentally beneficial. For example, one Greyhound bus takes an average of 34 cars off the road.

Cost

Bus lines are known as an affordable travel option, for example, in 2008, the average one-way Greyhound ticket cost $53.

Expanding Customer Services

Bus companies, besides passenger service, also provide a number of other services for their customers such as package delivery and passenger charters. For example, Greyhound PackageXpress service offers value-priced same-day and early-next-day package delivery to thousands of destinations. Also, the company's Greyhound Travel Services unit offers charter packages for businesses, conventions, schools, and other groups at competitive rates.

Major bus lines also have interline partnerships with a number of smaller independent bus lines across the United States. These bus companies provide complementary service to existing schedules and link to many of the smaller towns in a major carrier's national route system.

Bus lines continue to find new ways to cater to their customers' needs. For example, in 2008, Greyhound partnered with Peter Pan Bus Lines to launch BoltBus, a new curbside express service with a unique set of amenities. BoltBus offers at least one seat on each schedule for $1, and passengers can enjoy free Wi-Fi, power outlets, extra legroom, and comfortable seats. BoltBus has daily express service from Washington, D.C., to New York, and service from D.C. to Baltimore and Philadelphia to Boston with a stop in Cherry Hill, New Jersey. Also in 2008, Greyhound Canada and Adirondack Trailways launched a curbside express service, similar to Bolt-Bus, called NeOn. NeOn has schedules from New York to Toronto with a stop in Syracuse, and service from New York to Buffalo.

The introduction of these carriers, and their subsequent success in terms of ridership, has shown that more people are choosing intercity bus as a travel option.

PASSENGER—COMMUTER TRAINS
by MTA Long Island Rail Road

The top priority of passenger rail companies is getting customers where they are going on time and safely.

Service Quality

On-time departure and arrival are extremely important to today's busy consumer. On-time performance is accomplished by continuously purchasing up-to-date reliable equipment, continuously hiring and training the best employees, and moving managerial decision making as close to the consumer needs as possible. The Long Island Rail Road (LIRR) set a modern-day on-time performance record in 2008 with 95.1 percent of the more than 300,000 trains that operated that year reaching their destinations within six minutes of their scheduled arrival times. More than 87 million passengers used the LIRR in 2008, the most in almost 60 years. In its 2008 Customer Satisfaction Survey, the LIRR received high marks from thousands of customers who participated. The survey found that 89 percent of customers who responded were satisfied with the overall quality of LIRR service. Personnel courtesy and facilities cleanliness are also very important elements of service quality. The survey reported 95 percent satisfaction rating for train crew courtesy. Many customers did, however, find fault with the cleanliness of Penn Station restrooms. The restrooms are now undergoing a $5 million renovation program.

Safety

Safety is a main concern for passengers, and every effort is being made to eliminate all potential hazards. A major effort to reduce the space between LIRR station platforms and train doors and educate the public "to watch the gap" has resulted in a decrease in gap incidents.

Environment

Traveling by public transportation uses less energy and produces less pollution than comparable transportation in individual vehicles. Public transit also reduces highway congestion and is essential to energy-efficient land use patterns. A public transit system recycles many materials and wastes produced by its operations. For example, the LIRR recycles a variety of materials including fluorescent bulbs, used oil, batteries, scrap metals, obsolete computer equipment, and used office paper.

Locations

In the competitive passenger transportation industry, it is important to offer the highest number of service locations possible. For example, LIRR passengers have access to service at 124 stations over 319 route miles.

Costs

Although public transit systems are less expensive per passenger mile to operate than cars, the upfront costs are immense. For example, a major new LIRR terminal is being built, and the project, including the use of two tunnel-boring machines, has been budgeted at $7.2 billion.

PASSENGER—SHIPS
by Carnival Cruise Lines

Introduction

According to the latest economic impact statistics available, direct spending by the North American cruise industry and its passengers totaled $18.7 billion and the industry was directly and indirectly responsible for generating 354,700 jobs in the United States.[5] This doesn't factor in the tens of thousands of people who are employed aboard the ships. Carnival Cruise Lines alone has approximately 36,000 crew members, many of whom have worked for the company 10, 20, and, in some cases, even 30 or more years. When asked what has kept them in the cruise business for so long, the answer is inevitably the same—the chance to travel and to work and form close friendships with people from around the world who represent a variety of vastly different cultures and backgrounds.

Costs

Much of the cruise industry has consolidated in the past 20 years with larger companies buying smaller ones. The larger an organization the greater its purchasing power, which lowers operating costs and makes a company more competitive.

Pricing

Among many trends that have reshaped the modern cruise industry is technology. Automated reservations systems enable cruise lines today to manage millions of passenger reservations simultaneously. Computerized yield management systems, the most sophisticated of which came into being around the mid–1990s, allow cruise lines to adjust pricing for each voyage according to sales activity to maximize profitability. Although the cruise experience has evolved substantially, the cost of a cruise vacation has not changed dramatically over the past few decades. The inherent, all-inclusive value of a cruise accounts, in large part, for cruising's immense popularity today as a mainstream vacation choice and is one of the industry's core marketing messages.

Marketing

Cruise lines' marketing activities today heavily integrate technology. Targeted e-mails promoting pricing offers and product enhancements, along with Internet advertising, play a huge role in marketing efforts today. For example, Carnival's Web site receives over 1 million visitors per month. The cruise industry remains unique in the travel industry because the majority of business is still booked through travel agents whereas airlines, hotels, and rental cars are primarily booked directly by the consumer. Based on the more involved nature of a cruise reservation, such as choosing the right cruise line and cabin, it is anticipated that travel agents will continue to be the main distribution source for cruises.

Service Quality

Along with changes in ship design has come a huge array of new activities both complementary and revenue-generating, such as spa treatments, video arcades, shopping malls, specialty restaurants, golf lessons, art auctions, children's programming, outdoor movie screens, and massive water slides.

Locations

Another major factor contributing to the growth of cruise lines has been the industry's close-to-home ship deployment strategy. In earlier years there were only a handful of ports in North America equipped to host a cruise ship operation. Among the primary ports were New York, Miami, Fort Lauderdale, and Los Angeles. However, as other port cities began to realize the economic benefits of the cruise business and cruise lines sought to expand their operations, many ports began building docking facilities and terminals to accommodate cruise operations. Carnival Cruise Lines led the charge in expanding to alternative homeports, believing that if it became easier for people to get to a ship's departure port, more people would give cruising a try.

Environment

The future of the cruise industry depends on the health of the world's oceans. Cruise lines take an aggressive approach to both high- and low-tech solutions to mitigate their environmental impact. Massive recycling programs, advanced wastewater treatment systems, improved engine efficiencies, reduced power usage through energy-efficient lighting and appliances, reduced fuel consumption, and reduced emissions are some of the areas where cruise lines are heavily focusing their environmental initiatives.

Safety

The safety of passengers and crew is the number one priority of cruise line operators. The industry has an enviable record when it comes to safety and security and works closely with federal, state, and local law enforcement agencies. A cruise ship is inherently secure because it is a controlled environment with limited access. Cruise lines have established strict ship security procedures that are, in part, outlined in internationally agreed-upon measures set forth by the International Maritime Organization, which is a body of the United Nations.

TRANSPORTATION—INTERNATIONAL
by John Deere

Introduction

The goals of transportation and materials-handling specialists in every factory throughout the world are the same: get the item to its destination as fast and inexpensively as possible, with zero damage. All of these important variables must be considered when a company selects materials-handling methods and develops a delivery schedule.

Speed of response is very important in the global marketplace because of the increased number of competitors over purely domestic competition. Products must be delivered on time to meet the expectations of the customer. For example, new combines sold to farmers, whether they are in Africa, Asia, Europe, or the Americas, must be in the field and in top working condition when crops are ready for harvest. Delivery speed also is important because companies continue to pay interest on the capital they borrow to build a machine until it is delivered to the customer and paid for.

International infrastructure standards, including roads, railroad gauge (rail width), port depth, and airport length, are fairly standard.

Transportation Modes

Companies should be familiar with the idiosyncrasies of international truck, rail, ship, air cargo, and barge transport. It may be necessary to use all of these methods to get a product to its destination. The type of carrier chosen affects the final cost of a product and often plays a big role in customer satisfaction and, ultimately, customer brand loyalty.

The key to coordinated transportation is the use of software programs that allow manufacturers or suppliers to communicate with all of the transportation companies and the export/import officials in the countries through which their products will be passing. Electronic Data Interchange (EDI), for example, uses electronic translators to organize data so it can be used by everyone involved in the transport. Once communication has been established, the type of transport can be chosen.

International shipments also require shipping marks for identification. These marks, along with EDI and Global Positioning Satellite technology, help shipping agents track the shipment throughout the transporting process anywhere in the world.

Truck Lines

Long- or short-haul truck lines have become the most popular intracontinental method. Trucks, in comparison to railroads, are faster and less damaging to the product, but are more costly. Domestic trucking fees typically are charged by weight; international fees are typically by volume. For example, a box of feathers that is 10 cubic feet and a box of nails the same size may incur similar transportation costs. Also, well-developed shipping rates in the U.S. trucking industry allow a shipper to accurately and conveniently bill costs to the customer before the product is shipped. International shipping rates are not yet as accurate and require a second bill after the shipment is complete.

Rail

Rail transport can be a time-consuming process. Products are often loaded at a factory, shipped to a terminal, railroaded to a hub, and switched to another line. This process may occur many times before the product reaches its destination. The gauge (track width) of the railroad tracks in one country may not be compatible with those in another country. The rails in Russia, Finland, and Portugal are a different gauge than those in surrounding countries. Trains facing this dilemma must be unloaded and repacked before crossing into these countries.

Ocean Freight

Exporting products over the oceans takes much more time per mile than ground transportation. Not all ocean lines ship to every port. The destination of the shipment determines which line will transport the product. For example, a tractor going to Australia may be sent first by rail to Savannah, Georgia, before it is loaded onto a ship. Tractors going to Germany may leave on a line that has its point of origin in California. Some importing

countries require the manufacturer to have the more expensive shipments inspected before they are loaded onto the oceangoing ship. For example, Argentina and Ecuador require a complete inspection, including proof that the cost of shipping the product has been paid by the manufacturer.

Air

Air is the most expensive transport medium. The time element is of primary importance, and the size, shape, and weight are extremely important cost factors. Even with high rates, airfreight has become a necessity in some situations. If a $125,000 machine is out of service and needs a critical part that is not available locally, the part can be shipped by air to the customer overnight.

Barge

Barge traffic on inland waterways, such as the Ohio, Yangtze, and Rhine rivers, is still cost-effective for bulkier materials. Manufacturers rely on the European waterways more than they do the U.S. inland waterway system. In general, barge traffic is slower than the other transport methods and is tied closely to the weather and seasonal changes.

Intermodal

Intermodal transport is an effective way to interface barges, trucks, trains, ships, and, in some situations, planes. For example, a truck trailer could be unhooked from the truck bed and transferred as a large, rectangular container onto a flatbed railroad car. At the next terminal, the trailer could be lifted from the train car and set on the deck of a ship. After the voyage, it could be transferred to a barge and moved inland before it is again hooked to a truck for final delivery.

Product Handling

Material is packaged, crated, and protected in a number of ways to ensure a zero-defect delivery to the destination point. Poorly packaged products run the risk of transport damage, vandalism, and pilferage at switching points and sidetracks.

Some problems and solutions are unique to international transportation. For example, specialized crates with inner supports are sometimes constructed for higher-cost items. Although this method is expensive, it may be the only answer for machines that are shipped on long hauls, such as cross-country trucking or on ocean transports. Some manufactured items made of metal, such as farm tractors, run the risk of rusting in the salt-laden air during ocean voyages. For this reason, the machine industry has developed specialized coatings that can be sprayed onto exposed surfaces before a product is crated and placed in, or driven into, the ship's hold. In another example, plastic shrink-wrap that can seal out sea air from products, such as stereo equipment, on an ocean voyage may itself trap moisture and cause damage. The product must be properly dehumidified or water-absorbing material such as silicate must be packed inside.

The legal requirements set by an importing country sometimes cause problems. For example, Australian law prohibits the import of nonfumigated wood. Pallets, freight boxes, or any wood products exported to that country must be exposed to a fumigant to kill fungus, bacteria, and insect larvae. Some fumigants can harm surfaces of a machine or a metal product.

In every form of international shipping, the shape and weight of the product is important. There is a disproportionately costly surcharge due to any extra space used in addition to the standard container size of 40 ft. × 8 ft. × 8 ft. For example, a company may ship a machine that is 225 cubic meters in volume. If a small eight-inch diameter pipe sticks out of the top of the machine five feet and hangs over the side five feet, the shipper will pay a considerable added cost for a machine that is now an additional 100 cubic meters in size. At an additional cost of $50 per cubic meter, or $5,000, it might be less expensive to remove the pipe, secure it within the main unit, and install it after the crossing.

International shipping is expensive due to the long distances covered, and economics dictate that containers should be as full as possible. Partially filled shipping containers are billed the same as a full load.

TRANSPORTATION—CASE STUDY (PASSENGER)

by Carnival Cruise Lines

Company: Carnival Cruise Lines
Case: Passenger Ship Industry Growth

Cruise liners began serving as modes of transportation in the mid–1800s. These vessels were the main means by which immigrant populations moved between the United States and Europe and also a primary mode of long-distance travel in general. These transatlantic liners were a source of pride for many countries, which competed with each other to build vessels that could sail at the fastest speeds.

In the mid–1960s, cruising had an elitist reputation. It was viewed as a vacation only for honeymooners and the well-to-do. It took many years for the modern-day cruise industry to effectively overcome this perception and establish cruising as an affordable, mainstream vacation choice.

Businessman Ted Arison saw the potential in remarketing the industry and negotiated a financing deal to purchase a transatlantic liner. Renamed the *Mardi Gras*, it became the first ship for the newly formed Carnival Cruise Lines and entered service in March 1972. However, hasty

(Continued)

arrangements to launch the company and start generating a return on investment proved disastrous. Also, the ship ran aground off Miami on its maiden voyage. The fledgling company was so cash-strapped that on that first cruise, it was necessary to empty out the cash registers from the bars and casino to pay for fuel for the return trip to Miami. The company's unreliable cash flow, however, unwittingly led to something extraordinary. To save money on fuel, the ship operated at slower speeds, which meant passengers were on board for extended periods rather than in port. To keep them busy, it was necessary to provide an exciting shipboard experience that included extensive entertainment and activities. The ship became the destination—a floating resort—and people began referring to the *Mardi Gras* as "the fun ship." It was a groundbreaking concept for its time and the beginning of a transformation. Cruising was about to evolve from a niche vacation to eventually become a multibillion-dollar mainstream industry that attracts millions of people a year from all walks of life.

Shortly thereafter, the company's financial fortunes began improving and the home office had picked up on the "fun ship" moniker, turning it into the cruise line's official marketing slogan. Many view Carnival's "Fun Ship" slogan as the single, most effective marketing tool in the history of modern-day cruising. Carnival expanded through the acquisition of existing ships.

In 1984, Carnival Cruise Lines became the first cruise company to launch a network television advertising campaign.

The cruise industry continued to build larger, more modern ships throughout the 1980s and 1990s. Soaring glass atriums, expansive spas, a multitude of bars, high-tech show lounges, and cabins with balconies eventually became the norm. A common hull platform approach to new ship construction gained popularity. Companies began building several ships in succession based on the same hull and structural design but with vastly different interiors. These are commonly referred to as sister ships. A common hull platform saves money and enables cruise ships to be built in more rapid succession. The longest series of ships based on a common hull platform is Carnival Cruise Lines' 70,000-ton Fantasy class, which includes eight ships constructed between 1990 and 1998.

By the late 1980s there were many different cruise lines in operation catering to a variety of different market segments. Carnival Cruise Lines, the leading mass market operator by then, began expanding through the acquisition of other cruise lines. The ultimate goal was to create a portfolio of brands targeting different demographics.

Over the next two decades, the company embarked on an extraordinary expansion course. Carnival currently owns the largest cruise vacation group in the world, with a portfolio of cruise brands in North America, Europe, and Australia.

In late 2008, Carnival Cruise Lines launched a new branding campaign centered around the tagline "Fun For All. All For Fun." The campaign aims to capture the spirited and spontaneous fun at the core of the Carnival vacation experience. More than three decades after the "Fun Ship" slogan first came into being, fun remains the core marketing message that enabled Carnival to evolve from a fledgling one-ship company to the world's most successful cruise business.

by SkyHook

Company: SkyHook
Case: Delivering Cargo "Beyond the Last Mile"™

The Problem/Market Need

Transportation or logistics managers often need to get equipment, materials, and consumables to very remote locations. Often the equipment and materials are heavy and the remote site is well beyond the last mile of traditional roadways or water routes. Getting the freight to these destinations can be dangerous, time-consuming, unreliable, environmentally damaging, and expensive. This is usually the case in the Arctic, mountains, deserts, or other undeveloped regions where infrastructure is often lacking. For example, in the arctic, heavy equipment, materials, and consumables are typically hauled in by barge or ship during the summer months as open water permits. Since overland transportation during the summer is not permitted to avoid environmental damage to the soft tundra and vegetation, materials are stockpiled until freeze up occurs and an ice road to the work site can be built. The construction of an ice road not only delays the start of operations, it has to be rebuilt every winter before operations at a worksite can resume. Not only are ice roads limited to seasonal use, they are unreliable due to the unpredictability of the spring thaw which, if it starts early, results in supplies and equipment being left stranded at the worksite until freeze up.

The Solution/Market Opportunity

A market for a heavy-lift, short-haul aircraft will exist as long as industry continues exploration and development of remote regions throughout the world and conventional means of transport in those remote regions are cost-prohibitive, unreliable, or environmentally burdensome. To make this market economically feasible, a whole new type of transportation needed to be developed.

SkyHook aircraft will revolutionize the manner in which operations and logistics are carried out, particularly in remote or undeveloped regions of the globe. SkyHook will enable delivery of cargo for at least 200 miles beyond the end termination of a road, rail line, navigable river, or shoreline. SkyHook technology represents a solution for companies' heavy-lift, short-haul challenges; this technology is the only way many projects will be able to progress economically. This technology will circumvent significant capital, manpower, time, and unreliability associated with road construction and use. SkyHook aircraft will be utilized in a variety of applications where the lift capabilities of existing VTOL (vertical take-off and landing) aircraft are inadequate, such as logging and civil construction, or where ground transportation is precluded by environmental concerns.

SkyHook International Inc. filed an International Patent Application titled Hybrid Lift Air Vehicle in 2007, and will now pursue transportation opportunities in the Americas, Africa, Europe, and Asia.

The lifting forces are provided by four lifting helicopter blades. The aircraft will be propelled laterally through the air by four ducted propellers located below the main rotors. Precise hover positioning will be obtained by using thrust vanes located behind the ducted propellers. Because

(Continued)

the empty weight of the JHL–40 is supported by aerostatic lift, the aircraft reverts to near neutral buoyancy once the load is set down and rotor lift is reduced. Consequently, it does not require ballast exchange.

SkyHook Applications

Oil and Gas Seismic Surveys

Seismic surveys require roads that, unfortunately, result in significant disturbance to soil, water, vegetation, and wildlife. In many instances, use of JHL–40s may be the only way to conduct seismic surveys compliant with environmental regulatory requirements.

Oil and Gas Exploration and Well Drilling

In northern areas, drilling/service rigs and operating consumables such as fuel, pipe, mud, cement, chemicals, and water are transported to the well site by truck on seasonal ice roads. Because ice roads must be built before the rigs and materials are hauled to their respective well site and because the rigs must be removed before the ice road starts to melt in the spring, drilling operations are currently limited to approximately 70 to 90 days per year. This narrow window can generate intense competition for manpower and resources. In the case of an unexpected early thaw, rigs can become stranded and remain idle until the next season's freeze at a cost of hundreds of thousands of dollars per day in standby fees.

Pipeline Construction

In remote pipeline construction areas, in many cases, lay down yards at the staging point do not exist and have to be constructed in order to receive pipe and equipment during the summer. In the winter, an extensive network of ice roads is required so that pipe and material can be moved to the pipeline right-of-way and distributed along the pipeline route.

Mining

Production mines depend on ice roads to service their logistical needs. The weather-dependent nature of ice roads, however, makes this mode of transportation highly unreliable and sometimes cost-prohibitive. SkyHook aircraft will enable the mining industry to begin work immediately on new sites without waiting for a new road to be constructed.

Civil Construction Projects

SkyHook aircraft will enable the construction industry to lift prefabricated sections, equipment, and materials to construction sites where access constraints preclude the use of cranes.

Forestry—Selective Logging

Due to a much larger payload, the JHL–40 will allow more efficient harvesting as well as harvesting of more valuable logs that are too massive for current helicopter technology to claim.

Firefighting

The JHL–40 will greatly enhance forest firefighting capability due to its payload capacity (water or water/foam-retardant combination) and be able to operate at night since they will be equipped with stadium lighting to safely navigate through various terrains and precisely release their loads.

Humanitarian Relief

Hauling in relief supplies such as food, water, shelter, and clothing can be accomplished where roads and airports have been rendered impassable by storm, floods, earthquakes, and so forth.

Marketing Strategy

SkyHook will market the services of JHL–40s on a fee-for-service basis, and deploy the aircraft, crew, and all logistical support necessary to satisfy the customers' needs. SkyHook anticipates a steady increase in demand for SkyHook aircraft as the technology is proven and customer confidence and respect grow. SkyHook plans to preserve its reputation by ensuring that service contracts are executed in a manner that meets or exceeds customer expectations. The own-operate strategy enables SkyHook to exercise complete control in this regard.

Development

SkyHook has teamed with and hired The Boeing Company to design, build, and commercially certify the JHL–40 aircraft. At the time of writing, the program is in the design phase and will subsequently transition into the build, test, and certify phases. By utilizing as many commercial off-the-shelf (COTS) components as possible, the program will greatly reduce the time to market compared with traditional aircraft design and build timelines. Currently SkyHook is forecasting the first JHL–40 to enter service in approximately 2014.

TRANSPORTATION—CASE STUDY (PASSENGER)

by Amtrak

Company: **Amtrak**
Case: **Passenger Trains—Value Creation through Service Enhancement—2008**

The National Railroad Passenger Corporation (Amtrak) began operation on May 1, 1971, to provide intercity rail passenger services throughout the United States, supported in part through congressional capital and operating grants.

The project that resulted in Acela Express was a by-product of various attempts to reduce Amtrak's need for a federal operating subsidy. When confronted with a need to reduce operating costs in 1994, the company first attempted to reduce or eliminate services on the worst-performing routes. The results were unsatisfactory; the company's large fixed costs were hard to shed and had to be spread over a smaller revenue base when routes were reduced.

In 1997, Congress passed legislation requiring Amtrak to be operationally self-sufficient by the end of 2003. Amtrak was faced with a serious challenge. Revenues in recent years had been increasing at a steady rate, but not one that promised revenue adequacy.

Amtrak eventually adjusted course and focused on growing ridership on its remaining routes and, through economies of scale, reducing its losses. However, the significant revenue increases required

(Continued)

to drive improved operating performance would be extremely difficult to achieve with Amtrak's existing services, particularly in a travel environment dominated by low-cost air fares and inexpensive gasoline. It was clear that Amtrak had to develop major new sources of business. Given the size of the northeastern travel market and Amtrak's strong asset base, it had two major strategies for doing so.

- Reduce travel times between New York to Boston and New York to Washington, D.C.
- Improve service, including on-time performance

Reduce Travel Times

In 1997, Amtrak enjoyed a 36 percent share of the total air/rail market between New York and Washington, D.C. where it connected two city centers on a three-hour schedule. A reduction in trip time between New York and Boston, which at that time required between four and five hours, would improve Amtrak's competitiveness with airlines, its market share, and its revenues. Amtrak's major competitors in both markets were the Delta and U.S. Airways shuttles operating out of Washington Reagan, LaGuardia, and Boston Logan airports, although other airlines also operated to and from nearby airports. Even though at three hours, the train schedule was two hours longer than the shuttle, the ability to detrain in city centers (avoiding a long cab ride) was compensation for a large percentage of travelers. Amtrak also enjoyed a competitive advantage in terms of customer experience since travelers are able to work, talk on their cell phones, or meet with their associates while on board the train.

The public had expressed interest in higher speed of rail travel, more departures, and an improved level of service. Specifically, there was strong interest expressed in improving travel times in the New York to Boston and New York to Washington, D.C. routes.

Accomplishing this between New York and Boston would require substantial investment: electrification between New Haven and Boston, straightening of curves, and significant upgrades to existing track to handle higher operating speeds. Early on, the ideal solution—much straighter rights of way—was ruled out due to the high cost of land acquisition. Therefore, in addition to the infrastructure upgrades, Amtrak would have to build highly sophisticated tilting trains that would be capable of moving on curved tracks at high speed. Engineering studies showed that these improvements could reduce the trip time between New York and Boston from nearly five hours to between three and three and a half hours. By using new high-speed train equipment for the New York to Washington, D.C., trip, Amtrak could also reduce the three-hour schedule time by approximately 15 minutes.

To determine if the additional speed and frequency associated with high-speed service would generate an increase in ridership and revenue sufficient to justify the capital investment, Amtrak developed a series of demand models. The finding was encouraging: additional passenger and yield (revenue per passenger mile) growth could add $180 million per year to the bottom line. To capitalize on this prospective demand and thus realize its revenue potential, Amtrak elected to double the number of planned New York to Boston frequencies.

Amtrak presented these projections to Congress, which authorized the capital required to complete the project supplemented by private financing. By 2000, the infrastructure and equipment were in place to begin the rollout of the next generation of U.S. passenger rail service.

Improve Service

In addition to improving trip times through higher speeds, transformation of all customer service within the corridor would be needed. Amtrak conducted extensive research with its customers and employees to help guide the design of the new trains, services, and amenities. A wide-ranging effort would be undertaken to improve the quality of all aspects of customer service, including reservation booking, station visits, and trip quality.

Service enhancements included improvements to reservation and customer service systems. Call centers were reengineered to provide faster, more efficient service with reduced customer wait times. Amtrak had for many years been successful in attracting business customers to its Metroliner service, but now sought to improve its access to this customer base. It did so through enhancements to its corporate booking tools and its Web technologies. Amtrak also upgraded its station ticket office technology and continued to improve and expand its Quik-Trak self-service ticketing machines. Amtrak also undertook an extensive customer service training program with all Amtrak employees.

Responding to marketing research that showed a desire for assigned seating among high-end travelers, Amtrak upgraded its reservation system to assign seats for first-class passengers on Acela Express trains. Assigned seating would later be withdrawn as Amtrak discovered that passengers still preferred to pick their own seats—and often did not understand that in an assigned seat environment they could not change seats at will, not realizing that passengers boarding at later stations may have already been assigned those empty seats.

Recognizing that the customer loyalty programs offered by the airlines placed Amtrak at a competitive disadvantage, Amtrak introduced its Guest Rewards loyalty program in July 2001. This program offered points for travel and was linked with airline programs to give customers a full range of redemption options. In addition, the existing Metropolitan Lounges were improved and rebranded as ClubAcela for the complimentary use of best Guest Rewards members and First Class travelers.

To capitalize on all these changes, management realized it needed to reposition the Amtrak product in customers' minds. Consumer research showed that while Amtrak enjoyed near-universal name recognition in the marketplace, its brand image did not fit with the modern look and feel of the new services. A new Amtrak subbrand was seen as a way to communicate the emergence of a new level of service to customers.

Amtrak developed a new brand name and color scheme to replace the existing Metroliner and Northeast Direct monikers. The name Acela was developed to highlight acceleration and excellence. A two-tiered subbrand structure was initially planned to differentiate each service operated under the Acela brand. The new high-speed trains would be known as Acela Express, and all other Amtrak trains operating in the corridor between Washington and Boston would become known as Acela Regional.

To roll out the new brand image, Amtrak began an innovative advertising and promotional campaign in the months leading up to the launch of the new brand. The campaign began with subtle advertising in movie theaters and used outdoor media to provocatively introduce the new brand name in an offbeat but attention-getting manner that did not specifically show the product itself. As the launch got closer, more traditional newspaper, radio, and television advertising was introduced to announce the features and benefits of the new service. Interestingly, the Acela branding campaign was so successful that customers called both the Express and Regional trains Acela. Therefore, Acela

(Continued)

Regional trains were rebranded as simply Regional trains, The terms Acela Express and Acela are now used interchangeably. Regional trains would later themselves be renamed Northeast Regional to give the product clearer differentiation in the marketplace.

The new Acela trains were at the time and remain today quite distinct from the equipment already in service on the Northeast Corridor. Amenities include conference tables throughout the train, at-seat electrical outlets, oversize luggage storage, and upgraded food and beverage services.

The new service began in December 2000 and was an immediate success, significantly improving Amtrak's competitive positioning in the Northeast. The product itself continued to attract growing ridership, while external factors also favored rail travel, including the rise in gas prices and growing airport congestion.

Amtrak's market share on the Northeast Corridor rose sharply between 2001 and 2008. Amtrak's share of the air/rail market between Washington, D.C., and New York was 45 percent in 2001; by 2008, it had risen to 62 percent. The growth in the New York to Boston market was even more dramatic. A service that was responsible for only 27 percent of the market share in 2001 grew to 48 percent in 2008. The Acela service was proving its value. In FY 2008, Acela generated 26 percent of Amtrak's ticket revenue. Total systemwide ticket revenue rose from $1.2 billion in FY 2002 to $1.7 billion in 2008. These were significant gains, but after financial difficulties in 2002, it was generally acknowledged that a goal of Amtrak profitability was not achievable, and the requirement was eventually repealed by Congress in 2008.

During this period, Amtrak made a number of changes in its corporate practices that were designed to build on its improved service; some changes were designed to specifically improve Acela service, other changes were designed to incorporate lessons learned from the phase-in of the new equipment to improve all of its Northeast Corridor services. Track and infrastructure were extensively improved. Equipment maintenance procedures were enhanced so that equipment could be replaced quickly and operated with improved reliability. After substantial investment in infrastructure and equipment maintenance process improvements, Acela on-time performance rose to 90 percent, which further contributed to the service's popularity. Partly in response to its growing market strength, in late 2002 Amtrak began the phased introduction of more sophisticated pricing and revenue management processes for Acela Express. Until that point, Amtrak had maintained 2 price points for Acela departures (peak and off-peak). Over the next three years, Amtrak would expand that to 5 price points that were revenue-managed based on demand for each specific departure. This allowed Amtrak to introduce lower prices for trains with low demand, and higher prices for the most heavily used peak trains. Ultimately, this pricing flexibility has improved Amtrak's ability to respond to the competitive forces in the market and earn the most revenue per departure.

The public perception of Acela's success has often rested heavily on those aspects of the train that are more generally known, such as its speed or tilting capability. However, its success has ultimately depended on the convergence of a number of marketing and operational initiatives that resulted in a frequent, reliable, comfortable, and competitively priced service.

AMTRAK

The National Railroad Passenger Corporation (Amtrak), established in 1971, is the main provider of intercity passenger rail services, and is an important component of the nation's transportation industry. Amtrak, headquartered in Washington, D.C., has over 18,000 employees and annual revenues of $2.4 billion. Visit Amtrak at www.amtrak.com.

Robert M. Ripperger

Robert Ripperger is in the Government Affairs and Corporate Communications Department. Prior to this, Mr. Ripperger served in the Army and worked for several defense contractors. He received his BS from the US Military Academy and his MA from the Fletcher School at Tufts.

ATLAS AIR WORLDWIDE HOLDINGS, INC.

Atlas Air, founded in1993, is the leading provider of freighter aircraft leasing and operating solutions in the United States. Atlas is headquartered in Purchase, New York, has annual sales of $1.56 billion (2007), and has 1,725 employees (2007). Visit Atlas at www.atlasair.com.

William J. Flynn

William Flynn is the President, CEO, and a member of the Company's Board of Directors. Before joining AAWW in 2006, he served as President and Chief Executive Officer of GeoLogistics Corporation, a leading global freight forwarding and logistics company. Prior to this, he was the Senior Vice President of the Merchandise Service Group of CSX Transportation. Mr. Flynn received his BA, *summa cum laude*, in Latin American Studies from the University of Rhode Island. He received his MA in Latin American Studies from the University of Arizona.

BNSF RAILWAY COMPANY

BNSF, founded 1849, is among the world's top transporters of intermodal traffic, moves more grain than any other American railroad, carries the components of many of the products we depend on daily, and hauls enough low-sulfur coal to generate about 10 percent of the electricity produced in the United States. BNSF, headquartered in Fort Worth, Texas, has 41,000 employees and annual sales of $18.0 billion (2008). Awards include Fortune's Most Admired Companies (Most Admired Railroad) (2008), *G.I. Jobs* Top 50 Military Friendly Employer (2005–2008, No.1 in 2007), and *ComputerWorld* Best Places to Work in IT (2008). Visit BNSF at www.bnsf.com

Patrick Hiatte

Patrick Hiatte is the General Director Corporate Communications and has held various communications positions in various locations over 35 years. Mr. Hiatte received his BA in Journalism from the University of Missouri.

CARNIVAL CRUISE LINES

Carnival Cruise Lines, headquartered in Miami, Florida, is the largest cruise line operator in the world. Carnival, founded in 1972, has 81,000 employees and annual sales of $13 billion. Visit Carnival at www.carnival.com.

Jennifer de la Cruz

Jennifer de la Cruz is Director of Public Relations. Ms. De la Cruz began her public relations career as an account executive at the Miami-based P.R. firm of Al Wolfe Associates, which specialized in travel and tourism accounts, including Carnival Cruise Lines and Carnival's Crystal Palace Resort & Casino. She is a member of the Cruise Lines International Association's Public Relations Committee and is an occasional speaker on public relations and cruise industry panels. She has participated in nearly a dozen Hospitality Management Training programs through Johnson & Wales University, one of the nation's leading hospitality management schools. Ms. De la Cruz received her BS in Public Relations with a minor in Journalism from Florida State University. She is actively involved in Carnival's "Friends Uniting Neighbors" (FUN) Team, an employee volunteer group, and is also active in Hands On Miami, another volunteer service organization in South Florida.

COLONIAL PIPELINE COMPANY

Colonial Pipeline, founded in 1962, delivers each day an average of 100 million gallons of gasoline, kerosene, home heating oil, jet fuel, diesel fuel, and national defense fuel to shipper terminals in 12 states and the District of Columbia through the 5,519-mile Colonial system.

Colonial Pipeline, headquartered in Alpharetta, Georgia, has annual sales of over $800 million and over 600 employees. Visit Colonial Pipeline at www.colpipe.com.

Steve Baker

Steve Baker is the Manager of Media and Marketing at Colonial Pipeline. Prior to this, Steve was a journalist with The Associated Press. Steve received his degree in English from the Washington and Lee University.

Additional Pipeline material provided by:

Don Santa, Interstate Natural Gas Association of America.

CON-WAY FREIGHT

Con-way Freight, founded in 1983, is headquartered in Ann Arbor, Michigan. Con-way Freight was the company that launched the first broad-based overnight service for regional LTL freight in the United States. Con-way Freight has annual sales of $2.8 billion and 18,250 employees. Con-way Freight has won many awards including American Trucking Association, 2008 Fleet Safety Award; Logistics Management, Quest for Quality Award, Top Regional Carrier; Information Week, No. 1, Information Week 500 Rankings, Best Technology Success.

Visit Con-way Freight at www.con-way.com.

David L. Miller

David Miller, Vice President, Global Policy and Economic Sustainability, is a 34-year veteran of the freight trucking industry, the last 25 years with Con-way Freight. In his current role, he is responsible for directing Con-way Freight's strategies and programs related to legislative, regulatory, public policy, and corporate sustainability affairs at local, state, national and international levels. Mr. Miller was named the company's top policy executive in 2008, joining the corporate executive staff from Con-way Freight, where, since 2007 he served as chief operating officer. Mr. Miller started his trucking industry career in 1972, joining Con-way Freight in 1983 as a freight operations supervisor in Cincinnati, Ohio. He has served in a number of increasingly responsible positions over his career, including service center manager, region manager, director of quality and vice president and director of strategic planning. He also was president of Con-way Southern Express, one of Con-way's three regional LTL carriers, and later became president of Con-way Central Express, the company's largest regional LTL operation. Among his professional affiliations, he is a member of the American Trucking Associations' Cross-Border Operations Policy Committee and its Highway Policy Committee. He sits on the Board of Directors of the U.S. Chamber of Commerce, serving on the Board's policy committees for Environment & Energy and Regulatory Affairs, and is a member of the Chamber's National Security and Emergency Preparedness Department. He also is a member of the Transportation Research Board's (TRB) Trucking Industry Research Committee. Mr. Miller received his MBA from the Executive Management Program from the University of Chicago Graduate School of Business.

Additional Trucking information provided by:

Ted Scott

Ted Scott is the Director of Special Projects at the American Trucking Association. He received his Civil Engineering degree from the University of New Mexico and his MS in Business Administration from Boston University.

JOHN DEERE

Deere & Company, collectively called John Deere, was founded in 1837. The company has grown from a one-man blacksmith shop into a corporation that today does business around the world and employs approximately 56,000 people. John Deere consists of three major business segments (agriculture and turf, construction and forestry, and credit). Those segments, along with the support operations of parts and power systems, are focused on helping customers be more productive and improve the quality of life for people around the world. Visit John Deere at www.JohnDeere.com.

Eugene F. Standaert

Eugene F. Standaert, prior to his retirement in 2000, was a transportation team leader for John Deere. He was responsible for optimizing product transportation to customers. Mr. Standaert attended St. Ambrose University in Davenport, Iowa.

FEDEX TRADE NETWORKS

FedEx Trade Networks, Inc., headquartered in Memphis, Tennessee, is a subsidiary of FedEx Corporation, and was founded in 2000 (with international freight forwarding and customs brokerage antecedents going back to the 1890s). FedEx Trade Networks is one of the largest customs entry filers in North America, clearing through Customs a significant portion of cargo moving into the United States, and Canada and provides international freight forwarding around the globe.

FedEx Trade Networks has approximately 3,250 employees (part of FedEx Corporation's 290,000 team members around the globe), and is the winner of Logistics Management's *Quest for Quality* top five international forwarders for the past several years. Visit FedEx Trade Networks at www.ftn.fedex.com.

Janice Prezzato

Janice Prezzato is the Managing Director, Marketing and Communications. Prior to this, Ms. Prezzato was Director, Logistics; VP Traffic and Transportation. She has

twice received the FedEx Five Star Award, and is a member of the National Industrial Transportation League (former member of board of directors and executive committee) and Council of Supply Chain Management Professionals (CSCMP) Ms. Prezzato received her BA in Journalism/Communications from Wayne State University, Detroit, Michigan.

GREYHOUND LINES, INC.

Greyhound, founded in 1914, is the largest provider of intercity bus transportation, serving more than 2,300 destinations with 13,000 daily departures across North America. It has become an American icon, providing safe, enjoyable, and affordable travel to nearly 25 million passengers each year. The Greyhound running dog is one of the most-recognized brands in the world.

Greyhound, headquartered in Dallas, Texas, has 9,700 employees and a fleet of more than 1,300 buses. For more information about Greyhound, BoltBus or NeOn, please visit www.greyhound.com, www.boltbus.com, or www.neonbus.com.

Abby Wambaugh

Abby Wambaugh is the Lead Spokesperson for Greyhound. Prior to this, Ms. Wambaugh worked in communications at Walmart and the Oklahoma State University Office of Communications. Ms. Wambaugh is a member of the International Association of Business Communicators. Ms. Wambaugh received her BS in Journalism and Broadcasting from the Oklahoma State University.

INGRAM BARGE

Ingram Barge, founded in 1946, is headquartered in Nashville, Tennessee. Ingram Barge is the largest U.S. inland barge carrier with sales of over $1 billion and over 2,300 employees. Visit Ingram at www.ingrambarge.com .

Jerry Knapper

Jerry Knapper is the AVP of Planning and Analysis. Mr. Knapper received his MPA from Drake University.

MTA LONG ISLAND RAIL ROAD

The Long Island Rail Road (LIRR), founded in 1834, is the largest and oldest commuter railroad in North America, carrying more than 300,000 customers daily (2008). The LIRR is part of the Metropolitan Transportation Authority (MTA). The MTA is the largest transportation network in North America serving 14.6 million people in the 5,000 square mile area encompassing New York City, Long Island, southeastern New York State, and Connecticut. MTA railroads, subways and buses account for approximately one of every three users of mass transit in the United States. The MTA LIRR, headquartered in Jamaica, New York, has 6,800 employees and a budget of $1.5 billion (2008). Visit the MTA LIRR at www.mta.info.

Michael Charles

Michael Charles is the Manager-Media Relations, and has served as media, community, and government liaison for LIRR for almost 29 years. Prior to this, Mr. Charles was a news reporter at various radio and television stations in the New York City area. Mr. Charles received his BS English and Speech from the State University of New York at New Paltz, New York.

OVERSEAS SHIPHOLDING GROUP

Overseas Shipholding Group, Inc. (OSG) is a market leader in global energy transportation services. Overseas Shipholding Group owns and operates a fleet of more than 120 International Flag and U.S. Flag vessels that transport crude oil, refined petroleum products and gas worldwide. Visit Overseas Shipholding Group at www.osg.com.

Jennifer L. Schlueter

Jennifer Schlueter is Vice President, Corporate Communications and Investor Relations. In this capacity she has oversight of investor relations, crisis communication, executive communications, employee communications, media relations, and is responsible for the Company's public Web sites. Prior to joining OSG she held numerous positions at Gartner, Inc. a research and advisory firm that tracks the technology industry. She began her career as a financial analyst. Ms. Schlueter received her BS in Finance from Portland State University. She is a member of the Investor Relations Association and a past board member of the Westchester/Connecticut chapter of NIRI.

SOUTHWEST AIRLINES

Southwest Airlines, founded in 1971, has the best Customer Satisfaction record of any airline (Department of Transportation records since 1987). Also, Southwest carried more domestic passengers than any other airline in 2008. Southwest Airlines, headquartered in Dallas, Texas, has 35,000 employees and annual sales of $11 billion (2008). Visit Southwest Airlines at www.southwest.com.

Linda Rutherford

Linda Rutherford is the Vice President of Communications and Strategic Outreach. After a successful newspaper career, Ms. Rutherford joined Southwest Airlines Public Relations Department in 1992. In her current position, her team relates the Southwest Airlines story to the public through traditional media channels, through the online Emerging Media Team, and through various community outreach efforts.

SKYHOOK

SkyHook, founded in 2006, is headquartered in Calgary, AB, Canada. For an illustration and more information, visit www.skyhookintl.com

Pete Jess

Pete Jess, Founder, President and COO, is the innovator and visionary behind SkyHook. Over the course of his thirty-five year career in the Canadian high arctic, he has overseen various projects in the transportation and logistics field such as remote area oil rig moves, ice road and runway construction, and development of oil spill response methods. His private ventures include designing and manufacturing underwater ROVs used around the world in many applications and by the U.S. Navy. He also founded Jessco Logistics Ltd. which specializes in the supply and support of remote services and infrastructure for aviation, oil exploration, scientific research, engineering, film, and television. His contracts with the scientific, military, engineering, and nuclear industries have dealt with logistics, specialized equipment design and development, project management, and remote area guiding and outfitting.

NOTES

1. *Dictionary of Marketing Terms*, Peter D. Bennett (Chicago, IL: Marketing Association, 1995).
2. ATA Transportation Loss and Security Council.
3. AAR.
4. USDOT.
5. Cruise Lines International Association, 2007.

24 RETAILING

by Saks Fifth Avenue, Costco, Sears, Patagonia, and Trader Joe's

THE ESSENTIALS OF RETAILING
by Saks Fifth Avenue and Costco

Introduction

The primary goal of a retail operation is to make a profit while fulfilling the last step in the manufacturing/distribution chain—place products in the hands of customers. A retail operation, through its marketing efforts, can increase or even create a perceived need for products. Ultimately, however, the retail world is captive to the principle of supply and demand as much as any other part of the manufacturing/distribution chain. As the last link in the chain before the consumer takes possession of a product, the retailer must be keenly aware of consumer demands. In the past, retailing was almost entirely a one-direction endeavor where there was virtually no feedback from the customer. Today, retailers are involved in a constant two-way dialogue with their customers in order to narrow down the wide possibilities of what a customer might buy.

Definition

Retailers are "establishments that sell merchandise and related services to the public for personal or household consumption." (U.S. Department of Commerce). The retailer can be either a physical location or on the Internet.

RETAIL OWNERSHIP

The first step in retailing is to determine the method of ownership, operational policies, and organizational structure.

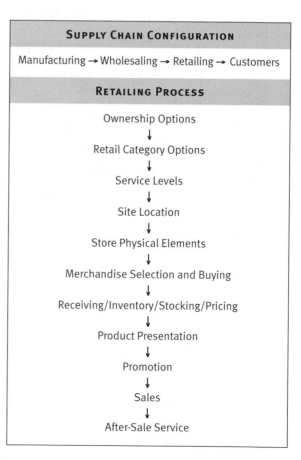

SUPPLY CHAIN CONFIGURATION

Manufacturing → Wholesaling → Retailing → Customers

RETAILING PROCESS

Ownership Options
↓
Retail Category Options
↓
Service Levels
↓
Site Location
↓
Store Physical Elements
↓
Merchandise Selection and Buying
↓
Receiving/Inventory/Stocking/Pricing
↓
Product Presentation
↓
Promotion
↓
Sales
↓
After-Sale Service

Methods of Ownership

There are several methods of retail ownership, including independents, retail chains, franchises, and cooperatives.

Independents

Independent retail operations are not affiliated with other retail operations. The owners are the sole proprietors or operate in partnerships. Often these establishments are operated by families who provide a personalized environment and service.

Owned and operated independently, these owners have the advantage of running the businesses according to their own tastes and preferences and controlling the profits. The disadvantages are that independent stores do not have the name recognition or experience the economies of scale in product purchasing of a large-scale operation.

Retail Chains

A corporate *retail chain* is comprised of multiple retail stores under common ownership and management. These stores offer similar merchandise assortments, have similar appearances, and use a centralized buying system. Chains vary in size from two stores to hundreds. Examples of large retail chains include Sears, J.C. Penney, Wal-Mart, and Home Depot.

The advantages of operating a chain store include centralized management, larger computer systems, purchasing bargaining power, and economies of scale. The disadvantage of chains is that they usually have less local flexibility in management style and product selection.

Franchises

A *franchise* is an association of independent retailers that each pay for the right to distribute established products or services, use well-known trademarks, and use a successful business format. Companies are willing to operate their business as a franchise because this allows the firm to increase their sales and market penetration without having to raise their own capital. Franchise buyers typically pay an initial franchise fee, lease a store, buy their own equipment and inventory, and pay a royalty based on sales.

The advantage to the consumer is the known standard of quality and service from store to store. The advantage of franchise ownership is selling an established product or service with a proven method, thus eliminating many start-up problems. Additional advantages include the economies of scale in product purchasing and advertising, and afford company representatives the availability to detect problems and provide advice on how to solve them. The disadvantage is that some franchises are unable to cater to local preferences.

Cooperatives

Cooperatives are independent retail operations that combine their buying resources in order to achieve purchasing economies of scale. These members cooperate in buying and transporting the merchandise. For example, cooperatives are prevalent in the men's clothing industry.

Operational Policies

Operational policies refer to practices such as hours of operations, general pricing levels, ambiance, and organizational structure.

Hours of Operations

The hours of operation selected help to provide time value to the customer and may help to differentiate one store from another. There are three categories of time: seasonality, days, and hours.

- **Seasonality.** The retail establishment typically operates all year long with the advantage of constant availability to the customer. However, some stores operate only seasonally, such as farmers' markets, beach rental facilities, and Christmas tree lots, with the advantage of providing customers' seasonal needs without paying for rent on a year-long basis.
- **Days.** Most stores are open seven days a week with the advantage of constant availability to the customer. However, some stores are open only a few days a week, typically only those days most shopped by their customer base, with the advantage of minimizing operational costs, which fits

with their discount pricing strategy and helps to differentiate the store in marketing communications efforts. For example, Frugal Fannie's Fashion Warehouse is open on weekends only.

- **Hours.** Most stores operate from approximately 9 A.M. to 9 P.M. However, to provide additional time value, some stores are available 24 hours a day, such as convenience marts (7-Eleven), catalog shopping (L.L. Bean), and Web sites (J. Crew). In addition, some stores now operate on an extended schedule, such as from 6:30 A.M. to 12:00 midnight, to accommodate today's customers who typically work during the day. Some stores are open by appointment only for valued customers to shop at their convenience.

Pricing Levels

Pricing levels depend on the type of store category, type of customer sought, type of merchandise carried, store image, and the amount of competition in a given location. Pricing strategies are discussed in detail in Chapter 18, "Product Pricing."

Organizational Structure

Every employee in a retail organization is focused on how the retailer's various functions will get products into the hands of customers. Primary positions include buyers, visual merchandisers, retail sales reps, the marketing staff, operations staff, and human resources.

RETAIL CATEGORIES

The next step is to determine which category of retailing is the most appropriate. There are two main categories: in-store retailing and nonstore retailing.

In-Store Retailing

There are several different types of retail stores, including department, specialty, warehouse clubs, *convenience, outlet, and super centers* or hypermarkets.

Department Stores

A *department store* is typically a large-scale retail operation that offers a diverse assortment of merchandise in varied price ranges. The stores feature merchandise for the individual and the home that may be arranged in separate departments according to each product line. Department stores typically have a main or flagship store, usually the original store in a downtown setting, whose sales are extended through branch stores established in suburban shopping malls. Examples of leading national department stores include Sears, Macy's, J.C. Penney, and Nordstrom.

The primary advantage of department stores is the convenience of one-stop shopping for the entire family. The primary disadvantage is the lack of depth within the product lines carried in many departments. Hoping to capitalize on this disadvantage, the dominance of department stores constantly is being challenged by the increase in other types of retailers such as mass merchandisers, specialty stores, television shopping networks, catalogs, and the Internet.

Specialty Stores

A *specialty store* sells one or a few specific product lines within a broader category such as apparel, furniture, appliances, or toys. These stores focus on meeting the needs of a particular customer segment and competing for this customer base through a unique merchandise assortment rather than price. This merchandise is narrowly focused but offers a depth of selection within the merchandise category. In doing so, specialty stores have become a fast-growing sector of the market. A disadvantage of the specialty store may be the lack of a diverse assortment of products to support the business if the market for the main specialty product diminishes. Examples of specialty stores are Saks Fifth Avenue, a fashion retailer; F.A.O. Schwarz, a toy retailer; and Lane Bryant, an apparel retailer for plus-size women.

Several specialty stores have become category dominant, also known as category killers, because they are so successful within their niche that many department stores have given up competing with them: for example, Toys"R"Us in toys and Bed Bath & Beyond in linens.

Mass Merchandiser/Warehouse Clubs

A *mass merchandiser* is a retailer that attempts to reach the largest audience through low pricing. The main advantage to the consumer is the extremely low price of the merchandise. The main disadvantages are that not all brands are carried, the lack of service, and the lack of consistent selection.

There are three main varieties of product selection:

- A wide variety of products with a medium depth of selection, such as Wal-Mart, Kmart, and Target
- A wide selection with limited product categories, such as Best Buy and Staples
- A limited width and depth of categories but a variety of bulk purchases, such as Costco and BJ's Wholesale Club.

Convenience Stores

A *convenience store* is "a retail business with primary emphasis placed on providing the public with a convenient location to quickly purchase from a wide array of consumable products (predominantly food, beverages, snacks, and gasoline) and services."[2] The advantages include the convenient parking and locations, and extended hours of operation. The disadvantages include the lack of depth of merchandise and the relatively higher prices. Examples include 7-Elevens and mini-marts in gasoline stations.

Outlet Stores

Outlet stores are retailers that sell overruns, out of season products, or unpurchased merchandise from national manufacturers and national specialty store chains. These were formerly known as clearance centers. The primary advantage is the low price. The disadvantage is the typically far away locations. Examples include National Liquidators, Syms, Loehmann's, The Gap Outlet, and Levi's Outlet.

Super Centers

Super centers are mega-supermarkets and large general merchandise stores that offer everything from food to appliances under one roof. For example, Target, Kmart, and Meijer super centers are the size of six football fields and can have as many as 60 checkout counters. Wal-Mart's Super Stores have 35 merchandise departments ranging from apparel and fine jewelry to automobile servicing and seafood. Super centers in the United States are very similar to European hypermarkets.

Nonstore Retailing

There is a large and growing segment of retailing that in broadest terms is called nonstore retailing. Each retailer within this segment avoids one of the largest expenses in retailing: rent. Nonstore retailing includes the Internet, temporary retailers, and vending machines. Other sales methods such as catalog marketing and home shopping networks formerly were grouped under retailing but now are more accurately grouped under direct marketing.

Internet

Internet retailing is described in detail in Chapter 25, "Internet Retailing."

Temporary Retailers

Temporary retailers include bazaars (church and school), flea markets, farmers' markets, garage sales, and seasonal kiosks in malls. These retail outlets are usually owner-operated, in temporary locations, and may be outdoors. A temporary tenant leases temporary space in malls for a short duration, either seasonal or until a full-time tenant selects the space. Temporary tenants include booksellers, jewelry sellers, and promotional sellers of long-distance telephone services. The advantages of this type of temporary retail arrangement are the low prices, seasonal assortment, and unusual items. The disadvantages include unknown locations, nonwarrantied merchandise, and discontinued operations.

Vending Machines

Vending machines are nonattended devices that mechanically distribute a product. The predominant products distributed through vending machines include sodas, candy/snacks, hot beverages, and newspapers. However, high-priced items also are sold. For example, in Japan, where retail store space is at a premium, vending machines sell designer ties and cameras. The predominant locations for vending machines are in or near manufacturing/warehouse sites, office buildings, and retail locations. The advantages for the consumer are the convenient locations and 24-hour availability. The advantage for the manufacturer is the accessibility to relatively inexpensive additional distribution points. The disadvantages for the consumer are the relatively higher prices and the limited selection of products.

Direct Store Delivery

Direct store delivery offers a lifestyle solution that meets the needs of busy people, typically marketed to suburban families juggling time-intensive demands of family and dual careers. The direct store delivery company receives orders from customers via telephone, fax, or the Internet and then picks the ordered products in largely the same fashion a consumer would. The company then delivers the order to the home at a prescheduled time. If delivery depends on the customer being at home for the delivery, it is called attended delivery. If the customer is not required to be at home, it is called unattended delivery. The advantage of this method of shopping is the time saved for the customer. The disadvantage is the additional cost of the service.

RETAIL SERVICE LEVELS

Different types of retailers provide different levels of service to customers. The current trend in retailing is to offer either upscale full-service shopping or low-cost self-service shopping. Retail operations generally can be categorized as either full service or self-service.

Full Service

Full-service stores provide a breadth of amenities and attempt to make customers' lives easier through a variety of services. Full-service retailers create an atmosphere that will encourage customers to return for more enjoyable shopping experiences. Full-service retailers generally offer services from four classifications: sales assistance, services that provide convenience, services that facilitate sales, and auxiliary services.

- **Sales Assistance.** A full-service store provides sales assistance to the customer in order to answer questions, find the correct merchandise, offer merchandise suggestions, and transfer title.

- **Services That Provide Convenience.** Services that provide convenience are basic services offered by most stores and are used by all shoppers. Examples of this type of service include ideal store location, effective store layout, pleasant store appearance, and accommodating store hours.

- **Services That Facilitate Sales.** Services that facilitate sales are offered in addition to the most basic services. Such services include credit, delivery, installation, and engraving. These services can be especially helpful if the merchandise is a specialty or high-priced luxury item.

- **Auxiliary Services.** Auxiliary services are secondary to the full-service retailer's operation of the business, but make shopping in the store more convenient or enjoyable for the customer. Examples of auxiliary services include gift-wrapping, layaway plans, special orders, gift certificates, fashion consulting, and children's play and babysitting areas. Some retailers may offer such auxiliary services as valet parking, coat and package check, priority alterations, and personal shoppers.

Self-Service

Self-service stores generally offer as few amenities as possible in order to provide customers with the lowest possible cost. Self-service customers recognize that the trade-off for low costs often results in minimal assistance in stores, inconvenient store locations (in order to lower rent), a warehouse ambiance, cash-only policies, and lack of dressing rooms. Often self-service stores sell items in bulk quantities or sell off-brand or discontinued merchandise.

RETAIL LOCATION

The primary goals of the retail location are to site the store as close as possible to customers, where they are accustomed to shopping and at the lowest cost of real estate. Retail location consists of the site selection process and store site configuration options.

Site Selection Process

Store location is one of the most important elements that go into the success of a store. Even a store with the right products at the right prices will find it difficult to overcome an inappropriate site. Each site should be able to accommodate, and is dependent on, a geographic consumer base, known as a trading area, specified by population size and drive-time to store location. The typical goal when selecting a store site is to find a location that has potential for high foot traffic (the number of people who will be passing near and, hopefully, through the store). Store site selection today focuses on community traffic patterns.

The first step in determining an appropriate location is to define the store's trading area. The *trading area* is the geographic area from which the store will draw its customers. Physical characteristics are a key part of this determination. These include the nature of the trading area's road system (the presence of freeways, one-way streets, etc.) and geographic obstacles (lakes, mountains, etc.). Then an analysis must be made of the competitive situation. Finally, consumer behavioral issues are studied to determine the size of the trading area. For example, elderly residents often prefer to do their shopping close to home. This could indicate locating several smaller stores near bus routes rather than one large store farther away from elderly communities.

The next step in site selection is to find locations in which the demographics of the trading areas match those that the retailer is trying to reach. Large retailers do this through sophisticated computer modeling. Small retailers rely on government statistics, library research, and a personal knowledge of the area in which they are planning to locate.

Having focused on one or several potential sites, the next step is to begin work with the city planning department and other government agencies to see if the plan for the store fits the community's general plan and zoning requirements. This step generally is taken before the retailer buys or obtains an option on the real estate or building. Although most cities generally welcome the prospect of increased sales tax and payroll tax revenue, some overbuilt communities have placed stringent restrictions on new development that could make it too expensive or otherwise impractical for a retailer to locate there.

Store Site Configuration Options

There are two main site options: freestanding stores and shopping centers.

Freestanding Stores

Freestanding stores are physically separate from other retail stores and constitute about 44 percent of all retail space as defined by sales volume.[2] Usually, retailers who use this format select convenient locations for their customers, such as a site along a major highway.

The advantages of the freestanding format are that these locations usually offer greater visibility from the road, easier parking, greater proximity to target market neighborhoods, and determination of their own hours of operation. The freestanding format also can have a more flexible physical layout. For example, fast-food restaurants can increase their seating capacity and add a drive-through window. The disadvantages of the freestanding location are fewer shoppers and added expenses. Shoppers have to make a special trip to go to this type of store, and freestanding stores do not gain customers from the foot traffic generated by other stores in a shopping center location. A freestanding store may need a larger promotional budget than a shopping center store in order to attract customers.

Shopping Centers

A *shopping center* is a cluster or grouping of stores physically connected to one another or to a common public space. There are several advantages for stores located in shopping centers. Stores are able to benefit from joint promotional activities with the other tenants in the center. Similarly, the parking requirements for a shopping center store may be shared with other tenants, leading to cost savings over the freestanding store. Shopping centers have another advantage in that they generally will work to have a balance of the types of retailers within the center. This helps limit competition to some extent. In 1997, there were 42,874 shopping centers in the United States, representing 53 percent of total retail sales.[3]

There are two types of shopping center configurations: malls and strip centers. Malls typically are enclosed with two rows of stores facing a common walkway. A *strip center* is an attached row of stores configured in a straight line or an "L" or "U" shape without enclosed walkways. Shopping malls typically have large anchor stores such as Sears or Macy's, located at either end, and smaller shops such as book, gift, and specialty stores located in the middle.

There are several types of shopping centers: the neighborhood shopping center, the community shopping center, the regional shopping center, and the superregional shopping center.[4]

- **Neighborhood Shopping Center.** A neighborhood shopping center usually consists of several small stores offering convenience products and personal services such as a dry cleaner or video rental store and anchored by either a grocery store or a drugstore.
- **Community Shopping Center.** A community shopping center typically offers a wider range of stores than the neighborhood center. Community shopping centers typically are anchored by a well-known specialty store offering sporting goods, apparel, electronics, home furnishings, or toys, for example, Bed Bath & Beyond or Kohl's.
- **Regional Shopping Center.** Regional shopping centers are comprised of two or more full-line department stores, such as Macy's, that anchor the center and are supplemented by several apparel stores, shoe stores, furniture stores, appliance stores, and drugstores. This type of shopping center typically is enclosed with an inward orientation of stores connected by a common walkway.
- **Superregional Shopping Center.** Superregional shopping centers, also known as mega malls, have hundreds of stores, three or more major anchor department stores, restaurants, and entertainment centers.

RETAIL STORE PHYSICAL ELEMENTS

Consumers see and judge the physical elements of a retail store every day, so these elements are important to design correctly. The main physical elements of the retail store focus on three areas: architecture, signage, and the floor layout and fixtures.

Architecture

Prior to the 1950s, the exteriors of most retail establishments only needed to appear clean in order to convince people to enter the store. The store sign, the display of merchandise, and the reputation of the merchant were more important than the style or design of the building in which the store was located. In the 1950s, architecture began to play a significant role in store design. One of the most outrageous examples surviving today is the donut shop in the shape of a huge donut. This Los Angeles landmark has been seen in many movies (thus garnering additional sales due to free publicity).

The importance of a store's exterior stems from the fact that first impressions are important. Often, the exterior of a building will be the first impression the shopper has of the retailer's approach, either a bare-bones discount operation or a lavishly conceived boutique.

Signage

The store sign, known as *signage*, includes the name of the store and occasionally a logo and advertising tagline. High-end stores may be bold enough to just display a logo for which they have become known, although smaller stores may still open without a professionally designed sign. Most stores today invest thousands of dollars in creating a unique way of presenting themselves. These efforts may coordinate the entire image of the retailer so that all of its signs, exterior and interior, are synchronized with its advertising and direct-mail efforts. Signage may have to comply with local aesthetics requirements that are determined by town councils or local architectural review committees.

Floor Layout

Floor layout is the positioning of fixtures and merchandise and the flow of foot traffic to direct customers to specific point-of-purchase areas. Floor layout is important as most consumers seek convenience and time-savings during shopping. Certain boutique clothing stores will greet customers at the door, ask them what they would like to see, have them sit down, and then bring a particular product or products to them without having the customers walk through any aisles.

Fixtures

Fixtures usually are the second largest initial expense, after the building itself. *Fixtures* are the display materials, lighting, and operational furniture required by the store and include everything from shelves to dressing room mirrors. The fixtures should reflect the image of the store and allow the customer to feel at ease with his or her shopping experience. For example, the bare cement floors and steel fixtures of Old Navy reflect the store's low prices, and the wood paneling enhances the quality image for Polo. Ralph Laoren.

RETAIL MERCHANDISING SELECTION AND BUYING

Retail buyers are the employees who search wholesalers, merchandise marts, and sometimes the world for the right products to offer to customers. Buyers travel to trade fairs, meet with manufacturing salespeople, tour manufacturing facilities, examine catalogs and price lists, sample and test products, and then select the products that seem most appropriate. A buyer's role has always been to purchase at a low price and sell high, but today this often involves financial arrangements (rebates, cooperative advertising allowances) that go beyond the instinctive recognition of a good buy.

Buyer Responsibilities

Retail buyers have several responsibilities, such as:

- Understanding and identifying the needs and wants of their target consumer
- Maintaining awareness of economic conditions
- Making regular trips to the manufacturer, trade shows, and fashion shows
- Watching for product trends
- Selecting merchandise assortments
- Negotiating with vendors for favorable terms and services
- Pricing merchandise to generate desired profits
- Maintaining well-balanced stocks and assortments

Merchandise Selection Determinants

Product selection, as determined by senior management and retail buyers, is dependent on three main factors: consumer needs, the type of merchandise offered, and the size of the retail operation.

- **Consumer Needs.** The product mix is always changing as consumers' needs and the competition require.
- **Type of Merchandise Offered.** The type of merchandise offered can drastically change the responsibilities of the buyer. For example, selecting and buying basic merchandise is extremely different from buying fashion merchandise. Basic products have a relatively constant demand, and the sales for these products vary only slightly from year to year. A buyer for fashion merchandise, however, realizes that fashions change continually, and merchandise that sold well last season may not be popular the next season. A buyer for fashion merchandise depends more on forecasting consumer demands and market trends than on the analysis of the prior year's sales.
- **Size of Retail Operation.** The size of the retail operation also determines the buyer's responsibilities. His or her duties in a small retail store may include selecting and buying the merchandise for several departments, whereas buyers' duties for larger stores are more specialized. These buyers are responsible for a particular product category rather than every product in the store.

RETAIL RECEIVING/INVENTORY AND STOCKING/PRICING

Receiving and Tagging

Goods are shipped from the manufacturer or the wholesaler to the retail store's distribution facility and from there sent to the individual store location, usually at a receiving dock. Some retailers still use the laborious process of giving each item a store label, a store-supplied stock keeping unit (SKU), and a store price tag. However, this tagging process is rapidly being replaced by the Universal Product Classification (UPC) bar-code system supplied by the manufacturer. The *bar-code system* is a series of computer-read symbols that increases reliability and decreases time spent during the consumer purchasing process.

Inventory and Stocking

Buyers must always be acutely attuned to the marketplace and ready to adjust to the constantly changing demand and supply conditions within the market. This is especially true in planning merchandise assortments. To help accurately plan inventory levels, buyers consider two important elements: sales forecasting and stock planning.

Most retailers will develop a sales forecast and then plan the amount of inventory required to meet the forecast. The difficulty of making an accurate forecast depends on the type of merchandise being considered. Buyers may use past sales figures as a guide in making a forecast for basic merchandise, such as toasters or chairs. However, for fashion merchandise, a thorough knowledge of market trends is needed.

Once the forecast is made, the buyer can plan the inventory levels. The objective is to have enough merchandise in stock to meet sales expectations along with unanticipated customer demand. A prime reason for lost retail sales is lack of stock, known as a stock-out. However, it is important to maintain an inventory level small enough to ensure a reasonable return on the store's investment in inventory.

One way to determine whether there is too little or too much invested in inventory is to determine the rate of stock turnover (compute the number of times the stock turns over in a given period). Before the rate of stock turnover can be found, however, the average inventory must be calculated (add the inventory at the beginning of the period and the inventory at the end of the period and divide by two). The average inventory is then used to find the annual rate of stock turnover (in retail dollars) by dividing the net yearly sales by the average inventory on hand (in retail dollars). All businesses use the rate of stock turnover as a gauge to assess the optimal level of inventory.

INVENTORY COMPUTATIONS

Total Inventory = Beginning Inventory + Ending Inventory
Average Inventory = Total Inventory ÷ 2
Rate of Stock Turnover = Yearly Sales ÷ Average Inventory

To attain the very delicate balance of inventory and sales, many buyers use the stock-to-sales ratio method. This method maintains inventory in a specific ratio-to-sales. Stock-to-sales ratios are calculated by dividing the dollar value of the stock on hand by actual sales in dollars. For example, if a department had merchandise valued at $40,000 at the beginning of the month and sales for that month amounted to $20,000, the resulting stock-to-sales ratio would be 2. This ratio is then used to calculate stock levels needed at the beginning of the month. The stock-to-sales ratio for the month multiplied by the planned sales for the month determines the inventory level needed at the beginning of the month.

Inventory security is important as retail theft is an expensive problem. There are several methods for providing physical safekeeping of the merchandise. These include locked storage rooms, guarded store entrances, locked display cabinets, and electronic article surveillance tags (EAS). Marketing should try to minimize the intrusion of each of these methods on customer shopping.

Pricing

The pricing aspects of merchandising include pricing strategies and pricing methods.

Retail Pricing Strategies

Regardless of the individual product strategy followed, retailers hope to set average prices high enough to cover costs and make a reasonable profit. In determining price strategies, retailers have three pricing choices: pricing under the market, above the market, or at the market.

- **Pricing under the Market.** Merchants that want to appeal to value-conscious customers price their products under the market. These retailers advertise and promote their stores on the basis of price and offer merchandise at a price with a lower than usual markup. An individual product that is priced under the market is called a *loss leader*, typically a staple item such as milk. The goal of the loss leader is to lure customers into the store who are specifically attracted to low-price staples. Other high-price items in the store compensate for the loss leaders. Pricing below cost is illegal.
- **Pricing above the Market.** Other retailers consistently price merchandise above the market. These stores offer exclusivity, quality, convenience, and service in return for the price asked.
- **Pricing at the Market.** Still other merchants price at the market, believing that a significant number of customers neither look for the lowest prices nor are willing to pay for the highest prices. The customer this store attracts is concerned with price, convenience, attractiveness of the store, and the attitude of the sales personnel.

Retail Pricing Methods

There are several pricing methods, including markup, dollar margin, markdown, unit, and item.

- **Markup.** *Markup* is the retail price after a specific percentage profit has been added to the price of the product received from the manufacturer or wholesaler. For example, the markup typically has been $33 \frac{1}{3}$ percent for electronic goods, 40 percent on shoes, and 50 percent on clothing.
- **Dollar Margin.** An alternative to the standard percentage markup is the dollar margin concept. This method prices merchandise according to demand, appeal, and competition rather than pricing to achieve a given profit on each item. The price is determined by the value a particular item has to the customer. Depending on the price, the item does not always make a profit by itself, but these items are offered to provide a wide selection for customers, drawing customers into the store who will buy many other items that will make a profit.
- **Markdowns.** Retailers may use markdowns to increase sales of poorly moving merchandise or old stock to make room for incoming items. Markdowns are sometimes implemented in stages. In some retail categories such as fashion, a 50 percent reduction is often necessary to sell goods at the end of a season.
- **Unit Pricing.** *Unit pricing* is the quotation of prices given in a common standard of measurement (weight, size). Using unit pricing, the consumer may easily compare prices of dissimilar product weights or sizes. This practice is used predominantly in grocery stores in response to consumer requests.
- **Item Pricing** Item pricing occurs when every item sold has a price tag as opposed to a common tag located on a shelf or wall near a display of products.

RETAIL PRESENTATION OF PRODUCT ASSORTMENT

Retailers should try to meet the customers' need for a large assortment of merchandise (always in stock) while being aware of the financial constraints of the company's merchandise buying plan. Presentation has two parts: what is presented (model stock) and how it is presented (visual merchandising).

Typically the retailer makes the decisions as to which specific products to place on the shelves and how to display them. However, in some stores, there is another approach called category management, which is a strategy used when the retailer allots a certain amount of shelf or floor space to the manufacturer or wholesaler's products to use as the manufacturer or distributor chooses. An example of this is the magazine racks at the grocery store.

This approach is being used extensively today in other product categories, especially those in which a dominant manufacturer or distributor has a large number of items. What the retailer gives up in control, however, usually is gained back in terms of efficient restocking practices and lower labor costs.

Model Stock

Retailers strive to maximize the sales and profits from the store's inventory investment with the establishment of an ideal assortment, or model stock. In preparing the various assortments of merchandise for sale, stock is broken down according to factors important to the target market, such as brand, price, material, color, and size. Once the general product categories are decided upon, retailers then present the merchandise (model stock). For example, if the store offers women's, men's, and children's apparel, the retailer then further divides these classifications into subclassifications. Women's apparel can be broken down into categories (or designers) such as suits, dresses, coats, shoes, and handbags. Then the merchandise in each category can be sorted according to brands carried and price points offered. Items are also sorted according to general characteristics such as different colors, sizes, material, and styles. Increasingly, buyers work closely with the retail operators to determine the most effective way to display and offer the product in the store. Finally, the retailer presents the assortment that displays the most important characteristics in relation to the targeted customer. Some stores showcase every possible product while others try to present fewer but better selling items.

Visual Merchandising

Visual merchandising places emphasis on how a product is displayed. Displays present the store's merchandise in a manner that will draw in customers and call attention to specific merchandise, either seasonal or sale items.

The most common example of visual merchandising is the window display. Whether in a high-fashion salon on New York's Fifth Avenue or a sewing machine store on Main Street, U.S.A., a retailer with a creative sense of design can significantly increase the number of people coming into a store by developing eye-catching window displays. However, a recent trend by some stores removes the window displays in favor of allowing potential customers to see directly into the interior of the store. The hope is that the whole store will be more of a draw to customers than any one piece of merchandise displayed in the window.

Another method of visual merchandising is the use of end-of-aisle displays (also called endcaps) to call attention to products, typically sale items. By placing products in a special display at the end of an aisle, along one of the main concourses of a store, retailers and manufacturers are almost certain to sell the product more quickly. It is a simple matter of visual exposure to the product. This is such a proven technique that most retailers charge manufacturers an extra fee for such placement.

One of the more extreme examples of a store that relied on visual merchandising in recent years was Incredible Universe, the electronics superstore started by Radio Shack in the mid–1990s. Shoppers were greeted with a massive array of hundreds of large-screen televisions, stereos, and appliances. Consumers found that such a mind-numbing array of sights and sounds was overwhelming and complained that it was difficult to find the products that were for sale. The store concept lasted approximately six months and lost millions of dollars.

RETAIL PROMOTION

Retailers must put forth their best efforts in order to turn potential customers into actual customers.

Store Marketing Communications

Retail advertising provides significant revenue for most daily and weekly newspapers and radio and television stations. Most television advertising, primarily placed by brand manufacturers, is designed to drive viewers into local retail establishments. Sales promotional activities have proven effective and may include book signings, special celebrity appearances, children's events, taste samplings, store ambiance, and even the Macy's Thanksgiving Day Parade.

Manufacturer—Retailer Co-op Advertising

An interesting retail trend is the decreasing reliance on cooperative advertising funds. These funds traditionally have been allotted by manufacturers to retailers so that the retailer will have money specifically earmarked for advertising the manufacturer's product. Thus, if the retailer is placing three pages of ads in the Sunday newspaper, the funds provided by the manufacturer may pay for one of those pages, as long as the page features the manufacturer's brand. These cooperative advertising funds usually are paid to the retailer in the form of deductions from the manufacturer's invoice. In recent years, there has been a trend to net out, or eliminate, the cooperative advertising allotment and simply lower the cost of the product. The retailer then can lower its retail price in order to attract additional customers.

Store Ambiance

The style, ambiance, and atmosphere of a store can play a major role in where the customer is willing to shop. The ambiance of a store is created by its physical attributes and by intangibles such as the music being played and the demeanor of the staff. For example, Bloomingdale's has long been known for attracting customers by its theater approach to shopping. Theater retailing means always having something happening, whether it is cooking demonstrations or spritzing free samples of perfume.

RETAIL PERSONAL SELLING
by Sears

The retailer provides a source from which the customer takes possession and title of purchased products. Sales clerks, also known as sales associates or team members, attend to the needs of the store's customers. Knowledge of the store's product line and courteous service are the key elements of retail sales. Greeting the customer, determining the customer's needs, obtaining the desired merchandise, completing the financial transaction, and bagging the merchandise is the usual sales process.

The sales clerk often is the primary contact between the retailer and the customer. The ways a retailer handles financial arrangements for customer sales has become very important to its success. For a small merchant this can be as simple as providing a credit and debit card machine at the sales counter. Larger-scale retailers may provide an array of financial arrangements for customers. For example, retailers of expensive products such as automobiles or large appliances often arrange financing.

It is impossible to define a single model that fairly represents the selling process across the proliferation of retail formats such as warehouse clubs, mass-market merchandisers, category killers, specialty merchandisers, and department stores. Creating a superior selling organization begins with selecting salespeople who are enthusiastic about the prospect of helping customers purchase items that meet their needs. Extensive interviews, often involving current sales staff and sometimes customers, are common among stores that consider service to be a key part of their value offering. Skills sought include effective interpersonal communication, stress tolerance, self-confidence, and a customer service orientation. The selection process also may include detailed role-plays and simulations of common selling situations using trained observers or, more recently, computer-based simulation.

There are some common steps that provide an effective framework for creating a positive buying experience across a wide range of merchandise and retail formats. The retail selling process is a step-by-step process that includes preparation, relating, discovering, suggesting, advocating, supporting, closing the sale, and extending the relationship.

1. **Preparation.** Salespeople do a lot of preparation before the customer walks in the store. Preparation includes attention to a high level of personal appearance, maintenance of superior merchandise presentation in the store, and setting measurable sales goals.

2. **Relating.** Customer satisfaction depends on their interaction with the retail salesperson. Consumer research has shown that in most store situations, customers expect to be acknowledged within 20 seconds of entering the store department. Effective selling focuses on some very basic procedures to cement a relationship with the customer from the start of the interaction. These procedures include making eye contact, smiling, and introducing oneself.

3. **Discovering.** This step focuses on uncovering through active listening what the customer needs, not what the salesperson wants to sell. This is initiated by an open-ended question such as "What brings you to our store today?" There is empirical evidence that increasing the time spent in discovery increases the close ratio (the number of sales successes to sales opportunities) significantly.

4. **Suggesting.** Based on the information gained through discovery, the salesperson should suggest items (typically two or three) that meet the customer's needs.

5. **Advocating.** In this step, the salesperson moves to a demonstration of the items he or she has suggested, with the goal of helping the customer make a selection. The emphasis in successful advocacy should be on the benefits the customer will derive, such as saving time or energy, reducing aggravation, or enhancing self-esteem, not on the features of the item. This subtle distinction focuses the tone of the dialogue on the customer's point of view.

6. **Supporting.** It is not uncommon that customers may express some objection to the product. The supporting step is designed to help salespeople respond to these objections while continuing to move toward a sale that will satisfy the customer. The general process used to handle objections includes clarifying the objection; cushioning it by tempering its impact (such as a company price-matching policy or further explanation of item benefits); answering it in an honest, direct fashion; and then seeking agreement with the customer.

7. **Closing the Sale.** There are a variety of ways of asking for the sale, the final critical step in the retail sales process. Methods of closing include summarizing the item's benefits, presenting alternate choices (with the assumption that one will be selected), or simply asking for the sale directly. The timing of this process is critical, and should not happen until the previous steps have been executed. Salespersons also should listen for verbal buying signals such as asking if the item is in stock or when it could be delivered. The salesperson should reinforce the buyer's decision immediately after the sale in order to avoid the problem of buyer's remorse, when a purchase decision may be undone.

8. **Extending the Customer Relationship.** It is crucial for a company's long-term success to extend the customer relationship after the sale. This might include keeping in touch by calling to check on delivery, installation, or product performance, or sending a thank you note. Research across a variety of industries has shown that it is the delighted customer, not merely the satisfied one, who will return for repeat business and actively recommend the store to others.

RETAIL AFTER-SALE SERVICE

After-sale service includes delivery, store warranties, and repair. Many retailers, large and small, go well beyond legal requirements in guaranteeing the quality and functionality of the products they sell. Often, the manufacturer's guarantee is relatively limited. However, in many cases, a retailer's guarantee may be unlimited: "If you buy it and it doesn't work, we'll refund your money." As more products become increasingly complicated, the after-sale function of installation also is becoming more important. Retailers often contract out this service, even if they are offering it for free to the customer.

RETAIL UNSOLD MERCHANDISE

Merchandise that is damaged, known as unsalable, returned, or unsold may be returned to the manufacturer, discounted in-store, transferred to the outlet store, or sold to a discount retailer. Returned merchandise frees up space for newer merchandise.

RETAILING—INTERNATIONAL
by Patagonia

Retail stores bring products to the consumer in convenient locations. Retail stores should seek to create their own global brand image by bringing the retail store philosophy to life. Creating a store's own image builds brand recognition and loyalty. Both depth of inventory selection as well as style selection offer the customer a more complete representation of the store brand and product line. International retail stores typically are managed under regional entities, such as Patagonia Europe. Each operation has a general manager that has overall responsibility for the direction of the retail division. This allows retailers to adapt the retail philosophy that was developed in the home country to local market conditions, while still preserving the operational and philosophical direction that is highly effective for the store. Standardization procedures reduce costs and create a more efficient business; however, the retailer must meet the needs of customers in different markets.

International stores are for the most part in-line stores (full price, not discount) that offer a complete selection of products. Each market should have at least one outlet store to manage discontinued products, overstocks, and out-of-season styles. The level of presentation and service in the outlet stores should be the same as in-line. Store size and location tend to be a step down from in-line criteria.

There are several areas in which international retail stores can adapt to local market conditions in order to become highly successful. Local store managers should have responsibility for store configuration, merchandising, and staffing.

Store Configuration

Retail stores, on a global basis, may vary in size depending on local real estate conditions. The stores in Japan are smaller than in Europe or the United States, due to the higher costs of real estate. This requires that stores operate in a more efficient manner than in the United States, such as giving up gathering spaces and space between items. Smaller stores also operate with fewer personnel, and store presentation tends to be sparser.

Store design and construction (build-out) requirements vary by country. Best practices from the strictest country requirements should be incorporated into all stores. For example, due to environmental requirements in some countries, Patagonia recently has increased its use of recycled materials, low-environmental impact paints/floor finishes, energy-efficient lighting, and heating/cooling systems in its stores in every country.

The retail store concept may be licensed to the local distributor in markets that are too small to be economical for the retailer to set up their own operations. The stores use the same design principles in fixtures, layout, and presentations. In general, the stores do not require as significant an investment as directly owned stores, due to lower real estate costs, as well as lower standards on build-out. The objective with these stores is to come as close as possible to the experience of shopping in one of the original stores.

Merchandising

Local market merchandise buying and inventory management is operated out of a logistic function center located in the local market (country or region). This allows retailers to take advantage of local inventory management needs on a rapid basis. Inventory selection and replenishment may vary by store size. Most international retail stores work with twice-a-week restocking programs; however, restocking may be as frequent as twice a day in smaller high-volume stores such as in Tokyo. Inventory needs are established by in-store point-of-sale (POS) systems that automatically download sales data to a central computer. Inventory is shifted among stores based on sales, weather, and other local factors. In addition, each international retail store should support the warranty and service levels of each product on a consistent basis. The customer must be satisfied with the product that they receive from the store regardless of its location.

Staffing

International consumers may be introduced to new products in the retail store; therefore, stores should be staffed with sales associates who use the products and are well versed in how they work. For example, Patagonia stores serve the function of steering the customer to guides, trips, schools, and other resources that can serve to maximize their product experience in the outdoors. All stores should reflect the language requirements of the customer base. For example, Patagonia stores in Europe have multilingual staff. This adds to the complexity of hiring and training needs for the retail locations.

RETAILING – CASE STUDY

by Costco

Company: Costco
Case: Merchandise Selection — Expanded Product Mix

Even a highly successful business sometimes needs to reassess its basics if it wants to continue being a strong competitor. In 1988, having achieved one of the most meteoric rises in retailing history from the time of its founding just four years before, Costco realized that it was facing some very tough competition from the Price Club, Pace Club (a division of Kmart), and Sam's Club (a division of Wal-Mart).

Each warehouse club required a fee and certain qualifications before an applicant could become a member and shop. Each club operated in a big box warehouse environment with an absence of fancy fixtures, few or no sales clerks, and a self-service approach. And, most importantly, each stressed everyday low pricing on nationally known brand products. In fact, both consumers and stock analysts seemed to be of the opinion that there were very few distinguishing features among the key competition in the warehouse club industry.

Costco's management became convinced that it would need to do something dramatic to distinguish itself within the industry. And whatever it did would have to be substantive, not just a short-term promotional blitz. The company had based its success on its mission to provide brand-name merchandise at the very best value. But it was already selling products from Michelin tires to Pert shampoo, just about everything short of fresh food. And there was the answer.

The fresh food idea had several key advantages for Costco. For example, with many meat and produce items, quality and freshness could be seen and understood immediately by the shopper. A fresh-from-scratch bakery, in addition to adding important products such as bread and pastries, could add a whole new dimension to the warehouse environment, the pleasing aroma of fresh-baked goods wafting throughout the building. Butchers working in a well-run meat department could be seen by the public through windows, adding a sense of theater and excitement to the shopping experience.

Costco set about carefully investigating, in order not to tip off the competition, how it could fit perishable items into its efficient operating systems. Perishables would require a significant increase in the equipment costs of operating a warehouse store, including such items as refrigerator and freezer compartments. Another key factor would be finding ways to eliminate the much larger spoilage factor that goes with fresh food, compared to the dry foods the company had been selling.

Fortunately, several key managers in the company had worked in the grocery business and were able to assist in working with quality suppliers to find cost efficiencies, such as better freezer systems.

Despite its efforts to figure out as many of the potential pitfalls as possible, Costco knew that it was taking a big risk in treading this new path within its industry. Would consumers used to buying their fresh foods primarily in nationally known supermarket chains really consider switching to making their purchases in the warehouse environment? What would convince people to do this? Once again, the answer seemed clear to all of the company's managers: if the products are of unquestionably high quality and if we sell them at unquestionably the best value, then we will have the same kind of success with fresh foods that we have had in other product categories. That is exactly the approach the company took, applying all of its operating disciplines to the fresh food business, and modifying none of the company's core. For example, using the time-honored 80/20 rule, Costco chose to focus on the 20 percent of the fresh food items that account for 80 percent of any fresh food operation's business, proving again that less can be more when it comes to warehouse merchandising.

It is hard to realize today how revolutionary this new approach was at the time it was implemented. The statistics do paint a clear picture, however. In 1987, the year before Costco began adding fresh food to its product mix, the majority of all fresh food shopping was done in supermarkets. By 1998, that percentage had changed significantly, Costco alone was selling $1.8 billion in fresh food items, approximately 10 percent of the company's total sales. By 2008 that figure had risen to roughly 50 percent.

The success of Costco's move into fresh foods precipitated an industrywide movement. It is an example of a company understanding consumers' needs and taking the proactive steps necessary to fulfill those needs.

RETAILING – CASE STUDY

by Trader Joe's

Company: Trader Joe's
Case: Customer Focus

In 1967, the first Trader Joe's opened in Pasadena, California. Their goal was to develop a small format store that was unlike any of the convenience store outlets cropping up across Southern California at the time. They would replace the somewhat cold convenience format with a romantic, travel, and leisure image of the South Seas and of international living. They would play exotic music and wear Hawaiian shirts, in an effort to add a sense of fun and adventure to their small retail business.

As with any new format, some things worked and some things didn't. For example, they had planned on being a strong discounter of hosiery and phonograph records. These programs were not successful. On the other hand, to their surprise, their program of carrying wines from small, obscure California wineries was tremendously successful. They were intent on paying attention to their customers, and letting them dictate what products succeeded and what products failed. It was at this

(Continued)

point that Trader Joe's developed the mindset that with their small format stores, all products needed to continuously earn their place on the shelf.

In 1970, they introduced the *Insider Report on Food and Wine.* This publication was so well received by their customers that they realized the best marketing approach was to talk openly and honestly to their customers about the products that they sell.

At one point in the 1970s, Trader Joe's carried every wine available from every producer in California. Their selection of wine, combined with their willingness to talk in depth about what they sold, helped to establish Trader Joe's as a trusted retailer.

In addition to being passionate about wine, they also became passionate about food, and began writing about their food products with the same in-depth, behind the scenes knowledge that they used for marketing wine—all the while remaining true to a culture of adventure and fun. They traveled the world to find unique and interesting food and drinks people couldn't get anywhere else. When they returned, they always had a number of stories to tell. They encouraged customers to try new products, and if they didn't like them, they could bring them back for a full refund. Trader Joe's used limited mailings of their *Insider Report* and customer word of mouth to build a small, but vocal cult following in Southern California.

In 1985, they changed the name of the *Insider Report* to the *Fearless Flyer.* With its in-depth stories about the products they carried, plus a unique blend of irreverent, self-deprecating humor, the *Fearless Flyer* quickly became a marketing icon and remains their most important marketing tool.

Over the years, Trader Joe's has grown and evolved simply by listening to their customers, staying true to their original values, and by being passionate about the products they sell. They communicate that passion through their *Fearless Flyer* and through the fun experience within their stores.

CORPORATE PROFILES AND AUTHOR BIOGRAPHIES

COSTCO

Costco Wholesale, Inc. headquartered in Issaquah, Washington, operates an international network of more than 550 membership warehouse clubs. Visit Costco at www.costco.com.

David W. Fuller

David W. Fuller is Assistant Vice President, Publishing, for Costco Wholesale, Inc. His responsibilities include the publishing of *The Costco Connection,* a monthly magazine produced in several international editions for 8 million members of Costco. He attended Chapman College.

PATAGONIA

Patagonia was developed as a brand for outdoor clothing in 1973. Patagonia has 53 stores in the United States, Europe, Japan, Korea, Chile, and Argentina. Visit Patagonia at www.patagonia.com.

Nate Smith

Nate Smith was formerly Vice President, Patagonia International. Mr. Smith received his BS from the United States Naval Academy. He received his MBA from the University of Chicago.

SAKS FIFTH AVENUE

Saks Fifth Avenue has 53 stores throughout the United States. Visit Saks Fifth Avenue at www.saks.com.

Kimberly Grabel

Kimberly Grabel is Senior Vice President and is responsible for consumer research, brand strategy, advertising, direct and database marketing, customer development and loyalty programs, and PR and events. Ms. Grabel received her BA from the University of Pittsburgh. She received her MBA from the American Graduate School of International Management.

SEARS, ROEBUCK AND CO.

Sears, Roebuck and Co. is the nation's largest provider of home services, with more than 13 million service calls made annually. Visit Sears at www.sears.com.

Steven P. Kirn

Steven Kirn was formerly Vice President on Innovation and Organization Development. Mr. Kirn received his BA from Bellarmine College. He received his MA and Ph.D. from the University of Florida.

TRADER JOE'S

Trader Joe's Company operates over 305 neighborhood grocery stores in 25 states plus Washington, D.C. Visit Trader Joe's at www.traderjoes.com.

Trader Joe

This case study was submitted by a Trader Joe's executive who wishes to remain anonymous. The culture of Trader Joe's is an inverted pyramid, where executive Crew Members support the stores so the stores may support the customers. Individual Crew Members, especially executives, do not seek individual recognition, biographies, or bylines, and rarely contribute to outside publications of any kind.

NOTES

1. U.S. Department of Commerce.

2. National Association of Convenience Stores.

25 INTERNET RETAILING

WELCOME TO INYOURFACEDUDE.COM!!

by Staples.com, Lulu.com, Toysrus.com, and Bloomingdales.com

THE ESSENTIALS OF INTERNET RETAILING
by Staples.com

Introduction

Definition
Internet retailing is the sale of merchandise via a commerce-enabled Web site. For a site to be considered an online retailing site, it must make a substantial portion of revenue from the sale of merchandise and a consumer must be able to select merchandise online and complete the transaction online without intervention by the retailer.[1]

Internet Retailing Growth

1969   Internet first started

1995   First Internet retailer, 0 percent of total retailing

2008   Unknown number of Internet retailers, $161 billion industry, 7 percent of total retailing[2]

Advantages

There are many advantages of shopping online. The consumer can quickly access a wide variety of Web sites, shop 24/7, compare prices, get much more information about products than can be gotten offline, learn how other consumers rate products, and save time by not having to trek from store to store. The primary reasons consumers buy online are (1) the convenience, (2) the ability to save time, and (3) the ability to find a low price.[3]

Disadvantages

Some customers shy away from Internet retailing due to some perceived disadvantages. Some customer concerns are

- They have to wait for merchandise to be delivered (although many customers opt for overnight delivery).
- They want to touch certain merchandise such as clothing before they buy (although clear pictures and detailed descriptions address this).
- They often have to pay for shipping (although some companies pay for shipping).
- They feel that returning a product can be a hassle (although online retailers are making improvements in this area; see the "Purchasing Process" section below).

ORGANIZE THE BUSINESS

The question that every company, including an Internet retailer, must ask is "What is it that I want to sell and who do I want to sell it to?" The first step in setting up an online store is to define the retailing goals. Having a plan in place before utilizing the technologies and marketing capabilities of the Web is essential.

Develop the Business Plan

If the Web site is a spin-off of an existing retail operation, then most business administrative requirements have already been taken care of. If this is a new stand-alone Web site, then it will be important to research several areas, including legal, financial, and administrative. (See Chapter 3, "Strategic Planning.")

Determine the Product

Typically the first step in establishing an Internet retail site is to determine the product to be sold. There are several options that can determine product selection.

- **Goods vs. Services vs. Information.** The site may sell physical goods or services or provide information.
- **Existing Store vs. Startup.** The product offering may be predetermined by the existing store structure or franchise license. However, an Internet site will allow an existing store, whether stand-alone or franchise, to sell the existing product line and expand into additional product lines.
- **Unique Products vs. Standard Products.** A start-up company may offer unique products to meet their niche market or it may offer a huge variety of mass market products.
- **Product Sourcing.** The site may offer proprietary products or act as a reseller of another company's products.

Determine Target Market

Determining the target customer from the start will help in developing the site and the marketing communications strategy. Specific markets to determine include:

- Niche markets versus a more general public
- Domestic markets and/or international markets

Determine Type of Site

The next step in building a Web site is determining whether to have a stand-alone site or create a Web site using an established, third-party e-commerce platform provider such as Yahoo, Amazon, or eBay. The advantages of a stand-alone site are the ease of access and site flexibility. The disadvantage is the cost of setting up the site and promoting the site. The advantages of piggybacking on an existing site are that these third-party platforms can support a range of retailing operations, including order management, payment processing, and Web content management. They can also provide online marketing tools and services.

DEVELOP THE SITE

The following steps are required to create an online retail store.

Determine Domain Name

The first step is to pick a domain name (the Web site address or locator). There are two parts to the Web address: the domain name (typically the company name) and the domain name extension.

Domain Name
The name should be unique and easy for people to use (avoid adding unnecessary punctuation). (See discussion about the name selection process in Chapter 4, "Branding.") The simpler the domain name and the more indicative of the product line the more likely people will find the site. Once the name has been selected, it must be registered in order to keep others from using it. There are many services that register domain names for minimal fees, such as NetworkSolutions.com.

Domain Name Extension
In addition, one must select an extension that helps delineate the background of the company. There are over 300 domain name extensions. The most frequently used extensions include:

- .com (company)
- .biz (company)
- .org (nonprofit organization)
- .gov (government)
- .int (international organization)
- .tv (television)

- .pro (credentialed professional)
- .net (typically network providers)

There is a small annual fee to own the domain name.

Determine Domain Host

It is also necessary to select a domain host, which is an organization dedicated to storing Web sites in their vast computer system and making them available to users through the Internet. Major domain host companies include NetworkSolutions.com and GoDaddy.com. Besides hosting, the companies also can provide additional services such as e-mail routing. There is a monthly fee for the hosting service, and the cost varies depending on the size of the Web site and amount of hosting services provided.

Determine Creative Look of Site

An important step is to determine the creative look of the site. The look can be anywhere from plain and simple to upscale. This choice should support the brand, the goal of the site, and the needs of the target customer. The look should be uniform as it applies to the text, the pictures, and the videos. The creative look should balance between expressing the image of the brand with the need to create a functional selling platform.

Home Page

The next step in setting up an e-commerce site should be designing the layout of the site's home page. The home page is an important focal point for the site, as most traffic comes in through the home page, although many site visitors go directly to a product page through a search engine. Once people have found the site, make sure it is easy for them to find what they are looking for. The aesthetics and visuals of the site should primarily focus attention on the product. Therefore, it should be uncluttered, attractive, and engaging. For example, Amazon.com has chat rooms where readers can discuss books with others.

Navigation (Search and Browse Paths)

Products or information may all be available on the home page and in many instances there will be multiple products that require multiple pages (some sites have thousands of pages). A retail Web site has dozens, hundreds, or even thousands of product pages, far too many to list on the home page. Typically, then, the home page lists conveniently grouped product categories that the consumer may search or browse. Categories may include product type, product price range, gender, and so forth. For example, Staples.com lists thousands of products under the easy-to-navigate main sections such as Office Supplies (paper, pens, etc.), Technology (computers, printers, etc.), and Furniture (chairs, desks, etc.).

Product Page

Many Internet retailers believe this is the most important page. The goal of the product page is to convert the browser into a buyer. The product page should display everything about the product in order to help the potential buyer. The product page should be informative and easy to understand and include price, size, colors, availability, material, shipping cost, assembly requirements, cleaning requirements, and so forth. This can be accomplished through text, pictures, video, or a combination of all three. The customer has a natural tendency to desire to see and touch the product. Because the customer cannot directly examine the product, the quality of the picture and product description is very important.

Purchasing Process

The site should make it easy for customers to purchase a product through simplicity, shopping carts, and assurances of information security. Purchasing simplicity means that products can be purchased in as few clicks as possible.

- **Shopping Carts.** Shopping carts, or purchasing icons, allow the customer to automatically hold a product for purchase while scrolling through other product categories. This can also allow for automatic billing totals and shipping fees. A customer must be able to clearly see product cost, shipping fees, and delivery times.

- **Payment Options/Payment Systems.** The Web site should provide flexibility for the customer by providing as many payment options as possible. Payment options include credit cards, gift cards (your own retail gift card or other companies' gift cards), or payment systems such as PayPal or Bill Me Later.
- **Customer Trust/Security Systems.** Asking customers for payment requires the establishment of trust. There are several ways to help accomplish this.
  - Show clearly that the site is legitimate by displaying membership in trade associations and business groups such as the Better Business Bureau.
  - Show clearly all costs and fees (products, shipping, taxes, etc.).
  - Indicate clearly that the site is administered/monitored/certified by a third-party organization such as VeriSign.com or epubliceye.com.
- **Order Status.** Customers should be kept informed about their order. Many Web retailers send out an e-mail confirming the order has been shipped. In addition customers may be able to log in or call with their order number and track their order.
- **Order Returns.** Web retailers, like store retailers, should realize that a certain percentage of all merchandise will be returned. To keep customers happy, the return process should be as easy as possible. Many Web retailers guarantee free returns, supply a preprinted return label, and, if they have a retail store, allow returns to be made directly to the store.

Customer Service

It is very important that customers feel comfortable and confident in their purchase. Customers should be able to request information through mail, e-mail response systems, or toll-free telephone numbers. A customer-focused return policy is also an important factor.

Distribution

Distribution of purchased items may be done in-house or through a fulfillment house.

- **In-house.** The advantage of in-house capabilities is the control of operations and product shipping. The primary disadvantage is the lack of economies of scale, which can make it difficult to operate cost-effectively.
- **Fulfillment House/Drop Shipping.** There are many companies that are geared to servicing the distribution needs of Internet retailers. The benefits of using a fulfillment company are the experience and the in-place systems. These companies typically charge on a per shipment basis. Shipments are managed through data feeds from the Web site and can be as simple as a batch process nightly feed or sophisticated real-time tracking for the customer.

Test Phase

Once a site has been developed, it should be tested prior to a final launch. The site should be tested page by page for content accuracy, spelling, navigation flow, links, printability, and so forth. Mistakes are less costly to correct in a prelaunch test. Initial testing may be simple, as with a group of friends and employees, or more rigorous, as with professional Web management companies such as Gomez.com, Keynote.com, and TestComplete.com.

Soft Launch

A soft launch occurs when the company starts selling on their Web site slowly without any PR or advertising promotion. The benefit of this method reduces the cost of promotion and allows a small number of initial real customers to place orders so that any problems can be corrected before the site is officially open.

Launch

A launch means the site is open for business and the marketing campaign has started to increase traffic to the site.

PROMOTE THE WEB SITE

The Web site can be promoted through traditional marketing communications and Web-based communications, such as banner ads, direct e-mail, and search engines.

Banner Ads

Banner ads may be located on portals or on other Web sites that have similar customer interests. For example, if a company sells gifts, it should advertise on a site where people shop for gifts. The advantages of banner ads are that they increase brand awareness, but a disadvantage is that they may be expensive on a cost-per-click-thru basis.

Direct E-mail

The advantages of direct e-mail are that a large targeted customer base can be reached at a low cost, and lists may be compiled quickly through a list rental company. The quality of the list is improved if it is opt-in. The disadvantage is the typically low response rate unless the e-mail creates a sense of urgency, such as with a good sale offer. Sites may add appeal to the customer shopping experience through e-mailing new site offerings, membership programs, and loyalty programs, such as Click Rewards.com.

Search Engines

If potential customers do not know of a particular domain name, they may search their service provider for key words indicative of their needs. In order to make the site search engine optimizer (SEO)–friendly, the Web site should register, or embed, key words that customers would naturally look up with search engines such as Google.com and Yahoo.com to accommodate customer searches. The cost to be included in a search engine is on a pay-per-click basis.

Affiliate Marketing

A cost-effective way to build brand awareness may be achieved through affiliate marketing programs, which find appropriate partners that will advertise the site based on a revenue share model. Companies that provide affiliate marketing include LinkShare.com, CommissionJunction.com, and Google.com.

Portals

A *portal* is a price comparison shopping site from which the customer can go to the selected site. Portals include companies such as PriceGrabber.com, Shopzilla.com, and Shopping.com.

Off-line Marketing

Offline marketing is discussed in detail in Chapter 10, "Advertising"; Chapter 11, "Public Relations"; Chapter 12, "Promotional Marketing"; and Chapter 13, "Direct Marketing."

WEB SITE ANALYTICS/FEEDBACK

The primary indication of customer service quality is revenue. One of the main benefits of Web site retailing is the ability to receive continuous and instantaneous customer and financial feedback.

In order to continuously improve the Web site and customer shopping experience, it is helpful to use a customer online shopping reporting system that reports the number of hits, customer behavior, and navigation. Companies that provide feedback systems include eGain.com, Kana.com, GoogleAnalytics.com, Omniture.com, and CoreMetrics.com.

Depending on how the site is performing, you can continuously improve and upgrade the site. (See Chapter 19, "Product Quality.")

INTERNET RETAILING—INTERNATIONAL
by Lulu.com

Introduction

The Internet is a new medium with its own rules and behaviors and is unique because of its ability to connect everyone on the planet at a low cost. From blogs to peer-to-peer sharing to YouTube, the Internet makes it easy to give things away for free. The problem with "free," as economics dictate, is that if you create something of real value, then you need to earn money in order to continue creating things of value. For example, Lulu's business model involves the creation and utilization of Internet tools that enable authors, photographers, and others to sell their creations as opposed to giving them away. There are several important differentiating factors for facilitating international sales on the Internet.

Differentiating Factors

- **Language.** The Internet goes everywhere; that is why it is an exciting place for opportunity. Marketers will encounter users of all dialects, and differences in colloquialisms can generate problems. Merely translating a site from English does not localize that site for a respective market. One must use quality automated translation tools and hire customer service staff that can read and write in any supported languages. That still does not account for visual elements, however. For example, in France an "A+" does not mean anything, but a check mark next to an "A" means "job well done." For example, when displaying bestsellers, Lulu had to create a method for displaying only best-selling French titles. Displaying American titles was poorly received.
- **Payment.** Dealing in international markets means dealing with a variety of currencies. Although credit and debit cards are held as the standard for e-commerce, there are regions where this is not the case. The bank-transfer method used throughout Europe is sometimes viewed as intrusive in America. PayPal, which has international capabilities, may be shunned in favor of homegrown national solutions such as the Netherland's iDeal. Some major banks have set up online banking options to aid in this area.
- **Shipping.** The world is far from having a standardized format for addresses. Issues arise due to customs, duties, taxation, and language barriers. Also, differences in standard product size, weight, color, and word-processing software settings can pose variations in product consistency. However, there are now many Internet infrastructure suppliers and global express shipping companies that can help with many of the tasks of distributing a solution globally.
- **Legality.** Doing business on the Internet requires a membership agreement between the company and users, and a privacy pledge that establishes user rights as well as outlines what users can and cannot expect on any given site in terms of behavior and activity. Establishing agreements with members in international markets can introduce differing laws governing inclusion and privacy. To be safe, marketers should obtain legal advice with respect to specific regional markets.
- **Research.** When dealing with such a vast audience, the question becomes "How to conduct research on customers that have never purchased the kind of service that is being offered?" Research must be more general in nature than routine marketing research. You cannot simply ask a focus group which product they like better when the competition for that product does not yet exist. The answer is to find prospective customers who indicate an interest in your solution, build it for them, launch it, and then study the behaviors of the early adopters. Then, redesign it and relaunch it and, most likely, repeat that process.

by Toysrus.com

Company: Toysrus.com
Case: **Winning Customers through Great Service**

As the Internet age came alive in the late 1990s, Toys"R"Us established a presence online and launched the world's largest toy and baby products store—Toysrus.com—to offer busy moms and dads a convenient shopping experience, 24 hours a day, seven days a week. As consumers became comfortable with the simplicity of shopping online, demand for access to all the products that lined the shelves of Toys"R"Us and Babies"R"Us stores increased. Toys"R"Us responded by expanding its e-commerce offerings to include an Imaginarium category so customers would have online access to the finest learning and specialty toys available and a sports category that addressed the more physical aspects of fun.

By the summer of 2000, the popularity of online shopping continued to evolve. To better meet the needs of new and expectant parents, the company launched Babiesrus.com to deliver convenient access to informational resources that support parents throughout pregnancy and their child's first year. The site also enabled customers to access the company's best-in-class baby registry, which has been used by over 10 million parents to date. Since more than 40 percent of all "R"Us baby registries created in 2008 were through Babiesrus.com, the increased popularity of the online baby registry became apparent.

It also became apparent that the Web site offered more than just a sales platform. The site became an opportunity to foster community, connect and communicate with customers, and provide them with valuable information as they research products and services that would ultimately bring them into the stores or motivate them to make a purchase.

Recognizing an opportunity to enhance its e-commerce site and empower its customers with more product information and decision-support tools, in 2008, Toysrus.com underwent a complete redesign. The site today looks and feels vastly different than it did at its launch. A fun new look, with bold colors, interactive graphics, and the recognizable Toys"R"Us branding, is the first thing visitors notice when they come to the site. They also will find enhanced tools and services such as pricing, guest ratings, and buying options. Web site visitors also can locate Toys"R"Us or Babies"R"Us stores in their area by simply entering their ZIP code and then seeing real-time stock information for the in-demand toy or baby product they are seeking through the "Want It Today?" feature. These features and functionality provide customers with an exceptional online shopping experience that helps them select the right gifts with ease.

Just as Toys"R"Us shoppers have long relied on the company's knowledgeable store associates to help them select the right products in-store; Toysrus.com allows them to take advantage of that expertise in the comfort of their own homes. The Toys"R"Us Gift Finder application takes the guesswork out of shopping for a present by asking online shoppers to answer a few simple questions about the child for whom they are buying (e.g., age, gender, activities, interests, and skills) and providing a set of recommended presents with access to key product information.

And, with the site's Wish List feature, an online gift registry for kids, wishes can be granted the easy way. Whether for holidays, birthdays, or special occasions, the Toys"R"Us online Wish List lets parents and caregivers browse products with their kids to create and update a running list online of their most desired presents. Wish Lists can be shared with friends and family, updated online or through in-store purchase, and printed from home or at any store service desk.

The site's advanced navigation also makes selecting merchandise and learning about products easier than ever. On Babiesrus.com, shoppers can choose items from featured collections simply by scrolling their mouse over catalog photos or fully decorated nurseries, eliminating the need to find each product separately on the Web site.

In addition, there is a strong online presence for circulars, safety messages, and baby registry. For example, the baby registry features a Quick Start Registry to provide first-time parents with a list of basic essentials by product category, enabling them to build their registry quickly and effortlessly. The popular Mom's Favorites community where moms can rate products and share valuable information with others has been placed in a prominent position, and makes it easy for shoppers to view favorites by category, comment on merchandise, and review what other parents and caregivers are saying about individual products.

Toysrus.com also offers services such as e-Invite, which allows parents to order printed personalized announcements, invitations, and cards in celebration of special occasions and milestones in their child's life. By simplifying and enhancing the look of its e-commerce site, fostering a sense of community, and adding helpful tools that make it easier than ever for customers to select and purchase the perfect gifts for their loved ones, Toys"R"Us continues to provide its customers with an unbeatable product selection and exceptional shopping experience.

As the organization continues to grow, Toys"R"Us will expand its online presence, offering shoppers, parents, and caregivers the most extensive, trusted information about toy and baby products on the Web and maintaining its unrivaled position as the world's largest toy and baby products store.

INTERNET RETAILING – CASE STUDY

by Bloomingdales.com

Company: Bloomingdales.com
Case: Internet Retailing — Site Redesign

Promoting the Store (2000)

Bloomingdale's began in the late 1800s as an East Side of New York bargain retailer of women's apparel and accessories and has grown into a full-line department store catering to the fashion needs of the entire family and their home. By the 1980s, Bloomingdale's had earned a global reputation of being "Like no other store in the world" through the concept of "retailing as theater." Still, discovering what value means to the customer and delivering it on a day-to-day basis are ongoing challenges for Bloomingdale's. As if the saturation of the retail market did not create competition enough for a share of the consumer's wallet, the Internet opened literally a world of options to satisfy the shopper's quest for value. Bloomingdale's, like every other retailer in the world, is faced with delivering the key elements of the value equation (desirable merchandise, appropriate price, convenience, service, entertainment, information, relevance, and fun) in a competitive environment of ever-rising customer expectations.

(Continued)

Keeping pace with customers requires information from a constant dialogue through a variety of research methodologies, such as surveys (mail, telephone, and online), intercepting customers in the stores while they shop, and through focus groups (both the formal behind-the-glass variety, as well as an informal gathering in the stores). Analysis of this customer data linked to past purchase history provides a strong predictor of future buying behavior. However, customers today, with their many shopping options, are less predictable than ever.

With today's highly mobile and time-pressed consumers, marketers need to utilize any and all available media to create a customer relationship with their brand. Since Bloomingdale's roots are solidly based in brick-and-mortar retailing, the company has always promoted its Web site using conventional as well as online media. Retailers' profits depend on promotion, so Bloomingdale's incorporates Bloomingdales.com into newspaper ads and inserts, magazines, catalogs, and direct mail. In addition, in-store media, such as signage, register receipts, credit card statements, package inserts, and even the legendary Big Brown Bag, is used. Bloomingdale's wants its customers to know that they can communicate with their brand 24 hours a day, 7 days a week, from anywhere in the world where they have Internet access.

Direct online marketing also is essential to attracting new customers and supporting a successful Web site. Bloomingdale's uses banner ads on selected sites where targeted customers are likely to go. Direct e-mail notices are effective in sending relevant messages and offers to targeted individuals.

It is important to note here that the log files that individual visitors create as they migrate from a banner ad or e-mail to a Web site and then through the site are huge and encrypted. They need to be condensed and translated before they even approach usefulness from a traditional marketing standpoint. This has led to the development of new intelligent modeling applications, such as collaborative filtering, in which customer and marketer communicate with each other. In this manner, true one-to-one marketing occurs.

Through the Internet, Bloomingdale's has an opportunity to truly bring Fifty-ninth Street to the world, while making each individual customer feel as if he or she has the store all to themselves. The challenge then is to deliver on the promise.

Promoting the Brand (2006–)

In 2006, Bloomingdale's decided to move their Internet business from under the umbrella of the Marketing Department to a separate division, called Bloomingdale's Direct. In 2008, Bloomingdale's closed the catalog and renamed the business Bloomingdales.com. The main difference is that Bloomingdales.com is now run as a separate business that collaborates closely with the store instead of a business run by the Marketing Department. It is now under the direction of the Vice Chairman/GMM of Ready to Wear and Bloomingdales.com. Bloomingdale's main goal in doing this is to become a great multichannel retailer.

CORPORATE PROFILES AND AUTHOR BIOGRAPHIES

STAPLES.COM

Staples is the world's second largest e-tailer. Staples, the world's largest office products company, is committed to making it easy for customers to buy a wide range of office products, including supplies, technology, furniture, and business services. Visit Staples at www.staples.com.

Pete Howard

Pete Howard is Senior Vice President of Staples Business Delivery, which provides office products and services to small and medium-sized businesses throughout North America via Staples' e-commerce sites and catalogs. Mr. Howard received his BA and MBA from the University of Chicago.

LULU.COM

Lulu.com, founded in 2002, has created a platform for authors to publish their work for free and profit from it in Lulu's global marketplace. Visit Lulu at www.lulu.com.

Bob Young

Bob Young is the founder and CEO of Lulu.com. Mr. Young received his BA from the University of Toronto.

TOYSRUS.COM

Toys"R"Us, Inc., founded in 1948, launched Toysrus.com in 1998 to cater to busy moms, dads, and other toy-buying adults who would appreciate access to the world's largest toy store at their fingertips. Visit Toys"R"Us at www.toysrus.com.

Michael Scharff

Michael Scharff was appointed Vice President, General Manager e-commerce in December 2007. In this role, he is responsible for all of the company's Internet operations and provides leadership for all online merchandising and marketing initiatives, as well as the company's cross-channel programs.

Additional information provided by:

Kurt Peters, Editor-in-Chief, *Internet Retailer.*

BLOOMINGDALES.COM

Bloomingdale's, headquartered in New York, was founded in 1872. Visit Bloomingdale's at www.blomingdales.com.

NOTES

1. InternetRetailer.com, 2009. Used with permission.
2. Ibid.
3. Nielsen Online report, InternetRetailer.com, November 21, 2008.

INDEX

Network television, 186
New markets, 43
New product uses, 290
New products, 294*f*
News media, 218–221
Newsletters, 221–222
Newspapers:
   advertising in, 187
   direct marketing with, 262
   promotional marketing with, 244
New York Times, 249–250
NGOs (nongovernmental
   organizations), 212
Niche marketing, 42
Nike, 91–92, 284
NME (National Medical Enterprises), 30
Nondurable goods, 284
Nongovernmental organizations
   (NGOs), 212
Nonstore retailing, 427–428
Nordstrom, 276–278
Nordstrom, John W., 276
North American Industry Classification
   System (NAICS):
   and direct marketing, 258
   and market segmentation, 135

O

Objective-and-task method, 185
Objective performance indicators, 52
Observation (marketing research),
   100–101
Occupational Safety and Health
   Administration (OSHA), 28
Ocean shipping, 404–405, 412
Odd-number pricing, 333
The Office (television show), 206
Office Depot, 376
Off-line marketing, 446
Oil, 406, 416
Oligopoly, 134
1–800-Flowers.com, 168
One-time advertisements, 183
Online auction bidding, 141, 373
Online job sites, 156–157
Online media, 264–266
On-packs, 237
Open bids, 141
Open branding, 69
Open loop systems, 365
Open rate (e-mail analysis), 261
Operating leases, 140
Operating Profits (OPs), 39
Opinion formers, 212
Opinion leaders, 120–121
Opportunity costs, 325
OPs (Operating Profits), 39
Order bias, 103
Order status/returns, 445
Organizational information, 104
Organizational management, 345–346
Organizational markets, 42
Organizational offering, 43–44
Organizational purchasing, 133–150

buyers/purchasing departments,
   136–137
defined, 133
demand types in, 133–135
DuPont case study, 148–150
and environmental responsibility, 26
ethics issues in, 12
IBM case study, 146–148
international, 144–146
process of, 137–144
segmenting demand in, 135–136
types of, 137
Organizational responsibility, 10–36
   economic responsibility, 10–11
   environmental responsibility, 20–30
   ethical responsibility, 11–18
   international environmental
     responsibility, 29–30
   international ethical responsibility,
     17–18
   international social responsibility, 20
   legal responsibility, 11, 18
   Pfizer case study, 33–35
   social responsibility, 18–20
   Tenet Healthcare case study, 30–33
   Xerox case study, 35–36
Organizations, 5–6
OSHA (Occupational Safety and Health
   Administration), 28
Outbound telephone selling, 263
Outlet stores, 427
Out-of-home media, 188–189
Outside sales representatives, 160–161
Outsourced logistics, 387
Owens-Illinois, 306, 320
Owned media, 265
Ownership (customer value), 4
Ownership of goods, 401
Ownership methods, 424–426
Ownership options (transportation), 395
Ozone depletion, 25–26

P

Pabst Blue Ribbon, 273–274
Package mail, 259
Package pricing, 333
Packaging, 305–321
   aluminum, 309
   aspects of, 305–307
   branding with, 70–72
   Dean Foods case study, 319–320
   defined, 305
   and environmental responsibility, 27
   ethics issues in, 13
   flexible, 310–311
   glass, 307–308
   international, 315–317
   labeling, 312–315
   Owens-Illinois case study, 320
   paperboard, 308
   rigid plastic, 311–312
   steel, 309–310
   Tanimura & Antle case study, 317–318
Packing list, 398

Paid media, 265
Pallets, 398
Papa John's, 336–337
Paper manufacturing, 337–338
Paperboard packaging, 308
Parity, 297
Partnerships, 363–364, 367, 390–391
Parts, 138, 283
Passenger transportation, 407–411
Payment options (Internet retail), 445,
   447
Pay per click (PPC) advertising, 244
PEDIGREE, 201–204
Peer review, 15
Penetration pricing, 332
PepsiCo:
   packaging by, 61
   product testing by, 296
   products of, 284
   promotional marketing case study,
     250–252
Percentage-of-sales method, 185
Perception management, 210
Perfect competition industries, 134
Performance measurement:
   of branding, 75–77
   indicators for, 51–52
   in supply chains, 362–363
Periodic sales, 333
Permission marketing, 245
Personal interviews (marketing
   research), 100
Personal reference groups, 120–121
Personal selling, 153, 156, 435–436
Personnel, 47
Persuasive advertisements, 182
Pfizer, 33–35, 295
Pharmaceuticals, 382
Philanthropy, 19, 215
Physical address validation, 257
Physical distribution, 380
Physical environment, 121
Pick orders, 384
Pick and pack function, 370
Pipeline transportation, 396, 406–407,
   416
Place (customer value), 4
Plank, Kevin, 80, 81
Planning, 39–56
   for advertising, 181–185
   and customer needs, 42–44
   defined, 39
   defining organizational offering in,
     43–44
   determining strategies in, 48–51
   ethics issues in, 11
   and feedback, 52
   goals of, 39–40
   and implementation, 51–52
   international, 54–56
   situation analysis in, 44–48
   structures for, 40–42
   of transportation, 395–398
Plastic packaging, 311–312